KAREL ČERNÝ

INSTABILITY IN THE MIDDLE EAST
STRUCTURAL CHANGES AND UNEVEN MODERNISATION 1950–2015

CHARLES UNIVERSITY
KAROLINUM PRES 2017

Reviewed by: Prof. Dr. Luboš Kropáček (Charles University, Department
of Near Eastern and African Studies, Prague)
Jaroslav Weinfurter, M.Sc., M.A. (Metropolitan University Prague)

This book was supported by research project GAČR no. 13-35717P "Arab revolutions
and Political Islam: A Structural Approach", carried out at Charles University,
Faculty of Humanities."

CATALOGUING-IN-PUBLICATION – NATIONAL LIBRARY OF THE CZECH REPUBLIC

Černý, Karel
  Instability in the Middle East : structural changes and uneven modernisation
1950-2015 / Karel Černý. – First English edition. – Prague : Charles University in Prague,
Karolinum Press, 2017
ISBN 978-80-246-3427-2

321.01-025.16 * 316.42 * 316.422 * (5-15)
– 1950–2012
– political stability – Middle East – 1945–
– social change – Middle East – 1945–
– modernization – Middle East – 1945–
– monographs

316.4 – social processes [18]

ISBN 978-80-246-3427-2
ISBN 978-80-246-3191-2 (pdf)

CONTENTS

INTRODUCTION: CHRONIC INSTABILITY IN THE MIDDLE EAST

MODERNISATION AS THE CAUSE OF INSTABILITY IN THE MIDDLE EAST – TOO SLOW OR TOO FAST?

The academic, media and public discourse regarding the development of the post-colonial Middle East has long featured two viewpoints that, on the face of it, are diametrically opposed. The first claims the region is backward and rigid, with change taking place too slowly, if at all. The second believes that the region is transforming too quickly and that this is traumatising and destabilising local societies.

This book offers an alternative way of looking at the issue that brings together these two apparently contradictory viewpoints. It conducts a theoretically original and empirically substantiated analysis of the structural causes of Middle Eastern social and political instability, an instability manifest externally in many different forms: the protracted crisis of governing regimes and their ideologies and legitimacy; an upsurge in different ideologically driven opponents of these regimes in the form of oppositional political Islam and pro-democracy movements; a surge in political violence in the form of terrorism, civil wars or revolutions during the Arab Spring; the chronic post-revolutionary instability of the region, the collapse of many local states and the erosion of social order resulting in chaos, anarchy and interregnum.

Monitoring these external, constantly changing manifestations of pan-regional instability means understanding the Middle East as a dramatic chessboard full of constantly materialising and disappearing state and non-state actors enforcing their interests, promoting their ideologies, and competing with each other, while at the same time entering into often unexpected coalitions or, indeed, dissolving them equally unexpectedly. However, the aim of this book is to offer an explanation of the deeper causes of a chess game that is being played ever faster and during which new pieces are being added and the chessboard itself being redrawn, along with the very rules of the game. A new Middle East is emerging, one completely different to that which we have been accustomed to for decades.

How is it possible that, while over the last fifty years the Middle Eastern political chessboard was one of the most stable, predictable and boring in the world, controlled as it was by the same figures playing in accordance with the same strategies, over the last few years the pace of history has sped up beyond recognition? I will argue that this is the consequence of the impacts of long-term, subterranean social changes that have been taking place over the last fifty years but have been hitherto unobserved, since most observers have concentrated on the political game and not on the changes to its deeper demographic, social, economic and political determinants. And yet the character of these changes is strikingly reminiscent of what was a politically and socially destabilised Europe during the 19th and early 20th centuries. Reminding ourselves of recent European demographic and social history offers the possibility of better understanding the causes of the current turmoil in the Middle East.

EXCESSIVELY SLOW SOCIAL CHANGE

Those subscribing to the first viewpoint referred to above see the Middle East as an underdeveloped region, in which islands of modernity, progress, education and Western culture are surrounded by an ocean of medieval ignorance, obscurantism and Islamic-backed reactionary forces. According to this analysis, the region is experiencing a form of schizophrenia, with one leg in the camp of modernity, and the other still firmly planted in tradition (e.g. Longrigg, Jankowski 1963). More sophisticated versions of this line of argument describe the Middle East as a region inhabited by people who for the most part have not yet adapted psychologically to the modern world. Mentally they languish somewhere in the Middle Ages and its traditions. They cannot be described as "modern" because they are not sufficiently educated, socially mobile and informed. The boundaries of their community are the boundaries of their world. They are stuck in a time warp of tradition. They are walking backwards into the future, as it were, so as to replicate as faithfully as possible the patterns of behaviour, identities and aspirations of previous generations, which represent their role model and authority. They do not possess new, expanding consumer and career aspirations, and as a consequence lack an advanced sense of empathy, namely the ability to imagine alternatives to their life and the organisation of their community or wider society. They do not perceive themselves to be an active subject capable of changing the course of history according to a programme conceived of in advance, but as a passive object simply being dragged along by history and destiny (e.g. Lerner 1964, cf. Bah 2008). The more vulgar, borderline racist interpretation of the immutability of the region speaks of what it calls the "Arab mind", a specific, unchanging personality archetype common to all Arabs characterised by an aversion to manual work, an obsession with sexuality, an overabundance of pride, a partiality for conspiracy theories, a reluctance to accept reality, an unwillingness to submit to anything other than power, and a comprehensive backwardness (e.g. Patai 1973, Friedman 2006).

The latest perspective on the region is the influential series of studies entitled the Arab Human Development Report (2002, 2003, 2005, 2009), compiled under the auspices of the UN by Arab scholars and intellectuals. These reports traced the deeper cause of the backwardness of the Arab world back to a *combination of three deficits*: the freedom deficit, women's empowerment, and the knowledge deficit. Democratisation and the promotion of constitutional liberalism are not taking place, while, on the contrary, authoritarian and oppressive regimes persist. The status of women is not improving fast enough. The participation of women in different social spheres remains low, while oppression and discrimination remains high. As a consequence the human potential of an entire half of the population lies idle. Finally, the reports' authors say, the region is unable to mount an effective fight against illiteracy and to produce a sufficiently well educated population. It is unable to generate innovation and new knowledge. On top of this it is unable to avail itself of the innovations and knowledge generated elsewhere in the world. The Arab world lags behind other global regions in all respects.

One of the consequences is a lack of economic growth. In addition, what economic growth there is fragile, since it is wholly dependent on the export of raw materials, a burgeoning, ineffective state sector, and on family businesses from the informal sector on the boundary of the grey economy that are incapable of generating stable jobs or expanding because they cannot apply for bank loans. By contrast, the sophisticated output of stable firms with high value added plays a minimal role. Job creation is sluggish and the region is unable to compete within the global economy. Another consequence of the three deficits is the lack of functioning state institutions that would ensure effective, transparent and high quality governance and thus a reliable framework for economic development and a tranquil, safe life for the population. Quality of life lags behind other regions of the world because of the ongoing risk of poverty, poor health and deteriorating nutritional and ecological standards (AHDR 2002, 2003, 2005, 2009).

The approach taken by the Arab Human Development Report team selects developmental indicators from the many gathered by the World Bank and highlights those that show the Arab world to be lagging behind other regions. Not only does the Arab world occupy a lowly position in these rankings, but the situation is improving at a slower tempo (cf. Amin 2006). Such studies point out with relish that not a single Arab university features among the 500 top universities in the world. The Arab publishing market represents only 1% of global book sales, a figure completely incommensurate with population statistics. While Turkey and Iran have multiplied several times over their scholarly output over the last decade as measured by specialist articles, the Arab world does not research or publish and is stagnating academically. The Arab world has low newspaper circulation per capita, limited telephone coverage, and translates only one book a year per one million of the population: in Hungary and Spain these figures are 519 and 920 respectively. All of this is intended to illustrate the region's intellectual stagnation and its aversion to new ideas (e.g. Zewail 2011).

One variant of the argument that the Middle East is developing too slowly involves a narrative of chronically unsuccessful modernisation projects and developmental strategies imposed on a top-down basis by enlightened dictators on a subservient and backward population. This often involves reformist leaders recruited from the army, who, face to face with military defeat and their country's obvious technological and economic inferiority as compared to the West, attempt to implement a *defensive modernisation strategy aimed at closing the gap*. Above all they attempt to establish a modern, powerful army and to embrace new technology so as to be able to resist the pressure of the West and play a commensurate role in international politics. However, generally speaking they are only able to create a strong army having first established a functioning secular education system and an effective state bureaucracy based on a codified, Western-style legal system. This strategy, based on the assumption that successful modernisation also requires a certain degree of cultural Westernisation, was first attempted by the Ottoman Turks, followed by the Arabs, Iranians, and Afghans. However, for the most part the strategy failed and encountered opposition on the part of a population unsettled by attempts at what they saw as excessively rapid change. What ensued were repeated waves of Islamic fundamentalism driven by the belief that, on the contrary, the region lagged behind the West because it had deviated from its own culture and religion (e.g. Lewis 2003a, 2003b).

Both the more sophisticated scholarly and the more vulgar non-academic versions of the slow-development theory of the Middle East region and its allegedly medieval character are often close to the *discourse of orientalism*, i.e. the set of widespread and deeply entrenched Western ideas, clichés and stereotypes regarding the Orient. Orientalism is based on the binary opposition of two interdependent categories – the Occident and the Orient, civilisation and barbarism – each of which makes no sense on its own. The idea of a Muslim Orient as the antithetical image of Europe, and later the United States, had always enabled the West to define itself by virtue of what it was not, locate its essence, and confirm its positive self-image as being in contradistinction to that of the Other, Oriental and inferior. This stereotype views a citizen of the West as broadminded, rational, active, industrious, peace-loving, progressive, dynamic and civilised, while the Oriental is prone to despotism, slavery, irrationality, savagery, fanaticism, indolence, violence, unbridled sexuality, primitiveness and barbarism (Said 2008, Halliday 2005, Barša 2012). The basis of the Orientalist discourse is *essentialism*, i.e. the idea that the present attributes of Oriental people are determined by an ancient barbaric culture of primitive desert Bedouins, whose influence they cannot shake off, and that these attributes are intrinsic, not subject to historical development, and fixed in time. The only thing that can liberate the Oriental from being suspended in timelessness and stagnation is an external shock or intervention in the form of colonialism or neo-colonialism (Abdel-Malek 1963).

In Western popular culture Orientalism is manifest, for instance, in television programmes and Hollywood films in which for a hundred years Arabs have been depicted as one of the "three Bs": belly dancer, billionaire or bomber (Shaheen 2001, 2008). In Western politics Orientalism is then manifest in the justification of military intervention (Afghanistan, Iraq) in order to spread democracy, freedom, human rights and the emancipation of women. It is assumed that any change to this inflexible region can only come from without, and it is emphasised that the backwardness and absence of democracy in the region breeds violence and terrorism (Amin 2004, Amin 2006, Zogby 2012). The first to come up with the argument, still being recycled to this day, that justifies Western political violence against non-Western parts of the world was Napoleon Bonaparte during his expedition to Egypt in 1798 (Said 1981, Wallerstein 2008).

The basic premise of this book will perhaps seem counterintuitive in that it takes Middle Eastern societies to be relatively modern, a viewpoint at odds with the discourse of Orientalism. The fact is that over the last few decades Middle Eastern societies have changed far faster than have Western ways of thinking about the Orient, which remain rigid and incapable of adapting to the new reality. This is why we have a problem in understanding and correctly analysing the *new* Middle East.

EXCESSIVELY RAPID SOCIAL CHANGE

The opposite opinion views the Middle Eastern region as changing rapidly, a fact that over the last few decades has traumatised the population and driven them into the arms of both moderate and militant Islamists. For instance, in the religious revivals and the creation of new movements and sects, Saïd Amir Arjomand sees a globally intensifying process taking place in parallel not only within the framework of mainly Muslim regions, but within the framework of many other religious traditions. The common denominator is excessively rapid social change that all over the world sees the recycling of local versions of traditional fundamentalisms. This flies in the face of mainstream modernisation theories. The processes that were supposed to lead inevitably to secularisation and the death of religion have instead resulted in a renaissance and even the politicisation of Islam and other religions (cf. also Huntington 2001).

In the case of Muslim societies this involves, in approximately chronological order, the following processes, now running in parallel and overlapping, that escalated after World War II: (1) the integration of the Islamic world into the international economic and political system in the form of colonialism, imperial intervention, Christian missions, and economic, cultural and political globalisation, (2) the expansion of communication and transport technology and infrastructure, (3) the acceleration of urbanisation, (4) increased literacy and greater access to education in general, and (5) the creation of centralised nation states and the politicisation of the masses accompanied by repression on the part of regimes (Arjomand 1986, 2006). While the first four processes follow a similar trajectory in all countries and lead, arguably, to the unification of revivalist religious movements, the last factor is variable and leads to diversification as the character of political regimes forms to a significant extent the character of Islamist movements within each nation state (Arjomand 1995).

An approach that emphasises the rapid *social change* taking place in the Middle East often attempts to use this fact in order to explain the rise of oppositional political Islam, which has been going on since the 1970s. Though Islamic movements are highly heterogeneous internally and the formative influence of the specific national context in which they are rooted can be tracked down in the case of each, this is a phenomenon of international dimensions. The main causes of this upsurge must therefore be common to all movements (Dekmejian 1995). Individual writers then argue as to whether affinities and analogies can be found between current Islamism and earlier European Marxism (Gellner 1995, Roy 1992, 2004, Eisenstadt 2003), Russian anti-Tsarist anarchism (Gray 2004), German Nazism (Lewis 1990, 2003, Buruma and Margalit 2005), or secular nationalism (Juergensmeyer 1994). However, they all agree that the broad and internally highly differentiated current of Islamism is far more the product of the modernisation of the Middle Eastern region in the same way that the European political movements referred to above were the product of modernisation in their time, and not the consequence or residue of the Middle Ages, as proponents of the secularisation theory still thought until recently. I would agree with Shmuel Noah Eisenstadt (2000, 2003) that these movements possessed significant ambitions to define themselves in respect of the Western version of modernity, to be inspired selectively by it, and to come up with an alternative version or variation also inspired by domestic tradition, be this "invented" or genuinely authentic.

This was the approach I myself highlighted (cf. Černý 2006), when, using empirical data, I operationalised Zbigniew Brzezinski's theoretical concept (1993, 2004) of the *global political awakening* of modernising societies. Developing countries of the Global South are at present describing a similar trajectory to the fast social change that Europe experienced during the 19th and early 20th centuries: a growing population with an ever larger proportion of young people and a consequent pressure on resources; an exodus from over-populated rural and peripheral areas to cities and central regions making political organisation easier; a more educated population and the expansion of mass media accompanied by a rise in career, consumer and political aspirations; and the development of market economies creating visible inequality. In 19th and early 20th century Europe these processes led to the deracination of populations from traditional social and normative structures. The resulting vacuum was filled by new political movements offering new social frameworks, identities and orientation in a rapidly changing world. This all culminated in the expansion of mass political movements, the wholesale political mobilisation of the population in the name of new ideologies, and considerable political destabilisation. And so we had a century of nationalism and revolutions (the 19th century) and a century of killing sprees in the name of utopian ideas promising to create heaven on earth (the 20th century). This was the "Age of Extremes", the "short 20th century" (1914–1989) (cf. Hobsbawm 1998).

Fig. 1 The political awakening of world macro-regions 1975–2003

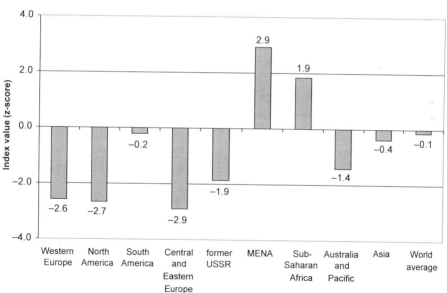

N.B.: The resulting synthetic index of political awakening is the arithmetic average of dimensionless quantities (z-score) taking into consideration the rate of population growth (1975–2003), the pace of urbanisation (1975–2003), the rate of the intergenerational increase in literacy (adult population versus the young), and the rate of economic growth (1990–2003). Unweighted population sizes of individual states. The author's calculations.
Data source: UNDP Human Development Report 2005; cited in Černý (2006: 117).

By the same token, moving forward in time we find rapid social change bringing analogous political destabilisation in developing countries. While mass political movements in the Global South are not obliged to seek their raison d'être in secular ideologies, the structural sources of their expansion are identical to those of the movements of European modern history (Brzezinski 1993, 1999, 2004). And so the Middle East, along with Sub-Saharan Africa, finds itself in a stage of history in which it is experiencing the most powerful combination of rapid demographic, social and economic change. This is why the political awakening is so strong here in comparison with other world macro-regions, where the process of political awakening has already subsided or is subsiding (see fig. 1, cf. Černý 2006).

However, for a long time the problem with this type of analysis was that subterranean demographic, social and economic changes were being played out beneath the surface of Middle Eastern political systems that on the surface appeared to be stable and displayed no visible signs of political awakening. Individual countries were ruled for decades by the same dictators, and the political and economic power in a country was divided up among cronies of the same families, tribes or religious beliefs (e.g. Hybášková 2004). In the meantime, beneath the smooth political surface invisible social and demographic changes were simmering and gathering momentum. The attention paid by researchers to visible events in the political sphere and their orientation on the chessboard of political actors meant that these deeper, inconspicuous and less easily grasped structural changes were overlooked. They were also underestimated because, given their fundamental character, they progressed in slow, gradual accretions, over decades rather than years. As a consequence, there was an overemphasis placed on stasis in the Middle East and a focus on explaining the causes of this anomalous stability (cf. Gause III 2011).

CREATING AN ALTERNATIVE THEORETICAL MODEL: UNEVEN MODERNISATION AND ITS CONTEXT

Both the viewpoints outlined contain an element of truth. However, by looking at things selectively and focusing only on particular aspects of Middle Eastern reality, neither viewpoint captures the whole picture. The fact is that certain aspects of Middle Eastern reality are indeed changing very quickly, with, for instance, sharp increases in the population, urbanisation, media diffusion, and education. However, other aspects are changing very slowly, if at all. For instance, over the last fifty years political regimes have been rigid and the capacity of states to govern effectively and discharge basic functions in their own territory has been eroded. And the modernisation projects initiated by enlightened dictators have often failed, in the process discrediting the secular ideologies they had drawn on to justify their actions.

FIRST THEORETICAL INSPIRATION: UNEVEN MODERNISATION

For this reason, this book will pursue an alternative approach that to a large extent integrates the two positions referred to above. It will do this by emphasising the highly *uneven and asynchronous pace* of development in individual *dimensions* of Middle Eastern social change (see fig. 2). In this alternative approach Middle Eastern modernisation in the post-colonial period is characterised by (1) a very high pace of *socio-demographic modernisation*; a demographic revolution characterised by sharp population growth and a greater proportion of younger generations within the population as a whole, urbanisation, an intergenerational increase in education, and the expansion of the media and other means of communication. These swift changes are accompanied by (2) a slower, irregular pace of *economic modernisation*; economic growth made volatile by external influences and deformed by its unbalanced dependence on natural resources, the slow diversification of economic sectors, and an ailing labour market and hence the absence of social mobility. And finally by (3) a very slow, non-existent or even regressive rate of *political modernisation*; the erosion of the ability of Middle Eastern states and their institutions to govern effectively, to enforce their own laws and to discharge basic functions in their own territory, including the state monopoly on violence; and the absence of democratisation and constitutional liberal principles making it impossible to co-opt ever more modern populations into political systems.

The result of the collision of the divergent, mutually unsynchronised pace of development in these three basic dimensions of social change is a region with sizeable and relatively *modern societies* living in *rigid and non-functional states* controlled for decades by the same archaic monarchies or military republican dictatorships, and populations that are unable to find sufficient life chances in *deformed rentier economies* that fail to generate suitable job opportunities and distribute the nation's wealth evenly throughout society. In other words, the Middle East is a region full of modern, metropolitan, educated, media savvy and mainly young people with high consumer, career, professional, civic and political aspirations. However, closed, inflexible economic and political systems are unable to meet the growing demand in people for upward social mobility and self-fulfilment and *co-opt* these populations into an economic and political system. Modern societies are therefore excluded from participating in economic and political systems and stand outside them. This generates instability in the Middle East.

Fig. 2 Model of uneven modernisation: The interaction and tensions of the three dimensions of social change

Political modernisation (stagnating or even regressing)
Economic modernisation (unstable, slow or stagnating)
Social and demographic modernisation (very fast)

N.B. Possible interactions and tensions are shown by the arrows.

The mutually unsynchronised rate of development in these three basic dimensions of social change gives rise to *three general deficits*: a prosperity deficit, a democratic deficit, and a security deficit. The *prosperity deficit* is due to the excessively rapid rate of change in the socio-demographic sphere that developments in the economic subsystem cannot keep up with; a surfeit of well educated, urbanised and informed people are acquiring professional and consumer aspirations that outstrip the possibilities of the economic subsystem. The *democratic deficit* is due to the excessively rapid rate of change in the socio-demographic sphere that developments in the political subsystem cannot keep pace with and which remains closed to the majority of the fast growing population and is unable to co-opt new political actors and the ever larger group of politically mobilised masses. The *security deficit* is again due to the excessively rapid rate of change in the socio-demographic sphere that developments in the political subsystem cannot keep pace with. This results in weak, unreliable and unpredictable states unable to perform basic functions and enforce law and order, ensure internal and external security, and provide adequate infrastructure and a social safety net for all social strata. The combination of these three deficits is the source of the frustration and political instability in the region. In addition, the interaction between the political and economic system needs to be taken into account: the formation of a rentier economy retrospectively shapes the character of political systems in the direction of rigid authoritarianism. These steps in the analysis mean moving from the macro to the micro level, from an examination of the development of structures to an examination of how these uneven social changes impact on the frustration, motivation and actions of political actors (this theme is addressed in more detail below).

Our alternative model is inspired by a *critical* reading of *modernisation theories* (cf. Knöbl 2003, Lorenz 2006, Wucherpfennig and Deutsch 2009). The concept of modernisation is taken to be a *value-neutral* analytical tool that enables us to distinguish between individual dimensions of the modernisation process, e.g. the technological, economic, demographic, social, political, cultural, value or psychological changes (e.g. Apter 1968, Smelser 1959). However, while classical modernisation theory assumed synchronised, interconnected development in individual, mutually dependent spheres – the development of education or the media was to result in the development of the economy and social structure, which would in turn culminate in democratisation and secularisation (e.g. Lerner 1958, Lipset 1959, 1994, Rostow 1960) – this book will, on the contrary, emphasise the *divergent tempo and inconsistencies* in the development of individual spheres. While classical modernisation theories assumed the smooth, harmonious and peaceful development of modernising societies as opposed to the revolutionary development of Marxist analyses, this book will emphasise the discontinuous, reversible and nonlinear character of modernisation and above all its many unintended consequences and politically destabilising potential (cf. Sztompka 1993, Keller 2007, Arnason 2010).

A key author in this respect is Samuel P. Huntington and his classic text *Political Order in Changing Societies* (1968), which, reacting to the first wave of modernisation theories, showed that the pace of development tends to be very uneven and mutually conflictual in individual social dimensions. For this reason the internal dynamic of emergent modernising countries – previously European countries, at present developing countries – generates intense political conflict and instability. This is due to the mismatch between the excessively rapid pace of socioeconomic change and the slow rate of change to rigid political systems. During modernisation, socioeconomic changes produce a mass-mobilised population and more and more political actors entering into contentious politics with each other: intellectuals, the middle classes, students, workers and finally peasants. However, the rapid politicisation of society is usually played out in the absence of adequate political institutions that could co-opt political actors into the political system and offer them rules and mechanisms for non-violent contention and the promotion of their interests. Political actors are banished to the peripheries of the political system. Their pursuit of political participation is then realised on the streets in the form of direct action: demonstrations, strikes, violent protests, coups and revolution. And so while traditional societies are (still) politically stable, modern societies are (again) politically stabilised. However, *modernising* societies are politically destabilised, with a higher risk of coups in the first stage of modernisation and a higher risk of revolution in the second stage, when a genuinely mass political participation has already been achieved. In short, *tradition* and *modernity* are accompanied by stability, and modernisation is accompanied by instability and escalating conflict (Huntington 1968, cf. Fukuyama 2006). Huntington comes up with a counterintuitive finding: without commensurate political development, modernisation may result in tyranny, political and social chaos, civil war, and outbursts of political violence (cf. Fukuyama 2011).

In this respect the Middle East is no exception. It is politically destabilised for the same reasons as Europe was in the past and other regions of the post-colonial world later on. The analyses of the rise of oppositional Islam by writers such as Vallerie Hoffman (1995) and Sami Zubaida (2009) focus on the uneven pace of change in the Middle East in individual social dimensions. In his essays on the Arab Spring, Francis Fukuyama (2011) examines the mismatch between the pace of social, economic and political developments and explicitly highlights the topicality of the approach taken by Samuel P. Huntington. Fukuyama also describes his teacher as one of the last researchers who attempted a genuinely comprehensive overview of social change and tried to create an all-encompassing theory of political change. According to Fukuyama, most theoreticians these days are specialised in one dimension of social change and do not try to understand the relationship between its political, economic and social dimensions. For this reason we have a problem understanding the Middle Eastern world (Fukuyama 2011).

However, Huntington conspicuously overlooked the role of *external factors* in the destabilisation of modernising post-colonial countries, above all the role of the geopolitical context characterised by the Cold War with its bloody, proxy conflicts being played out in the early stages of the modernisation of the Third World. In addition, he overlooked the role of premodern culture and above all *religion*, since he was writing in the spirit of the secularisation theory prevalent at that time, which anticipated a decline in the influence of religion in modernising societies. However, these factors can be consistently built into our provisional model of uneven modernisation, and we shall look to the latest theory of multiple modernities for inspiration.

SECOND THEORETICAL INSPIRATION: MULTIPLE MODERNITIES

Classical modernisation theory mistakenly assumes the existence of only a single universal model, applicable to all societies, of the modernisation process, which reads from the same script all around the world and culminates in an identical way of organising society in an identical version of modernity. According to this narrative the Western version of modernity ought to be asserting itself globally, since modernisation and Westernisation are seen as synonymous. However, the competing concept of *multiple modernities*, based on a comparative analysis of different forms of modernity in various parts of the world and in different stages of the development of individual societies, emphasises the existence of multiple models of modernity and the existence of multiple paths to modernity. In addition, modernity itself is never definitive but contingent upon self-reflection and critical questioning. Instead of "the End of History" we are witnessing rather the historical stratification of different models of modernity in the manner of geological strata (cf. Arnason 2009, 2010, Eisenstadt 2003, Spohn 2001).

What are the reasons for the institutional and ideological diversity of modernity? Firstly, multiple versions of modernity are the outcomes of conflict between different social and political movements promoting their own, mutually competing concepts of modernity, their own *programmes of modernity*. Islamists are an example of such a movement. They are both the product of swift social change and, through the promotion of their own project, the driver of accelerated change, as when, for example, they approach political power as an instrument for the radical transformation of society. Their utopian programme promises to create a new man and a new society, and even a new international order and a new collective identity that bridges the fragmentation of society into different national, ethnic, social, or regional identities. At the same time they have a predisposition toward totalitarianism, when, like the communists or Nazis, they deem the interest of the collective to be superior to that of the individual (Eisenstadt 2000).

Secondly, different versions of modernity are the outcome of a *positive or negative* profiling in respect of the Western model of modernity. The Western model operates as a *reference point* by virtue of its historical primacy, and as a consequence cannot be ignored but must be addressed head on, whatever the consequences (Eisenstadt 2000). Furthermore, individual versions of modernity cannot be studied in isolation because their *interdependence* is increasing and because non-Western versions of modernity are often the result of disparate reactions to the rise and global expansion of the Western version that they have had to confront (Arnason 2010). The Western version of modernity is regarded with ambivalence in the non-Western world, which is why we see there a "continuous selection, reinterpretation and reformulation of these imported ideas". For instance, Islamists define themselves in relation to the Western model of modernity. They attempt to select and adapt certain of its elements. However, they also reinterpret them within the concepts of the Islamic religious tradition: "These movements have attempted to dissociate Westernisation from modernity, denying the Western monopoly on modernity and rejecting the Western cultural program as the epitome of modernity." (Eisenstadt 2000: 15, 22).

Thirdly, different versions of modernity are the consequence of the interaction of universal modernising processes on the one hand, and local traditions, value systems, cultural assumptions and specific historical experience, including the experience and legacy of colonialism, on the other. For this reason, in the colonial and post-colonial period, modern and traditional sources are connected and combined, and this results in the formation of an ideological and institutional diversity of forms of modernity (Eisenstadt 2000). The relationship between and compatibility of more or less reconstructed or even invented traditional components and modern elements adapted to a varying degree to the local cultural context differs in individual versions of modernity.

Traditions can be used to legitimise modernity or to subject it to harsh critique. Temporarily suspended or repressed traditions can be rediscovered in reaction to modernity. Viable aspects of tradition can adapt and evolve and even prosper in symbiosis with modernity. Tradition itself therefore appears to be diverse, in the same way as modernity, and different elements of tradition interact with modernity in different ways (Arnason 2010). The fact that different pre-modern traditions and historical experiences (cultural zones) lead under the same degree of socioeconomic development to a different outcome in terms of value-based, and subsequently institutional (secularisation and democratisation), change has been empirically documented by the team led by Ronald Inglehart using data from the World Values Study (Inglehart and Norris 2004, Inglehart and Welzel 2006).

If, therefore, the classical theory of modernisation ignored or at least underestimated the role of the cultural and geopolitical context in which modernisation takes place, my model of uneven modernisation rectifies this state of affairs. A comparative analysis of the Middle Eastern pattern of modernisation will therefore take its context and the interaction of individual levels of uneven modernisation with this context into consideration (see fig. 3).

Firstly, we highlight the interaction of the modernisation process and the pre-modern cultural substrate, i.e. the primordial tribal or ethnical identities and above all the Islamic religion within the context of which uneven modernisation is taking place. In this respect Islam is co-forming and modifying modernisation. At the same time, however, within the context of objective experience with uneven modernisation certain aspects of Islam are being promoted to the detriment of others. Yet Islam is providing inspiration to opposing political actors and is becoming a source of the political imaginary, criticism and mobilisation. However, the point is not to ascertain what Islam says about current modernising processes and the impacts thereof and to become caught up in a never-ending dispute led by Orientalists and primarily Muslims themselves (cf. Roy 2004), but to attempt to indicate what Islamists and other inhabitants of the Middle East facing the impacts of uneven modernisation are saying about what Islam has to say about their experience that is relevant. The attempt, therefore, is to show what Islam-inspired discourses are being generated by uneven modernisation within the geopolitical context under consideration.

In this respect Islam is not to be seen as the main, or even sole, *independent* variable determining political instability, the character of political conflicts, and the repertoires of contention. Similarly, it is not the main variable determining the growth of political Islam. I do not subscribe to those culturological arguments proclaiming that Islam is showing its true face and is the cause of all problems. However, it is also not to be taken as a completely *dependent* variable, as a passive victim of cold-blooded abuse in political rivalry being driven by social, economic and political circumstances and therefore vulnerable to the doctrinaire interpretations of a range of different interest groups. These two extreme positions either claim that Islam is responsible for everything or for absolutely nothing (cf. Juergensmeyer 2004). However, alongside uneven modernisation and the geopolitical context, I take Islam to be one of the independent variables that *only* in mutual *interaction* is playing a role in the growth of political Islam, shaping the character of political conflicts and the overall (in)stability of the region. The question of whether Islam has a destabilising or stabilising effect within the context of uneven modernisation will be put under the spotlight. At the same time, I incline to the hypothesis that, without Islamic social ethics and institutions, the Middle East would be unable to withstand the onslaught of uneven modernisation and there would be destabilisation and a far more dramatic breakdown of social order.

Secondly, I take into account the broader international political context of uneven modernisation in the region. This has long been characterised mainly by the effects of European *colonialism*, which created artificial, weak and unworkable post-colonial states. Beginning in the 19th century, French, British and Italian territorial expansion led to the creation of colonies, protectorates and other dependent zones. After the First World War this process culminated with the break-up of the Ottoman Empire and the carving up of its territory by the Europeans, with France and Great Britain, under the terms of a secret agreement (the Sykes-Pikot agreement of 1917), leading the way. The establishment of Middle Eastern states failed to respect the right of local peoples to self-determination and was driven purely by the interests of the great powers. As a result, local populations feel only a limited allegiance to their states, i.e. to their borders, power elites and institutions. Geographical boundaries do not respect the boundaries of particular communities. While in Europe a strong national identity tended to precede the emergence of an independent nation state, in the Middle East new artificial states often came into being that then retrospectively attempted to shape the national identity of the population. This also led to peoples being left without their own state (e.g. the Kurds, Palestinians, Druze, Yazidis) or, conversely, the existence of many different groups forced to live within the boundaries of one highly heterogeneous state (Libya, Lebanon, Syria, Iraq) with which they do not identify. Exceptions to this model are Egypt, Turkey, Iran, and perhaps Morocco, with their long traditions of statehood, or Tunisia with its relatively homogenous population. What we see are artificial and unclear borders that do not respect natural historical boundaries (e.g. of the Ottoman provinces), which lead to interstate conflicts, separatism, or the poor management of shared watercourses and irrigation systems (cf. Barr 2012).

The international political context of Middle Eastern modernisation is also characterised and shaped by the Israeli-Palestinian and the *Arab-Israeli conflict.* This conflict has generated wave upon wave of refugees, repeatedly destabilised the region, and stood in the way of its economic and political development. Dictatorships have justified restricting political rights and civil liberties, increasing the defence budget and even their own failure by appealing to a state of war or the threat posed by Israel (cf. Hourani 2010, Laurens 2012). The international context of Middle Eastern modernisation is also characterised by the fact that, unlike the historical modernisation of Europe, it is not taking place in a global core, but on a *periphery*. If the core region of the world system is above all the geopolitically dominant West, Middle Eastern countries (with the exception of Israel) are located on the periphery or semi-periphery of the world system. For this reason, modernisation is not accompanied by world dominance, which would allow some of the proliferating population to be exported in sufficient numbers to other continents, as happened in the case of modernising Europe. Within the context of uneven modernisation, population pressure is generating social tension and political instability in the Middle East.

Finally, the Middle East is characterised by important natural resources (oil and natural gas), a geostrategic position between Europe, Africa and Asia, strategic routes of oil pipelines and sea lanes (Suez, the Strait of Hormuz), and the ensuing emergence of *rentier states* and strong interference on the part of the superpowers during the Cold War and significant external interventions after it ended. Colonialism and the intervention of the West in the affairs of the Islamic world had always provoked a response in the form of religious revivals (Kropáček 2003, Lewis 2003a, Dekmejian 1995). Thanks to its strategic sources of oil (two thirds of global reserves), after the Second World War the region became the leading battleground of the Cold War and remains a geopolitical epicentre to the present day (Brzezinski 1999, Amin 2004, Robejšek 2006, Šlachta 2007, Tomeš et al. 2007, Fawcett 2009).

However, Middle Eastern regimes have long feared the invasion of foreign ideas more than military invasion (Huntington 2006). The most elite military units are not created and trained to protect the nation from an enemy from without but opposition from within (Klare 2004). The vast oil wealth and other unearned income of rentier economies, combined with imports of the latest Western military and police surveillance technology, have allowed Middle Eastern regimes to create a sophisticated repressive apparatus that has no analogy in history or in other regions of today's developing world (Zakaria 2004).

Fearful of losing power, dictatorships alienated and isolated from the majority population (Saudi Arabia, Kuwait, Egypt, Jordan and Iran up till 1979) have long counted on the comprehensive military, diplomatic, food and financial support of the West. However, the increasingly visible presence of American soldiers and Western companies in individual countries is itself becoming an important factor in the destabilisation and delegitimisation of the regimes. It forces Western governments to intensify their activities in the region and to step up support for authoritarian regimes (Klare 2004, Pfaff 2010). This then plays into the hands of Islamists and other opposition groups, which criticise the West for its alliance with unpopular dictators while loudly proclaiming its support for democracy, freedom and human rights. A typical example of how this narrative is played out was the CIA-orchestrated overthrow of the democratically elected prime minister of Iran in 1953. More recently, the discrepancy between pro-democracy rhetoric and the realpolitik of the USA was clearly manifest in Washington's dismay at the success of Islamists in elections in Morocco, Kuwait, Jordan, and especially Egypt and Palestine. On the other hand, Middle Eastern regimes can easily be denounced by pointing to their links with the USA, a tactic frequently used by opposition groups in individual countries (Lewis 2003b, Ottaway 2010). The West thus becomes a secondary enemy of Islamists and other opposition groups, while the primary enemy remains their own regimes (Juergensmeyer 1994, 2002).

A NEW THEORETICAL MODEL OF MODERNISATION IN THE MIDDLE EAST

The new theoretical model that will inform all the analyses conducted in individual chapters of this book encompasses the mutual and multiple interaction of the following independent variables (see fig. 3): (1) Islam and its politically relevant imaginary, concepts, symbols and meanings, (2) rapid demographic and social modernisation; population explosion, swift urbanisation, a rise in literacy, a boom in higher education and the expansion of the media, (3) slower, fluctuating economic modernisation; the development of the labour market, economic growth, economic diversification, (4) negligible, even regressive political modernisation; a weak state and a lack of the democratisation that would enable ever larger numbers of new political actors to be assimilated into the political system, (5) the unfavourable broader international context of social change in the Middle East; the existence and maintenance of artificial post-colonial states, support for authoritarian regimes by the superpowers, the oil factor creating rentier political systems blocking democratisation and economic diversification, the Israeli-Arab conflict and geopolitical tensions disrupting stability and long-term development, and limited channels for sufficient emigration abroad (cf. Černý 2014).

I work on the assumption that primordial identities and Islam, with its politically relevant concepts, the unfavourable international and post-colonial historical context, rapid demographic and social change, slower economic

Fig. 3 A model of Middle Eastern modernisation and its context: the interaction of independent variables

| International context (post-colonialism, oil, the Arab-Israeli conflict) |
| Political modernisation (stagnating or regressing) |
| Economic modernisation (slow or stagnating) |
| Social and demographic modernisation (very fast) |
| Islam and primordial identity – pre-modern cultural substrate (a source of political symbols, meanings, language, imaginaries, historical memory) |

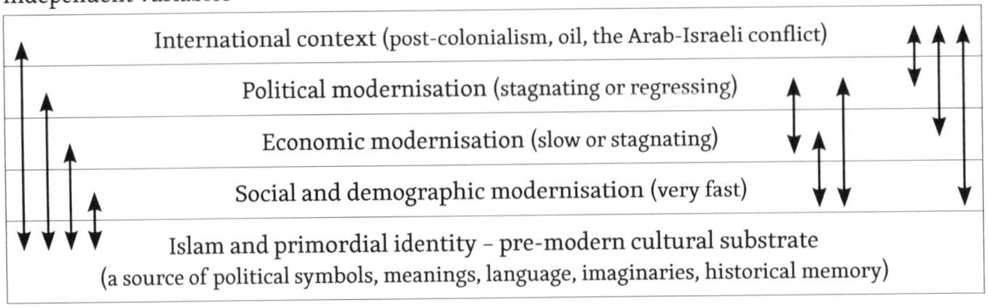

N.B. Possible interactions and tensions are shown by the arrows.

development that is unstable over time, and a rigid political system, are *independent variables* that can *in themselves* only partially and *inadequately* explain the instability of the Middle East. For this reason, I do not consider analyses working in isolation with individual independent variables as effective. What is important is the overlapping and intersecting of these variables at a given time and space. Only the *mutual interaction* of independent variables generates the ensuing instability of the region. All variables are equally important in the model of mutual interaction; both the more or less static (the international context and political systems), and the relatively dynamic (demographic and social change). Overall, then, this is not a model that offers a mono-causal explanation of political instability (e.g. Islam/the demographic explosion is responsible for everything). On the contrary, it is a theoretical model that operates with multi-causal explanations.

This theoretical model is a somewhat approximate but necessary generalisation of a far more complex reality. It is an abstract construct emphasising those aspects of reality and the changes thereto that I deem important when analysing the causes of instability. Conversely, I leave to one side other aspects of reality in order to make sense of what would otherwise be an unmanageable complexity. The theoretical model therefore represents a kind of Weberian *ideal type*, which, albeit in simplified form, provides a basic guideline for orientation within a far more complex reality. In addition, an ideal type in the form of a theoretical model can be compared and contrasted with empirical reality and its legitimacy ascertained.

FOUR POSSIBLE MACRO COMPARISONS OF THE MIDDLE EASTERN PATTERN OF MODERNISATION

The theoretical model allows us to analyse the degree of unevenness of modernisation of the Middle East as a region, while taking into account the broader context. However, it also provides a framework for four types of grand historical-sociological comparisons. This is made possible by the fact that the modernisation process represents a relatively universal historical phenomenon, which nevertheless has specific historical and geographical variations. The comparison will be both *synchronous* and *asynchronous*, i.e. it will compare processes running in parallel at any given time, as well as ana-logous processes running at different times or according to different phases. The purpose of these comparisons will be to determine in what respect the model of post-colonial Middle Eastern modernisation is *specific* and in what respect it is *universal* and comparable with other modernisation patterns.

Firstly, the main focus will be on a systematic comparison of the pattern of post-colonial Middle Eastern modernisation (1950–2015) and the moderni-sation pattern in other global macro-regions, especially post-colonial (Sub-Saharan Africa, South America, Asia, etc.) or post-communist. Here the main hypothesis will be that Middle Eastern modernisation has been significantly uneven over the long term in respect of the individual dimensions of social change in comparison with other macro-regions. This explains the current relatively high instability of the Middle East compared with other macro-regions, where modernisation over the last few decades was not as uneven, mainly because democracy's third wave was taking place in these regions or they reported stronger economic growth.

Secondly, the individual phases of post-colonial Middle Eastern mod-ernisation will be compared in terms of how uneven the pace of develop-ment is within individual dimensions during individual periods. The main hypothesis here will be that the unevenness in the pace of development in individual dimensions has increased over time. In the 1950s and 60s it was less pronounced, but then peaked at the start of the 21st century, a fact that in part explains the timing of the Arab Spring. The Arab world especially, as a subset of the Middle Eastern region, stands out for the way the gap has inexorably widened between the pace of development of individual dimen-sions of modernisation.

Thirdly, the degree of unevenness will be compared of the post-colonial modernisation process across individual countries within the Middle Eastern region. Emphasis will be placed on a comparison of the Arab countries. The main hypothesis here will be that the degree of political stability/instability of individual countries during the course of the Arab Spring (2011) is par-tially explained by the degree of unevenness of the modernisation process of these countries.

Fourthly, I will conduct an additional historical comparison of current post-colonial Middle Eastern modernisation and early Western European modernisation. One of the premises of this book is that we achieve a bet-ter understanding of the contemporary Middle East through a deeper understanding of our own modern history. The better we understand European modernisation, the better we understand its Middle Eastern counterpart. Furthermore, we will be in a position to see their similarities and differences. European modernisation took place in an analogous way from the end of the 18th century to the beginning of the 20th century and was accompanied by similar political destabilisation. However, while modernisation in the Middle East is being accompanied by a crisis of most secular ideologies and the rise of political Islam, early European modernisation was accompanied by heightened social and political conflict that was manifest externally by the dominance of secular ideologies, though conservative Christian ideology also played a role: from the French Revolution in 1789 via the revolutions of 1848 to the rise of communism and explosive nationalism at the start of the First World War.

My main hypothesis here is that the pace of social and demographic change in the Middle East is significantly faster than it was in modern Europe, when all changes took place at a more relaxed tempo. On the other hand, the pace of economic and above all political modernisation in the Middle East lags behind that of the historical development of the economic and political subsystems of early modern Europe. A historical comparison with Europe reveals the overall asymmetry of Middle Eastern modernisation to be greater. Western European modernisation was also uneven across its main dimensions, but *to a lesser extent*: there was a greater *cohesion* between rapid social and demographic change and economic change (the Industrial Revolution) and political change (the creation of centralised national states and rule of law, democratisation). *Structurally* speaking, then, a Middle Eastern region destabilised by internal conflict is more reminiscent of early, albeit less uneven, Western European modernisation with all of its secondary, unintended consequences than medieval Europe (a popular cliché).

However, a historical comparison with Europe reveals the broader geopolitical context of Middle Eastern modernisation to be extremely unfavourable. The process is being played out on the post-colonial *periphery* and not at the core of the global system during the era of colonial expansion, as it was in the case of Western Europe. For example, it was this fact that enabled European colonies to absorb the increased numbers of European citizens caused by demographic growth: migration to non-European continents effectively released the pressure of accumulating social and political tensions.

On the other hand, a cultural context characterised by the dominance of Islam, clearly absent in the case of early European modernisation, has ambivalent outcomes. For this reason we cannot say that, with its imaginary and institutions, Islam represents an incontrovertible factor in the political instability differentiating the Middle Eastern pattern of modernisation from its Western counterpart, which is often the conclusion of Western analysts.

Indeed, within the context of Middle Eastern uneven modernisation, Islam is often a stabilising factor. Primordial identities such as extended family, clans and tribes operate in a similarly ambivalent way.

OPERATIONALISATION OF THE MODEL OF UNEVEN MODERNISATION AND SOURCES OF EMPIRICAL DATA

The aim of *operationalisation* is to link up theoretical and empirical findings by converting a theoretical model into empirically comprehensible, investigable and falsifiable form. The individual dimensions of modernisation and its broader context will be represented by empirical indicators so that it becomes possible to examine the degree of unevenness of Middle Eastern modernisation and undertake the relevant comparisons where appropriate. In order to operationalise and verify the model, many indicators will be used in the form of time series charting the development of the political, economic, social and demographic dimensions of modernisation.

The indicators will be presented in *non-aggregated* form, especially when comparing the unevenness of the development of individual countries in the region. They will also be presented in *aggregated* form when comparing the unevenness of the development of individual global macro-regions or the unevenness of individual stages (five-year periods or decades) of the modernisation of the Middle East. Similarly, I shall use *simple* statistical indicators (e.g. population growth rate), as well as *synthetic* indices I have calculated from several simple indicators (e.g. a state's capacity to govern).

Firstly, the relevant data will cover two sub-dimensions of *political modernisation*: the extent of political rights and civil liberties, and the capacity of a state to govern effectively within its territory. The first sub-dimension will draw on indices used by the organisations Freedom House and The Economist Intelligence Unit. It will also use data on the perception of corruption gathered by Transparency International and data on the freedom of the press gathered by Reporters Without Borders in its World Press Freedom Index. The capacity of a state to govern effectively within its territory will be covered by the many indicators of the World Bank (the World Governance Indicators, or WGIs).

Secondly, the dimension of *economic modernisation* will be examined using data on the overall pace of economic growth, the degree to which an economy is dependent on exports of natural resources, and Gross Domestic Product per capita figures as provided by the World Bank and the United Nations Development Report. Key data will include information on unemployment in general and youth unemployment in particular provided by the International Labour Organisation (ILO). Additionally, I will attempt to take into account data on the level of social inequality and the proportion of the population living in absolute poverty. This data indicates the degree of inequality in the distribution of economic resources within a society and is reported by the World Bank. I will also look at the development of world food prices (the Food and Agriculture Organisation, or FAO) and the proportion of a family's budget that goes on buying food (United States Department of Agriculture, Economic Research Service).

Thirdly, the *social dimension* of modernisation will be examined using data on the development of educational systems, urbanisation, and the expansion of the media. Indicators will be used charting the quantitative expansion of *educational systems* as a proportion of the literate adult population, the proportion of children attending primary schools, and the number of young people attending secondary schools and universities. This data is updated every year by UNESCO. The quality of education is in part examined using data on the international testing of the knowledge and skills of pupils provided on a regular basis by two international research organisations: the Programme for International Student Assessment (PISA) and Trends in International Mathematics and Science Study (TIMSS). I will also work with other data, e.g. with the share of gross domestic product that a government allocates from the state budget to the educational sector. The World Bank periodically provides indicators charting the development of *urbanisation*, i.e. the number of people from the population as a whole living in cities. I shall also draw on the United Nations Development Report that shows the percentage of an urban population living in slums. The proliferation of the media will be illustrated by a host of indicators. The spread of television, the internet and mobile TV is monitored by the World Bank. The circulation of daily newspapers per thousand inhabitants is monitored by UNESCO. In addition, I shall draw heavily on representative sociological surveys examining individual media ratings (Pew Center, Zogby International, TESEV).

Fourthly, I will examine the *demographic dimension* of modernisation using indicators reported by the World Bank on the population growth rate and the proportion of young people (aged 15–24) of the population as a whole. I will also refer to the age pyramids provided by the UN demographic agency POPIN.

I believe that this is the first time the Middle East has been charted and compared so comprehensively and systematically. However, I was greatly inspired by the political economists Alan Richards and John Waterbury and their classic study entitled *A Political Economy of the Middle East* (3rd edition, 2008), in which, using numerous statistical indicators, they operationalise their own theoretical model and systematically compare the region of the Middle East with other world macro-regions. Similarly, the Russian team headed by Andrej Korotajev, Julia Zinkina and Alexandra Chodunov (2012) attempted using a mass of statistical data to analyse systemically the causes of the Arab Spring.

FROM THE MACRO-LEVEL OF STRUCTURES TO THE MICRO-LEVEL OF ACTORS AND THEIR ACTIONS: MECHANISMS OF DESTABILISATION

The last step in our analyses entails a transition from the *macro-level* of uneven structural change to the *micro-level* of social and political actors and their actions, i.e. the transition from relatively long-term and gradually escalating and accumulating processes, summarised here as uneven modernisation, to the social and political consequences ensuing therefrom that generate social conflict and instability. This also involves the transition from *independent* variables to *dependent* variables, from causes to effects. In addition, it reflects the transition from less observable and relatively inconspicuous long-term trends to their visible, often dramatic and externally manifested impacts.

Fig. 4 Relationship between the macro and micro levels: from structural change to the actions of individuals

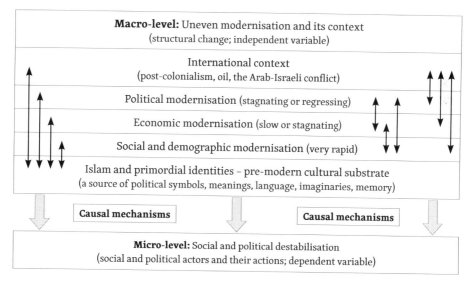

This step in my analysis will involve a detailed inventory wherever possible of all relevant *causal mechanisms* by which macro-processes can influence micro-reality and the actions of actors. It will therefore be a systematic inventory of particular causal mechanisms that, through a logical chain of cause and effect, link up uneven modernisation and its broader context with the accumulation of frustration and social conflict, the decline of regimes, the rise of opposition groups, and social and political instability. I will therefore investigate systematically all the individual relevant interactions between the individual dimensions of uneven modernisation and its broader context, and trace on a micro-level the concrete social and political consequences of these uneven processes and the interactions between them (see fig. 4).

At this point the theoretical model of uneven modernisation and its context will provide us with a clear framework and a sound basis for a systematic investigation of the concrete causal mechanisms that can be identified in a highly confusing, almost impenetrable reality. For this reason the theoretical model will determine the structure of this book, the logic of its interpretation, and the sequence of individual analyses. When indentifying individual causal mechanisms I shall draw on the literature that already exists from a range of specialised fields, the field research conducted, and detailed case studies of individual countries of the region of the Middle East or of individual phenomena and the sub-processes being played out in this region. Though my work is based on comparative historical sociology analysing long-term historical processes, this level of analysis will also deploy to the full an *interdisciplinary approach* that will draw on Middle Eastern Studies as well as the sociology of religion, political sociology, political economy, social geography, demography, history and political science. I believe this approach to be valuable and innovative in that it identifies several dozen specific causal mechanisms of destabilisation in already existing literature that are often published in a highly implicit form and within very diverse research contexts. I bring together these causal mechanisms by embedding them within the framework of the theory of uneven modernisation, and in doing so clarify and systematise the interpretation of the multiple causes of instability in the Middle East. However, by investigating individual causal mechanisms I also justify and defend the relevance of the uneven modernisation model as a general explanatory framework for the interpretation of Middle Eastern instability.

Individual causal mechanisms will be gradually discussed in the subchapters of the book. For instance, the interaction of rapid demographic growth, behind which lags economic development and job creation, leads within the conservative cultural context of Islam, which emphasises the value of marriage and large families, to the demographic marginalisation of an entire generation of young people who do not have sufficient funds at their disposal to start a family. Such people no longer have the social status of children, but are still not regarded as adults, and this makes for uncertainty, disaffection, and potential political radicalisation. Similarly, the discrepancy between the rapid pace of demographic growth and closed, rigid political systems results in predominantly young populations being governed by ever older dictators.

The generation gap between the power elite and the majority population thus increases. This leads to mutual alienation and increases the potential for conflict. An analysis of these very concrete causal mechanisms will form the main part of this book.

Finally, mention must be made of the nature of the relatively *loose* relationship between macro-reality and micro-reality, between structure and action, between uneven modernisation and social destabilisation. By *social structure* we have in mind the complex of *relationships* between individual components of the social whole, i.e. an aggregate of relations by which partial components within one social system are connected. For this reason, my analysis of social structure will focus on the method by which the social whole is formed. It will analyse the set of mutual relationships between elements or the mutual *configuration* of individual parts of this whole; in this case the configuration of and relations between individual dimensions of the modernisation process and its broader cultural, historical and geopolitical context. These elements – and above all the relations, configurations and interactions between them – characterise the nature of the entire social system and differentiate it from other systems. That is why it is possible to undertake a comparative analysis of societies of a similar historical and cultural type; in our case of modernising societies. Although social structures are relatively *stable* in time, they too are subject to long-term, gradual historical change that I shall monitor using many different macro-indicators. This means that by focusing on social structure it is possible to analyse the development of a given society in time. The transformation of the main structural features of a given society then gives us a clue as to the character of the overall social change of this society; in our case the character of change in the Middle East is characterised by the high unevenness of the pace of the development of individual elements or social subsystems (cf. Velký sociologický 1996: 1239–1241, Giddens 1971 and 1976).

The key thing here is to understand structures as relatively stable *frameworks* for the actions of both individual and collective actors. The existence of structures precedes that of actors. Structures are external to actors and *shape* their *actions*. Structures do not determine the actions of actors, but place certain limitations on their freedom of choice and autonomy. However, they create *pressures* that mean that a certain mode of action is more probable than another within the framework of the structure in question. This leads to the formation of certain prevailing patterns of behaviour within any one structure. However, if actors and the patterns of their behaviour are directly observable, the same cannot be said of structures. If we want to explain the observable actions of actors, we must determine the concrete form of structural pressures acting upon them, and thus determine the status of a given actor within the social structure as a whole (cf. Arnason 2010, Giddens 2009).

In my analysis those structural pressures shaping the actions of individual and collective actors are causal mechanisms. Specific causal mechanisms can be traced within the structure of relationships and configurations of the individual elements of uneven modernisation and its context, and thus the origin of these structural pressures, i.e. causal mechanisms, can also be explained. However, causal mechanisms create only pressures and do not ever in themselves directly and unambiguously determine actions. If, therefore, the social structure does not directly determine social action and allows for considerable latitude in terms of response, this will result in a relatively high variability of responses on the part of actors to uneven modernisation.

Uneven modernisation in the Middle East is thus the most general common cause of the many diverse forms and external manifestations of the region's destabilisation: increased frustration and latent social tension and visible social conflicts; the collapse of the legitimacy of post-colonial regimes and a rise in the popularity of oppositional political Islam and pro-democratic liberal movements attempting to replace these regimes; mass migration and political terrorism on the part of people excluded from the economic and political subsystems; and unarmed but often violent revolutions and bloody civil wars fought by those who want to change the status quo or offer a new meaning and direction to their lives.

Similar structural pressures characteristic of the entire region are manifest at different times in different places. Different national contexts, with their own historical and political dynamic, also play a crucial role. And above all we must not overlook the freedom of choice of individuals, for instance socio-economically and demographically marginalised young people, who are unable to realise their potential in professional or family life and may find alternative means of self-realisation and sources of positive self-esteem as much in a militant religious movement as in a community of opposition bloggers and civic journalists. Similarly, the alienation of a predominantly young population from ageing dictators can be manifest in an apolitical stance and distaste for politics as such, as well as a tendency to subscribe to opposition movements comprising generationally closer activists.

The starting point of all individual analyses of the causal mechanisms leading to political destabilisation that form the subject matter of each chapter involves embedding these mechanisms within the structure of unequal modernisation viewed within its broader cultural, historical and geopolitical context. However, this structuralist approach is then combined eclectically with other theoretical approaches and paradigms that are relevant to the examination of individual dimensions of the process of unequal modernisation and endeavour to explain the conduct of political actors within this framework.

METHODOLOGICAL, TERMINOLOGICAL
AND PERSONAL OBSERVATIONS

When the social sciences use the term "society", they are often implicitly referring to the nation state. The state as the basic unit of analysis prevails. The aim of this work is to overcome a *state-centric* and politico-centric perspective and think primarily in the category of the broader *macro-region*. This does not possess a unified political organisation or clearly and unequivocally defined borders. However, it shares a similar historical, geopolitical, cultural, demographic, social, economic and political *profile* (cf. Mauss 1929/1930, Durkheim and Mauss 1913, Arnason 2009). Furthermore, the Middle Eastern macro-region is so interconnected internally in terms of migration, communication and media, and local people identify with it to such an extent, that an event in one of its parts often unexpectedly influences events in other parts. As the leading American researcher in the field, F. Gregory Gause III, said self-critically of mainstream political science and Middle Eastern studies (2011): "What happens in one Arab state can affect others (...) As a result, scholars and policymakers can no longer approach countries on a case-by-case basis."

This is why in this book I work on the assumption that offshoots of instability in different parts of the region grow from the same structural roots, though at the same time they are modified by specific local, national and historical circumstances and also by the dynamics of a different form of reaction on the part of the relevant actors, above all governments. For instance, the Arab Spring (2011) had the same structural causes everywhere, which is why it resonated powerfully throughout the entire region. Nevertheless, its course and results differed dramatically in individual parts of the region. Generally it can be said that, though we observe symptoms of destabilisation across the entire region, these appear in very diverse forms in different places. This book aims to offer a common denominator in the shape of uneven modernisation and its broader context.

However, there is no consensus in the academic community as regards a precise definition of the Middle Eastern region. The region cannot be simply equated with the Islamic world or the Arab world (Šanc 2011). Some writers argue that the very unstable and variable borders of the region are what characterises the Middle East, a claim that clarifies nothing and if anything makes things even more obscure. They also speak of a dry climate and a lack of water, the existence of ancient civilisations, and the fact that the region is the birthplace of the three great monotheistic religions. In modern times, the character of the region has been shaped by a high level of religious, ethnic and cultural pluralism, which has generated disputes, conflicts and instability. Another feature attributed to the region is its rich reserves of oil (De Blij and Muller 2006).

From a slightly different perspective the historian Nikki Keddie (1973) identifies the Middle East with the territory that the Arabs acquired during the expansion of the 7th and 8th centuries. This territory is characterised by a desertified and semi-desertified environment where irrigated agriculture or a nomadic way of life predominates. The Middle East is clearly separated from neighbouring regions by impenetrable deserts and high mountain ranges (according to Šanc 2011). Politological definitions emphasise the authoritarian character of the local regimes, the rentier character of economies dependent on the extraction and export of oil, the spread of Islam, the long-standing Israeli-Palestinian conflict, and the geopolitically strategic location of the region at the intersection of Africa, Asia and Europe (cf. Sorli, Gleditsch and Strand 2005). Any definition of the region therefore tends to be arbitrarily adjusted to suit the character of the research objectives (Kropáček 1999, Šanc 2011).

For the purposes of this work I will use the definition of the region used by the United Nations, namely, the region of the Middle East and North Africa (MENA) containing the following countries: Israel, Iran, Turkey and predominantly Arab countries beginning with Morocco, Algeria, Tunisia and Libya (the Maghreb countries), via Egypt to Saudi Arabia, Kuwait, Bahrain, Qatar, United Arab Emirates, Oman and Yemen (countries of the Arabian Peninsula), and ending with Lebanon, Palestine, Syria, Jordan and Iraq (the Mashriq countries). In individual analyses and interpretations I shall look at the subset of Arabic Middle Eastern countries. Wherever the region is to be understood in a different way, the reader will be clearly alerted.

A second brief comment relates to the difference between the scholarly perspective of the insider and *outsider*, i.e. the difference between immanence and transcendence (cf. Šubrt 1996). Though I travel frequently and often to the Middle East and have friends there, I am not a permanent inhabitant of the region, something I regard as an advantage when getting to know the region. The role of Central European outsider makes easier a disengagement from vested interests and ideologies that I would be embroiled in if I lived in the region. Another great advantage is the fact that the Czech Republic was never a colonial or neo-colonial power. If, therefore, knowledge and the means of its production tends to be strongly linked to power structures (cf. Said 2008), a Czech perspective on the region is not as encumbered and deformed by such power relations, bloodshed and historical grievances, notwithstanding the fact that the Kingdom of Bohemia used to be part of the Habsburg Monarchy, which for centuries competed with the Ottoman Empire (cf. Mendel, Ostřanský, Rataj 2007).

However, the role of outsider above all means being able to take a detached view of Middle Eastern society free of emotional baggage. When a researcher is part of a society and the very problems he is researching, his ability to step back and look at things from a distance without emotion is severely compromised. It is more difficult to achieve a neutral, balanced analysis. A classic example of the potential effectiveness of the expert view of the outsider is the still unrivalled analysis of American exceptionalism written by the French aristocrat Alexis Tocqueville (1992), to which we might add the famous analysis of American racism written by the Swedish Gunnar Myrdal (1944).

My third observation relates to the conceptual definition of political Islam. The rise of Islamic movements took place to varying degrees, with various twists and turns, within roughly the same time period (from the start of the 1970s) in all countries of the Middle East. This mainly involves the Egyptian Muslim Brotherhood and its offshoots present in most Arab countries. It would also include, for example, the Turkish conservative AK party and its numerous predecessors, the Algerian Islamic Salvation Front, the Tunisian Ennahda Movement, Palestinian Hamas, Lebanese Hezbollah, and the many Iranian revolutionary movements. It also involves a host of smaller militant groups, including Al-Qaeda and Islamic State (Kepel 1996, 2002).

What do these movements, organisations and political parties have in common? What alternative do they offer? There is no complete consensus in this respect. For instance, Mark Juergensmeyer (1994, 2008) classifies most Islamists within the broad category of *religious nationalism*. He views this as a new type of nationalism, one reacting to the crisis of secular ideology and resorting to traditional culture, values, and especially religion. The ambition of this global trend, which is not restricted to the Islamic world and the Middle East, is to bring together modern politics and traditional religion, thus arriving at its own version of modernity. Religious nationalists argue that the nation should be defined and the nation state legitimised using the religious traditions of the majority. At the same time this movement campaigns against unsuccessful secular ideologies and corrupt politicians, who, it claims, have failed utterly. Its political conflict with the latter is often seen as part of a metaphysical conflict between good and evil (cf. Černý 2009).

Other writers speak of *Islamist movements* and take these to be "activist groups that see both a political ideology and a religion in Islam", in order, paradoxically, that they may "part company with their own religious tradition". They are pitted against both the West and the regimes in their own countries, and offer as a remedy to both society and politics a return to what they perceive to be the true Islam. However, the question is to what extent visions are being propounded that are feasible, constructive, and applicable in practice (Roy 1992: vii). Common to all is an endeavour to replace existing corrupt political elites, the promotion of a conservative socio-political agenda, and a strong nationalism (Roy 2004). Simply speaking, Islamism can also be defined as the reduction of Islam to a politically and socially relevant range of themes and problems (Kepel 2002, Hoffman 1995). Islamism sees Islam as a "total way of life", which does not distinguish between the private and public spheres, religion, politics, and the economy. It also assumes that the new challenges of our times call for a prudent reinterpretation of the basic sources of Islam. The main objective of the Islamists is to see Muslims return to their faith: hypocritical Muslims, religious in name only, must become "true" and devout believers (Kouřilová 2007).

The protracted political conflict between the corrupt, unsuccessful and unpopular political and economic elites and the emerging opposition Islamists has been playing out in all Middle Eastern countries since the start of the 1970s. One group attempts to hold onto its positions of power, the other seeks a radical transformation of the social order (Kepel 1996, 2002, Roy 1992, Ottaway 2010). At the same time, both parties increasingly compete for the support of the general public, which is then drawn into the political fray. Both parties then, in an attempt to reach the masses and mobilise supporters, increasingly seek refuge in Islam. This reinforces a long-term, deep change in political discourse in favour of the Islamic narrative (Starrett 1998).

Instead of the "bloody borders of Islam" and the conflict between civilisations (cf. Huntington 1993, 2001), in the region of the Middle East we are more witness to the rivalry *within* the borders of individual nation states, and the confrontation between Islamists and governments is sometimes violent (Sorli, Gleditsch, Strand 2005). Instead of the competing secular elites and counter-elites anticipated by half a century's classical modernisation theories (cf. Lerner 1964, Huntington 1968, Brzezinski 1993), we are witnessing de-secularisation, de-privatisation and above all the re-politicisation of religion (cf. Swatos 1999, Stark 1999, Lužný 1999, Halík 2003, Nešpor and Lužný 2007, Arjomand 1986, Kepel 1996). The causes of the rise of opposition Islamist movements in the Middle East, and their conflicts with the post-colonial power elite, will therefore form an important part of this book.

POLITICAL MODERNISATION:
WEAK AND AUTHORITARIAN STATES

"You know what? These policeman are going to beat you until nightfall, when they will return home to eat and sleep. And then other policeman will arrive and will beat you until sunrise, when the first policemen will come into work and beat you until nightfall. Compared to us you're nothing. We are the government. Would you like to return to your family? Your mother and father must be worried about you…"
(Alaa Al-Aswany, The Yacoubian Building)

"System? What system? I am the system!"
(Habib Bourguiba, President of Tunisia)

"Where there is no tax, there is no need for representation. In the Middle East there is no need even for a population, which simply reduces the oil wealth of those who control them. Why share this income with a population they do not need? Why look after their safety? Why inform them? Why cultivate them? Why employ them? The Arab masses must be consolidated, stabilised, controlled and maintained on an income of between one and two euros per day."
(Jana Hybášková, Ambassador of the European Union in Iraq)

"I got to know another Morocco. A Morocco of poverty, shame and desperation. Examinations in the state hospital were free, but we had no drugs."
(Tahar Ben Jelloun, The Last Friend)

"We do not reject America, but we have the feeling that America is rejecting us. This isn't about envying America but more the feeling that we are hated by America. We want to be recognised and respected by America. But we feel that this isn't the case. We feel like rejected lovers."
(An Educated Lebanese)[1]

Although national service did not officially exist in Morocco at the end of the 1960s, barracks in the Sahara operated as boot camps for opposition-
-minded students flirting mainly with Marxism. In one of them, Sergeant Major Tadla, a bald, semi-literate ogre, welcomed new "conscripts" with the

---

[1]   Al-Aswani 2002: 160, cited by Gombár 2007: 62, Hybášková 2006b: 2, Jelloun 2011: 105, Zogby 2012: 90.

following words: "I'm in charge here. I report to no one, not even the camp commander. You are just ninety-four spoiled kids. You're being punished. You wanted to be smart-asses, and I'm going to teach you a thing or two. There's no daddy and mommy here. You can yell all you like, nobody will hear you. In this place, I will dress you and change you. You'll no longer be spoiled kids, queers, children of the rich. Here Commander Tadla rules. Forget all that liberty-democracy crap. Here the slogan is: 'We belong to Allah, our king, and our country.' Repeat after me..." This is how the Moroccan writer Tahar Ben Jelloun evokes the authoritarian character of his country in the novel *The Last Friend* (2011: 87), a country that, as well as repressing its population, does not even respect its own rules and laws, while resorting to religion as the source of its own fragile legitimacy.

Modernising Middle Eastern societies continue to be governed by *weak* yet *authoritarian* regimes that over the last fifty years have barely changed, are ideologically burnt out, and are consequently incapable of co-opting newly emerging political actors. When I speak of rigidity and the stagnation of political systems, I am referring to the rigidity and stagnation of their structural parameters, which relates to the ability of regimes to survive, the ongoing preponderance of authoritarianism, and the low capacity over the long term of Middle Eastern states to govern effectively in their territory and to carry out the basic functions for their populations. Within the framework of these relatively unchanging political structures there are of course fascinating activities being played out on the part of politically relevant actors. However, the given structures do not have to take these into consideration and so certain patterns of behaviour are more probable than others. For instance, political regimes are willing to change almost everything in order that the political order remains the same and the political elites retain their power. They co-opt a minority while attempting to control, discipline or suppress the rest of the population.

In this chapter I shall examine the mechanisms by which an interaction takes place between corrupt Middle Eastern political systems and the Islamic political imaginary. I shall also look at the mechanisms that lead to conflict between these rigid political systems and the far more dynamic demographic and social developments taking place in the region, as a consequence of which these regimes and their cronies are becoming increasingly alienated from the rest of the population. The aim of this chapter, therefore, is not only to analyse the prevalent character of political regimes in the Middle East, but above all to examine the complex, agonistic interaction of this political system with other dimensions of the uneven modernisation process and its broader context (as played out in culture and on the international stage). This objective is shown in fig. 5.

Fig. 5 The interaction of the political system with other independent variables examined in this chapter

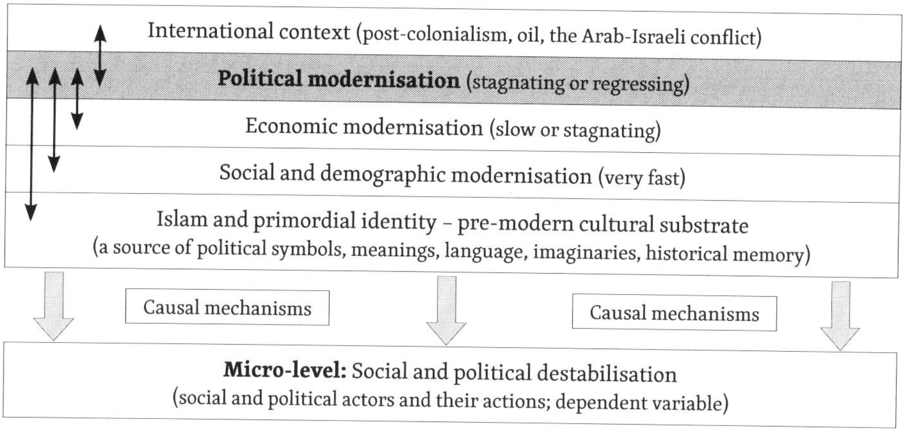

N.B. Possible interactions and tensions are shown by the arrows.

FROZEN POLITICAL MODERNISATION IN AN INTERNATIONAL COMPARISON: THE DEMOCRATIC DEFICIT

When we think of repressive regimes, what countries spring to mind? Russia, controlled by elites drawn from the secret services, the mafia, and gas company oligarchs? China, where a billion people are controlled by the million-strong caste of the communist party? Communist Cuba, bankrupted and crushed by economic sanctions? Belarus, over which the European Union is forever wringing its hands? Or famine-struck, fortress-minded North Korea? These regimes certainly have their problems. However, there is a blank space in our mental map where the West has long overlooked, downplayed or even justified repression in the name of preserving stability: the Arab world.

According to the *democracy index* published by *The Economist* (Democracy Index 2010), Kuwait, Morocco and Jordan are even more repressive than Russia (see table 1). However, they are long-term strategic allies of Washington in a geopolitically key region, and so the West conveniently ignores the undemocratic nature of these monarchies and, on the contrary, offers them support.

Similarly, the much maligned Cuba is actually slightly more democratic than the pro-American regime of Bahrain, where an American naval fleet has been based since 1971. The minority Sunnis have long persecuted the majority Shiites, who have been deprived of their political rights and a share in the country's oil wealth. In 2011, with fraternal Sunni military assistance provided by Saudi Arabia, Bahrain massacred demonstrators calling for fairer treatment and democratisation. Likewise, communist Cuba is a freer place to live

Table 1 Democracy Index: The Middle East and comparable countries 2015

Country	Overall ranking out of 167 countries evaluated	Final score and description of regime
Israel	34	7.77 (flawed democracy)
Tunisia	57	6.72 (flawed democracy)
Turkey	97	5.12 (hybrid regime)
Lebanon	102	4.86 (hybrid regime)
Morocco	107	4.66 (hybrid regime)
Palestine	110	4.57 (hybrid regime)
Iraq	115	4.08 (hybrid regime)
Mauretania	117	3.96 (authoritarian regime)
Algeria	118	3.95 (authoritarian regime)
Jordan	120	3.86 (authoritarian regime)
Kuwait	121	3.85 (authoritarian regime)
Bahrain	122	3.49 (authoritarian regime)
Comoro Islands	125	3.71 (authoritarian regime)
Qatar	134	3.18 (authoritarian regime)
Egypt	134	3.18 (authoritarian regime)
Oman	142	3.04 (authoritarian regime)
Djibouti	145	2.90 (authoritarian regime)
United Arab Emirates	148	2.75 (authoritarian regime)
Sudan	151	2.37 (authoritarian regime)
Libya	153	2.25 (authoritarian regime)
Yemen	154	2.24 (authoritarian regime)
Iran	156	2.16 (authoritarian regime)
Saudi Arabia	160	1.93 (authoritarian regime)
Syria	166	1.43 (authoritarian regime)
Selected predominantly Muslim countries		
Indonesia	49	7.03 (flawed democracy)
Malaysia	68	6.43 (flawed democracy)
Bangladesh	86	5.73 (hybrid regime)
Bosnia and Herzegovina	104	4.83 (hybrid regime)
Pakistan	112	4.40 (hybrid regime)
Afghanistan	147	2.77 (authoritarian regime)
Regimes most criticised by the West		
Burma	114	4.14 (authoritarian regime)
Cuba	129	3.52 (authoritarian regime)
Belarus	127	3.62 (authoritarian regime)
Russia	132	3.31 (authoritarian regime)

China	136	3.14 (authoritarian regime)
Uzbekistan	158	1.95 (authoritarian regime)
Turkmenistan	162	1.83 (authoritarian regime)
North Korea	167	1.08 (authoritarian regime)
Selected Western democracies		
Norway	1	9.93 (full democracy)
United States of America	20	8.05 (full democracy)
Italy	21	7.98 (flawed democracy)

N.B.: The Economist's Democracy Index ranks countries from 10 (democratic) to 1 (authoritarian). Ranked in descending order.
Source: Economist Intelligence Unit, Democracy Index 2015

than the military dictatorship in Algeria supported by France, where in 1991 the army annulled the results of democratic elections won by the opposition Islamic Salvation Front, so plunging the country into civil war (1991–1997).

One might, for instance, compare China, long subject to criticism, with the degree of repression in Qatar and Egypt. Since the 1980s, Egypt has been receiving financial, military and food aid from the United States every year in exchange for peace with Israel and calm operations in the geopolitically strategic Suez Canal. The authoritarian states of Oman, United Arab Emirates, Tunisia and Yemen are considerably less democratic than China.

Finally, Saudi Arabia, constantly pampered and protected by the Americans and possessing the largest oil reserves in the world, has long been the least democratic Arab state of all. Along with North Korea, Turkmenistan and Burma it is the most repressive state in the world, less free even than the endlessly criticised Iran. The Saudi regime has no respect for human rights. No opposition whatsoever is permitted in the country. School textbooks are crammed full of intolerance and hatred for otherness. Not only the representatives of other religions are persecuted (Christians and Jews), but even Muslims simply professing a slightly different concept of Islam (including Shiites). The large numbers of foreign workers in the country are treated almost like slaves, women are subject to discrimination, and torture in prisons is rampant. Mutilation as a penalty is still practiced, including the medieval punishments of flogging, stoning or decapitation by sword (Human Rights Watch 2010).

Middle Eastern societies that in most respects are modern and undergoing rapid transformation are ruled by "archaic" political systems that have remained virtually unchanged for the last half century (Roy 1992). Even before the arrival of Islamists on the political scene, these regimes were incapable of co-opting newly emerging political actors and regulating the

Fig. 6 Development of political rights and civil liberties in global macro-regions 1973–2015

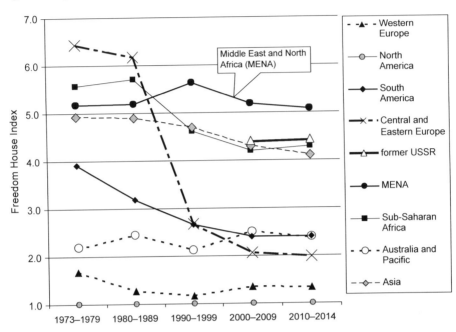

NB.: The author's calculation of the arithmetic average of individual macro-regions (unweighted by the population size of particular states). This is a synthetic index. It is the arithmetic average of indices measuring civil liberties and political rights. Turkey is included in Western Europe and Israel in the MENA region. The Freedom House index ranks individual countries from 1 (a democratic, free country) to 7 (not free).
Source: Freedom House

conflicts of interest groups (Lerner 1964). It was the slow pace of change in the political subsystem, which lags behind the rapid changes taking place in other spheres, which became the source of destabilisation and tension in the region. Middle Eastern regimes are *praetorian*: they exclude political actors from the system, exiling them to the street and illegality. The fact that the politically mobilised masses are unable to participate legally in politics leads to a higher incidence of political violence (Huntington 1968).

The Middle East has long been the least free and democratic macro-region in the world. Conversely, Sub-Saharan Africa, Asia, Latin America and post-communist Europe are these days incomparably more democratic (see fig. 6 and table 1). In terms of established politological typologies we can divide Middle Eastern regimes into *secular republics* where the president occupies a privileged position (Syria, Iraq, Yemen, Algeria, Egypt, and Tunisia up until 2011), and *republics combining* secular and religious sources of legitimacy (Libya and Yemen). We can also distinguish between *traditional monarchies*

(Morocco and Jordan) and *conservative monarchies* (Bahrain, Kuwait and the United Arab Emirates) (Kropáček 1999, Ehteshami 1999, Guidére 2012). However, all of these regimes share something in common: they are all authoritarian. From the point of view of their oppressed citizens and opposition groups it is irrelevant whether civil and legal rights are being trampled over by a republic or a monarchy.

The Middle East is also unique in that *democracy's third wave*, which began with the Carnation Revolution in Portugal (1974) and was accelerated by the fall of the Berlin Wall (1898), totally passed it by. In addition, along with the post-Soviet republics of the Caucasus and Central Asia, it is the only world macro-region where repression actually intensified during the 1990s (see fig. 6). Not even the attempt to democratise Iraq, when the American-led invasion anticipated a democratising domino effect spreading across the entire region, had a positive effect (cf. Huntington 2008, Zakaria 2004, Jamal, Tessler 2008, Braizat 2010, 2013).

Over the last four decades the degree of political rights and civil liberties in the Middle East has stagnated and repression remains high: the index varies between 5.3 and 5.6 according to the author's calculations. In contrast, democratisation has been taking place over the long term at various different speeds in all other world macro-regions. For instance, Sub-Saharan Africa has witnessed significant democratisation since the 1990s (from 5.5 to the current 4.3). Democratisation is also taking place in Asia (from 4.2 to 3.5) and Latin America (from 3.7 to 2.8). And this is not to mention the robust democratisation of the former Eastern bloc (from 6.5 to 3.4; cf. fig. 6).

So democracy's third wave bypassed the Middle East. Instead, during the 1990s, faltering regimes oscillated between partial political liberalisation and repeated de-liberalisation (cf. figs. 7 and 8). They also inclined pragmatically toward greater religious legitimisation directed inward, and to legitimisation through democratic rhetoric and the doctrine of the war on terrorism directed outward. Furthermore, they attempted to expand somewhat the social base of power elites to include technocrats and business circles. At the same time they started to emulate Western democratic institutions and their formal procedures, while preserving informal power structures. They co-opted some of the opposition into power elites by offering them political perks and privileges in exchange for loyalty. At the same time they were happy to see them scrap over the favour of the elites and thus become internally divided. The remaining opposition was harshly suppressed. Regimes made a great play of reshuffling things simply in order to maintain their grip on power (Albrecht, Schlumberger 2004, Ottaway 2010). It is too early to evaluate definitively the outcome of the Arab Spring. However, many dictators once again proved to be proficient Machiavellians capable of anything if it meant holding on to their power (cf. Stacher 2012, Noueihed, Warren 2012).

REGIONAL COMPARISON: THE DEMOCRATIC DEFICIT OF MIDDLE EASTERN REGIMES

Though the Freedom House index (2010) shows that the level of repression differs slightly between individual countries of the region, none with the exception of Israel and Turkey can be deemed democratic. Regimes that have long been the most repressive in the world can be found here: Libya (7.0), Sudan (7.0), Saudi Arabia (6.5), Syria (6.5), Tunisia (6.0), Egypt (5.5) and Algeria (5.5) (see table 2 and figs. 7 and 8). We can confidently rank these countries alongside the most notorious dictatorships in the world, such as North Korea (7.0), Burma (7.0), Cuba (6.5), China (6.5) and Belarus (6.5). The freest countries in the region are Lebanon (4.0), Kuwait (4.5) and Morocco (4.5).

Table 2 Level of political rights and civil liberties in MENA countries 1973–2014

Country	1973–1979	1980–1989	1990–1999	2000–2010	2011–2014
Algeria	6.1	5.9	5.7	5.5	5.5
Bahrain	5.0	5.0	6.1	5.2	6.1
Egypt	5.1	4.6	5.7	5.7	5.4
Iran	5.6	5.5	6.2	6.0	6.0
Iraq	6.9	6.8	7.0	6.1	5.8
Israel	2.4	2.0	2.0	1.8	1.5
Jordan	6.0	5.5	4.1	5.0	5.5
Kuwait	4.3	4.8	5.2	4.3	4.9
Lebanon	3.1	4.7	5.4	4.8	4.5
Libya	6.5	6.2	7.0	7.0	5.4
Morocco	4.5	4.4	4.9	4.7	4.5
Oman	6.3	6.0	6.0	5.5	5.5
Palestine	---	---	5.5	5.5	5.5
Qatar	5.3	5.1	6.4	5.7	5.5
Saudi Arabia	6.0	6.4	6.9	6.7	7.0
Sudan	5.8	5.2	7.0	7.0	7.0
Syria	6.3	6.4	7.0	6.8	7.0
Tunisia	5.5	5.1	5.4	5.7	3.0
Turkey	2.7	3.7	4.1	3.4	3.0
United Arab Emirates	5.4	5.1	5.6	5.7	6.0
North Yemen	5.0	5.2	---	---	---
South Yemen	6.9	6.6	---	---	---
Yemen	---	---	5.4	5.3	6.0

N.B.: The Freedom House index ranks countries from 1 (a democratic, free country) to 7 (not free). The author's calculation of the arithmetic averages of countries for individual decades.
Source: Freedom House

Fig. 7 Development of political rights and civil liberties in Arab monarchies 1973–2015

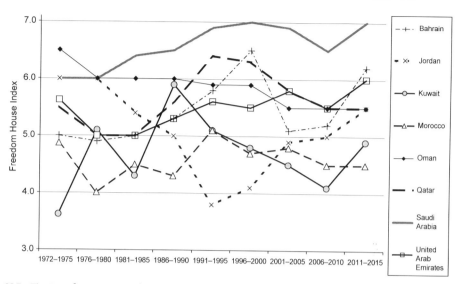

N.B.: The Freedom House index ranks countries from 1 (a democratic and free country) to 7 (unfree). The author's calculation of the arithmetic averages of countries for individual five-year periods.
Source: Freedom House

The following graphs (cf. figs. 7 and 8) also show that the level of repression in individual Arab countries changes over time, especially if we look at trends over shorter five-year periods rather than decades, which have a tendency to "smooth out" the fluctuations of individual years. However, long-term oscillations remain within the authoritarian zone and do not involve qualitative transitions from democracy to authoritarianism or vice versa (with the exception of Lebanon and Kuwait). In other words, most countries do not follow a clear, long-term trajectory, but feature a temporary relaxation of repression followed by its consolidation. In addition, we see that this relatively variable degree of repression applies to both monarchies and republics alike. We cannot therefore conclude that, generally speaking, republics are more repressive than monarchies or vice versa. In each type of polity we find highly authoritarian regimes and less authoritarian or hybrid regimes.

Finally, there is no direct relationship between the level of political repression and its evolution over time in a country and whether that country participated in the Arab Spring or not (2011). Among Arab monarchies, revolutionary Bahrain is a moderately repressive regime and over the last decade has if anything relaxed its restrictions on freedom. As far as republics are concerned, while revolutions took place in Syria and Libya, highly repressive countries, they also took place in the slightly less repressive Egypt, Tunisia and Yemen. And while repression has increased significantly over the long term in Tunisia, in Egypt and Yemen it has stagnated or even decreased slightly over the short term. On the other hand, there have been no revolutions in the highly repressive Saudi Arabia, and this is also true of the relatively liberal monarchies of Jordan, Morocco and Kuwait. The only relatively stable republic was Algeria, with memories still fresh of the bloody civil war (1991–1997) that followed an unsuccessful attempt at democratisation at the start of the 1990s.

At first sight, then, we see that, rather than the level of political rights and civil freedoms, it was more the type of political organisation and legitimacy of a regime – republic versus monarchy – that made the difference between stability and instability during the Arab Spring. At the same time it is clear that revolutions did not take place in the following least repressive regimes: Lebanon, Kuwait, Morocco and Jordan. Although mass protests were held in these more open regimes, the governments did not react with brutal violence against the demonstrators, but with dialogue, compromise, and an offer of political and constitutional reforms.

Fig. 8 Development of political rights and civil liberties in Arab republics 1973–2015

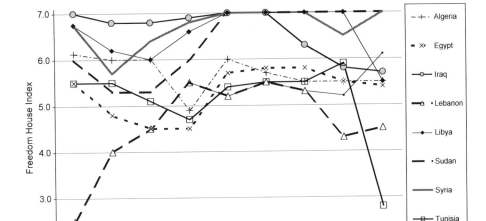

N.B.: The Freedom House index ranks countries from 1 (a democratic, free country) to 7 (unfree). The author's calculation of the arithmetic averages of countries for individual five-year periods.
Source: Freedom House

LOGIC OF THE INDEXES: HOW THE LEVEL OF FREEDOM
AND DEMOCRACY IS MEASURED

Several teams of experts are involved in the attempt to quantify qualitative phenomena and to determine the level of democracy and human rights in individual countries of the world. Though there is no consensus among them regarding methodology or even how to define democracy, the results they arrive at in terms of the rankings of individual countries end up being almost identical.

Perhaps the most frequently cited ranking is that conducted by the American non-governmental organisation Freedom House, which has been assessing the level of democracy in the world since the 1970s. A panel of experts on each country scores 25 topics covering two sub-dimensions: civil liberties and political rights. These scores are added up and the result is an overall ranking of each country. Countries are ranked from 1 (most free), 3 to 5 (partly free), up to 7 (least free). A table is then compiled. For the sake of transparency and intelligibility a detailed verbal assessment is offered of each country describing the 25 topics under consideration. The Freedom House index is not content with a minimalist, formal definition of democracy involving universal voting rights and competing political parties. Likewise, it is not confined to a merely formal wording of constitution and laws, but evaluates the way regimes actually operate.

As regards the dimension of *civil liberties*, the panel of country experts assesses on an annual basis whether there genuinely exists freedom of assembly, freedom of association, freedom of speech, and independent media. It looks at whether citizens are safe from the arbitrary power of a political, religious or power-based majority, whether independent trade unions and professional organisations have the right to exist, and whether the justice system is truly impartial and ensures that laws are enforced and that citizens enjoy equality before the law. They also decide whether there is freedom of religion. The evaluation of regimes from the point of view of *political rights* is similarly detailed. The experts decide whether people are free to organise themselves into political parties, movements or interest groups and whether there exists a genuine opposition and real alternation of power. They also look at whether executive and legislative bodies are elected by the people in fair, free and universal elections, whether power is not being usurped by the army or an oligarchy, and whether minorities have a share in power.

The Freedom House index thus measures two dimensions of each regime: the degree of constitutional liberalism and the level of democracy. Though there tends to be a correlation between these dimensions (cf. Tilly 2006b) and they are often conflated in public awareness, both factually and historically they represent two independent characteristics of political regimes. While

political rights are related to the ability of the public to co-influence government decision-making, civil liberties are more about the protection of the individual against the potential tyranny of the majority, an all-powerful state,
or an intolerant church (religion). The punishment meted out to Socrates,
who was sentenced to death by drinking a cup of hemlock, was therefore
supremely democratic, but utterly illiberal, because the majority violated
the basic human right of every person to the protection of life. Conversely,
early modern England was relatively liberal, since it guaranteed everyone
basic civil rights and equality before the law, though relatively undemocratic,
because the right to vote was possessed only by a minority of wealthy men
(cf. Zakaria 2004).

The Freedom House index can be criticised for exhibiting *ethnocentrism*
or for its positivist attempt to evaluate qualitative phenomena that, by their
very nature, are difficult to measure and define precisely. However, it can be
defended on the basis that, in addition to a reductive, one-dimensional index
that simplifies the multidimensional reality of regimes, it offers a detailed
verbal assessment of individual dimensions and therefore justifies the final
score awarded in a transparent fashion. The *validity* and objectivity of the
index can further be verified by virtue of its correlation with other rankings,
such as the *Democracy Index* published by *The Economist*. For instance, in addition to the level of civil liberties and political rights, the competing team
of The Economist Intelligence Unit also evaluates the functioning of government, the level of political participation of citizens, and the state of political
culture as revealed by a respectable 60 evaluation criteria. What this shows
is that different teams of experts employing different methodologies arrive
at similar conclusions. The Freedom House index also enjoys the advantage
of examining what is unquestionably the longest time frame, which stretches
back to 1973 (Freedom House 2010; for a discussion see Tilly 2004b, Inglehart
and Welzel 2005, Tomeš et al. 2007). Finally, the index can be defended by
virtue of the fact that extensive, representative sociological surveys of the
opinions and attitudes of populations in the Middle East reveal a similar
understanding of democracy and civil rights as is common in the West. The
index is therefore not necessarily Western-centric (cf. Braizat 2010, Jamal
and Tessler 2008, Dixon 2008, Esposito and Mogahed 2007).

THE SECOND DIMENSION OF POLITICAL MODERNISATION: A WEAK STATE AND A GOVERNANCE DEFICIT

A starving Suleiman stumbles and falls into a cage containing a hungry
tiger. In order to cut down on costs, the tiger is fed only donkey meat, which,
though cheap, is unfortunately similar to human flesh. The tiger does not

hesitate and bites off the leg of his keeper. The newspapers later carry the shocking news that, though Suleiman has worked for the national circus for more than thirty years, he lives modestly and devoutly, sleeps on a mattress between cages, and has no savings to pay the cost of medical treatment. In pre-revolutionary Egypt his story became one of the first metaphors for that half of the population struggling on the border of poverty. During the 2000s, the incident redirected the attention of the media, until then focussed on the middle and upper classes, to the problems of the lower classes.

However, the condition of the national circus could be seen as a metaphor for the decline of the entire state and the erosion of its institutions. Older Egyptians remember a similar tragedy dating back to 1972, when a lion tore the director himself to pieces in front of horrified spectators. At that time the country also found itself gripped by despondency. This was brought on by the war with Israel (1967), which occupied the oil fields in the Sinai. Investors and tourists fled in the face of military tensions. The state treasury was bankrupt due to the loss of income from oil exports and the closure of the Suez Canal, as well as the cost of resettling war refugees and the creation of a new army. The result was that for several years the upper floors of houses had no running water, garbage collection collapsed, electricity supplies and telephones functioned only sporadically, street lights remained unlit, and roads were pitted with potholes (cited by Amin 2004).

Along with political rights and civil liberties, the capacity of states to govern within their territories represents the second main dimension characterising political regimes. And just as the liberal-democratic dimension can be expressed on a scale from democracy to authoritarianism, so the dimension of governance can be expressed on a scale ranging from strong and effective centralised states to weak if not failed states, i.e. on a scale of political order versus political anarchy (Huntington 1968). In the analyses conducted by the social sciences, the capacity of states to govern was long ignored, with emphasis being laid on democracy and democratisation. And yet a certain level of state power is a condition for democracy, and indeed for dictatorship. Said power allows for implementation of the will of the majority (in a democracy) or the dictator (in a dictatorship). In addition, the capacity of states has a crucial influence on the form of repertoires of contention and the level of violence in political conflicts (Tilly 2006b).

In his theory of the civilising process, Norbert Elias (1994), for example, emphasises that the concentration of the means of violence in the hands of a centralised bureaucratic state during the course of European history forced, and at the same time permitted, the gradual pacification of the rest of society. A change of social structures (sociogenesis) led to a change of the psychological structures and habitus of individuals (psychogenesis), and these two mutually dependent processes were both conditional upon and constitutive of the other. Political rivalry in the courts of absolutist rulers was then played out in a far more sophisticated manner, with the winner being the party that best managed to suppress its aggression and emotions. Manifestations of violence gradually became a source of shame and condemnation amongst the lower classes too.

Max Weber (1997) also emphasised that the modern European state is above all an institution with a monopoly on the legitimate use of physical force. It prohibits other actors from using violence and instead provides rational rules for resolving social conflicts by promoting through its bureaucratic apparatus legal norms binding upon all citizens that create a clear, stable and predictable environment that nurtures the safety of citizens and long-term economic development. On the other hand, a weak and dysfunctional state, which adopts new laws but fails to enforce compliance with them, was identified (cf. Myrdal 1968, 1970) as the main obstacle to the economic development of post-colonial countries. A weak state creates rules that are subsequently breached, and this allows those who breach them to become rich. A weak state is incapable of collecting the taxes necessary if it is to function and pay its employees adequately. As a consequence it generates corruption, which then weakens the state still further. Control over positions in a weak state becomes a source of power and wealth, and allows its holders to profit from corruption and clientelism. Public employees and politicians relinquish their social responsibility and sacrifice the pursuit of the public weal for the pursuit of private profit. The rich and powerful are then able to buy goods that are not for sale or should be available to all without exception, and this flies in the face of the principle of social equality. A weak state is therefore unreliable in times of social strife and is unable to enforce its will even on a day-to-day basis.

For example, in Egypt during the era of Mubarak the weakness of the state was manifest in a relinquishment of many state *functions*. The state did not invest in increasingly obsolete infrastructure and provided insufficient protection for historical monuments, the environment, and the security of its citizens. It failed to enforce building regulations, and this resulted in the construction of new but poor quality, unsafe buildings. Likewise, it failed to prevent the illegal seizure of state land, something that not only the poorest without the opportunity of finding affordable housing resorted to, but also the upper classes, who built palatial villas on state land and speculated in real estate. The state not only failed to enforce the repayment of state loans provided to the private sector and the enforcement of legal judgements, but even failed to compel compliance with the most basic rules of the road, such as respect for traffic lights. The biggest scandals revealing the impotence of a weak state were to be seen in how state institutions responded to national catastrophes. They were unable and unwilling to help victims of the Cairo

Fig. 9 The capacity of states to rule their territories in world macro-regions 1996–2015

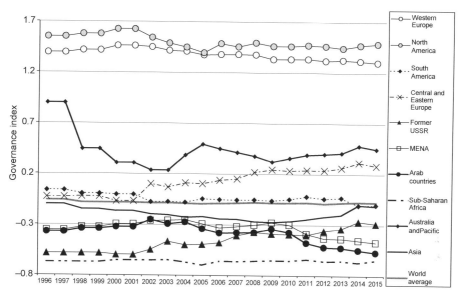

N.B.: This synthetic index of the ability of a state to govern is the arithmetic average of five separate indices: Political Stability and Absence of Violence, Government Effectiveness, Regulatory Quality, Control of Corruption, and Rule of Law. The author's calculation of the arithmetic averages of individual states and macro-regions (unweighted by state population size).
Source: World Bank 2015, World Governance Indicators (WGIs).

earthquake of 1992, during which many people died or were made homeless due to poorly constructed buildings (Amin 2011). Many of these widely reported catastrophes involved huge traffic accidents in which many lower class people died and were injured, and during which the police stood by idly until the last minute, ambulances were slow to arrive, and hospitals refused to accept patients, arguing that "their injuries were too serious", while the state was unable so much as to organise a dignified burial, provide compensation to survivors, and apprehend all the known culprits (Amin 2004).

The capacity of post-colonial developing countries to govern is generally speaking far lower than that of developed countries. And yet convergence is not taking place between the Global North and South. On the contrary, individual indicators reveal that the chasm is widening (Kauffman et al. 2009). The Middle East fits into this general model and even belongs among the weaker regions within the context of the Global South, since the ability of Middle Eastern states to govern has long been significantly below average according to international comparisons (cf. fig. 9). Only the poor countries

Fig. 10 The capacity of Middle Eastern states to govern in their territory 1996–2015

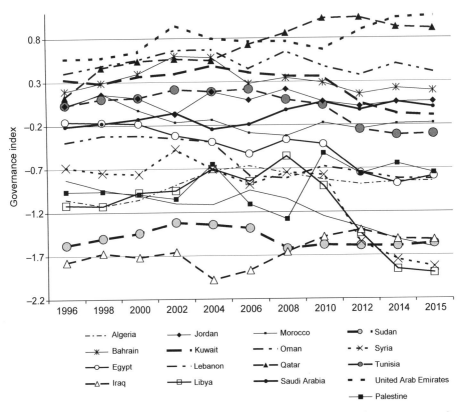

N.B.: This synthetic index of the ability of a given state to govern is the arithmetic average of five separate indices: Political Stability and Absence of Violence, Government Effectiveness, Regulatory Quality, Control of Corruption, Rule of Law. The author's calculation of arithmetic averages for individual states.
Source: World Bank 2015, World Governance Indicators.

of Sub-Saharan Africa are less able to govern, and these are often on the threshold of collapse. Conversely, post-colonial countries in Asia and South America have a greater capacity. Similarly, the post-communist countries of the former USSR also enjoy a greater capacity to govern, even though after the breakup of the USSR in the 1990s that capacity was less than in the Middle East. There has been a sharp upward trend during the same period in post-communist Central and Eastern Europe. In addition to the low capacity of state institutions, another characteristic of the Middle East is the long-term stagnation of this dimension of political modernisation. If there has been any change at all over the last few years, it has been for the worse, towards the further erosion and weakening of state institutions.

In terms of capacity to govern, there are greater differences between the post-colonial developing countries of the Global South than between the developed countries of the Global North, which are relatively homogenous in this respect (cf. Kauffman et al. 2009). The post-colonial Middle East again fits into the general pattern. The local states differ considerably in terms of capacity to govern and are relatively heterogeneous (see fig. 10). Along with Turkey and Iran, the small, oil-rich monarchies of the Gulf have a high capacity to govern. This especially applies to the ever stronger Qatar, but also the United Arab Emirates, Oman, Kuwait and slightly declining Bahrain (in that order). However, not even these states can be ranked alongside the advanced countries of Western Europe or North America in terms of capacity to govern. On the other hand, the world's weakest states have long been mainly republics: Iraq and Sudan, ground down by civil war, as well as Yemen, Libya, Syria and declining Lebanon and Egypt. By Middle Eastern standards the monarchies of Jordan, Morocco and Saudi Arabia, along with republican Tunisia, display a medium capacity to govern.

LOGIC OF THE INDEXES: HOW AND WHAT MEASURES A STATE'S CAPACITY TO GOVERN

The capacity to govern reflects the ability of state institutions to implement policy that provides benefits and services to individuals and businesses (Besley and Persson 2011: 2). Charles Tilly (2006b: 16) defines it similarly as the ability of the state to influence and control effectively the distribution of people, activities and resources in the territory under its legal jurisdiction. The concept of state capacity relates to different functions of the state, while accepting that in reality states will only perform these functions to a certain extent. For instance, the *bureaucratic and administrative capacity* of the state refers to the ability of its bureaucracy to put forward and subsequently implement state policy, and is therefore closely associated with the competence and professionalism of the state bureaucracy, especially its ability to deal effectively with taxes to the benefit of the people (cf. Rauch and Evans 2000). On the other hand, a state's *legal capacity* relates to its ability to enforce security, compliance with contracts, and the rule of law, i.e. to manage public property that the private sector would find difficult to oversee (Collier 2009). *Infrastructural capacity* relates to the territorial range of state institutions, i.e. the extent to which a state is able to control its entire territory, including the peripheries or separatist regions, and enforce its policy. Inter alia, therefore, this capacity is associated with the transport and communications infrastructure covering the whole country (Soifer 2008). In addition, we can distinguish, for example, *fiscal capacity*, i.e. the ability of the state to collect taxes, and *military capacity*, namely the ability of states to ensure not only external but internal security, including the suppression of rebellion and civil wars (Hendrix 2010).

There exists a range of indexes quantifying the ability of individual states to govern. The longest time-series (since 1996) covering the largest number of countries (more than 200) is contained in the World Bank's programme stipulating the annual World Governance Indicators (WGIs) for individual states. These are based on almost forty individual indicators from data sources produced by approximately thirty non-governmental organisations or academic institutions. These indicators are based on *subjective perceptions* of the ability of individual states to govern; the perceptions of companies, investors, citizens, political leaders and NGOs. These perceptions are ascertained using a range of empirical surveys. Five of a total of six indicators relate directly to the ability of states to govern (Savoia and Sen 2012).

Firstly, the *Political Stability and Absence of Violence* indicator measures perceptions of the likelihood that a government will be destabilised or overthrown by unconstitutional or violent means, including politically-motivated violence and terrorism. The *Government Effectiveness* indicator details perceptions of the quality of public services and how independent they are of political pressure, the quality of policy formulation and implementation, and the credibility of the government's commitment to such policies. The third indicator, *Regulatory Quality*, examines perceptions of the ability of the government to formulate and implement sound policies and regulations that permit and promote private sector development. Then there is the *Rule of Law*, which measures perceptions of the extent to which agents have confidence in and abide by the rules of society, and in particular the quality of contract enforcement, property rights, the police, an independent judiciary, and the likelihood of crime and violence. Finally, *Control of Corruption* measures the perceptions of to what degree public power is exercised for private gain, as well as "capture" of the state by elites and vested interests (Kaufmann, Kraay and Mastruzzi 2010).

The rule of law, the quality of regulation and the effectiveness of government reflect the level of the state's legal, infrastructural and administrative capacity. Political stability and the control of corruption in turn correspond to the bureaucratic capacity or the fragility of the state (Savoia and Sen 2012). For the purpose of this analysis I use the five World Governance Indicators shown above, from which one synthetic index was compiled allowing for an international comparison of individual world macro-regions, as well as individual states within the Middle Eastern macro-region.

THE CHARACTER OF MIDDLE EASTERN REGIMES AND THE CHARACTER OF POLITICAL REPERTOIRES OF CONTENTION

From the point of view of their citizens, Middle Eastern regimes exhibit the *worst combination*, namely *weakness* combined with *authoritarianism*. A citizen cannot depend on a weak and dysfunctional state to guarantee its basic functions. He cannot rely on state institutions to provide sufficiently accessible, good quality public goods (a police force, healthcare, education, administration, an independent judiciary and law enforcement, sanitation and a healthy environment). On the other hand, he can rest assured that if he wants to express his displeasure regarding the state of public services and the dysfunctionality of the state, he will not be offered any legal avenues and will be silenced. If he attempts to reform a dysfunctional state by organising collective action, he will be persecuted. And given the rigidity that has characterised current political systems for several decades in both dimensions, he can feel confident that not even the gradual reform of one of the two dimensions is very likely. As a consequence, any change to the political system is most likely to be violent.

INTERNATIONAL COMPARISON: THE MIDDLE EAST AND OTHER WORLD MACRO-REGIONS

During the course of its history, every political regime in the world can be assigned to one of four basic *types* (cf. Tilly 2006b). In the upper left quadrant (see fig. 11) are the world macro-regions where *low-capacity undemocratic states* predominate. As well as the Middle East we see Sub-Saharan Africa, the post-communist countries of the former USSR, and Asia. And within the context of the Middle East, Arab countries tend to be even more undemocratic and possess lower state capacity. The mirror image of this type are *high-capacity democratic states* located in the lower right quadrant. Here we see mainly North America and Western Europe. However, we also find the post-communist countries of Central and Eastern Europe and the territories of Australia and the Pacific. *Low or medium-capacity democratic countries* are more common in South America and are to be found in the lower left quadrant. Finally, a macro-region composed mainly of *high-capacity, undemocratic countries* does not exist for the period of time under examination. The closest to this theoretical type, to be found in the upper right quadrant, are those regimes in the Middle Eastern sub-region formed by the oil monarchies of the Gulf States.

Fig. 11 Character of state regimes in world macro-regions 2006–2010

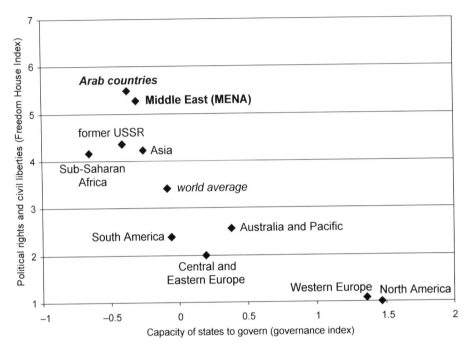

N.B.: The author's calculation of the arithmetic averages of individual dimensions of political regimes in individual world macro-regions 2006 to 2010 (unweighted by state population size). The higher the Freedom House index, the more unfree and undemocratic the macro-region. The higher the World Governance index, the greater the capacity of states to govern inside the macro-region is.
Source: Freedom House, World Bank.

REGIONAL COMPARISON: INDIVIDUAL MIDDLE EASTERN REGIMES

A similar comparative typology can be carried out of the Arab countries of the Middle Eastern macro-region (cf. fig. 12). This region is not completely homogenous. Though all of the local states are undemocratic, they differ only in terms of the degree of political repression. However, when it comes to the ability of individual states to govern, there is greater variability: from low--capacity states, to medium and even relatively high-capacity states. Firstly, republican Lebanon and monarchist Morocco are relatively less repressive states with low to medium capacity to govern. Secondly, monarchist Kuwait and Jordan are relatively less repressive states with medium or higher capacity to govern. Thirdly, decidedly undemocratic states with higher capacity to govern are the small oil monarchies of the Gulf: Bahrain, Oman, the United Arab Emirates and Qatar. This would also include republican Tunisia.

Fig. 12 Character of political regimes in the Arab world 2006–2010

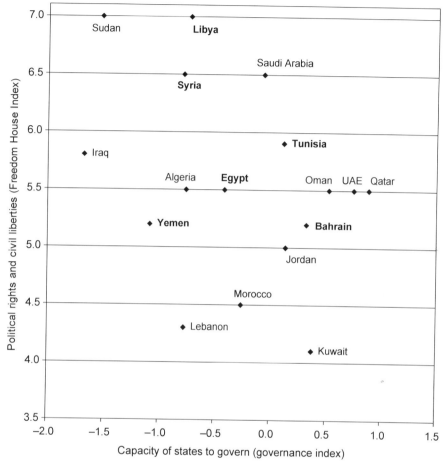

N.B.: The author's calculation of the arithmetic averages of individual dimensions of political regimes in individual Middle Eastern states from 2006 to 2010. The higher the Freedom House index, the more unfree and undemocratic the country. The higher the World Governance index, the greater is the capacity of a state to govern. The states shown in bold are where revolution, mass protests or civil war took place during the Arab Spring (2011). Source: Freedom House, World Bank.

Fourthly, in the last quadrant containing undemocratic, low-capacity states we see republics that are often on the threshold or beyond of civil war: Iraq, Sudan, Yemen, Algeria, Libya and Syria. Republican Egypt and monarchist Saudi Arabia are markedly undemocratic states with a moderate capacity to govern.

Could the character and dynamic of a regime explain the political instability of Middle Eastern countries during the Arab Spring? The theory that revolutionaries availed themselves of the *opportunity* created by the diminished ability of a state to govern (Tilly 1978, Goodwin 1997) is most pertinent to the situation in pre-revolutionary Yemen, and somewhat less so in Libya and Syria. These states have long featured a low ability to govern and in the Arab world are the lowest along with Sudan and Iraq, countries riven by civil war for years or even decades. In addition, prior to the revolution there was a further, albeit slight drop in state capacity in Yemen, Syria and Libya. Egypt was also relatively low in terms of ability to govern. However, pre-revolutionary Tunisia and Bahrain were medium-capacity, and the situation did not change over time in Tunisia. In the past there had also been a significant downturn in Lebanon's ability to govern, a phenomenon accompanied by the Cedar Revolution of 2005 (cf. figs. 10 and 12).

On the other hand, those countries with higher state capacity are significantly more stable: Qatar, United Arab Emirates, Oman and Kuwait. It would appear that state capacity enables us to differentiate between politically stable and unstable Arab countries more accurately than changes to this capacity in time. Change in the Middle East tends to be less pronounced and less frequent. On the contrary, the rigidity of political regimes and the absence of any change to their ability to govern is characteristic of the region.

Revolutions and civil war also failed to materialise in the relatively freer Arab countries: Kuwait, Lebanon, Morocco and Jordan. Instead, they took place in the most repressive, i.e. Syria, Libya and Tunisia, as well as in the slightly less repressive countries, namely Egypt, Yemen and Bahrain. Those repressive countries that managed to avoid revolution are the oil-rich monarchies with moderate or higher capacity: Saudi Arabia, Oman, Qatar and the United Arab Emirates. What this means is that revolutions and civil war were more likely to break out in poorer and more repressive countries with low or moderate capacity to govern.

POLITICAL REGIMES AND POLITICAL REPERTOIRES: A WEAK AUTHORITARIAN STATE, REVOLUTION AND TERRORISM

What is the relationship between the character of political regimes and the predominant repertoires of contention? A state-centric approach analyses the repertoires of contention with a reductionist focus on events in the political sphere. It regards the state as an autonomous institution relatively independent of classes and civil society. The character of the state and the governing regime in turn influences the actions of political actors and the likelihood of revolution or other repertoires of contention. The practice of the state fundamentally shapes the strategies of social groups and their potential politicisation (Goodwin 1997).

REVOLUTION

The state-centric approach sees revolution as the culmination of a changing balance of power accompanied by a struggle for power in the state. It does not see it as a deviation, but more as an extreme form of conflict, a continuation of politics by other means (Sztompka 1994). The state finds itself at the centre of analysis simply because revolutions themselves are concentrated around it. Revolutionaries want to control a modern centralised state and thereby mould society. Conversely, states obstruct radical change, acting as an instrument of social control that safeguards the existing order. The struggle for power in a centralised state explains why, as opposed to other forms of social conflict, revolution is a modern phenomenon, and why in history revolutions only appeared as late as the 17th century along with the emergence of centralised states, reaching their zenith in the 19th and 20th centuries. The state is also at the centre of analysis because the character and practice of the state impacts fundamentally on the possibilities of revolutionaries, the mobilisation or demobilisation of the public, and the dynamic shaping revolutionary coalitions (Goodwin 1997).

According to this narrative, a precondition for revolution is the emergence of *multiple sovereignty*, i.e. two or more alternative power centres, the government and its challengers, who lay claim to power in the state. The challengers create organisations and introduce their leaders and ideology. Intellectuals play a key role in this phase. However, the government can prevent revolution if it succeeds in *co-opting* the challengers, while the challengers can only succeed if they do not allow themselves to be co-opted and a sufficiently large section of society switches its loyalty over to them. The challenger must also *mobilise* the human and material resources needed to lead a political conflict, and create a sufficiently broad revolutionary *coalition* by appealing to the common interests of all. They must sideline particular identities or opposing interests within the ranks of a socially heterogeneous coalition. On the other hand, they must emphasise the lowest common denominator, i.e. the overthrow of the government. The more social groups join a revolutionary coalition, the greater is the pressure on government and the more likely a transfer of power. However, it is difficult to maintain the unity of such a coalition (Tilly 1978).

The creation of a broad-based coalition requires the mass *dissatisfaction* of the population with the existing government. The government must either be seen as unsuccessful in meeting the legitimate needs of the population or as disproportionately increasing the pressure on individuals through tax increases, military conscription, land annexation, or blocking the means of subsistence. It must be perceived as the initiator of unfair and unpopular measures. Otherwise, the discontent will focus on other targets (Tilly

1978). *Culture* is important for such an oppositional *framing*, with the help of which people can come to perceive objective reality as subjectively unfair and changeable. However, for this they need new cognitive frameworks and discourses that can generate new meanings for reality and conduct. Nevertheless, it is often states that form and construct identities, ideas and emotions. Often, however, they generate discourses that eventually turn back on themselves (Foran 1997). In this phase an endeavour to implement reforms can be risky for a government (the *too-little-too-late syndrome*). The government thereby admits its weakness and confirms that it is to blame for the discontent (Goodwin 1997).

However, latent discontent is always present in a population. This is why another precondition for the success of revolution is the appearance of a *political opportunity*, within the framework of which the political mobilisation of the population can take place. Such an opportunity is represented above all by the inability of a government to use force to the extent necessary to suppress a challenger and demobilise his supporters, i.e. the absence of the means of repression, a loss of control over these resources, or a lack of political will or consensus inside the political elite to use such resources. The breakdown and collapse of state power tends to be caused by geopolitical factors or domestic political crisis: a gruelling war, the pressure of a superpower in favour of a challenger, fiscal crisis, conflict between the political elite and the dominant social class, internal conflict dividing and weakening the political elite, or a situation in which the challenger finds an ally within such a divided political elite. What is crucial here is how the *army* reacts. The chances of the revolution proving successful increase if the army does not display sufficient loyalty to the old regime: it waits, remains neutral, or even deserts the government and adds its weight to the challengers. The concept of *political opportunity explains why some challengers successfully exploit frustration in order to form a revolutionary movement and others do not* (Tilly 1978).

At the same time, the likelihood of a political opportunity arising and spreading relates to the *low capacity of the state* to govern, i.e. to the material and organisational (in)ability of the government to promote and enforce its policy notwithstanding the resistance of a challenger, civil society, and other actors. The infrastructural power of such a state tends to be weak or geographically uneven. Revolution then starts at the peripheries, beyond the reach of state institutions. The bureaucracy, army and police are ineffective, corrupt and underfunded. This is sometimes at the behest of a dictator, who systematically sets out to undermine the power of the bureaucracy and army so that they are incapable of generating alternative power centres potentially threatening his own. Such a state will easily collapse when exposed to external pressures or internal crisis (Tilly 1978).

Exclusive regimes with an inclination towards authoritarianism tend to have many motivated opponents and few dedicated supporters willing to stand up and be counted. Autocratic or neo-patrimonial dictators, regarding the state as part of their household, *systematically alienate, weaken and divide the counter-revolutionary elites*, elites drawn from the ranks of officers, the public administration or businesspeople, who, along with dictators, share latent anti-revolutionary feeling and whom dictators often regard as their main rivals. Such dictators fear the creation of alternative power bases and the possibility of a coup, and so they use their power against the elite unpredictably, arbitrarily and intensively. In addition, they live by the motto "divide and rule", and this leads to the further fragmentation of the elite. The outcome is that the *regime has a narrow social base*. It cannot rely on the support of a larger number of loyal groups that, under normal circumstances, would be politically conservative and counter-revolutionary. The counter-revolutionary elite is thus in a situation in which, when revolution genuinely breaks out, it is slow to repress it and barely motivated to act at all. However, it is equally weak when it comes to the opportune removal of the dictator and the implementation of preventative reforms that would prevent revolution. The likelihood of the outbreak and success of a revolution thus increases (Goodwin 1997).

Exclusive authoritarianism, on the other hand, generates a broad social base of opponents. It creates radical enemies by *excluding* most of the mobilised groups from *power and resources*. De-radicalisation happens when mobilised groups are *incorporated* into the system and acquire a share of power and resources, or at least the feeling that they have a realistic chance of acquiring such a share in the future. Incorporation holds out the hope that the state might be reformed without resorting to violence. It creates the feeling that government is not simply the domain of a small clique that excludes all others. This is why there has never in history been a revolution in *democracies*. All revolutions during the 20th century took place in authoritarian regimes, which are the incubators of radical collective action. Revolutionaries and other specialists in political violence thrive. They are regarded as realists by a society excluded from a share in state power and resources. Their repertoires of contention are regarded as being the only effective ones, while the position of moderates in authoritarian regimes is systematically eroded. Society regards moderates as ineffective and impractical idealists incapable of pushing through policy. And so by virtue of its blanket exclusion of citizens and resources, the authoritarian regime vindicates radical ideology, radical identities, and radical political action. It offers no alternative to the political violence of revolutionaries.

An authoritarianism generating many enemies will tend to use excessive *state violence* against mobilised groups and opposition leaders. Similarly to the exclusion from power and resources, state violence also legitimises and popularises the idea that a regime that kills its own citizens must be overthrown and radically reorganised, thus lending weight to ideologies speaking of the intolerability of a continuation of the status quo. If people are being murdered, piecemeal reform measures will not suffice, but only the complete transformation of the state and society. What is more, state violence acts as a boomerang. Even those who have hitherto been moderate or apolitical become politicised and arm themselves simply for the sake of self-defence, or join already armed, organised militants. The upshot is that revolutionaries often win over hearts and minds not because their ideology is especially attractive, but because the population feels the need to protect itself against a brutal state. In addition, mobilised revolutionary groups resort to violence after discovering that their demands for change cannot be met through legal, peaceful means, since such endeavours encounter state violence and repression. The unintended consequence of exclusion and regime-sponsored violence is to strengthen the position of challengers (Goodwin 1997).

A state-centric approach therefore reveals some *types of state* to be more prone to collapse and the creation of opportunities can then be exploited by revolutionary challengers. Such states are also more prone to the formation and mobilisation of a cohesive revolutionary movement. Certain types of state provide a space for the organisation of a revolutionary movement, weaken the counter-revolutionary elite, contribute to the politicisation of the population's dissatisfaction, choke off all possibilities of non-violent reform, force people to take up arms in order to defend themselves, and lend a veneer of seriousness to radical ideologies and identities (Goodwin 1997).

Types of state can be differentiated using two dimensions. The first dimension is a state's *capacity to govern* as measured by the degree of control it has over the resources, activities and population in its territory. High-capacity states are able to effectively promote officially approved collective action and suppress conduct defined as banned. They are able to use state violence effectively, make more demands of their populations, monitor them more closely, and enter more often into conflicts and social interactions. The second dimension is the *level of democracy* as measured by the degree of control over the government and state resources enjoyed by the population, and the degree of freedom protecting them against the wilfulness of the state. Democracies offer space for a wide variety of tolerated behaviour, and only limited examples of conduct are banned or compulsory (Tilly 2006b, Huntington 1968).

This means that *revolutionary situations* arise more frequently in undemocratic states with a low or moderate capacity to govern. Revolutions are pointless in democracies: the functioning of the state can be influenced by many non-violent means. They are equally ineffective in collapsed states, where the grip of the central government exerts no pressure. Finally, they are too risky in non-democratic regimes with a high capacity to govern, since the state is too strong an adversary (Tilly 2006b). Lewis Coser (1956) employs a similar argument when he claims that democracy, as opposed to authoritarian regimes, does not suppress the majority of conflicts but allows them to be played out in full. Minor conflicts balance each other out in terms of sheer numbers and, acting as a safety valve, allow for the continuous release of accumulated tensions in society. Authoritarian regimes on the other hand attempt to suppress all conflict and their governments tend to collapse in the face of one large, uncontrolled conflict after a period of apparent stability (Coser 1956).

Since the 17th century Europe has followed a historical trajectory from non-democratic regimes with a low capacity to govern to high-capacity democracies. The historical drop in the incidence of revolutionary situations corresponds to this, and in any case a revolutionary situation in itself does not in most cases lead to a *revolutionary outcome* (Tilly 1993). However, empirical evidence indicates that the post-colonial Middle East follows a completely different historical trajectory leading from weak, non-democratic regimes to even weaker and more authoritarian ones. As a consequence, revolutions seem to be one of the very few ways of pushing for change.

TERRORISM

However, the state-centric approach does not regard revolutions as a disparate and isolated repertoire of contention. On the contrary, it sees them as part of a cluster of related, mutually interpenetrating repertoires of contention, a cluster formed by the concurrence of a high level of violence, a relatively high level of coordination, and a relatively high level of asymmetry of the competing parties: terrorism and civil wars. Something else revolutions have in common is that they are least likely to occur in democratic regimes with high-capacity governments, but most likely to occur in non-democratic regimes with low-capacity governments. Political rivalry in this type of regime displays a dynamic in which terrorism becomes revolution and revolution can become civil war. However, the sequence can also be reversed. Challengers may resort to the parallel utilisation of multiple repertoires, with one of the repertoires temporarily prevailing at any given point in the conflict with the government (Tilly 2006b). Robert Pape (2003, 2006, 2010) described this dynamic using the example of suicide terrorism as a method of asymmetrical warfare against foreign occupation by a militarily more powerful opponent, and showed that a campaign of suicide bombings tends to represent the culmination of other forms of violent resistance against a real or imagined occupation.

According to Charles Tilly (2006b), *terrorism* is therefore not as frequent in high-capacity regimes, because strong states keep a firm grip on their monopoly on violence and are able to pacify the society within their jurisdiction. Similarly, they are able to keep at bay terrorism organised and supported from without by a competing state or non-state group. They control effectively the means of violence and specialists in violence. The prevention, monitoring and repression of potentially violent actors is relatively high, and the state is therefore able quickly and effectively to nip potentially violent conflict in the bud. The state is highly involved in political rivalry either as the main participant attempting to eliminate open political conflicts (in non-democratic regimes), or as an independent third party attempting to moderate such conflicts (in democratic regimes). Under such conditions a highly secret organisation and very careful planning is necessary for a terrorist attack, as in the case of the attacks in New York and Washington (2001), Casablanca (2003) and Madrid (2004).

Terrorism is also not so common in democratic regimes because democracy offers a wide range of approved or tolerated repertoires of contention. Indeed, it proscribes only a small set of repertoires, above all violent ones. There exists therefore a host of non-violent and legal alternatives to collective action, amongst which political actors may choose and using which they may issue publicly their political demands. This diverts political actors from needlessly risky, illegal and violent terrorism, which within the democratic context is no longer an effective, rational method of political participation (Tilly 2006b). Similarly, democracy tolerates or even supports a range of political actors. It bans only a small number of them and pushes them outside the system or into illegality (Tilly 2006a). Finally, the police and the armed forces are under greater and more transparent control in democracies. They abide by laws, do not breach the human rights of certain groups, and do not provoke opposition groups to resort to terrorism. Overall we see that there is the least pressure to resort to terrorism in democratic regimes. The mirror image to this state of affairs is to be found in low-capacity, non-democratic regimes that, on the contrary, generate the most terrorism (Tilly 2006b).

CIVIL WAR

The state-centric approach analyses the incidence of *civil war* in a similar way. Civil wars have been on the increase since the end of the Second World War due to the process of decolonisation, during which a large number of new independent states came into being that tend to be undemocratic and whose capacity to govern is weak and gradually diminishing. In addition, decolonisation takes place against the backdrop of an expansion of both the legal and illegal international trade in arms and commodities (drugs and raw materials), which permits not only governments but opposition groups to buy weapons, and within an international political context in which strong superpowers intervene in the internal affairs of weak post-colonial states, especially in the conflicts taking place inside these states (support for opposition groups, coup d'états, separatism, etc.).

Civil wars are rare in strong democracies. The mechanisms of democracy mean that opposition groups or separatist movements can draw on a wide range of legitimate or tolerated non-violent repertoires of contention in order to achieve their goals. In turn, the strength of the state ensures a monopoly on the use of violence in its territory. It does not allow the internal opposition or a foreign state to destabilise the government or to arm or train challengers. In contrast, politics in weak, non-democratic states is a "non-repeating zero-sum game", in which the winner takes all and the loser loses everything, because there is no sharing of political power and economic resources. The winner garners all power and economic resources for themselves and their cronies by filling all the key positions in the administration. Seizing power in a state is all the more tempting when the country is poor, lacks a diversified economy, and where there exist no alternative means for achieving wealth and social advancement. The losers, on the other hand, are completely excluded from power and economic resources for good, or at least until the next civil war or revolution. As a consequence any conflict over power in such a state is extremely intense and violent (Tilly 2006a).

POLITICAL REGIMES AND POLITICAL REPERTOIRES: PARTIAL CONCLUSIONS

The Middle East is full of undemocratic states with a moderate or low capacity to govern. The assumption of the state-centric model, namely that the character of a political regime forms the character of its prevailing repertoires of contention, explains why the region generates high levels of political violence. In this respect the post-colonial Middle East differs from other modern macro-regions, including post-colonial and post-communist regions, as well as from the historical development of modernising Western Europe, where there was a gradual transition from weak, undemocratic states to strong democratic states, a process accompanied by a reduction in the frequency of political violence and a transition to non-violent forms of political contention.

We need not, therefore, resort to clichés regarding Arab culture or Islam, such as the "bloody borders of Islam", the "religion of the sword" or a "yearning for martyrdom", in order to explain the causes of the high level of political violence in the region, even if culture is always a source of the meanings, motivations and rationalisations of interested parties. Culture tends more to be an important independent variable caught up in political conflicts already underway. Cultural and political systems interact and come into conflict.

However, the state-centric analysis is less adroit at explaining the *dynamic transitions* between the individual repertoires of contention within the framework of individual Middle Eastern regimes: between coups, terrorism, revolution and civil war. It finds it equally difficult to explain the *timing* of the occurrence of specific violent repertoires of contention or the absence thereof. While the character of Middle Eastern political regimes over the last twenty years has been relatively static, the same period has witnessed great variety in the prevailing repertoires of contention, from terrorism and sporadic outbreaks of civil war during the 1990s, to the Arab revolutionary domino effect of 2011; from what appears to be political stability following the era of military coups lasting many decades, to the chronic instability at the start of the 21st century culminating in the collapse of certain states and the creation of large pockets of anarchy often extending beyond the borders of individual states (especially Libya, Syria, Iraq, and Yemen).

The reason for these analytical lacunae is that the state-centric perspective is resolutely reductionist. It focuses on developments in the political sphere and seeks to explain politics from within politics. It thus ignores parallel developments in the economic, social and demographic spheres and the discrepancy between the rapid pace of developments in these dynamic spheres and the sluggish changes taking place to rigid political systems. It is for this reason that the most unstable societies are those in which this development is most uneven, i.e. it is in non-democratic regimes with a low capacity to govern and in non-diversified economic systems characterised by slow economic growth unable to generate sufficient attractive jobs that a more modern, larger, younger, more educated, more urbanised, more media-savvy and politically mobilised society is coming into existence. This society feels the prosperity deficit and democratic deficit more and more keenly, while at the same time becoming more skilled at mobilising politically and organising itself around collective action upon realising that individual strategies of social mobility are unavailable. The state-centric perspective can thus be constructively incorporated into our general model of uneven modernisation, notwithstanding that fact that it examines only one level of uneven social change extracted from the overall context.

For this reason the following sub-chapters place the political level of social change within the broader context of uneven modernisation and analyse the many interactions that take place between the political system and changes in the economic, social or demographic spheres. They thus identify the many mechanisms transforming divergent and uneven social changes on the macro-level into political action and instability on the micro-level.

(1) THE BIRTH OF POLITICAL ACTORS: MASS POLITICAL PARTICIPATION AND RIGID POLITICAL SYSTEMS

Many political scientists, historians and sociologists have shown that, from the mid-20th century onwards, the regions of the post-colonial developing world, including the Middle East, are undergoing a socio-political development similar to the one experienced from the 18th century to the beginning of the 20th century by a modernising Europe (cf. Huntington 1968, Brzezinski 1993, 2004, Kennedy 1996).

The deeper structural causes of the current instability in the Middle East are therefore analogous to those that led to the rise of European mass movements, revolutions, and intense social and political conflicts, though the outward manifestations and ideological discourses of these structural transformations may differ. For instance, in Western Europe, opposition to monarchies and later liberal democracy was usually voiced by leftist or fascist secular doctrines. In the Middle East, on the other hand, from the 1970s onwards opposition was spearheaded mainly by various versions of political Islam, even though during the Arab Spring (2011) the discourse of liberal democracy resonated strongly. And so the more we remind ourselves of the course and political problems associated with European modernisation in the early modern era, the better grasp we will have of what is going on in the modernising Middle East today.

The spread of literacy and education, the dissemination of the means of mass communication, rapid urbanisation, industrialisation, the creation of centralised nation states and the demographic revolution culminates in the political awakening of what was previously a politically passive and conservative majority of the population. This majority lives in isolated and uncoordinated communities scattered across rural areas, abides by unchanging customs and traditions, and respects traditional authorities (Brzezinski 1993).

So while *traditional societies* are composed mainly of apolitical segments, modernisation is the process by which politically aware *actors* are formed, starting with intellectuals and reform-minded elites of the bureaucratic and military hierarchies, moving on to students and an ever more assertive urban middle class, followed by revolutionary workers and finally the rural masses. Since rural communities in modernising societies represent the largest mass of the population with the greatest political potential, many opposing actors, from conservative groups or military juntas to reform-minded urban factions and revolutionaries seeking to overthrow the system, make strenuous efforts to win them over to their side. This accounts for the conflicting perceptions of the role of the peasantry in political conflict, which can either be regarded as a conservative force or, on the contrary, as the standard bearer of revolutionary ideologies (Huntington 1968).

Within the ruins of disappearing or weakened traditional social structures, disoriented and alienated individuals seek new groups and *identities* that could replace these structures. There is shift of identity from *small groups* typical of traditional societies (family, tribe, congregation, village, etc.) to an identification with *large groups*, such as class, race, region, political party, social or religious movement, professional group, nation, or even civilisation (Huntington 1968). Charles Tilly (1983) points out that the shift in identities and loyalties towards larger groups is also related to the creation of modern centralised states, since the most important political decisions (tax collection, military conscription, the handling of property rights, etc.) more and more take place on a national level. For this reason individual interest groups must mobilise and engage on this national level.

Mass *political participation* represents a key defining feature of modern politics. This fact has to be confronted by authoritarian regimes in which the government controls a population whose political activity destabilises the regime, and also by democratic governments where, on the contrary, the masses control the government and their political activity increases the stability of the system. The political systems of modernising countries must therefore gradually come to terms with the three main waves of political participation: the urban middle classes, workers, and the rural population.

Praetorian regimes resolve the problem by escalating their repression of newly formed or newly aware groups with ambitions to enter politics. The disparity between ever more modern societies and insufficiently developed political institutions then grows larger, resulting in greater political instability. In contrast, *civil regimes* draw on increasingly sophisticated political institutionalisation in an effort to achieve the non-destructive incorporation and political assimilation of new political players into the political system, mostly through political parties. They create conditions and rules for the non-violent resolution of ideological differences and they promote a sense of community that shares core values and goals. The most propitious situation is one in which the creation of political institutions is one step ahead of growing political participation, since it means that institutions for the assimilation of the politicised masses are prepared even before their forceful entry onto the political scene, and so the socio-economic and political dimensions of modernisation are in harmony with each other (Huntington 1968).

If, therefore, the pace of political modernisation and *institutionalisation* (political parties and institutionalised methods of resolving conflicts between actors) corresponds to that of political mobilisation and the participation of new actors, a society is relatively stable. Conversely, if new actors cannot be assimilated within the existing political system and socio-economic modernisation is excessively divorced from political modernisation, there is a greater threat of social instability and violent conflict. Politics and political actors are forced into illegality and onto the street. During the first stages of socio-economic modernisation this then increases the risk of military coup, which is an expression of a conflict between the elite and a small counter-elite composed of the middle classes. In subsequent stages of socio-economic modernisation, when politicised workers, students, peasants and the urban poor are becoming involved in political rivalry, the likelihood of revolution and civil war increases. The politically awakened masses now participate in conflicts and political rivalry, with bloodier outcomes (Huntington 1968).

APPLICATION TO THE MIDDLE EAST: TRADITIONAL AND MODERN PERSONALITY TYPES

Daniel Lerner (1964) charted the interim stage in the emergence of modern political actors empirically using pioneering sociological research in several Middle Eastern countries (Egypt, Lebanon, Jordan, Turkey and Iran). Working on the premise that "modernity is primarily a state of mind" (ibid: viii), Lerner's heroes are three distinct and psychologically alienated personality types, whose proportional representation in the population gradually changes during the process of modernisation: (a) traditional, (b) transitional, and (c) modern.

The traditional and modern types differ in respect of their values, opinions and mentality. This applies above all to their capacity for empathy and the sophistication of public opinion. The man of tradition cannot imagine living differently. He rejects otherness, innovation, experimentation or deviation from the norm, and, on the contrary, places great store by loyalty, obedience, passivity, and the absence of change. As he sees it, in an ideal world every future generation would live by the same principles as the previous.

The traditional type is not psychologically capable of moving beyond his limited experience and is unaware of the alternative directions that not only his own life could take, but the development of society as a whole. These limited horizons are connected with the *absence of empathy*, namely the ability to see oneself potentially in very different social roles, to strike up contact with new people, to be inspired by different models of behaviour, and to be capable of adapting to new social situations and changing environments and planning for the future. The traditional type is unable – at least without consternation or even outrage – to answer projective questions such as: what he would do if he was president of his country or editor-in-chief of its most influential newspaper; if forced to, what country he would emigrate to or what kind of life he would wish for after moving to a capital city or even the USA. Typical replies to such questions were: "I'd rather die than imagine life elsewhere", "God would punish me if I even had such a thought", or "What kind of stupid question is that?"[2]

Most Iranians, for instance, displayed no interest whatsoever in the nationalisation of the *Anglo-Iranian Oil Company*, the most dramatic event at the time. Likewise, the Syrians completely ignored a series of military coups caused by rivalry among narrow elites and counter-elites. The King of Jordan ruled uninterrupted over a scattered population in rural and nomadic regions until the exodus arrived of politicised and relatively urbanised, literate and informed Palestinian refugees. Traditional Turks were fond of declaring: "Politics doesn't concern us", "You can't change anything so it's stupid to even try", "Our leaders know best what to do", or "It is not for us to judge our leaders".

An *apolitical* stance and the absence of opinions can be due to many factors. It may be a fatalistic form of piety ("Everything is God's will", "I am satisfied with what God gave me."), or a conviction that problems have no resolution and that the current situation will persist forever. It may be an inability to place personal problems within a broader national or even international context. For instance, respondents said that poverty was their biggest problem, though were unable to identify it as a problem for the entire country. It may also reflect an inability to understand fully a person's own interests and because of limited empathy to perceive possible alternatives to the social order in which these interests would be better met. Finally, the horizons of the world of a traditional man end at the borders of a nomadic tribe, village or urban neighbourhood, which is also where his identity and loyalties end. Such a person is very difficult to mobilise politically using modern political symbols of the nation or class. Traditional masses without opinions and formulated political stances are thus ideal fodder for political elites, who can rule undisturbed while the masses at most look on passively (Lerner 1964).

A re-orientation from tradition and the past to the future is closely linked with the emergence of an empathetic personality type able to imagine themselves in various different new roles and situations. This is the psychological basis of modernisation itself (cf. Eisenstadt 2000). As a result public opinion arises relating firstly to local and regional affairs, but more and more frequently to matters of national or even global significance. This can then lead to the mass politicisation of a people, who are now able to see the connections between their personal situation and the state of society as a whole. They begin to form opinions regarding a range of issues and seek to apply these opinions in practice (Lerner 1964).

---

2   However, Lerner underestimated the context of repressive regimes during his questioning carried out at the end of the 1950s. Respondents might well have been afraid to express their opinion (Bah 2008).

The mass entry of previously traditional populations into the political arena represents a historically new situation and a fundamental challenge to regimes of all types. A narrow political elite divorced from the rest of society is no longer able to rule without interruption, at most challenged from time to time by a similarly isolated counter-elite. Socio-economic and demographic modernisation has become detached from the pace of political modernisation. As a consequence, mass political mobilisation comes into sharp conflict with highly repressive and authoritarian regimes, which do not offer institutionalised methods of resolving proliferating conflicts between interest groups and ideologies. The vast majority of the population continues to be excluded from political systems and participation. The inability to co-opt new political actors into the political system represents a fundamental source of political tension and destabilisation across the post-colonial Middle East.

(2) THE DISCREPANCY BETWEEN PREFERENCES AND REALITY: THE DESIRE FOR DEMOCRACY, PROSPERITY AND CONSERVATIVE MORALS

There is strong support for democracy, political rights and civil liberties in Middle Eastern societies fully comparable with other regions of the developing world and even the West. This is reliably borne out by a vast number of representative sociological surveys carried out in the region over recent years by academic institutions, non-governmental organisations and reputable commercial agencies, e.g. the Pew Research Center, the Gallup World Poll, Zogby Polls, the World Values Survey and the Arab Barometer.

All these surveys arrive at the same conclusions: in the Middle East there is the *greatest rift in the world* between the pro-democracy opinions of the public and the repressive character of regimes. Political preferences diverge most radically from political reality, while elsewhere in the world the character of regimes corresponds more closely to the prevailing attitudes of populations. Herein lies the potential for instability (Inglegart and Welzel 2006). The result is an intensely experienced *democratic deficit*. Nevertheless, with the exception of the oil-rich and sparsely populated monarchies of the Gulf States, people in the region are also aware of the *prosperity deficit* (Pew Center 2007). The combination of these two intensively experienced deficits is at the root of the increase in political tension. The Arab public evaluated the Arab Spring (2011) using the same logic, namely as an endeavour on the part of ordinary people to achieve dignity, freedom and a better life (57%). Only a minority interpreted it as an attempt by opposition or sectarian groups to seize power (16%) or an attempt on the part of the superpowers to plunge the region into turmoil (19%). It was for this reason that the vast majority of

Arabs supported the uprising of populations against authoritarian regimes in Syria (89%), Yemen (86%) and Bahrain (64%) (Zogby 2011).

However, the Middle Eastern public has long been deprived of an opportunity to say what they think and what they want (Zogby 2012). In the meantime, there has been speculation in the West regarding the incompatibility of Islam and democracy and a supposed inclination on the part of Arabs towards authoritarianism: these speculations have no backup in data (cf. Kedourie 1992, Esposito and Voll 2001, Bukay 2007).

In traditional or early modern societies, where most of the population are not interested in politics, have no firm political opinion, and do not participate in political rivalry, the competing elites and counter-elites are unconcerned by what the majority think. Public opinion only makes an appearance with the advance of modernisation, especially thanks to the expansion of the media, an increase in education, and urbanisation, along with the creation of centralised nation states and the spread of political propaganda (cf. Lerner 1964, Šubrt 1998). With modernisation more and more classes – the intelligentsia, students, the middle classes, workers and finally peasants – enter the political arena (Huntington 1968). A national awareness arises and the idea of a nationally defined political community takes root (Gellner 1993, Anderson 2008).

The transformation of an apolitical, traditional population into a politically aware, self-confident and active public is something that Middle Eastern authoritarian regimes and traditional religious and opposition groups, including Islamists, are having to react to. If they seek the support of the general public, they have to react to the deeper ideological shifts in public opinion and adapt their policies and rhetoric accordingly. Regimes, religious leaders, opposition groups and Islamists have to respond to the demand for democracy and openness if they want to ride the wave of a modernising population. So what opinions, attitudes and values must political elites and counter-elites respect if they are to win public support?

FOLLOWERS OF THE PROPHET: PIETY, TRADITION AND CULTURAL SUPREMACY

Since the 1970s, the Islamic discourse has become the main language of Middle Eastern politics, to which many different political actors with a variety of different interests and visions have claimed allegiance (Eickelman and Piscatori 1996). Religion, tradition and culture are important sources of identity. For this reason, the religious and cultural substrate, within the context of which rapid and uneven modernisation is taking place, is becoming a source of politically relevant symbols (the devil, the Crusaders), popular role models (the Prophet, *salaf*, ibn Taymiyyah), imaginaries (the "golden age", *Jahiliy-*

yah), and concepts (*Jihad*, Islamic law, *fitna*). These are concepts (cf. Lewis 1988, Mendel 2008) carrying a strong emotional and political charge that both authoritarian regimes and opposition groups attempt to control and reinterpret to their own ends.

Using data from four waves of the World Values Survey, Pippa Norris and Ronald Inglehart (2004) claim that a *value gap is opening up* between a demographically stagnating *minority* of ever more secular, advanced and wealthy parts of the world living in safety and prosperity (the West with the exception of the USA) and the rest of the world, demographically dynamic but living in poor, less advanced and strongly religious regions at constant threat from an unpredictable natural, political and social environment. For this reason most of the world's population places its faith in supernatural forces and certainties in the form of religion. This involves almost all societies of the developing world, including those that are predominantly Muslim. There is no intergenerational reduction in faith or religious practice. Indeed, in the generation born in the 1960s there has been an intensification of religious sentiment (Inglehart and Norris 2004).

The most religious regions in the world are the poor societies of Africa and the whole of the Middle East. The least religious are the wealthy countries of Western Europe. The USA and certain countries of Eastern Europe are located somewhere between these two extremes (Pew Center 2007). Instead of secularisation, over the last few decades what we are seeing is more a *global religious revival* (Moghadam 2003). Some countries of Western Europe are an exception, though not the USA (Davie 2009).

If Muslims are asked to state their core values, they usually place faith in God and their family in first place. For the vast majority of Muslims faith is an important aspect of everyday life: from 98% in Egypt to 86% in "secular" Turkey. In the USA this figure is 68%, and in Western Europe it is significantly lower (28% in Great Britain). Most Muslims believe that their life has an important goal and a deep meaning (90% of Egyptians and Saudis). They also claim that regular prayer helps reduce personal fears, stress, and the anxiety caused by everyday worries (from 83% in Morocco to 53% in Turkey) (Esposito and Mogahed 2007).

Muslims are also significantly more likely to believe that faith in God is a necessary precondition for the *morality of the individual*: 99% in Egypt and 97% in Jordan, though only 66% in Lebanon. In Europe, on the other hand, this opinion is shared by only 20% of the population (Pew Center 2007). At the same time, the majority of Middle Eastern Muslims see no contradiction between their religion and life in a modern society (Pew Center 2006).

Muslims also view customs and traditions as crucial to their life (approx. 90%). In contrast, Americans (54%) and post-traditional Europeans (approx. 20%) are considerably more reserved in respect of their traditions

(Esposito and Mogahed 2007). However, a slight majority of Muslims are concerned about the decline of their traditional way of life and culture, though an international comparison reveals these concerns to be less acute than in other parts of the world. Internationally, Muslims are among those most strongly convinced that *their way of life must be protected against foreign influences* (between 80% and 90%). If, then, Muslims are in favour of economic globalisation, rating international trade, multinational corporations and economic migration highly, the same cannot be said of the globalisation of culture, which they perceive as a threat (Pew Center 2007).

Muslims believe their culture is *superior to others*. However, this applies mostly to large, populous nations beyond the borders of the Arab Middle East. The Arab world is more restrained in this respect. While this opinion is shared by 89% of Indonesians, 82% of Pakistanis and 80% of Turks, it is true of only 59% of Jordanians and 55% of Kuwaitis. A feeling of cultural exclusivity sets Muslims apart from the highly self-critical Western Europeans, with the exception of the culturally proud Italy. Conversely, Muslims, including Arabs, share a sense of exceptionalism and uniqueness with Americans, and above all with the heirs to the large historical civilisations of all continents (Pew Center 2007).

In conclusion, as far as religiosity and cultural pride are concerned, the Middle East is similar to the USA, where religion has played a crucial role since the arrival of the first Protestant settlers determined to establish a New Jerusalem. To this day in the USA many different brands of political actor incline towards the religious imaginary. However, it would be untrue to say that this makes Americans less modern or less democratic. Modernity and democracy can take different forms, and the paths to them can also be convoluted and articulated in different ways (cf. Kepel 1996, Juergensmeyer 2000, Huntington 2005, Kohut and Stokes 2007).

PAN-ARAB AND PAN-ISLAMIC IDENTITY

Human identity is always multi-layered and an emphasis on its individual dimensions can vary depending on a person's life experience or situation at any given point in time. What is typical of the Middle East is that, as well as identifying with the nation state, Arabs identify equally strongly with other Arabs and Muslims. When asked to choose their primary identity, approximately a third opt for nationalism, a third pan-Arabism, and a third pan-Islamism. Their identity as Arabs (2010) is important for 100% of Palestinians, 99% of Egyptians, 90% of Jordanians, 88% of Saudis, and a lukewarm 72% of Lebanese. Similarly, Arab unity is personally important for the vast majority of Arabs: from two thirds of Moroccans to over 90% of Saudis (Zogby 2012).

This multi-dimensional identity is then projected into political preferences. Arabs believe that if their government reaches a decision, it should above all be in the interests of their country (58%). However, a fairly large number of respondents think that the government should be looking after the interests of all Arabs (23%), or even all Muslims (20%) (Zogby 2011). The political implications of Arab identity also relate to the question of Palestine and the occupation of Iraq. By far the majority of Arabs consider these issues important (2007). However, the main motif running through these findings was not religion or the fact that the Palestinians and Iraqis are victims of occupation. The main motif was that "they are Arabs like me" (Zogby 2012).

ATTITUDE TO THE WEST: ADMIRATION OF INSTITUTIONS, ANTIPATHY TO FOREIGN POLICY

Arabs are allegedly not like us. They hate our way of life. They dislike freedom and feel contempt for democracy. They are submissive in the face of authority and see no value in the individual or individual freedom. Dictatorship is the default setting for Arab societies. However, these and similar stereotypes are simply a reflection of the Western discourse of *orientalism* and in no way represent the reality of Arab societies (Halliday 2005, Said 2008).

Muslims in Western countries most admire the level of technical development, a stable standard of living, freedom of speech, and a functioning democracy (Esposito and Mogahed 2007). Similarly, Arabs living in the USA emphasise scientific and technological development, the quality of the educational system, goods, films, and freedom and democracy (Zogby 2012).

Muslims are most irritated by the West's foreign policies, especially its support for authoritarian regimes, its partisan support for Israel, and its military interventions (Esposito and Mogahed 2007). After the invasion of Afghanistan and Iraq, Arabs regard the USA along with Israel as their biggest threat, far greater, for instance, than the threat represented by Iran (Zogby 2010, 2011). Most inhabitants of Muslim countries are even worried that the USA might soon attack their own country: 74% share this concern in Indonesia, 72% in Nigeria and Pakistan, 71% in Turkey (a NATO member), 57% in Lebanon and Jordan, and 53% in Kuwait. Only in Morocco does the majority of the population find little credence in such a threat (Kohut, Stokes 2007). A large number of Arabs believe that the guiding force behind American foreign policy is not simply the desire to control oil supplies (53%) or to protect Israel (44%), but also a religious rivalry that is attempting to weaken the Muslim world (32%) and maintain its own dominance in the region (29%) (Zogby 2011). When Arab respondents are offered the opportunity to send a message to the US, one of the most frequent pleas is "Stop killing us!" These ambivalent attitudes towards America were summed up by one Lebanese as follows: "We don't reject America, but we feel America is rejecting us. It's not that we hate America, but that we feel that America hates us. We want to be recognised and respected by America and we feel this isn't the case at present. We feel like a spurned lover" (Zogby 2012: 90).

SUPPORT FOR DEMOCRACY, AVERSION TO AUTHORITARIANISM

The vast majority of Muslims believe that *democracy is not simply a matter for the West*, but that it could operate equally well in their own countries: in Kuwait 81% hold this opinion, in Jordan 70%, and in Egypt 59% (Pew Center 2007). A preference for democracy can, of course, change over time. For example, in spring 2011 support for democracy in Egypt grew considerably. As elsewhere in the world, Middle Eastern public opinion is not monolithic and incapable of change (Pew Center 2011).

Democracy is not perceived by Muslims as an exclusively Western and culturally alien institution. To most people, *democracy, for all of its shortcomings, is the best form of government.* This view is held by between 92% and 99% of Egyptians, Moroccans and Turks. Indeed, there is greater support for democracy in the Arab countries than anywhere else in the world. Western Europe and the USA are next, followed by other Muslim countries, Latin America and Sub-Saharan Africa. The least support for democracy is to be found in post-communist Eastern Europe and above all in Eastern Asia (Inglehart 2007). If we examine the influence of socio-economic or political development in a comparative multiple regression analysis, we arrive at the startling conclusion that democracy in predominantly Muslim countries is considerably more attractive than in the societies of other religious traditions. In other words, if Muslim societies were socially and politically more advanced, support for democracy would be even higher (Inglehar, Norris 2002, 2003, Dixon 2008).

The Arab Barometer also identifies a high level of support for democracy. Despite its flaws, democracy is regarded as being the best system of government by 86% of Arabs on average, with this figure applying to 92% of Moroccans and 83% of Algerians and Palestinians. Likewise, a majority of Arabs (90%) want to see democracy in their own country: 96% of Moroccans and 81% of Algerians. Interestingly, there is *no relationship* between religiosity (frequency of reading the Koran or visiting a mosque) and support for democracy. The religious and secular factions of society support democracy equally strongly (Jamal and Tessler 2008). Egypt is an exception, where more religious people incline towards democracy, while secularists lean towards authoritarianism. Overall, then, the region's democratic deficit cannot be explained by culture, Islam or the piety of Arabs. On the level of individuals it does not seem that Islam operates as an obstacle to democracy (Tessler 2007).

Muslims are also aware of the possible shortcomings of democracy in terms of its indecision, ineffectiveness, and its inability to maintain law and order and to ensure stable conditions for the healthy functioning of the economy. In this respect their mild scepticism is comparable with that of the Western public. However, the day-to-day *functioning of democracy*, if not the idea itself, is rated positively (Inglehart and Norris 2002). As a consequence, a majority of Arabs (83%) pronounced themselves in favour of gradual reform and democratisation (Jamal and Tessler 2008).

At the same time, most Muslims, like most Westerners (61%), *reject authoritarian forms of government*, or to put it more precisely, they reject the idea that a strong leader who did not have to worry about elections and parliament would be good for the country. Although this type of regime is disproportionately represented in most of the mainly Muslim and Arab countries, in this respect too there was no great discrepancy between Islam and the West. Significantly greater support for strong leaders was found only in the Sino-Confucian civilisation (Inglehart and Norris 2002, Pew Center 2007).

Other surveys conducted in Arab countries are consistent with these findings. Only 17% of Arabs believe that an unelected authoritarian leader unrestricted by parliament would be good for their country. Again, there is no correlation between support for authoritarianism and religiosity. Somewhat paradoxically at first sight, this opinion does not even correlate with the level of support for democracy as the best form of government. It is often held by people worried about the chaos that might ensue from rapid democratisation, something they have seen take place in Algeria, Palestine and Iraq, i.e. by people who are in favour of gradual democratisation. This is often the opinion expressed by the people of Morocco and Jordan, i.e. countries with relatively popular and reform-minded monarchies. According to this minority segment, the long-term political transition to democracy must be implemented and overseen by a strong leader (Jamal and Tessler 2008).

CONSTITUTIONAL LIBERALISM: POLITICAL RIGHTS AND CIVIL LIBERTIES

Muslims around the world support the basic liberal principles without which democracy cannot exist, since it would otherwise be under constant threat of becoming distorted into a tyranny of the majority, dominant religious group, or state power. Extremely important in this respect is freedom of religion, an impartial judiciary and media, free and fair electoral competition, and freedom of speech. More problematic, however, is the lukewarm support shown for the principle of civilian control over the army, and above all attitudes to women.

Support for liberal principles is above average even within the framework of an international comparison: "In general, the emerging democracies of Africa and the Middle East offer the strongest support for the six principles tested, while Eastern Europeans and Asians express the least." At the same time, not only individual geographic and cultural regions differ, but variability reigns even within these regions and states themselves, again demonstrating that the Middle East is not some homogenous monolith (Pew Center 2007: 58).

The freedom to practice religion is deemed "a very important" principle, with support ranging from 90% of the inhabitants of Kuwait and Egypt to 70% in Turkey. A fair and impartial judiciary is deemed very important by the vast majority of Egyptians and Lebanese (almost 90%) (Pew Center 2007). In this respect, Arabs are angered by the corruption that inhibits the impartial rule of law in which the same rules would apply to everyone. For example, Egyptians believed that their biggest problem, along with a lack of democracy, was corruption (53%). Alongside the improvement of economic conditions (82%), they therefore felt the top priority was the creation of a fair judicial system (79%) and the impartial rule of law (63%) (Pew Center 2011).

Free and fair elections in which several political parties compete for voter preferences is seen as very important, as is freedom of speech (Pew Center 2007). The majority of Muslims around the world agree with the proposition that a citizen must be able to express freely his opinion of political, social and economic topics, with 94% of Egyptians and 93% Iranians espousing this view (Esposito and Mogahed 2007). The opportunity to speak one's mind and to criticise the government freely is deemed "very important" by 86% of Lebanese and 80% of Egyptians, the highest level of support for freedom of speech of all 35 post-colonial and post-communist countries (Pew Center 2007). After the fall of the Mubarak-led regime, a total of 63% of Egyptians saw freedom of speech as a priority. This was the third most urgent priority after improvements to the economic situation and the creation of a fair judiciary (Pew Center 2011). Similarly, an independent media free from government censorship is considered "very important" for 75% of Egyptians, 72% of Lebanese, 62% of Moroccans, and 50% of Turks. Conversely, a free press is least supported by Muslims from South and Southeast Asia, i.e. far beyond the borders of the Middle East. The willingness in this region to accept censorship is very similar to that of the Russians and Poles (Pew Center 2007, Jamal and Tessler 2008).

Civilian control of the military is generally viewed as less important than other democratic principles. However, this is a worldwide phenomenon not restricted to the Middle East. The principle is seen as very important by 57% of Lebanese, 50% of Moroccans and 47% of Turks, but only by 15% of Kuwaitis and a measly 3% of Jordanians (Pew Center 2007). The much debated issue of the separation of Islam and politics in the Middle East is in fact overshadowed by the problem of the separation of the military and politics. The absence of civilian control over military budgets and the "tradition" of military coups in the region is problematic. Middle Eastern regimes largely arose from the officer class, with generals comprising the upper levels of the pyramid of power. As a consequence, the armed forces are sometimes perceived as the guarantor of secularism or the supremacy of an ethnic, religious or tribal minority over the rest of the population.

However, attitudes to the army could change quickly. For instance, shortly after the overthrow of President Mubarak the army was the most popular institution in Egypt, with 88% of Egyptians convinced of its positive role in spring 2011. The police, who were beating protesters at the time, were viewed negatively. Field Marshal Mohamed Tantawi, despite being linked to the old regime, enjoyed the confidence of 90% of the population, making him the most popular personality. As a result, only 27% of Egyptians deemed control of the military by civilians to be a priority, very much at the tail end of a total of nine key tasks for the new regime (Pew Center 2011). However, by the end of the year most Egyptians perceived the army in a negative light, with 43% believing that it was trying to slow down or even reverse the results of the revolution, and only 21% thinking that it was trying to support the revolution (Zogby 2011).

A less well explored liberal principle is that of the *rights of ethnic and religious minorities*. For instance, in post-revolutionary Egypt religious freedom was not deemed a priority even in the face of attacks against Coptic Christians. Only 36% of the population rated it a priority, which made it the issue least perceived to be a problem after control of the army (Pew Center 2011).

The *democratic deficit* felt by Middle Eastern people who are committed to liberal principles while being suppressed by authoritarian regimes is the highest in the world. Only Palestine is an exception. The biggest discrepancy between the ideal and the reality is felt most intensely by Moroccans, Egyptians and Turks. This applies to all the liberal principles tested, with the exception of the free practice of faith, which is apparently a reality for 40% to 80% of respondents. The people questioned said that under no circumstances did liberal principles correspond to conditions on the ground in their countries. There is a large democratic deficit in the region and widespread frustration at the repression practiced (Pew Center 2007).

STATUS OF WOMEN

In addition to control of the military and the status of minorities, the most problematic opinions aired relate to women and their role in the public sphere (studies, work and politics). Furthermore, many studies conducted by Arab intellectuals emphasise that the unequal status of women is a major factor in the stagnation of the Middle East (AHDR 2002, 2005).

The chasm in values separating Islam and the West relates to gender equality, the status of women in society, and sexual freedom, and is not the consequence of divergent opinions regarding the best form of government and organisation of the political scene. Differences cannot be accounted for simply by virtue of lower socio-economic development or political oppression. A key role is played by cultural difference. If the West can be deemed most liberal in the world in respect of gender, Muslim societies are to be found at the other end of the scale. In addition, individual generations of Westerners are becoming more and more liberal, while in the Islamic world we find hardly any shift in values whatsoever. The chasm grows ever deeper (Inglehart and Norris 2002, 2003).

In predominantly Muslim countries there is far greater agreement than in the West – an extra 30 percentage points – with the following statements: men make better political leaders than women; where there is a lack of jobs, men have more right to work than women; a university education is more important for a man than a woman; a woman must have children if she is to be fulfilled in life; women should not live with their children in a household without a husband. These statements are rejected by, on average, 82% of Western populations, but only 55% of Muslims.

There is far less tolerance in the Islamic world than in the West of divorce, abortion, and especially homosexuality, though figures were similar in Sub-Saharan Africa and Asia (Pew Center 2007). Ronald Inglehart and Pippa Norris (2002, 2003) consider tolerance of sexual minorities to be a critical indicator of liberal attitudes, while at the same time recalling that only a few short decades ago you could not speak openly of sexual freedom and the equality of women even in the West.

Surveys also point to a *split* in the Muslim world as regards gender. For example, in roughly half of the countries (Morocco, Lebanon and Turkey) those who believe that women and men are equally good *political leaders* were in the majority. However, in the other half (Palestine and Kuwait) the view prevailed that men made better leaders. Notwithstanding this, women have held the post of president in Turkey, Pakistan and Bangladesh, something that cannot be said of the United States and other Western countries (Pew Center 2007).

Although young girls are traditionally encouraged to pursue activities at home and all sorts of prejudices reign regarding the *employment of women* (cf. Frouzová 2005), young Muslim women want the right to decide for themselves whether to seek work corresponding to their qualifications (76% of women in conservative Saudi Arabia, 88% in Egypt). In this they are supported by men (62% in Saudi Arabia, 73% in Iran) (Esposito and Mogahed 2007). However, the public in individual countries is divided as to whether men and women should be separated on the workplace. In most countries women are more in favour of non-segregated workplaces than men (Pew Center 2010).

Most Muslims believe that it is equally important to provide an *education* to both boys and girls, though the figures are lower in the Islamic world than in other countries, ranging from 73% of Egyptians and Jordanians to 94% of Kuwaitis (Pew Center 2007, 2010). However, this is not the result of culture or religion, but rather a general characteristic of developing countries without functioning social services and health and pension provision. It is usually the son who looks after sick or aged parents, while the daughter goes to live with her husband's family. This is why poorer, larger families, who cannot afford to provide an education to all of their offspring, make the oldest son the priority. His higher education is the precondition for better paid work and thus more secure provision for the parents in old age (Frouzová 2005, Richards and Waterbury 2008). Despite this, in many Middle Eastern countries women are now achieving higher qualifications than men. More women than men study at university in the United Arab Emirates and Iran, while more girls than boys are studying at secondary schools in Jordan, Algeria, Lebanon, Kuwait and Libya (Esposito and Mogahed 2007).

Most Muslims agree that women should have the right to decide whether or not to wear a headscarf. Women are slightly more in favour, and over the last few years there has been a growing trend in the Muslim world supporting the freedom of women to decide whether to cover their bodies or not. The actions of militant Islamists forcing women to cover up has if anything been counterproductive, since it is in these countries that the belief is growing most rapidly that women should decide for themselves (Pakistan, Bangladesh, Indonesian Aceh) (Pew Center 2007).

Overall, as far as all aspects relating to equality between women and men or the role of women in the public sphere (education, work and politics) are concerned, we see a polarisation of opinions rather than a clear consensus. A small majority of Muslims is advocating greater *equality of women* and men: women should have the same rights as men; they should have the right to vote independently in democratic elections without being pressured by the male of the household, to occupy positions in politics, and to be able to drive or work outside the home without being restricted by their surroundings or their husband and his family. The greatest support for emancipation is in Turkey, Lebanon and Iran. In most of the Arab world it is lower. However, it represents the views of the majority in all countries (Esposito and Mogahed 2007).

A UNIVERSAL AND CONSENSUAL UNDERSTANDING OF DEMOCRACY?

The cardinal question remains as to what people in the Middle East understand by the concept "democracy" and what they expect of it. Does everyone understand it in the same way or are there differences of opinion among segments of the population as to what it means? And is it a similar idea of democracy to that in the West?

When Arabs were asked to rate the level of democracy in selected countries, including their own, on a scale of 1 to 10, their opinions agreed with those of Western political commentators or human rights organisations such as Freedom House: Saudi Arabia, Syria and Iran always came out worst, while the United States and Japan were rated top. In addition, respondents were able to distinguish subtler nuances between Arab regimes (e.g. Algeria, Yemen, Jordan and Lebanon). They even conceded a realistic degree of democracy to the otherwise negatively ranked Israel. The survey's authors conclude: "Arabs rank democracy in individual countries the same as experts and international organisations. Their understanding of democracy is therefore based on a *universal* perspective." (Braizat 2010: 136).

The fact that Arabs regard democracy as do Westerners is borne out, for example, by analyses of the open question "What does democracy mean?", which offered respondents the opportunity to reply in their own words (the Jordanian survey *The State of Democracy*). Most (63%) equated democracy with political rights and civil liberties. Most frequently they employed words like freedom of speech, an independent press, free and fair elections, the rule of law, the accountability of politicians to citizens, and freedom of association. A smaller section of opinion (21%) emphasised themes linked with justice and social equality. A minority (11%) believed that democracy was about economic prosperity, well-being and economic development.

Similarly, when Arabs were asked which of the attributes offered were important for democracy (*The Arab Reform Initiative*), most (80% to 100%) emphasised freedom of the press, freedom of movement, thought and religion, and the freedom to organise public discussions or demonstrations. They also highlighted guaranteed property rights, the right to elect their representatives and the right to be a member of a non-governmental organisation and to work in civil society or become a member of a political party. Democracy, therefore, is not an *ethnocentric* model foreign to the population of the Middle East (Braizat 2010, Esposito and Mogahed 2007).

FIRST MISUNDERSTANDING: DEMOCRACY AS A MEANS OF ACHIEVING PROSPERITY

However, the tendency of Middle Eastern people to regard democracy *instrumentally* could be problematic. Apart from the democratic deficit they are also experiencing a strong *prosperity deficit*, measured as the difference between the subjectively perceived importance of prosperity and an evaluation of whether their country is actually prospering. In Egypt and Lebanon frustration at economic backwardness was highest of all thirty-five post-colonial and post-communist countries surveyed. It was noticeably lower in oil-producing Arab countries (e.g. Kuwait). Differences in the degree of frustration were considerable between individual countries of the Middle East, and on average did not diverge significantly from Latin America, Africa and post-communist countries (Pew Center 2007).

The prosperity deficit is also evident in the responses to an open question asking what respondents regarded as the main problem in their country (the *Arab Barometer*). Half (51%) of Arabs cited problems of an economic character, especially inflation, unemployment and poverty. Only 5% mentioned an authoritarian form of government. Other respondents reported problems related to international politics, above all the American occupation of Iraq (8%) and the Arab-Israeli conflict (7%). The Arab public experiences the prosperity deficit more intensely than the democratic deficit. From democracy they often expect a more effective resolution of economic problems that authoritarian regimes are incapable of dealing with (Jamal and Tessler 2008).

Many Arabs seem to believe that the establishment of democracy will automatically resolve the social and economic problems of their countries, since institutionally they will be comparable with Europe or the United States. Democracy is not only equated with the regular changing of government by means of free elections or the freedom to criticise the government, but equally strongly with the gratification of the basic needs of the population, who are often living on the breadline. Likewise, democracy is often equated with a small gap between rich and poor (cf. Braizat 2010).

The problem associated with an instrumental understanding of democracy is picked up by Inglehart and Welzel (2006: 270) using data from the World Values Survey: "The modern world is no longer divided into those who are for democracy and those against: most people support it. The main difference now is *why* people actually support it." Pro-democracy enthusiasm can often entail the expectation that democracy will also bring prosperity, security, or even success in international relations. Civil liberties and political rights often take a back seat. All this means that attitudes towards democracy in parts of the population are often inconsistent, with people who claim to support democracy often coming out in favour of an authoritarian government or technocrat who promises to resolve poverty and kick-start economic growth.

The risk associated with an instrumental understanding of democracy derives from the fact that democratic transformation is not guaranteed to meet unrealistically high hopes for social and economic progress quickly and easily. The resulting frustration may lead to disillusionment with democracy and the emergence of radical ideologies, including militant Islamism.

SECOND MISUNDERSTANDING: ISLAMIC OR SECULAR DEMOCRACY?

The second problem is the absence of a consensus regarding what type of democracy is desirable if it is to meet the needs of a largely religious, conservative majority of the population, ensure the rights of minorities, and be fair and functioning. Above all, it is unclear as to what role Islam should play.

Muslims are slightly clearer in their heads as to what their democracy should not be. They do not want *American-style* democracy. However, it should be pointed out that American-style democracy is also strongly rejected by Western Europeans along with Turks and Jordanians, while Lebanon is relatively more open (Kohut and Stokes 2006: 129). Similarly, Muslims in most countries do not believe that "adopting Western values would help the development of our country" (Esposito and Mogahed 2007: 107).

On a general level, Muslims claim that Islam already plays a major role in the political life of their country: 89% in Indonesia, 69% in Turkey, 54% in Lebanon, 48% in Egypt and 34% in Jordan. In several countries they are convinced this is a good thing: 91% in Indonesia, 85% in Egypt and 76% in Jordan. Elsewhere, opinions regarding the influence of religion on politics are more ambiguous, though those who are happy with the current influence of religion are still in a slight majority: for example 58% in Lebanon and 38% in Turkey (Pew Center 2010).

This general configuration of attitudes is already opening up the space for receptiveness towards the linking of Islam and democracy, religion and politics. The Middle East differs above all in respect of opinions regarding to what extent Islamic clerics or Islamic principles should influence executive power and the legislative process, as well as what the religious profile of politicians and public officials should be.

It seems, then, that Muslims differ from Westerners by virtue of their greater readiness to *link religion and politics*. They differ less from citizens of other culturally distinct regions of the world, though here too their attitudes cannot be fully explained simply by the lower level of socio-economic or political development. A different culture plays a role. Muslims are more likely than Europeans, though not Americans, to believe that people who do not believe in God are not fit for public office. This relates to the preferred profile of politicians and public officials. Only 39% of Muslims disagree with these statements, while the figure in the West is 62%. These attitudes probably reflect a wish to find a solution to the pervasive corruption in the region and are based on the conviction that religious people are not so easily corrupted because of their ethical principles (Inglehart and Norris 2002, 2003).

However, most Muslims have no desire for Iranian-style theocracy. They do not want clerics to be directly involved in (joint) decisions on the constitution, laws, foreign policy, what women are allowed to wear, or what is allowed to be shown on television and what the newspapers can write about (Esposito and Mogahed 2007). The right of clerics to participate in lawmaking is opposed by 74% of Turks, 56% of Iranians, 53% of Indonesians and 44% of Palestinians. In some Arab countries around a third of the population believe that clerics should be allowed to advise elected politicians. However, only a minority of the citizens of all countries want the clerics to have a dominant role during the drafting of laws. For the sake of comparison, only 65% of Americans are against clerics having a say in the way that laws are written, i.e. fewer people than in secular Turkey and approximately the same as in theocratic Iran (Mogahed, Rheault 2007).

However, as far as the influence of clerics on government decision-making is concerned, the Arab population is divided into two equally strong camps, with 56% thinking that clerics should have the opportunity to influence government decisions and 44% against. Some Arabs are in favour of a consultative role for religious authorities. This polarisation persists even among supporters of democracy. Around half advocate Islamic democracy and half its secular version. This provides the potential for political conflict over the future concept of Middle Eastern democracy.

Nevertheless, there are no differences amongst supporters of Islamic and secular democracy in respect of tolerance towards other political opinions and ethnic or racial otherness, or opinions relating to equality between men and women. Support for Islamic democracy is not bound up with a person's own religious practice. It is more about an evaluation of the political reality of a given country. It is people who are worried about the possible chaos linked with democracy and people with little confidence in government who could envisage clerics occupying a advisory role (Jamal and Tessler 2008).

Generally speaking, people in the region believe that government decision-making should take account of religious imperatives. Support for the secular principle of the separation of religion and state as expressed in the statement "religion is a personal matter and should not be part of government policy" is lower in Muslim countries than in Western Europe. Nevertheless, around half of Middle Eastern Muslims agree with the principle (60% Kuwait, 58% Lebanon, 55% Turkey, 47% Egypt). Again for the sake of comparison, only 55% of Americans advocate the separation of church and state, a position that puts them closer to populations of the Middle East. Of the 47 countries spread around the world where the survey was conducted, Jordan was the exception, with only 17% of the population adhering to this secular principle. There is also very little support for it in Morocco and Palestine (Pew Center 2007).

Influenced by the secular camp, most Muslims ask that Islamic law (*Sharia*) be *one* of the sources – by no means the only – of legislation. This is the demand of 66% of Iranians and 46% of Palestinians. Laws should not be at odds with Islam but should be inspired by it. This demand is already enshrined in the constitutions of most regimes or is met in family law. The Egyptian Muslim Brotherhood then pushed through the creation of an elected Islamic council that would oversee compliance of acts passed with Islamic law. Liberals in the country were against this and favoured a concept of Sharia as the orientational and general interpretative framework of the law, a kind of counterpart to European common law.

In some countries a majority of people believe that Islamic law should be the *sole* source of lawmaking. This applies mainly to Egypt (67%) and Jordan. In contrast, in Turkey a clear majority is against Islam playing any role whatsoever in legislation (57%). This secular camp finds a certain level of support in other Middle Eastern countries. The role of Islamic law is therefore the second point of conflict relating to the concept of Middle Eastern democracy.

At this point it is worth pointing out that as many as 46% of Americans would like to see the Bible being *one* of the sources of the laws of the United States, and a tenth of the population would like it to be the *only* source. This is exactly the same distribution of opinion as in Iran in relation to the role of Islamic law. Sharia law clearly attracts support by virtue of the fact that it promises to create barriers restricting the potentially unlimited power of dictators. It becomes easier to understand the preference some Muslims have for an advisory role to be taken by the clergy, in order that it exert an influence over government decision-making (Esposito and Mogahed 2007, Mogahed and Rheault 2007).

Just as American and European versions of democracy differ, so the Middle East may come up with its own model. Support for democracy, liberal principles, conservative social values, and a limited role for Islam in politics cannot be ignored by regimes that wish to maintain their legitimacy and stability. But neither can it be ignored by opposition groups, including Islamic groups, if they want to compete for public support. Both regimes and opposition groups will therefore have to bring their policies in line with the values prevailing in rapidly modernising societies if they want to retain influence and relevance. If not, they will have to fall back on manipulation and violent coercion. The oppositional potential of the public is then weakened by being split into two groups, namely supporters of the Islamic and secular versions of democracy respectively, i.e. into an Islamic and liberal-democratic opposition. This split of the public and main political actors is accompanied by the absence of a consensus regarding the ideal way of organising society constitutionally and results in paralysis and the escalation of political conflicts during post-revolutionary transformation and democratisation (e.g. Tunisia, Egypt and Libya).

(3) THE DISCREDITING OF UNSCRUPULOUS DICTATORS, THE INVENTION OF TRADITION AND THE MORALISING DRIVE OF ISLAM

The famous hadith attributed to the Prophet claims that we know when God is pleased with Muslims by the person of their leader. If he is pleased, the best will rule. If not, the worst. Muslims accordingly always have the leader they deserve (Esposito and Mogahed 2007).

Middle Eastern authoritarians are seen by their populations as corrupt, unjust and wicked tyrants. This perception is based on reality. In addition to a high level of political repression, the region objectively suffers above average corruption in world rankings. Though the data published by *Transparency International* is incomplete, does not cover all countries in the region and is above all concerned with *perceptions* of corruption, it nevertheless shows that

Fig. 13 Perceptions of corruption in world macro-regions 2001–2015

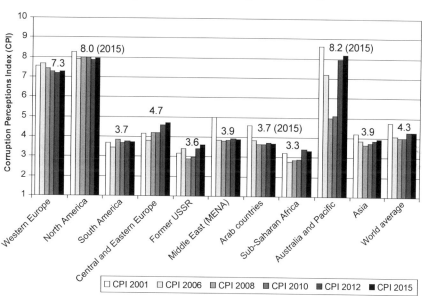

N.B.: The Corruption Perceptions Index (CPI) ranks countries from 1 (highly corrupt) to 10 (very clean). The author's calculation of the arithmetic averages for selected years and macro-regions. Unweighted by individual state population size[3].
Source: Transparency International (www.transparency.cz).

---

3   The number of countries differed in each year of the survey: N(2001) = 91, N(2006) = 162, N(2008) = 178, N(2010) = 174. To begin with advanced OECD countries were disproportionally represented to the detriment of regions of the developing world, and it is therefore difficult to reconstruct reliably a long-term trend, especially in the case of developing countries, including the MENA region.

corruption is as widespread in the Middle East as it is in Asia, Latin America and post-communist Central and Eastern Europe (see fig. 13)

One explanation regularly offered as to why the region's countries are ruled by incompetent, corrupt dictators, and an argument these days deployed by political Islam, relates to the alleged apostasy not only of elites but of the whole of society. If in the classical bipolar concept of Islam the world is divided into two parts, dar al-Islam (the "abode of Islam") and dar al-Harb (the "house of war"), Islamists have now added a third category, dar al-Kufr (the "land of disbelief"). This land is populated by Muslims only in name, hypocrites who have rejected their faith. This modern innovation implies that it is no longer a matter of urgency to Islamise the non-Islamic parts of the world (dar al-Harb). Instead, Muslims should put their own house in order, i.e. re-Islamise Middle Eastern society and thus reform local power elites. The solution to all problems offered by Islamists is a complete return to faith and strict Islamic morality (Lewis 2003b, Mendel 2008). This is a similar appeal to that heard, for instance, in the USA or Poland, from Christian-based parties and movements urging the re-Christianisation of society, i.e. strict observance of the Ten Commandments as a guaranteed way of rectifying problems that the current secular establishment is unable to resolve (Kepel 1996).

Islamists disagree amongst themselves as to whether it is only the political elites that are morally degenerate or society as a whole, and whether a remedy is to be sought through the revolutionary overthrow of godless rulers, the initiation of terror, sectarian isolation from mainstream society (hijra), or by means of non-violent, patient missionary and charitable activities aimed at the moral revival of a degenerate society (dawah). Moderate attempts to re-Islamise society on a gradual, bottom-up basis are often joined by the endeavours of certain Islamist factions to seize power by force or to be co-opted into the regime by means of democratic elections, and thus to accelerate "top-down" re-Islamisation from a position of state power (Kepel 1996, Burgat 2002). For mainstream Islamists, then, the West is not the main interest or target for confrontation or re-Islamisation. Instead, it is a secondary enemy, since it keeps in power corrupt secular dictators, who themselves represent the primary enemy (Juergensmeyer 2008).

Islam has many black-and-white, moralising dichotomies at its disposal in order to describe rulers and their policies: truth-falsehood (batil-haqq), permitted-prohibited (halal-haram), enjoining good-forbidding wrong (ma'ruf-munkar). The strict application of these oppositions to political reality in the Middle East leads to criticism and negative evaluation (Bureš 2007). Another criterion by which today's leaders are measured is the government of the Prophet and the first four "rightly guided" caliphs from the Golden Age of Islam (632–661). Looked at from a purely historical perspective, the rule of these immediate successors of the Prophet Muhammad (Abu Bakr, Umar, Uthman ibn Affan, Ali) was no idyll. Three died a violent death leaving behind a legacy of regular civil war between Sunnis and Shiites. However, an *idealised* vision of their reign has taken root in the Muslim imaginary. Contemporary Islamists contrast today's dictators with the idealised construct of a purported history. This was characteristic of the approach taken by the darling of the Islamists, Rashid Rida (1865–1935). There is no way that dictators can measure up to such a comparison. The chasm between the ideal of an invented tradition and reality on the ground is too wide (Eickelman, Piscatori 1996).

The dominion of modern authoritarian regimes is receding from the ideal of the Golden Age according to Islamists. On the contrary, it more and more resembles its repugnant antithesis, the dark era of pre-Islamic barbarism, ungodliness and ignorance (*jahiliyyah*). At that time people did not behave in accordance with God's good tidings. Either they had not heard them them or had incorrectly understood them or wilfully ignored them (in the case of the good tidings brought by Abraham or Jesus). Dog eats dog was the only law. Everything was permitted. The absence of rules and a life of illusion without any ethics led to violence, anarchy and lawlessness. As a consequence life was hard, cruel and short. This was brought to an end only with the coming of Mohammed and the emphatic promotion of Islam as a reformist force for civilisation in contrast to barbarism.

Today, however, according to the Islamists we are on the path of decline and degeneration in the direction of modern barbarism. This idea of *modern jahiliyyah* is at the same time a recent innovation unknown to classical Islam and traditional clerics. The term was coined in response to the development of society by modern activists such as MohammadibnAbd al-Wahhab, Maududi and Sayyid Qutb. This new perspective maintains that things are simply getting worse: from the Golden Age of Islam to contemporary *jahiliyyah*. Indicators of moral degeneration include shocking phenomena such as the spread of banned alcohol, drugs, pornography and prostitution (Kepel 2002, Mendel 2008). A symptom of modern idolatry is the blind obeisance paid to one-party rule, which is widespread in the region, or the uncritical worship of authoritarian leaders in the form of personality cults or a ban on criticism. The same goes for the deification of the nation by secular nationalism and above all the worship of money and mindless consumerism. These modern idols compete with God, thus seriously undermining *monotheism* and leading Muslims away from Islam. Governments are mostly to blame, since they have accepted and even encouraged this decadence and abandoned their duty to protect the Islamic faith and morals and to reward virtue and discourage vice (cf. Qutb 2013).

THE CONCEPT OF RULER:
FLAWED DICTATOR VERSUS THE SUPERMAN OF ISLAMISM

Contemporary Middle Eastern leaders cannot begin to compare with the ide-alised rulers of Islam's Golden Age, nor even with the ideal ruler promised by the Islamists. The latter reduce political theory to personality and identify in detail the personality traits of a suitable leader (*emir*). They derive them from the presumed and idealised characteristics of the Prophet himself and the first four "rightly guided" caliphs. The only way to guarantee sound govern-ment is to leave it in the capable hands of an exceptional individual, who will represent political, legal, religious and moral authority for all citizens.

For instance, the Pakistani Islamic leader Maududi states that any adept for the post of ruler must be a healthy, adult man, as well as an active Muslim who has undertaken the pilgrimage to Mecca (the *hajj*). This guarantees that he does not come from the largely corrupt society of Muslims in name only. He should fear God, be wise and trustworthy, and should not yearn for power (Roy 1992). Shiite political Islam asserts that a ruler should be a charismatic philosopher king. Imam Khomeini demanded that such a ruler be above all a wise and just legal expert: "We need a ruler who enacts laws rather than promoting his own desires and passions. A leader for whom all people are equal before the law, a leader for whom all people have the same duties and the same rights, a leader who does not offer preferential treatment to or dis-criminate against anyone." (Khomeini 2004: 124).

The call for morally pure leaders and uncorrupted officials to replace the current compromised officials of state institutions may be attractive for broad swathes of the Muslim population, including those who are not dyed-in-the-wool supporters of the Islamists but are disenchanted after decades-long rule by incompetent dictators. For instance, the opinion that insufficiently reli-gious people are not suited to hold public office is shared by the majority of the public. Personal devoutness appears to be a guarantee of moral qualities (Inglehart and Norris 2004).

According to Islamists, the social and political hierarchy should faithfully reflect the virtues and moral profile of individual believers. The ascent of an individual to higher social strata within the framework of the ideal Islamic society should therefore reflect his moral quality and capacity for self-im-provement. Such self-improvement and self-cultivation on the direct path of Islam (*as-sirat al-mustakin*) is called jihad of the heart/soul or sometimes "greater jihad". It appears that these principles are already being applied with success within the Islamist movement. This is how the elitist Egyptian Muslim Brotherhood or the Pakistani *Jamaa Islamiya*, which are not interested in mass membership, perceive their own groups. At the same time, the movement is viewed and presented as the seed and embodiment of the principles of a future ideal Islamic society. It is seen as a refuge from a corrupt society, an island of purity in an ocean of corruption and ignorance, and a training ground for perfecting the virtues of its members. As opposed to secular parties, the movement's leaders are not simply politicians but moral instructors (Roy 1992).

However, with its emphasis on personal qualities, political Islam overlooks the constitutional and institutional order of society. *Hakimija*, the alternative it offers of Islamic rule, is another new term that is unknown to classical Islam but forged in the workshop of the Islamists, which is why it remains relatively vague. Institutions such as government, courts, media, schools or the police are good or bad according to how virtuous and devout are the people leading them and what sort of people work for them. The priority here is that these institutions fulfil the Quranic principle of promoting the virtuous and preventing vice, and not the configuration of a system for their operations and control. Political Islam can thus be achieved against any constitutional backdrop, including democracy, which for the Islamists is of secondary importance (Roy 1992).

Islamists promise to resolve complex problems through a simple infusion of religious morality into politics and the public sphere. Unlike Judaism and Christianity, Islam holds that Man is not burdened with original sin. For this reason, the tendency to concentrate power, money and fame at the expense of others, or to be dragged along by emotions and ambitions, is not the necessary outcome of human nature. It is simply the result of insufficient piety in an individual, something that can be relatively easily remedied. Islamists repudiate the findings of history and anthropology. For this reason, for instance, they do not agree that power corrupts and that absolute power corrupts absolutely (cf. Popper 1994). They therefore see no need to create institutions that would automatically take into consideration the weakness of people and create safeguards in the event of their failure. As far as the key social and political positions are concerned, it is simply necessary to find the right people and to install them in place of the current deviant dictators and their networks of cronies (Roy 1992).

The sole external constraint on a ruler is respect for agreements entered into and a reverence for God's decrees handed down in the form of Islamic law (Mendel 2008). The call by Islamists for the introduction of stricter morality and Islamic law (*sharia*) can thus be seen as an attempt to build barriers against the arrogance of power and the abuse thereof. Islamic law performed a similar function in history, partly protecting communities against headstrong Sultans. This is another reason why Islamists are often supported by broad swathes of the population, who see in the strict application of Islamic law a way of reining in the limitless power of dictators and ensuring some semblance of equality before the law and justice for all (Esposito and Mogahed 2007).

THE LOSS OF DICTATORS' LEGITIMACY

Political Islam, then, claims to know the criteria for distinguishing between good and bad Muslims, something that from the perspective of traditional Muslims is absurd, as well as the criteria for distinguishing between virtuous and corrupt leaders and legitimate and illegitimate regimes. According to classical Islam, a ruler should enforce Islamic law, promote virtue and discourage vice. Ruling in accordance with God's law and protecting the Muslim community (*umma*) against external enemies forms the basis of the *legitimacy* of a ruler's power. This legitimacy is put at threat when a ruler is manifestly godless and morally compromised (Roy 1992).

The current elites are unable to meet the morally exacting requirements of Islam. Islamists then show that the rulers are not governing in accordance with God's law (*sharía*), and they remind their followers that the duty of all Muslims under such circumstances is to overthrow such elites, because they have ceased to execute the task entrusted to them by God to the benefit of mankind. There is a risk that the final opportunity that God offered mankind through the prophecy delivered by the last in a long line of prophets will be lost. These prophecies are contained in three consecutive revelations in the form of the Torah, the Bible and the Quran. Seen from this perspective Muhammad is the ultimate "seal of the prophets" (Kropáček 1996).

However, removing an unsuccessful ruler gives rise to the threat of internal upheaval, civil war or anarchy (*fitna*), as well as the concomitant external threats. For this reason, neither in history nor in modern times have traditional Sunni clerics ever called for armed jihad against oppressors. At most they urge rulers to display greater humility and the population as a whole to display obedience and to maintain order. However, the right to declare jihad against godless dictators has now been expropriated by more radically-minded Islamists, who regard the clerics as failing in their traditional roles and responsibilities. Likewise, lay Islamists have arrogated to themselves the right to interpret Islam (*ijtihad*) and the right to promulgate rulings on points of Islamic law (*fatwa*). Traditionally, this was also the exclusive domain of the clerics and is yet another innovation. According to these new interpretations, expressed in the moralising language of Islam, rulers are now seen as disrespectful to God, as arrogant and unjust tyrants (*taghut*), as apostates from Islam (*kafírs*), and above all as the instigators of the decline of Muslim societies into a state of barbarism analogous to the period prior to the arrival of the Prophet (modern *jahiliyyah*). These rulers have abdicated their duty to protect morality, faith and the laws of Islam and have become the primary enemies of political Islam. For their sins they are often excommunicated (*takfir*) by those Islamists promoting a revolutionary "top-down" re-Islamisation of Muslim societies. This creates the rationale for an armed struggle to be prosecuted in order to overthrow these rulers (Ibrahim 1980, Kepel 2002, 2004, Bureš 2007, Mendel 2008).

A CLASH OF RELIGIOUS IDEALS AND POLITICAL REALITY: A TWOFOLD INTERPRETATION

The de-legitimisation of regimes and the rise of Islamism can be seen as an *interaction* between the politically relevant imaginary of Islam and the reality of incontestably corrupt authoritarian regimes. Like other religions, Islam (cf. Juergensmeyer 1994) offers more than merely different visions of a better society and ideal governance. It also offers a moralising language as the basis for a harsh critique of existing society and government. Religion is not destined to operate solely as Marx's "opium of the people". It is not obliged to assist in the justification and conservation of the existing allocation of power, but can operate as a tool for political mobilisation or as a stimulant for revolutionaries. So this is not simply about competing ways of interpreting Islam as liberal or conservative, political or apolitical, moderate and militant, etc. To the same extent it is also a way of *interpreting social and political reality* through the prism of faith. The emergence of certain interpretations of Islam, especially those pertaining to its political dimension, is not the only factor in political destabilisation and the rise in the popularity of political Islam, but also the growing corruption and brutality of power elites.

Reality prompts a certain reading of Islam at the expense of others. Similarly, Islam prompts a certain reading of reality at the expense of others. The changing political, social, historical and cultural *context* influences the interpretation of the revealed text as much today as it did in the past. The basic equation applies: "text + context = interpretation". In our case, for instance, this might read: "Quran and sunnah + politico-social reality = political Islam". However, political reality may equally well represent the text, and Islam and its politically relevant imaginary the context within which this text is to be read. The outcome is a critical interpretation of the reality of godless, corrupt regimes: "Quran and sunnah + politico-social reality = critique of reality and the search for alternatives".

In this respect the French sociologist Francois Burgat (2002) compares political Islam to a river. It is as misleading to generalise the character of the river in terms of the cascading waterfalls and dangerous gorges in its upper reaches as it is to draw overarching conclusions from the slow-moving current of the same river several kilometres downstream, or even from the same place several years later, when the river might be being used for the irrigation, transport and modernisation of a country. As far as the interpretation and re-interpretation of Islam is concerned the social and political context is crucial and leads to a variability of Islamism in time and space. For instance, the radicalisation of the Egyptian Muslim brotherhood under the presidency of Gamal Abd al-Nasser was due more to the arrest and torture of its members rather than a study of the Quran and its politically relevant principles. Conversely, at the start of the era of President Mubarak the same brethren adopted a more moderate stance and joined in parliamentary elections. There are clear differences between the Iranian Shiite revolutionaries, the Afghan Taliban, Palestinian Hamas, the Egyptian Muslim Brotherhood, the Algerian Islamic Salvation Front, the Turkish ruling AKP or the Bosnian Party of Democratic Action led by Alija Izetbegovic. The differences are the result of the divergent contexts from which these movements emerged and developed, albeit cleaving to the same Islam.

Islam is a diverse historical and cultural tradition comprising highly complex and sometimes contradictory systems of ideas. What is important is which elements and emphases prevail at any given point in time, and which will be subject to suppression by political actors and interpreters. Hence the ancient Muslim adage: "Islam is a sea in which you can catch any fish you want." (cited in Kropáček 2002: 79). Islam does not *in itself* play a role in the rise of political Islam and political destabilisation. As the sociologist Olivier Roy (2004: 10) points out: "The key question is not what the Quran really says, but what Muslims say the Quran says". And this always depends on the broader political and social context. It is for this reason that Islam, like other religious traditions, always developed dynamically and underwent a variety of interpretations and re-interpretations.

THE INVENTION OF TRADITION

The results of these new Islamist interpretations of the Quran and the Sunnah is a new emphasis on a politically relevant dimension of classical Islam, along with significant semantic shifts in its terms and even the birth of new terms and concepts: *dar al-Kufr*, Islam's Golden Age, a new *jahiliyyah*, *hakimija*, and the right of laypersons to proclaim *jihad* and issue *fatwas*. According to the Orientalist Miloš Mendel (2008), these innovative concepts comprise some eight percent of the conceptual framework of a movement like Hamas, Hezbollah or the Muslim Brotherhood. However, within the framework of the *invention of tradition*, Islamists propagate these innovations as an authentic part of their religion so as to ensure their credibility and acceptance in society, even though their continuity with the past is, in fact, fabricated. The paradox then becomes that, though the Islamists pass themselves off as a revivalist movement attempting to purify Islam of the deposits and deformations of the all-too-human proclivity for fabrication and innovation (*bida*), they end up creating new deposits of their own (Eickelman, Piscatori 1996, Barša 2001).

Traditions (Hobsbawm 2000, Giddens 2000) have always been invented and initiated. They have always been an instrument of power, because they favour certain actions, interpretations of the world or identities at the expenses of others. Tradition lends legitimacy to a certain type of social organisation by invoking its alleged longevity and thus its successful validation by time and the accumulated experience of previous generations. At the same time a generally accepted tradition puts power into the hands of its guardians and exegetes, who no longer have to resort to brute force and coercion in order to impose their will, as we know from Max Weber (1997). The struggle for historical memory thus enters the political arena (cf. Kropáček 2002).

Contemporary Islamism also fashions the past in order to influence the present and future. It excavates history in order to formulate and build a vision of the future. In this respect it brings to mind the era of the national revival of European nations, which manipulated the past and invented their own "glorious" history in order to justify their claim on the present and future existence. An extreme example in the current world of Islam would be the deliberately falsified and manipulated wording of hadiths by Saudi or Iranian propaganda (Beránek 2007, Mendel 2008). Middle Eastern regimes also invent and manipulate tradition in their battle with the Islamists, though as opposed to the Islamists they do this in order to maintain the political and social status quo, i.e. in order to maintain their privileged position. The history and tradition of Islam is becoming a proxy battleground of the regimes and opposition groups fighting for the imaginary of the Muslim public.

According to the historian Eric Hobsbawm (2000), new traditions or the revival of old and half-forgotten traditions in modernising societies serve to establish and reinforce the *social cohesion* of newly formed and still insufficiently established groups, parties and movements. Islamists, for example, appeal to the tradition of the caliphs of the Golden Age and attempt to organise mutual relations drawing on this model. Members of militant organisations regularly come together in order to commemorate the death of martyrs or visit the tomb of their movement's founder. Invented traditions also establish and *legitimise new institutions*. For instance, Islamists promote the idea of an Islamic state as a supposedly authentic, time-proven model for the organisation of society. Using the Islamic principle of *shura* (consultation) they then justify new democratic mechanisms within the movement. Tradition also facilitates the *socialisation* of members through the passing on of faith, values and conventions. Hobsbawm thus sets straight simplistic sociological models that create a strict differentiation between traditional and modern societies and speak of the "decline of traditions" during the modernisation process. In fact, traditions remain important in the political sphere. The process of modernisation, involving rapid social change and a need for fixed points of reference, can lead to the reinforcement and revitalisation of traditions rather than their decline (cf. Bauman 1997, Sztompka 1993). This is what is taking place in the Middle East at present.

Not only members of Islamist movements, but broad swathes of Middle Eastern populations react positively both to the politically relevant classical concepts of Islam and to the newly formulated and interpreted traditions. Unlike secular political actors, these traditions speak in the familiar language of Islam. Middle Eastern societies are religious and secularisation has not taken place (cf. Inglehart and Norris 2004, Espozito and Mogahed 2007). Moreover, with its emphasis on individual morality and the resurgence thereof, the ideology of Islamism is intellectually undemanding and accessible. In a vaguely formulated alternative it offers simple solutions to a wide range of complex problems. However, the major cause of the rise of political Islam over the last few decades is the prevailing conviction in Muslim societies of a deepening crisis and the moral degeneration of their political elites. Here is where the political potential of Islam is realised, at the point of intersection between Islam and reality in the Middle East. In post-modern Europe a moralising discourse is regarded as ridiculous, embarrassing and almost indecent. On the contrary, in the Middle East and in the Christian United States, the political discourse is full of terms like good and bad, God and Satan. And this language resonates amongst a segment of the politically aware public.

(4) COSMIC WAR AND THE SATANISATION OF POLITICAL ENEMIES

What this means is that not only Islam, but quotidian existence and a frustrating political reality may provide a text suitable for interpretation, especially for Islamists, in whose attitudes and activities this world and its politics are often more important than a transcendental faith (Kepel 2002, Juergensmeyer 2008). For the Islamists, Islam, with its social critique and politically relevant imaginary, is becoming the context for a critical reading of the corrupt world in which they live. Culture, including religion, is a storehouse of interpretations and meanings for understanding and making sense of everyday life, apparent social chaos, and life on the margins. The social appeal of political Islam does not therefore derive simply from a propagandistic popularisation of a specific interpretation of Islam, but above all from the popularisation of a critical interpretation and moralising reading of the real condition of society and its powerful elites.

For moderate, let alone militant Islamists, this world is a place where "cosmic war" is being waged[4]. Islamists share a tendency to read the world in this

---

4   This way of reading the world is common to all religious and nationalist terrorist movements and is by no means restricted to Islamist circles.

way, a reading that differs substantially from the rest of the Muslim population, especially from apolitical fundamentalists, official clerics, power elites and secular movements. While to the rest of society the world might appear peaceful, from the perspective of militant Islamists a fundamental conflict has long been underway, sometimes open, other times cunningly concealed and insidious. Ordinary people have not woken up to the fact yet or prefer to avert their gaze from signs of conflict. However, that which people outside the Islamist movement understand simply as an individual social problem or an ordinary political skirmish over power, fame and fortune, the religious militants see as part of a far broader moral and spiritual struggle. Everything is to play for and there is no room for compromise. In the momentous clash between good and evil, either the forces of light or darkness, order or chaos, God or Satan, will prevail. But they cannot coexist.

Current earthly conflicts and political problems are placed by Islamists within a broader *transcendental* context that surpasses the particularity of the "here and now". They view such problems as part of a more general, *metaphysical* and universal conflict between good and evil, the pure force of God and the impure forces of Satan, order and chaos, light and darkness. They also regard them as part or the culmination of a mythological historical struggle winding its way through the history of Islam (Juergensmeyer 1994, 2000).

One and the same conflict between good and evil is taking place on all levels of reality. On the individual level it is seen as a struggle between faith and the temptation to sin. In the social world it is manifest in a moral conceptualisation of politics as an uncompromising battle between good and evil. And on the metaphysical or cosmic level it is manifest in the struggle between God and Satan. While most believers understand the conflict between good and evil present in every religious tradition to be metaphorical, religious militants regard it as literal. While most believers begin the fight against evil by looking within, i.e. by avoiding sin and bettering themselves in accordance with the jihad of the heart, militants believe that evil is all around us, it is an external force working upon us. It can therefore be attacked with force and destroyed once and for all (Juergensmeyer 2004).

What *function* does such a concept of the world fulfil? A belief in an ongoing cosmic conflict offers confused people *orientation in the world*. It acts as a compass, providing information as to who I am, why I am suffering, and why the world is moving in the wrong direction. It is a compass that tells me on whose side I stand and against whom I am fighting. Activists therefore experience their awakening as a form of enlightenment. It offers relief and the end of confusion and frustration at not being able to understand the world. However, unless this moment of enlightenment can be elicited in the rest of society it can lead to new frustrations.

This view of the world leads to *symbolic empowerment*. The individual now regards himself as part of a grand cosmic struggle between God and Satan that exceeds the merely ephemeral. By participating in this struggle he stands on the side of truth, love, light and God. Life and death take on a deeper meaning. In life he becomes a warrior of God fulfilling a historical mission for the good of mankind, and in death he becomes a martyr. This is both a source of self-esteem and provides the motivation for maximum commitment.

The idea of a cosmic war also *justifies the use of violence*, something that would be impossible under conditions of peace. The duty of the believer is to stand his ground in *defence* of good against the advancing forces of evil. The idea that the world has long been at war – even though the deluded majority have perhaps not yet caught on – and that religious movements are on the side of the victim and not the aggressor, allows the classical religious concept of a *just war* to be dusted down and deployed. Violence is permitted for the purpose of defence if all non-violent ways of resolving a dispute have been exhausted. While for people outside the movement its militant acts may seem confusing, shocking and unjustifiable because they disturb the peaceful, seemingly non-violent course of the world up till now, from the point of view of activists theirs is a legitimate, responsible and morally laudable effort to resist the advancing forces of evil in all the forms it takes in a world understood through the prism of cosmic war. Moreover, terror and armed struggle are seen as a "message" sent to mainstream society, an attempt to lead it out of passivity and lethargy, an endeavour to reveal clearly that the world has in reality long been the theatre of a fierce battle between God and Satan. This message aims to assert an opposing interpretation of the world and to show that peace does not reign – on the contrary.

Finally, the concept of cosmic war offers *hope*. It holds out the promise of relationships being repaired and a final victory being attainable in situations that seem hopeless, irresolvable and already lost. The vision of a cosmic war includes an eschatological narrative regarding the final victory of good, truth and God, and the promise of positive changes in personal as well as political and social life. Because religion offers cosmology, history and eschatology, it contains a powerful mobilising element that secular ideology does not offer to the same extent. Islamists have the advantage of being able to connect up and multiply the politically mobilising potential of nationalism and religion.

Both moderate and militant Islamist movements build their political career on the extent to which, faced with various earthly problems and political conflicts, they identify convincingly the advancing dark forces of Satan, place them within the context of cosmic war, and promulgate this specific method of reading the world throughout society as a whole. The outcome of a religious reinterpretation of political conflicts is a transformed understanding of the enemy. Every group engaged in the public sphere has enemies. But now the adversaries find themselves on opposite sides of the barricades of the cosmic war and not merely on different sides of a prosaic ideological conflict or a dispute between different interest groups regarding their share in power or resources. The rivals are no longer even people, but puppets embodying the forces of Satan, who manipulates them behind the scenes. In consequence, the enemy is labelled using stereotypical, collective and anonymous categories: they are the "infidels", "apostates", "crusaders", "Jews". This enables the individuality of the enemy, his existence as a flesh-and-blood individual, to be denied. Instead, the concept of cosmic war contributes to the *Satanisation* and *dehumanisation* of the enemy, which in turn contributes to the escalation of conflict and facilitates the act of killing.

When people are experiencing oppression and injustice the enemy is easily identifiable. Otherwise he must be creatively invented. In Middle Eastern societies the *primary enemy* of the Islamists are discredited governments and their godless and corrupt representatives, who stand on the side of the devil (Juergensmeyer 2000). Through the explosive lens of cosmic war rulers are seen as the devil incarnate: according to classical Islam, the fallen angel *Iblís* has in his job description the task of exposing the individual to temptation and thus sowing the seeds of confusion amongst the populace as a whole. This is the devil's way of competing with God: by deflecting Muslims from their faith. Islamists also portray dictators as the embodiment of the *Antichrist*, who, according to eschatological visions, will appear on earth before the Day of Resurrection. This is how President Anwar al-Sadat of Egypt and Shah Reza Pahlaví of Iran were regarded by militants. In the wake of these dictators will come the Mahdi or Jesus, who will kill the Antichrist in the Great Battle. In this Islamic variation on the end of history, the arrival of the Messiah and the establishment of a just world may be accelerated still further by the unleashing of jihad against evil (cf. Mendel 2008).

The allies of what are now regarded as the Satanised governments of the Middle East become the *secondary enemy*. First and foremost this refers to the United State of America, but also to many Western European countries. By this logic even official, pro-regime clerics can be the secondary enemy. They too work in the service of Satan; the USA is sometimes seen as the Great Satan and Israel as the Little Satan (Juergensmeyer 1994, 2000, 2008). Islamic State of Iraq and Syria (ISIS) is the most recent group to formulate its ideology within the logic of cosmic war. As W. F. McCants shows in his book *The ISIS Apocalypse* (2015), the group's ideology emphasises the apocalyptic course of the modern degenerate, chaotic and broken world and promises an early end of history in the form of a final battle between good and evil. According to the tradition of the prophets this is to take place somewhere near the Syrian city of Dabiq.

The advancement of the concept of cosmic war throughout society is the consequence of the *interaction* of the religious imaginary and political reality. From this perspective the Middle East is ruled by corrupt despots standing on the side of Satan in his battle with God. If political Islam, especially its militant offshoots, is to be successful, it is necessary that mainstream society embrace fully this diagnosis of a corrupt world, i.e. the concept of cosmic war. The world then becomes a text full of hidden meanings that must be deciphered with the aid of a religious imaginary derived from the *mainstream* Islamic tradition and its founding sources (the Quran and Sunnah), and not from marginal, extreme interpretations of Islam. The ethical maxim of classical Islam that states that a Muslim must dedicate his life to doing good and resisting evil creates the conditions for the involvement of a large part of the population in the political struggle against godless rulers, i.e. on the side of the Islamists (cf. Juergensmeyer 1994).

(5) THE CURRENT CONFLICT AS A CONTINUATION OF HISTORY

The second context within which the modern world is interpreted is the history of Islam. The current terrestrial struggle is not then simply part of a metaphysical war between good and evil, but also the continuation and culmination of the legendary battles of history fought by pious Muslims since the time of the Prophet Muhammad up to the present (Juergensmeyer 2000). Viewed in this light, contemporary Islamists see themselves as successors of the Prophet and a long line of historical reformers courageously standing up to the arrogance of power and campaigning for the moral rehabilitation of society within the framework of revealed Islam (Dekmejian 1995). This perspective serves to situate Islamists within a longer-term framework that offers orientation. It also provides symbolic empowerment by portraying the current struggle as the continuation of a grandiose historical mission following in the wake of the famous heroes of yore. In addition to the *cosmological* perspective (cosmic war and the metaphysical battle between good and evil) and the *historical* perspective (historical rebels against godless rulers as the forerunners of today's Islamists), there is also the *eschatological* perspective, which looks with hope to the future yet often oscillates between pessimism and belligerent optimism (Juergensmeyer 1994).

The Islamist understanding of history breeds anxiety. The Golden Age of the Prophet and the first four "rightly guided" caliphs is a thing of the past. Since then, because the people have deviated from Islam, we find ourselves on the path to modern barbarism (*jahiliyyah*). There is a risk that we will squander the last chance that God gave Man through Muhammad's teachings, this time irrecoverably, because after Muhammad, the "seal of the prophets", there will be no further prophet (Kepel 1996, Lewis 2003b). On the other hand, many Islamist movements – more in the Shiite than Sunni tradition – envisage an imminent end of history that, thanks to the arrival of a Messiah (the Mahdi, the "hidden Imam", Jesus) and his battle with evil, will end in victory, especially if people join forces on the right side of the barricades and do not simply look idly on from a distance as the Antichrist in the form of a local dictator or foreign power attempts to win (cf. Dekmejian 1995, Mendel 2008).

The history to which Islamists claim allegiance has been being written since the crisis of succession and the internal struggle over who would lead the Muslim community after the death of the prophet Muhammad. Sunni fundamentalism claims that the undisputed model for all Muslims, including future generations, should be the Prophet Muhammad and the first rightly guided caliphs from the Meccan Quraysh tribe. In contrast, Shiite fundamentalism locates its role models in Muhammad and the descendants of Imam Ali, cousin of Muhammad and husband of the Prophet's daughter Fatima.

Soon after this schism, the Umayyad dynasty (660–750), the first of many such Sunni dynasties, comes into being. The principle of the transfer of political power and amassed wealth in a family line results in the caliphates being ruled by generations of hypocritical and godless rulers elevating their own egoistic interests above those of the Muslim community and, from the perspective of Islamists, over the spirit of God's law. Genuine faith is thus shunted to one side in favour of a soulless technology of power that will stop at nothing.

A similar moral degeneration, spiritual burnout, corruptibility of power and crisis of legitimacy then afflicts the dynasties of the Abbasids, Fatimid Caliphate and the quarrelling caliphates in Andalusia, and later on the stagnating and declining late Ottoman Empire (1699–1922). The fragile legitimacy of these dynasties often culminated in the use of force as the sole means of preserving the status quo. It also saw the relentless persecution and exemplary punishment of religious critics of the rulers. In the eyes of contemporary Islamists, these critics then become forgotten and rediscovered martyrs, heroes and inspiring role models, who did not hesitate to stand up to the ruling power and to lay down their lives for the truth. The crisis par excellence, highly reminiscent of today's situation to modern Muslims, would be the invasions of the godless Mongolian hordes of the lands of the Muslim world (1258). These invasions led to a temporary breakdown of society, a threat to Islam, and anarchy.

During difficult periods for the Islamic Ummah, self-proclaimed saviours would periodically appear in the form of adherents of strict fundamentalism calling for an uncompromising return to roots, i.e. to the life and faith of their pious predecessors (the *Salafis*). In this respect the pioneers include the Imams Hanifa and Malik. Despite the risk of persecution, these founders of the two Sunni schools of law criticised the abuses perpetrated by the Umayyad dynasty. Ibn Hanbal, founder of another Sunni school of law and a believer in strict orthodoxy, aimed his criticism at the Abbasids dynasty. He became a martyr and to this day remains a model of courage in the face of unjust, tyrannical power. Ibn Taymiyyah also stands out in the long line of opposition rebels (cf. Ibn Taymiyyah 2013, Ťupek 2015) who as a matter of principle refused to acknowledge any authority but that of the Quran and the Sunnah. Despite being repeatedly imprisoned he never stopped promoting jihad against all manifestations of heresy amongst Muslims (the Sufi brotherhoods), as well as against infidels (the Mongols, Druze and Alawites). In modern history we can add to the large and still growing pantheon of champions of fundamentalism Rashid Rida, al-Wahhab and Sayyid Qutb, the latter tortured and executed by the authoritarian Egyptian regime (Dekmejian 1995).

The overall *pattern* of periodic *religious rebellion* against corrupt power and enfeebled social relations is characterised by an uncompromising dedication to the *restoration of the Islamic Ummah* by means of a return to the true Islamic faith and a search for constant inspiration in the life of the Prophet Muhammad; it is worth both living and dying for this truth. Theories exhibiting different degrees of sophistication go hand in hand with practical activism. Devotion to God then goes hand in hand with devotion to the world and a sensitive perception of its problems. Ultimately, the rebels stand against the existing authorities, both political and religious. From time to time they promote armed jihad as an instrument for the defence of the revealed faith, which is in danger.

Historical dissidents are perceived by contemporary political Islam as inspiring role models. In a famous hadith, Muhammad said that every hundred years a charismatic leader – though not a prophet – would appear in order to defend Islam against degeneration and to fight against the malevolence of godless tyrants (Dekmejian 1995, cf. Lewis 2003a, 2003b). Contemporary Islamism, which arrived on the scene during the 1970s, sees itself as continuing these periodically emerging historical struggles. Its leaders are regarded as descendants of a line of martyrs who dedicated their lives to the cleansing of Muslim societies and the fight against godless tyrannies. There are numerous parallels between historical crises and the dramatic present: the corruption of today's dictators corresponds to the apostasy of former caliphs, while occupation by the Israelis or Americans corresponds to the historical threat posed by the Mongols, Crusaders and colonialists. History becomes a matter of interpretation in exactly the same way that religion is: "The burden of history lies heavily on Islamic ideologues, who in the current crisis are trying to reconstruct the past in order to influence the future" (Dekmejian 1995: 36).

Modern discredited authoritarian regimes are interpreted within the context of the politically relevant religious and historical imaginaries. The concurrence of a desolate political reality and Islam stimulates a specific cosmology, history and eschatology (Juergensmeyer 1994, 2000). Religion and history provide the context for a particular reading of reality. The fortunes of political Islam then depend on how widely this interpretation of reality can be popularised within society. How convincing this reading of the world proves to be depends not only on the propaganda of the Islamists, but above all on the state of Middle Eastern political and social reality. If signs of a breakdown of society and failure on the part of its elites (cf. Kepel 1996) are most visible in the Middle East, the region also possesses the greatest potential for the re-politicisation of religion and history.

(6) THE DECLINE OF SECULAR DOCTRINES: AN IDEOLOGICAL VACUUM AND ISLAM AS AN ALTERNATIVE

The course of Middle Eastern secular ideologies can be summed up as follows. After the fall of the caliphate, what took its place was either a weak, non-functioning and superficially implanted interwar liberalism (Egypt and Lebanon) or military secularism (Turkey and Iran). Both ideologies rejected a more significant role for Islam in political thinking and practice. Since at least the mid-20th century, the post-colonial Middle East has been dominated by Arab nationalism, pan-Arabism, and an Arab socialism occasionally invoked by Marxists. Apart from rhetorical flourishes and symbolic references to Islamic civilisation, religion continues to be pushed to the margins of these ideological systems or an attempt is made to tame and control it. The trajectory of these secular ideologies follows that of classical theories of modernisation: a rapid rise in optimism is followed by gradual disillusionment and decline. In the early 1970s, modernisation theories, like Middle Eastern secular ideologies, lost their appeal and persuasiveness. Since then political Islam has moved in to take the place of the discredited secular ideologies (Barša 2001).

POST-COLONIAL ENTHUSIASM AND DISILLUSIONMENT

The same fate has been met by Middle Eastern regimes adhering to secular doctrines. Though these found favour to begin with, people today are tired of them and disenchanted by their weak performance when in power. The progress promised by these regimes has diverged more and more visibly from reality in the form of post-colonial stagnation. Rather than the fruits of modernisation being enjoyed by the region, it was more the negative effects that accompany such a process: the disintegration of traditional bonds, increased instability, inequality, criminality and vice (cf. Sztompka 1993, Keller 2007).

The leaders of the emerging independent countries were masters in raising unrealistic expectations in the population. For instance, the Shah of Iran promised a standard of living comparable with Germany, and the country was to become a military superpower balancing India in the Indian Ocean and the USSR in Central Asia. To begin with President Nasser of Egypt received the support of the masses for megalomaniac projects like the Aswan Dam and industrialisation on a massive scale. However, these high expectations were inevitably followed by even greater disappointment. The aspirations awakened by populism came into conflict with reality (Lerner 1964). The country failed to catch up with the social and economic level of the West, which served as a *reference point*. Furthermore, the Middle East lagged behind even other post-colonial regions, despite having originally enjoyed something of a head start (Juergensmeyer 1994, Zakaria 2004).

Instead of the economic growth and prosperity comparable with the West that had been promised, Middle Eastern regimes and their secular doctrines brought poverty and stagnation. Instead of the freedom that had been promised, they brought repression, state terror and fear. Instead of social justice and national unity, they brought polarisation, visible inequality and political tensions. Instead of military strength, national security and a respectable role in the world befitting the legacy of a once powerful civilisation, they brought simply military defeat and irrelevance in international politics. And instead of a gradual expulsion of religion into the private sphere, they contributed to the revitalisation of Islam and its radical politicisation (Lewis 1990, Juergensmeyer 2008).

THE TRAUMA OF MILITARY DEFEATS AND NEO-COLONIAL HEGEMONY

A critical turning point was the shocking defeat of the Arabs in the war with little Israel (1967), notwithstanding the fact that propaganda had heralded a swift, easy victory (Smith 2008). This defeat was seen as evidence of the incompetence of regimes and the non-functioning of models of development inspired by foreign secular ideologies that had been applied until then. However, the loss of Jerusalem, the third holiest place of Islam, was also seen as a religious defeat caused by deviation from Islam (Esposito 2003). While the attacking Egyptian soldiers in the war of 1967 were still chanting nationalist slogans like "Earth, sea, air!", during the following war in 1973 they were now shouting "Allahu Akbar!" (Kepel 2002). A similar reversal of fortune was experienced beyond the boundaries of the Middle East during the humiliating defeat suffered by Muslim Pakistan in the war with India (1971). These failures contributed to the discrediting of what had until then been the dominant secular ideologies in the wider Muslim region (Kropáček 2002).

Nikki Keddie, an American expert in Eastern and Iranian history, notes that the consequence of military defeats suffered by Muslim societies has always been the rise of radical, intolerant interpretations of Islam and a tendency to reject everything non-indigenous or Western. This began as far back as the first losses suffered by the Ottoman Empire, as well as by the Persian, Moroccan, Egyptian and Indian Mughal Imperial forces. The same reaction was later provoked by European, Zionist, Russian and Soviet, as well as Indian and Chinese colonialism. And there are similar repercussions arising from the current neo-colonial interference on the part of the United States. In addition, at present we see an *interaction* between the humiliating international politics being prosecuted by non-Islamic powers (Europe, the USA and Israel) and a historical substrate in the form of a self-confident, assertive Islam that sees its non-Muslim opponents as morally inferior. The result is a growing criticism of the hitherto dominant secular doctrines and an inclination towards more radical versions of Islam. International political reality is at odds with the Quran, which states: "You have been the best nation that has been raised up for mankind. You enjoin what is right, forbid what is wrong and believe in Allah. If the People of the Book believed in Islam, it would be better for them; among them are believers, but many of them are transgressors" (Quran 3: 110) (cited in Kropáček 2002: 71).

These military, international political and economic failures are interpreted as the result of Muslims straying from God. Success in these areas would, on the contrary, confirm the rightness and strength of their faith. During the Golden Age, Muslims were devout believers and this went hand in hand with their military expansion. They dominated the world at that time, both culturally and economically. This was seen as evidence of God's favour and confirmation of the integrity, strength and superiority of their faith (Esposito and Mogahed 2007). An essential prerequisite for the success of Muslim societies these days, therefore, must be the re-Islamisation of society (Kepel 1996). On the other hand, it is not becoming for the *heirs to a famous civilisation* to continue to copy slavishly Western secular ideological models (Fukuyama 2002, cf. Chátamí 2001). These models have been discredited if only by virtue of having first arrived in the Middle East with European colonial dominance. And they were imposed in the region from a position of strength, whether by Europeans and their collaborating lackeys, or later by local post-colonial dictators (Kropáček 2002, Mendel 2008).

A DISPLACED IDEOLOGICAL PENDULUM: A MINORITY IMPOSES SECULARISM ON THE MAJORITY

In addition to failures resulting from the promotion of the wrong models of development, or the right models but applied wrongly (Zakaria 2001, 2004), secular ideologies found themselves on the defensive because they were from the start *imposed on a disorganised majority* by a well organised *minority*. The regimes imposed secularism on a top-down basis. While in Europe emancipatory secular ideologies expanded the rights and freedoms of all citizens at the expense of the dominant religious and political powers, in the Middle East secular doctrines have served only a minority. Above all it has been the post-colonial political elite that has benefitted in its struggle with traditional tribal, ethnic and religious authorities and identities. During the centralisation of state power and the creation of national unity, these elites have attempted to bypass such authorities. Similarly, secular doctrines benefited religious minorities (Christians, Jews, Shiites, Alawites and foreigners), to whom they guaranteed equality, and the embryonic post-colonial middle classes, which as their wealth and influence increased were reluctant to be restricted by religion, for them a matter of personal conscience (Juergensmeyer 1994, Kepel 2002).

Initially, the *apolitical* and passive segment of traditional society that had had Western-style secularism imposed on it did not mount any *organised* resistance. However, many instances of individual and isolated resistance have been documented (Huntington 1968, Roy 2005). This segment of the population was accustomed to accepting the decisions of political power uncritically. It was scattered among small, isolated communities of farmers and nomads that were turned inwards and reliant on tradition (cf. Gellner 1993). The devoutness of the traditional segment of the population contributed to its political passivity and fatalism: "Everything is the will of God" (an Egyptian farmer), or "I am satisfied with what God has given me" (a Jordanian nomad). These traditional peoples were unaware both of their own interests and any possible alternatives to it. The horizons of their world ended at the boundaries of the nomadic tribe, village or traditional urban neighbourhood. The same boundaries marked the end of the sources of their identity and loyalty. It was therefore very difficult to mobilise them politically using symbols of the nation or class that extended beyond traditional identity and required an identification with the wider community. For instance, most Iranians took no interest in one of the most dramatic events of modern Iranian history: the nationalisation of the *Anglo-Iranian Oil Company* (1955). Moving to Turkey, during the mid-1950s, a time during which their country was continuing with secularisation and had sent the third largest military contingent to participate in the Korean War, traditional Turks would typically declare: "Politics doesn't relate to us", "There's nothing we can change in any case – it's just stupidity to get involved at all", "Our leaders know best what is to be done", or "It is not for us to judge a leader". Traditional apolitical masses lacking informed opinions did not participate in public opinion or political decision-making (Lerner 1964: 301, 318).

This situation favoured the political elites, which were able to govern unimpeded and faced competition only from a narrow counter-elite (Huntington 1968). However, the hitherto passive and apolitical majority gradually experienced a *political awakening* (cf. Brzezinski 1993) and discovered that they were living in a state with whose ideology they were unable to identify and whose political language they could not understand. They did not recognise their own country and did not feel at home in it. The result was the emergence of conservative ideologies, including political Islam. This was an attempt to correct the displaced ideological pendulum and return it from the Western or Soviet-style secularism being promoted by a minority to an ideology intelligible to the majority, a majority that now demanded a voice in political life and a share in the shaping of the political discourse (Burgat 2002). Indeed, Islamists view democratisation as the process of ensuring the dominant political ideology complies with the values of mainstream society (Juergensmeyer 1994, 2008).

DECLINE OF THE WEST, DECLINE OF THE MODEL

Finally, the appeal of secular ideologies of Western provenance is declining because of the crisis that has been taking place since the start of the 1970s in Western societies themselves, be this a genuine or presumed crisis. If the messenger lacks credibility, then so does his message. It makes no sense to be inspired by something that has been proven not to work.

The Muslim world first gazed with surprise upon the economic recession in the West provoked by the 1973 oil crisis. It also marvels at the West's inability to reproduce itself demographically, the intensification of consumerism, materialism and individualism, and the emphasis on the freedom and rights of the individual at the expense of duties, responsibilities and obligations towards others and society as a whole. The Middle East also perceives with alarm Western epidemics of drug addition, alcoholism, suicide, criminality, prostitution and pornography. It observes with consternation the crisis of Western families and the disrespect paid to old age. It finds the existence of orphanages and old people's homes particularly difficult to understand.

During the seventies, Muslims were also horrified by the wave of left-wing terrorism that swept across Western Europe, notably that carried out by the Red Army Faction in Germany and the Red Brigades in Italy. This is ironic from today's vantage point, when it is the West that links terrorism with the Middle East, Muslims, and the Arab world. Western doctrines were also discredited by the Cold War, which was perceived as a kind of family quarrel between competing Western ideologies, between the Soviet and capitalist models. In addition, the Cold War was accompanied by an irrational and potentially self-destructive arms race between the USSR and the USA. For these reasons, the USSR and later the USA and Europe ceased being attractive models (Kropáček 1996, Etzioni 2004, Kouřilová 2007).

Ideologists and leaders of Islamist movements are very familiar with the advantages and disadvantages of Western societies. Many of them are widely travelled and have studied in the West, and others have lived there in forced exile, for instance the Tunisian Rachid Ghannouchi, the Egyptian Sayyid Qutb, and the Iranians Imam Khomeini and Ali Shariati (Burgat 2002). To a certain extent, then, the Middle Eastern diagnosis of the strengths and weaknesses of Western models is based on genuine knowledge. However, political Islam is to a degree subject to distorted images of Western societies that spread around the global village thanks to the expansion of virtual reality and the *simulacra* produced by the mass media. To take an example: not every American lives like the heroes of the series *Dallas*. Not everyone worships wealth and sexual licence (Eickelman and Anderson 2003, Hoffman 1995). The Islamists are able to alarm the population of the Middle East with the threat of a moral decline associated with the promotion of secular models, while at the same time promising to protect the people against the scourge of Western decadence through the application of their own alternative (cf. Buruma and Margalit 2005).

IDEOLOGICAL VACUUM AND THE SEARCH FOR AN ALTERNATIVE: "CHANGE" AS THE SLOGAN OF THE DAY

The *multiple* discrediting of secular ideologies has created an ideological *vacuum* that has been filled by political Islam. Islamists propound their vision as the only, and diametrically opposed, *alternative* to the secular models of burnt-out dictators, many of whom have ruled for decades. For instance, the Egyptian Hosni Mubarak ruled from 1981, the Tunisian Ben Ali from 1987, the Libyan Colonel Gaddafi from 1969, and the Yemeni President Saleh from 1978. The rest of the authoritarian rulers in the Middle East generally came to power after the generational change of the power elite at the turn of the millennium (Morocco, Jordan, Syria).

As a consequence, a disillusioned and weary Middle Eastern population is eager for *change*. They want to see the replacement of both the power elite and the style of government and ideology to which that elite subscribes. Under these circumstances the Islamists find support among wide swathes of the social spectrum, both rich and poor, the highly devout and the religiously half-hearted, men and women, the pro-democracy oriented and those suspicious of it, supporters and opponents of the emancipation of women, etc. This is not simply a disciplined cadre of supporters or the highly devout and more conservative segments of the population. However, their support *for* political Islam is a protest *against* the existing regimes. The Islamists are regarded as an *alternative* to economically ineffective, politically repressive and culturally alien regimes (Rivero and Kotzé 2007, Jamal and Tessler 2008).

The sources of development and modernisation are now to be found not only in Western ideas, but in cultures and traditions closer to home. *Cultural decolonisation* is perceived by Islamists not only as the culmination of political and economic decolonisation, but as the condition thereof (Juergensmeyer 2008). In contrast, secular doctrines have had the tendency to believe that only the most rapid Westernisation of society and the displacement of tradition and Islam into the private sphere will bring about modernisation (Lewis 1990, Zakaria 2001, Eisenstadt 2000). The mistake is no longer perceived to be the slow pace of Westernisation, but, on the contrary, an undiscriminating fascination with everything Western accompanied by a deviation from Islam (Lewis 2003a).

(7) THE CHRONIC CRISIS OF THE LEGITIMACY OF REGIMES: THE CAREER OF MIDDLE EASTERN IDEOLOGIES

Over time, Middle Eastern regimes tried out just about all of the secular ideologies that were available on the market for political ideas. However, in the end they discredited each of them. A sure-fire way of compromising all of these ideologies, however attractive they may originally have been, was to link them with unsuccessful and unpopular regimes. These regimes wrapped themselves in the blanket of secularism in an attempt to legitimise their privileged status and to mobilise the support of a politically awakening population.

Over the long term, no regime can rely simply on brute force and coercion, but must convincingly *vindicate* itself in the eyes of the population using an appropriate and sufficiently attractive *ideology*. No amount of political and socio-economic inequality per se will become the cause of rebellion. Inequality is rejected only when it is perceived as unfair, unjustified and illegitimate (Keller 1997).

At the same time, people cannot live without ideology. They cannot live without concepts that allow them to interpret the society in which they live, as well as their own past, present and future. They cannot live without ideas that give their lives meaning, motivate their actions, and offer them hope. People need ideas about the world that *orientate* them in a chaotic and unintelligible reality. Liberation from one ideology will therefore always involve a shift in the direction of another ideology (Berger and Luckmann 1999).

Ideologies must therefore correspond to the needs of both power elites and individuals in a given society. It is not important whether an ideology is "true". An ideology is a form of false consciousness defending the interests of certain social groups while at the same time providing a means of orientation to individuals in a given society. Far more important for all involved is that there be a compelling doctrine to hand. If the dominant doctrine collapses, an *ideological vacuum* arises and political instability increases. The demand then grows amongst both political elite and the population at large for the vacuum to be filled by a new and credible ideological alternative (Giddens 1999: 376, 550).

The secularisation thesis holds that the modern ideological history of Europe (though not of the United States) can be described as the gradual displacement of religion by its secular substitutes, which performed and continue to perform the same psychological and social functions. These *secularised religions* often managed, under the advertising banner of progress and in the name of creating of an earthly paradise in the form of a classless or racially pure society, to wreak historically unprecedented violence that culminated in the Gulag and the Holocaust. Instead of religious festivals and the cult of prophets, Europe demanded obeisance to a leader, party, nation or single truth (cf. Aron 2001). In contrast, the post-colonial Middle East is moving in the opposite direction: from an initial enthrallment with Western secular ideologies to political Islam. The career path of Middle Eastern political ideologies can be read as a story in which periods characterised by the dominance of a certain "grand narrative" regarding the legitimacy of political and economic inequality alternate with periods during which this narrative is challenged and the consensus collapses. For instance, the once dominant idea of the caliphate was replaced by the idea of Arab nationalism, pan-Arabism and Arab socialism. These were later replaced by new and persuasive doctrines that appeared to be better aligned with the changed political reality: political Islam or religious nationalism, and most recently democracy or Islamic democracy.

THE CALIPHATE AND PAN-ISLAMISM

In the Middle East the caliphate as an ideology and political system enjoyed legitimacy in the eyes of the population for centuries. In his ideal form as inspired by the example set by the Prophet Muhammad, the *Khalifa* was to embody religious, political, military and legal functions in one person. The political theory of the caliphate was formed 100 to 150 years after the death of the Prophet and was based on the idea that only God had power over the *ummah*. God was also the sole lawmaker. Allah delegated his power to the Khalifa, who was his sole representative on earth, his one and only local shadow. The Khalifa is here in order to enforce God's law (*sharia*), but not so that he might invent laws or enact the will and wishes of the people. His duty is to govern and to reach decisions in accordance with the revealed law of God, and to defend the community of believers (*ummah*) against the infidel (*kuffar*) and against internal unrest or rebellion (*fitna*), apostasy, heresy, sin, and any inclination to polytheism. The legitimacy of the Khalifa could be obtained by the most religious and just being "elevated" to the head of the community on the basis of the mechanism of pre-Islamic Bedouin democracy, in which origin does not play a role (Kharijites) or through the consensual selection of a Khalifa from the ranks of the influential Meccan tribe of the Quraysh, whence came Muhammad himself (Sunni). Either that, or he must be a direct descendant of the "House of the Prophet" (Shiite), beginning with Fatimah (daughter) and Ali (cousin and son-in-law of the Prophet) (Bureš 2007).

The legitimacy of the Caliphate was long manifest in the fact that most of the apolitical and illiterate population, scattered around rural areas, did not become involved in politics. Although the day-to-day functioning of the Caliphate significantly diverged from its ideal, internal pressures did not generally represent the main threat to its power. In the end, the Caliphate collapsed under the pressure of European colonialism. When European colonialism itself quickly collapsed after the Second World War, there was an urgent need to justify the power of the newly emerging domestic regimes taking the place vacated by the foreign powers. The Middle East experienced the first threat of ideological vacuum (Dekmejian 1995). However, at the start of the 21st century the idea of the Caliphate became attractive for some Muslims. It was to be built on the ruins of secular ideologies and regimes that had attempted to replace it over the recent decades but had failed woefully. To this end, in 2014 the leader of Islamic State, Abu Bakr al-Bagdadi, declared from the pulpit of a mosque in Mosul, Iraq, that he stood at the head of a Caliphate that had been destroyed in 1924, since when not even the most radical fundamentalist had dared announce it anew. Al-Bagdadi declared himself the Caliph, i.e. a representative of the Prophet Muhammad, who embodied both worldly and spiritual power in a single person. He stated that Islamic State would enforce a strict interpretation of Allah-inspired Islamic law (*sharia*), including *hudud* punishments such as chopping off limbs or stoning. His aim is to reconstruct the Golden Age of Islam, i.e. his idealised conception of the era of the Prophet Muhammad and the first generations of Muslims (*salaf*). This was a time when Islam was supposedly unsullied by human fabrications, the faith of Muslims was pure and the Muslim community (*umma*) was not divided into Sunnis and Shiites. Islamic State therefore demands submission and a pledge of allegiance (*baja*) of all Muslims in the world. Al-Bagdadi also requires them to leave their corrupt countries and, following the example of the Prophet, migrate (*hijra*) to his exemplarily led territory, change their lives, and put themselves at the service of the Caliphate and Allah. Islamic State declares that its aim is to destroy all impediments to God's rule on earth and to protect Muslims against infidels and apostates.

However, the ambitions of Islamic State are, at least rhetorically, global and expansionist. It wants to conquer and unite all territories where Muslims live. It rejects utterly the legacy of European colonialism in the form of the carving up of the Middle East and the splitting up of the once united community of all Muslims (the *umma*) into individual nation states advocating the foreign, toxic idea of nationalism. It reserves particular hatred for the secret Sykes-Picot Agreement (1916) entered into between Great Britain and France, which continues to influence the political map of the region, which the Islamists want to redraft root and branch. Like other totalitarian movements Islamic State wants to create not only a new kind of person and a new type of societal utopia, but also a new organisation of international relations (Weiss and Hassan 2015). However, in its effort to unite Muslims it is polarising further Middle Eastern societies. The Islamic State project is being condemned by religious authorities as non-Islamic or even anti-Islamic (cf. Open Letter to Baghdadi 2014).

On the other hand, individual nation states are also revamping and promoting the idea of pan-Islamic unity. The most obvious example is the Organisation of the Islamic Conference (founded 1969), renamed the Organisation of Islamic Cooperation (2011), which brings together 57 mainly Muslim countries. Officially it tries to represent the voice of Muslims the world over, to defend their interests and to push for world peace. It was established in response to the Arab-Israeli conflict and supports the two-state solution. It also serves as a platform for criticism of Israeli policy. In fact, it is a free association of nation states, a kind of debating union without any real integration potential and without any impact on international affairs (cf. Kropáček 1999).

THE TWO FACES OF ANTI-COLONIAL RESISTANCE: ISLAM AND NATIONALISM

Resistance to colonialism took two different ideological forms. On the one hand it looked to the nomadic and peasant classes of remote areas and attempted to unite them by appealing to an Islamic religion intelligible and common to all. References to jihad and sharia law were intended to unite the tribes in the struggle against the Europeans, often under the leadership of a charismatic cleric or acknowledged sheik of the Sufi Brotherhood, such as Kadir in Algeria, Abd el-Karim in Morocco, Shamil in the Caucasus, or the mystical sect of the Sanusiyya in Libya. It was only important clerics or sheiks of brotherhoods that had the authority that transcended individual tribes and regions. On the contrary, the colonialists, with their strategy of divide and rule, used traditional Middle Eastern tribalism (*badawa*) to their own advantage by encouraging tribal conflict on the one hand, and solidarity (*asabiyya*) with the state on the other (Roy 1992).

The second current of resistance looked to the less numerous literate urban classes. It attempted to bring together fragmented society in the struggle against the Europeans not by drawing on Islam, but under the banner of Western-style nationalism. Both Muslims and prominent Christians figured in the resistance movements (Roy 1992). At that time the example of Germany and Italy, two countries that during the 19th century had successfully united previously fragmented and weak political formations in the name of nationalism in order to become strong and widely respected political and economic players in the world, served as a powerful role model. Although religious nationalism played a role in the struggle for independence, in the post-colonial era it was secular nationalism that prevailed (Juergensmeyer 1994, 2008).

Most nationalist leaders had attended colonial schools providing a Western-style education. Some had even lived and studied in Western cities, especially Paris and London. There they were inspired by the European concept of history as the narrative of nations and nation states. Similarly, they acquired an understanding of international relations as involving a balance of power and clusters of international treaties concluded between individual sovereign states and nations. They picked up terms such as nation, nation state, national identity, sovereignty and independence from their European university lecturers. The first generation of the bilingual intelligentsia was infected with the nationalist way of thinking. However, this was alien to the remnants of "indigenous" societies, from which the new intelligentsia was alienated. Members of the indigenous intelligentsia often worked as lower-grade civil servants, performing the role of middleman between the European colonial administration and the colonised population. Initially, therefore, the new intelligentsia was unintelligible and culturally alien. However, over time the idea of a unified national community was popularised. This was helped by the increased *circulation* of people within the territory of the colony. Improvements were made to means of transport, and "career fairs" were organised around a colony offering education or jobs in the public administration or capitalist corporations. In the end, the concept of nationalism turned against colonial power and led to the creation and spread of the idea of a national community and the mutual solidarity of its members. After independence was acquired, Western-style nationalism, an *ideological import* from Europe, became the starting point for the creation of new nation states (Anderson 2008).

Ernest Gellner (1993), an expert on Muslim societies and a theoretician of nationalism, highlights the deeper *structural conditions* for the emergence and spread of nationalism. Nationalism only comes into existence with the transition from an agrarian to an industrial society. This profound transformation began in Europe, and it was here that nationalism first arose. In the Middle East the era of nationalism arrived later, along with industrialisation and modernisation often initiated by the European colonialists. Former peasants and nomads began to settle in cities. The city began to function as a huge *melting pot*. People arriving from all corners of the world gradually set aside their local cultures, which took the form of different languages, incomprehensible dialects of Arab, and manifold versions of folk Islam with its own idols and cults of the saints. The *circulation* of individuals in different roles and positions encouraged by a changing *division of labour* contributed to *cultural unification*. If in the agrarian era the individual inherited their work from their ancestors and performed it in a given place in a given community in unchanged form for the whole of their lives, in the modern, industrial age they changed it many times during their life, just as they changed their colleagues and workplaces. Increased specialisation leads to the *interdependence* of people within the framework of the national economy, which now exceeds what had until that time been self-sufficient traditional communities.

In order for people to be mutually *interchangeable* so as to be able to perform various roles and functions in economic life, they must also be as *similar* as possible to each other. Above all they should have gone through an identical and *standardised education system*. Each can then be quickly and easily trained to perform a specific job. In addition, education systems produce and distribute socially a unified *high culture*, e.g. a standardised literary language, standardised concept of history, and standardised heroes and role models. This replaces the fragmentation of different local traditional cultures. Likewise, *mass communication* is now *standardised* and transmits unified content from a single media source to an extensive mass audience. Until then societies had had to rely on face-to-face communication and content did not have a unifying impact. All of these changes contribute to a feeling of a united national community, while the hitherto dominant smaller local units between the individual and the state begin to disintegrate and become more and more difficult to identify with.

Prior to the era of nationalism, the predominantly rural Middle Eastern population identified with the community of all world Muslims (*ummah*), but in particular with small and mutually isolated or antagonistic local communities of traditional tribal societies (*Asabiyyah*). The ideology of nationalism emerged from the conflict with ethnically, culturally and linguistically dissimilar Europeans, who monopolised economic and political power. More educated urban segments of Arab societies arrived with nationalism. However, they gradually spread further, especially into those parts of society that had already been affected by modernisation. It was no coincidence that the proponents of secular Arab nationalism were Arab speaking Christian minorities who were generally speaking better educated with greater links to Europe (Gellner 1993). Arab Christians remain the main proponents of nationalism to this day. In the past they contributed significantly to the revival of Arab culture and often stood at the forefront of anti-colonial resistance. Under no circumstances, therefore, did they represent a fifth column that would be tempted to collaborate with the European powers for religious reasons. Furthermore, Arab Christians regard secular nationalism as an ideology that, unlike Islamism, poses them no threat as a religious minority and is not interested in making second-class citizens of them (Mendel 2014).

ARAB NATIONALISM AND SOCIALISM

Secular nationalism provided legitimacy to anti-colonial movements and newly established regimes. In its official form it emphasised an ancient, pre-Islamic history and supported archaeological research and the restoration of ancient cultures. Post-colonial regimes also validated themselves with socialist rhetoric and reforms. At the same time there is an ideological transformation to *Arab socialism* with a strong nationalist tinge (Arjomand 1986, Dekmejian 1995). With its emphasis on redistribution and solidarity, Arab socialism was presented to the conservative population of Egypt, Syria and Iraq as properly understood Islam. For instance, the regime in Algeria claimed that it was building an authentic domestic version of socialism based on the "specific character of the nation" and compatible with a "specifically Arabic-Muslim civilisation" (Gombár 2007). Elsewhere even Islam and its spiritual and religious endowments (*waqf*) and Quran schools were exposed to head-on ideological attack and openly condemned as representing the main impediment to progress within the framework of social engineering. This took place in Turkey and later in Iran, Algeria and Tunisia (Kepel 2002).

The legitimisation of political power during the post-colonial period relied on a negative definition of the nation based on its external rivals, and in addition tried to reach out to a population displaying no especial love of nationalism with an ambitious programme of national development that promised rapid prosperity comparable with the former colonial powers. These powers were a source of historical grievance but also admiration and imitation. Every citizen of a nation was therefore called upon to make sacrifices when building the national state. The watchword in Egypt was "Unity, discipline, work!" (Richards and Waterbury 2008).

Although "secular" Turkey tends to be interpreted as a specific model, in the post-colonial period it was seen as an inspirational template for other states. Most states reflected the "six principles" of the development of the Republic of Turkey in their national socialist programmes, above all the emphasis on building strong industrial sectors and a powerful army as guarantees of international independence, territorial integrity, and as a prerequisite for an end to foreign interference. The Turkish emphasis on the revolutionary role of state power, which would fashion a completely new type of westernised, modern and secular citizen on a top-down basis, also resonated powerfully. This ties in with the creation of a unified modern nation at the expense of the traditional faith-based, ethnical, regional or tribal stratification of society. Hence the emphasis on social equality through the redistribution of resources and the airbrushing out of potential conflicts. National unity was also to be ensured by the dominance of a single omnipotent party. Marxist theories of class struggle or the competition between different political parties in a liberal democracy were seen as a threat to national unity. Like Turkey, post-colonial regimes also placed an emphasis on mass, state-accredited standardised education for everyone, and on a centrally planned economy with an important role for state-owned enterprises, including nationalisation (a popular measure at that time), the creation of trade tariffs, the replacement of imports with a country's own production, and industrialisation or land reform (cf. Richards and Waterbury 2008).

However, national socialist leaders were similarly inspired by the model of the economic development of post-war Europe, which had seen an emphasis placed on the key role of the state in the economy. Middle Eastern leaders were well informed of events in Europe, which left a strong impression on them. President Nasser of Egypt, for instance, wore a tailor-made suit in the European style and was an avid reader of the British leftwing magazine *The New Statesman*. The Jordanian royal family maintained the tradition of studying at Oxford University (Zakaria 2004). Finally, the emerging Middle Eastern states also looked to the United States and the Soviet Union for inspiration (Lewis 2003b).

Post-colonial nationalism also sought legitimacy by *distinguishing itself from* the former colonial states, especially France and Great Britain, despite often being inspired by these countries when modelling its reforms. By means of this demarcation, post-colonial regimes issued a reminder, for instance at the Bandung Conference (1955) and in the Non-Aligned Movement, that they were leading their countries to an independence that was far from being self-evident. Nationalism also set itself in contradistinction to Israel, which it regarded as a continuation of European colonialism. America, on the other hand, which did not initially intervene in the internal affairs of the region, was viewed as a friendly country (Hudson 2009). In addition to defining themselves in opposition to imperialism, Middle Eastern nationalist movements distinguished themselves from each other. Arabs saw enemies in their historical rivals, especially the Turks, whom they blamed for the era of Ottoman rule, and Iran, successor to the historically competitive Persia. The Turkish and Iranian variants of nationalism were also imbued with mutual antipathy (Lewis 2003b, Hinnebusch 2009).

THE CHRONIC WEAKNESSES OF NATIONALISM

The confrontational tendencies of newly established nationalist regimes in relation to a range of internal and external enemies stemmed from the fact that their very existence was fragile and could not be taken for granted. Initially, in the eyes of the population the legitimacy of these regimes and states was weak and remains so to a certain extent (Esposito 2003). To begin with post-colonial regimes and states enjoyed far more *international legitimacy* as guaranteed by international law, organisations and powers. *Internal legitimacy* on the other hand lagged behind (Albrecht, Schlumberger 2004).

The reason for this was that Middle Eastern populations continued to claim allegiance to sub-state identities and societies, for instance the extended family, clan, tribe, ethnic group, region, Sufi brotherhood, religious group or sect, or, on the contrary, to supra-statist units and identities, e.g. pan-Islamism with the all-Islamic ummah or a pan-Arabism embracing all Arabs. Pan-Turkism and pan-Iranism were analogues in this respect. Both sub-state and supra-state identities are so strong that they undermine any identification with the nation state. The outcome is a different configuration of political identity than is common in Western Europe, where sub-state and supra-state loyalties are politically far weaker than identification with the nation state and the nation state is consequently stronger and more stable (Huntington 2001).

In surveys of public opinion only slightly more Arabs identify primarily with their state (39% on average), while approximately a third prioritise their affiliation with the Islamic world (33%). Slightly fewer people incline towards an all-Arab identity (28%). Identification with the nation state is stronger in the small city-states of the Gulf, where the population does not want to share the profits from oil with the broader Arabic and Islamic communities (Kuwait, Qatar and the United Arab Emirates). It is relatively strong in countries with deeper historical roots, longer continuity of statehood, and a relatively homogenous population in which a particular ethnic group predominates (Turkey, Iran, Israel, Egypt, Morocco and Tunisia). In these countries democratic mechanisms contribute to a consolidation of national identity and unity. In contrast, artificially created states whose populations are fragmented along ethnic, linguistic and religious lines are weaker and less unified, since individual parties tend to self-profile using ethnic or religious discourses (Iraq, Lebanon) (cf. Hinnebusch 2009, Zogby 2012).

The *artificial character of states* created during the era of European colonialism therefore represents a weak point of Middle Eastern nationalism. These states were born with a chronic deficit of legitimacy. Their boundaries were basically drawn by France and Great Britain, and these boundaries did not respect the ethnic and religious stratification of society or the historically established administrative units. An example of this would be Lebanon, created on the initiative of France by being split off from Greater Syria, an unnatural, religiously highly heterogeneous unit including Sunnis, Shiites, Druze, and various Christian groups. Iraq, whose borders were drawn with set square and which is highly diverse in terms of religion and ethnicity, was to become similarly fragile, with Christians, Sunnis and Shiites, Arabs, Kurds and Turkmens living cheek-by-jowl. During the era of Saddam Hussein, unity was maintained by means of terror perpetrated against the country's own population and an aggressive foreign policy: the attempt to participate in the Arab-Israeli conflict, rivalry with Egypt over leadership of the pan-Arab movement, and finally war with Iran and Kuwait over disputed borders drawn by the Europeans. The Arab Peninsula was divided up similarly. As well as the state boundaries, local royal dynasties were arbitrarily chosen and appointed by France and Great Britain (Iran, Syria, Jordan, Iraq, the Arab Peninsula) that often had no roots in and were alien to the countries in question, or members of collaborating minorities (Christians, Jews) were elevated to the head of the colonial administration, resulting in disunity after independence had been achieved. Nation states were therefore often viewed as a negative consequence of European colonialism by their citizens, the bastard offspring of the great powers governed by the logic of divide and rule. It was difficult for local populations to identify wholeheartedly with nation states and the associated ideology of nationalism. At the same time an alternative was on offer in the form of a unified *ummah* driven by a restored caliphate or a single pan-Arab state (Esposito 2003, Hinnebusch 2009).

MARXISM AND PAN-ARABISM

The baton of opposition to chronically weak nationalist regimes was initially taken up by *Marxism*. However, it should be pointed out that Marxism was regarded in Arab countries as a strictly economic doctrine and its concept of historical materialism rejected as atheistic. To begin with this was the movement feared most by the political establishment within the context of a heightened Cold War, though in the end Marxists seized power only in Yemen and Afghanistan. In response, regimes began to support Islam, initially convinced that it was an apolitical and harmless counterweight to the revolutionary left that could neutralise the popularity of the Marxists (Arjomand 1986, Kepel 1996).

Regimes also attempted to co-opt certain Marxist concepts into their rhetoric and even their political programme. Above all, however, regimes monitored the ambitious idea of Arab political integration under the banner of *pan-Arabism*, a philosophy that promised to resolve the weakness of Arab nationalism, namely its political fragmentation: "one nation, many states".

While nationalism defined itself in opposition to the colonial powers, pan-Arabism mobilised support thanks to the escalating conflict with Israel and the charisma of its main propagator, Gamal Abd al-Nasser. The question of Palestine became a matter for all Arabs. The unity of Arabs artificially divided by European colonialism was then interpreted as the prerequisite for strength, stability and rapid prosperity.

However, pan-Arabism did not prove its worth in practice. It suffered from conflicts between ambitious rulers, each of whom fancied themselves as leader of all the Arabs. The Federation of Arab Republics enjoyed but a brief existence before disintegrating into the original states. Nobody actually wanted to relinquish national sovereignty and sacrifice their power for the good of a higher unit. Frustrating attempts at pan-Arab integration were experienced by Libya, Egypt, Syria and Iraq. The only relatively successful merger of Arab countries was that of North and South Yemen, though this remains fragile and threatened by chronic separatism to this day (cf. Lewis 2008). Pan-Arabism was definitively discredited by the military losses in the wars with Israel, during which the Arab states were incapable of coordinating their actions. As a consequence pan-Arabism was revealed to be an impracticable chimera. Dreams of pan-Turkism and pan-Iranism suffered the same fate (Barša 2001, Hinnebusch 2009). These days the flame of political pan-Arabism flickers weakly in the form of the interstate organisation the Arab League (founded 1945), which aims to draw closer the relations between its member states and co-ordinate collaboration between them, to safeguard their independence and sovereignty, and to consider in a general way the affairs and interests of the Arab countries (Kropáček 1999). However, there are disagreements caused by divergent interests, the breakdown and implosion of many states, an increase in sectarian tension between Shiite and Sunni Arabs, economic crisis and a lack of funds for development projects caused by the fall in the price of oil. An example of just how insignificant is the League was its most recent summit (2016), to which only seven of twenty-two heads of states bothered to turn up. Most of these were unable to travel elsewhere because of the problems they face at home (the presidents of Yemen and Sudan) in countries that are not deemed important. The undiplomatic statement by the Moroccan minister of foreign affairs apologising for the absence of the king speaks volumes: "Given the absence of important concrete initiatives which could be submitted to Arab Heads of State, this summit will only be an occasion to take ordinary resolutions and deliver speeches which pretend to give a false impression of unity and solidarity between Arab States." (cf. The Economist, July 30th 2016).

And thus another ideological vacuum has opened up in the Middle East since the 1970s. Ideological helplessness and exhaustion has culminated in a shift towards multiple versions of political Islam. Opposition groups, often former Marxists, have formed an attachment to Islam having seen secular ideologies discredited. However, in an attempt to legitimise their power, Middle Eastern governments, often comprising confirmed secularists, have combined Islamic elements with their former nationalism. Opposition groups and the regimes they oppose thus compete for the support of an ever more religiously and politically active population (Dekmejian 1995, Kropáček 1996, 1999, Kepel 2002).

POST-ISLAMISM?

However, in the meantime even political Islam has lost its sheen. Despite its original self-confidence and dynamism, it has almost never managed to seize power, or even convince most of the population that it represents a real alternative to secular ideologies. A key reason was the discrediting of the Iranian revolutionary movement, which along with Islamist Sudan and the Taliban in Afghanistan is not viewed as an attractive alternative in the Middle East. More appealing is the model of development applied by conservatives from the Justice and Development party, or AKP, in Turkey, or that of the democratising Asian economic tigers Malaysia and Indonesia.

In many Middle Eastern countries the popularity of Islamist ideology has also dwindled because of the *co-opting* into coalition governments of Islamists, who have consequently assumed a degree of political responsibility for the development of their countries and have had to make concessions in the name of political compromise (Jordan, Morocco, Bosnia). The terrorism of radical factions (Egypt, Algeria) has similarly discredited Islamists. In the era of Post-Islamism, moderate Islamists have become simply one of many political forces that combine party politics in the fashion of European conservative Christian parties with the activities of affiliated charities and educational organisations operating in the sphere of Islamic civil society (Kepel 2002, Roy 2004, Barša 2011). However, in light of the electoral successes of the Muslim Brotherhood in post-revolutionary Egypt (2011 and 2012) and Tunisia (2011), and less so in Libya (2012), it is open to question as to whether Islamism has gone out of fashion. The future, therefore, remains open, and it seems more likely that this is a flexible ideology and relatively durable movement that manages to adapt to dramatically changing conditions.

MACHIAVELLIANISM I: THE SEARCH FOR ALTERNATIVE SOURCES OF LEGITIMACY

This story of the rise and fall of individual ideologies is reflected above all in the development of secular presidential *republics*: the ideological shifts in Egypt are exemplary in this respect. To a lesser extent it corresponds to the ideological development in *monarchies*, whose political legitimacy is based primarily on *traditional authority*, i.e. the claim that political power is derived from the sanctity, inviolability and antiquity of a monarchical dynasty whose reliability has been confirmed by history and previous generations. However, in monarchies too the story of the rise and fall of individual ideologies is important, because it mirrors the changes of discourse within the framework of the anti-monarchy opposition.

Along with the collapse of every other ideology – the caliphate, constitutional liberalism, nationalism and Arab socialism, pan-Arabism, Marxism – there has been a gradual *political awakening* of the Middle Eastern population and the arrival of new political players in the political arena. The age of mass ideologies begins when competing political doctrines do not compete only for the favour of minority segment of society, but reach out to the majority of a hitherto apolitical and passive population. The time when Arab nationalism, pan-Arabism or Marxism was in the ideological ascendant has changed and no longer resembles the modern day, when political discourse has been reoriented in the direction of Islam and democracy. Gradually a mass political public has been born. Most of the population must once again search on the market for political ideas for a credible political doctrine and the persuasive legitimisation of social order. A regime must convince not only the most modern strata of society of its legitimacy, but society as a whole, while the opposition must convince the whole of society that the current political establishment is illegitimate and offer an alternative that will find favour amongst broad swathes of the population.

However, despite their ideological burnout and permanent crisis of legitimacy, Middle Eastern regimes have been surprisingly stable for decades and have managed to avoid democracy's third wave. In this respect they have displayed the greatest long-term stability, not to say rigidity, in the world (Albrecht, Schlumberger 2004, Huntington 2008, Inglehart, Welzel 2006).

The fact is that, despite a chronic crisis of political legitimacy combined with economic difficulties and international pressure, Middle Eastern regimes have proved themselves capable of *adaptation* (cf. Albrecht, Schlumberger 2004, The Economist, February 2011). Since the end of the 1980s, when the third global wave of democratisation accelerated, they have made a series of incremental changes, the purpose of which has been to transform everything while retaining the most important thing of all: the power elite. We are not talking here of regime change, but changes *within the framework* of the political system.

Above all, the strategy for ensuring legitimacy was amended. Dictators now justify themselves in the eyes of the superpowers (the USA and the European Union) and international organisations (the UN and NATO) by means of a newly acquired *democratic rhetoric*. After 11 September 2001 there was much talk of the *fight against international terrorism*: in the name of the "war on terrorism" inconvenient opposition groups with nothing in common with terrorism were liquidated without a word of protest from the international community. The same strategy was employed by China in its Eastern Muslim provinces, Russia in the Caucasus, and the dictators of Central Asia. Dictators also achieved *external legitimacy* thanks to a reinstituted promise to maintain *stability*, namely "cold peace" with Israel, a safe environment for foreign investment, secure oil supplies, and the prevention of mass exoduses of economic migrants to the West. Colonel Gaddafi, for instance, vindicated his power in the eyes of Europeans by preventing the potentially devastating mass movement of migrants from Sub-Saharan Africa to Europe.

External legitimacy is particularly important for the *weaker countries* of the region. It ensures diplomatic, financial, military and food aid is provided by superpowers acting as the patron of the respective regime. Also important is the *moral effect* of the external recognition of and support for a regime by a superpower. The domestic population is cognisant of the external support enjoyed by their government, and this weakens opposition appeals for its overthrow, since a powerful external patron stands behind the regime that would be reluctant to let it simply topple.

More important, however, is *domestic legitimacy*, i.e. the tolerance of power disparities by the majority of the local population. The *charismatic legitimisation* of dictators relying on a *cult of personality* that emphasises their outstanding attributes, moral rectitude and wisdom is for the most part a thing of the past. In their time a cult of personality was enjoyed, for instance, by President Nasser of Egypt, King Hussein of Jordan, the Tunisian dictator Bourguiba, or the respected King Faisal of Saudi Arabia, as well as the Iranian revolutionary leader Khomeini. Collectivist secular ideologies promising rapid development and prosperity have also failed, as we saw in the previous chapter.

Another mechanism for obtaining the consent of the population to its division into the privileged and the rest involves the redistribution of the financial resources acquired from the extraction and export of oil or natural gas. Using this undeserved natural wealth, regimes either buy the blanket support of the entire population most often by means of subsidies for food, electricity, housing or fuel, or at the very least they bribe a loyal clientele with immediate links to the power elite. This applies, for instance, to "second-order" rentier states, which do not themselves extract and export oil to any great extent, but receive a brokered rent from their neighbours for its extraction, for example in the form of remittances. This represents the Middle Eastern form of an *unwritten social contract* that says that rulers will be tolerated if they allow at least some of their oil riches to trickle down to the lower reaches of unprivileged society. However, even this method of buying stability became problematic during the 1980s and 90s because of economic difficulties and demographic growth. As well as the dwindling revenues resulting from the low price of oil, it was necessary to "bribe" a larger and larger part of the population. For this reason the subsequent increase in oil prices to over USD 100 a barrel was a godsend for the dictators and enabled them to remain in power (Albrecht, Schlumberger 2004). In this respect the American-led invasion of Iraq (2003), which promised to elicit a domino effect leading to the democratisation of the Middle East, had unintended consequences. Contrary to expectations the invasion did not weaken the dictators, but strengthened their hold on power, since they saw their oil revenues multiply almost overnight. For instance, in 2002 Algeria's oil rent was USD 12 billion: in 2004, for the same amount of oil extracted, this figure was USD 23 billion. Saudi Arabia saw its revenues leap from USD 64 billion to USD 115 billion, Kuwait from 14 billion to 27 billion. Alongside the effect of the economic growth of China and India and the failure to invest in the oil industry during the 1990s when oil prices were low, the war in Iraq contributed to an increase of the price of oil on jittery markets (Laurens 2013).

However, the price of oil on global markets remains unstable. For this reason regimes are again turning to *traditional methods of legitimising* their power, for instance by appealing to the Bedouin model of unquestioning respect for authority and social hierarchy. In particular, they are resorting to religion and attempting to enlist the support of official clerics or ostentatiously resorting to religious rhetoric and highlighting the personal devoutness of their leaders. A fundamental source of legitimacy involves *scaring* a population by raising the spectre of Islamic terrorism, which allegedly only a strong, repressive regime is capable of standing up to (Albrecht, Schlumberger 2004, Stacher 2012).

MACHIAVELLIANISM II: INVENTING SCAPEGOATS AND PROXY CONFLICTS

Discredited, unsuccessful Middle Eastern regimes with limited legitimacy and support from their populations are using propaganda, a censored media, various one-off campaigns and the judiciary to divert attention away from the question at the back of everyone's minds: *"Where did we go wrong?"*, a question with implications in terms of reform and even revolution. And so regimes are attempting to introduce into public discourse a subtly different question: *"Who brought this upon us?"*, while in the same breath answering their own question by blaming foreigners for their problems. In this atmosphere, typical of repressive and closed societies, *rumours and conspiracy theories* thrive that unerringly uncover the most diverse culprits for problems that the regimes in reality have brought upon themselves. These *scapegoats* are then blamed for everything from poverty and unemployment, the inescapability of repression and a ban on opposition groups, to military losses and a lack of economic competitiveness. Everything is the fault of other parties. The regimes thus redirect the accumulated frustration and aggression of their populations onto proxy targets. Using the mechanism of a safety valve unsuccessful regimes deflect criticism and regularly release the accumulated frustration of their populations, and in doing so they avoid any outbreak of open conflict with opposition groups that would lead to a loss of power. There are many entrenched areas of debate that can be deployed to initiate a wide range of proxy conflicts (Lewis 2003a, cf. Coser 1956).

The decline and current stagnation of Islamic civilisation and individual states is often attributed to the invasions of the nomadic Mongols of the 13th century. After the arrival of nationalism in the Middle East, mutual recriminations have circulated between the Turks, Arabs and Persians, each of whom blames the other for their backwardness. Turkey, for instance, has long explained its stagnation as the historical consequence of the "burden" of uncivilised Arabs that the Ottoman Empire had to shoulder long ago. According to this narrative, the Turks, an advanced nation, paid the price for its attempts to civilise backward Arab regions of the empire while receiving no thanks in return. The Arabs, on the other hand, put the blame for their current problems on Turkish colonial domination, oppression and exploitation. For their part, the Shiite Persians regard their current situation to be the outcome of injustices long perpetrated by Sunni Turks and Arabs (Lewis 2003a).

The latest tactic is to blame French, British and American *colonialism* and *imperialism* for all their woes. There is hidden potential in an anti-imperial discourse for the legitimisation of regimes. Indeed, when these regimes take the side of the West (e.g. during the Gulf War, 1991), they face a crisis of legitimacy and increased opposition (Hinnebusch 2009). The causes of all today's problems are traced back to European colonial rule, which supposedly distorted the culture and economy of Middle Eastern societies in readiness for its takeover in more sophisticated form by American neo-colonialism. While after World War II the United States was popular and welcome in the region because it had not yet been sullied by any association with European colonialism, this is no longer the case (Lewis 2003a and 2003b). After the collapse of the USSR and the end of the Cold War, when the USA became the sole superpower with global reach, it became de rigueur to see the hand of America behind everything negative taking place in the world[5]. Paranoid

---

5   However, the tendency to see the "hidden hand" of the USA and the CIA behind all problems was typical even previously and beyond the boundaries of the Middle East. During the 1970s India popularised such conspiracies when it unsuccessfully experimented with a third way (Zakaria 2008: 150).

fears of American control of the world stem not only from the dominance of the USA in the military sphere, but also in the political, economic and cultural spheres. Globalisation is seen as a tool for achieving American control of the world (Juergensmeyer 2000).

America is criticised by the Middle Eastern public for deepening global inequality, damaging the environment, and unfairly favouring Israel in the conflict with the Palestinians. After the invasions of Afghanistan (2001) and Iraq (2003) especially, the United States was regarded by the Middle East as the greatest threat to world peace, and the populations in countries such as Turkey, Lebanon, Jordan and Kuwait were worried that the USA would attack their countries too. The discredited "war on terrorism" was regarded in the region as a pretext to pursue American interests, i.e. to control the sources of oil, acquire geopolitical dominance, settle old scores with disobedient dictators and non-state actors, and support Israel (Kohut and Stokes 2007).

In addition to anti-Americanism, there has been a boom in *anti-Semitism*. As in the case of nationalism, this is a European ideological import. It was first spread by European consulates and the Christian Church in the 19th century. Until then the Ottoman Empire, the Kingdom of Morocco and the caliphates in Andalusia had been prominent havens for Jews fleeing from Europe in the face of medieval pogroms and the Holocaust. The culmination of anti-Semitism in the Middle East would only arrive after the formation of the Zionist movement and the subsequent Jewish migration to the British Mandate for Palestine. Anti-Semitism then intensified after the declaration of the establishment of the State of Israel (1948). Middle Eastern anti-Semitism is thus the effect and not the cause of hostility towards the Jewish state. However, Middle Eastern regimes continue to nourish it and manipulate it in order to achieve their main objective: the maintenance of their own power.

The State of Israel is regarded as a loose continuation of European colonialism and the never-ending series of expulsions of Muslims from their homes: from the Iberian Peninsula (1492), Greece (1830s), the Balkans, and India (1947). In this atmosphere the cause of all of these failures is sought – and found – in all-powerful, international *Jewish conspiracy* (Lewis 2003a, Laqueur 2007, Öz 2006). Deep-rooted *conspiracy theories* are being elaborated and popularised in countless Arab, Persian and Turkish versions inspired by classic European anti-Semitic writings. The paradigms are *The Talmud Jew* by August Rohling (orig. 1700) and the *Protocols of the Elders of Zion* from the end of the 19th century by an unknown Russian author (Laqueur 2007).

In addition to the mass media, regimes use the state *education system* with its centralised curriculum and textbooks in order to encourage a self-image among Muslims as being the *eternal victims* of various *internal and external enemies* (Starrett and Doumato 2007). Entire generations become the target of propaganda that popularises the question "Who brought this upon us?"

at the expense of the more dangerous and self-critical question (from the regimes' perspective): "Where did we go wrong?" The concept of religious education differs in the curriculum of individual countries. However, the underlying message of the *founding story* of the Muslims is the same everywhere. The adventure story of the Prophet Muhammad and his companions presented by religious education textbooks recounts how good, peace-loving and upstanding Muslims have from the very beginning had to be on guard against attacks by a long list of treacherous enemies. For instance, the idolaters of Mecca, the Jewish traitors of Medina, and the wild, aggressive tribes of Arabia. The story then serves as the basis for an analogous explanation of history: the Crusades, the Mongol invasions, European colonialism, traitors and apostates from their own ranks, etc. It also contextualises the present in the form of Jewish Zionism and American imperialism. Muslims must therefore be increasingly on their guard against various threats from both internal and external enemies (Starrett and Doumato 2007). Iranian textbooks, for example, with extensive reference to Russian, French and British imperialism and the subsequent interference of Israel (Mosad) and the USA (whose military presence and support for Shah's dictatorship predates 1979), depict Iran as a *vulnerable country under permanent siege* (Freedom House 2008).

Regimes facing an internal crisis of legitimacy also have a tendency to prosecute international disputes or aggression against an external enemy. By escalating a conflict with a foreign enemy, often embodied by a former colonialist, regimes can temporarily unite an otherwise divided society. A hostile public and competing political movements can rally behind the regime in the face of a common external enemy, mobilise in support of the government and expect protection and leadership from it. This strategy has often been observed and described outside the Middle East (cf. Huntington 2008, Kazancigil 2006, Smith 2009). The slow pace of domestic reforms led President Nasser of Egypt and the Iranian premier Mosaddegh, for example, to become more involved in foreign policy, and this included an intensification of their confrontation with the West (Lerner 1964). Colonel Gaddafi too bolstered his legitimacy in the eyes of the domestic population through permanent confrontation with external enemies and an almost conceited self-stylisation as an internationally recognised leader (cf. Gombár 2001).

Israel especially has long been the universal military foe. Arab dictatorships adopted the hardest stance to the country at the beginning of their existence. The newly created Arab states and their power elites were not yet consolidated and felt the weakness and uncertainty of their status. They sought to enlist the support of their populations through conflict with an external enemy in the form of Israel, which appeared weaker and was therefore an ideal target. In contrast, Turkey, already internally consolidated with a recognised government, did not need to become embroiled in the conflict.

Practically all Arab regimes from the start used the question of Palestine to their own ends, profiling themselves to their domestic public in the role of champions of the interests of all Arabs and all Muslims. At the same time they often competed with each other for leadership of the Arab anti-Israel coalition (Egypt, Syria, Jordan, Iraq, Libya). However, as their power was consolidated and they were unable to defeat Israel, regimes became more moderate in their outlook. Nonetheless, diplomatic negotiations with Israel or the signing of peace treaties had a tendency to weaken the legitimacy of regimes and destabilise them. For instance, the assassination of President Anwar al-Sadat (1981) followed the signing of a peace treaty with Israel (1979). The assassination of King Abdullah of Jordan (1951) took place because of negotiations with Israel. The subsequent civil war in Jordan (1970) broke out because of the truce called between Jordan and Israel. Jordan was again destabilised after signing a peace treaty (1994) (Smith 2009, Hinnebusch 2009). Syria remained Israel's main enemy. Like Iran, the regime attempted to win the support of an otherwise divided population through confrontation (Gombár 2001).

A particular tactic employed by Middle Eastern regimes is the artificial inducement or at least exploitation of different international controversies that prey on the sensitivities of a religious population. Controversies that are interpreted as manifestations of Muslim fanaticism often have deeper political causes. Regimes ostentatiously set themselves against the neo-colonial West using international affairs. Confrontation with colonialism and imperialism was always the main and often sole source of their legitimacy. For this reason, when faced with a threat to their own power, regimes resort to a tried-and-tested tactic and profile themselves as indispensable defenders of Islam against godless foreign forces. At the same time these controversies allow them to deflect the attention of the population away from domestic problems and to release the accumulated frustrations these problems caused (cf. Burgat 2002).

The forerunner of all following controversies involved the mass protests against the book The Satanic Verses (1988). The affair was stirred up by the Iranian revolutionary regime, facing a serious political crisis after an exhausting war with Iraq (1980–88) over the successor to the ageing charismatic leader of the revolution Khomeini. This was followed by disputes relating to offensive statements made about Islam by Theo van Gogh (2004), the controversy provoked by the publication of caricatures of the Prophet Muhammad in European newspapers (2006), and the clumsy statements by Pope Benedict XVI in Regensburg (2007). Clashes ensued from the anti-Islamic campaign organised by the Dutch populist Geert Wilders (the insulting film Fitna, 2008) and provocative episodes of the serial South Park (2010). The regimes themselves, especially Iran, in turn caused offence by denying the Holocaust had taken place.

MACHIAVELLIANISM III: PLAYING AT DEMOCRACY

From the end of the 1980s onwards regimes experimented with *partial political liberalisation*. They relaxed repression, increased the space for a free press, legalised the operation of non-governmental organisations and increased the plurality of elections. However, contrary to the expectations of opposition groups and foreign governments, liberalisation did not lead to gradual democratisation. That would have entailed a change in the type of regime and increased the likelihood of the political elite being toppled. And so each wave of liberalisation was followed by a tightening up of repression as soon as the regime had regained its self-confidence and security. These waves of de-liberalisation were accompanied by the arrests of opposition figures, the falsification of elections, the liquidation of disloyal movements and press censorship. The strategy of oscillation between temporary liberalisation and repeated de-liberalisation helped co-opt some of the opposition during times of crisis. It enabled regimes to win time, mitigate the onslaught of criticism, and survive politically until they had consolidated anew their position. However, certain particularly repressive regimes such as Syria and Saudi Arabia were reluctant to use this strategy (Gombár 2001, 2004, 2007, Ottaway and Choucair-Vizoso 2008).

Regimes attempted to prop themselves by creating a semblance of *democratic legitimacy*. They attempted to persuade their populations that their power derived not only from *care for the people*, but from the *will of the people*. This sleight of hand had been obvious in the past after states had won independence, but was applied far more emphatically from the 1990s onwards, with dictators imitating Western democratic institutions and introducing new "democratic" institutions. New political parties, non-governmental organisations, ministries with new names, ombudsmen, commissions, advisory committees and second parliamentary chambers were created. A conveyor belt churned out hitherto unprecedented regulations, laws and procedures based on Western democratic models. This mostly involved, for instance, the decentralisation of decision-making and a shift of powers to the regional and local levels and formal supervision of the impartiality of elections and constitutional reforms.

In reality these were simply rhetorical, superficial and *formal changes*. Real power and the ability to take decisions remained concentrated in informal institutions such as the family, tribe and cronies surrounding the first circle of power. The vast *disparity between formal and informal political institutions* made the Middle East exceptional on the international scene. For instance, in Tunisia for many decades the government of Ben Ali reached informal decisions within the family circle in the presidential palace in Carthage, while the formal political institutions with no real power were based in the centre of Tunis. The purpose of this democratic "facade" was to create the semblance

of democracy in the eyes of Western governments and regimes' own populations. These populations no longer believed in the previous, now bankrupt,
ideology that rulers had used to legitimise their power for many decades and
yearned for democracy. The rulers had to react. In addition, the introduction of formal democratic procedures allowed regimes to detect earlier than
previously the mood of those social segments that kept dictators in power.
Parliaments elected on a partially free basis acted as weather vanes tracking
the variability of public opinion. Though they had no real power or legislative
authority, they served as a discussion forum in which a plurality of opinions
and interests were heard.

Expanding formal "democratic" institutions also served as a *channel for
social mobility* into the politico-economic elite for especially ambitious and
capable individuals who would otherwise have created an effective counter-
elite and provided dangerous reinforcements to opposition groups. Regimes
relied on the *inclusive co-optation* of individuals and entire social groups,
especially political and economic. This was not a case of *co-optation based on
allocation* by means of the redistribution of the revenues from oil or other
rents, as described above. After many decades of little or no movement,
the *social base* of regimes was now broadened, taking in business leaders
especially. Economic crisis led to the dismantling of the public sector and
privatisation, thus creating a more powerful private sector. In addition, the
power elite expanded to take in loyal political parties and movements that
were offered restricted room for criticism of individual measures taken by
the regime, though still forbidden from attacking the regime as such. Finally,
the elite was joined by highly educated technocrats, whom regimes increasingly needed for their operations and effectiveness and who were often delegated with the management of ministries.

Broadening the social base of the regime allowed for the reapplication
of the old strategy of *divide and rule*. The co-opted groups and individuals
occupied the second and third concentric circles of power, while at the same
time being encouraged to compete amongst themselves and seek the fickle
favour of the power elite. This balanced the influence of individual groups
and prevented them from unifying against the regime. For instance, in Egypt
under President Mubarak, instead of calling for root-and-branch change, the
co-opted opposition was for a long time mired in never-ending internecine
squabbles between secularists and Islamists, conservatives and liberals, left
and right, etc. The fomenting of disputes among the co-opted opposition stabilised the political system in the same way as another tried-and-tested strategy of dictators: when things went wrong blame, criticise, recall and change
ministers, civil servants and other representatives of formal institutions.
Though in reality these officials did not enjoy real power or the opportunity
to exert any significant influence on the way their institutions were run, they

were useful as scapegoats and could be blamed for the hardships suffered by the population.

These Machiavellian innovations were supplemented by the old practices of the internal dynamic of the power elite, which relied on the *rotation* of individuals around various functions. This included appointing the most ambitious individuals to be merely ceremonial ambassadors and despatching them to the most remote countries possible. This process of rotation also prevented the creation of an independent opposition centre within the framework of the second and third circles of power that could have threatened the first circle. These tricks helped boost or replace the teetering legitimacy of regimes and maintain their power so that they did not have to resort to blanket repression of the population or the suppression of the opposition as an example to others. This pragmatic Machiavellianism and the flexible search for alternative sources of legitimacy partially explains the long-term political stability in an era of the mass political awakening of the population of the Middle East and global democratisation across all the other continents (Albrecht, Schlumberger 2004, Ottaway 2010, Stacher 2012).

DEMOCRACY: MIDDLE EASTERN IMITATIONS

Notwithstanding what has been written above, alongside political Islam the main opposition alternative remains pluralist democracy. However, the bloom of democracy and free-market capitalism can fade when local populations do not assess it against the yardstick of its Western originals, but against its Middle Eastern *imitations* with which they have direct experience. The misuse and confusion of terms on the part of authoritarian regimes served to discredit democracy. Instead of being disappointed by the incompetence of authoritarian states, populations were disappointed by democracy itself (cf. Zakaria 2004).

One pillar of democracy is the free competition of *political parties* in a pluralist system. However, in the Middle East the institution of political parties was discredited from the very moment independence was won. Authoritarian systems and their ruling parties often designated themselves as "democratic". However, the concept of democracy was always used very vaguely and expediently. In addition, legal political parties are often created artificially and on a top-down basis by the regime itself, whose instructions they then follow. The aim is to create a semblance of democratic competition and thus boost the legitimacy of the regime. For instance, the regime of the Shah of Iran founded a monarchist party while at the same time organising for the creation of what was ostensibly an opposition party. These two loyalist parties quickly became known as the "Yes!" party and the "Yes sir!" party (Richards and Waterbury 2008).

Under the pressure of their own populations, Western governments and international human-rights organisations, most other authoritarian rulers began staging similar political theatre. They spent money organising elections, and then even more money on rigging the results. They would ban the candidates of strong, popular parties, often the communists and Islamists. Popular candidates would be intimidated and arrested. Electoral lists would be manipulated and impediments created to the registration of voters from regions known for their opposition to the regime. Pro-regime propaganda became the norm and fear of change was whipped up. The results of elections were brokered behind the scenes and known long in advance, something that happened in Egypt for instance on a massive scale in 2010. The "fairness" of elections was often attested to by their results, in which the establishment won 99.9% of the votes. Regimes were also fond of the institution of the referendum, largely in order to push through anti-democratic constitutional changes, for instance to extend the term of office of presidents in Tunisia and Egypt (Ottaway 2010, Burgat 2002).

The regimes then back this up by ensuring that the elected governments, parliaments or local authorities have no real power. At most they participate in decisions on social, educational or cultural policy, but not in decisions taken by the ministries of the interior, defence and foreign affairs or in matters bearing upon finance and the extraction of oil. They function far more as advisory committees or toothless discussion forums. The outcome is a stage set, with formal democratic institutions, rhetoric and rituals, which is then presented by authoritarian regimes as though it were genuine democracy (Zakaria 2004, Richards and Waterbury 2008). However, one unintended consequence of the attempt by authoritarian regimes to ensure democratic legitimacy for themselves can be the popularisation of the idea of democracy and the subsequent de-legitimisation of the regime, whose government is seen to be acting at variance with the principles it preaches.

CORPORATISM

The historical roots of the rejection of pluralist democracy among some segments of the population relate less to Islam than to European *corporatism*. This was inspired by Italian and German *fascism* and spread to the region along with German philosophy popular at the time (Lewis 1990, 2003b). Corporatism regards society as analogous to the human body or organism. The government is the brain. The workers are the hands and the peasants the legs. If a complex organism is to function, all of its parts have to work in harmony. The ideal is *government by one all-inclusive party*. Conversely, the class warfare promulgated by Marxists or the free competition of political parties promoting the particular interests and values of subgroups as articulated by liberals is an undesirable pathology paralysing the collective body.

This view of society was particularly espoused by active or retired *military officers*, who after independence found themselves at the head of Middle Eastern states. Corporatism corresponds well to the strict division of functions between individual military units such as navy, army and air force. These are not interchangeable and only their mutual operations contribute to the functioning of the whole. A well integrated social organism is also analogous to military hierarchy and a vertical command structure. This coordinates the activities of individual military units and requires unqualified loyalty to the whole and unconditional obedience to commanding officers (Richards and Waterbury 2008).

Middle Eastern authoritarianism thus clearly follows the ideological sources of European corporatism, which is close to the worldview of army officers. It was these officers who, during the first stages of Middle Eastern modernisation, represented the vanguard and the most powerful of the reform-minded social segments of society (Huntington 1968). The roots of authoritarianism in the Middle East do not therefore have to be located purely in the history of the Islamic religion or Muslim societies. It suffices to look at developments in the 20th century, when the assumption was that a precondition of the rapid evolution of society and successful modernisation that would close the gap on the industrialised world was social unity and the suppression of internal conflict (Richards and Waterbury 2008). Moreover, the United States and the Soviet Union supported this stance taken by their Middle Eastern clients during the Cold War (Kropáček 1999).

The *one-party model* was supported in the Middle East in line with corporatism, and failing that the model of a *united front* comprising several parties and movements, for instance the Arab Socialist Union in Egypt, the FLN in Algeria, and the Ba´ath party in Iraq and Syria. However, the purpose of this kind of party was not to mobilise the population and control the power elite, but to demobilise and control the politically active population. As remuneration loyal cadres were awarded positions in the party and the public administration. Their task in these positions was to control the membership base and their subordinates and denounce critically-minded members and colleagues (Richards and Waterbury 2008). Talented and ambitious party members were co-opted into the government or ended up in the diplomatic service. The embassies of most Arab regimes represented the career "grave" of ambitious politicians (cf. Gombár 2007). With the aid of party technocrats reforms initiated by narrow political elites could also be effectively implemented. Parties thus served as a transfer mechanism within the framework of the state machinery and a sophisticated technology of power (Richards and Waterbury 2008).

(8) THE TURN TO RELIGION: OFFICIAL ISLAM AND THE RISKY STRATEGY OF REGIMES

In the era of Arab secular nationalism, Saddam Hussein emphasised the Mesopotamian roots of the identity of post-colonial Iraq. He provided generous financial support for the reconstruction of ancient Babylon and profiled himself publicly as the successor of pre-Islamic colossuses such as Hammurabi, Assurbanipal and Nebuchadnezzar. However, from the 1980s onward he began to look for religious sources of the legitimacy of his power. The *turn to Islam* took place during a period of economic crisis and a draining war with Iran (1980–88). For instance, a television film was made depicting Saddam as a hero fighting for the faith. The cult of personality no longer works purely with an image of the leader in military uniform, but in a pilgrim's robes at prayer. The hitherto secular president also "discovered" in his family tree a line leading back to the Prophet himself. During the Gulf War (1990–1991) he added the inscription "God is great" to the flag and portrayed the conflict with Kuwait and the international coalition as a religious war against Christians, Jews, and their minions from the ranks of Muslim apostates (Gombár 2001, Kropáček 1996).

After defeat in the war and international sanctions, Iraq was on the verge of collapse. And so Saddam allowed Sunni and Shiite charities, until then persecuted, to go about their business. He also permitted Islamists to lead the Friday worship in mosques. In the meantime, the structures of the secular ruling Ba´ath party were Islamised. The exhausted regime also announced its intention to construct the largest mosque in the world in Baghdad. It was for this reason that, after the American invasion and the overthrow of the regime (2003), it was Sunni and Shiite Islamists that managed most effectively to fill the ideological vacuum and power vacuum thanks to the upswing in their fortunes at the end of Saddam's reign (Kepel 2004, Hybášková 2004).

Most Middle Eastern regimes underwent a similar turn to Islam in an effort to secure *religious legitimacy* for themselves. For instance, Algeria, Tunisia, Egypt and Syria were secular until the 1980s, after which they passed themselves off as promoters of Islam. They insisted on compliance with fasting during Ramadan. State television and radio broadcast Friday prayers, recitations of the Quran, and highly popular quizzes on the subject of Islam. The governments financed the construction of mosques and representatives of the regime, accompanied by television cameras, attended Friday worship and pilgrimages to Mecca (Gombár 2001, 2007, Kropáček 1996).

It is for this reason that Islam is enshrined as the state religion in all countries of the Middle East. Most constitutions pointedly refer to sharia law as the source of legislation. An attempt was made to ensure that state laws were not in conflict with Islam. Sometimes this was simply a case of rhetoric addressed to conservative segments of the population. However, generally speaking Islamic law is applied at least in family, inheritance and endowment law. The upshot is that most Middle Eastern countries have a *dual* legal system. Certain areas are dealt with by rules based on Islamic law, while other regulations draw on European secular models, such as British common law or the French Napoleonic Code. However, a certain duality had always been present in the law. There had always existed a potential conflict between the worldly legal system approved by rulers and the eternal law of God. However, these had been in symbiosis: the sovereigns enforced laws that at least partially found their inspiration in Islamic law. From the 19th century onwards, the duality of worldly and eternal law had been emphasised along with the permeation of Western constitutionalism guaranteeing civil rights, including equality before the law and the rights of minorities (Arjomand 2004).

However, the efforts being made by regimes to secure political legitimacy through the allegedly Islamic character of their legislation are double-edged. Opposition Islamists warn that these measures are insufficient and promise that they would apply Islamic law in all spheres of life across the whole of society. Governments then respond by attempting to Islamise the law still further in order to pre-empt criticism from the Islamists and refute accusations of religious apathy. This vicious circle ensures the penetration of Islam into the law and constitution (Kropáček 1999, 2002, Arjomand 2004).

Ostentatious government campaigns represent a specific way of demonstrating the Islamic character of regimes. Campaigns against alcohol, such as those in Libya (1969–74), Egypt (1981), Sudan (1983) and Pakistan (1978–84), have been associated with re-Islamisation. In certain less advanced countries regimes like to demonstrate their orthodoxy by coming down hard on adultery (Iran, Pakistan, Afghanistan under the Taliban, Sudan, Nigeria and Somalia). Certain regimes occasionally organise show trials of moral delinquents. An example would be the chopping off of the limbs of shoplifters, public flogging for drunkenness, or stoning for adultery. This is true of countries such as Saudi Arabia, Libya, Pakistan, Iran and Sudan (Mendel 2008).

Authoritarian regimes also attempt to give the impression of being genuine fighters for Islam through populist attacks on apostates, heretics and dissenters. This would include the persecution of Shiites in Saudi Arabia, the oppression of the Ba'athists in Iran, and the death penalty for critics of Islam and apostates in Sudan. It would also include the trials of Christians and Muslims "insulting Islam" in Pakistan and the annulment of the marriages of converts from Islam in Egypt. The violation of religious freedoms and the persecution of minorities is more a consequence of the crisis of legitimacy of local regimes than the Islamic religion. It is analogous to the policy of many conservative populists in the West, who push for the death penalty as a simple solution to complex problems. Middle Eastern regimes use Islamic law in an effort to demonstrate their Islamic character, to please the conservatives, and to compete with opposition Islamists whose aim is to implement sharia law through state power (Arjomand 2004, Kropáček 1999).

According to Islam, a key function of the state is to promote virtue and forbid vice (Esposito and Mogahed 2009). Therefore, if the state fails in all of the modern functions it has arrogated to itself in the post-colonial era (ensuring prosperity, social justice and a respected status in international relations), it can attempt to legitimise itself in the eyes of the Muslim population by placing an emphasis on the ostentatious enforcement of Islamic principles and public morality. Instead of economic and social development, a regime can now set itself the task of re-Islamising society, something that to populist despotic rulers seems an easily attainable goal. In addition, an emphasis on Islamic morality as opposed to political and economic liberalisation would not appear to threaten the position of the power elite. Finally, an emphasis on moral and legislative themes in public discourse diverts attention away from economic, social and political problems. While regimes (Kepel 2002) suffering a crisis of legitimacy during the Cold War era turned to Islam out of fear of Marxism, later they sought recourse in Islam in an ideological battle with opposition Islamists, who in the intervening period had become the best organised opposition group.

The unintended consequence (Starrett 1998) of this strategy, however, was the long-term popularisation of Islam in the public sphere, especially in politics. States thus inadvertently propagated the rhetoric, way of thinking and arguments of the Islamists. They began to play the game according to the rules of the Islamists, who insist that all of politics must be discussed and justified by means of and in accordance with Islam. However, it is difficult for regimes to meet these strict religious criteria (Burgat 2002). Their rhetoric and perfunctory measures encouraging Islamisation lack credibility and come across as hypocritical. For instance, from time to time a state will conduct a campaign against alcoholism, but at the same time will licence and tax the production and sale of alcohol. Or it will enter into an alliance with the godless West or Israel. The continued popularisation of the political dimension of Islam then simply increases the visible discrepancy between the religious ideal and the worldly reality of regimes, these contributing to their de-legitimisation.

At the same time fears of the Islamisation of the Middle East must be relativised in the event of the Muslim Brotherhood seizing power. Islamisation has been going on for at least three decades on the initiative of authoritarian regimes that are often secular in origin. However, the distrust and fear of the more secular section of society regarding the country's future direction played a crucial role in the military coup (2013) in post-revolutionary Egypt and the removal of the democratically elected Muslim Brotherhood.

The Brotherhood itself did not help by failing to seek broad-based support in society but polarising it through Islamic rhetoric. In contrast, after the revolutionary overthrow of the dictatorship in Tunisia (2010–2011) the Islamists were more willing to compromise and cooperate with political actors across the entire spectrum. Nevertheless, there too the secular section of civil society, fearful of Islamisation, have forced many concessions and remain deeply distrustful of the Islamists (Hamid 2014).

(9) DOMESTICATED CLERICS AND THE DECLINE OF THE TRADITIONAL RELIGIOUS AUTHORITIES

One reason why regimes have turned to religious sources of legitimacy is in order to curry favour with Islamic clerics (*ulama*). Traditional religious authorities are to re-enter the service of political power and save it by means of an infusion of religious legitimacy (Mendel 2008). Prior to the 1970s many Middle Eastern rulers, fired up by the secularisation thesis, assumed that the political role of clerics during modernisation would fade into the background. However, since that time they have once again been resorting to the political potential and relevance of the clerics, hoping that they will use their *fatwa* (religious legal opinions regarding controversial questions) to explain intelligibly any contentious actions taken by the regime to the largely god--fearing majority of the population. Similarly, they expect them to deploy Islam in support of the regime in their Friday sermons (*khutbah*) (Starrett 1998, Berkey 2007).

In addition to manipulating interpretations of Islam to meet the momentary needs of power, official clerics have the task of promoting a moderate, non-violent, non-revolutionary and strictly apolitical version of Islam. They are to be assisted in this by the education system and a state-censured media. This strategy views Islamism as the *heroin* of the Arab streets, while an Islam that conforms to state power is its attenuating *methadone* (Doumato and Starrett 2007). However, the coexistence of Sunni clerics and unpopular political power, the *traditional pattern* up till now, is disintegrating, and the clergy and its prestige being discredited.

THE COEXISTENCE OF RULERS AND SUNNI CLERICS: THE TRADITIONAL PATTERN

The particular social status of *Shiite* clerics and their different relationship with political power is the reason for their greater revolutionary potential. They often stood at the head of modern rebellions, for instance the Iranian Constitutional Revolution (1905), rioting against the Shah (during the 1960s), and the Iranian Revolution (1979). In contrast, from the very beginning of

Islam the *Sunni* clergy occupied a *bipolar or ambivalent position* between the people and political power. In the name of God it asked the ruler to be fairer in his treatment of his subjects. From time to time it reproached him for his excesses and interpreted God's law (*sharia*). It at least formally required rulers to govern in accordance with these laws and to enforce them within the state. In this way the clergy placed limits on potentially unrestricted, arrogant worldly power, which it then in recompense legitimised in the eyes of the citizenry. The Muslim community was exhorted to be obedient to its rulers and to have respect for the existing social order, rules and authorities (Juergensmeyer 1994, Kepel 1996). Under Islamic law, an uprising on the part of the population against a ruler was not regarded simply as a venal sin worthy only of general condemnation, but as a *great sin* equal in importance to apostasy, blasphemy or desertion (Mendel 2008). For instance, the Hanafi school of law (*mazhab*) refers to an eloquent surah of the Quran: "Oh ye who believe! Obey Allah and obey the Messenger and those in authority among you!" (cited in Bureš 2007: 43).

The most powerful weapon used by clerics against political power was the *exclusive* authority to *declare jihad* in order to overthrow a godless ruler whose power was threatening to spiral into unjust tyranny that failed to respect any of the rules and ethical norms derived from Islam. However, clerics have virtually never used their monopoly on calling jihad against tyrants in history for fear that society might fall into the chaos of civil war (*fitna*). Anarchy was interpreted as a far worse alternative than government by a tyrant; a day of anarchy far worse than a hundred years of tyranny. This would open up a society weakened by internal conflict to external attack. Moreover, the absence of state power would make it impossible to enforce any of God's laws. In addition, the interdependence of the clerics and rulers meant the former were reluctant to enter into open opposition (Kepel 1996, 2002).

THE ASYMMETRIC COEXISTENCE OF MODERN STATES AND TRADITIONAL CLERICS: SUNNI CATHOLICISATION

The relationship between modern regimes and the traditional *ulama* is *asymmetric*. As opposed to medieval khalifas, modern regimes have a strong tool for controlling the clerics, namely the modern centralised state with its extensive bureaucratic apparatus.

Modern states have often disbanded or nationalised Islamic endowment foundations (*waqf*). Generally speaking the assets of these foundations took the form of real estate, the revenue from which financed religious institutions independent from the state such as schools, mosques, spas and charities. In addition to their earnings, the foundations received gifts from the faithful and rulers seeking the favour of the clergy. The post-colonial loss of the economic independence of clerics led to a situation in which, for the first time in the history of Islam, they became state employees working for a salary financed from the public budget, in the same way as civil servants and teachers. As a consequence, the clerics became more loyal to the regimes, on which they were now dependent for a living.

Governments also began building, organising, financing and operating a *network of mosques* that were then under their control. The state then took control of the comprehensive *education of the clergy*, including Islamic lawyers and judges, the imams of mosques, Quran reciters, and teachers in Quran schools and madrassas. It determined the curriculum of schools teaching the clergy and promoted its own conception of Islam across the board, so crowding out other views. The centralised education of clerics is historically completely unprecedented. For most of history Sunni clerics were not centrally organised in any way and their education differed depending on the personality of their teacher. This led to what was a traditional *plurality* of opinions of individual ulama regarding theological, political and legal questions. For instance, their fatwa might differ and even contradict each other, and this was not considered strange.

The Supreme Council of Clerics and the Supreme Mufti, established by the state, supervise the centrally organised clergy. These institutions are authorised by states to issue authoritative fatwa or to resolve disputes relating to the compatibility of state legislation and Islamic law. The state's interests within the context of the centralised organisation of clerics is then monitored by the Ministry of Religious Affairs with its regional branches, offices, officials, circulars, forms, notices, regulations, and above all its budgets, on which the clerics depend. What resulted was something hitherto alien to Sunni Islam, namely a regimented hierarchical organism reminiscent of the Catholic Church but run by the state (Berkey 2007, Hefner 2007).

The official ulama influences believers through public speeches on general topics relating to ethical, religious or current social issues (*khutbah*). These are traditionally included as part of the regular Friday prayers. The state controlled media then disseminates the speeches from the state controlled mosques to the public, so that they are brought to the attention of those who do not regularly attend the mosque, for instance women. In the early days of Islam the authority to deliver *khutbah* belonged to the Prophet. It was then delegated to the Khalifa or city governors. The themes addressed in the *khutbah* always pertained to fundamental practical and political matters linked with the life of the community and not only doctrinal matters. This rhetorical authority, though swiftly transferred to the clergy, nevertheless retains its function of social control and political orientation to this day.

The other traditional means by which clerics are able to influence believers is through religious-legal opinions given on important political or social events or as answers to specific queries posed by believers (*fatwa*). These are available on many websites in the form of frequently asked questions (FAQs). Television and radio also broadcast programmes dedicated to the opinions of clerics regarding political problems and the everyday concerns of the faithful. In their legally oriented analysis, *fatwa* thus provide a religious justification of important measures being taken by regimes. For this purpose regimes usually appoint a reliable cleric screened in advance to the rank of supreme *mufti* of the country. This function has been established by both monarchies such as Saudi Arabia, Morocco and Oman and secular dictatorships like Algeria, Egypt, Syria and Iraq (Mendel 2008).

Middle Eastern "political commissars" in the form of official clerics thus legitimate all sorts of issues in the post-colonial region in the service of the regimes. In Egypt, they were called upon by President Nasser (1952–70) to explain to the country's more conservative citizens the necessity for family planning and why they should deposit their savings in banks working with interest, or to create an enthusiasm in the population for the building of Arab socialism as the correct interpretation of Islam. His successor, president Anwar al-Sadat (1970–1981), had a religiously justified argument drawn up by the ulama in support of the unpopular peace treaty with Israel (1979) and the neoliberal economic reforms imposed by the International Monetary Fund (Starrett 1998).

AL-AZHAR UNIVERSITY BROUGHT UNDER CONTROL

The Egyptian government used similar means to bring into line the hitherto independent, thousand-year old *Al-Azhar University* in Cairo. This institution had always been regarded throughout the Sunni world as the leading centre of Islamic education. The government turned its lecturers into state employees, and the management of the university was now no longer selected by an academic community independent of the state, but was appointed by the president (after 1961). For instance, the loyal Sheikh Tantawy (1996–2010), appointed the university's highest representative, was well known for his liberalism in respect of criticism of the pre-Islamic custom of female circumcision and advocated greater representation of women in senior governmental and official positions. He also banned female students from wearing the niqab on campus, arguing that Islam required nothing of the kind and that wearing the niqab could be construed as a sign not only of religious belief but also political conviction, namely sympathy with the opposition Muslim Brotherhood. It took the Egyptian courts to overturn the ban in the name of religious freedom. However, greater controversy was provoked by the Sheikh's justification of diplomatic talks with Israel, and he even ostentatiously shook hands with the Israeli President Shimon Peres in front of the cameras. Chaos ensued when the Sheikh justified the use of interest in the banking industry or threatened journalists writing critically about President Mubarak and his poor health, for which he demanded a punishment of eighty lashes (Hefner 2007, Kepel 2002).

The next Sheikh of Al-Azhar, Ahmed al-Tayeb (from 2010), then personified the complete domestication of the Egyptian clergy. He was a personal friend of President Mubarak, a senior member of the governing National Democratic Party, and for many years served as supreme mufti of Egypt. His animosity towards the opposition Muslim Brotherhood was well known at the time and when dean of the university he had had one of their demonstrations on campus broken up (2006). After taking office he was heard to say that Al-Azhar would be a bastion of tolerance and moderation in the face of extremism and fanaticism and stressed that his decisions would be reached for the good of Al-Azhar, Egypt and Islam. Notwithstanding these proclamations, his career seemed more based on the logic that what was good for Mubarak's regime was good for Egypt, Al-Azhar and Islam. Any opposition to the regime was denounced with the labels "extremism" and "fanaticism" (Hackensberger 2010).

In an effort to subjugate and control the clerics of the prestigious Al-Azhar University, the Egyptian post-colonial regime replicated a strategy going back two hundred years to the time of Napoleon's expedition to Egypt (1798–99). Aware of the relative weakness of his army, and thus the lack of brute force need to occupy the country's vast tracts, Napoleon first turned his sights on the sixty highest ranked clerics of Al-Azhar. He attempted to win these over to his side on the basis that they would then justify the French colonial presence to the population as a whole in the language of Islam and from the position of religious authority. Napoleon himself took on the role of devout Muslim, though ultimately his efforts met with failure (Said 2008).

THE MULTIPLE CONNECTIONS BETWEEN STATE AND CLERGY: FROM TURKEY TO SAUDI ARABIA

The forerunner of modern efforts to quell the power of the clerics and create an official religion compatible with the interests of the political elite is republican Turkey. Though the Republic of Turkey tends to be viewed by academics as a specific and exceptional secular model in the region, as far as quelling the traditional clerics is concerned most republican and socialist regimes underwent a similar development.

Turkish *secularism* (Massicard 2005, Pirický 2006) by no means entails official atheism or the separation of state and religion, since in Islam there can be no talk of the separation of church and state because Sunni Islam does not recognise the institution of the church. It also does not mean the equality of all faiths and their recognition by a neutral state. Islam is the official religion of Turkey. Every Turk is officially labelled a Muslim upon being born. Turkish secularism is therefore mainly about rigorous state control of religion, i.e. the regime's monopoly on the promotion of an official version of religion, namely the Sunni Islam of the Hanafi *mazhab*. This is done at the expense of other schools of law and tendencies that are officially declared to be undesirable and banned.

A crucial element of Turkish laicism is the substitution of Islamic law, the judiciary and education with secular and Western-inspired institutions, something that took place somewhat later in most Middle Eastern countries. The Turkish state controls religion by means of the all-powerful Directorate of Religious Affairs (*Diyanet İşleri Başkanlığı*, 1924), which reports directly to the premier. The directorate trains future preachers in state schools. It makes them public employees paid from the state budget and working with the state's permission. It also influences and controls the content of Friday's sermons delivered by a cleric. The institution has a larger budget than the Ministry of Industry (EUR 400 million, 2002) and runs a network of 75,000 state mosques. It employs 90,000 officials and another 75,000 people in various positions, making it one of the largest employees in the country. Yet the purpose of the directorate from the start was to train clerics in such a way that they justify the governing regime and the republican system.

The antithesis of Turkey and its domesticated army of official clerics is clearly these days Saudi Arabia. This is a Middle Eastern country where the ulamas retain a central role and relative independence from political interference. However, here too the clerics are for the most part loyal to the regime and offer legitimisation of government measures. Indeed, the unification of the Bedouin tribes and the establishment of a monarchy took place thanks to the symbiosis of the royal family of Al Saud and the movement of orthodox clergy led by Mohammad ibn Abd al-Wahhab. For this reason, the legitimacy of royal power rests on loyal clerics united on the Council of Senior Scholars and on the Supreme Mufti, who support the policies of the monarchy by means of fatwas issued in a religio-legal language (Beránek 2007b).

The reformist King Faisal (1964–1975) turned the clerics into state paid employees. These then used their fatwas to justify controversial innovations such as the start of television broadcasting, which always began with a recitation from the Quran, or the opening up of primary and secondary school education to girls. A famous fatwa is that defending the hitherto blasphemous idea that the Earth orbits the Sun. Crucial from the perspective of the regime and the official clerics was the Iranian revolution (1979), which inspired Islamist critics of the monarchy expecting the imminent arrival of the Mahdi and the end of the world at the end of the century: according to the Islamic calendar this was the first day of 1400. The Islamists' rebellion against the monarchy culminated in the occupation of the Grand Mosque in Mecca. In the end it was only with American assistance that they were expelled from the sacred precinct, where violence is not permitted. The Supreme Mufti Abd al-Aziz ibn Baz had to endorse this scandal in one of his fatwas. The mufti found himself in a similarly unenviable situation after the invasion by Saddam Hussein of neighbouring Kuwait (1990), when Iraqi tanks threatened the Saudi Eastern Province with its abundance of oil fields. He very reluctantly issued a fatwa justifying the expeditious deployment in Saudi Arabia of an American army numbering half a million in the immediate vicinity of the holiest sites in the Islamic world as part of Operation Desert Shield. The fatwa argued that the Prophet himself had requested assistance from non-Muslims. The controversial deployment of American troops subsequently incited terrorist attacks on the American embassies in Kenya and Tanzania (1998), carried out on the anniversary of the arrival of the military in the country. At the same time terrorists belonging to al-Qaida called for the speedy withdrawal of the Americans (Kepel 2004).

For this reason, the rising political tension in the monarchy brought about by the unequal distribution of oil revenues, the presence of foreign armies in the proximity of holy sites, and scandals involving several hundred princes, was diverted in the direction of another target with the aid of further religio-legal expert statements by clerics loyal to the regime. Like Iran, Saudi Arabia issued a fatwa (1989) calling for the death of Salman Rushdie, author of the provocative The Satanic Verses. True to the logic of the scapegoat, the Shiites and competing Iran were also labelled arch-enemies.

However, the most dramatic consequences followed in the wake of ibn Baz's fatwa calling for anti-Soviet jihad in Afghanistan as the collective religious duty of all Muslims. The Saudi state supported the struggle against the USSR both financially and logistically. The regime attempted to obtain religious legitimacy through ostentatious support for the Afghan jihad and to divert criticism of its young generation away from the Saudi family to a new enemy in the form of the Soviet Union. However, an unintended consequence was the wave of terrorism that ensued after the return of Saudi veterans from Afghanistan at the start of the 1990s. Another wave of terrorism followed the fall of the Afghan Taliban (2001), when more veterans returned home and continued the fight under the banner of al-Qaida in the Arabian Peninsula. These boomerang effects were the consequence of a strategy that involved boosting the role played by the discourse of religious clerics in society pursued by the state after the occupation of the Grand Mosque by religious opposition groups (1979). This in turn reinforced the popularity of religious arguments within the framework of political affairs. However, it also eroded the prestige of the pro-government clerics at the expense of clerics and self-proclaimed preachers critical of the monarchy (Kepel 2004: 152–196, Beránek 2007, Ťupek 2007).

The reliance of Middle Eastern regimes on the authoritative voice of traditional clerics was apparent during the organisation of the international anti-terrorist summit in Egypt (1996). This took place against the backdrop of a wave of suicide bombings by Hamas against Israelis. It was also when the satellite station Al-Jazeera was beginning its activities and among other things covering in detail events taking place in Palestine. The growing popularity of the Palestinian Islamic movement across the region, combined with the jihad led by opposition Islamist groups in other countries (Egypt, Algeria), gave regimes cause for concern. And so they approached top Islamic jurists, though these occupied different positions in their fatwas. Either they denounced suicide attacks under all circumstances, as in the case of the Saudi Abd al-Aziz ibn Baz, who consistently defended the interests of a Saudi Arabia yearning for stability and other regimes concerned by the spread of armed jihad, or, as for instance in the case of the Egyptian Sheikh Tantawy, they carefully distinguished between support for the Palestinian struggle and the methods of the suicide bombers in other cases.

However, the genie had been let out of the bottle. For the first time in the centuries-old history of Sunni Islam, a group of *mainstream* ulamas embarked on a tortuous justification of suicide bombers, albeit applied to the particular situation in Palestine. Above all they pointed to the extreme nature of the Israeli occupation that, they argued, required extreme forms of opposition. They also highlighted the defensive character of the resistance, in which all less violent methods up till that time had failed. Moreover, the Palestinians were protecting the most fundamental values such as land, Islam and honour. However, it was not long before other groups of militants began to perceive similarities between their situation and that of the Palestinian resistance, claiming that elsewhere too what was involved was a defence of Islam and orthodox Muslims against oppression. Gradually the arguments of religio-legal experts originally deployed to justify only the Palestinian jihad came to be applied flexibly to other situations in other parts of the region, and were again used not to interpret Islam itself but political events on the ground as examined above (Kepel 2008).

CLERICS VERSUS ISLAMISTS

The decline of the traditional religious authorities and the end of their monopoly on the interpretation of Islam was also related to the expansion of education systems and the proliferation of new media. A highly educated and self-confident stratum of the population took the opinion that they could do without the clerics and were capable of interpreting Islam just as well for themselves. The internet and satellite TV stations currently feature a wide range of interpretations of Islam originating in both clerics and the laity, and it is now possible to choose that interpretation that best meets the needs of a particular group. Believers no longer need to rely on the viewpoint espoused by their local imam (Kropáček 2002, Starrett 1998).

However, the decline in the prestige enjoyed by traditional clerics was hastened by their collaboration with unpopular regimes, which responded to the crisis of legitimacy they faced by resorting to clerics and their religious arguments, i.e. no longer by appealing to secular ideology but Islam. During the second half of the 20th century traditional clerics found themselves in thrall to political power. This was especially visible in Morocco, Saudi Arabia, Egypt and Turkey, where clerics discredited themselves by abnegating their traditional function, namely to criticise the transgressions of rulers from the perspective of Islam.

The space opened up was soon filled by lay Islamists criticising authoritarian rulers and questioning the legitimacy of their government by highlighting the discrepancy between their policies and Islam (Kepel 2002: 48–54). At the same time, Islamists also began criticising traditional clerics for collaborating with despots and arrogating to themselves a monopoly on the interpretation of Islam. The Islamists now found an audience among those who were not content with the hypocritical or humdrum Islam being promulgated by the official ulamas. In this respect political Islam is similar to the Christian Reformation, during which Protestants declared themselves to be against the traditional religious authorities (the Catholic church), which were distorting faith in favour of political power and overlooking God, salvation and morality (*Goldberg* 1991).

However, most traditional Sunni clerics still refuse to countenance rebellion against even the worst despots, and herein lies the core of the dispute between radical Islamists and traditional clerics loyal to state power. Their conflicting attitudes towards power leads each to accuse the other of the most serious sin, that of heresy and apostasy. The clerics accuse Islamists of being apostates because they incite what for Islam is risky and deadly insurgency against current rulers. This would result in chaos and the liquidation of the community of believers by enemies attacking from without. Conversely, Islamists accuse pro-regime clerics of hypocrisy, seeing them as analogous to the members of the Prophet's community, who pretended to follow Muhammad while in reality supporting the powerful Quraysh. In addition, they accuse the clerics of the sin of apostasy, since they have relinquished what is both their right and sacred duty to declare jihad against apostates from the faith, including apostates from the ranks of godless and unjust tyrants (Dekmejian 1995).

The darling and role model of the Islamists became the long forgotten "Jan Hus of the Middle East", Ibn Taymiyyah (1263–1328). Faced with internal decline and the external threat from the barbarian Mongols, Taymiyyah had not been afraid to stand up to the dominant practices of his colleagues loyal to power. He criticised the discrepancy between the demands of Islam and the visible excesses of the political elite and societal morality. He pointed out that the duty of clerics in this situation was to urge believers to rise up against their godless rulers and overthrow them. He was not afraid to take risks, was persecuted and for a long time forgotten. For Islamists this was a powerful, inspiring story relevant to the present day, which was popularised by the leading lay theorists of Islam in the 20th century such as Hassan al-Banna, Sayyid Qutb, Maududí and Mohamed Farag, who contrasted the ethical consistency of Ibn Taymiyyah with the embarrassing obsequiousness of modern clerics towards political power (cf. Mendel 2008, Ťupek 2013).

However, consensus is lacking among Islamists. Moderate mainstream thinking tends to renounce violent rebellion against godless despots. For instance, Egypt's Muslim Brotherhood distanced itself from violence in the influential manifesto contained in the text "Preachers, not Judges" (1969) by their moderate leader Hassan al-Hudaybi. Deciding who is a true Muslim and who a heretic deserving of the death penalty is something that should henceforth be left to God, and people should desist from their amateur dabbling in the question (Pargeter 2013, Zahid 2010).

Another unintended consequence of efforts to achieve religious legitimacy by *co-opting* clerics into the service of the regime is the popularisation of the religio-political method of argumentation in public sphere. Official ulamas publicly justify government policy by appealing to Islam. At the same time, a loyal ulama is now caught up in distinguishing between an Islam that is moderate or revolutionary, apolitical or political, open or fanatical, violent or non-violent, tolerant or intolerant, correctly or poorly understood, etc. The endeavour of those in power is to condemn inappropriate interpretations of Islam and enforce those that will operate as an instrument of the internalised discipline described by Michael Foucalt, as Marx's opium of the people, i.e. as a form of false consciousness serving the interests of the ruling class. If Islamism is understood as the heroin of Arab streets, Sufism and other seemingly apolitical forms of Islam are to be its methadone. If Muslims are incapable of ridding themselves of their dependence on religion, and secularisation has proved to be a chimera, then a substitute therapy must be found that at least blunts the social appeal and political dimension present in Islam (Doumato and Starrett 2007).

In fact, official Islam as promulgated by the pro-regime ulamas does not perform the function of political anaesthetic, but gradually popularises the Islamic discourse as such. And this will always be potentially political. Islam thus becomes the language of all the key political battlegrounds. The rule now is that everything must be discussed, explained and justified in the light of Islam, and this means that various different groups use the religion for the purpose of self-legitimisation and thus popularise still more a political reading of Islam (Eickelman, Piscatori 1996). Official ulamas have created a powerful Islamic discourse regarding politics but are no longer capable of monopolising and controlling it, since it has entered the public domain and taken on a life of its own (Starrett 1998).

Finally, clerics and authoritarian regimes are in conflict with opposition Islamists over the interpretation of reality itself and not just Islam. Even if the clerics manage to push through an apolitical conception of faith, Islamists can successfully point to the fact that all is not well in the real world, that there is a conflict between good and evil, God and Satan (Juergensmeyer 1994). All interpretations of Islam, therefore, contain within themselves the potential for an apocalyptic reading of the everyday world and a call to believers to defend themselves against the forces of evil and decline. The success of the Islamists is measured in terms of to what extent and how widely they manage to popularise this perspective. In the Middle East, therefore, in their struggle with opposition Islamists, pro-regime ulamas face two conflicting lines of interpretation operating in parallel: the conflict over the interpretation of political reality and the conflict over the interpretation of the Islamic religion.

The unintended long-term consequence of co-opting the clerics into the service of regimes is thus the loss of their authority and their monopoly on the interpretation of Islam and political reality. Running in parallel with this is the popularisation of Islamic discourse in politics, a fact that opposition Islamists and other political actors are quick to seize on. As a result, both regimes and clerics find themselves at the mercy of an increasingly pronounced interpenetration of politically and religiously based arguments that they themselves originally created. In the service of political power the clerics were first supposed to emphasise the Islamic character of increasingly feeble authoritarian regimes. However, these days disputes being conducted in religious language are moving beyond their control, while they conduct the most fierce political battles with the opposition in the language of Islam.

(10) OIL RENT, THE POWER PYRAMID AND THE SOCIO-ECONOMIC ALIENATION OF REGIMES

A *rentier state* and its economy resemble a parasite. They stand and fall along with a non-productive type of economic activity, such as income from the export of natural resources (oil, natural gas, diamonds, timber) or collection charges for the transit of these raw materials. Egypt, for instance, controls the Suez, and Syria or Jordan are located on the routes of oil and gas pipelines.

Similarly, massive foreign aid from a superpower can also represent a rent, for instance the financial transfers from the USA to Egypt, Jordan and Pakistan. It is typical of a rentier state that *a substantial part of its income is from abroad*, and that these *financial flows are under the direct control of the government* and derive from highly *non-productive activities* that require only a *minimum workforce* (Ross 2001, Luciani 2009).

Middle Eastern regimes are rentier states. They accumulate political power and economic wealth through the control of revenues from the extraction and export of oil. This applies above all to Iran and the Arab states of the Persian Gulf, though almost all countries in the region have smaller stocks at their disposal. A pivotal role here is also played by the extraction and export of natural gas, especially in the case of Algeria and Libya (Klare 2004, Richards and Waterbury 2008). Two thirds of the global reserves of conventional oil and a significant amount of extraction capacities are found in the Middle East (Brzezinski 1999, Bičík 2000, Cílek, Kašík 2007). However, even those regimes that are barely involved in extraction are also indirectly dependent on oil. These are known as *second-order* rentier states (Albrecht and Schlumberger 2004), which every year receive something in the order of EUR 22 billion through the regional redistribution of oil wealth (Hybášková 2006). The post-colonial extraction of oil allows Middle Eastern dictators to consolidate their political position. This has maintained regimes into the 21st century that would in all likelihood have not survived without oil rent. A *dependence* on the flow of oil is therefore two-sided and interdependent: it is not a necessity only for the West, but for the survival of authoritarian regimes in the region (Luciani 2009).

However, Arab regimes that enjoy a monopoly over a different form of rent than oil are also rentier states. For instance, Morocco is the world's most important exporter of phosphates, accounting for 40% of global exports. Along with the annexed Western Sahara (1975) it possesses 75% of world deposits. Every year, the Egyptian political elite awards itself around USD 2 billion received from the operation of the Suez Canal. A further approximately USD 2 billion arrives in Cairo every year from the United States in the form of foreign aid. The secular dictatorship in Egypt was long considered the most important ally of the USA in the Arab world because of its unique strategic location, powerful army, the size of its population, and its role as mediator in the Israeli-Palestine conflict and the peace concluded with Israel (Ottaway 2010). In addition to military and financial assistance, Egypt also receives food aid, part of which the regime distributes to the needy and the rest sells on the black market to groups close to the regime (Cílek 2011). We find a similar situation in Jordan, where foreign aid from Washington represents around six percent of the country's gross domestic product (Zakaria 2004).

Middle Eastern regimes without significant mineral resources have also learned how to avail themselves of international money transfers known as *remittances*. These are sent by people who have emigrated to the West or have gone to work in the wealthy Gulf monarchies to their relatives back home. These two directions of Middle Eastern migration are roughly equal in strength, and equally important in terms of remittances. In smaller, poorer countries without abundant natural resources and with a significant *diaspora*, these remittances play a key role. This is especially true of Jordan, where financial transfers from abroad represent 22.7% of GDP, and Lebanon (24.4% of GDP). Remittances are also important in Morocco (9% of GDP), Yemen and Egypt (6% of GDP) and Tunisia (5% of GDP). In contrast, remittances sent home by the Turkish diaspora represent only 0.2% of the country's GDP (Human Development Report 2009).

OIL RENT AND AUTHORITARIANISM

Of the twelve member countries of the Organisation of the Petroleum Exporting Countries (OPEC), not one is democratic (see tab. 3). Indeed, they have long ranked among the most repressive countries in the world (cf. Baňouch, Fedorko 2000). Other key non-OPEC exporters are also often non-democratic

Tab. 3 The Organisation of the Petroleum Exporting Countries (OPEC) and political repression (2013)

Country	Level of repression
Algeria	5.5
Angola	5.5
Ecuador	3.0
Iran	6.0
Iraq	6.0
Kuwait	5.0
Libya (*)	4.5
Nigeria	4.5
Qatar	5.5
Saudi Arabia	7.0
United Arab Emirates	6.0
Venezuela	5.0

Source: Freedom House, 2013 (www.freedomhouse.org)
N.B.: Every year the Freedom House index ranks 25 criteria of political rights and civil liberties. The scores awarded range from 1 (free) to 7 (not free).
(*) Up until 2011 Libya had the worst score possible (7.0).

states: Russia, Columbia, Oman, Yemen, Syria and Sudan. Where democracy is in place (Norway, Great Britain), oil began to be extracted and exported in quantity long after democratic institutions were established and had become sufficiently entrenched. Similarly, one hundred years after the first borehole was put into operation in Pennsylvania in 1859, the USA was the largest oil producer and exporter in the world. However, democracy had been established many generations prior to the oil boom (Cílek and Kasík 2007, Friedman 2010).

Tab. 4 Dependence on oil exports and the absence of democracy (1995)

Country	Share of oil in exports (%)	Level of repression (Freedom House ranking)
Brunei	47.6	6.0
Kuwait	46.1	5.0
Bahrain	45.6	6.0
Nigeria	45.4	7.0
Congo	45.1	6.5
Angola	45.0	6.0
Yemen	38.6	5.5
Oman	38.4	6.0
Saudi Arabia	33.9	7.0
Qatar	33.9	6.5
Libya	29.7	7.0
Iraq	23.5	7.0
Algeria	21.4	6.0
Venezuela	18.8	3.0
Syria	15.0	7.0
Norway	13.5	1.0
Iran	12.0	6.5
Ecuador	8.5	2.5
Malaysia	6.0	4.5
Indonesia	5.7	6.5
Cameroon	5.6	6.0
Kirgizstan	4.2	4.0
Netherlands	3.1	1.0
Columbia	3.1	4.0

Source: Share of oil revenue in national wealth Ross 2001, Freedom House level of repression. N.B.: Every year the Freedom House index ranks 25 criteria of political rights and civil liberties. The scores awarded range from 1 (free) to 7 (not free).

Closer analysis shows that the character of a political regime correlates more precisely with the relative *share of oil exports of the overall economic performance* of the country than with oil exports. If, then, the extraction and export of oil dominates the economy, the regime is likely to be strongly authoritarian (see tab. 4). Extraction in sufficiently developed and diversified economies does not destabilise the democratic system to such an extent. Conversely, in poor, economically backward countries the expansion of extraction leads inexorably to the degeneration of fledgling democracy and the gradual onset of authoritarianism, or blocks the possible emergence of democracy in the case of, for instance, monarchies or dictatorships. This relationship also applies outside the Middle East and is valid for several other raw materials (e.g. natural gas and diamonds). The significance of these statistics continues to apply even after account is taken of the influence of other oft-discussed characteristics, e.g. the predominant religious tradition. Therefore, the cause of the ongoing authoritarianism in the Middle East is not Islam, but the rentier character of the local states (Ross 2001).

The causal relationship between a *rentier state* and an authoritarian regime is manifest across three general mechanisms: the rentier effect, the repression effect, and the modernisation effect. The *taxation effect* ensues from the fact that a normal nation state acts as an instrument for the taxation of the population. It is dependent on society and the state of health of the economy if it wants to finance its own operations. In contrast, a rentier state is not dependent on the tax it receives from its population. On the contrary, state control of oil rent and the redistribution thereof means that society tends to become dependent on the state. Understanding the tax effect is made easier by examining the contrast between the political development of today's rentier states and the historical development of modern Europe. The ongoing and costly wars being waged by rulers (France, Great Britain) saw an increasingly intolerable tax burden placed on the population, and eventually the citizens in these countries reacted. They demanded a share of power so as to be able to play a part in decision making and to oversee how the state would deal with "their" money: *No taxation without representation!* According to this narrative logic, the right to vote was first won by those citizens whose tax burden was the heaviest, gradually trickling down to those with fewer assets, and finally to those with none, at which point we see the introduction of universal suffrage (cf. Tilly 1986). The effect of increasing taxes *subsequently* leading to gradual democratisation in the 20th century has also been empirically demonstrated outside Europe (Ross 2001). However, today's oil rentiers do not need to tax their populations thanks to their high oil revenues. Indeed, they have no need of their populations at all, and would be happier and better off without them. If, therefore, the population of an oil state is taxed minimally or not at all, it does not have the same immediate need for representation in government, where it could control and influence the handling of the state budget. The population does not feel that the government should be explaining its finances and being accountable for the transparent management of the state treasury. The pressure of the population on its government is minimal. The government feels the same and sees no reason why the people should have a say in government when they do not pay tax: *No representation without taxation!* Authoritarian rulers have a tendency to regard the rentier state with its mineral wealth as their personal property, almost a part of their household assets, similarly to the way medieval European feudal lords regarded their land and subjects. As a consequence, the rentier state is associated with *neopatrimonialism* (Lewis 2003b, Luciani 2009).

The associated *spending effect* then says that oil revenues allow authoritarian regimes to bribe the population by means of higher social spending and other advantages that people in other countries can only dream of: subsidised or free energy and public services. The state literally has the population on its payroll. Dictators may long to win the population over to their side, but only rentiers have sufficient fiscal resources to make this happen. The legitimacy of power is therefore not derived from the will of the people, but from the generosity and method of redistributing petrodollars. Oil states thus become potentially omnipotent patrons who take care of their people, or at least those loyal to them, from the cradle to the grave. The financial clout of rentiers minimises social tension and smoothes out the sharp edges of criticism. It eliminates the support and attractiveness of opposition groups, whose career depends on a persuasive critique of existing living conditions and the dissatisfaction of the masses. If demands for a change of regime begin to grow, it suffices to increase social spending and a political crisis is usually averted. This was how the Gulf regimes headed by Saudi Arabia, for instance, reacted to the wave of Arab revolutions after 2011 (Ross 2001).

The *effect of the formation of independent groups* is again often contrasted with the historical development of modern Europe and the United States. The emergence and expansion of an economically independent bourgeoisie (France, Great Britain) assisted the process of democratisation. The economic autonomy and confidence of this layer of society gradually tipped over into political autonomy and power that balanced the hitherto dominant influence of the aristocracy (Moore 1968). In rentier regimes, on the other hand, civil society is regarded as an independent sphere between the state and the family that is structurally weak because it has nothing to fall back on economically. Social capital in the sense of a dense network of relationships and trust between citizens is in deficit. The state and the oil industry it runs completely dominate the economy, so preventing the seeds of alternative economic and political power centres independent of government from putting out shoots.

According to this narrative, all that exists between the state and the family is a barren wasteland (Ross 2001).

Another telling argument involves the *repression effect*. Every authoritarian regime fears the threat from its own population and a potential opposition more than an external enemy. It dreams of creating a heavily armed, perfectly trained, lavishly paid and thus unconditionally loyal and obedient *repressive apparatus* (Huntington 1968). However, it is above all the oil rentiers that are capable of making this dream come true by means of their oil revenues. It is for this reason that we speak of "national security states" (*mukhabarat*) in the Middle East, characterised by bloated secret services, police forces, and all-powerful military institutions. The most elite military units are created in order to suppress domestic opposition rather than to repel foreign invaders. This state attempts to monitor all social activity and dominate society (Zakaria 2004, Luciani 2009). Wherever oil, natural gas or another lucrative resource represents more than 50% of a country's exports, wealth is generated to the benefit of the power elite that suffices to create and finance a sufficiently repressive apparatus. This apparatus can then suppress any kind of opposition, while controlling deposits, extraction, refining and exports. Once it has expropriated power, oil rent is able to acquire yet more power and accumulate wealth (Tomeš et al. 2007).

However, the effect of repression is not only manifest in the fact that rentiers *can* afford to sponsor powerful, extensive repressive apparatuses. As opposed to other authoritarian regimes, rentiers *must* create such apparatuses. He who controls geographically concentrated natural riches wants to maintain this control. However, the idea of seizing the revenue from oil rents is also attractive to potential challengers, who want to distribute the profits from extraction and export to their own benefit. Challengers may arise in the form of foreign governments or separatist movements provoking border disputes in the regions of oilfields. More often they appear in the form of tribal, ethnic, religious or regional groups that are excluded from the distribution of oil rent, even though this wealth is located within their territory. This then creates the need for an extraordinary militarisation of oil regions, as well as the construction of the repressive apparatus needed to police potentially rebellious segments of the population that are excluded from the distribution of profits from oil (cf. Klare 2001, 2004, 2008).

Finally, there is the *blocked modernisation effect*. This is based on the classic assumption that a certain level of socio-economic development creates favourable conditions for the spread of democracy in a given society (Lipset 1956, 1994). However, economic growth does not in itself lead to democratisation. What is needed is economic development that stimulates the emergence of a strong middle class, the migration of the population from rural to urban areas, the expansion of a well educated and critically-minded public and media, and the specialisation of the professional structure. In other words, democratic institutions will find it difficult to put down roots in a highly rural, agrarian and illiterate population, unconnected to the media. Having said that, democratisation will not be helped by an "artificial" economic boom based not on education, skills and the professional specialisation of the middle class, but on non-productive rentier activities (Inglehart and Welzel 2006).

The effect of the oil rent was demonstrated during the course of the Arab revolutions. While densely populated republics with little in the way of rent collapsed, all those regimes exporting oil in large quantities and with smaller populations held onto power and remained relatively stable. The only exception was the Libya of Colonel Gaddafi, who did not distribute the rent among the population in order to ensure the wider loyalty of clients beyond the framework of the three (of a total of 200) allied tribes. Instead, he spent a substantial amount of the rent on the creation of megalomaniac projects in the Sahara or supporting his foreign policy centred around pan-Africanism (cf. Gause III 2011).

OIL RENT AND THE THREE CIRCLES OF POWER: THE POLARISATION OF POWER

The power structure (Gombár 2001, 2007) of most Middle Eastern regimes can be simply described as comprising concentric circles if the aim is to emphasise the horizontal dimension of the distribution of power, or as a pyramid if we want to emphasise the vertical dimension. This anatomy of regimes, based on *informal relationships* and political *clientelism*, is in stark contrast to the formally declared power structure enshrined in constitutions.

The core of the *first circle of power* generally comprises the family and large extended family of the president (in secular dictatorships) or king (in monarchies). It also usually involves top military leaders, often allied by kinship or arranged marriage with the head of state, or at least along a common line of tribal or clan affiliation, which functions as a cement binding together the first circle of power. It is here and nowhere else that the most serious decisions are taken, collectively, consensually and informally, regarding politics, business and the allocation of key posts in the country. The logic of the thinking of this inner circle of power can be summarised by the answer given by Habib Bourguiba (1956–1987), dictator of Tunisia for thirty years, when asked how he would describe the political system of his country: "System? What system? I am the system!" (Gombár 2007: 62).

Moving outwards from the first circle of power there is the clientele, comprising elite military units, intelligence services, secret police and other key security agencies, above all the officer corps. The *second circle of power* also represents an interest group capitalising on the economic and political order in question. Any political change, economic reform or liberalisation potentially threatens the privileged position of the first and second circles of power.

In addition, the first and second circles of power are often linked not only by shared interests and clientelism, but tribal, clan, religious and regional ties. For instance, in the Libya of Gaddafi, the regime relied on just three privileged and therefore loyal tribes comprising the individual circles of power: the Qadhadhfa, Magarha and Warfalla. In Morocco the three concentric circles comprise the royal family and rural elites, along with privileged Berber tribes that formed the core of the police, military and secret services. Algeria is ruled by the army standing in the centre of three circles of power, which owns the state-run oil giant Sonatrach. Civilian ministers here constitute only the second circle of power recruited from the revolutionary rural elite, above all from the Oujda tribe, which in the war of independence removed French domination and in the parallel civil war the competing traditional urban elites. Tunis is formally speaking the capital of Tunisia where the government sits, though in reality the family of the president rules from the top level of a three-level power pyramid from its palace in Carthage. On the first level of this pyramid is concentrated the hard power of key ministers of the armed forces and secret services, economic power in the form of representatives of the main business families, and the necessary expertise in the hands of leading technocrats and specialists. In Syria we find a four-level power pyramid, though pivotal from the regime's perspective is the Alawite sect, from which is recruited the family of the presidential dynasty of Assads (Gombár 2001, 2007).

A relatively heterogeneous *external (third) circle of power* comprises most of the ministers, with the exception of the ministers responsible for the security and military services and foreign affairs, along with experts and technocrats, the top bureaucrats and pro-government parties, and wealthy businessmen capitalising on government contracts or the monopolies acquired thanks to their connections. It also includes some of the co-opted opposition groups comprising a number of small and insignificant parties and movements, from the heads of co-opted trade unions, pro-regime clerics and loyal journalists (Gombár 2001, 2004, 2007).

Authoritarian regimes divide most of the rent among the top of the power pyramid. Less wealth trickles down to the lower levels. However, the majority of the population, who are not part of the network of cronies and informal links with direct or indirect connections to the tip of the pyramid, are excluded from the fruits of the rent. Inequality of power is accompanied by socio-economic inequality.

In many Middle Eastern countries, for several decades the polarisation of power accompanied by the socio-economic division of society has threatened to culminate in what is known as the *Iranian scenario*. Social tensions (Kepel 1996, 2002) leading to revolution in Iran (1979) caused a skyrocketing increase in revenues from oil exports, especially after the oil crisis (1973). The expectations from all levels of society rose similarly fast. However, the material situation of the majority was in contrast to the prosperity of the Westernised elites, the military-industrial complex and groups close to the regime of Shah Pahlaví. The unequal distribution of petrodollars and intensified social polarisation was escalated by the dip in oil prices in the aftermath of the oil crisis. This sparked the revolution that promised that there would be a more just distribution of oil revenues amongst all levels of society, thus mobilising people against the regime.

OIL RENT AND THE SEGMENTATION OF SOCIETY: SOCIO-ECONOMIC POLARISATION

The distribution of petrodollars contributes to the *segmentation* of society within the environment of authoritarian regimes, since it tends to be highly *unequal* in terms of regions, tribes, clans and social and religious groups. Privileged segments of the population close to the regime support the ruler because they profit from the distribution of oil revenues. Unprivileged groups without family or other ties to the regime find themselves in opposition, having been excluded from the distribution of the revenues. Oil rent results not only in the authoritarian character of regimes, but deepens the segmentation of society, which in turn leads to *latent political instability*.

Authoritarian rulers redistribute oil revenues within the framework of a relatively narrow, isolated power elite, which means that loyal segments of the population and kinship networks from which members of the regime are recruited profit most from the influx of petrodollars. The state bureaucracy, police, secret services and the army also profit from oil revenues. However, most of the population is excluded from the distribution of the rent. The resulting segmentation and polarisation is the consequence of a combination of oil rent and authoritarian regimes that do not distribute this rent democratically, but in accordance with the logic of clientelism.

Social segmentation and polarisation result in political destabilisation. Regimes fear disloyalty from groups excluded from the rent, and so they often resort to the protection of a strong *external patron* (the United States, Russia), hoping that such a patron will defend them in the event of rebellion by their own population. This often leads to the permanent deployment of foreign armies in a country or in its territorial waters and the construction of military bases or outposts in the wider region.

However, these alliances, motivated by the endeavour to stabilise regimes with the help of external forces, become counterproductive over the long term and tend to intensify instability still further. Regimes begin to face criticism of a different kind. Voices are raised asking whether it is appropriate to sell the country's mineral wealth abroad to the benefit of the external patron, which is allegedly the biggest beneficiary from exports of raw materials. The accusation that regimes are collaborating with godless foreigners leads to a further drop in their legitimacy. The presence of foreign soldiers is also highly provocative (Klare 2004, Zakaria 2008, Pfaff 2010, Pape 2003, 2006, 2010).

The extraction of oil and natural gas is technologically complex and sophisticated. These resources are located deep underground and require huge initial investment and an extensive extraction and transport infrastructure. Unlike diamonds, coffee, tropical wood, rubber, and plants for the manufacture of drugs, deposits of oil and natural gas are highly concentrated geographically. It follows from this that a conflict over the control of oil rent is usually played out in two ways. Firstly, it is a struggle for control of the state (revolution, coup, civil war), especially if the deposits are geographically close to the central regions of a country. Secondly, when oil-rich regions are located on the peripheries of a country far from the reach of central government, an attempt is made to gain autonomy or complete independence by means of separatism; think South Sudan, Iraqi Kurdistan, Indonesian Aceh, post-Soviet Chechnya, Cabinda Province in Angola (Klare 2001, Tomeš et al. 2007, Šmíd et al. 2010).

OIL RENT AND POLITICAL IDENTITY: THE POLARISATION OF PARTICULAR GROUPS

In most countries of the Middle East *identity politics* plays an important role. And yet according to modernisation theories racial, ethnic, tribal, clan, linguistic, regional and religious identities are supposed to have faded in significance. However, in the Middle East their political significance is if anything increasing with the emergence of modern states, especially when membership of a tribe, ethnic group or religion intersects with power imbalances and socio-economic inequality in post-colonial states, i.e. in situations in which members of the power pyramid linked by informal client networks are recruited from a specific tribal, religious or regional segment of the population, while the rest of the excluded population, outside the power pyramid and the redistribution of rent, is recruited from different tribes, regions or ethnic and religious groups. Particular identities overlap with identities based on social class and multiply their political potential.

Particular identities are reinforced by the collective experience of political exclusion and social deprivation. This means they can be used for the effective political mobilisation of groups excluded from power and resources.

If the power elite is alienated from the rest of society not only in terms of class but also in terms of ethnic, tribal, regional or religious identity, an opposition is easily mobilised against it within the excluded segments of the population. These traits are to be seen in Turkish Kurdistan, Sudan, Lebanon, Yemen, Iraq, Libya and Syria (Richards and Waterbury 2008). Religion or ethnicity thus serves as a political catalyst in class conflict (Gellner 1993).

The same kind of multiple overlap of particular identities along the lines of class and power inequality is also to be found in the oil-rich monarchies of the Gulf. Tribal, ethnic and religious groups bereft of power and oil revenues can thus attempt to change this unfavourable situation. They mobilise politically by appealing to shared interests, but also to shared tribal, regional and religious identities. However, the power elite wants to maintain its privileged position, and thus mobilises its clientele in its defence, a clientele whose informal network also replicates the tribal, regional or religious segmentation of society. Particular identities thus contribute to both the internal cohesion and solidarity of groups in opposition and those in power (Klare 2004, Hybášková 2006). The intensity of the conflict over power in a rentier state grows along with the increase in total wealth that could be acquired by seizing power and redistributed to affiliated groups along the lines of client networks and consanguinity. The oil rent means there is more and more at stake. In addition, in authoritarian regimes we are talking of a zero sum game: the winner takes all. Everything is to play for, but everything is to lose. This ratchets up the intensity and violence of conflict when it comes (cf. Olson 1963, Huntington 1968).

The political scientist Michael T. Klare (2001, 2004, 2008) warns that the Iranian scenario, combined with the effect of political identity, puts the Gulf oil monarchies led by Saudi Arabia most at threat. In Saudi Arabia the unequal division of oil revenues props up a royal family comprising 7,000 princes, plus their cronies, above all the many loyal clerics, since the Saudi regime came into being via a symbiosis of the warriors of the Saud family and the religious followers of MohammadibnAbd al-Wahhab. A key role in protecting the regime and the royal family against opposition is thus also played by the National Guard, which is recruited from affiliated tribes and is trained and provided with modern equipment with the aid of the United States and its training personnel. Large numbers of American training personnel have maintained an ongoing presence in Saudi Arabia since 1951. From 1990 to 2003 a huge contingent of the American army operated in the country after the operations Desert Shield and Desert Storm. A similarly privileged status to that of the National Guard is enjoyed by the police force, with regular salaries and the most up-to-date equipment and weaponry.

Some of the Saudi-Arabian Sunni tribes, as well as approximately 15% of the Shiite minority, are excluded from the division of power and thus the oil rent. This applies mainly to the Sunni tribes from the Hejaz and 'Asir regions. It is here that one finds a bastion of moderate and radical Islamists who oppose the monarchy, and above all a strong anti-American sentiment. This is why Saudis applying for a visa to the USA after 2001 were obliged to state their tribal affiliation, since the Saudi Arabian internal political conflict is increasingly manifest externally. It is no mere coincidence that those who occupied the Grand Mosque, under the leadership of Juhayman al-Otaybi (1979), came from Hejaz and 'Asir. As indeed did the Saudi terrorists who attacked the United States on 11 September 2001 and some of the members of al-Qaeda expanding their activities on the Arab Peninsula, especially after the invasion of Iraq by the Americans (2003). The uprising by ostracised Shiites (1979), long excluded from power and petrodollars, in the Eastern Province, where the largest deposits of Saudi oil are to be found, represented the most serious threat yet to the regime (cf. Baer 2003, Klare 2004, Beránek 2007).

(11) THE CULTURAL ALIENATION OF WESTERNISED REGIMES: CULTURAL DECOLONISATION

The post-colonial division of power and wealth in Middle Eastern societies is shadowed by the cultural division. On one side there is a small, *westernised*, secular elite profiting from the existing order. On the other there is the rest of the population, cut off from power and wealth, but more firmly anchored in domestic culture and traditions. This clash of cultures within a state can be taken advantage of by opposition groups, including Islamist groups. The *duality* of society in terms of power, wealth and culture creates a space for the emergence of opposition ideologies that profile themselves as explicitly anti-Western and anti-secular. As an alternative (cf. Juergensmeyer 1994) they offer *cultural decolonisation*, a return to supposedly authentic domestic culture, values and traditions. This cultural clash manifests itself as a conflict between the discredited *secular nationalism* of the elites and the *religious nationalism* of the opposition. At the same time (cf. Eisenstadt 2000) an attempt is being made at a reinterpretation of modernity within the context of the indigenous culture, rather than its wholesale rejection. The endeavour is to offer an alternative programme for modernity in opposition to the prefabricated Western version.

The power elites are alienated from the rest of the population not only because of their power, wealth and particular identity (tribal, religious or regional), but also by virtue of their education, lifestyle, manner of dress, consumerism, language and culture. They usually represent the most westernised segment of the population, set apart from the majority and difficult to understand. However, even the relatively small counter-elite claiming allegiance to the secular opposition, from liberals to communists, can be similarly unintelligible and culturally alien. As a result, the political language of the power elite and part of the counter-elite can be more remote from the tradition-based masses than that of political Islam.

Both the power elite and some of the secular opposition can thus appear to be collaborating with an alien Western world with which they share cultural similarities. They can give the impression of being the successors to the European colonial administrators. Opposition Islamists on the other hand are closer to the people not only in socio-economic terms but cultural terms also. They are easier to understand and are in immediate daily contact with the people and speak their language. This makes them more trustworthy and their propaganda more effective (Lewis 1990, 2008, Esposito 2003).

It was only after independence had been acquired that the mass westernisation of post-colonial societies began. It was not overseen by Western colonialists or imperialists, but by the newly established regimes, which generally speaking were of the opinion that a necessary condition for the modernisation of society was its cultural westernisation and assimilation into the international community headed by Europe, the United States and the Soviet Union. The regimes moved in this direction as a vanguard and example to the rest of society.

The small politico-economic elite, speaking French or English fluently, had studied at Western-style schools at home or in some cases abroad. Members of this elite displayed their admiration for the West by regularly reading the European press and driving American cars. They were not often to be seen in mosques and considered the West to be their point of reference. However, they controlled a society that mostly spoke Arabic, Persian or Turkish, a society that was more rooted in tradition and had never studied or travelled abroad. As the moderate Tunisian Islamist Rachid Ghannouchi was heard to say, the westernisation of education, the legal system, the media, public administration and the arts had taken place so rapidly that "people wondered whether they were still living in their own country" (cited in Burgat 2002: 29).

It was only after independence had been won that translations of foreign literature, mainly from English and French, began to appear on the bookstands. The number of French or English speaking citizens rose and were recruited as loyal employees of the newly created administrations. It was in fact the domestic regimes, and not the Europeans, that abolished traditional Islamic schools and religious institutions, while everything Western was supported. As a result, people began to ask whether their regimes were not actually assisting in the dominance of the West. It seemed to them that domestic rulers had not prevailed over Western colonialism, but rather over their own Arab culture and Islamic civilisation, which they were now suppressing. The new Middle Eastern elites began to be seen as "alien", in the same way as had the former European colonialists (Burgat 2002).

THE REPUBLIC OF TURKEY AS FORERUNNER

The first person to attempt westernisation on a large scale in the Middle East was Mustafa Kemal Atatürk. He also tried to set an example to others in his personal life. After the overthrow of the Sultanate (1922) and the war of independence (1918–1923), an elite group was formed of politicians, businessmen and military personnel that had received a Western secular education. They came from Istanbul, Ankara and the West Coast. The state abolished traditional Islamic institutions such as Islamic law, the judiciary, caliphate, religious schools, endowments and Sufi orders. Western fashion was also promoted by the state. Men were forbidden from wearing the fez and advised to wear Western-style suits, while women were discouraged from wearing the veil. The state radio station broadcast only Western classical music and the country transferred over to the European Gregorian calendar (Montran 2005, Massicard 2005).

A major reform measure aimed at hastening westernisation was the abolition of the Arabic alphabet and its replacement by the Latin (1928). This impeded the access of all succeeding generations of Turks and Kurds to the many centuries of intellectual and religious heritage recorded and refined in the Arabic script. The new elites deemed this cultural heritage to be reactionary, and believed that mastery of the Latin alphabet would open the way to Turks to the rapid acquisition of European languages, and through them to the intense transfer of Western ideas and technology (Huntington 1968).

A rival political project responded to this radical westernisation by attempting to achieve a synthesis of Islam and modernity, Islam and democracy. The opposition *Progressive Republican Party* (1924) promoted a platform that would introduce reforms more gradually and "respect religious thinking and feelings" (party statutes, Article 6). However, the party was unable to find favour among voters because it was banned by Atatürk when, soon after the Republic of Turkey was created, the country introduced a single-party system of government (1925–1950). More conservative thinkers were only to have a voice in politics with the creation of the new opposition *Democrat Party* (1950) led by Adnan Menderes, whose ten years in government were brought to an end by a military coup (1960) supported by the secular and westernised Kemalist elite recruited from the state bureaucracy, universities, the judiciary and the army. An attempt was later made to rehabilitate the Ottoman era and Islamic religion by President Turgut Özal (1983–1993). However, this did not involve a radical rejection of the West, but more an endeavour to strike a new balance between different sources of Turkish identity. Indeed,

Menderes promised to turn Turkey into a "little America", accepted the Marshall Plan, led his country into NATO and focused his international attention on the democratic West. Of the economist Turgut Özal, who worked for a long time in the United States, it was said that "he loved reading the Quran and watching popular television serials and he enjoyed bowing his head to the carpet in ardent prayer in the Sufi mosque, after which he would set off for a Texas barbecue" (Akyol 2012: 75).

Islamists from the Refah party led by Necmettin Erbakan and later from the governing Justice and Development Party (AKP) led by Tayyip Erdogan also reacted to the radical cultural westernisation of their country and continued their efforts to rehabilitate Islam in the public and political sphere. However, their struggle also represents a struggle for a share of state contracts for the economic counter-elite in the form of "green capitalists" or "Anatolian tigers". These are small and medium sized family firms forming the major dynamic of the Turkish economy, whose interests in the political sphere are represented and defended by Islamists. The contracts had for a long time been monopolised by the westernised secular power elite along with the army, i.e. by firms affiliated with the secular Republican Party. This "culture clash" also conceals a conflict over the redistribution of the national wealth to the benefit of farmers, the conservative peripheral regions and the poor regions of Anatolia, which is a stronghold of Islamists. This is at the expense of more secular regions and cities, and the westernised social strata (Pirický 2007, Tiosavljevičová 2007, Tunkrová 2007).

IRAN AND "WEST-TOXICATION"

A similarly militant top-down process of westernisation was played out somewhat later in Iran. Reza Shah Pahlaví introduced secular reforms and cultural westernisation immediately after his coronation (1926). He attempted to outwit the clerics and westernise education and the legal system. He also attempted to emancipate women by decree. While after the Iranian Revolution (1979) the morality police patrolled the streets of cities arresting insufficiently veiled women, during the reign of the pro-Western Pahlavi dynasty the army hunted down women deemed to be excessively veiled. However, traditionally dressed or unshaven men were also the target of repression. Shocking manifestations of rapid "west-toxication" of a hitherto mainly traditional society included the spread of the "degraded" culture of Western provenance, such as American films, discotheques, rock music and bars selling alcohol. Interestingly, this culture was being consumed mainly by groups close to the power elite and not by ordinary Iranians. Another cultural shock was caused by the arrival of many privileged Westerners, employees of oil companies, diplomats and soldiers who did not worry too much about their culturally insensitive conduct and ostentatious show of wealth. American soldiers enjoyed complete immunity from the country's legal system. On a cultural level the power elite surrounding the Shah merged too visibly with these "godless" foreigners. The Islamic Revolution can thus be seen as a reaction to the culture shock engendered by excessively rapid westernisation (Juergensmeyer 1994, Kepel 2002, Cvrkal 2007).

THE POST-COLONIAL ARAB WORLD

The idol of the newly emerging Arab post-colonial elites was President Gamal Abd al-Nasser of Egypt. He was born in Egypt under British administration and grew up in Alexandria, i.e. in a more Mediterranean than Arabic urban culture. He spent his formative years in the army, the most westernised segment of society, whence he acquired his fascination with all things Western, from tailor-made suits, American sunglasses and cigars, to British newspapers (Zakaria 2001).

The elites of other secular dictatorships or monarchies also lived in a kind of ivory tower culturally separated from the rest of the population. For instance, the current leaders of Morocco, Syria and Jordan were educated in Europe and enjoy Western hobbies. The Moroccan king loves skiing in the Alps and the Jordanian kings are passionate motorists. Similarly, the gilded youth of Egypt or Saudi Arabia, recruited from the power elite, live like their contemporaries in American or European smart sets.

A critical opposition is thus in a position to highlight the foreign origin of the culture of the elites and its allegedly toxic effects on society. They believe that Western culture leads to arrogance, a loss of social cohesion, mindless consumerism, a loss of faith, disrespect for authority, and decadence, and when presenting their alternative vision they position themselves against the wholesale acceptance of everything Western. On the contrary, they offer a return to indigenous cultural sources and a new synthesis of these sources with selectively and prudently selected Western influences (Etzioni 2004). In this respect, secular intellectual and opposition groups are at a disadvantage in that on the cultural front they are too similar to the compromised power elite (cf. Juergensmeyer 1994).

Though the post-colonial conflict was seen by both regimes and their secular challengers mainly as a conflict between progressive and reactionary forces, as a rivalry between avant-garde modernisers and conservatives stuck in the Middle Ages, with the rise of political Islam the conflict comes to be seen as a struggle between authentic home-grown ideas and toxic foreign ideas, as a conflict between a country's own cultural patrimony and imported Western influences (Burgat 2002). While the first stage of decolonisation was associated with the acquisition of political independence and the creation of a new state, and the second stage linked with economic modernisation via economic reform, these days Islamists are talking of a third stage of decolonisation, by which they mean independence from Europe and the USA in terms of culture, values and ideology as a necessary condition for a definitive break with the legacy of colonialism (Juergensmeyer 1994, 2008).

It should be pointed out that the return to an indigenous culture is a phenomenon that affects most post-colonial and post-communist societies. It is not unique to the Middle East, but the consequence of the ideological exhaustion of anti-systemic movements of the 20th century, i.e. communism, socialism and national liberation. These failed either because they were unable to seize power or because, having seized it, they handled it incompetently and were discredited (cf. Wallerstein 2005). According to the Russian sociologist Aleksandr Panarin (2003), in the Second and Third World we are witnessing a *new revolution in consciousness*. First there was an attempt to completely discard a country's own culture and join the prosperous Western club as soon as possible. However, after a few decades this was shown to be a completely unsuccessful strategy for many reasons. The current response is a return to a country's own culture, traditions and roots. Culture is regarded as a source of dignity and positive identity, but above all as the basis of a people's own version, interpretation and mastery of modernity.

However, what is crucial in the Middle East is that the very different culture of the westernised and often secularised elites overlaps with many other lines of sharp social stratification, especially lines of a power-based, economic, tribal, regional and ethnic character. This overlap and the multiplication of the different identities of both privileged and unprivileged groups makes for potentially intense, even violent political conflict and casts a more favourable light on the arguments used by the opposition (cf. Dahrendorf 1959).

(12) CLIENTELISM AND THE ALIENATION OF THE REGIME FROM THE REST OF THE POPULATION

Clientelism is based on a personal, asymmetric and reciprocal relationship between the patron and his clients. This relationship is one of mutual dependence and convenience. The patron offers his less powerful clients protection, material resources and support in critical situations, while the clients repay their patron in a different form, such as by providing votes in elections. They also boost his prestige by showing him respect in public and by acquiring new clients. The higher the position of the patron in society, the greater the privileges for his client network, and vice versa.

Clientelism does not disappear during the transition to a modern society. It flourishes in many different social situations and survives as an important part of modernising and modern political systems. During modernisation, the model of traditional clientelism proves itself to be highly flexible and adapts to the new conditions of the political structure of modern states. As far as political clientelism is concerned, the Middle East is thus not unique.

Given his position in the power pyramid of modern states, a modern patron has exclusive access to goods and services that are much in demand but scarce. The resources under his control are not for sale. Instead, the patron distributes them to an extensive and loyal clientele in order to reinforce his position. The clients receive them only by virtue of being part of a network that has access to them through the good offices of the patron. Clientelism is thus a multilevel institution comprising politically and economically powerful patrons, ranks of middlemen with many contacts at their disposal, and a large group of clients. This network carries out the informal but effective distribution of goods, allegiances and services on a quid pro quo basis. The status of each person is decided on the basis of how powerful the clientele they are part of is and what position they occupy in it. The situation of those who are not part of any clientele is the most precarious (Keller 1997: 77–81, 161–163).

Clientelism in the Middle East was traditionally based on the unequal relationship between landowners and peasants. The landowner represented the local monopolist, who controlled the land in any given region and was the only party in the community with disposable income. He was thus able to assist the peasants in crises caused by drought, crop failure or sickness. Every year he provided grain and occasionally offered loans. In return, the peasants worked for him or voted for him or supported him in some other way in politics. Poor peasants had no choice but to seek the support of a patron. The post-colonial land reforms damaged the traditional relationship of mutual obligations. After the nationalisation of land, the state became the general patron (Richards and Waterbury 2008: 327).

In post-colonial Middle Eastern states clientelism maintains the internal cohesion of regimes and their individual circles of power and contributes to stability and unity. The distribution of sought after resources trickles down from the centre of power via the client networks to the lower ranking members of the power elite, i.e. to the second and third circles of power and their diversified clients, who are usually recruited from family groups and affiliated sects, tribes or regions, which thus comprise the regime's support. A member of the inner circle of power is thus the patron of clients from the larger second circle. The members of the second circle of power then act analogously as patrons of clients from the third circle of power (Roy 1992, Gombár 2007).

The power of modern Middle Eastern patrons is primarily based on their control of political power and key positions in the state. It derives secondarily from the support and ongoing renewed and reinforced loyalty of the clientele. The lower an individual stands in this hierarchical network, the fewer scarce resources "trickle down" to him. Nevertheless, such an individual is still better off than those who do not belong to a clientele with connections to political power. Hence the vested interest of all those "inside" the system in the operation and consolidation of the client network, and the vested interest of those "outside" the system in its dissolution (collective strategy) or in joining its ranks (individual strategy).

Most Middle Eastern states have been taken over by modern predators recruited from certain regions, ethnic groups or tribes, for instance in Libya, Algeria, Tunisia, Jordan, Saudi Arabia, Yemen and Turkey, or from minority religious groups, as in the case of Lebanon, Syria, Iraq and Bahrain (Roy 1992). In addition to the traditional solidarity based on blood, regional or religious ties, of equal importance to the client network are contacts established during studies in military academies, universities, during childhood in the same street, in the anti-colonial resistance movement, religious seminars or cells of the ruling party. These modern links are maintained and buttressed over the long term by means of marriage, kinship alliances and services rendered (Richards and Waterbury 2008).

The function of a patron in the Middle East is to procure public goods for his clientele, goods that in theory should be available to the same extent to all citizens of the state without exception. This involves, for instance, arranging such matters as the procurement of a passport, entry to a good quality school, a low-interest loan from an agricultural bank, a highly sought, lifelong position in the state sector or army, a trade licence, food aid, or the allocation of state contracts. Middle Eastern pro-regime political parties soon degenerated into an important vehicle for clientelism, which means that their members and supporters are not mobilised en masse for a radical transformation of society, but, on the contrary, rewarded for remaining passive and doing nothing whatsoever (Richards and Waterbury 2008: 328).

The modern state has become a major universal patron. This is visible in its most extreme form in the oil-rich monarchies of the Gulf. In Kuwait, for instance, the population receives free water, electricity and petrol from the state in return for its obedience. As a consequence, this desert monarchy has the highest consumption of water per capita in the world. The average urban family owns several large gas-guzzling cars. In return, the regime expects from its many clienteles that they will not interfere in politics and accept their constitutionally enshrined second-class standing, in which the constitution distinguishes between five categories of people with varying degrees of status. At the top there is the ruling royal family, and on the bottom there are Arabs from other countries and non-Arab foreigners. In the spirit of the royal mechanism of divide-and-rule, old merchant families and traditional nomadic tribes are set in opposition to each other, while the status of both is subservient to the royal family (Hybášková 2004).

However, most Middle Eastern regimes do not enjoy the luxury of being able to provide such generous "bribes" to their own populations, and if the role of universal patron-state deteriorates, a space opens up for Islamists oriented on the provision of social services (Lubeck and Britts 2002, Kepel 1996). This leads to a situation in which, alongside the dominant client network with tentacles reaching the very tip of the power pyramid, there exist parallel client networks that are relatively independent of the power elite. The Islamists or other contra-elites are thus able to create their own client network (cf. Clark 2004).

However, in a rapidly modernising society, the decline of state power also increases the scope for the renaissance of *traditional small groups*. Small groups such as the extended family, clan, or rural community relocating via chain migration to cities do not disappear from the scene. On the contrary, in the 21st century they are assuming a new importance and social function. In an era of economic deregulation and the penetration of market principles into all spheres of life, they protect their members against the unpredictable fluctuations of capitalist markets and the unpredictable repression of volatile regimes. This is a kind of "insurance" based on the mutual obligations, trust and support of equal partners with similar interests. The modern significance of these old groups in new form is down to the weakness of the social agencies of the state, civil sector and political parties. However, it also intensifies this weakness, competes with it, and undermines its attractiveness by offering alternative identities and allegiances (Richards and Waterbury 2008).

Traditional rural tribalism in the modern state and politics is dramatically restructured and intertwined with the economic mafia and political godfathers. During the second half of the 20th century, new client groups took over all states in the Middle East, live off them parasitically, and use them to their own advantage and to the detriment of most of society. Resources are distributed mainly among the clientele and not, for instance, in order to improve education, healthcare or an infrastructure for all. Unlike traditional medieval or early modern clienteles, they have control of a centralised state and repressive apparatus. In addition, they have the support of the West and connections to global markets and the monopolisation of rents ensuing therefrom, which they use to consolidate their power (cf. Tomeš et al. 2007).

The swollen parasitism of a small "decadent" elite accompanied by the modern breakup of society into clans and clienteles is the focus of the attention of opposition Islamists. Their ideal is a *unified* umma of brothers and sisters based on the principle of the oneness of God and His Creation, including society (*tawhíd*). The current fracturing of society they regard as a dangerous and unacceptable internal division (*fitna*). State revenues should be distributed fairly and in accordance with Islamic social sensitivity (see the state redistribution of *zakat*). Islamists also promise to stand on the side of the downtrodden (*mustadafun*) in their conflict with arrogant and unjust rulers (*taghut*) and oppressors from the ranks of the privileged classes (*mustad'afín*). Islamists speak on behalf of the majority and denounce the multiform polarisation of society and inequality of the divided *umma* in the language of Islam (cf. Roy 1992).

(13) MILITARY CLIENTELE: CO-OPTING OF THE ARMY, POLARISATION OF SOCIETY

The role of the army and the armed forces in a power structure is crucial. This is often the consequence of the historical origin of Middle Eastern regimes, which emerged in the wake of military coups (Heydemann 2000, Cook 2007). The ongoing rule of military and semi-military regimes to this extent is unparalleled in any other post-colonial regime, making the Middle East the most militarised region in the world (Sorli, Gleditsch, Strand 2004).

As a consequence, military budgets take up a significantly larger share of the national wealth than is common in the rest of the world. On average, Middle Eastern governments spend 3.75% of gross domestic product (GDP) on their armies. In other regions of the developing world military budgets are substantially more modest: in South Asia the figure is 2.5% of GDP, in Central Asia 2.25%, in East Asia and Sub-Saharan Africa 1.75%, and in South America 1.25%. For the sake of comparison, military spending in the richest countries of the world is 2.5% of GDP.

However, though most countries in the Middle East spend significantly more on the military than the world average (2.7% of GDP), levels of spending vary. Without doubt the record holders have long been Saudi Arabia (11.2% of GDP), Jordan (6.0%), the United Arab Emirates (5.6%) and Syria (4.2%). In absolute terms Turkey and Iran also spend lavishly on the military. Though Egypt (2.2%), Morocco (3.4%) and Algeria (3.8%) are somewhat more frugal by the standards of the region, they nevertheless spend more than is common in the rest of the world. It should also not be forgotten that until recently these figures were even higher. Tunisia spends least of all on its armed forces (1.4%) (World Bank Indicators 2010).

A role is played here by the geopolitically strategic location of the Middle East as the focal point of tensions of global significance, as well as the existence of regional armed conflicts. This is another factor leading to the militarisation of the region (Tomeš 2009, Šlachta et al. 2007). However, Middle Eastern regimes are fearful less of invasion by foreign armies than by foreign ideas (Huntington 1968), and their most elite units are not created, armed and trained in order to defend the nation against an external enemy but against an internal opposition (cf. Klare 2004). This function of armies as the ultimate guarantor of civil peace is accepted even by many intellectuals and opposition politicians. As the Egyptian satirist and writer Ali Salem once replied (1994) when asked whether Islamic fundamentalists would ever achieve power: "No, the Egyptian army would never allow it" (cited in Barak 2011: 407). The oil rent, combined with imports of the most up-to-date military and police technologies, have allowed Middle Eastern regimes to build a sophisticated repressive apparatus that is unprecedented in European history or other regions of the post-colonial world (Zakaria 2004).

The huge funds allocated to the military contribute to the unequal dispensation of resources among segments of the population loyal to the regime and the rest of unprivileged society excluded from the redistribution of resources. The army's control methods then systematically generate social segmentation and polarisation. Three basic mechanisms are responsible for this. As an important client of the power elite, the army receives a substantial share of the rent in the form of generous defence budgets. This form of co-optation is used by very rich, sparsely populated oil states, mainly the Gulf monarchies. The second mechanism is the provision of economic privileges that allow the army to create an extensive empire comprising a fundamental part of the national economy. This form of co-optation is used mainly by republics with fewer natural resources (Egypt, Iran, Sudan, Syria, Algeria). The third mechanism involves recruiting officers and rank-and-file soldiers from specific tribal, regional, religious and ethnic groups that are then loyal to the regime. This method is used by regimes comprising an ethnic, tribal or religious minority controlling a different ethnic, tribal or religious majority (Syria, Bahrain, Jordan).

However, most regimes to some extent or other combine all three approaches, the aim being to ensure the army has a vested interest in the survival of a regime. While this assists co-opt the army into the regime, it also contributes to the visible polarisation of society and the alienation of the elite from the rest of the population. Over the short term, the effort made by regimes to co-opt other groups linked to the army had a stabilising effect by eliminating coups they might organise. However, over the long term it systematically created favourable conditions for the emergence of widespread dissatisfaction with the social exclusion that ensued. Though this strategy managed to co-opt particular groups, this was at the expense of alienating everyone else. There was a reliance on the strategy of co-optation, which had proved its worth in the past, even within the context of a changed situation in which new actors had gradually entered the political arena that nobody had attempted to co-opt.

ORIGINAL SIN: THE EMERGENCE OF REGIMES FOLLOWING MILITARY COUPS

The first army to seize power was that led by Atatürk in Turkey, and this heralded developments in other Middle Eastern countries. The Turkish army was later to organise four coups against democratically elected politicians. Similar developments soon followed in Iran, where Reza Shah, installed and supported by the British, recruited followers from the elite Cossack officer class and sought inspiration from Kemalist reforms in Turkey. The army was the bulwark of the regime during its internal political crisis right up until the revolution (1979) (Richards and Waterbury 2008).

The military also began to play a key political role in the post-colonial Arab world, where army officers achieved power by means of a series of military coups in the 1950s and 60s. Though historically speaking the first was General Bakr Sidqi in Iraq (1936), who overthrew the monarchy installed by the British, the model for other officers in the region as a whole later was the charismatic Gamal Abd al-Nasser, who after assuming power swapped his uniform for a suit, created a cult of personality, ruled in an authoritarian style in the name of the revolutionary liquidation of the old order imposed by foreigners, and based his legitimacy on a pledge to raise Egypt's economic and international standing. This model was to inspire military regimes in Sudan, Syria, Iraq, Yemen, Algeria and Libya (Owen 2011).

Following the example set by Atatürk and Nasser, the army was regarded as the *most advanced stratum*, as the sole force capable of enforcing modernisation reforms, defending the interests of the weak middle classes and preventing revolution or the collapse of social order, a distinct possibility in the wake of the coups in Syria, Egypt and Iraq. The officer class were members of the most educated segments of the population and were often among the few people to have been educated in the West or the USSR. The compatibility of their outlook with modernity was to be seen in their code of ethics, which emphasised promotion based on meritocracy, in which qualifications, effort, performance and diligence played a role, and not simply their readiness to trust in fate and God. It was also to be found in their self-discipline, organisational skills, and in values such as honour, efficiency, order, asceticism and a code of ethics that was offended by corrupt, inefficient governments. In addition, the officers identified with the ideals of progress, reform, nationalism and patriotism. For this reason the ethics of the officer class in post-colonial countries has been compared to the Protestant ethic of early European capitalists. The expectation was that this code of ethics had the potential to transform radically hitherto backward societies.

The army as an institution was regarded in this optimistic spirit as a melting pot, uniting heterogeneous nations comprising various ethnic, racial, linguistic, religious and tribal groups (Huntington 1968, 2005, 2008). However, its progressive potential was quickly exhausted and it became more of an impediment to the political and economic modernisation of Middle Eastern countries (Richards and Waterbury 2008). The armies themselves gradually began abdicating responsibility for the salvation of the nation, a project to which they had claimed allegiance during the 1950s and 60s. Furthermore, regimes increasingly prevented the armies from constructing an ideology based on self-sacrifice for the public weal and on a sense of mission in the name of the nation. And so the armies resorted to looking after their own particular interests (Droz-Vincent 2011). As a result, the social prestige of the army waned, and this reduced the chance of success of possible military coups (Hertog 2011).

In Turkey, the Arab countries and Pakistan the separation of the army and politics represents a similarly serious problem as the separation of politics and religion. Armies represent a kind of state within a state. They tend to protect the power elite against its own population rather than the population against an external threat, or they act as an autonomous political player protecting their own interests above all others. However, the population is insufficiently aware of the importance of strict control of the army by civilian politicians (see the surveys examined in this chapter), and this has long represented an impediment to the democratisation of the region.

THE ARMY AS A CLIENTELE

Military presidents promoting a republican regime gradually converged with monarchies. They now aspired to terms of office lasting a lifetime and, in accordance with the dynastic principle, attempted to pass on the reins of government to their son or other relative. They too now found themselves facing the problem of how to control the army and prevent their own overthrow by military coup orchestrated by a competing clique of captains (Owen 2011).

An extreme method was introduced by Gaddafi in Libya, who deliberately disbanded the regular standing army and during the course of political crisis (2011) relied on foreign mercenaries from the Islamic Legion (Chad, Sudan) that he remunerated from oil rent. The running down of the army was a strategy resorted to by Tunisia and several small Gulf monarchies apprehensive of any threat to their power. For example, the regime in Bahrain counts on the presence of the headquarters of the US Fifth Fleet on its territory, assuming that its strategic alliance with the US will mean it will be defended if faced with a threat. For this reason it has not created an army that corresponds to the genuine scale of potential threats that the country faces (mainly from Iran). Another strategy pursued by several Gulf regimes involves outsourcing units of the regular army to allied countries (Yemen, Pakistan), which on the basis of regular rotation are assigned as part of a relatively small national army (Droz-Vincent 2011).

Regimes often attempt to control the army through intelligence and to rotate cadres rapidly within various positions and entire units on different missions, so that it is impossible to establish a cohesive core that might form an alternative centre of power. A system of frequent and regular promotions is another method employed to ensure the loyalty of officers.

However, the most general mechanism for controlling the army is clientelism. Though military units are separated from day-to-day politics, senior officers gradually become an integral part of the political regime. The ties of kinship connect the families of the dictator, top civil servants, leading businesspeople, politicians, clerics and senior officers. The position of individual officers then depends more on their informal or family relationship with the head of state than on their professional skills and the formal relationship they have with their immediate superiors. A currently very relevant example is the control of most of the leadership positions, elite units and intelligence services enjoyed by the minority Alawites in an otherwise majority Sunni Syrian army mostly made up of conscripts. Assad's Syria arose out of a military coup d'état by the Ba'ath Party (1963), and though the Assad clan is recruited from the Alawite minority, by means of nepotism and cronyism it has gradually taken over control of the army and other security institutions. This seizure of power by the minority Alawites was manifest during the brutal suppression of the uprising by the Sunni population in Hama (1982), during which the entire city was bombarded. Historians to this day argue about whether the military operations were led by the then dictator Hafez Assad or his younger brother Rifaat Assad. Similarly, at present the concentration of political and military power in the hands of the minority Alawites is the cause of the brutal civil war (beginning 2011). The military regime has long been against the majority Sunni Syrian society, which it is forced to co-opt, pacify or intimidate. For this reason it can only hold onto power at the expense of the mass killing of its opponents from mainstream society and with the risk that the entire country will disintegrate. However, the regime controls the means of state violence and is prepared to use it, because everything is in play. Its defeat would represent the death sentence for the minority Alawites (cf. Stacher 2012).The best known example here would be the Egyptian General Abdel Hakim Amir, who was promoted because of his loyalty to the regime and not because of his abilities. The country paid heavily for this in the fiasco of its involvement in the war in Yemen (1962) and above all in its crushing defeat in the war with Israel (1967). In its efforts to control the armed forces, patronage undermines their professionalism and effectiveness.

The patron in the form of dictator looks out for the interests of his client in the form of the army. The army's interest as a corporation involves regular, generous financing from the state budget, expensive "toys" for soldiers in the form of modern weaponry, and privileges in the form of non-interference on the part of the state in how the military spends its budget. The private interest of individual officers involves their occupying key positions in the army or in politics and business. The relationship of the army with the regime is thus similar to that of the co-opted clergy and represents a balance between the interests of the regime, army and, on rare occasions, society at large. In return, the army leadership ensures for its patrons that there is calm in the barracks and loyalty in military units. Its approach to politics is similarly conservative and cautious, and it has no great desire for regime change or the increased influence of opposition groups (Droz-Vincent 2001, Gombár 2001, 2004, 2007).

CO-OPTATION BY MEANS OF RENT AND THE BALANCING OF PARALLEL FORCES

Another common strategy deployed by republics and monarchies is the creation of parallel military forces. This results in *dual armed forces* composed of mutually independent parts that compete with each other for the favour of the regime and, by extension, the distribution of state resources. This system of divide and rule means that the influence of individual units is balanced: the army patrols the army. Syria employed such a system by creating elite units reporting to officers recruited directly from the president's family. Yemen created a similarly extended parallel Praetorian force, trained by the United States and officially designed for use in the fight against terrorism (Droz-Vincent 2011).

However, the system was perfected by the Gulf monarchies, which have sufficient rent at their disposal to enable them to create and finance genuinely thriving parallel structures. This then allows the monarch to resolve conflicts and to satisfy the ambitions of the many members of the royal family as well as those of feuding family factions. By creating more and more new armed forces and new positions within them, the monarch also builds alliances with those occupying these positions. For example, the parallel system of security forces in Saudi Arabia was created in 1962/63, when the conflict over succession between King Saud and Crown Prince Faisal reached its peak. Faisal rewarded his individual allies by appointing them Minister of the Interior and Minister of Defence and the National Guard. He gave them a relatively free hand in management of the ministries, so that gradually a state within a state was created with its own parallel, mutually competing armed forces, institutions and the infrastructure securing units and their families (housing, education, healthcare). Clientelism is also based on nepotism. Ministers and senior commanders remain unchanged and employ their sons and brothers, who then employ their own relatives. The result is that hundreds of princes from the extended royal family and other groups connected with the regime have built a career for themselves in the security services. In addition, the units recruit rank-and-file soldiers from allied tribes and regions of the Central and Western part of the Arabian Peninsula. These days the Ministry of the Interior alone employs 750,000 people, of which 60,000 are in "military positions". The elite National Guard recruits soldiers from the loyal tribes allied with the Saudi royal dynasty. However, the rest of the population is excluded, and people outside the kinship network have no chance of working their way up into the command structures.

As a result the regimes are less vulnerable to coups, the last serious attempts at which in the Gulf were in the 1970s. However, the system is extremely costly and accounts for the largest part of the state budget (25%). This applies even during times of economic recession, when the military budget is not cut at all. Cuts in spending would put at threat the loyalty of individual security forces during times of potential crisis by creating conflicts over resources and privileges. The system also leads to the unrestrained, disorganised creation of overlapping state institutions, thrown together on an ad hoc basis whenever the regime is in crisis and someone must be co-opted. It becomes impossible to coordinate individual units and there is no integrated defence planning. As a consequence the armed forces are ineffective when it comes to providing security because their main function now is to provide jobs to clients linked to the regime (Herb 1999, Hertog 2010, 2011).

A THREAT TO THE UNITY OF THE REGIME: THE RIVALRY BETWEEN THE ARMY AND INTERNAL SECURITY FORCES

The creation of parallel structures leads potentially to rivalry between the army and the internal security services. Security forces are rife in the Middle East. They expanded during the post-colonial period and led to the creation of a police state. They place a high demand on the state budget, for which they compete with the army. However, the powers of the army and police forces are not clearly defined, and this intensifies the conflict between them. There is a confusing overlap between their spheres of legal competence. Constitutionally armies are supposed to ensure not only external but also internal security.

Conversely, the police and the interior forces are often so militarised that at first sight they could be mistaken for the army and often supplement the army's work in regions afflicted by civil war (Turkey, Algeria) or in the war against terrorism (Morocco, Yemen). The legal duty of many other paramilitary forces armed with heavy weapons is to protect the regime against a mass uprising. Such militia, linked to the ruling Ba´ath party and reminiscent of the communist militia of the Eastern bloc, were created by both Syria and Iraq, while Colonel Gaddafi of Libya and the Saudi royal family created revolutionary guards or National Guards, independent of the army, for their personal protection (Sayigh 2011).

Because of its structural conflicts with the internal security forces, whatever the patronage it enjoys the army is not always completely loyal to the regime. The internal unity of seemingly homogenous regimes has its limits (Gause III 2011), especially if a regime finds itself in a fiscal crisis accompanied by political crisis and begins to support a burgeoning police force and militarised interior services at the expense of the army, as happened in Egypt prior to the January 25 Revolution in 2011 (Soliman 2011).

In Egypt, for instance, an ever expanding Ministry of the Interior employs 1.4 million policemen, border guards and informers (2011). In Turkey this figure is 120,000, and in Yemen 150,000 people worked simply for the Political Security Organisation, reporting directly to President Saleh. The secret services expanded similarly. Fears of coups saw the creation of competing intelligence agencies subordinate to individual military units (the air force and ground forces), the governing party, and the president or monarch. The primary aim of these agencies is to monitor each other and hold the population in check, not to detect threats from abroad. Another trend involves the *militarisation* of the police and security services. Historically the police originated from colonial armies or from rebel armies that had won independence. The police therefore have a military character, i.e. similar training, weapons, ranks, internal organisation and a militaristic culture emphasising masculine values with a tendency to use violence against the population on a routine basis. The global war on terror has assisted the latest wave of militarisation of the internal security forces (Sayigh 2011).

CO-OPTATION ACROSS THE PRIVILEGED MILITARY-INDUSTRIAL COMPLEX

Sometimes a regime cannot or does not want to rely on co-opting the army by means of a system of patronage based on the redistribution of rent to the benefit of the armed forces. In this case it must ensure the loyalty of the armed forces by allowing officers to create an extensive economic empire that often becomes an important part of the national economy. The interest of the officer corps is then diverted away from political and security questions in the direction of business and private profit. In this way a regime is also able to ensure that the army has a stake in its survival and win it over to its side.

However, matters vary considerably in this respect in individual Middle Eastern regimes. The closest relationship between the army and the economy is to be found in Egypt and Iran and is manifest in both the public and private sector. In the public sector it involves an official and institutionalised economic empire of the army qua corporation, supervised in Egypt by the Ministry of Defence and the Ministry of Military Production. The army is involved in a wide range of activities, from industry and agriculture, to construction work, telecommunications and services. There are also activities that are relatively remote from the military, for instance the operation of tourist resorts. In addition, a parallel private economy has arisen run by retired officers. These use their connections to colleagues still serving in the army, or to politicians, mayors, governors and civil servants. In addition, they also enjoy considerable social capital since a lifetime's service in the army has bound them together, and on the basis of these firm informal relationships they create strong joint enterprises. All of this allows them to privatise state companies under advantageous conditions or to acquire state contracts (both civil and military) for their companies. However, both spheres of military business are based on the privileges guaranteed by the regime. The media, non-governmental organisations and the civilian section of executive power have no oversight over military business, and the legislation regulating the rest of the economy does not apply to it. If the state is not capable of providing generous subsidies to the army and paying its officers handsomely from the state budget, it ensures the loyalty of the armed forces by giving them a free hand to do what they want and earn as they will (Springborg 2011).

The army is involved in a similar way though not to the same extent in the public and emerging private sector in Sudan and Syria (and in Iraq up until 2003). Given the less developed economy and smaller domestic market and export potential, the military sector here is restricted more to activities it is directly involved in, namely weapons, munitions, construction, agriculture and foodstuff (Springborg 2011).

Turkey is located in the centre of this imaginary scale. The military-industrial complex is huge, advanced and highly diversified. However, it is clearly and institutionally distinct from the army. Companies are owned and managed by the military pension fund. For this reason, neither serving army officers nor civil servants from the Ministry of Defence sit on its supervisory boards, which are occupied by civilians. In addition, the salaries of officers on active duty are so generous and their professional honour so strong that they do not feel the urge to supplement their pay and retirement provision by means of business. Furthermore, the army orders most goods and services from firms owned by civilians, and not from army-owned, public-sector companies or officer-owned, private-sector companies, as is the case, for instance, in Egypt (Richards and Waterbury 2008).

The army is not much involved in the economies of Morocco, Jordan and Oman. The patronage of the king is discreet and restricted to individual officers and not the officer corps as a whole. The king ensures the loyalty of favoured officers in the future or rewards them for services in the past by means of shares in privatised companies, appointment to supervisory boards, or by allocating them positions on commissions managing state assets. The army is least involved in the economy in the rich monarchies of the Gulf and also in Tunisia. In general, the level of civilian control of the army and the level of military professionalism is highest in those countries where the army is least involved in the economy (Springborg 2011).

THE CO-OPTATION OF PARTICULAR GROUPS AND THE SEGMENTATION OF SOCIETY

If in societies divided by ethnicity, religion, region or tribe the ruling regime is recruited from a minority, this minority is also over-represented in the army. The army is then loyal to the regime thanks to shared ethnic, religious and tribal identity, as well as its interest in the stability and survival of the regime. If the majority were to seize power in the country, it would replace the army command and place its own members in charge (Gause III). Finally, recruiting officers and rank-and-file soldiers from a specific group leads to the social inclusion of this group and the exclusion of the rest of the population. Positions in the army can protect selected segments of the population against the most serious impacts of economic liberalisation or privatisation, while the remaining segments of the population face a drop in living standards (Sayigh 2011).

For instance, Bedouin tribes dominate the Jordanian army and loyally protect the royal family against the majority of the population comprising former Palestinian refugees, who have already once risen up against the monarch in a brief civil war (1970). In the Iraq of Saddam Hussein the leadership of the Ba'ath party and the army was recruited mainly from Sunni Arabs at the expense of the Kurds and Shiite Arabs. Conversely, religion plays a role especially in Bahrain, where Sunnis linked to the Sunni monarchy are disproportionately represented in the upper echelons of the army, which controls the majority Shiite population. This is true of Syria too, where the minority Alawites are favoured in the army and dominate its command, while the majority of the population is Sunni. Finally, regional and tribal membership plays a role in the composition of the military command in Yemen, which is deeply penetrated by tribal relations, while the majority of officers are drawn from the north of the country. A similar situation pertained in Libya under Colonel Gaddafi and in Saudi Arabia, where the elite National Guard is made up of privileged tribes from central and western Arabia, birthplace of the royal dynasty, while the army command is completely in the hands of members of the royal family (cf. Droz-Vincent 2011).

(14) TERRORISM AS THE CONTINUATION OF POLITICS BY OTHER MEANS

Another consequence of the long-term repression that began with colonialism and continues with the post-colonial rule of authoritarian governments is the blocking of the development of a *political culture* based on debate, tolerance, compromise, participation, civic responsibility and involvement. An authoritarian political culture and a tendency to political violence on the part of all concerned, both government and opposition, is therefore not a consequence of the nature of Islam but rather of modern politics (Esposito 2003).

Tab. 5 The history of colonial repression in the Middle East

Country	Period of colonial occupation	Duration of occupation (in years)	Colonial government
Algeria	1830–1962	132	France
Egypt*	1798–1801, 1882–1936	3+54	France/Great Britain
Iraq	1920–1932	12	Great Britain
Jordan	1922–1946	24	Great Britain
Kuwait	1899–1961	62	Great Britain
Lebanon	1920–1946	26	France
Libya	1912–1951	40	Italy/UN mandate
Morocco	1911–1956	45	France/Spain
Sudan	1898–1956	58	Great Britain
Syria	1920–1946	26	France
Tunisia	1881–1956	75	France
United Arab Emirates	1892/1916–1971	55/79	Great Britain
Yemen (North)	1839–1967	128	Great Britain

Source: Burgat 2002: 188
* Under the supervision of the Ottoman Empire (1882–1914), British protectorate (1914–1922). Only formal independence from 1922. The British army controlled the Suez Canal in 1936–1956.

The way the political system is set up means the opposition is condemned to illegality, secrecy and conspiracy. It does not enjoy basic political rights such as freedom of assembly, association, speech or thought. It then often resorts to direct action and violence as the only possible method of political participation, resolving social problems, enforcing its interests, and forcing social change. Terrorism then becomes a continuation of politics by other means. It becomes an extreme way of practicing politics under extreme conditions in which non-violent channels of political participation are closed.

Furthermore, when they find themselves facing political crisis, authoritarian regimes respond by increasing level of repression. For instance, in Egypt and Algeria during the global wave of democratisation during the 1990s, repression was cranked up against the most powerful opposition movements. These included largely moderate mainstream Islamists. Repression then drives opposition activists into the minority camp of militants. The polarisation between opposition and regime increases and it becomes increasingly difficult to maintain a moderate or neutral stance. A spiral of violence ensues. For instance, the frequency of suspicious deaths during interrogations at police stations in Egypt is in direct relation to the frequency of subsequent retaliatory terrorist attacks against the police. Recruitment into the ranks of radicals then rises. The subsequent wave of chaos and terrorist attacks against the government is used to justify the past and present repression of political challengers. And in the eyes of a terrified population this legitimises the regime, because only the regime promises stability and security.

The result is a *self-fulfilling prophecy*. Concerns regarding the onset of violent fundamentalism justify the repression practiced by regimes. This repression then strengthens the perception of violence as the sole effective instrument of politics among the ranks of opposition Islamists. The numerous militant acts committed by the opposition then retrospectively confirm the correctness of the original predictions made by regimes regarding the irredeemable violence and fanaticism of Islamists and the need to combat it (Barša 2001, Burgat 2002). As Robert Dahl puts it: "An opposition that would be non-violent if it were tolerated becomes violent because it is not tolerated" (cited in Anderson 1997: 17). The violence subsequently perpetrated by militants then discredits mainstream Islamists (Kepel 2004) and helps legitimise regimes, which avail themselves of the American "war on terror" to suppress moderate Islamist opposition (Ottaway 2010, Albrecht and Schlumberger 2004).

The relationship between authoritarianism and political violence in the form of a higher incidence of terrorist attacks is borne out by many statistical analyses of terrorism (Krueger and Laitin 2003, Krueger and Maleckova 2002, Abadie 2004, Krueger 2007, Piazza 2008). Comparative case studies lead to similar conclusions: non-violent political Islam is firmly established in less repressive regimes, while militant Islam is strong in repressive regimes. A contrast is often made between the tendency of political Islam to non-violence in Malaysia, Turkey and post-communist Bosnia and the greater tendency to violence in the authoritarian regimes of the Arab world. A similar methodological strategy used by case studies is to compare the development of opposition Islam in relation to the varying degree of state repression, e.g. the development of the attitudes of individual generations of the Muslim Brotherhood to violence in relation to the degree of political freedoms under individual Egyptian presidents (Arjomand 1995, Dekmejian 1995, Kepel 2002, Zahid 2010, Pargeter 2013).

As we saw at the beginning of this chapter, Charles Tilly offers a powerful theoretical tool for the analysis of political violence. Political regimes characterised by varying degrees of democracy and the capacity to govern determine the predominant repertoires of contention within their boundaries. Arab regimes are among the least democratic with only a medium capacity to govern, and it is precisely this type of regime that generates a higher incidence of terrorism aimed against the power elite (Tilly 2006a, 2006b). In other words, Arab regimes face the opposition they deserve, since the political methods employed by the opposition are defined far more by the political methods of those in power than they are by religion, culture or ideology. The state terror of repressive regimes and the terrorism of militant Islamist factions split off from the mainstream of opposition Islamists feed off and strengthen each other in a perverse symbiosis. One without the other could never achieve such an influence on society (Burgat 2002: 78).

ECONOMIC MODERNISATION: VOLATILE AND DISTORTED

"Bread, work and dignity!"
(Arab revolutionary motto, 2011)

"We want and need work. We need to respect ourselves,
devote our lives to work, create something."
(Amr Khaled, a popular Egyptian preacher)

"At the start of the revolution I swore that if we were successful,
I would do everything to rebuild this country as it deserves. I begin today."
(Egyptian revolutionary tweet, 11 February 2011)

"My granddad travelled by camel, my father by car,
I fly by jet, and my son will once again travel by camel."
(Saudi Arabian)[6]

OIL RENT AND DISTORTED ECONOMIC DEVELOPMENT: THE DUTCH DISEASE

The economy of a Middle Eastern rentier state resembles a parasite. In this respect the region differs significantly from other macro-regions, including post-colonial and post-communist. It also differs significantly from economic developments in the history of modern Europe.

Middle Eastern economies are to a considerable extent dependent on non-productive economic activities such as the export of natural resources (oil, natural gas and phosphates) or the annuities collected for the transit of these materials (as in the case of Egypt thanks to its control of the Suez Canal, Syria, and Jordan thanks to its location on the route of oil and gas pipelines). Similarly, the massive foreign aid from superpowers can also be regarded as a rent (e.g. the financial transfers from the USA to Israel, Egypt, Jordan, Iraq and Pakistan). It is typical of a rentier state that a substantial proportion of its

---

6   Cited in Amr Khaled 2011: 69, Idle and Nunns 2011: 217, Cílek and Kasík 2007.

income comes from abroad. These financial flows are under the direct control of the government and are derived from extremely unproductive activities requiring a minimum workforce (Luciani 1990, Ross 2001).

At first sight a surplus of oil might seem like an economic blessing, a firm starting point for sound, rapid economic growth. The economic rent is given by the difference between the low cost of extracting oil and its relatively high price on global markets. This difference is the biggest in the case of Arab countries, where the geological and geographical conditions are by far the most favourable, making the extraction of oil highly efficient economically (cf. Cílek and Kasík 2007).

In reality, however, it is a curse that chronically distorts the development of the economy and obstructs its diversification over the long term. Countries that are heavily dependent on oil exports (the Persian Gulf, Nigeria and Russia) are vulnerable to price fluctuations on the world markets for "black gold". They can be destabilised not only by a dramatic drop but also a rapid increase in oil prices. These fluctuations prevent the formulation creation of a long-term economic strategy on the part of the state and create an environment that is unpredictable over the long term. This then *deters investors* looking more for security and stability. It is common for rentier states to create sovereign investment funds (Kuwait, Saudi Arabia), though their investments are mostly directed abroad.

For the most part, however, the price of oil on global markets is stable, and this leads to stagnation caused by the *postponement of economic reforms.* If prices remain relatively high over the long term, politicians are reluctant to enact often unpopular reforms and take risky decisions. Attempts to diversify the economy so as to ensure it is not dependent on oil exports are put on the backburner and said dependency merely intensifies. Then, when prices collapse, there is no time for systematic, well prepared and thought-through reforms. For instance, the painful cuts in subsidies for basic foodstuffs and energy and the drastic deregulation of the labour market in Egypt during the 1980s was a reaction to a drop in the price of oil.

A surplus of mineral resources also leads governments to underrate the importance of investing in *human capital.* The feeling is that an educated, qualified workforce that would be competitive in the world is not necessary for prosperity. Neither the quality nor quantity of the workforce is deemed important. If we want to increase the national wealth, the argument goes, we simply drill another hole in the ground and the oil wealth will flow out of its own accord. Similarly, states deceive themselves into believing they do not have to *invest in the development of thriving, effective agriculture and industry.* They have no need of these sectors as sources of tax revenue and, by extension, power. They do not even need a taxable population. Rent replaces tax, while food and goods can be imported and paid for by petrodollars. From having been the cradle of agriculture, the Middle East has been transformed into the least food self-sufficient region in the world and the most dependent on imports. The population then sees that the pursuit of higher education and qualifications makes no sense, since there are no economic sectors and positions in which they might avail themselves of a good quality education (Richards and Waterbury 2008: 10–43).

In addition to the tendency to create mushrooming, cumbersome *state apparatuses* financed from rent, oil-rich countries often suffer what is known as *Dutch disease*. The massive influx of oil wealth undermines the long-term development and diversification of the economy. Governments begin to spend their oil revenues "generously", increasing wages without any rise in labour productivity. At the same time they invest primarily in infrastructure, construction projects and the state apparatus. In addition, exporting oil abroad sees the exchange rate of the domestic currency rise. Both processes – wage increases accompanied by lower productivity and a stronger domestic currency – result in the industrial and agricultural sectors being unable to assert themselves on global markets, hampered as they are by rising labour costs and the strong currency, which push up the price of exports in comparison with the competition. On the other hand, a strong currency and the purchasing power of the population make for cheap imports of goods and foodstuffs. Domestic industry and agriculture is then squeezed out of its own national market, having already failed on foreign markets. Under these circumstances industry and agriculture atrophy. The workforce and investors desert them and technological innovation is limited. Finally, fluctuations in world oil prices destabilise the exchange rates of rentier states. When oil prices rise, the currency strengthens. When they fall, the currency weakens. This makes investing in domestic industry and agriculture risky. The long-term unpredictability of exchange rates leads to unpredictable price competitiveness on global markets. This escalates the effect of the Dutch disease and undermines the overall competitiveness of a given country (cf. The Economist 1977, Richards and Waterbury 2008).

The Dutch disease explains the uneven development of three economic sectors: the internationally non-tradable production sector (services, construction) that is not exposed to foreign competition, the internationally tradable production sector (industry and agriculture) that is exposed to competition, and the extractive sector. The boom in the extraction of mineral resources creates a demand for labour, and the offer of higher wages redirects the workforce from industry and agriculture into extraction. The government's demand and spending also rise. Wages then rise in the non-tradable sector not exposed to direct international competition, and this drains more of the workforce from industry and agriculture, where labour costs are more flexible and cannot grow as fast because they are exposed to international competition. This change to the relative price of production leads to the re-location of capital, investment and workforce from agriculture and industry to services, construction and the public administration. The result is often de-industrialisation or the inability of a viable industrial sector to establish itself, something that applies to many Middle Eastern countries. Historical examples would include the huge influx of Latin American gold to Spain in the 16th century and the Australian gold rush of the 19th century. In the 20th century talk is mainly of the Netherlands and Great Britain, and these days of Russia, Azerbaijan, the Middle East, Indonesia and Africa (cf. Buiter and Purvis 1983).

INTERNATIONAL COMPARISON: THE MIDDLE EAST AND OTHER MACROREGIONS

An international comparison reveals the economic development of the Middle East to be extremely uneven over time. Throughout the 1960s and 70s the region reported by far the fastest year-on-year increase in gross domestic product (GDP) in the world: 7.3% and 7.9% respectively compared to the global average of 5.3% and 5.2%. However, during the 1980s there was a dramatic slowdown and rates of growth dropped below the global average: 2.4% compared to a global average of 3.0%. Over the next two decades the pace of economic growth then corresponded to the other regions of the developing world (cf. fig. 14).

It is no mere coincidence, then, that from the end of the 1970s Middle Eastern regimes faced serious political destabilisation. Mention should be made here of the Iranian Revolution (1979), the seizure of the Grand Mosque in Mecca (1979), and the assassination of the Egyptian president (1981). However, instability was also experienced throughout the 1980s by Algeria, Egypt, Turkey and Lebanon. It was during the period of the sudden slowdown in economic growth that political Islam arrived on the scene, though initially regimes were more fearful of opposition Marxist groups.

The rapid growth in wealth during the 1960s and 70s provoked exaggerated optimism among populations and an even faster increase in career and consumer aspirations. Against a backdrop of rapid economic growth, aspirations tend to outstrip increasing real living standards and the genuine development of the economy. The political potential of the resulting frustration also increases, especially when rapid growth is followed by stagnation or even reversal. At this point the economy describes the trajectory of an inverted "J" curve (growth followed by decline) and as progress is frustrated revolutions take place (cf. Davies 1962, Gurr 1970). This mechanism is applied with gusto to historical revolutions such as the French (1789), Russian (1917)

Fig. 14 Increase in gross domestic product in world macroregions 1960–2015 (in %)

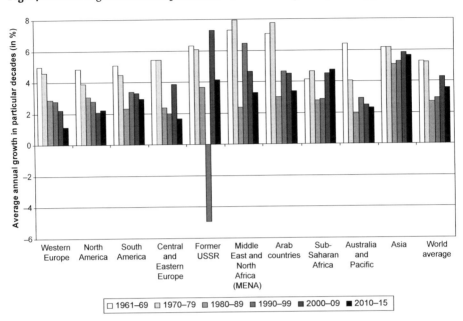

N.B.: The author's calculation of the average rate of growth of GDP for individual countries and decades. The resulting calculation of the average rate of growth for macroregions does not reflect the economic strength of individual states (unweighted averages of states). Central and Eastern Europe and the former USSR were excluded from the analysis of the 1960s and 70s (the statistics do not contain comprehensive data).
Source: World Bank Development Indicators 2016

Fig. 15 Ratio of rent from natural resources to total GDP in macroregions 2013

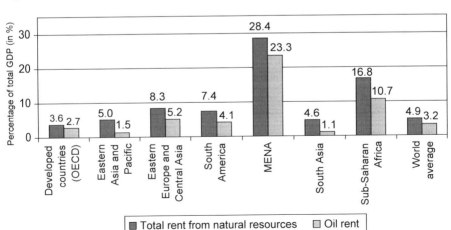

Source: World Bank Indicators 2015

and Egyptian (1952), or the last wave of global democratisation spurred by the oil-price shock (1973) that brought to an end the post-war meteoric growth of the world economy (*les Trente Glorieuses*) and created recession (Huntington 2008). The Iranian Revolution of 1979 and the destabilisation of the monarchies of the Gulf headed by Saudi Arabia can be explained using the same mechanism (Kepel 2002, Klare 2005).

Also highly problematic over the long term is the *structure* of economic growth, which is characterised by an extraordinary dependence on the extraction and export of oil (see fig. 15), as well as a dependence on tourism, transit fees for oil, natural gas and marine transport (Suez), the remittances sent home from abroad by economic migrants, and the financial aid provided by the United States (Egypt, Jordan). This makes Middle Eastern economies susceptible to external shocks, particularly to fluctuations in oil prices on

Fig. 16 The increase in per capita GDP in macroregions 1960–2015 (in %)

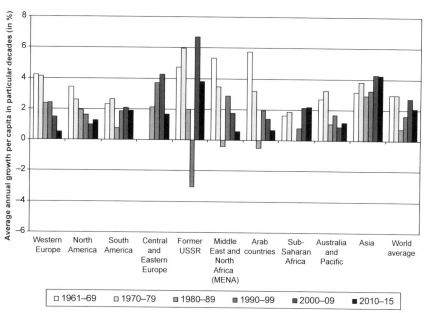

N.B.: The author's calculation of average rates of per capita GDP for individual countries and decades. The resulting calculation of the average growth rate of macroregions does not reflect population size or the economic significance of individual states (unweighted averages of states)[7].

Source: World Bank Development Indicators 2016

---

7   The number of countries differs in the decades and macro-regions under discussion (either because of a lack of data or the emergence of new states): N(1960s) = 105, N(1970s) = 120, N(1980s) = 146, N(1990s) = 172, N(2000s) = 175. The region of Central and Eastern European and the former USSR was excluded from the analyses for lack of data covering the 1960s and 70s.

world markets or the outbreak of armed conflict within the wider region. The most recent threat to the Middle Eastern economic model is the development of the extraction of unconventional sources of oil and gas from shale sands outside the region (Luciani 2009, Richards and Waterbury 2008, AHDR 2002, Bradshaw 2000).

Similarly problematic is the rate of economic development, which often cannot keep pace with demographic change (an increase in overall population size and the ratio of young people), social change (urbanisation and the expansion of the educated classes), and cultural change (a shift in values towards greater consumer and career demands in the case of educated men and women) (Lerner 1964, Roy 1992, Hoffman 1995, Hasso 2010).

The structurally uneven modernisation of the region is also clear from the long-term development of per capita GDP. From the end of the 1970s developments in the economic subsystem were unable to keep pace with the rate of population growth. As a consequence there was a drop in the absolute value of per capita GDP (see fig. 16), i.e. part of the population became poorer and their real living standards fell. Attempts were made to enact unpopular economic reforms, and the period witnessed increased political destabilisation. Bread riots and mass protests against cuts to food subsidies took place in Egypt, Turkey and Algeria. Similar protests were held against neoliberal reforms prescribed in tandem by unpopular authoritarian regimes and even less popular representatives of the International Monetary Fund. An opposition political Islam also began flexing its muscles more strongly (Kropáček 1999, Lubeck, Britts 2002).

Some sources hint at an even more dismal development of per capita GDP during the period 1970–2008, this within the narrower category of Arab countries (UN Human Development Report 2010, see tab. 6). However, according

Tab. 6 Per capita GDP and its increase in macroregions 1970–2008

Region	Per capita GDP in 2008 (in USD, current currency exchange rate)	Average annual increase in per capita GDP 1970–2008 (in %)
OECD	40,976	2.4
Arab states	4,774	−1.1
East Asia and Pacific	3,032	1.7
Eastern Europe and Central Asia	8,361	0.1
Latin America	7,567	2.0
South Asia	954	3.8
Sub-Saharan Africa	1,233	2.7

Source: UN Development Report 2010

to other sources between 1975 and 2000 Arab states fared slightly better than other developing regions and the overall development of per capita GDP was positive (UN Human Development Report 2005).

REGIONAL COMPARISON OF MIDDLE EASTERN COUNTRIES: A TWO-SPEED REGION

If we look in more detail at individual Middle Eastern states (see tab. 7) we see that the basic regional dynamic of economic growth applies to a certain extent to most of them. Despite this, after the start of the oil boom the region

Tab. 7 Average annual increase in GDP in MENA countries 1960–2015 (in %)

Country	1960–69	1970–79	1980–89	1990–99	2000–09	2010–15
Algeria	4.1	7.2	2.8	1.6	3.6	3.40
Bahrain	---	---	1.4	5.5	6.3	3.80
Egypt	5.4	6.2	5.9	4.3	4.9	2.90
Iran	11.6	6.2	–0.3	4.6	5.1	1.20
Iraq	6.1	12.1	–6.8	0.0	0.7	5.70
Israel	9.1	5.8	3.7	5.5	3.5	3.60
Jordan	---	15.2	4.0	4.9	6.4	2.60
Kuwait	5.7	2.3	–0.8	7.5	7.0	2.20
Lebanon	---	---	---	9.7	4.6	2.70
Libya	24.4	2.2	–7.0	---	4.3	–0.05
Morocco	5.0	5.3	3.9	2.8	4.8	3.90
Oman	22.8	6.8	9.8	4.1	4.8	3.50
Palestine	---	---	---	5.1	3.9	5.30
Qatar	---	---	---	---	8.8	8.40
Saudi Arabia	6.0	14.2	–0.6	3.1	3.4	5.00
Sudan	1.2	4.3	3.4	4.4	7.1	1.50
Syria	6.8	8.8	2.8	5.7	4.2	---
Tunisia	4.8	7.2	3.6	5.1	4.7	1.70
Turkey	5.7	4.7	4.1	4.0	3.8	5.20
United Arab Emirates	---	12.6	1.2	5.6	5.8	4.30
Yemen	---	---	---	5.1	3.9	–1.30

N.B.: The author's calculation of the arithmetic averages of the annual rate of growth for individual countries and decades.
Source: World Bank Development Indicators 2010 and 2016.

(cf. Fawcett 2009) represents a relatively heterogeneous "two-speed" region in economic terms. Most of the smaller, less populated Gulf States, abounding in oil reserves, fare better over the long term on the macroeconomic level: Bahrain, Kuwait and Qatar. On the other hand, densely populated countries without significant oil reserves are usually worse off: Egypt, Sudan and Morocco. The Middle East, therefore, is not an economic monolith, though it is possible to trace a common tendency given by the extraction of oil and the intra-regional labour migration and remittances related to it.

Many individual states also share a problem common to the entire region, namely that economic growth is not keeping pace with demographic growth: this is indicated by per capita GDP (see tab. 8). This is so especially in the

Tab. 8 Average annual growth of per capita GDP in MENA countries 1960–2015 (in %)

Country	1960–69	1970–79	1980–89	1990–99	2000–09	2010–15
Algeria	1.7	3.9	−0.3	−0.4	2.1	1.50
Bahrain	---	---	−2.1	2.5	4.0	1.40
Egypt	2.8	3.9	3.2	2.3	2.9	0.80
Iran	8.5	2.9	−3.7	2.9	3.6	−0.04
Iraq	---	---	---	---	−1.8	2.40
Israel	5.4	2.9	1.8	2.4	1.5	1.70
Jordan	---	11.0	0.1	0.6	3.9	−0.60
Kuwait	−4.8	−3.9	−5.2	−2.6	3.9	−2.80
Lebanon	---	---	---	7.1	3.3	−2.80
Libya	---	---	---	---	2.2	−0.20
Morocco	2.1	2.8	1.4	1.2	3.5	2.50
Oman	19.5	2.2	4.9	1.2	3.4	−4.50
Palestine	---	---	---	4.2	−5.3	2.20
Qatar	---	---	---	---	0.4	2.30
Saudi Arabia	2.1	8.8	−5.9	0.5	1.0	2.60
Sudan	−1.3	1.1	0.5	1.8	4.8	3.40
Syria	3.5	5.2	−0.8	2.9	1.5	---
Tunisia	3.3	4.9	1.0	3.3	3.6	0.70
Turkey	3.1	2.2	2.0	2.2	2.4	3.50
United Arab Emirates	---	−2.8	−5.2	−0.1	1.6	1.40
Yemen	---	---	---	1.4	1.0	−3.90

N.B.: The author's calculation of the arithmetic averages of the annual rate of growth for individual countries and decades. GDP based on constant local currency.
Source: World Bank Development Indicators 2010 and 2016

case of Yemen, Saudi Arabia, Qatar, Palestine and Iraq, where per capita GDP is rising most slowly and has dropped in certain decades, resulting in the absolute impoverishment of the population.

However, over the last few decades, even when economic growth has kept pace with demographic developments, we cannot speak of a rapid improvement in living standards in line with the optimism engendered by modernisation during the 1950s and 60s. For several decades the rate of economic growth in most countries has lagged far behind what would be necessary if the standard of living of the majority of the expanding populations were to approach the standard common in Western Europe or the United States, a frequent populist promise made by post-colonial secular leaders.

RAPID ECONOMIC DEVELOPMENT AS A POSSIBLE FACTOR IN POLITICAL DESTABILISATION

Mancur Olson (1963) came up with a counter-intuitive claim that rapid economic growth did not lead to political stability but instability, and sometimes even to revolution. Both individuals and entire societies are traumatised by rapid changes in the economic sphere. The vacuum that arises after traditional social structures and norms have crumbled can be filled by revolutionary movements that offer a recently uprooted people a new identity and sense of belonging.

Olson derived his hypothesis from early modern European history and recently independent post-colonial countries. For example, the English Revolution and Civil War followed a period of development. Further political instability in Britain coincided with the height of the Industrial Revolution (1750–1850). Both before and after Britain had been more politically stable. Olson follows Tocqueville (2010) in his interpretation of the French Revolution, which broke out at a time when France was experiencing dramatic economic developments. In Russia the frequency of strikes, rioting and revolution correlates with the accelerating pace of economic developments at the turn of the 19th and 20th centuries. Non-European post-colonial countries later followed the same pattern. Prior to its revolution, Cuba was the fastest growing economy in the developing world. The same was true of Argentina before Peron. Conversely, the most stable countries in Latin America were those lagging behind the rest (Paraguay, Peru, and Ecuador). In the Middle East after World War II, Egypt, the most developed country, was the least stable, while Saudi Arabia, where oil was not yet being extracted and which lagged behind the rest, was the most stable (Olson 1963: 545–550).

By means of what mechanisms does rapid economic development destabilise political systems? The most general is the *slackening of the bonds between individuals and the social groups* within which they had been most stably embedded: the extended family, established neighbourhoods, the traditional community or village, tribe, religious congregation or guild. This involves individuals (*déclassé*) who have lost their ties with existing social groups because these are disintegrating rapidly. Or it involves very socially mobile individuals (horizontally and vertically), whose position in the social order is changing quickly and who lose their clearly defined place in what had previously been a firmly established social order. They do not identify with the former primary groups but have not yet found new groups into which to integrate themselves. They drop out of the social order and suffer feelings of alienation and deracination, and are therefore more receptive to being approached, mobilised and organised politically.

Rapid economic development promotes *geographic mobility*. Certain urban and rural regions experience dramatic economic decline, others dramatic expansion. The geographical differentiation of income levels and life opportunities changes quickly and constantly and leads to the permanent search for new chances and repeated migration. The exodus from declining regions disrupts local communities and severs the links between members of extended families. Rapidly growing regions with high fluctuation and anonymous human relationships are incapable of creating a new, sufficiently stable social structure. *Urbanisation* operates in a similar way. Industrialisation creates new opportunities in rapidly expanding cities. People move from rural to urban areas in search of work. However, they are contracted to work in factories on an individual basis. Again they leave their extended family, tribe or village community. Their ties to these communities are weakened or destroyed completely. However, in an anonymous and rapidly expanding city they feel alone and alienated. They seek a new orientation and social role, something political movements can offer. In cities with spatially concentrated populations political agitation is cheaper and the spread of ideologies faster. It is technically easier to organise revolt. The stabilising traditional communities people leave behind in order to find work in a factory are also being eroded. Olson claims that sometimes these people feel nostalgic for a poorer but socially more secure and safer life in the country.

Those who *most benefit* from rapid economic growth also have a destabilising effect. The new distribution of wealth comes into conflict with the old distribution of political power and social prestige. The economic, social and political systems are in fact interrelated components of a single society. If one part changes, so must all the others. If a change to the economic system is too fast, the path to a new balance is unstable. The *nouveaux riches* are in an ambivalent position. They become alienated from the existing order because their newly acquired economic status does not correspond to their share of power and prestige. They are excluded from these spheres, and so they use their economic resources to change the social and political order so that it corresponds to their interests.

However, society is also destabilised by the volume of people who in an era of rapid growth become *absolutely poorer*. During such an era social *inequality* deepens because the profits of a small number of "winners" are highly concentrated, while the losses of the far larger numbers of "losers" are distributed widely (Olson 1963). Although average income rises in the early stages of fast economic growth, the median wage drops. Economic growth increases the number of those who are absolutely worse off: the minority becomes rich disproportionately to how the majority becomes poor (Kuznetz 1955). These *"nouveaux pauvres"* are not adapted to the existing order. Some have seen a drop in income, while others have become unemployed and lost their income entirely. For traditional peasant or nomadic communities "un-employment" is a meaningless concept. In a rapidly growing society it is the reality of those who lost out most to growth. They have become unshackled from the links of traditionally poor communities, while their aversion to poverty is greater, since they are aware of the possibility of the better life they longed for.

In addition, there are no *institutions* that would look after them. In traditional societies such institutions existed in the form of extended families, congregations or tribes, while highly industrialised societies already had a welfare state up and running. However, the early stages of industrialisation generates many new problems without having in place sufficiently advanced institutions that could replace traditional institutions and thus assist the less successful to adapt to their new circumstances. The result is frustration and insecurity.

As well as those who reaped absolute profit or suffered absolute loss from rapid growth, there also exist those who experienced *relative loss*. Though they saw an increase in absolute income, they feel left behind within the economic hierarchy. In their case, the income gained is insufficient to rid them of a feeling of dissatisfaction, since in comparison with those around them they feel unsuccessful. Furthermore, rapid growth generates *rising expectations*. This generates optimism and an awareness of the possibility of a better life and a constant rise in living standards. Such expectations may easily exceed the possibilities of the economy and find themselves in conflict with reality (Olson 1963, cf. also Davies 1962). Finally, economic growth can increase political instability by virtue of the fact that the profits to be gained from seizing power will rise proportionately to how the national wealth as a whole increases that a government can then control and redistribute as it sees fit amongst its cronies (Huntington 1968).

THE MODEL'S APPLICATION TO THE POST-COLONIAL ARAB WORLD: OIL RENT VERSUS NEOLIBERAL REFORMS

The model described by Olson corresponds closely to the development of Tunisia, which in late 2010 and 2011 triggered the wave of Arab revolutions. Over the last fifty years the country's per capita GDP has increased systematically, evenly and dynamically, actually accelerating from the 1990s up until the revolution. Olson believes that a society is exposed to the greatest instability, political fragility and likelihood of revolution during the economically most dynamic phase of take-off, during which a few leading industrial sectors generate the kind of prosperity that kick-starts the rest of the economy (cf. Rostow 1960). On the other hand, Tunisia also possesses a relatively diversified and therefore developed economy in all respects, and finds itself in the drive-to-maturity stage. Furthermore, the revolution began in the backward interior regions, not in the most dynamic regions, though it then quickly spread throughout the entire country. The example of Tunisia might also therefore correspond to the classical thesis of Samuel Huntington (2008) and Martin S. Lipset (1959, 1994), which states that the transition to democracy takes place in middle-income economies after they have reached a critical threshold of development (cf. Inglehart and Welzel 2006).

The revolutions that followed were also in accord with Olson's thesis. In the years prior to revolution, Egypt, Syria and Libya had experienced relatively dynamic economic development and an increase in per capita GDP. However, Algeria, Iraq and especially Jordan and Morocco had also experienced dynamic economic growth, and revolutions did not take place here, even though there were widespread protests in Morocco and Jordan that the regimes responded to in the form of concessions and constitutional reforms (see figs. 17 and 18).

Conversely, signs of the "J" curve leading, according to Gurr and Davies, to revolutions ensuing from rising expectations or frustrated progress were only to be seen in pre-revolutionary Bahrain and Yemen. However, this did not involve dynamic growth followed by a deep slump, but rather stagnation followed by a gradual decline. Therefore, although the Middle East was affected by the global financial crisis after 2008, there was no across-the-board economic slump tracking the trajectory of the "J" curve. Indeed, the "J" curve was only clearly apparent in Kuwait, Algeria and perhaps in Jordan. However, none of these countries experienced revolution or even significant destabilisation (see figs. 17 and 18).

Overall, however, the condition and development of the economy *does not differentiate* between Arab countries in such a way that it might *in itself* explain the outbreak of revolution and political instability. Revolutions

Fig. 17 Poorer Arab countries: per capita GDP 1960–2013

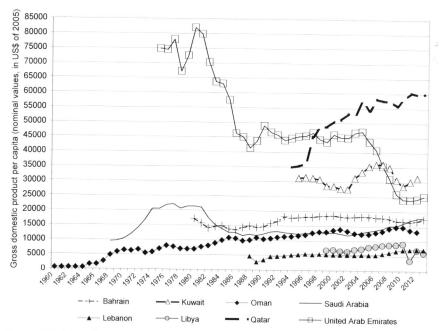

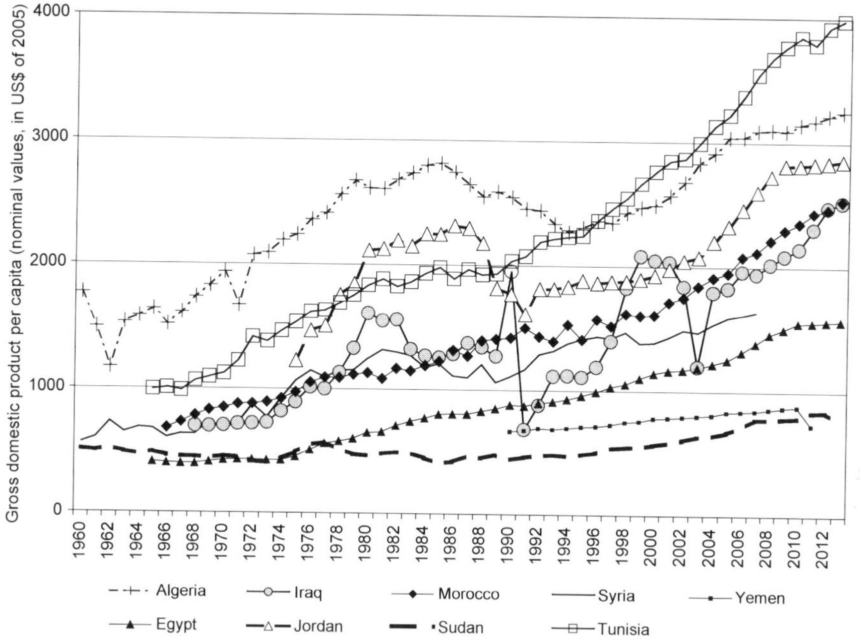

Source: World Bank

Fig. 18 Richer Arab countries: per capita GDP 1960–2013

Source: World Bank

took place under relatively variable economic conditions: in the rich albeit stagnating Bahrain, where the pace of growth over the last few years lagged behind the rate of population growth in such a way that there was a gradual drop in per capita GDP; in middle-income Tunisia with its long period of high and accelerating economic growth; and in middle-income Libya experiencing mild growth. However, there were also revolutions in Egypt and Syria, poor countries reporting only slight growth, and finally in the very poor Yemen, experiencing long-term stagnation, where the pace of economic development, as in Bahrain, was unable to outpace significantly the rate of population growth (cf. figs. 17 and 18).

It seems clear that the *absolute level* of a country's wealth differentiates the political development of Arab countries better than the *dynamic* of the economy emphasised by Olson. There was significant destabilisation in the form of revolution or civil war in the five poorest Arab countries: Sudan, Yemen, Egypt, Syria and Iraq. Conversely, five of the six wealthiest countries were politically stable: Qatar, the United Arab Emirates, Kuwait, Saudi Arabia and Oman. Poor Arab countries suffer political instability more than rich ones (see figs. 17 and 18).

This well highlights the dual economic character of the Middle East, divided into states with important oil resources and states without. Oil rentiers managed to survive the Arab revolutions and the overall destabilisation of the region thanks to their natural resources and the method by which the wealth flowing therefrom was distributed amongst individual loyal segments of the population. Libya is an exception. Colonel Gaddafi did not distribute the oil rent in sufficient quantities amongst the population and amongst a large enough clientele. Instead, he spent large sums on megalomaniac projects at home and abroad, and this did not create a loyal clientele on which his regime could rely during times of crisis (cf. Gause III 2011).

On the contrary, from the 1990s onwards, densely populated Arab states without significant oil reserves stepped up neoliberal-style *economic reforms* based on cuts to the welfare budget, the extensive privatisation of state enterprises, attracting foreign investment, the creation of incentives for the private sector, and the liberalisation of trade. These reforms were made necessary by external pressures in the form of the creeping globalisation of the world economy and the pressure of loan providers headed by the International Monetary Fund and the World Bank (cf. Lubeck and Britts 2002). There were also internal pressures, as regimes attempted to find a way of ensuring that their economies grew faster than their populations. At the same time they hoped that they would create a new social class profiting to such an extent from economic growth that it would become a new, loyal pillar supporting the regime during periods of potential political crisis.

The result of the reforms was solid economic growth, for which the Arab states were praised by the International Monetary Fund a few months prior to the revolutions. However, there was also an increase in visible inequality, since only a narrow stratum of businesspeople holding capital were able to benefit from the new opportunities created by neoliberal reforms, above all the friends and relatives of dictators, who enriched themselves during privatisation by means of bribes and asset stripping. Meanwhile, most of the population had neither the capital nor connections enabling them to profit from the new opportunities opened up by the free market. On the contrary, they were in the direct line of fire of the budgetary cuts and newly introduced, unregulated market forces. This new feeling of existential threat, accompanied by the sight of the "grand larceny" of the new millionaires, provoked indignation. The old social contract, based on the political loyalty of citizens to the regime in exchange for basic social provision and a feeling of economic security, collapsed. The Arab revolutions can thus be seen as an attempt to negotiate a new social contract with the regime (Gause III 2011). As Alaa Al Aswany, the Egyptian writer, activist and founder of the opposition Kefaya movement, was heard to say: "Egyptians could tolerate poverty. You can live with poverty as long as you think it's fair, as long as you think things will improve if you work hard. But what is intolerable is injustice, when you believe that what is happening is not fair and there is no hope for the future" (Aswany 2011: 88).

However, something else to collapse was the conviction shared by dictators that the new stratum of arrivistes benefiting from neoliberal economic reforms would create a reliable and loyal buttress of the regime. In fact, either they remained passive, fled the country, or even spearheaded protests, as in case of the Egyptian Wael Ghonim, working as the head of marketing for the international corporation Google as it was entering the Middle Eastern market. Contrary to the assumptions of regimes, activists from the new upper-middle class were often willing to risk their status and material benefits in the name of promoting freedom and political reform. In sum, therefore, regimes underestimated the importance of the manner in which economic reforms were implemented, especially the absence of a legal and institutional framework within which privatisation and the introduction of market mechanisms could took place. They also underestimated the political implications of the impoverishment of the masses and, on the contrary, overestimated the political potential of the new capitalists. A correction was made with the Arab revolutions, when the first reaction to the political crisis was the suspension of neoliberal reforms. However, political instability will not be resolved so easily, since the newly mobilised public is demanding a new social contract based on the redistribution of a wealth that governments do not possess, and the restoration of the old social contract that governments do not have the funds to finance (Gause III 2011).

THE INTERNATIONAL CONTEXT: THE FOOD CRISIS AND POLITICAL DESTABILISATION

With the possible exception of Turkey and Syria, no Middle Eastern country is food self-sufficient (cf. Bičík 2000: 88). The growing populations of the Middle East are highly dependent on food imports and therefore very vulnerable not only to price fluctuations on the world oil market, but also fluctuations on the world markets for agricultural commodities.

A lack of rainfall and fertile land, along with an excess of oil, is one of the main determinants of the economic development of the entire region. Since most of the Middle East is located in an arid region with annual rainfall less than 500 millimetres, an even greater problem is the irregularity of rainfall during individual years, from year to year, and even decade to decade. This results in frequent drought and unpredictable crop failures, as well as a dependency on irrigation. However, irrigation leads to gradual salinisation and land degradation (Richards and Waterbury 2008). Irrigation systems are fragile and vulnerable to political instability in the region, and need functional centralised states to ensure their operation and coordination. In addition, irrigation ratchets up international conflicts related to the distribution of strategic water sources in watercourses that flow through several countries, such as the Nile, the Euphrates, the Tigris and the Jordan (Klare 2001, Winterová 2010, Dohrmann and Hatem 2014).

Because of this dependency on irrigation, most of the fertile land, along with the populations, is concentrated in a very small area occupying only seven percent of the Middle East. The rest of the territory is neither inhabited nor put to economic use. For example, Egypt is spread over one million square kilometres, and yet the vast majority of its population of more than 80 million inhabitants (2006) live in the Nile Valley and Delta, an area covering only 39,000 square kilometres. This creates the highest population density in the world, far in excess of 2,000 persons per square kilometre, and puts it fully on a par with the most populated parts of India, China and Java. The pressure on food imports then grows because of the population explosion, which over the last three generation (60 years) has seen a twelve-fold increase in the Middle Eastern population. However, this population explosion is accompanied by the ecological degradation of fertile land caused by erosion, soil sealing, salination and contamination by pesticides, fertilisers and the waste water from industry and households (Richards and Waterbury 2008).

It should not be overlooked that the Middle East has several times in the past witnessed bread riots, when food subsidies were cut and prices increased (Richards and Waterbury 2008). If the repertoires of political contention are not new and have a certain tradition, they will most likely be repeated in similar situations (Tilly 2006). The Arab revolutions (2011) took as their motto "bread, work and dignity!", and both a temporal and causal link can be made with the scarcity of food.

Firstly, the Arab revolutions took place when world food prices were historically the most volatile and the highest ever since the start of measurements in the 1990s. From 2009 to the end of 2010, when the revolution began in Tunisia before spreading to other countries, both the nominal and real prices of food rose more rapidly than at any other time measured, and doubled in less than two years.

Secondly, different agricultural commodities rose in price at different speeds. The biggest increase in prices related to commodities of most importance for the poorest people, i.e. sugar, oils and cereals. Foodstuffs such as meat, i.e. commodities filling the shopping baskets of the middle and upper classes, rose only slightly. The impacts of price increases can thus be differentiated by social class (for the prices of commodities see FAO: The World Food Situation 2011; The Food Crises... 2011).

Thirdly, the global trend in rising agricultural commodity prices has the greatest impact in poorer countries, where spending on food represents a sizable part of the family budget. These countries include poorer, highly populated Arab countries such as Tunisia, Egypt, Algeria, Morocco and Jordan, i.e. basically the countries where revolutions or widespread protests and political destabilisation took place. Spending on food in these countries represents a significantly above-average proportion of a family's budget even on a global scale (see tab. 9). Conversely, the less populated and much richer Arab monarchies of the Gulf with their extensive mineral reserves do not conform to this pattern. Spending on food here accounts for a relatively small proportion of total household expenditure, in general fully comparable with the most advanced countries of the world, and so increases in food prices do not hit family budgets as hard. This means that, with the exception of Bahrain, revolutions did not take place here, political stability was higher, and these states used their wealth to further increase subsidies on basic needs.

Fourthly, the impacts of increased food prices in poor countries are differentiated by social class and inequality levels. They are most striking amongst the urban poor and lower-middle class without relatives in the countryside, who, as opposed to poor farmers, cannot rely on subsistence agriculture. As the Spanish proverb says: Civilisation and anarchy are only seven meals apart. The food crisis therefore clearly represented one of the powerful motives of active or at least passive support for the revolution, particularly amongst certain urban dwellers.

Finally, world food prices are closely linked to oil and gas prices. In the Middle East timber is expensive and unavailable. Food and drink therefore has to be prepared using gas. Increased food prices accompanied by a parallel increase in the price of gas means that the poorer classes are unable to make hot food and drinks. This problem is particularly acute in those Arab countries that do not posses significant oil and gas reserves and must for the most part import these commodities. On the contrary, the link between the price of oil and food helps the oil monarchies of the Gulf reduce instability: food prices may be rising, but the oil rent is too, and this can be used to subsidise imported foodstuffs.

Tab. 9 Spending on food 2008–2012 (% of total household expenditure)

Country	2008	2010	2012
Tunisia	35.8	23.3	35.5
Egypt	38.3	42.6	42.7
Algeria	43.8	42.7	43.7
Morocco	40.3	36.8	40.5
Jordan	40.8	35.0	32.2
Iran	26.3	26.3	25.5
Saudi Arabia	23.7	26.3	25.8
Turkey	24.5	22.4	22.2
Kuwait	14.6	18.7	18.6
Bahrain	14.5	14.3	13.9
Qatar	12.8	12.5	12.1
United Arab Emirates	9.0	14.5	14.3
USA	6.8	6.8	6.8
Germany	---	11.4	11.7
Czech Republic	---	14.2	15.5
Kenya	---	43.6	47.0
Pakistan*	---	46.2	47.7
Nigeria*	---	58.0	56.9
Global average**	---	23.4	23.4

Source: United States Department of Agriculture. Economic Research Service.
* Pakistan and Nigeria are the countries with the highest proportion of spending on food.
** The arithmetic average of a total of 86 countries for which data is available. The author's calculation.

The Egyptian revolution was predicted in a remarkable study by Václav Cílek, who showed that three years prior to the revolution the price of tomatoes fluctuated up to thirty times the base price. "Mad tomatoes" became a metaphor. The prices of other food behaved similarly. It was estimated that approximately two thirds of Egyptians spend 70–90% of their income on food (compared to an average of 43%, see tab. 1). Another slight increase in prices would plunge them into famine, since already stretched family budgets were unable to provide a "cushion" to cover any price rise. Similarly, the price of oil rose tenfold during the prerevolutionary year 2010. Millions of the poorest people were unable to cook hot meals for several weeks. The food crisis of 2008, when prices rose significantly for the first time, was repeated on a larger scale. Back then the Cairo newspapers had reported the shocking story of a man who had waited all day for a loaf of subsidised bread. When he failed to receive it, he returned home and out of desperation poisoned his starving family. Fights broke out in queues at government subsidised bakeries, while an estimated half of the state-subsidised grain was lost in the corrupt state apparatus (Cílek 2011). According to other commentators, the fact that a food and energy crisis took place simultaneously did not in itself cause revolution. This was due to an interaction with other factors (Friedman 2011; Kimball 2011). This book will therefore not only examine the politically relevant developmental tendencies within the framework of an economic system, but will systematically investigate the interaction and tension between the rate of economic development and the rate of development in other dimensions of uneven modernisation and its broader (cultural and geopolitical) context. It will attempt to show which concrete mechanisms leading to political destabilisation ensue from these structural pressures given by the unevenness of the pace of development in the political, economic and social system. The logical of this approach is summarised in fig. 19.

Fig. 19 The interaction of the economic system with other independent variables investigaed in this chapter

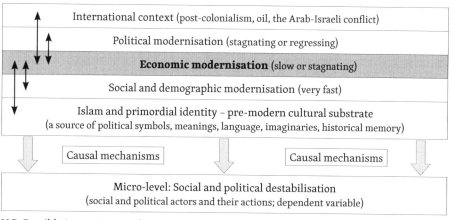

International context (post-colonialism, oil, the Arab-Israeli conflict)

Political modernisation (stagnating or regressing)

Economic modernisation (slow or stagnating)

Social and demographic modernisation (very fast)

Islam and primordial identity – pre-modern cultural substrate
(a source of political symbols, meanings, language, imaginaries, historical memory)

Causal mechanisms   Causal mechanisms

Micro-level: Social and political destabilisation
(social and political actors and their actions; dependent variable)

N.B. Possible interactions and tensions are shown by the arrows.

POPULATION EXPLOSION: THE MIDDLE EAST AND ITS ABANDONED YOUNG PEOPLE

"Nobody listened to the young. Nobody offered them hope. So much talent and energy that should be utilised in some way. No work. Not even a place to play football."
(The Egyptian preacher Amr Khaled)

"You have only four options: you can remain unemployed and single, because without work you can't have a family and find a flat; you can work on the black market and risk being caught; you can try emigrating to Europe and sweep the streets of Paris; or you can join the Islamic Salvation Front and vote for Islam." (A young Algerian man in the 1990s)

"All the respected and cultivated suitors that wooed me were finally revealed to be like the Egyptian General Assembly – to begin with the same promises, and in the end nothing but scandals." (Ghada Abdel Aal, I Want to Get Married)

"She could have been long married but she's too demanding. She studied and acquired many diplomas. That gives her the right to be choosy. But in his time girls didn't go to school. They were married off and got rid of." (Tahar Ben Jelloun, Silent Day in Tangiers)

"Perhaps you can see me, how I talk with my wife, listen to her, then answer her courteously, assess the situation from different angles as though we were in the British parliament? No!" (A traditional father admonishing his educated sons, Tahar Ben Jelloun, Silent Day in Tangiers)

"This country is not ours, Taha. This country belongs to those who have money." (a conversation between two young lovers, Alaa-Al-Aswany, The Yacoubian Building)[8]

INTERNATIONAL COMPARISON: THE MIDDLE EAST AND OTHER WORLD MACROREGIONS

The population explosion that has swept through the Middle East during the last fifty years has seen an almost fivefold increase in the number of people

---

8   Cited in Khaled 2011: 69; Booth 2002: 235; Aal 2010: 111, Jelloun 1990: 27 and 41, Aswání 2002: 75.

living in the region. In 1950 the Middle East was home to a hundred million people: at the start of the 21st century this figure was in excess of 440 million. By 2015 it is predicted that the population will number 639 million (Richards and Weterbury 2008). If we restrict ourselves to the Arab world (i.e. the Middle East without Israel, Turkey and Iran), we see an eightfold increase in the population during the whole of the 20th century. Around 1900 some 36 million Arabs lived here. One hundred years on and this figure is 280 million (Kropáček 1996).

According to the author's calculations, the dynamic of the demographic development of the Middle East over the last fifty years is unprecedented in comparison with other macroregions, including those of the developing world (Asia, South America, Sub-Saharan Africa, see fig. 20). A historical comparison with the demographic development of Europe reveals similar differences. Although from the end of the 18th to the beginning of the 20th century the same demographic transition basically took place in Europe accompanied by an increase in the size of its populations, the dynamic was less intense and the increase in populations spread over a longer timeframe. Furthermore, the political consequences of demographic developments in the Middle East are potentially more destabilising than they are in other regions of the world and than they were in European history.

Fig. 20 Population growth in world macroregions 1960–2015 (% per year)

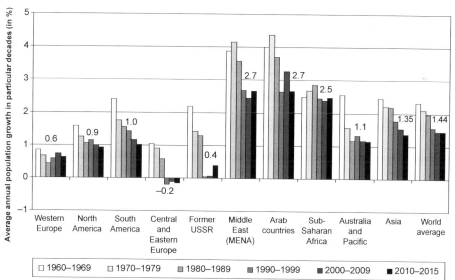

N.B.: The author's calculation of the average rates of population growth for individual countries and decades. The resulting calculation of the average rate of growth for macroregions does not take into account the population size of individual states (unweighted country averages).
Source: World Bank Development Indicators 2016

However, the course of demographic transition is not characterised only by an absolute numerical increase in the population. The overall demographic structure (pyramid) is changing in favour of a higher representation of young people, the proportion of whom is highest in the world along with Sub-Saharan Africa and South America (see figs. 23 and tab. 11). This is why over the last few years the oft-repeated mantra of Middle Eastern studies has been the observation that the current generation of Arab youth is not only the most numerous, but also the most educated, healthy, ambitious, informed, and globally connected generation in the whole of Arab history (cf. The Silatech Index 2011, Herrera 2009). At the beginning of the 21st century, around 100 million people aged 15–29 lived in the Arab world, i.e. some 30% of the local population. Approximately two thirds of the population are younger than 25 and therefore, as opposed to industrially advanced countries, comprise the vast majority of the overall population (Richards and Waterbury 2008).

REGIONAL COMPARISON: A COMPARISON OF MIDDLE EASTERN COUNTRIES

Though the overall population dynamic in the region is very high, the pace of growth differs country by country (see tab. 10 and fig. 21). For instance, the most dynamic populations of Kuwait, Yemen and Saudi Arabia will double over the next twenty years. The number of Iraqis, Jordanians and Syrians will double within three decades. However, population growth is slowing down in some small countries where the demographic transition has passed through both of its stages, namely a drop in the mortality rate followed by a drop in the birth rate: Lebanon, Turkey, Tunisia and Iran. Even here, however, the population will double over the next 50 to 60 years (Richards and Waterbury 2008). In much of the Middle East the birth rate has approached the level common in modern Europe to such an extent that several commentators are speaking of the gradual convergence of Arab and Western civilisations (Courbage and Todd 2011).

Are demographic trends in themselves sufficient to explain the degree of political destabilisation in individual Middle Eastern countries? The rate of population growth is not on its own sufficient to differentiate between Arab countries such that demography could be regarded as the sole variable explaining the occurrence or absence of revolution during the Arab Spring (2011). The fastest growth over the last decade was in the small, rich, highly urbanised Gulf states, i.e. Qatar, the United Arab Emirates and Kuwait. And yet not only did revolution take place here but these were the most stable countries. On the other hand, revolutions broke out in other countries with rapidly growing populations: Yemen (with an annual population growth

Tab. 10 Average rate of population growth in MENA countries 1960–2015 (% per year)

Country	1960–69	1970–79	1980–89	1990–99	2000–09	2010–15
Algeria	2.31	3.11	3.03	1.99	1.49	1.90
Bahrain	3.44	4.46	3.60	2.89	2.18	2.34
Egypt	2.50	2.21	2.62	1.98	1.87	2.15
Iran	2.71	3.13	3.43	1.67	1.48	1.26
Iraq	3.00	3.21	2.96	2.82	2.57	3.25
Israel	3.46	2.75	1.77	3.03	1.95	1.88
Jordan	5.78	3.78	3.74	4.25	2.40	3.20
Kuwait	9.99	6.29	4.58	1.68	4.41	5.01
Lebanon	2.66	1.52	0.51	2.40	1.28	5.60
Libya	3.85	4.25	3.78	2.04	2.02	0.19
Morocco	2.75	2.45	2.44	1.56	1.15	1.34
Oman	2.68	4.45	4.56	2.82	1.87	8.10
Palestine	---	---	---	4.05	2.62	2.96
Qatar	8.79	7.40	7.50	2.69	8.72	5.67
Saudi Arabia	3.32	4.95	5.48	2.52	2.29	2.34
Sudan	2.48	3.04	2.86	2.53	2.13	2.18
Syria	3.17	3.38	3.54	2.64	2.71	-1.76
Tunisia	1.94	2.11	2.46	1.71	0.97	1.03
Turkey	2.50	2.45	1.98	1.72	1.34	1.65
United Arab Emirates	8.22	15.53	6.53	5.48	4.06	2.88
Yemen	2.02	2.54	3.78	4.04	2.88	2.60

N.B.: The author's calculation of the arithmetic averages of the rate of population growth for individual countries and decades.
Source: World Bank Development Indicators 2010 and 2016.

of 2.9%) and Syria (with 2.7%), as well as in the relatively demographically dynamic Egypt (1.9%), Libya (2.0%) and Bahrain (2.2%). Conversely, within the wider region of the Middle East the lowest population growth was recorded in Tunisia (1.0%), which today, along with Lebanon, Morocco, Iran and Turkey, is completing the process known as demographic transition and in terms of demographic behaviour is beginning to resemble advanced Western countries. And yet the Arab Spring began in Tunisia. The only thing that all the revolutionary countries have in common is the gradual slowdown in the rate of population growth over the two to three decades prior to revolution. At first sight this would appear to be inconsistent with the theory that

Fig. 21 Average rate of population growth in MENA countries 1960–2015 (% per year)

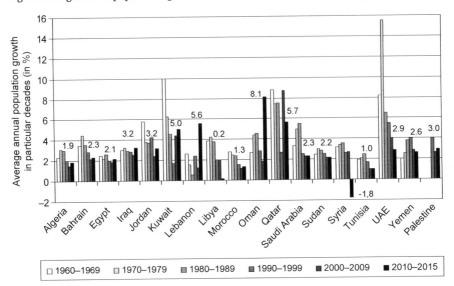

N.B.: The author's calculation of the arithmetic averages of the rate of population growth for individual countries and decades. The average rate of growth over the last decade is given numerically for each state in the graph.
Source: World Bank Development Indicators 2016

revolution is a consequence of demographic transition (cf. Goldstone 1997), since according to this theory the Arab revolutions should have taken place one to two decades earlier.

However, the vigorous population dynamic in *earlier* decades resulted in a high number and proportion of people *currently* in their twenties and thirties. This generation stood at the head of the revolution. The proportion of young people in the population was above average in four countries that experienced revolution: Yemen, Syria, Egypt, and Tunisia. The proportion of young people was somewhat lower in Libya and Bahrain. However, the politically far more stable Algeria, Jordan and Oman also had a high proportion of teenagers and people in their twenties. And so the representation of young people in the population as a whole is also not in itself sufficient to explain either the outbreak or the absence of revolution in individual Arab countries.

This chapter will contend that growing social tensions and political destabilisation are not simply the result of the dynamic of demographic change. A key fact is that neither the dwindling rate of economic growth nor the negligible tempo of change within authoritarian political systems is keeping pace with the population growth rate of the last 50 years. In terms of this disparity, the Middle East comes out top when compared with other macro-regions of the world. Furthermore, this discrepancy has if anything increased over time. It is also high if compared historically with early modern Europe, where disparities between demographic, economic and political developments also increased, though nowhere near as dramatically. For this reason the rapidly growing population, especially the up-and-coming generation of young people, has not been integrated into the economic and political system in the Middle East. So this chapter will not analyse demographic developments in isolation, but, on the contrary, will focus on the interaction of rapid demographic change and other dimensions of the uneven modernisation process within its broader cultural and geopolitical context. These conflictual interactions create areas of friction leading to destabilisation by means of various different causal mechanisms. This is summarised in fig. 22.

Fig. 22 The interaction of demographic change with other independent various examined in this chapter

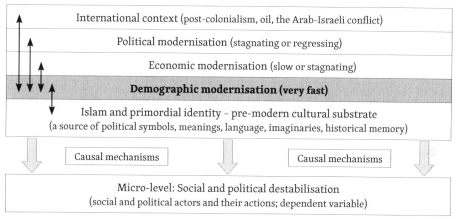

N.B. Possible interactions and tensions are shown by the arrows.

YOUNG PEOPLE CAUGHT IN THE TRAP OF UNEVEN MODERNISATION: DIVERGENCE IN THE RATE OF DEMOGRAPHIC, ECONOMIC AND POLITICAL CHANGE

Young people in the Middle East are caught in a trap of uneven development. Over the last half century demographic growth has been far faster than the sluggish developments in the economic, social and political system. This long-term and intensifying *structural* constellation has led to widespread dissatisfaction in the region with concomitant political consequences. These include the discrediting of the governing regimes and their ideologies to the benefit of opposition movements (including Islamists), the Arab domino revolutions of 2011, and the subsequent chronic post-revolutionary instability preventing the establishment of stable democracies.

The listless dynamic of Middle Eastern economies is failing to keep pace with a protracted population explosion that has seen a sharp rise in the number of young people. The situation is worst on the labour market, which is not growing fast enough and is overwhelmed by the influx of new job applications from graduates of what is historically the largest ever Arab generation. The creation of new entrepreneurial opportunities is also lagging behind. In addition, not only is the number of young people rocketing, but also their *formal* qualifications and the professional and consumer aspirations resulting therefrom. The conflict between these aspirations and the slow rate of economic growth and new job creation results in disappointment and frustration with the difficulties encountered in securing the dreamed-of career and moving upwards socially into the ranks of the white-collar, prosperous middle class.

Neoliberal economic reforms and austerity policies impact more dramatically on the large young generation than on comfortably established older people. Similarly, the global economic crisis of 2008 above all damaged the life opportunities of younger cohorts on the threshold of becoming employed or starting up a business. Any savings young people may have scraped together are often devalued by inflation before they are able to find a partner and get married. In addition, the rise in the number of young people is not matched by the construction of new, affordable housing, and this represents another fundamental barrier to marriage prospects. The supply of other services, such as urban public transport and the transport infrastructure as a whole, is also unable to meet the demands of demographic growth (Hoffman 1995, Swedenburg 2007).

The offer of *good quality* primary, secondary and tertiary education available to all is also unable to keep pace with the rising number of young people. State investment per pupil or student shows a long-term declining tendency. Though public expenditure on education has been relatively stable over the long term, the same cake now has to be divided up between more young people, who, furthermore, are opting to remain in the education system for a longer period of time because they can no longer be fobbed off with a basic education but hope to achieve higher qualifications. In over-crowded schools, maintaining a reasonable ratio between pupils and overworked teachers is proving to be a problem. The student-teacher ratio is if anything increasing, the quality of public education is deteriorating, and the question of social justice is becoming more and more acute. It is only the offspring of privileged social classes, who can pay for private tutoring and courses preparing them for the state examinations at the end of secondary school, who are able to study the most highly favoured disciplines at prestigious faculties (Booth 2002, AHDR 2002).

The rapid demographic changes in several regions have put huge pressure on scarce natural resources, such as fertile agricultural land, pasture, sources of drinking water, and timber for heating and cooking (Homer-Dixon and Blitt 1998, Kaplan 2003). This environmental pressure is compounded by the vulnerability of the region to the negative impacts of climate change, as manifest in desertification or more frequent fluctuations in weather patterns, drought, and crop failures in those regions economically and existentially dependent on agriculture (Dorte 2012). Falling domestic agricultural production is unable to keep pace over the long term with the breakneck tempo of demographic change. Food prices are rising. Food has to be imported to the region of the Fertile Crescent, which gave rise to the Neolithic Revolution and for thousands of years was one of the world centres of agriculture. This results in a negative agricultural trade balance (cf. Bičík 2000). Governments try to subsidise food prices in the hope of maintaining social order. A global food crisis accompanied by high or fluctuating prices on international markets, combined with the arrival of a large generation on the threshold of adulthood, has seen an escalation of political tension (cf. Cílek 2011). It was mainly young people without prospects who were drawn to the wave of self-immolation protests at the start of the Arab revolutions.

Finally, the values and attitudes of young people are changing and coming into conflict with authoritarian, overweening, and highly repressive regimes that are incapable of offering them any future prospects or providing them the space for economic or political inclusion within society. Such regimes are not even capable of finding appropriate ways of communicating with young people, and often appear to have no interest in the problems they face.

A HISTORICAL COMPARISON OF THE DEMOGRAPHIC REVOLUTION: EUROPE PAST AND THE MIDDLE EAST PRESENT

What are the causes of the current explosive demographic situation? It is the consequence of a universal process known as demographic transition, comprising a first stage during which mortality rates drop sharply, and a second stage during which there is a gradual reduction in birth rates. In the interim period therefore the population grows in size. Around the mid-20th century mortality rates fell sharply in the Middle East, though this was not accompanied by a comparable drop in birth rates. On the contrary, birth rates remained among the highest in the world for decades. At the start of the demographic transition they represented 50.5 newborns per 1,000 of the population (1950–1955). By 1970 this figure had dropped to 45. In 1992 it was only 34 and in 2003 there were approximately 27 newborns per 1,000 people. Despite this decline, fertility rates are still well above the global average (21 newborns per 1,000 people), and even above the fertility rates in the low development countries (LDC) with an average of 24 newborns per 1,000 people. The only macroregion with higher fertility rates is at present Sub-Saharan Africa with approximately 40 babies per 1,000 people (Richards and Waterbury 2008, World Bank 2010).

In a historical comparison of the demographic transition of the Middle East and Europe, where similar demographic developments took place between 1850 and 1950 (a little earlier in England and France), the Middle East also differs somewhat. Looked at broadly it behaves similarly to other macroregions of the developing world. Although the demographic revolution began here later than in Europe, its course was more dramatic and led to higher population growth within a shorter period of time (Toušek, Kunc, Vystoupil et al. 2008). Right up until the middle of the 20th century the increase in the world's population was caused by the population explosion in Europe and North America, and only then was it driven by the population explosion in developing countries, where the number of people more than tripled between 1950 and 2007 (Kalibová 2008).

The Japanese-Mexican type of demographic transition, characteristic of developing countries, including the Middle East, differs from the French and English type. In the first stage there is a rapid reduction in mortality rates thanks to better hygiene and the availability of inoculations, drugs, healthcare and food. However, in the meantime the traditionally high birth rate remains the same or even increases over the short term and only begins to drop gradually over a longer timeframe in the second stage of demographic transition. In the interim period, between the reduction in mortality rates and the subsequent reduction in birth rates, the population grows rapidly. In contrast, in the case of the French type of demographic transition the reduction in both mortality and birth rates takes place almost simultaneously and the overall growth in the population during the course of transition is not so dramatic.

In European societies the demographic transition lasted around a hundred years, and in the case of France, for example, the population increased "only" 1.8 times during this time. In contrast, in most developing countries it takes place in half the time and sees a doubling of the population every twenty years. Therefore, though Middle Eastern societies have undergone demographic transition over the last fifty years, here it has seen an approximately fivefold increase in the population, and in many countries it has not yet ended (Kalibová 1997, Richards and Waterbury 2008).

When the English pastor and economist Thomas Malthus (1766–1834) observed in amazement this universal process accompanied by population explosion in its less severe European variant, he predicted a bleak future for Europe. He noticed that, while resource growth followed a linear (arithmetic) trajectory, populations had begun to grow geometrically. The inevitable outcome of this conflict between demography, the limits of the environment and economic possibilities would appear to be social and political instability: population regulation by means of war, disease, famine, and other similar disasters (Malthus 2002). At present the Middle East faces the threat of being caught in a similar Malthusian trap, from which Europe eventually managed to wriggle free (cf. Brzezinksi 1993, 2004). As opposed to modernising Europe from the end of the 18th century to the beginning of the 20th century, the current Middle Eastern demographic revolution is not being accompanied by other parallel revolutions: (a) agricultural (an increase in the productivity of agricultural production and food self-sufficiency), (b) industrial (the employment of a surplus workforce released from rural regions), and (c) technological (international competitiveness thanks to innovation and increased productivity) (Kennedy 1996).

Compared to early modern Europe, the rate of population growth in poorer Middle Eastern countries has long outstripped the pace of economic growth (Egypt, Yemen, Jordan, Iran up until the 1960s). There has not been a rise in average income and effective demand and the creation of savings that could be used for investments and increasing productivity. Societies have remained caught in the *poverty trap* or the cycle of poverty. During the course of European modernisation, on the other hand, economic development was inextricably linked with demographic development. Economic growth was gradually initiated, the pace of which outstripped that of population growth. This led to a gradual increase in income per capita and rising living standards. This saw an increase in bank savings as well as increased consumption on the part of households with ever higher purchasing power. Household consumption fuelled demand, which stimulated a rise in production. Higher savings held in banks meant that credit was available to businesses, which were now able to invest in new capacities and technologies and thus increase efficiency and productivity. Further economic growth saw a further rise in income per capita, with all the reverse feedback impacts outlined above (Lerner 1964, Samuelson and Nordhaus 1995: 888). In addition, a higher standard of living helped slow down the rate of population growth, and this in turn increased further per capita income (Bičík 2000, Richards and Waterbury 2008).

Similarly, unlike the historical development of early modern Europe, the population explosion in the Middle East is not accompanied by comparable *international migration*. The geopolitical dominance and colonial rule of a more and more densely populated Europe meant that escalating political and social tensions could be released by "exporting" surplus yet ambitious segments of the population literally all around the world. The results of the European demographic transition can be seen in the predominantly European origin of the inhabitants of Northern America, Australia or New Zealand and the significant presence of descendants of European emigrants in South America and certain regions of Asia and Africa. For example, by 1900, i.e. the end of the demographic transition, without the mass exodus of people abroad the population of England would be almost double what it was: instead of 41 million it would have been in excess of 70 million (Kennedy 1996: 14). Without emigration, social and economic inequality between rich and poor Europeans would have been far greater. As it was, poorer citizens with fewer opportunities for upward social mobility in their own countries emigrated. This reduced the numbers of discontented, revolutionary minded European poor. International migration helped prevent the intensification of already serious social and political crises, a fact that is often underestimated (Sutcliffe 2004). Finally, the enlistment of potential "troublemakers" from the growing ranks of idle young men into colonial armies also acted as a safety valve that released population pressures in Europe. In addition to discipline and social control, active service in the army meant losses on the battlefield and disease. For instance, the death rate of British soldiers in Sierra Leone even during peacetime was thirty times that of soldiers serving in Europe (Kennedy 1996, Ferguson 2014). These days, however, individual continents are highly populated. And despite all talk of globalisation, the barriers to migration from the ever more densely populated countries of the Middle East are greater than they were in the past, when it was the population of Europe that was growing. The populations of Middle Eastern countries, which in the context of the world system are assigned to a subordinate peripheral status (cf. Wallerstein 1990, Holubec 2010), are thus held within the borders of national states, and only limited, insufficient migration takes place on a roughly equal basis to the West and to richer oil-producing Arab countries (cf. Richards and Waterbury 2008).

Population growth in the Middle East cannot therefore be explained as culture specific. It is a historically universal process that is linked with demographic transition, the basic mechanism of which – a falling mortality rate and subsequent drop in the birth rate – is the same everywhere. It took place first in Europe and then after a certain time lag in other parts of the world, including the Middle East. Here, however, the pattern differs from the European by virtue of a higher dynamic, lower integration with developments in other spheres (the economy, agriculture, politics and technological innovation), an unfavourable geopolitical context blocking significant migration, and also the high ethnic and religious heterogeneity of post-colonial states leading to imbalances between the different rates of growth of individual sub-populations. For this reason the domestic and international political impacts of the Middle Eastern population explosion are more dramatic than they were in the case of early modern Europe, which was also destabilised by the rise of radical ideologies and movements, revolutions, civil wars and external expansion, with the rapid increase in the size of the European population accompanied by a rise in the numbers of young people often cited as an important factor in this respect (Huntington 1968, 2001, Brzezinski 1993, Kennedy 1996, Goldstone 1997, Foran 1997, Tomeš et al. 2007). So what are the mechanisms of Middle Eastern internal political destabilisation caused by rapid demographic growth within the context of the sluggish development of the economic and political system?

(1) REBELLIOUS YOUTH: IDENTITY CRISIS, INTERGENERATIONAL CONFLICT AND ADOLESCENCE

We do not have to accept demographic determinism without so much as a murmur. Nevertheless, it is difficult to overlook the fact that destabilisation often took place when the numbers and proportion of the young within the population as a whole rose as a result of demographic growth: the Protestant Reformation in Europe, the wave of European revolutions at the beginning of the modern era, the rise of fascism in Germany with a majority of its population younger than 25, the protest movements and civil rights movements of the post-war baby-boom generation of the 1960s in the USA and Western Europe, the Iranian Revolution (1979), and the civil wars in Lebanon (1975–1990) and Algeria (1992–1997). In this demographic situation political regimes were exposed to the risk that the large numbers of young people would challenge the status quo (Huntington 2001). It was rebellious young people who most often managed to undermine governments in the Middle East, for instance in Morocco (1984), Sudan (1985), Turkey (the 1970s), Egypt (1968 and 1977), Iran (1978), and in the region-wide protests against the Gulf War (1990/1). This was especially the case when they managed to attract the urban poor or more reluctant middle classes to their cause (cf. Richards and Waterbury 2008). The Arab Revolutions (2011) were also sparked off by young people, who were then joined by their families and other segments of the population (cf. Mendel 2014).

A frequent objection (e.g. Richards and Waterbury 2008) throws doubt on the rise in the *proportion* of young people during the course of demographic transition and hence the political implications thereof, though these same critics often claim that the increase in the *absolute number* of young people has political consequences. They argue that a high proportion of young people in a population is typical of both traditional societies and of those undergoing demographic transition, and is therefore nothing new. However, they are mistaken. What is important is the *internal* age structure of these young

Fig. 23 Young people aged 15–24 as a proportion of the population as a whole in macroregions 1950–2015 (in %)

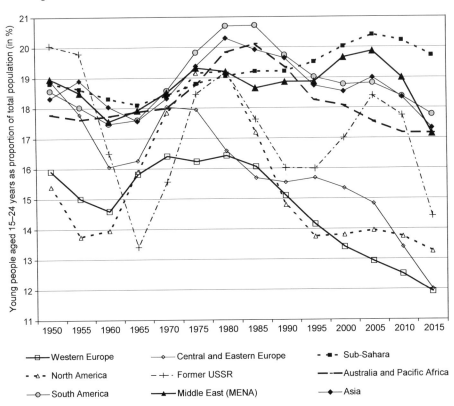

N.B.: The author's calculation of the average proportions of young people (aged 15–24) for individual macroregions and years. Unweighted country population size. Source: World Bank Development Indicators 2016

cohorts. In traditional societies the vast majority is formed by newborns, infants and children. A high neonatal, infant and child mortality rate means that many do not live to maturity. This explains demographers' obsession with detailed calculations of the neonatal, infant and child mortality rate. In contrast, during the demographic transition the neonatal and child mortality rate falls. Most survive and increase the proportion of older children or adolescents. The contrast with traditional societies does not therefore relate to the share of young cohorts (e.g. aged 1–25) but to the differences within this age group (e.g. a greater representation of the 15–25 age group). Graphically this development is clearly illustrated by age pyramids depicting the numerical makeup of individual cohorts during the course of demographic transition (see the POPIN statistics http://www.escwa.un.org/popin/members/egypt.pdf). Developments in the macroregions of the developing world are shown in graph 17.

From the 1960s to the end of the 20th century there was a rise in the proportion of young people aged 15–24 in Middle Eastern populations: from an average of 17% to almost 20% (see fig. 23). This makes the representation of young people in the population the highest in the world after Sub-Saharan Africa and almost double the levels of the politically stable and industrially advanced countries of Western Europe, North America and Japan. This is also why the region is unstable compared with others (see tab. 11).

However, the increased representation of young people in the region is not simply the consequence of demographic trends, but also social and cultural transformations: (a) the prolongation of studies, (b) the enforced postponement of marriage and parenthood for economic reasons in the lower and lower-middle classes (housing crisis, youth unemployment, inflation liquidating savings for a costly wedding), and (c) greater "choosiness" when selecting a potential life partner on the part of better educated and career oriented middle class men and women who do not wish to have the terms of an arranged marriage dictated to them by their parents. While a generation ago marriages were concluded by people aged 15–20, the current generation is often only entering into marriage after they turn thirty (Booth 2002, Kholoussy 2010).

Traditional Muslim societies are not given to recognising "adolescence" as a social category. It is, after all, a social and historical construct. Traditionally, swift on the heels of childhood followed adulthood, while "adolescents" represented a potentially problematic group and a threat to the social order. In an effort to neutralise unclassifiable "troublemakers" and ensure demographic reproduction in an era of high mortality rates, there was a tendency to marry off young people and burden them with the responsibility of adults as soon as possible (Swedenburg 2007). From the second half of the 20th century onwards, for the first time in its history the Middle East discovered, somewhat reluctantly, adolescence. The large number of young people who are no longer children but not yet adults is growing, and yet according to several authors Arabic has no suitable word to describe this stage of life. The term *murahaqa*, which is closest to our puberty, refers to developments up to the age of sexual maturity but is not often used in everyday language. *Fata* refers to a person on the path to marriage (aged 14–17). In contrast, *shabb* emphasises the formation of a sense of responsibility, obligation and duty to other people, family and community and is the most commonly used term (Booth 2002)[9].

---

9   Persian also lacks a direct equivalent of teenager. Small children and toddlers are called *nozad*, older children *koodak* or *bache*, adolescents *nojavan*, and young people still not considered adults *jovan*.

Up till the end of the 1960s, the modernising optimism of westernised elites in the region saw in young people the vanguard and future of the nation that would overcome the old-fashioned, backward-looking and conservative views of the older generations (Egypt, Turkey). However, with the rise of opposition Marxism and Islamism the potentially rebellious youth were redefined as a threat to social order, as a "problem", a group vulnerable to temptation and a "threat to national security" (Swedenburg 2007). As Mohamed Ali Mahgoub (1989), Egyptian Minister of Religious Affairs, said: "The problem with our young people is that they want to judge everything. As a result we have murder, strife, polarisation, destruction and fear. All this in the name of religion" (Starrett 1998: 175). How can we explain the radicalism and activism of young people? There are many answers to this question that are not mutually exclusive. Here we take them to be mutually complementary and relevant in different ways to the different sub-populations of young people and to different parts of the region.

Tab. 11 Proportion of people aged 15–24 in the populations of MENA countries 2010 and 2015 (in %)

Country	Population younger than 25 in 2010 (in %)	Population aged 15–24 in 2010 (in %)	Population aged 15–24 in 2015 (in %)
Algeria	47.5	20.5	16.6
Bahrain	43.9	17.9	15.2
Egypt	52.3	20.2	17.3
Iran	---	21.8	15.9
Iraq	60.6	19.9	19.6
Israel	---	15.4	14.8
Jordan	54.3	20.4	19.0
Kuwait	37.3	14.4	13.4
Lebanon	42,7	18.0	19.5
Libya	47.4	17.3	15.9
Morocco	47.7	19.7	17.7
Oman	51.5	20.6	16.3
Palestine	64.4	19.9	21.7
Qatar	33.8	17.9	14.6
Saudi Arabia	50.8	18.9	15.6
Sudan	59.0	20.3	19.9
Syria	55.3	20.5	20.0
Tunisia	42.1	19.3	15.6

Turkey	---	17.6	16.6
United Arab Emirates	31.0	11.9	12.7
Yemen	65.4	22.1	22.1
USA	**	14.0	13.7
Germany	**	*11.2*	*10.4*
Czech Republic	**	*12.6*	*10.1*
Japan	**	*9.9*	*9.5*

Source: World Bank Development Indicators 2010 and United Nations World Population Prospects: The 2015 Revisions. For the proportion of the population younger than 25 in countries of the Arab League The Economist Intelligence Unit 2011.

Firstly, young people without a family and a steady job are more likely to be drawn to opposition activism out of youthful rebelliousness, idealism, a tendency to criticise and a desire for adventure. Unlike adults responsible for children or aged parents, they have less to lose. In addition, their lack of experience means they are less able to assess risk (Richards and Waterbury 2008)[10].

Secondly, the crisis of adolescence can play a role and see rival political movements attempting to win over young people in search of an identity to their cause. The stage between childhood and adulthood in modern and modernising societies is a period characterised by a search for meaning in life and a place in the sexual, social, economic, religious and political world. This is accompanied by inner turmoil, insecurity and vulnerability (Giddens 1999: 55–56). As the sociologist Herbert Spencer observed: "All transitions are dangerous and the most dangerous is the transition from the restraint of the family circle to the non-restraint of the world" (cited in Starrett 1998: 220). Primary socialisation is culminating and is associated with the adoption and internalisation of the cultural patterns of behaviour characteristic of the society in question. These relate not only to language, but also to social roles, norms and values. The values are stabilised to which an individual will in all likelihood subscribe all of their life (Inglehart and Norris 2004, Inglehart and Welzel 2006)[11].

In addition to the protection provided by the family and the discipline of public education, a formative role is also played by peer groups, the media

---

10   Regarding the low age of militant Islamists see Ibrahim 1982, Krueger and Malečková 2002, Juergensmeyer 2000.

11   Empirical research shows that the basic value system of a generation remains relatively stable during the course of its life. However, changes can take place in the way a generation views political parties and movements if it seems that a particular group best embodies an individual's central values. For instance, during the 1960s and 70s the generation of young pan-Arabists and Marxists moved over to Islamism, which promised to respect their ideals the most.

and social movements. The influence of these secondary socialising factors gradually outweighs that of parents. Adolescents break free of the dominant influence of the family. They spend more time away from home in the company of their peers, begin to take note of political and societal problems, and are exposed to all kinds of competing ideologies and movements. This process is accompanied by experimentation in the sphere of social and sexual relationships, the lifestyle offered by subcultures, and religious and political ideologies. A young person often becomes a kind of nomad, trying out alternatives rather than pinning themselves down to one option forever. A young person is involved in an attempt to find themselves and create an identity. At the same time they long for recognition by others and the feeling of belonging to a group with which they can identify (Starrett 1998, Montoussé and Renouard 2005).

The influence of socialising factors in modern and modernising societies as opposed to traditional societies tends to be mutually opposed, even conflictual. In the Middle East a battle is being fought by state propaganda, official clerics, bloggers and opposition activists, including Islamists, for the hearts and minds of young people, whose political awareness is awakening and whose still malleable beliefs are crystallising. If (Kepel 2002, Roy 2004) up until the end of the 1960s young people rebelled under the banner of secular opposition doctrines (Marxism, pan-Arabism), these have been gradually discredited and political Islam has become fashionable. This fact calls into question the secularisation thesis. Most recently we see that large numbers of politically active young people are ideologically ambivalent. The rest are split between Islamist movements and liberal democratic thinking (cf. Bayat 2010).

For this reason, the psychological factors associated with a crisis of adolescence and an identity crisis are often cited as the reason why Islamists have been successful in recruiting disoriented youth, which is one of the important target groups of their propaganda (*da'wah*)[12]. According to Dekmejian (1995), this identity crisis is linked with feelings of alienation from mainstream society, which to the critical eye of a young person appears decadent, its leaders corrupt. It is also linked with feelings of loneliness, mediocrity, inferiority, powerlessness, insecurity, fears regarding the future and a loss of meaning in life. Subsequently, however, it is associated with idealism and a devotion to rediscovered ideals, activism, an attempt to put society and oneself to rights, a tendency to judge the world harshly in black-and-white terms, adherence to set principles and an unwillingness to compromise or to opt for easier paths

---

12   However, Islamists appeal to all generations. We should not forget that some secularly minded young people do not sympathise with the Islamists. These are the limits of a generational analysis and the conclusions are more probable than unequivocal.

through life. In this frame of mind adolescents sometimes incline toward ideologies that offer them a compass with which to orient their way through life, and can be drawn to charismatic leaders as role models. Political Islam, with what for Muslims is its comprehensible and comprehensive ideology covering all aspects of life, is capable, unlike secular doctrines, of uniting the ambivalent, faltering, insecure and disoriented personality of the adolescent. Conversion to Islam is, in the discourse of developmental psychology, a shortcut to adulthood catalysing the formation of an integrated, stabilised personality (Hoffman 1995). This individual reaction is thus analogous to a society's reaction when a turn towards fundamentalism is interpreted as the consequence of increasing uncertainty in an ever more changeable, complex, uncertain, dangerous, fragmented and globalised world without fixed points of reference (Kropáček 1996, Berger 1999, Robertson 2006).

Thirdly, intergenerational conflict with parents that exacerbates the crisis of adolescence can play a role in the radicalisation of young people under the banner of opposition ideologies. However, this element is not as powerful in the region as in the West, because Islam, with its emphasis on the family, cohesiveness and parental authority, operates as a social stabiliser (Booth 2002). In the Middle East, the developmental psychological factors referred to above are perhaps not as significant as the intergenerational estrangement and subsequent conflict caused and intensified by the completely different educational qualifications of illiterate or semi-illiterate parents on the one hand, and their educated offspring on the other, who at a critical stage of adolescent have the impression that their uneducated parents have nothing to tell them.

Urbanisation is another factor contributing to the weakening of parental authority. Parents acquire their attitudes from traditional rural communities, which to a young generation fully socialised in large cities can seem irrelevant and obsolete. The traditional Islam practised by parents creates the same impression, and in the eyes of young people seems full of pre-Islamic cults, prejudices and errors. Young people see it as their task to return Islam to the right track. The rapid modernisation of the Middle East in the second half of the 20th century is alienating the generations by driving a wedge between young people and their parents (Kepel 2002). Re-Islamisation is thus the consequence of a decline in the traditional values and structures associated with the traditional family, and not the result of ongoing continuity and the strength of tradition[13]. The growing call of Islamists for what they deem traditional Islamic values is above all an expression of nostalgia for a rapidly disappearing individual and social order (Roy 2004).

---

13 A manifestation of destructive mechanisms would be the sharp intergenerational conflict in Muslim immigrant communities in the West (see Roy 2004).

Generational conflict in an era of religious revival can lead to Islamic religiosity and argumentation being used to undermine parental authority by rebellious teenagers. The authority of Islam stands in opposition to that of parents, above all those parents who are either secularised or espouse vernacular versions of Islam. Parents are perceived to be hypocritical in failing to respect the principles they urged upon their adolescent offspring. It is difficult for adults to criticise adolescents for their religious ardour if religion is formally the core value of their own predominantly conservative communities. For instance, a young person living in Cairo, who along with his friends has rebelled against his parents, says: "Nobody from our nominally Muslim family is devout. But every day I got up early so that my friends and I could make morning prayers in the mosque. And sometimes I had to climb out of the window, because my father was against it." This conflict was played out when he was aged between sixteen and twenty. And with the abatement of adolescence it ended as quickly as it had begun. Some secular parents from the Egyptian middle classes, alarmed by and unable to explain the sudden turn to faith of their offspring, even packed them off to a psychiatrist (Starrett 1998: 171). Similarly, adolescent girls who insist on wearing a headscarf may be looking for self-expression, differentiation and a statement of pubertal protest against mothers and teachers who do not wear a scarf. Again the question arises as to whether this newfound attachment to Islam will be permanent or whether it is merely a phase on the stormy path to adulthood (Roy 2004).

However, intergenerational conflict characterised by a questioning of parental authority may drive young people permanently into the ranks of politically motivated religious movements. Organisations and movements offer individuals a "surrogate family", a feeling of belonging, the much sought after recognition of significant others, and positive emotional attachment. In the history of classical Islam, for instance, it is not common for members of a group to address each other as "brother", as it is today between Islamists. They call their basic organisation *usra*, or family. This lends legitimacy to Islamists in conservative societies (Eickelman, Piscatori 1996). The brothers offer appreciation and recognition, and thus dignity and the positive self-image that every young person going through the crisis of adolescence yearns for. Older, charismatic leaders offering new role models replace the eroded authority of parents. Movements that require the full participation of the entire personality, such as the Muslim Brotherhood, function as surrogate families[14] and satisfy similar psychological and social needs (Juergensmeyer

---

14   The family is the central value of Islam and the ideology of mainstream Islamists. It is regarded as a microcosm of the moral order and generally speaking Islamists do not attempt to compete explicitly with it. For instance, the founder of the Muslim Brotherhood declared: "When a man

2002, Kepel 2002). A similar search for meaning in life accompanied by partial disorientation can be manifest in the mid-life crisis. Either a person failed to realise their life project, or they did, but wonder whether it was worth the cost. They yearn for a new meaning, new points of reference, values and sources of positive self-esteem. Different versions of political and apolitical Islam can thus offer a positive identity and orientation in a hostile or incomprehensible society (Roy 2004).

Fourthly, some young Islamic activists display signs of a "Malcolm X syndrome". The first stage of life is devoid of religion (social deviation, criminality, nightlife, drugs and alcohol) and in sharp conflict with Islam, but is followed by a sudden turn to religion and a change of lifestyle on the threshold of adulthood. In extreme cases this conversion to what is often radical political Islam takes place in prisons, where a young person is isolated from the criminal sub-culture, experiences a guilty conscience, reflects upon a change of life, and in this state of mind is exposed to missionary activities. Malcolm X (1965) described his conversion as follows: "I had sunk to the very bottom of the American white man's society, when – soon now, in prison – I found Allah and the religion of Islam and it completely transformed my life." A similar path through life is to be found in the case of some of the terrorists who tried to blow up the Twin Towers in 1993 (Juergensmeyer 2002), as well as some of the attackers of 11 September 2001, the jihadist Richard Reid (Roy 2004), and the young and disaffected Algerian immigrant Khaled Kelkal, who launched attacks in France (1995) and who shortly before in a sociological survey had said (1992): "I want to do something. Leave France. Forever. This isn't the place for me" (Kepel 2002: 311). This pattern can be promoted in a world of intensifying globalisation, migration and rapid modernisation accompanied by the decline of traditional social and moral structures, including united families and communities, especially among uprooted and socially excluded minorities of Muslims in the West. However, it does not apply to most of today's Islamist youth.

Fifthly, and in contradistinction to the above, it tends to be well brought up boys of conservative families who are recruited. Middle Eastern Islamists of the first generations of the movement usually come from tightly-knit, functional, religious families in which the father has a strong influence. They spend their childhood and adolescence rooted in a stable, safe, conservative environment in urban neighbourhoods or villages with a high degree of social control. There are no signs of social breakdown or marginalisation. For instance, on the basis of detailed interviews with radical Islamists, Ibrahim (1982: 131) pointed out in his classic study that under normal circumstances

---

and women live together as a family, they create the basis of culture and civilisation" (cited in Eickelman and Piscatori 1996: 83).

they would be "ideal or model young Egyptians". Among Islamic militants the difference between the Malcolm X pattern and this pattern corresponds to the difference between the terrorism of the "socially uprooted" (e.g. the second generation of Al Qaida recruiting from communities living in the West) and the terrorism of the "socially rooted" (Hamas, Hezbollah) that is more embedded in local communities.

The identity crisis among youngsters from secure, conservative families is manifest when, during adolescence, they turn a critical eye on the world from the perspective of the religious values instilled in them by their family and become aware of a certain social *schizophrenia* in the form of a disconnect between genuine faith, with its exacting ethical precepts, and real life, with all of its compromises and expediency. They see a discrepancy between the ideal in the form of the life of the Prophet Mohammed, and their own life with its mistakes, ignorance and moral inconsistencies, between the organisation of an idealised Muslim society (*umma*) of the "Golden Age" of the Prophet and the first Four Rightly Guided Caliphs, and the functioning of today's corrupt and unjust society teetering on the brink of modern barbarism (*jahiliyyah*).

The conversion of young practising Muslims to political Islam is thus a process involving a *dawning* awareness of the social dimension of Islam and a reflection upon its politically relevant implications. It involves a reflection upon those aspects of faith that the traditional apolitical Islam of their conservative parents did not emphasise, because it was more interested in the relationships between Man and God and not in the organisation of relationships between people. Unlike their parents' religion, this is very much an Islam subject to reflection, that must be studied diligently, thought about, understood, embraced and applied, and this requires responsibility and active commitment. It is not a traditional Islam, which is unproblematic and passed down passively from generation to generation as part of the unquestioned tradition of the community that does not seek to understand it in more depth (Hoffman 1995).

The impulse to seek a non-traditional, holistic reading of Islam that includes all aspects of individual and social life arises when young people confront the imperfect and contradictory world around them. Empirical studies of the influence of Islamists on young people show that the arguments used to recruit them primarily highlight egregious examples of the moral "depravity" of the world and the eye-popping corruption of politicians. The second step is to assert that genuine Muslims must change this state of affairs, because Islam urges its follows to promote the honourable and suppress the reprehensible. According to research conducted by Samia al-Khasbah at Cairo University (1988), most students knew the name and objectives of several Islamist organisations. Most of them declared that Islamists took the interests of young people into account (75%) and were sympathetic to them. Most of them (82%) opposed attempts by the government to suppress Islamists, since Islamists genuinely wanted to improve Egyptian society (cited in Starrett 1998). Political Islam as an ideology of the young enjoys success because it seemingly connects to and develops the familiar foundations acquired from the family and school education, even though it represents discontinuity more than continuity, and also because since the end of the 1960s secular ideology has been discredited and has failed to offer a credible alternative (Hoffman 1995).

(2) THE LEISURE OF THE "ARAB STREET": A BLESSING OR A CURSE?

On his blog entitled Saudi Jeans (saudijeans.blogspot.com), the Saudi student Ahmad writes with frustration (8 May 2006): "Riyadh is a living hell for guys like me. There is nothing to do and nowhere to go: no cinema, no theatre, no parks, no nothing. The segregation of the sexes is way too extreme, and most people here think this is Islamic. I'm afraid it is not. In fact, it is pathogenic, psychologically and socially. The ban on entering shopping malls for young men makes it a challenge for those boys. So, sneaking in and hooking up with some girl has become an achievement that the boys show off and are proud of. Riyadh is a dead city from inside, and it really needs to get a life. Now, I just want to finish my studies and get the hell out of here" (Šisler 2006). The television preacher Amr Khaled (Khaled 2011: 69), popular amongst young people, explains youthful revolutionary feelings thus: "Nobody listens to them. Nobody offers them hope. So much talent and energy that has no outlet. No work. Not even a place to play football."

We see that, along with adolescence, leisure time is also making an appearance in this age group, until recently an unprecedented phenomenon in the Middle East on such a mass scale. For instance, in Algeria a term has been invented for the conspicuous and unsettling presence of groups of disaffected youths wandering the streets aimlessly and leaning against walls at every corner. The term is *"hitistes"*, or "those who lean against the wall".

The arrival of leisure time available to the masses also brought with it the danger of political destabilisation in modernising Europe of the 19th and early 20th century. In pre-modern Europe, with the exception of the aristocracy, leisure time was virtually non-existent. Even those times when work was not being directly performed were significantly associated with work and the physical reproduction of society (e.g. rituals invoking rain or a fine harvest). Leisure is a product of modern society: shorter working hours, a reduction in child labour, longer life expectancy and pension systems, as well as the forced unemployment of the proletariat (see Marx's "reserve army of labour").These days it is again being discussed as a danger of post-industrial societies[15]. What is important is whether this is forced leisure and therefore humiliating and frustrating (involuntary unemployment) or a chance for some well earned regeneration, entertainment and relaxation from work or studies. Also politically relevant is how such time is filled: by consumerism, sport, civil involvement or opposition activities (Kloskowska 1967).

Adolescence offers young people from well-off Middle Eastern families new opportunities. However, for the offspring of poorer people it entails frustration and a lack of hope regarding the future. While Egyptian teenagers from the new business classes ride around in luxury cars, wear the latest trends in designer clothes and spend the summer in seaside resorts, most of their peers cannot even rely on the traditional and until recently common expectation of finding accommodation and starting a family (Amin 2000, 2011). Similarly, the "gilded youth" of Casablanca in Morocco and Beirut in Lebanon lead an active nightlife, study at universities around the world and enjoy a similar lifestyle to young people in Western cities. However, the majority of their peers can expect only poorly paid and precarious work in the risky grey economy (Booth 2002).

A problem then arises when the poverty of one group comes into direct confrontation with the conspicuous consumption of the other (Booth 2002). One of the many reflections on this acute problem in literature is by the Egyptian writer Alaa Al Aswany in his novel *The Yacoubian Building* (2002: 104): "And in fact from the first moment, just as oil separates from water and forms a distinct layer on top, so the rich students separated themselves from the poor and made up numerous closed coteries formed of graduates from foreign language schools and those with their own cars, foreign clothes and imported cigarettes. It was to these that the most beautiful and best-dressed girls gravitated. The poor students, on the other hand, clung to one another like terrified mice, whispering to one another in an embarrassed way."

Leisure time reflecting social inequality leads to class *resentment*: that which forms the object of desire and admiration is also the target of criticism and rejection if it cannot be attained (Keller 1990). Conservatives of the lower and middle classes often believe that the model provided by the upper classes regarding how to spend free time leads to ennui, alcoholism, casual sex and sin: "Eyes born of the passion of the night. The voice of the sun. Passion. Whimsy. Satisfaction. Solar ardour. Pain. Boredom. Departure. Waiting for winter to wash away the sins of summer. This is the story of every year

---

15   The potentially destabilising consequences of shorter working hours and the expansion of the leisure sphere was written about by T. G. Masaryk, who wondered how leisure time would be filled. The risks of forced leisure in modern Western societies are examined by Ulrich Beck and Ralph Dahrendorf (Pongs 2000).

in Agami." This is a typically moralising report published in the magazine Rose al-Yūsuf on an Egyptian "prostitute", i.e. a young, single woman, from a private beach near Alexandria that was created after the neoliberal reforms (*infitah*). A contrast is provided with the "respectable" beach for the general public nearby, where bathing is a family affair, women cover themselves up, and Western bathing costumes, cigarettes and alcohol have no place (Armbrust 2007: 104).

The expanding mass of young people and their free time has a destabilising potential that regimes are attempting to neutralise. In order to do this, since the 1990s they have been establishing specialised ministries of youth and sports (e.g. the Palestinian National Authority in 1994, Egypt 1998) and creating national strategies to deal with the young. They want to employ young people *apolitically* by offering leisure programmes and channelling their energy in a harmless way. A similar function is performed by the legalisation of apolitical non-profit organisations that distance themselves from opposition activities and criticism of the regime. These can absorb the energy of an ambitious and active segment of the young that would otherwise tend to seek self-realisation in politics. For instance, the legalisation of the non-profit sector in Morocco (1999) keeps young people occupied during the "politically risky" summer holidays. The importance of ministries of youth for social control can be seen in the fact that positions in them are filled by leading figures of the power elite. These positions are not simply sinecures for politicians reaching the end of their career. They were filled, for example, by Hussein Uday, son of the Iraqi dictator, by Bouteflika before he became president of Algeria, or by the Egyptian Ali Disouqi, mentor and advisor to Gamal Mubarak. In addition, the regimes supervise, control and discipline the young by means of compulsory military service or civilian service in youth and student organisations. Dictators alarmed by the increasing numbers of disaffected youth act the part of a caring, protective Great Father and make every effort to appear as though they care for the future of the young generation (Swedenburg 2007, Youth Development in the ESCWA Region 2010).

However, in this respect, cumbersome, ineffective states lag behind the more active, flexible Islamists and other opposition groups. They failed to detect the development of leisure time soon enough. Islamists are in direct contact with the "Arab street" and have a head start over the dictators of several years when it comes to appealing to the young. For example, in Egypt both the Muslim Brotherhood and radicals such as *Gamaa Al-Islamiya organise attractive weekend trips for young people and summer camps for children similar to scout camps.* They offer opportunities to escape the city pollution, sightseeing trips, swimming in the sea and sports, all combined with interpretations of Islam and joint prayers. They also offer constructive afterschool activities such as Quran readings, special tutoring, clubs and sports. The state is often unable to compete and resorts instead to repression, arrests and propaganda campaigns aimed against the organisers and participants of such activities (Starrett 1998, Kepel 2002).

(3) THE ATTITUDES AND ASPIRATIONS OF YOUNG PEOPLE ON THE EVE OF REVOLUTION: THE CONFLICT BETWEEN HOPES AND REALITY

One young man from Algiers, caught in the trap of uneven modernisation, described his generation's experience on the eve of civil war in the 1990s: "You have only four options. You can remain unemployed and celibate, because without a family you can't start a family and find a flat. You can work on the black market and risk being arrested. You can try to emigrate to Europe and sweep the streets of Paris. Or you can join the Islamic Salvation Front and vote for Islam" (cited in Booth 2002). Since he said those words, the situation in the region has got worse. The frustration of young people in the lead up to the Jasmine Revolution in Tunisia was summed up by the rapper El Général. In his song *Rais Lebled* (Head of State) he declaims in outrage: "My President, your country is dead. People are eating from garbage, there is poverty everywhere you look. I'm speaking in the name of people who suffer. I have no fear, even though I know I will do myself harm". The song resonated with the feelings of the "lost generation" of the entire region, and was broadcast by the television network Al-Jazeera and played in Cairo's Tahrir Square during the Egyptian January 25 Revolution (cited in Turek 2011).

A unique sociological study entitled *The Arab Millennials* (2008) conducted on the eve of the Arab revolutions described in detail the aspirations and attitudes of young Arabs aged 18–24 (Egypt, Jordan and four Gulf states were compared with Germany, Great Britain and the USA) and with prescience stated: "Boosted by technology, this generation has unprecedented access to information and an unparalleled ability to communicate and organise by means of social networks. For this reason an inordinate ability is concentrated in its hands to influence politicians, who will have to take it seriously." A similar survey carried out by the Gallup organisation of young people (15–29 years old, 16,000 respondents in 20 countries of the League of Arab States) on the eve of revolution entitled *The Silatech Index* (2011) examined how they rated their career prospects and life opportunities. What do these surveys tell us about young Arab people?

Young Arabs do similar things to their peers in the West. They use the same technology and share the same lifestyle and aspirations. Most own mobile telephones (87%) and are in constant touch with friends or parents by text messages. Most (86%) check the internet at least once a day. They send emails, use social networks, surf for information, download photographs, music and videos, and follow the news as closely as their counterparts in the West. However, lower purchasing power and higher unemployment means that young Arabs do not use internet banking or buy goods via the internet as often. On the other hand they often look for friends and partners on the web.

Adolescent Arabs are equally fashion conscious as their Western counterparts. In their own words they are constantly worried about how they look. They spend most of their money on designer clothes and shoes, and on the contracts they have with mobile operators. Just like Western adolescents, Arabs look to global brands such as Nokia, Sony, Toyota, Nike, Macdonald and Toshiba. Local brands such as Emirates Airlines and Al Jazeera are only slightly less popular. However, a fifth of those questioned (23%) are frustrated that they do not have enough money for personal consumption (the figure is 10% in the West). Lack of money means that, compared to their Western peers, young Arabs go less often to the cinema, do not buy so much music, so many books, magazines, and do not own as many audio players. The gap between the Middle East and the West is smaller in terms of ownership of computers and laptops. Arabs do not save as much, and this unfortunately is a prerequisite for starting a family. The desire to travel and get to know foreign countries is as strong as in the West, though in reality Arabs travel far less (e.g. 70% of young Egyptians have never been abroad). Most would like to travel to Europe, though similarly popular are destinations in the Gulf and the Levant.

In terms of role models, young Arabs most often look to their parents (44%, in the West this figure is 67%). As opposed to the West, teachers, university lecturers and religious leaders play a significant role (31% versus 5% in the West), along with successful businessmen and politicians, who are far less popular in the West. Young Arabs consider the life coordinates defining the human personality to be mainly religious faith (68% versus 16% in the West), family (64%) and friends (61%). Similarly, the measure of success in life is deemed to be a healthy, happy family. However, unlike their Western peers, on the second rung of a meaningful life young Arabs place nonmaterial and spiritual matters, such as an attempt to improve the world (34% versus 12%) or "spiritual enlightenment". On the contrary, in the West young people see money and career as a successful measure of success in life.

As far as their professional aspirations are concerned, young Arabs are far more likely to dream of the technological and engineering sectors. A political career also enjoys far more popularity in the region than it does in the West. Conversely, law and the humanities are not popular. Young Arabs do not only expect a decent salary and self-fulfilment from their professions, but, as opposed to their peers in Germany, the UK and the USA, they would like to work for a firm that makes a contribution to the local community. They also want their work to contribute to the development of their country, with two thirds of respondents expressing this patriotic dream.

It is here that the sharpest conflict with reality takes place. Young people regard unemployment as the biggest problem (75%). Lack of freedom and the violation of human rights come a close second (71%). They are also concerned by the uncontrollable rise in inflation and the cost of living, the lack of affordable housing, the impact of corruption, and the erosion of traditional values. They rate the economic condition of their countries and their future with pessimism. Only a minority (41%) are convinced that they have sufficient opportunities for a successful career. And only a small majority (53%) believe that they enjoy greater opportunities than their parents did. In this respect education systems are seen as a key problem, which, they argue, do not teach the skills needed on the labour market and in the professions that degree courses are supposed to be preparing them for (86%).

Reality is frustrating for Middle Eastern young people. It does not offer sufficient opportunities for them to participate in economic and political life, which is what they yearn for. However, they are not apathetic or resigned. They do not yet seek escape in drugs, gangs and alcohol, nor do they offer blind allegiance to political radicals. Most young people (Esposito and Mogahed 2008) remain convinced of the need for basic justice, life opportunities, work, stability, and the possibility of marrying and starting a family. The modest aspirations of young Egyptians on the eve of revolution were summed up by Dina, a student: "Young people have modest ambitions. We want to live a normal, comfortable life, find a job and a partner and get married." However, even these modest dreams seem unattainable (Herrera 2009).

(4) A LOST GENERATION: THE POPULATION DYNAMIC VERSUS A COLLAPSING LABOUR MARKET

The websites and blogs of the up-and-coming generation of the Muslim Brotherhood in Egypt show that they have similar aspirations to those of young people in the West. They write of their families, friends, and their favourite films and music. However, in addition to religion they also often address topics such as unemployment, the economic situation, inflation or the housing crisis, which are not subjects that trouble the minds of most European and American teenagers (Lynch 2007). Young Arabs cite the lack of jobs as the most pressing problem of all seven social problems assessed (45%). Other problems, such as poverty and repression, come much further down the scale. Their lack of prospects sees every other Arab teenager longs to emigrate abroad, most often to Western Europe, the USA, or to wealthier Arab countries (AHDR 2002)[16].

The most dramatic expression of frustration was a series of self-immolations by men unable to find decent jobs (2010–2011). This is a phenomenon hitherto unknown in the region, and is all the more shocking because Islam forbids suicide under any circumstances[17]. The case of twenty-six year old Tunisian Mohamed Bouazizi was crucial, since it sparked off the domino effect of the Arab revolutions because millions of others identified with his fate. Since childhood Mohamed had studied at the same time as working in order to support his mother and sick father and to enable his younger sisters to attend school. Though he wanted to continue his studies, at the age of nineteen he was forced to leave school for financial reasons. He applied to join the army but was unsuccessful. Other attempts to find work in the formal sector were also unsuccessful. He supported himself and his family by selling vegetables on the street that he purchased with borrowed money. However, he had no business licence and thus operated like so many others in the grey economy, where he was vulnerable. He became the target of blackmail by the police and the authorities, who confiscated his goods and demanded bribes.

Tab. 12 Unemployment rate by macroregion in 2005 and 2011 (in %)

Region	2005	2011
Middle East (MENA)	13.2	10.2 (10.9)*
Sub-Saharan Africa	9.7	8.2
South America	7.7	7.2
Central Europe and CIS	9.7	8.6
East Asia	3.8	4.1
Southeast Asia	6.1	4.7
OECD	6.7	8.5

Source: ILO (2012). For 2005 cited in Richards and Waterbury (2008: 134)
* 10.2% relates to the Middle East and 10.9% to North Africa.

---

16 A survey of young people (aged 15–20) from Egypt, Jordan, Lebanon, Libya and the United Arab Emirates. However, the sample was not randomised and was limited in numbers (240 respondents). Though it included different classes and both genders, the results cannot be reliably generalised.

17 A similar innovation, controversial from the perspective of classical Islam, was the suicidal martyrdom of Iranian volunteers in minefields during the war with Iraq (1980–88), during which young people received the key to Paradise from the regime. Iran was thus able to compensate for the technical superiority of Saddam Hussein's Iraqi army, which was supported by the Arab and Western world. Hezbollah, allied with Iran, then used suicide bombings against the occupation by the USA, France and Israel. Palestinian organisations present in Lebanon then adopted the tactic and thus it entered the Sunni world, whence it ended up in Al Qaida (Kepel 2008).

His last conflict with the corrupt police and authorities ended when he set himself on fire on the steps of the Town Hall on 17 December 2011 (Ryan 2011).

The Middle East has the highest unemployment in the world, higher for a long time than other macroregions (tab. 12)[18]. It is the most serious problem facing the region and contributed to pre-revolutionary and post-revolutionary instability and radicalism. Most troubling is the status of young people, amongst whom there is higher unemployment than in the older generation, even on an international scale. This is a generational problem. The Middle East is facing huge influx of young graduates onto the labour market. Before the revolution (2010) youth unemployment stood at 27% in the Middle East and 20% in North Africa, compared to a global average of 12% (tab. 13). In the cities unemployment is in the tens of percentage points, and in poorer neighbourhoods the figure can be as high as 80% (ILO 2013, Richards and Waterbury 2008).

Tab. 13 Youth unemployment by macroregion 2008–2011 (in %)

Region	2008	2009	2010	2011
Middle East	25.3	25.5	27.4	27.7
Men	*21.7*	*22.2*	*23.7*	*23.8*
Women	*39.3*	*38.2*	*41.7*	*42.1*
North Africa	20.3	20.4	20.1	23.3
Men	*16.8*	*16.0*	*15.7*	*17.8*
Women	*29.1*	*31.7*	*31.0*	*37.1*
Sub-Saharan Africa	11.8	11.8	11.8	11.7
South America	13.5	15.4	14.0	13.3
Central Europe and CIS	17.0	20.4	19.3	17.9
East Asia	9.1	9.2	8.9	9.2
Southeast Asia	14.4	14.3	13.8	13.1
South Asia	8.5	9.4	9.7	9.2
OECD	13.3	17.4	18.1	17.6
World	11.7	12.7	12.5	12.3
Men	*11.5*	*12.5*	*12.3*	*12.1*
Women	*11.9*	*12.8*	*12.7*	*12.6*

Source: ILO, Global Employment Trends for Youth. A generation at risk (2013)
N.B.: The figures refer to young people aged 15–24

---

18 Unlike the International Labour Organisation, data from the World Bank puts the Middle East in second place after Sub-Saharan Africa because of a different methodology used. However, the gravity of the situation remains clear.

While a secondary or tertiary education represented a guarantee of finding work quickly, middle-class status, and lifelong affluence for the generations of their parents and grandparents, this is no longer the case. Yet young people's career expectations based on their academic qualifications remain as high as ever (Richards and Waterbury 2008). Young people (aged 15–24) account for half (44.7%) of all the unemployed, though the situation in individual countries differs (see tab. 14). For instance, in Iran, four times as many young people are unemployed as people older than 30, and this corresponds to the average in the Middle East (ILO 2012: 33). In Egypt, seven times as many young people are unemployed as adults. From 1998 to 2008 more than half a million young people have joined the ranks of the unemployed every year. After the start of the global economic crisis in 2008, this figure was 700,000 in the years leading up to the Arab revolutions (ILO 2013: 81). Conservative estimates believe that the next twenty years will see a further 50 million well educated young people join the ranks of the unemployed. Migratory pressures will increase (in the direction of the West and the Gulf States), as well as pressure for regime change (Laqueur 2004).

Tab. 14 Youth unemployment (among people aged 15–24) in selected Arab countries

Country (year of survey)	Unemployment level among men (in %)	Unemployment level among women (in %)	Proportion of young people of total unemployment (in %)
Bahrain (2001)	17.0	27.0	54.0 (2001)
Egypt (2002)	21.0	40.0	67.1 (2006)
Jordan (2005)	28.0	50.0	---
Kuwait (1995)	16.0	8.0	---
Lebanon (1997)	24.0	14.0	48.1 (2004)
Palestine (2004)	39.0	45.0	---
Qatar (2004)	8.0	30.0	70.4 (2004)
Saudi Arabia (2002)	25.0	39.0	50.9 (2007)
Syria (2003)	16.0	36.0	57.0 (2003)
SAE (1995)	6.0	6.0	33.4 (2005)
Yemen (2003)	21.0	14.0	---

Source: Youth Development in the ESCWA Region. ESCWA, United Nations, 2010.

Even though new jobs are being created in the region on a relatively dynamic basis (see tab. 15), supply is growing more slowly than the year-on-year increase in the demand of graduates seeking work. The divide between population growth, the numbers of ambitious young people with secondary school or university diplomas, and the absorption capacity of a labour market limited by the pace of economic growth is wider than for instance in Mexico, India, and other developing countries that face a similarly explosive situation. Compared to 1990, every year the labour market is being joined by 40% (Tunisia) up to 125% (Syria) more jobseekers. And yet simply to maintain the current, albeit critically high unemployment rate, the economy of the Middle East would have to create new jobs four times as fast as that of the USA, an unrealistic prospect to say the least (Richards and Waterbury 2008).

Tab. 15 The speed at which new jobs are being created by macroregions 2002–2011 (in %)

Region	Average annual rate 2002–2007	Average annual rate 2008–2011
Middle East	4.5	3.2
North Africa	3.4	2.0
Sub-Saharan Africa	3.1	2.8
South America	2.5	1.9
Central Europe and SNS	1.1	0.8
East Asia	1.2	0.6
Southeast Asia	1.8	1.9
South Asia	2.2	1.0
OECD	1.0	–0.3
World	1.8	1.1

Source: ILO, Global Employment Trends (2012: 38)

In addition, a new stratum is emerging of educated, ambitious young women, who do not want simply to spend their whole lives raising children and taking care of the household, as did their mothers. They want careers and are entering an already overburdened labour market. For instance, these days there are more women than men studying at university in the United Arab Emirates, and the situation is similar in Kuwait, Bahrain and Iran. In 1980 only 5.3% of women worked in the Emirates. In 1990 this figure was 16.3% and by the end of the millennium it had reached 40% (Hejlová 2004). In Turkey, though the proportion of women, especially poorer women, on the formal labour market has dropped over recent years, among the middle and upper classes women are highly represented in the prestigious professions; women account for 28% of Turkish lawyers and judges, 54% of doctors, and 45% of bankers and financial analysts. Many women are teachers and thus serve as a role model to the schoolgirls they teach, demonstrating in practice that a woman's place is not only in the home (Ayata 2004). Furthermore, urban middle class women are often forced to take a job because their husbands' income is insufficient to maintain the family's standard of living due to economic stagnation or neoliberal economic reforms (Lubeck and Britts 2002, Frouzová 2004). The impact of this social and cultural change on the growth of youth unemployment is gradually outweighing the influence of simple numerical demographic growth. A generational problem is also becoming a gender issue, since there are twice as many unemployed young female graduates (see tabs. 13 and 14) as male graduates in the region (Richards and Waterbury 2008).

Everything is complicated by the *dual* character of the labour market. Increasingly, young people occupy positions that do not correspond to their educational qualifications and do not ensure sufficient income to cover their basic needs, let alone to buy an apartment and start a family. Secondary school graduates are obliged to work as manual labourers, taxi drivers or hotel receptionists. University graduates often spend many years without work registered on waiting lists for the dreamed of positions in the public sector that were the very reason they pursued their studies (lifelong job security, guaranteed promotion and social prestige). The absorption capacity of a public sector that has been expanding for several decades has been exhausted due to overemployment or inefficiency, and this has made it the target of neoliberal reforms, deregulation and privatisation. Not even the region's private sector, which still comprises the smallest segment on the labour market, offers many opportunities. As a result, graduates are again being squeezed into the fastest growing *informal* or grey economy on the border of illegality, which accounts for 40% (Syria) up to 55% (Egypt) of jobs (excluding agriculture) and generates between a fifth and a third of gross domestic product. For instance, in Egypt in 1970 the informal sector created 20% of all new jobs: at the end of the 20th century this figure was 60%. Hazardous work in the unregistered and untaxed grey economy is characterised by low incomes, low qualifications, lack of career development, the absence of social security insurance and any legal protection, fluctuation, seasonality, and insecurity (Richards and Waterbury 2008).

Islamists create hope among young unemployed people with slogans such as "Islam is the solution!". Under the circumstances described their message can be appealing, since they often see the place of women as being in the home, while the man is the breadwinner. An obsession with the "woman question" then grows along with the arrival of women on an overburdened labour market, where they compete with their male peers (Hoffman 1995, Richards and Waterbury 2008). Iranian Islamists, for instance, issued the following warning: "Women want to control everything!" (Frouzová 2004)[19]. Nevertheless,

---

19 Iranian Islamists displayed the ability to adapt Islam flexibly to their needs. In the spirit of Islamic feminism during the revolution against dictatorship (1977–9) women mobilised on the

women are just as likely to sympathise with Islamists as men. The Muslim Brotherhood, Hamas and Hezbollah mobilise both sexes in their conflict with the enemy, while underplaying the emancipatory potential of Islam contained in the legacy of the Prophet and his wives and daughters (Mendel 2008). According to the movement's mainstream thought, women should study, fight, participate in the public sphere and work at least until their wedding, as long as they are appropriately veiled at all times (Roy 1992). The Muslim headscarf and attire thus serve as a way of permitting freedom of movement and involvement in modern society to women, and not as a medieval instrument of female subordination and enslavement (Burgat 2002, Pipes 1996).

The appeal of the Islamists derives more from their offer of experience or work to graduates in charity organisations (doctors, teachers, sharia compliant finance). Islamists also regulate relations in the informal economy ignored or criminalised by the state and operated outside of the rule of law. Vulnerable workers have no recourse to trade unions or the courts and are therefore exploited. The Islamists sometimes protect them, insist on informal contracts being enforced, and punish unscrupulous employers. Interest-free Islamic banking offers loans to those in the informal sector who would be overlooked by high street banks (Lubeck and Britts 2002, Kepel 2002). However, unemployed young people can be equally well radicalised in the name of liberal democratic or secular leftwing movements, or even in the name of anti-regime movements that have no ideology or leader, as the Arab Spring showed (cf. Bayat 2010).

(5) DEMOGRAPHIC MARGINALISATION AND THE MARRIAGE CRISIS

Not only are young people aspiring to a middle class status no better off than their parents or grandparents in terms of realising their modern dreams, they are actually worse off even in terms of traditional, conventional and hitherto easily attainable aspirations, since in addition to the crisis on the labour market, young people in the Middle East are facing a *crisis on the marriage market*. Socio-economic marginalisation is thus accompanied by *demographic marginalisation*[20].

---

streets. They justified their public activism with reference to the "emancipated" daughter of the Prophet, Fatima, or his granddaughter Zaynab, whom they took as their models. After the revolution, however, women were excluded from the public sphere, again in the name of Islam (Hoffman 1995).

20 Marginalisation is associated with the absolute or relative poverty of a section of the population of a given society. It leads to the deracination and social vulnerability of those whom poverty or unemployment pushes to the peripheries of society.

In conservative societies that place great store by large families (cf. Esposito and Mogahed 2008) and ascribe unambiguously positive status to children and adults, adolescence represents a sensitive period. Social status and an individual's prestige derive from their family and children, and a wedding is regarded as a clear and necessary rite of passage between childhood and adulthood. A functioning family is therefore the basic measure of success and a key objective of most young people. Until recently it was common for people to get married at a very young age, soon after reaching sexual maturity. Today the numbers of single people in their twenties and thirties who are caught in an ever-widening trap between childhood and adulthood is growing rapidly, and their social status in conservative societies is vague, and in the case of young women, a source of stigma. They are no longer children and yet do not have their own children and family. They therefore have nothing from which to derive prestige and social status, and this damages their self-image. They begin to regard themselves as failures, which is how they come to be perceived within their conservative community. Things are made more complicated by sexual frustration, since premarital and extramarital relations are strictly forbidden in conservative societies. On top of that, conservative cultures frown on the development of a culture of leisure time, during which young people might attain some kind of meaningful self-realisation (Juergensmeyer 2000). In Western liberal societies too, young people are opting to get married later in life. However, this is more about freedom of choice and there is no stigma attached.

According to the Brookings Institute (2007), delayed marriage affects approximately half of men aged 25–29. A census carried out in Egypt (2006) shows that a total of 5.7 million singles fall into this age bracket, while previous generations were already long since married at this age (Kholoussy 2010). In her Egyptian pre-revolutionary bestseller *I Want to Get Married*, later made into a successful TV serial, the pharmacist and blogger Ghada Abdel Aal says (2010: 88) that up to 15 million single young women longing to get married live in her country. In this autobiographical work she describes the desperation of young women with humour but also compassion: "In this situation I was willing to get married to any living multi-celled organism whatsoever as long as it was willing to snatch me out of the storefront of singledom."

Demographic marginalisation and the marriage crisis has been caused by (Starrett 1998, Kholoussy 2010): (a) the prolongation of studies, (b) the difficulty in finding a job that meets the relatively high aspirations of increasingly qualified graduates, (c) a focus on career in the case of both men and women, (d) an escalating housing crisis leading to the unavailability of affordable housing, (e) inflation devaluing savings for a wedding and a young couple's start in life, (f) the growing resistance of young people to marriages arranged by their parents and the new tendency for young women to be more selective when reacting to the advances of suitors, (g) the modern commercialisation of what were always costly wedding banquets, now serving as a status symbol (cf. Amin 2004), and (h) a trend toward exorbitantly expensive traditional gifts, jewellery and cash being showered on the bride that theoretically will secure her for life in the event of divorce.

Demographic marginalisation was long interpreted from the perspective of young men, who were regarded as its victim. However, single women without children and their own family are stigmatised even more in conservative societies: "From childhood onwards a young boy in Egypt is asked what he wants to be when he grows up. Girls of the same age are asked whom they want to marry. And to the general merriment of all, they normally reply their father" (cited in Aal 2010: 13). Single women are not fulfilling their clear social role and without a husband, family and children their social status is very low. Similarly, premarital sex is even more frowned on in adolescent females than men, since the honour and reputation of the entire family depends on the "purity" of its female members and the virginity of the daughters. A daughter's "purity" maintains her value on the marriage market. If she loses her reputation, her chance of marriage is even lower. As a result, girls wear headscarves and cover themselves up modestly so as to demonstrate their purity and increase their value on an overburdened marriage market. However, more and more women are insisting that society must accept them even if they remain single and childless, the likelihood of which for many people in their thirties in the Middle East is becoming greater and greater (Frouzová 2007, Kholoussy 2010).

Islamists view the marriage crisis as a sign of the incompetence of secular regimes and the dysfunctionality of their ideologies, or as the consequence of the pursuit of corrupt interests by a narrow elite that ignores the interests of the largest generation. Within the framework of Islamic civil society they offer newlyweds interest-free loans or organise joint weddings in order to cut costs. They inveigh against the trend for expensive wedding banquets and luxury wedding presents, and as part of the "discovery of tradition" emphasise the more moral virtues of discretion and modesty with appeals to the idealised beginnings of Islam. In some cases the movement functions as a kind of dating agency that searches out partners for its members. For instance, the Egyptian *Takfir wal Hijra* recruited many women as potential wives for its members. In a similar fashion the Muslim Brotherhood organises the Muslim Sisterhood, and weddings often take place between male and female members of the movement (Hoffman 1995, Kholoussy 2010).

Above all, militant religious movements offer single young men four alternative paths to self-realisation and *empowerment* instead of self-realisation in terms of profession, partner, family or leisure. Firstly, there is *psychological* empowerment. Militants are motivated to further action by the newly acquired feeling of power manifest in media interest and an influence on social and political events comparable with that of the state authorities (Treblin 2004: 127). Secondly, there is *symbolic* empowerment. By sharing an ideology of cosmic war, militants convince themselves they are virtuous warriors fighting on the side of God in a primordial metaphysical conflict with the advancing forces of evil in the variety of refined guises they take (e.g. in the form of a secular regime society or an occupying force). At the same time they are continuing the legendary battles fought by famous martyrs in the past, whose comrades-in-arms and successors they take themselves to be. They can thus change the course of history while giving meaning to their lives. Thirdly, there is the *social* empowerment made possible by the "surrogate family" of the organisation and comrades. This offers a feeling of belonging, success and recognition by others. The bonds formed between "brothers" are very strong, and this is manifest in increased levels of self-sacrifice and heroism in action and in the unleashing of a cycle of violence in an attempt to avenge the fallen. Also important, be it for real or assumed, is the approval of family and broader community from which the militants are recruited and in whose interest they feel they are acting. This too contributes to the social empowerment of terrorists, motivates them in action and drives them forward[21]. Fourthly, there may be *gender* empowerment in the form of "radical patriarchy", according to which the place of men is in the public sphere and the place of women in the home. Women are to admire men and look up to them, while men dominate women and protect them. This offers male militants additional self-esteem (Juergensmeyer 2000, 2006, 2008).

However, demographic marginalisation and the marriage crisis can give rise to a completely non-ideological opposition to compromised Middle Eastern regimes. For instance, the three most frequently chanted slogans by young revolutionaries on Tahrír Square after the resignation was announced of President Mubarak were: "Hold your head up high, you're Egyptian!" (a reaction to decades of humiliation and despair), "Everyone who loves Egypt, come and rebuild it!" (a patriotic readiness to sacrifice themselves for the nation), and "We're going to get married and have children!" (a reaction to the marriage crisis caused by the lack of housing and jobs as well as an expression of hope in a brighter future for the new regime) (cited in Idle and Nunns 2011: 9–10).

---

21   This applies to socially embedded terrorism (religious nationalists such as Hamas, Hezbollah and the IRA). This is integrated within communities and shares their values, including the culture of violence. The opposite is socially uprooted terrorism (the leftist, anarchist 1970s and 80s, Al-Qaeda), in which militants have severed ties with their communities of origin and do not share their values. Social empowerment is then provided only by their comrades-in-arms (Horgan 2005, Roy 2006, Pape 2006).

(6) THE GENERATIONAL ALIENATION OF THE POWER ELITE: THE OLD CADRES VERSUS THE YOUNG POPULATION

While 70% of Saudi Arabians are younger than 30 and the median age of the population is only 19, the average age of Saudi ministers is 65. The current King Salman is 80 years old and his predecessor King Abdullah reigned until he was 90 (2015). The ruling elite includes other members of the al-Saud family over 80 years old and suffering from Alzheimer's disease, diabetes and osteoporosis. Extreme cases include several princes who have occupied ministerial or gubernatorial seats for many decades. For instance, the governor of the Northern Borders Province has been in office since 1956 (The Economist, 5 March 2011). Similarly, at the start of the millennium the average age of ministers in Mubarak's government was 62, while half of the Egyptian population was younger than 25. In general, the president's closest collaborators and key figures in the first circle of power were of the generation born in the 1930s: the Ministers of Foreign Affairs Moussa and Maher, the Chief of General Intelligence Service Omar Suleiman, the Minister of the Interior Habib al-Adly, Prime Minister Ebeid, and the Minister of Defence and Military Production Tantawi. They entrenched themselves on the upper rungs of politics after the Arab-Israeli war of 1973 (Gombár 2009).

Governments in the region are alienated from young people not only because they did not come by their power through fair, democratic elections and have no idea how to solve their problems, but also because of the gulf dividing their generational experiences. While in the West, the former Soviet Union or Japan political leaders tend to share the same generational experience with most of the population they govern, in the Middle East ageing despots rule over extremely young populations (Richards and Waterbury 2008). One cannot help but observe that the Arab revolutions took place in countries where the heads of state have held onto power the longest: Tunisia (since 1987), Egypt (1981), Yemen (1978), Libya (1969) (see tab. 16). It was here that the largest collision took place between dynamic demographic growth and a rigid political system incapable of generational change and unable to resolve the problem of succession.

Parents and grandparents tend to support dictators or at least tolerate their corruption and failures. They received benefits from the new jobs created after independence was won and from the reforms being implemented at that time (land reform, seizure of the assets of colonialists). They remember the glorious beginnings of the era of dictatorships and the ethos of the struggle for national liberation during which several of the founders of the regime distinguished themselves (Kepel 2002). For instance, right up until the revolution the Egyptian regime attempted to maintain its legitimacy by appealing to its status as "the generation of October 1973", a reference to the

Tab. 16 Ageing Arab regimes and dictators in 2011 (countries of the League of Arab States)

Country	Head of state	Assumed power in	Year of birth
Algeria	Abdelaziz Bouteflika	1999	1937
Bahrain	Hamad bin Isa Al Khalifa	1999	1950
Comoro Islands	Ahmed Sambi	2006	1958
Djibouti	Ismaïl Omar Guelleh	1999	1947
Egypt	Hosni Mubarak	1981	1928
Iraq	Nouri al-Maliki	2006	1950
Jordan	Abdullah II	1999	1962
Kuwait	Sabah Al-Ahmad Al-Sabah	2006	1929
Lebanon	Najib Mikati	2011	1955
Libya	Muammar Gaddafi	1969	1942
Mauretania	Mohamed Ould Abdel Aziz	2009	1956
Morocco	Mohammed VI	1999	1963
Oman	Sultan Qaboos bin Said Al Said	1970	1940
Palestine	Mahmoud Abbas	2005	1935
Qatar	Hamad bin Khalífa Al Thani	1995	1952
Saudi Arabia	King Abdullah	2005	1924
Somalia	Sheik Sharif Ahmed	2009	1964
Sudan	Omar al-Bashir	1989	1944
Syria	Bashar al-Assad	2000	1965
Tunisia	Zine el-Abidine Ben Ali	1987	1936
United Arab Emirates	Khalífa bin Zayed Al Nahyan	2004	1948
Yemen	Ali Abdullah Saleh	1978	1942

Source: compiled by the author from different sources

famous war with Israel in which the country managed to cross the Suez Canal and to win back Sinai. During a time of political crisis, President Mubarak also wrapped himself in the flag and reminded people of his stint as a fighter pilot (Droz-Vincent 2011). However, there are fewer and fewer people with the same historical memories as the political elite. For the young majority of the population this is the past, which has nothing to say regarding the problems of today. And so unlike their parents they are more willing to listen to opposition leaders, including Islamists, who in addition are often closer in age to the young (Kepel 2002).

The generation gap is also reflected in the inability of the power elite to listen, understand, respect and communicate appropriately with the young, majority population, which is no longer willing to accept the traditionally patronising, directive and arrogant style of those in power, reminiscent of a patriarchal father admonishing a naughty child (Lindsey 2011). The most obvious intergenerational alienation from the power elite relates to young, well educated graduates from the upper middle class, who have managed to find a foothold on the global labour market. These are the computer programmers, bankers or advertising executives who are well versed in the corporate culture of Western firms, a culture that lays an emphasis on creativity, fair competition, self-confidence, and above all the principle of *meritocracy*, in which a person's work is assessed on an impartial basis and their remuneration based purely on performance. When such progressive groups of people leave work in the evening, they do not leave their acquired values behind them and have no intention of subordinating themselves to the authoritarian government, but instead call for fair governance, transparency, respect to be shown by rulers for their citizens, and their maximum commitment. This changed paradigm then comes into conflict with the authoritarian paradigm of the regimes, which are insulted by the criticism they hear rather than encouraged to reflect and reform (Bowker 2013).

This gaping generation gap only began to narrow at the end of the 1990s, when there was a generational transformation of the power elites in certain countries (Jordan, Morocco, Syria and Palestine). However, this involved changes to personnel at the top of the power pyramids and not to the entire political, economic elite, which remains closed and rigid in terms of generations (Richards and Waterbury 2008, cf. Gombár 2001, 2007). This situation (cf. Galeotti 1998) is reminiscent of the gerontocracy of senile apparatchiks and generals in positions of supreme power in the Soviet Union during the declining era of Leonid Brezhnev or the crumbling prerevolutionary era of the Eastern bloc (East Germany, Romania, Czechoslovakia). Although power was held onto by an ageing elite of governing parties as in the Middle East, the local populations were nowhere near as young as in the modern Arab world, and the historical memory of the power elites and their subordinate masses was not so divergent. Many people remembered the heroism of the Red Army during the Second World War or the era of post-war successes and prestige of the USSR.

A similar generation gap affects the labour market, where young graduates are disadvantaged and excluded by an older generation already ensconced in comfortable positions. A role is played here by legislation that has the effect of stifling the economy and creating an inflexible labour market. In particular, legal regulations preventing small and medium sized enterprises, i.e. the backbone of economic growth in the region as the economic success of Turkey shows, from laying off employees who have worked six months or a year, represent an impediment to their continued expansion.

Excessive employee safeguards result in even prosperous firms having to be very cautious when taking on new workers. Job seekers suffer the most, who find themselves outside the economic system (Richards and Waterbury 2008). Another problem is the clientelism and institutionalised corruption in operation when work positions in the public sector are being filled. This also leads to a sizeable segment of the young generation being excluded and exacerbates intergenerational alienation. As the Egyptian writer Alaa Al Aswany writes in his novel *The Yacoubian Building* (2002: 76), the central character of which is a young, talented secondary school pupil Taha, who is unable to study at police academy because his father is but a poor door-man without connections: "Taha, this country doesn't belong to us, it belongs to the people who have money. If you'd had twenty thousand pounds and used them to bribe someone, do you think any one would have asked about your father's job? Make money (...) He started to imagine fantastic scenes of revenge: he saw himself, for example, delivering the generals on the committee a speech about equal opportunity, rights, and the justice that God and his Prophet – God bless him and grant him peace – had bidden us to. He went on rebuking them until they melted in shame for what they had done and apologised to him and announced his acceptance into the college."

The domestic situation in the Middle East is riven by the generational conflict between young, well educated cohorts excluded from power and solid economic prospects, and less educated, older generations that nonetheless have solid jobs, opportunities and economic resources. On a national level (cf. Huntington 1968) this is analogous to the explosive situation that reigned within the framework of military and bureaucratic hierarchies during the 1950s and 60s and culminated in political instability manifest in a series of military coups organised by young army officers. Older generals and bureaucrats, often without qualifications or any special skills, had managed to occupy the top rungs thanks to their connections and the serendipity of being in the right place at the right time, whereas well educated and ambitious middle cadres made up of captains, colonels and civil servants came to realise that they would remain forever in their current posts under the current political system and would climb no higher no matter how hard they tried. As a consequence they were more willing to participate in dangerous conspiracies to overthrow the regime, in the hope that the cards would be reshuffled, this time more favourably, and they would obtain better positions in the military and bureaucratic pyramids.

(7) THE UNEVEN POPULATION GROWTH OF DIFFERENT GROUPS WITHIN A HETEROGENEOUS STATE

The borders of many Middle Eastern states were redrawn by set square by their European colonial powers and did not therefore respect the spatial distribution of tribal, ethnic, religious or regional groups (cf. Fromkin 1989, Gombár 1999, Barr 2010, Rogan 2012). As a consequence, the vastly different pace of population growth among different ethnic, religious and tribal subpopulations living together in the territory of one artificial and highly heterogeneous post-colonial state formation leads to an escalation of political conflict, above all in situations in which these subpopulations differ in terms of their share of power and the distribution of economic profits, or there are visible differences in living standards. Uneven demographic developments between individual subpopulations then disrupt and undermine the established balance of power (Richards and Waterbury 2008). Outside the Middle East, the classic example is the former Yugoslavia. The different rate of population growth in individual ethnic groups in the decades prior to the civil war in the 1990s resulted in the Slavic Muslim Bosnians reporting a higher birth rate than the Serbs and Croats. Yet these latter two groups had enjoyed political and economic domination in the country from the Second World War onwards (Huntington 2001, Vulliamy 1994).

Within the Middle East the classic example is the still destabilised Lebanon heading towards civil war (1975–90). Between the world wars the country was dominated both politically and economically by Christian groups, with the minority Shiites marginalised in the south. The still valid National Pact (1943), confirmed by the Taif Agreement (1989), was based on a census of 1932 and divided power according to a strictly sectarian key: the president must be a Maronite Christian, the prime minister a Sunni, the Speaker of the Parliament a Shia and the head of the army a Druze. However, these days the distribution of power and economic resources has not responded to the sharp increase in the number of Shias. The power balance has been disturbed and the pace of demographic development does not correspond to the tempo of changes to the rigid political system. However, the political elite refuses to have a new census carried out and to reform a now obsolete political system dating back to the 1940s (Kepel 2002).

Since the state of Israel was founded in 1948 there has been a power imbalance between the dominant European Jews (the Ashkenazi) and the growing number of oriental Jews arriving from the Middle East (Sephardim) or countries of the former USSR. Everything is further complicated by the status of the discriminated Israeli Arabs (second category citizens). These make up 20% of the population of Israel, though their numbers and share of the population are growing (Ježová 2011, Tureček 2011). There are political reasons within the context of the Israeli-Palestine conflict that play a role in the value ascribed large families on both sides. For instance, the Palestinians see their higher birth rate as an effective, long-term "demographic weapon", which over time will act as a counterbalance to Israel's current military superiority. Large families are also seen as prestigious and socially desirable for purely patriotic reasons (Kropáček 1996).

The oppressed Kurds in Turkey, Syria and Iraq have a similar demographic weapon at their disposal. Their numbers are rising faster than those of the political and economically dominant ethnicity in these countries (Richards and Waterbury 2008). In the case of the Arab revolutions (2011) this mechanism clearly did not apply within relatively homogenous societies with a historically strong national identity and a long tradition of statehood (Egypt, Tunisia and Morocco). However, it did play a role in Bahrain, where a poor, growing population of majority Shiites (70% of the population as a whole) live in a restricted space (the fourth most densely populated area in the world) governed by the minority Sunni royal dynasty. However, neither population censuses nor government statistics record this potentially explosive data on the demographic development of both religious groups, and so these are my own estimates. Similarly, it is possible that a certain role was played by the higher population dynamic of Sunni Muslims (currently 74% of the population) from the peripheries during the destabilisation of the political system in Syria, which for decades has been based on the governing clan of Assads recruited from minority Alawites (approximately 12%) supported by other minorities (Christians 10%, Druzes 3%).

However, the Lebanese model, in which thanks to the long-term difference in population growth of key sub-populations the power balance of a rigid sectarian political system collapsed, does not apply in crystalline form. Syria and Bahrain are evidence of the long-term potential instability of a political system given by the government of a religious minority. Instability can also intensify along with the different rates of population growth. This instability is in my opinion systemic. Sub-populations long excluded from power are also deprived of economic resources. However, because they are less developed and poorer, their birth rates tend to be higher (see Lebanon and Bosnia). Conversely, sub-populations with power are usually better situated in terms of the economy, and this results in a lower birth rate. The resulting difference in the population dynamic of privileged and non-privileged sub-populations then threatens the balance of power.

THE MEDIA REVOLUTION: THE MIDDLE EAST AS A RELIGIOUS MARKETPLACE

"The majority are still illiterate. But politically this plays a far smaller role than previously. Radio has changed everything. These days people in the most outlying villages listen to what is happening elsewhere and form their own opinion. Governments cannot rule as they used to. We are living in a new world." (President Nasser)

"Abdul Malik left school and wandered from coffee bar to coffee bar. He became our public scribe and epistoler. He read newspapers and magazines to us. When he read the political reports, the owner of the coffee bar switched the radio off and called for quit so everyone could hear his reading and commentary. Sometimes he left the newspapers to one side, stood up and gave a political speech." (Mohamed Choukri, For Bread Alone).

"I think I have made a mistake. I should never have left Morocco. Now I am confused, I have seen something else, I have seen how to live differently and better." (Tahar Ben Jelloun, The Last Friend).

"Films in cinemas are our teachers. They show us everything we can do." (Young Egyptian, end of the 1950s).

"A movie image of life in America, for all its documentary detail, is a radical 'theory' when it appears on the screens of Cairo, Ankara or Tehran." (Daniel Lerner).

"The telephone lines in Saudi Arabia are surely thicker and more abundant than elsewhere, since they must bear the heavy weight of all the whispered croonings lovers have to exchange and all their sighs and moans and kisses that they cannot, in the real world, enact." (Rajaa Alsanea, Girls of Riyadh).

"Dear people watching Arabs Got Talent, there's a better show going on called Tunisia's Got Freedom. Watch that" (Egyptian tweet of 14 January 2011).[22]

The population of the Middle East has a level of access to the media comparable with that enjoyed by people in the West: "If you walk into a cafe at any

---

22 Cited in Lerner 1964: 214; Šukrí 1980: 154; Jelloun 2011: 58, Lerner 1964: 54 and 11, Alsanea 2008: 162, Idle and Nunns 2011: 27.

time of day in any city in the Middle East, you'll see a typical sight – men sitting at a table with a cup of coffee or tea, smoking, reading a newspaper or playing a board game while listening with half an ear to a radio or television located in the corner of the room" (Lewis 1997: 5). And yet the media plays a political role. So what mechanisms are in play here?

The media contributes to the formation of modern and informed public opinion. It is one of the communication platforms for the dissemination of ideologies, including opposition ideologies. It is also a platform for the mobilisation and organisation of effective collective action, including revolution. Similarly, the media has the effect of shrinking the world. In doing so, it contributes to an increase in consumer aspirations, the visibility of illegitimate social inequality at home, and to an awareness of the existence of attractive reference countries that have managed to cast off the yoke of postcolonial backwardness (e.g. Turkey and China). New media have managed to overcome the censorship to which the traditional media is subject. They have helped to erode the monopoly enjoyed up till now on how the world is interpreted by both the regime's propaganda outlets and mainstream clerics. The new media has also increased awareness of the advantages of the democratic institutions operating in other countries, and satellites have reinforced a pan-Arab identity. It is used by many different political and religious actors to their own ends and the result is the emergence of a pluralistic political and religious marketplace. However, ideological pluralism is not for everyone. Some people long for a simple, transparent and stable world, and this is what the fundamentalists offer.

The role of the new media and social networks was looked at in detail in connection with the Arab Spring (Křížek and Tarant 2014). However, the expansion of the media was not in itself the critical factor behind instability in the Middle East. As table 17 shows, above-average viewing figures of several types of media were typical of Tunisia, Libya and Egypt, where revolution actually took place in 2011. However, similarly high figures were reported in the oil monarchies of the Gulf, which, with the exception of Bahrain, did not experience revolution. Conversely, a below-average exposure to media images was typical of the populations of prerevolutionary Yemen and Syria, and yet both these countries lived through bloody revolution. The expansion of the media, therefore, plays a politically relevant role above all *within the context of uneven modernisation* when the pace of economic growth or the development of legitimate and democratic political systems capable of effective governance in the territory of the state lags behind the expansion of the media. Furthermore, the broader cultural and international context within which the media is expanding in the Middle East is also important. All of these potentially conflictual interactions between the media revolution and other dimensions of uneven modernisation and its wider context will gradually be examined in this chapter with the aim of showing what mechanisms of political destabilisation give rise to this friction (see fig. 24).

Fig. 24 The interaction of the media revolution with other independent variables examined in this chapter

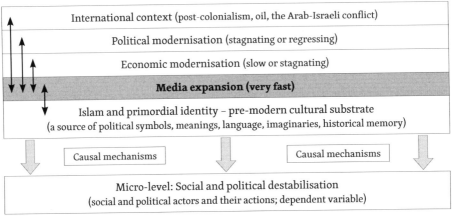

N.B. Possible interactions and tensions are shown by the arrows.

THE MEDIA REVOLUTION: AN INTERNATIONAL AND REGIONAL COMPARISON

An international comparison reveals the proportion of Middle Eastern households with a television to be very high, with 84% of families having a television at home (2005). This is higher than the global average (79%) and differs considerably from other regions of the developing world (in sub-Saharan Africa the figure is only 14%, in South Asia 32%, and in East Asia and Pacific 36%). On the other hand, the presence of televisions in homes is not much different from the wealthiest and most advanced macro-regions such as North America (97%) and Western Europe (96%) (see fig. 25). In the revolutionary year of 2011 (see table 17), 97% of the population watched television several times a week, and 86% every day. There was minimum variability between individual countries: from 92% who watched television every day in Libya to 79% in Palestine (TESEV 2012: 30).

As regards the media sources that people turn to for information regarding domestic and international current affairs, the Middle East shares the same model as the rest of the world. Television predominates (e.g. Turkey 97%, Jordan and Lebanon 96%, Kuwait 89%, and Egypt 87%). The picture is identical in the US (83%) and Western Europe (Germany 84%, Great Britain 83%). Newspapers used to be a secondary source of news reports around the

Fig. 25 Households with televisions in world macro-regions 2005 (in %)

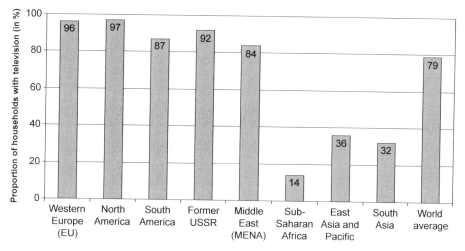

Source: World Development Indicators 2007

world. In the Middle East just under half of the adult population cite the press as an important source of information from home and abroad (from 63% in Kuwait, 49% in Turkey and 32% in Egypt and Palestine, to 20% in Morocco). In certain less advanced Middle Eastern countries with higher levels of illiteracy, radio continues to play a significant role (Egypt 57%, Morocco 54%, Jordan 44%). This is slightly similar to the media model of Sub-Saharan Africa, where radio dominates and is the main source of news reports for 90% of the population (The Pew...2007). However, the situation overall is changing fast in favour of the internet as the second main source of *international* news reports after television. The internet was the main source of news (2010) for 9% of Egyptians, Saudis and Jordanians and for as many as 15% of Lebanese or Emiratis (Zogby International 2010). In the revolutionary year of 2011, 20% of Arabs cited the internet as their main source of information from abroad (Zogby International 2011).

In the Middle East there is now a highly mobilised society exposed to many different forms of mass media. It is not simply interested in domestic issues but keeps a close eye on world events: 60% of Egyptians, 51% of Jordanians and Moroccans, 49% of Turks, 46% of Kuwaitis and Palestinians, and 43% of Lebanese. There is the same interest in information as there is in the West. For instance, approximately half of the adult populations of the United States (57%) and the Czech Republic (52%) say that they follow international events on an ongoing basis (The Pew...2007: 71). Satellite television stations are crucial in this respect, and of these Al-Jazeera has long predominated. In 2011, the year of the Arab Spring, Al-Jazeera was the station of choice for

Tab. 17 Media ratings in MENA countries 2011 (% of the adult population)

Country	TV viewing figures		Newspaper readership		Internet use	
	More than once a week	Every day	More than once a week	Every day	More than once a week	Every day
Egypt	97	82	74 (+14)	41 (+14)	69 (+11)	46 (+10)
Iran	96	90 (+4)	45	18	34	17
Iraq	100 (+3)	98 (+12)	42	8	53	13
Jordan	97	80	69 (+9)	38 (+11)	67 (+9)	46 (+10)
Lebanon	98 (+1)	88 (+2)	55	30 (+3)	59 (+1)	40 (+4)
Libya	97	92 (+6)	56	8	63 (+5)	38 (+2)
Palestine	96	79	66 (+6)	31 (+4)	65 (+7)	46 (+10)
Saudi Arabia	96	81	68 (+8)	35 (+8)	83 (+25)	58 (+22)
Gulf States*	98 (+1)	84	78 (+18)	46 (+19)	89 (+31)	70 (+34)
Syria	95	82	48	19	40	30
Tunisia	99 (+2)	85	64 (+4)	23	70 (+12)	50 (+14)
Yemen	95	85	63 (+3)	18	55	29
Total**	97	86	60	27	58	36

(*) Oman, Bahrain, Qatar, United Arab Emirates, Kuwait
(**) Regional average (weighted population size of individual states)
N.B.: The positive difference in percentage points against the regional average is shown in brackets.
Source: TESEV 2012

international news reports of 43% of Arabs. The second most popular station, Al Arabiya, was watched by only 14% (Zogby International 2011). However, the status of Al-Jazeera as favourite news station differs in individual countries: in Lebanon and Jordan it is preferred (2010) by only a fifth of the population, in Egypt by a third, and in Morocco by more than two thirds (Zogby International 2010).

As far as television entertainment shows are concerned, no station dominates as emphatically as Al-Jazeera does in the sphere of journalism. The most popular stations include MBC (most popular for 12%), Al Hayat (9%), Moga Comedy (8%), Rotana (5%) and Nile Comedy. However, Arabs do not only watch Middle Eastern television productions. Every day, half of the population watch American or European films, music videos and entertainment shows (73% in Morocco, 49% in Egypt, but only 26% in the Emirates and Saudi Arabia). In all, as many as two thirds of the region's population consume Western television culture at least every other day, and this phenomenon does not only apply to the young generation (Zogby International 2010).

Tab. 18 Newspaper circulation in MENA countries. Print run per 1,000 people

Country	1997	2000	2004
Algeria	26	---	---
Egypt	33	---	---
Jordan	76	---	---
Lebanon	63	57	54
Libya	14	---	---
Morocco	24	29	12
Palestine	---	---	10
Tunisia	---	23	---
Yemen	---	3	4
United Arab Emirates	206	198	193
France	145	157	163
Brazil	42	43	36
Tanzania	---	1	2
Mozambique	3	3	3
India	48	57	71
China	35	64	74

N.B.: These are the average numbers of newspaper copies calculated per 1,000 inhabitants. Data is unavailable for many MENA countries.
Source: UNESCO, World Bank

Newspaper circulation is not reliably charted in the Middle East. However, the statistics available indicate that newspaper print runs in relation to the population are significantly higher than Sub-Saharan Africa and comparable with Latin America, though still substantially lower than in the advanced countries of the world (see table 18). Even so, two Egyptian newspapers made it onto the *World Association of Newspapers* rankings of the top newspapers due their huge circulation. The Egyptian Al-Ahram was in 57th place with an average daily circulation of 900,000, and Al-Gomhuria made 77th place with 800,000 copies daily (2008). Top of the list are Japanese and Chinese newspapers. In 2011, the year of the Arab Spring (see table 17), 60% of the population of the Middle East regularly read a newspaper, with the daily readership standing at 27%. The figures were highest in Egypt (41%) and the Gulf States (46%), and lowest in the conflict ridden countries of Libya and Iraq (8%). A relatively small daily readership is also to be found in the most repressive countries such as Yemen, Iran (18%) and Syria (19%) (TESEV 2012).

Fig. 26 Freedom of the press in world macro-regions 2010 and 2015

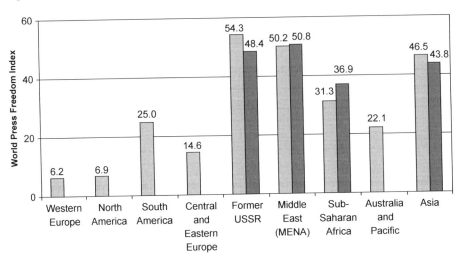

N.B.: The author's calculation of arithmetic averages (unweighted country population size). The values are arrived at every year for each country by a panel of experts from the organisation Reporters Without Borders using a range of criteria (e.g. the number of journalists imprisoned or killed, state laws regulating the press, etc.). The scores range from 0 (Finland and Island) to 105 (North Korea, Eritrea).
Source: Reporters without Borders. World Press Freedom Index 2010 and 2016 (www.rsf.org).

In certain poorer Middle Eastern states continuing illiteracy among older people and women may act as a barrier to the development of the press. High levels of censorship and political pressure on print journalists also plays a role (see tab. 19 and fig. 26). According to the press freedom index published by Reporters Without Borders (the criteria used when compiling the list include the number of murdered, missing or convicted journalists, the legislation regulating the press and its implementation in practice, etc.) a similarly poor situation is only to be found in the countries of the former Soviet Union (see fig. 26). The repression of journalists in the Middle East (50.2) is basically the same as it is in Russia (49.9). However, individual countries differ. Journalists are freest to write what they want in Lebanon, the Emirates and Kuwait. However, Iran, Syria, Yemen, Tunisia, Libya and Saudi Arabia persecute journalists as zealously as regimes such as Cuba (forever subject to criticism), Belarus (forever subject to European sanctions), China (always good for a scandal), and Burma, ruled by military junta (see tab. 19).

The communications revolution in the Middle East also encompasses computers, the internet, social media and mobile telephones. Prior to the wave of revolutions, ownership of computers (2007) was far more widespread in the Middle East than in other regions of the developing world such as Asia (37%

Tab. 19 Press freedom index in MENA countries 2010 and 2015

Country	Score 2010	Overall ranking 2010	Score 2015	Overall ranking 2015
Algeria	47.3	133	41.7	129
Bahrain	51.4	144	54.9	162
Egypt	43.3	127	54.5	159
Iran	94.5	175	66.5	169
Iraq	45.6	130	54.4	158
Israel	23.3	86	32.6	101
Jordan	37.0	120	44.5	135
Kuwait	24.6	87	32.6	103
Lebanon	20.5	78	32.0	98
Libya	63.5	160	57.9	164
Morocco	47.4	135	42.6	131
Oman	40.3	124	40.4	125
Palestine	56.1	150	43.0	132
Qatar	38.0	121	36.0	117
Saudi Arabia	61.5	157	59.7	165
Sudan	85.3	172	72.5	174
Syria	91.5	173	81.4	177
Tunisia	72.5	164	31.6	96
Turkey	49.3	138.	50.8	151
United Arab Emirates	23.8	87	36.7	119
Yemen	82.1	170	67.1	170
Other countries often criticised by the West				
Russia	49.9	140	49.0	148
Cuba	57.0	154	70.2	171
Belarus	78.0	166	54.3	157
China	84.7	171	81.0	176
Burma	94.5	174	45.5	143
North Korea (the worst)	105.0	177	83.8	179

N.B.: Overall rankings of all countries and dependent territories.
Source: Reporters Without Borders. World Press Freedom Index 2010 and 2016 (www.rsf.org).

of the population owns a computer in China and 14% in India), South America and Sub-Saharan Africa. However, the figures differ according to country. In poorer countries they are lower (11% of adults in Morocco, 18% in Egypt) than in more advanced countries (20% in Turkey, 44% in Jordan, 55% in Lebanon)

Fig. 27 Internet access in world macro-regions 1990–2015 (in %)

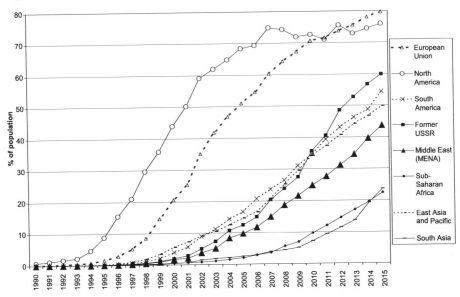

N.B.: The statistics show the number of people with internet access per 100 inhabitants.
Source: World Bank Development Indicators

or in the rich Gulf States (84% in Kuwait). The strong growth dynamic is perhaps more important. For instance, in Jordan the number of people owning computers rose between 2002 and 2007 from 31% to 44% of the population as a whole, in Lebanon from 49% to 55%, and in Turkey from 14% to 20% (The Pew…2007: 75).

In the MENA region, more people regularly use a computer (at work, school, in cafes, libraries or at home) than own one. There is also a sharp rise in users over time. In Lebanon on the eve of the revolution (2010) 52% of the adult population used a computer. In Turkey this figure was 42% (up from 23% in 2002), in Jordan 41% (30% in 2002) and in Egypt 32% (as opposed to 19% in 2006) (The Pew…2010: 20). An earlier survey (2007) reported 76% of adult users in Kuwait, 56% in Palestine and 23% in Morocco (The Pew…2007).

The number of internet users is rising sharply in the Middle East. In 2001 it was only one million. In 2010 this figure was 60 million and in 2014 around 120 million (Kropáček 2013: 106). This means the share of the population connected to the internet is double that of South Asia or Sub-Saharan Africa, and comparable with East Asia and South America (see fig. 27). This boom of recent years is summed up by Younes Zekri, a now bankrupt internet coffee bar operator, who claims that from 2006 to 2007 a new internet coffee bar opened every week in the peripheral Moroccan city of Zagora with its population of

30,000[23]. According to sociological surveys, then, a considerable segment of the population in the Middle East uses the internet on an *occasional* basis, though there is considerable variance between individual countries depending on the level of economic development: 71% of adults in Kuwait (2007), 48% in Palestine (2007), 35% in Lebanon (2010), 39% in Turkey (2010), 32% in Jordan (2010), 23% in Egypt (2010) and 22% in Morocco (2007). Email is occasionally used by slightly fewer people (The Pew...2007, The Pew...2010).

In 2011, 58% of the population of the Middle East *regularly* used the internet, with 36% using it every day. However, significant differences between countries persisted. Most of the daily users were in the rich Gulf States (70%), Saudi Arabia (58%), Tunisia (50%) and Egypt, Jordan and Palestine (46%), while the figures were lowest in Iraq (13%), Iran (17%) and Yemen (29%) (TESEV 2012). Middle Eastern users by no means restrict themselves to Arab servers. Some of them follow mainly French language sites (38% of users in Morocco, 6% in Egypt and 5% in Lebanon) or English language sites (10% in the Emirates and Morocco, 9% in Egypt, and 6% in Lebanon) (Zogby International 2010).

These differences are visible not only between countries but between generations. Young people (aged 15–29) use the internet more often, and this increases their access to all types of information, from political and economic data to information regarding education and careers. In the lead up to the Arab revolutions (2010), 22% of Arab young people had internet access at home and 62% within their community (in cafes and schools). Again, however, these figures differ according to country. For instance, as many as 71% of young people from high income countries had home internet access, but only 22% from middle-income countries and 9% from low-income countries (The Silatech Index 2011). Young and well educated people are again highly represented among at least occasional users of social media such as Facebook, MySpace and Twitter. In Turkey (2010), 55% of people aged 18–29 use social media (double the average of the adult population as a whole on 26%), in Jordan 47% (respectively 24%), in Lebanon 39% (18%) and in Egypt 37% (18%) (Pew Center 2010).

Use of mobile telephones is also increasing dynamically. In the MENA region the proportion of mobile operator customers of the population as a whole is almost comparable with North and South America and well in excess of South Asia and Sub-Saharan Africa (see fig. 28). While in 2002 only 35% of the adult Jordanian population owned a mobile telephone, in 2010 the figure was 94%. In Turkey during the same period the figure rose from 49% to 77% and in Lebanon from 62% to the current 79%. At present, 65% of Egyptian

---

23   Interview conducted by the author, Zagora, Morocco, July 2009.

Fig. 28 Mobile telephone use in world macro-regions 1980–2015 (in %)

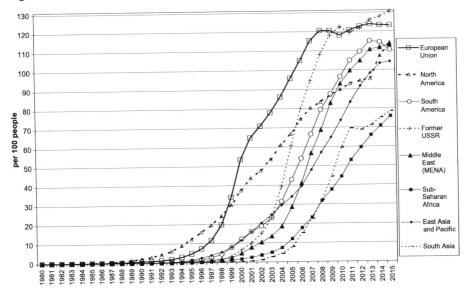

Source: World Bank Development Indicators

adults own a mobile telephone (The Pew...2010). In the lead up to the revolution the proportion of mobile telephone users among young Arabs (aged 15–29) was even higher (87%), and the difference between young people of poorer and wealthier countries was not as dramatic as in the case of internet access: from 81% using a mobile in low-income countries to 98% in high-income countries (The Silatech Index 2011). All in all the populations of the Middle East are far better informed, interconnected and politically mobilised than any time previously thanks to the rapid development of media and communications.

How does the Middle Eastern media revolution of the 20th century differ from the historical development of the media in Europe? And by what mechanisms could this rapid social change contribute to an increase in political instability within the context of significantly uneven modernisation?

THE MEDIA REVOLUTION: A HISTORICAL COMPARISON. MODERNISATION IN THE ERA OF THE GLOBAL VILLAGE

Mass media such as newspapers, radio and television offer real-time standardised content produced by a small group of people and aimed at a large, internally differentiated audience of relatively atomised individuals. The mass media first developed in Europe and the USA before moving to the Middle East. In Europe printing technology spread after 1450. The first pamphlets, the forerunners of newspapers, began to appear in the 18th century, and mass produced daily newspapers only started to be published at the end of the 19th century. Bestsellers had to wait until the 20th century (Kunezik 1995). The more gradual evolution of the print media was linked to pervasive social barriers that prevented the early adoption of the technological potential of the press. Levels of illiteracy were slow to drop. The sphere of mass leisure time brought about by shorter working hours, another precondition for the consumption of the press, was also slow in arriving. A more rapid development was prevented by the slow pace of democratisation, censorship, and the interventions of political power. Another barrier was the high price of newspapers on a still small market, which meant that economies of scale were not possible. In addition, a low level of urbanisation combined with an inadequate infrastructure did not allow for the fast, cheap distribution of newspapers to a population mainly scattered among rural areas. The concentration of large numbers of people within a small geographical area only took place later thanks to urbanisation (Kloskowska 1967). However, the press eventually became one of the first outputs of mass, standardised industrial production. Printers represented nascent capitalists (Keller 1999).

Compared to the press, film spread much faster in Europe. The first screenings took place in New York (1894) and Paris (1895) at the end of the 19th century, while cinema was at the peak of its influence between the world wars. Though radio technology was mastered around the same time, the first regular broadcast in the world was begun by the BBC as late as 1922. The development of television represents another stage. Again it was the BBC that was first to broadcast regular programmes (1936), though the boom in television only arrived after the Second World War (Kunezik 1995). In the development of Western media, therefore, the beginning of each new media revolution is phased, beginning at the moment that the previous subsides. Another characteristic is the gradual acceleration of the commencement of each new communications technology. It took the telephone approximately 20 years to find its millionth user, while television managed the same feat after only 15 years. This acceleration continued with cable TV (10 years) and the mobile telephone (less than five years) to the internet (two years) (Bičík 2000).

The Middle East experienced its own media boom some time after Europe during the 20th century. However, the spread of the media has been considerably faster. The development of printed media took 500 years in Europe, but only 100 years in the Middle East (Eickelman, Piscatori 1996). The leap from the first books and newspapers to telephones and satellites was even faster. What this means is that we do not see the gradual arrival of individual types of media spread over several centuries, as in Europe: first the printing press, followed by cinema, radio, television and the internet. In the Middle East the media revolutions took place in parallel, with individual types of media spreading more quickly and concurrently with others (cf. Lerner 1964). Many new forms of media, unavailable during the early phases of European modernisation, do not require a literate audience (radio, television and cassettes). There is an Arab saying that sums this up nicely: "Al-Jazeera even introduced satellite television into Bedouin tents". In many cases, therefore, Middle Eastern countries leapfrogged from a pre-literary stage (the dominance of oral communication) to a post-literary stage (new media not requiring a literate audience), with the result that not only the literate but even the illiterate segments of the population could be politically mobilised on a mass scale (Riesman 1964, Brzezinski 1993). Another crucial factor is the arrival of new electronic media, which are non-hierarchical and able to circumvent state censorship: the internet and satellite television. In the early stages of European modernisation this was not possible, and censorship was therefore more effective. The politically destabilising consequences of the media revolution are therefore potentially more powerful in the Middle East.

Career and consumer aspirations are stimulated by the rapid media revolutions. However, there has been no commensurate industrial revolution, as was the case in Europe, and as a consequence consumer demand is growing faster than the supply of economic opportunities. This results in frustration and political radicalisation far stronger than that in 19th century modernising Europe. In the West the relative interconnectedness of the development of individual social sub-systems was functional, and gradually rising aspirations stimulated, inter alia, by the media and advertising industries, encouraged motivation, entrepreneurship and economic growth. This was aided by the further expansion of the media, rising consumption and economic prosperity.

In addition, the speed of media expansion in the Middle East created greater potential for political mobilisation and organisation. The formation of mass public opinion and politically mobilised masses took place more quickly than in the West. However, it was not accompanied by democratisation. Political institutions were not created allowing the newly politicised and increasingly discontented masses to be integrated into the political system, with the result that, in contrast to modernising Europe, the development of the media system in the Middle East outstripped the development of both the economic and political systems (Lerner 1964, Riesman 1964, Huntington 1968).

Another crucial factor is the fact that during the course of the West's modernisation there existed no significantly wealthier and more advanced region that could have served as a reference point. Conversely, modernisation in the Middle East, indeed modernisation in the post-colonial world in general, is taking place at a time when Western countries are considerably more advanced both politically and economically. In a media connected world the West can therefore become a reference point. Different programmes of modernity are therefore obliged to profile themselves, either positively or negatively, in terms of Western modernity, and are not in a position to ignore it (cf. Eisenstadt 2000).

The modernisation of the West took place at a time when distances and state borders represented a serious obstacle to the dissemination of information. From the 16th to the start of the 19th century sailboats could not travel faster than 16 kilometres per hour. It was only in the mid-19th century that locomotives and oceangoing liners achieved speeds of around 40 km an hour. However, a trip around the world in eighty days, as undertaken by the hero of the novel by Jules Verne, was still verging on fantasy. In contrast, the modernisation of the post-colonial Middle East is taking place during an era of jet airliners, transatlantic cables, satellites and the internet, a time when, thanks to the development of transport and communications technologies, distances are being eradicated and the world is being compressed in terms of time and space (cf. Dicken 1992: 104). A consciousness of the world as a single place is coming into being, a place that is getting rapidly smaller. In other words, the modernisation of the Middle East is taking place at a time when the world is becoming a global village. In an era of high-speed electronic media, everyday life is experienced differently than in the era of the printed media. People all around the world are watching and experiencing the same events and can be informed in detail about affairs around the planet and in their own country, often in real time. You can hide nothing from your neighbours in the global village. This is stimulating the political and consumer aspirations of Middle Eastern populations, who are able to compare their life opportunities with those in other societies. Likewise, they can compare the political and economic systems in their own countries with those of the West or other advanced countries. This is adding to the de-legitimisation of Middle Eastern regimes, as well as offering a vision of alternative and inspiring models of development that have proven successful elsewhere (cf. McLuhan 1964).

(1) THE BIRTH OF PUBLIC OPINION: THE MASSES DISCOVER POLITICS

For a long time Su'ad Nawfal, a teacher from Rakka, took no interest in politics: "My private revolution began six years ago. Until then I knew nothing of Assad's crimes. At school we were told that our leader was flawless. But six years ago we bought a satellite and I learned of the massacres in Hama (1982) from television and a friend. I began to think more about the situation in Syria, about the ways that people must have suffered over the last thirty years. And when the revolution began (2011), a volcano inside me erupted. I was one of the first demonstrators" (Batistová 2015). The role of the media is regarded similarly by the Moroccan writer Mahi Binebine, who in his short story *Horses of God* (2014: 99, 110) reconstructs the life of suicide bombers from the slums of Sidi Moumen, a shantytown in Casablanca: "We had the TV tuned to a station airing wall-to-wall reports on the killing of Muslims in the world. This Palestinian boy must have died in his father's arms a hundred times. And each time it brought tears to our eyes." The hero of the slum was the kung-fu master Bruce Lee: "When they showed his movies, we ran into the cafe and followed them religiously. We also wanted to rectify wrongs, seek retribution on behalf of the weak, and fight for justice."

The spread of education and the mass media has contributed to the emergence of a new type of public that authoritarians cannot easily ignore (Eickelman and Anderson 2003). In contrast, the historical constellation in which most of the population was embedded in traditional, inward looking and mutually isolated communities was to the advantage of a narrow political elite, which was able to rule undisturbed. And occasionally an equally narrow contra-elite, alienated from the rest of society, took up the struggle. In the meantime the traditional masses gazed impassively at the occasional coup or attempted coup, or took no notice whatsoever (Lerner 1964).

The traditional peoples of the Middle East were in fact apolitical. For instance, on the threshold of modernisation most Iranians were not interested in the affair surrounding the nationalisation of the *Anglo-Iranian Oil Company*, nor even in the subsequent putsch against the democratically elected premier Mosaddegh (1953) carried out by the army, aided and abetted by the CIA and MI6. Events were followed by only a minority of Iranians. Similarly, during the 1950s neighbouring Syrians virtually ignored a series of military coups brought about by the rivalry of the narrow elite and counter-elite. When in the morning the mayors officially announced that yet another clique of officers now ruled the country, the villagers listened with resignation and then returned to their beds. The King of Jordan ruled without problem a traditional population scattered around rural and nomadic regions, but only until the exodus of politicised and relatively modern Palestinian refugees, who were urbanised, literate and informed. Similarly, in a pioneering public opinion survey, traditional Turks declared: "Politics doesn't concern us", "We can't change anything, so it's pointless to worry about it", "Our leaders know best what to do", and "It's not for us to judge our leaders". On the threshold of the media revolution the traditional masses did not participate in public opinion. They had no interest in events beyond the borders of their communities, had no opinions on these events, and were unable to place them within the context of their own situation. In answer to most of the politically inflected questions they were asked, they replied that they didn't know. They had no opinions regarding the main issues and problems of that time. In their feedback they rated the questions asked by the sociologists negatively for being too concerned with boring, irrelevant issues, while failing to address themes regarding which they would have had something to say, such as irrigation, nomadic life and the local community (Lerner 1964).

How can this apoliticism be explained? Firstly, the traditional form of devoutness probably promoted political passivity, even fatalism. As a traditional Egyptian peasant said in the 1950s: "Everything is God's will." Or the Jordanian nomad: "I am satisfied with what God has given me." This in turn gave rise to the belief that nothing could be done about problems such as poverty or Western interference. Everything was as it should be and the task of Man was to grin and bear it. The situation as viewed through this conservative lens could not be changed. History had not yet been invented and the ability to consider alternatives to historical development had not been born (Lerner 1964: 301, 318). Seen in this light, religion performed the function of Marx's opium of the people. It promoted a false consciousness serving the interest of the ruling class in maintaining the status quo. Religion only became a politically mobilising doctrine in the Middle East in the 1970s (cf. Kepel 1996 and 2002). Secondly, according to Max Weber (1998) the traditional legitimisation of the political order was based on a belief in the sacred bonds of historically established power relations and patterns of behaviour. The status of the privileged classes was thus based on an ancient, oft proven and unchanging tradition that everyone respected. In addition, tradition restricted the actions of the privileged and created limits on their conduct (cf. Bauman 1997, Keller 1999).

Thirdly, the apoliticism of traditional Arabs, Turks and Iranians was based on a mental inability to place their personal problems within the broader national and international context. In a survey conducted by D. Lerner, traditional respondents cited poverty as their biggest problem. However, they were unable to identify poverty as a problem of society as a whole. They were unable to view their situation in context or to generalise it, and were unaware of their own interests. A lack of empathy meant they were unable to formulate possible alternatives. The horizons of traditional respondents ended on the borders of their tribe, village or neighbourhood, which is where their identities and loyalties also ended. It is difficult to mobilise politically traditional people to act in the name of modern ideologies working with a concept of nation or class, i.e. in the name of identities and loyalties that transcend the hermetically sealed world of tribe, village or neighbourhood (Lerner 1964).

Mass politicisation only takes place with the transition from a mostly traditional to a more modern population. A new personality type is born. This process is facilitated by migration from rural to urban areas and increased levels of education, as well as by the spread of the media. At the same time, exposure to the influence of one type of media increases the demand for other types. For instance, reading newspapers prompts people to listen to the radio, read political pamphlets and watch films. A similar *multiplication effect* sees exposure to one newspaper or radio station increasing interest in the contents of other newspapers and radio stations, and modern public opinion begins to be formed. This opinion first takes note of local and regional affairs, but gradually moves on to national and international events. This then feeds into the mass politicisation of an originally apolitical population, which now understands the relationship between the situation on an individual level and that on a national and international level. People develop opinions regarding more and more subjects and want to apply these opinions in practice (Lerner 1964).

However, the influence the mass media has on public opinion is restricted in many ways. Firstly, modern media are in competition with persistent and extensive oral systems comprising informal networks of face-to-face communication, and opposition groups such as the Muslim Brotherhood or the communists have always exploited these systems. During the course of the Arab revolutions (2011), resistance was mobilised not only via the internet and mobile telephones, but also through face-to-face communication at Friday prayers. Chanting protesters in Cairo would often deliberately walk first through slums, where using direct communication they attracted as many people as possible to participate, especially in places where the regime had closed down the internet and mobile networks. Secondly, the regional reach of individual media at the start of the post-colonial era was highly erratic. It was concentrated in the major cities, where at the start of urbanisation only a minority of the population lived. Thirdly, the influence of the media continued to be restricted by illiteracy and low levels of education. Education is not only a tool for the consumption of media output, but creates the intellectual ability for it to be understood. The ability to spell out laboriously the contents of a newspaper provides no automatic guarantee that freshly literate villagers will understand those contents. For this reason, illiterate or semi-literate people often preferred to have newspaper read out to them by others, who then explained their contents in intelligible, simple terms. Similarly, an illiterate person with an awakening interest in politics prefers to listen to the radio in the company of someone who follows the reports with them and explains their significance. In addition, to begin with radio broadcasts were only in Modern Standard Arabic, which Arabs lacking a formal education did not understand. They therefore needed a "translation" into their local dialect from someone educated. As a consequence, each modernising community had its *opinion leader*, who enjoyed the confidence of the others and interpreted the information flowing from the media for them (Lerner 1964, Eickelman 2003). Such an opinion leader from Morocco of the 1950s was vividly portrayed by *Mohamed Choukri* (1980: 154) in his autobiographical novel *For Bread Alone*: "*Abdul Malik left school and wandered from coffee bar to coffee bar. He became our public scribe and epistoler. He read newspapers and magazines to us. When he read the political reports, the owner of the coffee bar switched the radio off and called for quit so everyone could hear his reading and commentary. Sometimes he left the newspapers to one side, stood up and gave a political speech.*"

Nevertheless, the birth of a new type of person and their entry en masse into politics represents a historical breakthrough and a major challenge to regimes. Politics is no longer something to be pursued unimpeded by only a narrow elite set apart from the rest of society, and public discussion is no longer dominated by a "creative minority" hoping to model the rest of society along their own lines. For instance, in Turkey this historical turning point ended the dominance of the Kemalists and the Republic Party (1950). The first free elections were unexpectedly participated in by those segments of the population that had never until then taken any interest in politics. They voted in the opposition Adnan Menderes and his Democratic Party, which was more receptive to Islam and to the mostly conservative population (cf. Huntington 1968). In Egypt, the politicisation of a hitherto traditional and apolitical population led to populism. Nasser's regime realised that it could no longer ignore the masses as it had done in the past. It was not possible to continue imposing reforms, the benefits of which were only to be appreciated retrospectively, because the people were still too backward in their thinking. And because the leaders did not want to allow the masses a share in power, they had to win them over with permanent propaganda (Lerner 1964).

The political consequences of the media revolution of the second half of the 20th century in the Middle East were therefore dramatic. As Nasser, who was one of the first to learn how to treat the media when building his personality cult, observed: "It is true that most of our people are still illiterate. But politically that counts far less than it did twenty years ago. Radio has changed everything. Today people in the most remote villages hear what is happening everywhere and form their opinions. Leaders cannot govern as they once did. We live in a new world." The Iranian premier *Mosaddegh* was the first to campaign effectively using radio. He was well acquainted with the political potential of the mass media having studied in France. During his overthrow, the army first occupied Radio Tehran on the principle that: "Without a microphone *Mosaddegh* is impotent" (Lerner 1964: 214)[24].

---

24   Ronald Inglehart (2002, 2006) does not agree with Daniel Lerner, who emphasises the synergy of media, education and urbanisation, that the media has the power to transform society deeply. Inglehart regards the media as catalyst of political changes but does not believe they influence

The modernising people of the Middle East exposed to the influence of the media are being politicised. They can see that politics is relevant because it affects their daily lives. They want to be informed, participate in public debate and play a part in forming public opinion. And because they have their own opinion, they also want to promote it and participate in power. Their political aspirations are growing. They understand that politics can be pursued in many different ways and that alternatives exist. They do not believe that the existing political order is the only one possible. They choose between competing role models, including political models. And now they are able to compare the political system in their own country with those of the West or the USSR (Lerner 1964). Since the population is influenced by the same media and themes, the feeling of a unified nation composed of people with common problems and a common fate is born and consolidated (Zubaida 2009).

(2) THE MOBILISATION AND COORDINATION OF COLLECTIVE ACTION: THE CASE OF THE ARAB SPRING

The media has the power to connect up previously isolated individuals and groups. It allows them to share and exchange political ideas and to form a consensus. It allows for the mobilisation of more supporters and can help in the organisation and coordination of very effective collective action. At the same time, the organisational potential of the media can be used by different political movements, be they secularist or Islamic, democratic or enemies of democracy, leftwing or rightwing. Marx and Engels had already remarked upon the role of the means of communication and transport spawned by the industrial revolution in the creation of the class consciousness and organisation of the working class. The railways, postal system, telegraph and telephone allowed for the connection of spatially separated places that nonetheless occupied an identical position in the social hierarchy and the same relationship to the means of production. The media thus helped transform a "class in itself" into a "class for itself". The latter is now aware of its class interests and understands who its enemy is. Thanks to the media, people now understand that they do not stand alone but share their class status with many others. They also share a joint organisation, programme and leadership (Marx and Engels 1973). The expansion of means of communication today is having similar political impacts in developing countries. Firstly, it simplifies and accelerates the dissemination of political ideas amongst large, geographically

changes in attitudes. Instead, long-term economic developments generating the division of labour, prosperity and security are decisive.

dispersed populations, thus streamlining agitation. Activists are no longer reliant on face-to-face communication when recruiting supporters. Secondly, the media expands the possibilities of political organisation. It increases the ability to mobilise and coordinate large numbers of people for collective action (Brzezinski 1993).

For instance, internet-based social media played an important role during the mobilisation of supporters and the subsequent organisation of protests during the course of the Arab revolutions. The media division of labour was as follows (cited in Kropáček 2013). Blogs and Facebook provided a platform for the creation of a consensus regarding the need for regime change. These discussions crystallised over several years. The Egyptian memorial page "We Are All Khalid Said" or the photography of the burned Tunisian *Mohamed* Bouazizi circulated on the internet sparked demonstrations against police corruption and brutality. Twitter in combination with smartphones then allowed for the rapid organisation of demonstrations and their flexible coordination in time and space. For instance, one of the first revolutionary Egyptian tweets read as follows: "The protests on 25 January will be held throughout Cairo, including the districts of Shubra, Mohandessin, Cairo University and in Arab League Street". It also helped spread practical tips: "Comfortable trousers, running shoes, fully charged mobile, some money, ID pass and enough cigarettes in case of arrest." It also spread warnings: "All the injured demonstrators who went to hospital have been taken away by the police." However, Twitter also contributed to the mobilisation of new demonstrators. For instance, on the critical day of 25 January, Wael Ghonim wrote: "Everyone come to Tahrir immediately. We need you now." It also mobilised other forms of support: "Several people died today. Hospitals need blood. Please tell everyone to donate blood." Meanwhile, YouTube offered detailed audiovisual testimony of events in the street that evaded the censor and called into question the official interpretation of events presented by the state media. The target group of the revolutionary propaganda was both an undecided and vacillating nation, as well as hesitant superpowers and foreign public opinion. In minimalist form Twitter also delegitimised regimes. For instance, Egyptian activists often tweeted in English: "I'll never get used to police throwing stones at demonstrators. Is it possible anywhere else in the world?", or threw down the gauntlet to the United States: "Teargas made in America rained down on unarmed, peaceful Egyptian demonstrators today simply because they seek dignity, justice and freedom. Mr Obama, are you listening?" (cited in Idle and Nunns 2011: 33, 40, 41, 45, 68). In addition, YouTube connected satellite television and the internet on a multimedia, bidirectional basis. For instance, the television coverage of Al-Jazeera was often converted into internet content and then disseminated and shared online. However, television also used social media to collect information and images published by citizen journalists.

It then used this material in its reports, especially where its reporters had been attacked and persecuted (Howard and Hussain 2011).

Digital media, mobile telephones and the internet have changed the way that political actors communicate in the Middle East. The synergy or interaction of a young, educated generation and new media has created a completely new political quality. Tension and dissatisfaction with regimes were present long before the revolutions. However, frustration was not sufficient in itself to spark off revolution. There first had to be "cognitive liberation". Mutually isolated individuals and groups had to be informed that they were not alone or in a minority with their critical opinions. They had to come to understand that they were individual parts of an extensive collective consciousness and that their outrage was shared by many others. An awareness of the prevalence of shared feelings and opinions was the first essential stage (cf. Havel 1990).

In the second stage, social media made it possible for hitherto isolated individuals and groups sharing similar opinions and emotions to find each other and join forces. They made it possible for dissidents who until then had been individualised, localised, and focused on a specific community or theme to network and join forces within an integrated movement with collective consciousness. Mutual solidarity is discovered and created and a strong feeling of a virtual community comes into being. During this phase the crystallisation of the consciousness of commonly shared problems is important. In the same way a consensus is formed in the emerging online public sphere regarding how to resolve these problems, i.e. a consensus regarding the necessity for regime change and effective ways of achieving this. Digital media allow vast networks between people to be created. These networks accumulate extraordinary social capital that can then be mobilised for real collective action.

It is in the third phase that the virtual networks materialise on the streets, spilling over from a virtual public space into a physical public space. The solidarity and trust created online tips over into solidarity between protestors. The speed of mobilisation is high, because relationships and contacts are being realised that have long been developed, deepened and prepared in advance on the internet. New media allows for the swift, effective coordination of protesters based on interconnectedness and a detailed familiarity with current developments on the ground. Demonstrators follow online news reports and adapt their tactics accordingly. Furthermore, the mobilisation and coordination of new protesters is made possible by virtue of the fact that networks of virtual friends on Facebook are already rooted in real friendship or kinship networks. This encourages trust among protestors and smoothes the path of their mobilisation and coordination.

What triggers mass mobilisation tends to be an incident that the government media ignores but which attracts the attention of the online connected public. In this case the icons of the protests were Mohamed Bouazizi in

Tunisia and Khaled Said in Egypt, who symbolised the brutality of the respective regimes and with whose fate everyone could identify: "The protesters were not inspired by Facebook. They were inspired by genuine tragedies and injustices documented by Facebook." Finally, a new, unique model of revolutionary leadership came into being in which no single charismatic leader or speaker stands at the head of the revolution, not even the leaders of classical opposition parties. On the contrary, the new media allows for informal, flexible, decentralised and broadly spread leadership. Regimes are helpless when faced by networks, because their proven strategy, which involves rounding up the leaders of the protests and decapitating hierarchical opposition organisations, no longer works.

During the fourth phase, with the help of the media protesters attempt to attract maximum attention from the undecided sections of the domestic public as well as the international community, i.e. foreign governments, international and non-governmental organisations and the media. The presence of mobile telephones, digital cameras and video cameras amongst the protesters can place restraints on the police and army. If the whole world is watching, they refrain from using maximum violence because this would elicit a negative reaction on the part of the domestic and foreign public. In Tunisia, Egypt, Morocco, Jordan and Algeria the army hesitated and did not crush the protestors by force. The soldiers in the streets were being constantly recorded and could not afford to be seen as being above the law. In addition, army conscripts belonging to the Facebook generation were well aware of their affinity with the demonstrators. The approach taken by the police could also have been far more brutal without the expansion of new media. And even if, despite this, the regimes in Syria, Libya, Yemen and Bahrain deployed the army, the violence was documented, spread through the media and provoked not only a critical reaction on the part of the international community, but also rifts within the army itself.

For these reasons, the regimes attempted to shut down mobile operators, disconnect the internet, and block access to Facebook, Twitter and YouTube. Bloggers and the administrators of the most popular Facebook accounts were arrested, and attacks were stepped up on domestic and foreign journalists. Facebook and Twitter were monitored in an attempt to anticipate future demonstrations and track down other internet activists that must be arrested. However, even after the overthrow of the regime the information war did not end. Political rivals vied for influence on post-revolutionary developments by seeking control over the revolutionary narrative. The winners generated more and more online content. The defeated regimes generated less and less, though attempted to cover their tracks and dispose of archives. Anything the activists managed to safeguard was usually published and disseminated on the internet immediately (Howard and Hussain 2011).

(3) A SHRINKING WORLD I: CONSUMER ASPIRATIONS AND THE REVOLUTION OF GROWING EXPECTATIONS

According to detailed surveys (Lerner 1964) conducted in the 1950s, i.e. on the threshold of modernisation in the Middle East, a traditional inhabitant of the region was basically happy. He was content with the little that he possessed as a member of the poorest social class. He was satisfied with the limited, unchanging world in which he lived in relative isolation like his predecessors before him. A traditional rural Lebanese father viewed the start of the changes that arrived in the region along with the media as follows: "In the evening he [the respondent's son] goes to the cinema. And immediately he wants a hat and new European-style trousers. He wants to buy a gun and heaven knows what else!" (ibid: 196). A recently urbanised nomad from Jordan expressed similar feelings regarding the changes: "He [the respondent's son] would like to visit the USA. He says that the prettiest girls, the best cars, and thousands of other wonderful things are to be found there" (ibid: 326).

The stance of a traditional inhabitant of the region is summed up by a Jordanian Bedouin, who has no idea that foreign countries exist and has never seen a city: "I am satisfied with what God has given me" (ibid: 318). However, the opinions of disaffected people on the borderline between the traditional and modern world were changing. Though they tended to be better off than the traditional nomad or peasant, this Jordanian farmer, exposed to the media and contact with people from the city, expresses a frustration common to many: "We live like animals. We do nothing but graft, eat and sleep" (ibid: 338). A traditional inhabitant of the region was concerned simply with survival, and their sole aim was to have enough work to buy bread. In contrast, the transitional inhabitant craved a better standard of living. The difference in attitudes could be summed up as "those who have nothing" versus "those who have (almost) nothing, but would like far more".

Lerner links modernisation with the emergence and spread of a new type of personality, one that comes into being because of newly created and subsequently growing aspirations. The transitional personality has one foot in the old world of traditional loyalties and identities and the other in the modern world, which shapes his attitudes and outlook on life. This is a "person in motion" or a "restless soul", whose curse is that what he has is never enough and he is not satisfied by what he is. Unlike previous generations, he wants to be someone else and have something else. While traditional man is sustained by the past and copies the needs and lifestyle of his predecessors, modernising man looks to a future full of dreams and expectations.

The increase in aspirations and a re-orientation from tradition to an open future is linked to the emergence of the *empathetic personality*. This is a person who is able to imagine themselves in new roles and alternative social positions. He is not fatalistic. He possesses psychological mobility, imagination and mental adaptability, and is therefore able to see the tension between what is and what might be. This is the source of the frustration of the modernising inhabitant of the Middle East. As a young Lebanese exposed to the influence of the media expressed it in the late 1950s: "If you are not aware of the existence of certain things, you don't crave them and miss them" (ibid: 177).

What leads to empathy and rising aspirations? Firstly, increased geographical and social mobility associated with urbanisation, i.e. with the move from the countryside to the city, where people encounter a range of hitherto unknown social roles and positions. Secondly, the populist and state-building rhetoric of authoritarians, who promise a high standard of living similar to that of the West. Thirdly, the spread of the media throughout the population. The media activates the imagination, recounting the stories of people representing hitherto unknown roles and potentially inspiring models. The public will never meet such people, but may yearn to become one of them: "Films are like our teachers. They show us all the things we could do" (ibid: 54). Radio is also referred to as the university of life (ibid: 346). At the start of modernisation, a media expanded that was based on the spoken word or graphic illustration that did not require a literate public (cinema, radio and posters). From the perspective of traditional classes this media was able to function as an inspiring "tutor in the correct way of life".

The attractive media image of the West has always played a key role in the Middle East. Europe, the United States and the Soviet Union were seen as a *reference group*. As a young Lebanese girl told the researchers in late 1950s: "America is a fantastic country. Americans have absolutely everything. Skyscrapers, zoos and lakes everywhere. It is a very rich country" (ibid: 202). The traditional inhabitant of the region had never heard of the existence of Western countries, ignored them, or knew very little about them, as in the case of this Jordanian nomad: "The USA? Is it like our encampment or more like Amman?" (ibid: 320). In contrast, modernising groups influenced by the media take an active interest in advanced countries and use them rather than other poor countries of the region as the yardstick by which to compare their own situation. As a young Syrian noted: "When we see the lives of people in the West and compare them with ours, we realise there is still a long way to go before we get to their level". Or a Lebanese of the same age: "I understand that, even if you come from a poor background, in America you can have a fantastic career and be top in your field. If you prove that you're really capable of it, you can work your way up to the top in a way that over here I can only dream of" (ibid: 400 and 210).

The ever growing masses of the Middle East want what they think people in the West have. However, their image of the West is distorted by the media. Perceptions of Western living standards are often idealised and exaggerated.

Under the influence of American films, the USA is often associated with a "clean and wealthy life", and this increases the frustration arising from a comparison of their own situation with the artificially confected image of the West. As Lerner concludes: "A film of the lives of ordinary people in the United States can be transformed into volatile radical theory on the screens of cinemas in Cairo or Tehran" (ibid: 11).

The expansion of the media within the context of uneven modernisation increases political tension. A hitherto humble and fatalistic population longs for a higher standard of living. More and more people expect more and more from life and want to participate in consumerism. They want to become like people from the West or the upper classes of their own countries. However, their needs tend not to be met and these new aspirations are contrasted with reality. Frustrations accumulate and threaten to escalate into revolutionary outbursts. Lerner maintains that happiness is a function of aspirations and the degree to which these aspirations are met. And in the case of a poor modernising population this discrepancy is the greatest, especially in economically stagnating societies caught in the poverty trap, or in societies where aspirations quickly spread to all classes and regions but wealth, albeit increasing, is distributed amongst a narrow elite. However, it is not the chasm in itself between a person's aspirations and their restricted opportunities to achieve them that represents the most politically dangerous situation, but the despair induced by the knowledge that this chasm will not be overcome in the foreseeable future (Lerner 1964).

In their well known interpretation of the revolutionary situation, James Davies (1962) and Ted Gurr (1970) work with the concept of *relative deprivation*. This involve an intensively experienced psychological distress stemming from the discrepancy between that which a person has in reality and that which they believe they should by rights have, i.e. between the perception of that which a person can realistically achieve in the current system and that to which they believe they are entitled. The subjective definition of the situation is important here: people must regard the political or economic reality of their lives as both unjust and at the same time changeable. However, this perceived injustice is always relative. It stems from a comparison of their current life opportunities and their "fair" aspirations, which are most often derived from the opportunities of a real or imagined *reference group*, i.e. a group with whose values, norms, patterns of behaviour, leaders or ways of life an individual identifies and accepts as their own. If a person is not part of such a group, they nevertheless long to be part and the conflict between desire and reality, between membership in their own group and the reference group is often hard to bear (cf. Merton 1957).

A revolution caused by rising expectations therefore arrives at that moment when, though the real economic or political conditions of the lives of the people are not changing, the aspirations that they believe are justified are rising sharply. If the discrepancy between aspiration and reality reaches a critical threshold, the accumulated psychological deprivation causes revolution. The swift rise in aspirations may be caused by the influence of a new ideology that offers a new (materialist) value system and sets a new standard as to what people can legitimately expect. It tells them how high their demands should be. By means of state propaganda, Middle Eastern secular ideology long promised its populations the imminent arrival of an affluence comparable with that of the West and the gradual liberalisation and democratisation of political regimes. However, in both spheres it simply aroused high expectations that it could not meet. The second mechanism behind the growth in aspirations is the *demonstration effect* of a reference group, i.e. the attractive example set by the high standard of living and opportunities on offer in other societies, or the lives of privileged groups inside a person's own society. At the same time, a parade of attractive models increasing existing aspirations and creating a need for the new and as yet unknown, burst upon the scene in the Middle East along with the media revolution. In the global village it is easy to identify with people living on the other side of the world and to deem it fair and legitimate to demand the same standard of living and level of political rights and civil liberties as they have.

(4) A SHRINKING WORLD II: VISIBLE DOMESTIC INEQUALITY

The arrival of a media that was difficult to censor was a headache for Middle Eastern dictators. It was not only the world as a whole that was becoming a transparent, shrinking global village. Individual countries could also now be examined in unprecedented detail. After the parliamentary elections (2006) in overpopulated Bahrain, the primary scandal was not only the unfair distribution of oil wealth, but the shortage of land. Young Shiites wanted to build homes and have families. But there was insufficient land. And so when Mahmud, who lived in an overcrowded building with sixteen of his relatives, saw satellite pictures of palaces and extensive land belonging to the royal family from the minority Sunnis on Google Earth, he, along with many of his peers, was furious, especially as right alongside he could see his poor, overcrowded suburb (Friedman 2011).

Investigative civil journalism has also arisen in Tunisia thanks to the blogosphere. Prior to the revolution, a video of President Ben Ali and his wife shopping in European capitals enjoyed great popularity (Howard and Hussain 2011). In the words of the Arabist Bernard Lewis: "Being abjectly poor is bad enough. But when everybody else around you is far from abjectly poor, then it becomes pretty intolerable." The new media tears the fig leaf from government propaganda and censorship that has concealed inequality up till now (cited in Petráček 2011).

However, inequality in itself does not generally lead to dissatisfaction. It only becomes the subject of criticism at the moment it is perceived as illegitimate and unjustifiable (Keller 1999). According to the Arabs, politics is about not only freedom, but also justice, about the contrast between justice and injustice, justice and oppression and corruption. Unjust inequalities arouse resistance (Lewis 1990). From the perspective of Islam extreme inequalities are immoral, and this is how they are being increasingly perceived in the region (Dekmejian 1995).

In my opinion, the new media has simply facilitated an explosive *interaction* between social reality characterised by extreme inequality and the social sensitivity of the Islamic imaginary. Crucially, Islam (Esposito and Mogahed 2007: 16) emphasises solidarity and assistance to the needy. It emphasises equality, humility and charity. Fasting during Ramadan tends these days to be seen as an opportunity for the wealthier classes to recall the hardship of the poor in society. The regular alms (*zakat*) taken from the property of every Muslim are intended for social assistance. They represent another pillar of Islam emphasising social responsibility and are regarded as a way of redistributing wealth from the rich to the poor. God does not want people to live in poverty. Destitution is not supposed to be their fate. In addition, charity work can be understood as a praiseworthy effort, as jihad of the hand. At the same time, however, the well known hadith attributed to Muhammad places an emphasis on hard work and activity: "The hand that gives is better than the hand that takes". Finally, the fifth pillar of Islam, the pilgrimage to Mecca, reminds Muslims that they are part of a close community that should not be divided by racial, tribal or class inequalities. Alongside a resistance to usury, Islamists sometimes work with an idea of property as a *means* of achieving the general welfare of the Muslim community, and not as an ostentatious *end* in itself. Similar discussions are taking place regarding the new role of the traditional *waqf*, namely collective ownership managed by a religious foundation for the sake of the common weal in the form of the building of schools, orphanages and spas (cf. Mendel 2008).

Some Islamists are also attempting to suppress manifestations of Western consumerism by highlighting the possibility of the intoxication and degeneration of Muslim societies by immoral Western culture (Chekroun 2005). However, this is often a sign of an ambivalent resentment: that which is vociferously rejected and condemned is often the subject of secret admiration and unfulfilled desire (Keller 1990). According to Islamists, the Western culture pouring out of films, television and video clips is promoting consumer norms, materialist values, a focus on the individual, and sexual abandon. All of this is regarded as being at odds with the spirituality, humility, thrift, responsibility and obligations of the individual to society preferred by Islam. The current epidemic of immorality is revealing the failure of secular governments. The function of the state is to promote virtue and discourage vice. It is to keep a watchful eye over the morality of its citizenry and to protect them against the temptations of toxic westernisation (Hoffman 1995, Etzioni 2004).

Political instability and a shift towards Islamism arise from increasing deprivation and not from absolute poverty. The modernising population of the Middle East yearns for the standard of living and level of consumption enjoyed by the upper classes in their own countries and by Westerners. They are familiarised with this way of living by the media, and it thus becomes difficult to continue to camouflage and conceal the extent of inequality. The media brings images into tea shops and living rooms of the wealth of the wealthy and the poverty of the poor. However, an awareness of inequality in itself does not usually lead to social conflict, but simply to an intensification of frustration. Inequality has to be understood as illegitimate and unjust. To this end the existing ideology, which attempts to persuade the lower classes in clear and convincing terms of the legitimacy of inequality, must be discredited. For instance, the Hindu concept of reincarnation justifies the caste system by referring to the conduct of an individual in a past life. Medieval Christianity defended inequality by calling it God's will. And the modern ideology of meritocracy points to the channels of mobility supposedly open to every hardworking, capable individual (Coser 1956, Gurr 1970, Keller 1999, Mareš 1999). However, in the Middle East the existing ideologies have been discredited, and it is Islam, including a political Islam emphasising its social dimension, that thanks to its social sensitivity provides arguments that throw doubt on efforts to legitimise the blatant inequality being reported on by various types of media.

(5) A SHRINKING WORLD III: THE TURKISH MODEL AND OTHER REFERENCE COUNTRIES

China and Egypt are the proud descendents of large civilisations. They are developing countries that self-profiled as anti-imperialist. Half a century ago China was poorer than Egypt. Today, however, after three decades of reforms and growth, China is the second most powerful economy on the planet, while Egypt is mired in poverty and has become dependent on the United States for financial and food aid. What went through the minds of Arabs as they watched the glitzy opening ceremony of the Beijing Olympics in 2008 on their televisions? It was galling enough comparing the backwardness of their own countries with Europe and America. But all the more frustrating now is the confrontation of their own lack of prospects with dynamically developing countries that fifty years ago stood on the same starting line with the Arab world (Friedman 2011). A sign of stagnation in a shrinking world is the flood of consumer goods from China. Inhabitants of the Middle East must be asking why it is not they instead of the Chinese who, thanks to cheap labour, succeeded against international competition (Friedman 2011b). What did our rulers do wrong? How did they squander the country's potential over the last fifty years? Ok, the Chinese surrendered their freedom. But in return they received economic growth, international respect and a functioning state. The Arabs also surrendered their freedom. But in exchange – apart from unemployment, stagnation and the Arab-Israeli conflict – they received nothing (cf. Petráček 2011, Lewis 2003).

When Iranians compare their country with more successful developing countries the result is also political tension. For many middle-class Iranians fond of Turkish beaches, Turkey is a success story worth emulating. Not everyone agrees. However, the "Turkish model" is fiercely debated by well informed Iranians[25]. Its supporters, known as internationalists (e.g. ex-president Khatami), demand the country open itself up to international influences, citing China, Malaysia, the Emirates and Turkey as inspiring models. They want Iran to engage in international trade, technology transfers, exchange trips by students and academics, and inter-cultural dialogue. They do not want isolation, but seek to be admitted to international organisations and to avail themselves of the positive aspects of globalisation. Integration into the global system will, they argue, bring security and prosperity, a claim contested by revolutionaries and conservatives (Sariolghalam 2008).

These examples illustrate the deeper changes in the orientation of the Middle Eastern public. They reflect the concurrence of the media revolution and a global realignment in the direction of a multipolar, post-American world (cf. Zakaria 2008). After the collapse of the alternative model represented by the USSR, the West remains the point of reference to which the inhabitants of the Middle East look and with which they compare their own countries. However, the West has lost the monopoly of a single attractive centre. New centres are emerging. And along with an increase in the *hard power* of these new centres in the form of economic, political and military power, there has been an increase in their *soft power*, i.e. the attractiveness of their institutions, cultures, values and lifestyle (cf. Nye 2004). Given the choice, most Jordanians would like to live in the United Arab Emirates. Lebanese would opt not only for France, but many successful Muslim countries. Pakistanis look to the emerging superpower of China. Turks regard Germany as their model and in Indonesia Japan is deemed the ideal. The American

---

25   A series of interviews conducted by the author, Iran, August, 2008.

Dream no longer predominates in the Middle East. Instead, Europe and increasingly Asia provide possible models of development. (Kohut and Stokes 2007).

THE TURKISH MODEL: UNIQUE OR UNIVERSAL?

Since the Justice and Development Party (AKP) came to power in 2002, it is the Turkish dream that, surprisingly, has found a home in the Arab public awareness. Though commentators often claim that the *Turkish model* is particular to that country and cannot be replicated elsewhere, they disagree as to wherein resides this particularity. Some believe it is the ninety years of a republic living in peace with its neighbours. Unlike the Arabs, Turkey has not been involved in draining conflicts with Israel and was able to concentrate on development. In addition, it did not experience a bitter and disruptive civil war, as did Lebanon, Yemen, Sudan, Algeria and, most recently, Palestine, Iraq, Libya and Syria (though the conflict with the Kurds is undermining development). An additional driver of government reforms is the prospect of integration into the European Union, something the Arab countries cannot even dream of. In particular, the country lacks exportable oil, and this obliges Turkey to develop a diversified economy. Another relatively unique factor is the historical continuity of statehood dating back to the Ottoman or even the Byzantine Empire, which established a strong state and national identity (Pope 2011, Fawsett 2009).

Some commentators, on the other hand, point to the highly reformist character of Ataturk, who, from the position of enlightened dictator inspired by the French Revolution, suppressed Islam and thus allowed for westernisation, economic development and democracy. Others claim that the history of the region yields many similar secular dictators (Bourguiba, Nasser, the Shah of Iran), and that this is not unique to Turkey. A competing legacy to Ataturk reconciles Islam with democracy and capitalism: from the Ottoman constitutional reforms (1876), via the banned Progressive Republican Party (1924), the government of Adnan Menderes (1950–60) and Turgut Özal (1983–93), to Tayyip Erdogan (since 2002). According to this interpretation the Turkish model differs from the rest of the Middle East by virtue of an established democracy and a capitalism unregulated by the state. The free rivalry of political parties only prevailed after Ataturk's death, and as a consequence devout Turks are not drawn to violence and radicalism, unlike sections of the religious Arabs. On the contrary, they support democracy as the surest guarantee of the freedom to practice their faith. The free market and the end of Ataturkian statism then assisted the creation of the Anatolian Tigers ("Islamic Calvinists"). This then levelled the typically Middle Eastern class gulf between wealthier secularists and poorer Islamists (Akyol 2012).

Finally, the uniqueness of the Turkish model is often associated with the active involvement of the army in politics and administration of the country. With its tradition of military coups, the army is regarded as a bastion and guardian of the secular republic tradition. However, opinions differ as to whether this is a good thing (Richards and Waterbury 2008). Ideas of Turkey as a model for Arab countries are often criticised as a sign of Turkish orientalism. The positive self-image of the modern Turkish nation is built upon a contrast being drawn with its own Ottoman past or with the backward Arabs and Kurds, who should learn a lesson from the Turks (Malečková 2013).

ARAB PUBLIC OPINION AND ITS FASCINATION WITH TURKEY

However, despite these disagreements regarding the nature of "Turkish exceptionalism" and despite Arab nationalism and historical grievances dating back to the time of the Ottoman Empire, an increasingly better informed Middle Eastern public regards Turkey with respect, as indeed did local reform-minded authoritarians in the past. In 2011 Turkey was the most popular country (78% of the population of the Middle East rated it positively), and this is a trend that has persisted for many years. Next were the Emirates (70%) and China (65%). The West cannot compete with Turkey (33% view the USA positively, 36% Great Britain and 46% France). Turkey's popularity was highest in Libya (93%), Tunisia (91%) and Egypt (86%), as well as in Palestine and Saudi Arabia (89%) (TESEV 2012). Premier Recep Erdogan has long been the most popular politician in the region (on 22% of the population) (Zogby International 2011).

Turkey is far and away the most popular holiday destination in the Middle East (30%; Lebanon is second on approximately 15%), and is even the second most popular destination in the world (with a 12% rating after France on 15%). Most of the population have experienced Turkish products (71%) and television serials (74%). And though Saudi Arabia is still regarded as having the strongest economy in the region (26% of respondents), Turkey comes a close second on 20%. Thanks to its dynamism it is most often seen as the future economic leader of the region (25%). Turkish foreign policy is also rated very highly and regarded as promoting peace in the region (77%). Its mediating role in the Arab-Israel conflict is supported (75%), and its reaction to the Arab Spring is also approved of (64%), most emphatically in Libya (89%), Palestine (81%), Egypt (80%) and Tunisia (75%).

Finally, Turkey is considered a *possible model* for Middle Eastern countries (61%), an opinion most widespread amongst Egyptians and Tunisians (78%), Palestinians (77%) and Libyans and Lebanese (75%) (TESEV 2012). For instance, most Egyptians (2011) expressed a preference for a post-revolutionary transformation of the political system along Turkish lines (44%), while far fewer came out in favour of the second-placed France (10%) or third-placed Saudi Arabia and China (8%), and almost none at all for the Iranian model (less than 1%) (Zogby 2011).

There are many reasons why the Turkish model should find such favour in the Arab world. A functioning democracy is most often cited (32%). Related to this is the fact that most Arabs see Turkey as a successful example of the coexistence of Islam and democracy (67%), again most often in Libya (91%), Tunisia (86%) and Egypt (80%). Supporters of the Turkish model also point to a booming economy (25%), as well as to the Islamic character of the country (23%), or, on the contrary, its secular political system (17%). We see, therefore, that ordinary Arabs select quite different, sometimes diametrically opposing, characteristics from the Turkish model – just like the academics and commentators discussed above. Conversely, opponents of the model (22% of all respondents) are most often vexed by the fact that it is not sufficiently Muslim (23%), by its alliance with the West (16%), its despised secularism (13%), its ethnic difference from Arabs (9%), and historical grievances from the era of the Ottoman Empire (7%). A positive perception of Turkey was strongest in Egypt, Tunisia and Libya, i.e. in those countries where the Arab revolutions began and were the most intense (TESEV 2012).

The Middle Eastern public is well informed about the Turkish economic miracle under the government of the AKP. After 2002 the Turkish economy recovered from crisis and grew by an average of 7% per annum, while exports rose fourfold and direct foreign investment twenty times over. Turkey is a newly recognised mediator between opposing parties, hosts prestigious summits, occupied the chair of the Organisation of the Islamic Conference (2005), is a member of the UN Security Council (2009–2010), and an observer in the Arab League (2010). Turkey won popularity through its confrontational approach to Israel and its support for Palestine. Arabs are also impressed by its ability to aspire realistically to membership of the European Union, a fact that implies an equivalence between Turkey and Western European countries. There are always hundreds of Arab journalists at meetings of Turkish and Western European countries.

This positive image of Turkey in the Middle East is completed by the free trade zone (Syria, Lebanon and Jordan, 2010), the abolition of visas for neighbouring countries, the opening of new border crossings, the flood of Arab and Iranian tourists, and the popularity of Turkish films, serials (over 70 of which have been dubbed into Arabic), music and goods. Finally, Arabs are impressed by Turkish democracy and the ability of the conservative AKP to reconcile Muslim faith with political pragmatism. The arrival of the AKP meant the disappearance of the old label of Turkey as an anti-Islamic and pro-Western puppet disappeared (Pope 2012). The regional attractiveness of Turkey is based, therefore, on a successful balancing act between the pitfalls of authoritarianism, militarism, military coup, a rigid statist mixed economy, religious fundamentalism, and a highly charged nationalism. These problems are universal to the region as a whole, and Turkey therefore provides appropriate inspiration (Pope 2011).

Turks also gained in popularity during the turbulent revolutionary year of 2011, when they were among the first to welcome the Arab Spring. Premier Erdogan quickly placed himself on the side of the Egyptian demonstrators when he declared that "we are with the people" and called on Mubarak to resign. The Turks were later to call for the departure of dictators in Syria and Libya. They subsequently encouraged Egyptian, Tunisian, Moroccan and Algerian Islamists to play their part in a parliamentary democracy (Aydintaşbaş 2012). And so Arab opposition groups and post-revolutionary governments claimed allegiance to the Turkish model, while Erdogan offered Turkey as an example (Malečková 2013). In an effort not to offend Arab patriotism, the Turkish foreign minister Ahmet Davutoğlu was more circumspect in his formulation, but said essentially the same thing: "We do not want to present Turkey as a model, even though others may see it in this way. However, the Turkish ability to find compatibility between democracy and secularism in a majority Muslim society could serve as inspiration for transforming countries of the region, including Egypt".

However, the Turkish model may become discredited. Turks have become involved in the transformations of individual countries, where they have selected partners and in doing so have been caught up in internal conflicts and lost their neutrality. Furthermore, an inclination to authoritarianism, the suppression of protests in Gezi Park (2013) and restrictions on freedom of expression throw doubt on the Turkish model (Malečková 2013). The possible transience of Turkey's popularity is well reflected in the triumphal tour by its leader Erdogan of the countries of the Arab Spring during autumn 2011, which contrasts with the gradual disillusion, almost disgust, that a large section of the Arab public feel towards him only a few years later.

(6) THE SHRINKING ARAB WORLD: THE DEMOCRATISING EFFECT OF AL-JAZEERA AND THE REVOLUTIONARY DOMINO

From the mid-1990s onwards, thanks to the arrival of the internet and satellite television, i.e. media able to circumvent censorship, the populations of the Middle East were better and better informed as to the functioning and advantages of democracy and could compare the corrupt dictatorships in their own countries with the politics of democratic countries. This has undermined confidence in dictatorships and, on the contrary, has popularised democracy as a realistic alternative. For instance, the innovative coverage by Al-Jazeera of events in hostile Israel has bolstered voices calling for change in the Arab world. Arab viewers watched with fascination the resignation of the Israeli premier Olmert, accused of corruption. Or the conviction for rape of the powerful ex-president Katsav by an independent court, which found in favour of ordinary female employees. Then there is the case of General Yoav Galant, who was not appointed chief of the General Staff because of allegations pertaining to public land. These scandals shocked Arab viewers because in Arab dictatorships similar abuses of power are commonplace and go unpunished. This increased awareness raised the bar of political culture and turned a spotlight on politics in their own countries. The new political style prior to the Arab revolutions was loudly proclaimed by the Palestinian premier Fayyad of the West Bank: "Don't judge me on how I fight against Israel, but according to the results of my government, according to how public services operate, how I serve our citizens, and the new jobs I create" (Friedman 2011, Boček 2006).

For a long time only a few radio stations circumvented censorship in the Middle East, mainly the *BBC World Service Arabic*, *Voice of America*, the French *Radio Monte Carlo-Middle East*, and the *Middle Eastern Radio Broadcast* transmitted from Cairo. However, the public only resorted to these news sources when conflict escalated. And so, apart from the internet, independent information on the democratic world only arrived with the satellite station Al-Jazeera. During the 1990s, the Saudi Arabian dictatorship, represented by Orbit Communications, backed down from a collaborative project with the British BBC that would have seen a documentary aired on executions in the desert kingdom. An itinerant team of journalists then received an offer from the reformist Emir Sheik Hamad bin Khalífa of Qatar, where the channel originated (1996) (El-Nawawy and Iskandar 2003). From the very start it made no attempt to hide its activism, its ambition to democratise a region intellectually isolated by censorship and political repression. The editorial board is made up of Arabs educated in the West (Al-Jazeera...2003). They come from a range of Arab countries and from tribal and urban backgrounds and represent both the left and right wing, the religious and secular, pro-Western and anti-Western thinking, and men and women. They are capable of working together because they share a respect for freedom of speech and for different opinions. For instance, the star presenter, the Syrian Faisal al-Qassem, sees the lack of freedom of speech as the major impediment holding back progress in the Middle East. He believes that Al-Jazeera is helping to build democracy in the region simply by doing its job well and teaching Arabs about free speech and openness. The station's motto has become: "The Opinion and the Other Opinion".

Al-Jazeera is the only news outlet unafraid to criticise dictators, and many of the opinions it broadcasts could see a person arrested in most Middle

Eastern countries. It thus has the effect of undermining the reverence with which the state media speak of Arab dictators. Rulers become accountable to the public. In contrast, state television coverage is restricted to a litany of official proceedings: a dictator's daily schedule, how he breakfasted with ambassadors, opened a new highway, in the afternoon offered paternal advice to students, and in the evening phoned his friend in the White House. Al-Jazeera also differs from the state media by providing a platform for all opinions, including opposition or decidedly minority views. Its code of ethics speaks of impartially offering various perspectives and opinions without prejudice. It offers a voice to all parties, something that is unprecedented in the Middle East (Kouřilová 2004). In doing so it finds itself at odds with the established approach of Arab journalists, as summed up by the editor of the pro-regime newspaper Al-Hayat: "The curse of democracy is that you have to include the views of both sides" (Boček 2006). Al-Jazeera flies in the face of this approach because it is not subject to censorship. The principles of its journalism abide by those of Western television (Kouřilová 2004), and the quality of its output far exceeds that of its rivals in the region. In 2007, even the official Israeli government spokesperson had this to say: "I deeply appreciate the manner in which Al-Jazeera reports on the Israeli-Palestinian conflict. I don't agree with everything it says, but at least it makes no attempt to misinform. In my opinion, Al-Jazeera is way ahead of the BBC or CNN" (cited in Boček, Vlnas 2007).

In addition to its news reports, Al-Jazeera's discussion programmes on sensitive topics have proved popular. These include *Bila Hudud* (No Limits) and *Akthar Min Ra'y* (More than an Opinion). The most popular and controversial talk show *Al-Ittijah al-Mu'akis* (The Opposite Direction), which pits guests with diametrically opposed views against each other, has become a legend. The programme also invites representatives of Israel and the United States, as well as atheists and Islamists. Al-Jazeera is breaking one taboo after another. Another innovation is the station's phone-ins. As one member of the editorial board puts it: "For Arabs this is revolutionary. They have waited so long for someone to listen to them. Letting people speak is important." Unlike state television, subject to the possibility of further censorships, interviews and commentaries are not filmed in advance. This makes for far more exciting live broadcasts, in which it is not clear until the last minute what the invited guests will say. In addition, the presenters make sure that the invited officials do not deviate from the topic in hand and demand that they answer the questions put to them. They also ensure that every guest is allocated the same amount of time (El-Nawawy and Iskandar 2003). Al-Jazeera's success shows that there has long been a demand in the region for independent journalism and for a discussion of topics that have long been only talked about in private. State television ignored this demand and the vacuum was eventually filled by Al-Jazeera. This saw an acceleration of nationwide discussions of crucial political and religious themes (Boček 2006, Kouřilová 2004).

The importance of Al-Jazeera is borne out by the reactions of panic-stricken Arab regimes, which for the first time in history lost control over the flow of information. Virtually every dictator in the Middle East is convinced that Al-Jazeera has a vendetta against them. They resort to shutting down its regional offices. They refuse visas to journalists. Guests slated to appear on programmes are prevented from travelling or their telephone connection is interrupted while live on air. On one famous occasion the electricity mains was switched off in Algerian cities, a measure taken by the government to prevent its people watching a programme on the country's civil war (1999). Most common are threats of severing diplomatic relations with Qatar, recalling ambassadors in protest against particular programmes, or stern communiqués addressed to the Qatar minister of foreign affairs (450 during the first five years of the station's activities). There is a boycott on advertising by media agencies usually owned by Saudi Arabia (Kouřilová 2004, 2006). Many large Middle Eastern and Western companies do not cooperate with Al-Jazeera for fear of losing the right to do business in the Arab world or a lucrative state contract. Instead they place their commercials on the state television. As a consequence of all this, Al-Jazeera has not been made a member of the *Arab States Broadcasting Union* (1998), and will not be unless it adapts to the "code of honour of the Arab media" and begins to respect the "brotherhood between Arab nations". In practice this refers to the gentlemen's agreement between Arab dictators not to criticise each other and to the fact that there exist taboos that are not spoken about (El-Nawawy and Iskandar 2003). However, the US military have also repeatedly attacked Al-Jazeera journalists in Afghanistan and Iraq. Controversy was aroused by George W. Bush's alleged plan to bomb the station's headquarters in Qatar in retaliation for a report on the civilian casualties of both wars. And a further scandal was the arrest of cameraman Sami al-Hajj, who was tortured, sexually abused and persecuted for his religion in Abu Ghraib prison, after which he was imprisoned in Guantanamo Bay. The organisation Reporters Without Borders and the International Federation of Journalists have protested against the intimidation of the station (Boček 2006).

The success of Al-Jazeera and the geopolitical importance of the region saw a struggle break out for the Arab television viewer. Major global players began competing for Middle Eastern public opinion. The Americans created the Alhurra TV station. The British BBC established an Arab channel. Every day for twelve hours the German Deutsche Welle broadcasts its roundup of world events in Arab, and the French government supports its interests by means of the project France 24. Even the European Union has started broadcasting Euronews in Arabic (Boček, Vlnas 2007). However, Al-Jazeera faces its stiffest competition from Middle Eastern satellite stations. A rising star in the region is the Lebanese Al-Manar, broadcasting from South Beirut (2000) and linked with Hezbollah. It is watched not only in Lebanon, but also in the Gulf States (Čečáková 2006).

Al-Jazeera has also reinforced a sense of pan-Arab unity and identity, an awareness that Arabs share the same fate and similar problems. For the first time since the time of the legendary singer Umm Khultum, whose performances during the 1970s the entire Arab world would listen to every first Thursday in the month, Arabs are watching the same programmes en masse (El-Nawawy and Iskandar 2003). The pivotal role of the new media in the Middle East is borne out by the domino effect that saw revolution spread from Tunisia to Egypt and the resonate with varying strength and impact in practically all countries of the region that share similar challenges, cultures and historical experience. This represents a repetition of the "television revolution" model known from the third wave of democratisation (1974–1990), which, however, had that time round avoided the Middle East. Democratisation in one country accelerates political change in other countries. It influences the way that power elites, opposition groups and undecided citizens think. Success in one country shows the rest that change is possible, and also shows them how it is to be achieved. The Carnation Revolution in Portugal and the overthrow of the military dictatorship in Spain (1974) inspired countries in former colonies bound by cultural links, migration flows and a similar historical experience, especially the culturally and linguistically affiliated states of Latin America and the Philippines, ruled over by sadistic military regimes. This model was later replicated in communist Eastern Europe, which shared the same historical experience, culture and problems. Samuel P. Huntington sees a snowball effect in the acceleration of the revolutionary process of television revolutions: "In Poland democratisation lasted ten years, in Hungary ten months, in Eastern Germany ten weeks, in Czechoslovakia ten days and in Romania ten hours" (Huntington 2008: 107).

The internet also contributed to a feeling of pan-Arab unity and solidarity. For instance, revolutionaries in different countries shouted slogans that had first been used in Tunisia. This phenomenon appeared unambiguously on the tweets of Egyptian demonstrators. On the very first day Hossam writes: "The demonstrators' slogan is the same as in Tunisia: Leave!" Mahmoud Salem reminds people: "A whole month of protests was necessary for success in Tunisia. Perseverance is the key." Sceptical voices are also to be heard: "This will go nowhere in Egypt: Tunisia is different, it's far more developed." On the other hand, from the very start optimists viewed the Egyptian revolution as part of a pan-regional revolt and as inspiration for other countries: "I hope this spreads to other countries. I'm tired of waiting for democracy from the West. It's time we took things into our own hands." And in a similar vein:

"Arab brothers and sisters. If you want to support our intifada, overthrow your own dictators. We need a pan-regional intifada." These pan-Arab considerations also heightened the motivation of demonstrators and their resolve, a resolve derived from a sense of responsibility for developments in other countries: "The hopes of the entire region now depend on the fate of a single square" (cited in Idle and Nunns 2011: 47, 57, 89, 108).

However, in a later stage of the revolution the pan-Arab media interconnectedness led to a dampening down of revolutionary fervour as news spread of bloody developments in Libya and above all Syria. This experience was no longer inspiring but discouraging. People began to perceive security and stability as more important than the risk-strewn path to democracy. Scepticism regarding change, as captured by the Arab proverb "one day of anarchy is worse than a century of despotism", helped many regimes survive (Lynch 2013).

(7) THE MEDIA AT THE SERVICE OF OPPOSITION POLITICAL ISLAM

After the Middle East achieved independence, the media was dominated by secular content. However, the current media discourse is more and more conservative and Islamic. The expansion of modern transport and communications technologies has led to the emergence and spread of a public sphere in which new social movements, including religious movements, can establish themselves. This option was long discounted by the social sciences, influenced by the secularisation thesis and a scientific preconception regarding the incompatibility of modern media and religious movements (Arjomand 1986). In today's media sphere a wide range of special-interest, ethnic and political groups are to be heard, which defend their often diametrically opposed views using the language of Islam. Gone are the days when only official religious and political authorities had access to a controlled and censored media (Eickelman and Anderson 2003). Furthermore, the effect of the media promotion of different forms of Islam, including political Islam, is compounded by the emergence of a literate, increasingly educated public that, unlike the illiterate traditional population, is exposed to the influence of a wide range of media (Hashem 2006).

Islamist reformists of the 19th century, like modern Islamists, availed themselves of the most advanced media. They are progressive in their utilisation of the printed and electronic media to reach the widest audience. From at least as far back as the 1970s there were to be found in their ranks many technically educated activists who understood well the possibilities and political potential of the media. Christian and Jewish groups have also been using the media intensively since the 1970s, for instance the charismatic television preachers in the United States (Kepel 1996). Journalists, well aware of the power of the press, television and internet, are often to be found in the leadership of these movements (Anderson 2003). From mobilisation that relied on charitable organisations based around mosques and took place on a face-to-face basis, these days Islamists are moving more in the direction of anonymous mass media (Kepel 2004, Roy 2004).

BOOKS AND PRINTING

As far utilisation of the media is concerned, Islamic revivalist movements were the accomplished predecessors of modern Islamists. In their time they were standing up to European colonialism and the spread of Christian missionaries. We find this, for instance, in British India in the 19th century. If the British introduced and promoted a hybrid "Anglo-Muhammadan law", Islamic movements in the 1920s and 30s countered by publishing traditional religio-legal tracts on social and political questions (*fatwa*). Now, however, these were published and distributed in bulk thanks to printing. Similarly, writings on reform orthodoxy were published in large batches that exist in several editions and remain popular to the present day. These include the books by Sayyid Ahmad *The Straight Path* and *The Strengthening of Faith*. These opposition publications helped foment anti-British armed jihad (Arjomand 1986, Kropáček 2002). The publication of books and pamphlets promoting Islamic reformism then spread from British India to the Middle East (Anderson 2003). During the 19th century books featuring Islamic themes also became more accessible in the declining Ottoman Empire. This allowed for the deeper penetration of Islam into ever broader classes that were no longer reliant on verbal instruction from clerics (Eickelman, Piscatori 1996).

An even greater transformation in the concept of Islam, which led to the mass religious revival of Indian Muslims, was wrought by the translation and mass publication of the Quran in Urdu, usually accompanied by an extensive commentary and explanatory notes. Collections of *hadith*, i.e. the sayings and deeds of the Prophet Muhammad, were also translated from Arabic to Urdu. In this way modern Islamic reformers were able to reach out to a wider public in their native tongue and bring them closer to Islam. Although the impact of the mass publication of the Quran on a largely illiterate and poor population might appear limited, the opposite was true. The Quran was read out loud to those who were unable to read and every copy was distributed and shared among a wide circle of people. Indeed, the impact of the first media revolution was so great that the Christian missionaries were appalled and reported back to Europe that the "Mohammedans are learning to avail themselves of the power of the press". The orthodox Deobandi movement (founded in 1867) was a past master at using the press. It propagated its strict concept of Islam using the most up-to-date period technology: the postal service, the railway, telegraph, cheap printing presses, bank transfers, the publication of annual reports with transparent financial reporting, and through media campaigns attracting sponsors. It was convinced that it could remedy the state of Islamic society through promoting a single correct version of Islam. The movement perceived British colonisation as the consequence of weakness caused by the apostasy of Muslims and a movement away from God's law. However, even then the movement did not restrict itself to attacking Islamic currents such as Sufism and Shi'ism, but, convinced of Islam's superiority as the last and most modern prophecy, also attacked Hindus and Christians (Arjomand 1986, Hefner 2007)[26].

In the Arab world too, the rise of Islamic reformism was a defensive re-action to the shock of European colonialism. The dissemination of its ideas was assisted by the development of the printed media and journalism, as well as the expansion of different means of transport. In interwar Algeria, for example, the Salafist movement for the defence of Islam was based around the magazine *Shihab*. Reformist ideas then spread geographically from the centre in the capital Algiers along the main railway line number one leading to Laghouat. After the Second World War, the ideas of Wahhabism in French Western Africa spread in a similar way along the main railway lines and high-ways. The movement's centres were to be found at transport intersections. However, though the Islamic reformists used the most up-to-date means of communication effectively, this does not mean that they themselves were modernists (Arjomand 1986).

At present a visible manifestation of religious revival is the boom in Is-lamic books. Sales of the Quran and books on Islamic history and religion have risen dramatically since the 1970s. It is now the done thing to exhibit the Quran in a place of honour in homes, offices and cars. In this way Muslims communicate with each other in an effort to establish trust in anonymous cities full of strangers (Dekmejian 1995). For instance, from 1954 to 1964 reli-gious publications accounted for only 10% of the book market in Iran. Prior to the Islamic revolution (1979) this figure rose sharply. In 1972 it was already 26% and in 1975 it represented a third of all books published, so making it

---

26   The promotion of a certain interpretation of a religious tradition is influenced by the social and political context. The network of schools run by the Deoband movement was originally highly sectarian and orthodox. It had arisen in the 19th century in shocked response to British colonialism and Christian missionaries. In the face of the Hindu majority Islam appeared to be in mortal danger. In post-colonial authoritarian Pakistan the movement self-profiled as intolerant and anti-democratic and allowed for the emergence of the Afghan Taliban. However, in secular, democratic and mostly Hindu India the mainstream of the movement and its schools transformed. It supports secular democracy and apolitical piety. It is endeavouring to raise educated, modern, prosperous and at the same time religious Muslims (Hefner 2007).

the largest category of books on the shelves of bookshops (Arjomand 1986). In the Middle East it is the predominant and fastest growing segment of the book market. In Arab countries it comprises 17% on average of annually published books, while the global average of religious books on the market is only around 5% (AHDR 2003). However, this boom is not simply the visible consequence of religious revival. It is also the instrument of religious propaganda (*dawa*) used by various rival factions (Eickelman 2003).

The success enjoyed by these new Islamic books is down to the historically unprecedented levels of education in the population (Starrett 1998). A book is seen as the expression of a non-consumerist, non-materialist culture, as a suitable gift, for instance at weddings. The book is accorded respect in the region, the predecessor of all books in the eyes of ordinary Muslims being the Quran. Islamic books – mostly collections of hadiths, selected fatwas addressing issues of the faithful and the advice of Sufi masters – are also published by wealthy patrons and distributed free. This enables the cream of society to demonstrate its piety, however dubious may be the origin of its assets (Hashem 2006). The advantage of this book segment, in addition to attractive dust jackets and graphic design, stems from its simple, accessible language, which meets the needs and possibilities of a mass public far more that the refined style of literary elites or the cumbersome, boring language of religious and political elites.

These new Islamic books encompass a range of genres. These include religious manuals on the proper upbringing of children, the concept of woman in Islam, suitable behaviour while on a pilgrimage to Mecca, or the relationship of Islam and science, politics and modern society. Saccharine romances for teenagers, "Islamic" novels adopting anti-secular stances, comics, children's books and non-fiction works interpreting dreams, genies or Israeli policy are extremely popular. Islamic books combine a certain interpretation of Islam with the rules of a given literary genre, while offering everything that the people are interested in. They are on sale everywhere: not only in bookshops or at the bazaar, but on street stalls, in public transport or in kiosks. They are ubiquitous and it is impossible to escape them (Eickelman 2003).

Finally, an essential feature of these books is their low price, often achieved by means of original business models. For instance, at the end of the 1980s a large collection of hadiths was published with minimum initial capital. Each of the eight volumes was first divided into five smaller sections. These were gradually published on cheap paper every month in serial form, making individual parts of the serial affordable even for the poorer classes, who would otherwise be unable to buy the entire compendium at once. The publisher did not have to take out a large loan and risk everything on publishing the complete collection, which in addition he would have had to store at some cost, with the worry that it might not sell. Furthermore, readers were motivated by the promise that if they purchased all the volumes, they would receive a discount. And in this way a collection of the sayings and deeds of the Prophet Muhammad, the sunna, found its way into the hands of ordinary Egyptians for the first time in history. This in turn kick-started a broad, nationwide debate on Islam, in which the intellectual elites and traditional authorities played second fiddle (Starrett 1998).

Although the Middle East is plagued by censorship and freedom of speech dare not speak its name, control of the media is usually selective. The state dominates television and radio. The monopoly on television broadcasting has only been surrendered in Lebanon. The press tends to be somewhat freer and private publishers are permitted, even though these are often puppet firms financed by the state (Eickelman 2003). The reason for this is that the power elite does not feel as threatened by the press and does not regard it as influential. Having said this, the regime of Saddam Hussein feared the printed word to such an extent that all typewriters had to be officially registered so that samizdat publications could not be distributed by means of carbon paper (El-Nawawy and Iskandar 2003). Banning certain publications would also run the risk of their being popularised and pirated. The print media that does not wish to find itself in conflict with the government may also resort to the tactic of formally "critiquing" the arguments of banned authors. The censors might not intercept this type of article, while a readership accustomed to reading between the lines is able to familiarise itself with the thinking of dissidents. An essential mechanism aimed at strengthening the internal cohesion of Islamist movements is the lending and sharing of illegal publications, as well as cassettes, floppy discs, CDs and DVDs. In less repressive regimes a network of people who consolidate their mutual trust and sense of community with each borrowed book would have no chance of coming into existence. With each loan they get to know one another better, encourage each other, and reinforce a sense of conspiracy and opposition to the regime. In a democracy each of them would acquire the given publication individually and anonymously. They would go to a bookshop or bazaar, where among other like-minded customers they would not have to share a secret and a common feeling of the dangers of impending persecution. A community formed and consolidated in this way can then be mobilised for collective action under the banner of Islam (Eickelman 2003).

CASSETTES, PHOTOCOPIERS AND FAX MACHINES

Audiocassettes and videocassettes are used by many different opposition groups in order to popularise their own version of Islam. They played a crucial role in the Iranian Revolution (1979). The Shah of Iran wanted the opposition cleric Imam Khomeini sent into the most geographically remote exile. He believed that by banishing Khomeini he would cut him off from his followers and that he would be unable to influence politics in Iran. However, for all his modernisation rhetoric and secularism, the Shah was far more old-fashioned that the Islamist opposition. Khomeini understood that the expansion in communications technology had shrunk the world and created a global village. Geographical distance no longer played such an important role. He dictated popular messages, sermons and instructions by telephone from exile. These were recorded and copied onto cassettes that circulated in Iranian society (Roy 1992). In pre-revolutionary Iran popular cassettes of the persecuted laic Islamist Ali Shariati had been circulated amongst the masses in a similar way. Shariati had combined Shiite Islam with Marxism and was looked up to, especially by young people and students (Turner 2007). Illegal media also gained in popularity because the Iranian state radio and television (*National Iranian Radio and Television*) became the mouthpiece of the hated SAVAK secret services. The performances of its officials and the reading out of long "confessions" by tortured opponents of the regime discredited the state media in the eyes of the public (Eickelman 2003).

Also popular in the Middle East are non-political recordings of the Friday sermons by clerical celebrities, or insightful theological commentaries on the Quran or the words of mystics, as well as subversive music or poetry with an Islamist message (Hashem 2006). Huge popularity is enjoyed by video-cassettes or DVDs containing recordings of programmes from the satellite channel Al-Jazeera, which can be obtained at bazaars even in the most repressive regimes. A talk show in which the Syrian secularist Sadiq Jalal Al-Azm launched an attack on the prophets, elevated Ataturk, and denounced Islam as "backward" became a legend. He was opposed by the highly regarded cleric Yusuf al-Qaradawi in what was historically the first (1997) encounter between an atheist and a cleric on TV screens in the Middle East (El-Nawawy and Iskandar 2003).

These recordings stimulate religious and political debate and erode the dominance of printed leaflets and brochures. For the first time in history "Islam of the word" (*al-Islam al-sawti*) begins to compete with "Islam of the press". Cassettes are cheaper than printed materials and can be easily copied, smuggled and distributed. They can be played in private and at public meetings. Listening to and sharing illegal recordings again creates a feeling of belonging and solidarity within an opposition community. Islamists are great fans of Friday's sermons given by self-proclaimed sheikhs or global celebrities from the ranks of clerics sympathising with the Muslim brotherhood. Yusuf al-Qaradawi occupies a privileged position in this company. Serious topics are examined from the perspective of Islam, while also making reference to classical writers such as Qutb, Maududi, Khomeini and Ibn Taymiyyah. Everything is accompanied by references to CNN or Al-Jazeera and spiced up with scandalous quotations from the memoirs of American presidents or references to Western leftwing intellectuals. In conclusion the idealised form of the Muslim community under the first caliphs is sketched out in order to highlight the contrast with the corrupt present (Eickelman 2003).

The anti-American recruitment videos put out by Al-Qaeda represent a similar hybrid. These criticised the suffering of the Palestinians during the second intifada, the poverty suffered by sanction-stricken Iraq, the deployment of American soldiers near holy sites in Saudi Arabia, the unfair division of the profits from Arab oil, and Western support for dictators. The videos attempt to be action filled and attractive in the same way as CNN, and use shots from the BBC and Russian television, as well as their own footage. Bin Laden gave context to his terrorism. Though the people of the Middle East were not in general in favour of terrorism, they condemned the injustices of the West (El-Nawawy and Iskandar 2003).

A small cassette thus became a nightmare for omnipotent Middle Eastern dictatorships. In a state of panic states confiscated and banned them at border crossings. *The Arab Postal Union* prohibited the despatch of audiocassettes and videocassettes abroad. Parcels were inspected and confiscated. A recipient would often receive their parcel unwrapped after a delay of several months, or would be officially informed that it had been lost (Eickelman and Anderson 2003). During the 1990s regimes faced other headaches. The start of the decade was marked by fax and photocopy, but by the end of the decade satellite television and internet had appeared. For instance, from the safety of London the exiled Saudi *Committee for the Defence of Legitimate Rights* cast doubts on the Islamic character of the Saudi government. It sent revolutionary texts from "Londonistan" accusing the royal family of corruption. It proclaimed confidently that "While Khomeini's revolution had been cassette based, ours will be fax" (Norton 2003, Beránek 2007). The fact that new electronic media cannot easily be inspected is a problem for regimes. If a dictator decides to block faxes, the internet or a mobile signal, the economy is threatened with collapse and he risks losing the support of the classes that have up till now supported the regime, e.g. business circles. It is therefore difficult to prevent imports of printers, photocopiers, cassettes and CDs (Eickelman 2003, Lindsey 2011).

SATELLITE TELEVISION: OSAMA BIN LADEN AND YUSUF AL-QARADAWI

In response to the Gulf War (1990–1991) and what was at that time the complete media dominance of the American CNN, the first Middle Eastern satellite, *Middle East Broadcasting Centre* (MBC), owned by Saudi investors, began broadcasting from London. Orbit, another of its satellites, broadcasts from Rome, as does ART (Arab Radio and Television Network). The Egyptians launched their own project entitled *Egyptian Satellite Channel*, and the United Arab Emirates came up with *Emirates Dubai TV*. Other satellite television stations are the political projects of specific power groups. For instance, the Lebanese *Future TV* was owned by the former premier Rafic Hariri. ANN (Arab News Network) is run by the cousin of the Syrian dictator Bashar al-Assad (Gonzales-Quijano 2003). Later on the "politically correct" Television Abu Dhabi was a hit, as was the popular Al-Arabiya based in Dubai (Boček, Vlnas 2007).

However, by offering a voice to anti-government dissidents, including Islamists, and even to militant Islamists living in exile and under sentence of death at home, the phenomenon that broke the silence in the region was Al-Jazeera. The station has become a discussion platform for a wide range of opposition groups that are persecuted in their own countries and often isolated from the population. It has also become a communication channel between opposition groups and their sympathisers, and has been unsparing in its criticism of official clerics, often disclosing their close connections with regimes. News and current affairs programmes examine taboo issues linked with Islam. Is Islam an obstacle to success? What does it have to say about human rights, female circumcision or polygamy? What nonconformist interpretations does it offer today? What are the causes of religious terrorism? What is the programme of banned organisations? Is Hezbollah really a terrorist organisation? (Kouřilová 2004). When Middle Eastern regimes attack Al-Jazeera, they stylise themselves as defenders of Islam, culture and the religious sensibilities of their people. A pro-government Saudi newspaper is typical in this respect (1998): "How dare representatives of Al-Jazeera attack Islam and the holy Quran? How can they invite atheists to make fun of our religion in the name of freedom? What effect will this have on young Arabs? And what effect will it have on people who don't know enough about Islam? (El-Nawawy and Iskandar 2003: 116).

For instance, Al-Jazeera offered a platform to bin Laden at a time when he was virtually unknown in the West. In his very first broadcast interview (1999) he spoke of the duty of every Muslim to fight for the liberation of their country from a possible American occupation. "What we demand are rights for all people without distinction. We want liberation from the Americans. God gave people the instinct to reject foreign domination and oppression." In other statements bin Laden drew attention to unjust Western policies, while at the same time attempting to interpret the political and military aggression of the West as basically a clash of religions. In a half-hour message soon after the American attack on Afghanistan (2001) he declared: "Recent events have confirmed a great truth. Today it is clear that the West in general, and the United State in particular, feel tremendous hatred towards Islam. Terrorism against the USA deserves respect, because it is in response to injustice and is an attempt to bring an end to American support for Israel, which is killing our nation." After broadcasting such a video, Al-Jazeera has always organised a large panel discussion in which space is made for the official position of the United States and other critics of Al-Qaeda, so that the opinions of bin Laden are balanced by other voices. Despite this, Al-Jazeera has been accused of becoming a mouthpiece for terrorists. It has defended itself by pointing out that these materials are then used by leading Western television stations, including CNN. It has also pointed out that during the Gulf War (1990/1991), CNN would regularly broadcast the hate-filled speeches and press conferences given by Saddam Hussein. However, the main argument has been around the issue of balance. As Al-Jazeera's director Muhammad Jasim Al-Ali has said in defence of the station (2001): "We learned about an independent media from the United States. And now the Americans want us to give up what we learned from them? Our critics forget that bin Laden is one of two sides in this war, both of which we are presenting to viewers. How could the news be balanced without a presentation of the perspectives of both sides?" (El-Nawawy and Iskandar 2003: 149, 155, 176). However, the problem remains that the spectacular operations mounted by Al-Qaeda are conceived of as extravaganzas for a global television public (Kepel 2008). The terrorists do not only want many people to die but many people to see them die. The rise of Middle Eastern terrorism may therefore be related to the spread of television. If, hypothetically speaking, television ceased to exist, the number of attacks would probably drop (Juergensmeyer 2000).

However, Al-Jazeera also provides media space to so-called moderate Islamists. Thanks to Al-Jazeera and its regular programme *Sharia and Life* (*Al-Shari'a wal-Hayat*), Yusuf al-Qaradawi, the Egyptian preacher living in exile in Qatar, has become a global celebrity. By the standards of Sunni clerics al-Qaradawi advocates an unusually oppositional approach close to that of the Muslim Brotherhood. While Sunni clerics are usually conformist and support regimes, al-Qaradawi criticises both radical Islamists and dictators (Mendel 2010). The programme's audience is estimated to be 60 million, and perhaps every Muslim has read, heard or seen something by him. He studied at religious seminary at the Al-Azhar University, where he was top of his year. He regards a turning point in his life to be his meeting with Hassan al-Banna, founder of the Muslim Brotherhood: "It was love at first sentence."

In Egypt, al-Qaradawi was repeatedly imprisoned for his affiliation with the Brotherhood (1949, 1954–56, 1962). His books are required reading for the many members of the movement, and this has ensured them the status of bestseller. The Brotherhood has repeatedly offered him a leadership role. Even though he is not an official member of the organisation, he is more in the position of its uncrowned head-ideologist, hence the correspondence between his opinions and those of the Brotherhood. At Al-Jazeera he promotes a view of Islam as an all-encompassing system, something Banna had already claimed. As he said in his programme (2004): "I believe in the totality of Islam. Islam is not simply spirituality. Islam is exalted religion and the earthly world, missionary work and secular power, a religious creed and law. Islam is industry and agriculture. Islam is even art. Islam is in everything" (Belén Soage 2010: 20, 29).

Also in line with the position taken by the Brotherhood, al-Qaradawi advocates the modernisation of Islamic law so as to meet the requirements of today. At the same time, like the Brotherhood he sets himself against conservative clerics who support the regime in Saudi Arabia and other dictatorships. However, he often comes out against Western interference (2000): "In the Quran there is no mention of women not being able to stand for election, drive a car or acquire a doctorate. These people want to suspend time, they regard everything as banned (haram). They mix local traditions and customs with Islam. The real threat is more the growing military presence of the United States in the Gulf. Wherever the American army goes it insists on establishing nightclubs, bars selling alcohol and discotheques. And these things are genuinely forbidden in Islam" (El-Nawawy and Iskandar 2003: 80). And it was al-Qaradawi who from the 1990s onwards popularised the term "moderate Islamists" (al-wasatiyyah), in addition to whom there are apparently intellectually inflexible conservatives, violent jihadists, and excommunication Islamists (takfiri) accusing Muslims holding a different view to theirs of apostasy. In his programme he speaks of moderate Islamists (2003) as of the Muslim community of the golden mean (ummatan wasatan): "The centre is the balance between reason and revelation, body and spirit, rights and obligations, individualism and collectivism, inspiration and devotion, the sacred texts of the Quran and the Sunnah and individual interpretations, the ideal and reality, the eternal and the ephemeral, a reliance on the past and looking to the future." It is the search for this balanced centre that has become part of the discourse of the Muslim Brotherhood (Belén Soage 2010: 30).

However, during the search for a golden mean moderation often falls by the wayside. For instance, in his programmes al-Qaradawi defends the death penalty for apostates (Lafond 2013) or flogging as a punishment for homosexuality (MEMRI 2006). However strongly he condemned the attack of 11 September 2001 by claiming it was incompatible with Islam, he did not reject the general idea of aggressive jihad. Instead, he said that such jihad should involve spreading the message of Islam by using satellite television and the internet, i.e. that it should be jihad by tongue, and that the task was not to fight terror with terror, but by persuasion and superior arguments and by understanding the roots from which terrorism grows. As far as the conflict with Israel is concerned, al-Qaradawi deems "electronic jihad" using the media as far better than armed struggle. He also speaks of "economic jihad", by which he means a Gandhi-inspired rebellion based on a boycott of the enemy's goods: "Every riyal spent on Israeli or American goods will eventually become a bullet shot into the hearts of our brothers in Palestine" (Mendel 2010: 259). Nevertheless, al-Qaradawi has said that the Palestinian suicide bombings represent "legitimate terrorism" and has quoted from the Quran where it suggests sewing fear and terror into the heart of infidel enemies during wartime. He regards the Palestinian attacks as an extreme form of defence of the nation and state against oppression and a legitimate form of resistance to a humiliating occupation. However, by defending specifically Palestinian terrorism he released the genie from the bottle. Mainstream Sunni clerics had never in history advocated suicide attacks. The legitimisation of Palestinian martyrs legitimises other would-be attackers, in whose cause, given a degree of interpretative flexibility, it is possible to find an analogous defence of Islam, honour and homeland (Kepel 2008).

INTERNET

Lebanon is the centre of the "Arab information highway". For decades the saying went that Egypt writes, Lebanon prints, and Iraq reads. Most innovations in communications technology found their origin here. However, the Middle East was first connected to the internet in Beirut (1995) immediately after the end of the civil war (Gonzales-Quijano 2003). The opportunities opened up were first seized upon by a small circle of programmers and engineers with an interest in Islam and politics. As unorganised individuals they published the Quran, collections of hadiths and the works of classical Islamic scholars on the internet. Next in line were members of the educated middle classes. The social range of internet users gradually expanded, along with the range of interpretations of Islam and views on politics. In the next stage organised activists of all kinds appeared, from secularists and feminists to Islamists. For instance, the Lebanese Hezbollah was among the first. Its Sheikh Hussein Fadlallah published his Friday sermons online along with fatwas examining different issues. The Muslim Brotherhood has its own website, as does Yusuf al-Qaradawi, e.g. the IslamOnline.net project and the personal site qaradawi.net. Islamists are also withdrawing into cyberspace under pressure from regimes forcing them out of the public sphere. Last to go online were official circles. Governments, Shiite clerics from Qom in Iran, the Saudi Wahhabis and international organisations such as the Organisation of the Islamic Conference (renamed the Organisation of Islamic Cooperation in 2011) all now have their own websites (Anderson 2003, Lynch 2007).

The internet offers a wide range of Islamic topics of interest to the lay faithful and not only intellectuals or clerics. In addition to polemics and a defence of Islam, a new form of apologetics is appearing, often basing its arguments on modern science, thus evincing the infinite wisdom of an Islam capable of anticipating any scientific discoveries. A complete collection of hadiths, the top reciters of the Quran, and the Friday sermons of many different clerics are now to be found on the internet, as well as practical information on prayer times, the nearest mosque, and shops selling halal food (Anderson 2003). Religio-legal expert opinions (fatwas) taking the form of FAQs examining issues raised by believers are very popular. While traditionally such analyses were tailored to a specific person and their problem, today's trend is to make things as general as possible, leaving space for individuals from the mass audience to reach their own interpretation (Eickelman, Anderson 2003). As well as emails, thematically organised chats, blogs and Facebook groups are becoming more and more popular. By virtue of its form the internet offers a range of genres, from "conversations" within more or less open communities, to "publishing" activities if we assume that websites are the equivalent of printed books. What is important is that, thanks to the internet, a new public space has been opened beyond the control of regimes, a space in which people can meet, exchange opinions and information, and make connections between discourses that have until now been separated (Anderson 2003).

The internet has also been adopted by global jihadists fighting against Middle Eastern dictators and their Western allies. After the fall of the Afghan Taliban (2001), Al-Qaeda moved into cyberspace, becoming cyber-jihadists. Because it is encrypted, the internet allows them to coordinate preparations for attacks. The linking up of individuals and groups from all around the world reinforces an awareness of the global character of the movement for the protection of the Muslim community (umma) against a common enemy. Propaganda plays a crucial role in making possible the relatively safe recruitment of new supporters. Prior to 11 September 2001 there were only a handful of extremist websites: these days there are thousands of them. Though most are in Arabic, more and more are being written in English and French (The Economist 2007). This is a reflection of the importance of the second generation of Al-Qaeda, which arose in reaction to the occupation of Afghanistan (2001) and Iraq (2003) by the West and recruits from Muslims born to immigrants in Europe and the United States, as opposed to the first generation, which arose in reaction to the invasion of Afghanistan by the USSR and recruited from within the Arab world (Roy 2004).

The handheld camera and the internet have become as important a weapon as the machine gun or bomb. The media battle includes shots from conflict zones. Shots of a dying enemy accompanied by shouts of *Allahu akbar!* appear on the internet only minutes after an attack. Another video will describe the pleasures awaiting the martyr in paradise. The internet is flooded with press releases of insurgent groups giving the background of their attacks. As one jihadi magazine urges its readers: "Brothers, do not despise taking film. Each frame of a film has the same worth as a rocket fired at the enemy Crusaders and his puppets." The internet has thus become an open university of jihad, an ideological and practical guide on how to kill (The Economist 2007).

The most prolific author up till now is the jihadi veteran Abu Musa al-Suri. His six-volume opus *The Global Islamic Resistance Call* (2004) is the best read jihad manual. It is an electronic book containing many audiovisual pre-sentations that are reminiscent of a distance learning textbook. Its strategy for world domination involves a number of small, independent terrorist cells. These have a shared ideology, but promote terror around the world indepen-dently of each other. Suri also analyses the failure of militant Islam. In his "Report on the State of the Umma" he blames it on the apostasy of the Muslim elites and the broader masses: "The umma is facing an invasion by Ameri-can Zionists and Crusaders supported by collaborationist governments and hordes of Muslim hypocrites" (cited in Kepel 2008: 162).

Simona Hlaváčová (2006) sums up the situation as follows: "Surfing Muslim virtual reality offers an idea of the pluralism of the Islamic identity and the mutually competing movements in Islam, and deconstructs both the stereotypes of the Western media and the myths propagated by conservative Salafism about the one and only true Islam, the vision of which scares West-erners." The expansion of means of communication as part of modernisation does not have to result in the decline of religion, its privatisation and de-politicisation, as posited by the secularisation thesis. Within the context of modernisation in the Middle East it may, on the contrary, result in its revival and re-politicisation (Arjomand 1986).

Competing interpretations of the world and Islam vie for the public's at-tention via new media. Islam is thereby popularised and a shift takes place in the direction of the political. This becomes an alternative to traditional orthodox folk and scholarly versions of Islam as presented by the masters of mystical orders, ministers of religious affairs, and official clerics (Anderson 2003). In the mid-20th century, post-colonial governments decided that the mass media was an excellent tool for enforcing their own version of apolitical Islam, along with their own ideas of national community, secular identity and positive role models. However, subsequent media revolutions undermined the media dominance enjoyed by official political and religious authorities up till then. The arrival of new symmetrical media (the internet, fax cassettes, photocopiers) hastened this process of erosion, and the relative importance of asymmetrical media that could be controlled from a single centre and be used to influence the masses fell. (Eickelman, Anderson 2003). The vacuum left by traditional clerics and Sufi masters was then filled by Islamists offer-ing their own interpretation of Islam (Roy 1992).

(8) THE RELIGIOUS MARKET AND THE EROSION OF TRADITIONAL AUTHORITIES: THE STRUGGLE OVER HOW TO INTERPRET ISLAM

Fatima, a university student from Shiraz in Iran, loves the Prophet and Ali. It is for this reason that she covers herself up. She is also proud of Persepolis and the glory of pre-Islamic Persia. Furthermore, she is learning English so as to be able to read Harry Potter on the internet before it gets translated into Farsi[27]. The multilayered identity of Iranians is often based on various, mutually conflicting, cultural sources. Sariolghalam (2008) has concluded that the "intertwined sources of the Iranians' identity – nationalism, Islam and westernisation – remain an uncomfortable mix." Marjane Satrapi outlines the dilemma of the Iranian identity in a similar way in her famous comic book *Persepolis* (2006): "Sometimes it is really hard to choose between the fatalism of one (the clerics) and the arrogance of the other (the West)." Most educated people with access to the new media experience their own private "clash of civilisations". However, this is not just a private matter with a happy ending, as in the case of Fatima. It is also a political matter.

Politics can be understood as embodying a rivalry for the distribution of scarce resources in society, as an answer to the questions: who will receive what, when and how? However, politics is not simply a struggle for power, wealth and prestige, but also for the interpretation of identities and symbols and thus for control of those institutions that produce said identities and symbols and subsequently interpret their significance. There is also a fight for the imaginary of the people. After the fall of the secular doctrines, many different political actors claimed allegiance to Islam, which became the language of politics. In an effort to legitimise their power, governments resort to religion. Coercion on the part of the police and army is in itself insufficient. The opposition, on the other hand, offers a competing interpretation of Islam with the aim of delegitimizing the government (Eickelman, Piscatori 1996). Governments discredit the opposition's tactics by claiming that their interpretation is heretical, a case of religious deviance. The opposition in turn accuses the government and ulama of heresy when deeming its version of Islam to be apostasy (Mendel 2008).

A new religious sphere is formed through the combination of the arrival of new media, a new educated public involved in struggles for interpretation, and a new concept of Islam at a moment in time when demand is increasing for readings adapted to contemporary problems. The monopoly that governments and official clerics used to have on the interpretation of Islam

---

27   An interview by the author with Fatima, a university student, in Shiraz, August 2007.

is being eroded, because regimes are losing the ability to censor effectively and to dominate the media space (Eickelman, Anderson 2003). The clash of different interpretations relates to a question that is absurd for a traditional Muslim, the question of who is and is not a true Muslim. Who is entitled to answer that question? In other words, who can represent and interpret Islam? Official clerics and regimes emphasise that only clerics with a classical religious education are such authorities. However, Islamists and new Islamist intellectuals claim that every lay autodidact has a potential right to interpret if they acquire sufficient erudition and win the trust of the community of followers (Roy 1992, 2004; Starrett 1998).

Bryan S. Turner (1974, 2007) goes so far as to claim that the newly expanding public sphere undermining existing authority is based on the interaction of new media and a new public with what was traditionally a highly heterogeneous Islam. Islam was always open to discussion, both non-hierarchical and inclusive, and therefore internally diversified. In this respect it differed from hierarchical Catholicism with its homogenising inquisition, churches and councils. As opposed to Catholicism, and to a lesser extent Protestantism, Islam knows no sharp division into the clergy and the laity. The authority of Islamic legal and religious scholars (*ulama*) was always rooted in the local. It was based on bonds within the community on the level of neighbourhood, tribe or village. It was not based on membership in an organisation, as in the case of preachers in the Catholic Church, but on a consensus reached by the community to the effect that a given individual was sufficiently devout, that he was a good teacher and mentor in matters pertaining to both faith and everyday life. He knows things that others do not but appreciate are important. In addition, different legal schools (*madhhab*) always coexisted side-by-side in Islam. Dissenting views from different clerics were commonplace and the formal religio-legal opinions (*fatwa*) addressing such problems often reached different conclusions, sometimes diametrically opposed conclusions. The modern media simply expanded the space for a traditionally open interpretative discussion that had lasted fourteen centuries. The new media platform for the continuation of age-old debates breathed new life into the traditional model of religious pluralism (Turner 2007).

If anyone who enjoys a natural respect from believers because of their erudition can be a cleric, the internet has made a potential mufti of everyone. It has made available to anyone who can read literary Arabic an extensive collection of religious texts and a centuries-old tradition of interpretation. Everyone can now engage in contemplation and interpretation of Islam, everyone can speak on behalf of their religion and publish fatwas. The expansion of education, new media and the market for religious ideas has created a new public and a new class of competing interpreters. A new reflective, self-aware religiosity is being promoted and religion can no longer be passed down unquestioned from previous generations. On the contrary, the prevailing notion these days is that the interpretation of meanings must be actively sought and justified (Turner 2007), in order that everyone can construct their own concept of Islam (Eickelman 2003). The result is a pluralism of Islam, while the traditional clerics are being circumvented, since the new public no longer needs them (Eickelman, Anderson 2003).

The new media lead to a paradoxical development. They contribute to the downfall of traditional religious authorities, while stimulating a religious revival. The gates to *ijtihad*, i.e. independent reasoning in cases in which the holy texts do not offer a clear answer, have reopened (Turner 2007). Disputes on the interpretation of Islam are becoming democratised, with more and more people participating and providing their own readings. Interpretations are appearing on the religious market that suit people in light of their situation and social status. The increased diversity of interpretations is also the consequence of the growing class, cultural and political diversity of people participating in the discussion (Eickelman, Anderson 2003). Above all, the internet has created a democratic religious market. It has smoothed out the unevenness between state, civil society groups and individuals. Everyone has the right to speak and everyone's word carries the same weight. On the web people can assemble, associate and express themselves even in regimes that crack down on basic freedoms in public space. It is difficult to censor the internet. Conversely, the cost of publishing on the internet is minimal if compared with the press or radio. Alongside mosques and universities, the internet has become an island of freedom in an ocean of oppression. Everything under the sun is talked about on the web, and the official clerics usually keep away. This means there is a chance for science, Western culture, secular ideologies and competing religions to come into contact and permeate the Islamic imaginary (Turner 2007).

University students frustrated by the failure of modernisation in their countries are the new Islamic intellectuals. As regards faith they are autodidacts offering their own concept of Islam. First they spoke out against secular intellectuals and regimes, and later against traditional clerics. They call for an interpretation of Islam that would recognise and respond to their problems. What tends to result is a reinvention of tradition (Roy 2004, Turner 2007). As opposed to the historical development of the West, the Middle East has been unable economically and politically to integrate the rapidly expanding educated middle class. As a consequence, in debates with the clergy, this "lumpen-intelligentsia" focuses on political and social themes. Alienated from the system, it is critical, and opposition Islamism suits its needs. Islamism fills the ideological vacuum left by the discredited clerics. At the same time it is establishing itself successful thanks to the new media (Roy 1992).

Religious market theory explains how an increase in the plurality of mutually competing versions of Islam leads to its vitality (Turner 2007). The theory assumes that the spiritual dimension of a person is a universal anthropological constant. Peoples' demand for religion is unchanging. Yet as customers of the "religious supermarket" they are considering which forms and interpretations religion would suit them best. Where there is a monopoly, preachers and religious organisations are like passive, "lazy corporations". They do not have to compete, they do not attempt to offer specialised "products" and meet the diversified demands of potential believers. There is a mismatch between supply and demand, individual religiosity remains on a latent level, and religion withers and fades. Conversely, a plurality of competing religions and interpretations does not have to lead to limitless relativism and scepticism of any and every faith and therefore to secularisation, but can lead to religious revival. Competition compels religious movements to work harder to appeal to the population. Many specialised "products" continuously fill gaps on the market and increase the likelihood that everyone eventually finds what they are looking for within a culturally and socially diversified society (Finke and Stark 1992; Lužný 1999).

The religious market theory was originally created in an attempt to explain the increased vitality of religion in the United States, with its religious pluralism and competition, as compared to the secularisation of Western Europe, dominated by specific churches in individual societies. An oft-heard criticism of the theory points to the high level of religious feeling in the Catholically homogenous Ireland, Italy and Poland. Furthermore, in the US the religious scene exhibits plurality only on a national level: in individual regions (e.g. the Southern states) it tends more to be homogenous. As a consequence, there is not much in the way of competition on the level of community, and most people remain with one version of faith for the whole of their lives. Furthermore, it is not clear what is cause and what effect: the vitality of a religion may stimulate religious activity and pluralism. Finally, the effect of religious pluralism operates to a certain extent. Excessive pluralism can weaken and discredit religion as a whole. The applicability of the theory is therefore restricted to certain cases. The Middle East tends to be classified as a religious monolith dominated by Islam (Hamilton 2001). It is claimed that religion is vital and experiencing a resurgence in Muslim countries, even though there is no competition between different religions on the religious market. This fact is used as an argument against the validity of the religious market theory (e.g. Norris and Inglehart 2004).

I believe that this chapter has shown that the Middle East is not such a monolith. There is considerable religious pluralism in the region and new interpreters asserting themselves alongside conventional religious authorities. They offer interpretations that deviate from traditional and mainstream thought or create new traditions whose authority is said to derive from their links to the Golden Age of Islam. The population of the Middle East is becoming more diverse: from traditional, illiterate nomads with transistor radios, to confident university students following the internet and satellite television on a daily basis. More and more interpreters of Islam are offering a plurality of visions in an attempt to attract attention, above all states, traditional clerics, and new Islamic intellectuals, including Islamists. A precondition for the emergence of a "religious supermarket", where supply and demand can intersect, is free access to religious products on the market. This has taken place thanks to the expansion of new media that circumvents censorship and the state-controlled mass media.

(9) PLURALISM AND FUNDAMENTALISM

The modernisation of Middle Eastern countries has not yet led to secularisation. On the contrary, it has contributed to a strengthening of religious faith. Increasing pluralism accompanied by greater contact between people with different views of religion was made possible by virtue of urbanisation, rising educational standards, geographical and social mobility, international migration, and the spread of free markets. However, it was also made possible by the spread of the media. The recognition that a hitherto unquestioned worldview is not the only one represents a threat to *feelings of security*. While in traditional societies most people lived in a culturally unified and religiously integrated environment, these days they are being permanently confronted with otherness and cultural strangeness. Yes, traditional Middle Eastern societies often included many religious communities living side by side, for instance Jews and Muslims. However, this physical proximity was accompanied by social and psychological distance and a minimum of interaction: the communities did not mix and did not share so much as a table or bed. An active search for certainty is only typical of modern man. Traditional people were not discomforted by the ongoing need to select from a surplus of possibilities. Their lives were not accompanied by anxiety and doubts regarding the meaning of life. They did not have to question the values to which they cleaved.

In addition to uncertainty in the cognitive sphere, parallel uncertainty resulted from the breakdown of social bonds. Individualisation leads to the "liberation" of the individual from the fixed bonds of family, tribe or village. Most people are no longer firmly integrated within their community from birth to death, as they were in traditional societies. Modern man is freer. However, the flipside of freedom is alienation and a desperate need to belong somewhere. In the face of boundless freedom some experience fear and disorientation and make a rush towards groups that offer fixed rules, security and a sense of belonging (cf. Fromm 1993). Anomie accompanied the modernisation of the West and these days the same is true of the Middle East. The clear rules and social bonds and groups within which people had been entwined are weakening.

A tense pluralism is accompanied by disturbing and genuinely modern questions. What should one believe in? How should one live? Reactions to these questions may range from tolerance to extreme nihilism, a feeling of resignation in the face of any search for truth and a rejection of its existence. Or conversely, a highly charged fanaticism wrought by a desperate yearning for security, truth, indisputable values, a clear meaning of life and instructions on how to live. This reaction is in the background of the contemporary rise of religious movements and fundamentalism in rapidly modernising Muslim and Christian societies. It defines itself in relation to doubts regarding its truth, but takes different forms, from the defensive ghetto of true believers who isolate themselves from the rest of a corrupt and hypocritical societies and live without compromise in accordance with demanding and strict rules, to offensive movements favouring the tactics of a "crusade" with the aim of conquering and reforming the whole of society, which has deviated from God and in its disoriented state does not know what is best for it.

However, supporters of secular cults also tend to be fundamentalists convinced of their truth and superiority. Secular ideologies often hold out the promise of heaven on earth, for instance in the form of a classless society, salvation during the course of life on earth. They create cults of saints and rituals. They demand the sacrifice of "believers" and an uncritical acceptance of dogma. Europe above all has experience with this reaction to modernisation. However diverse religious and worldly orthodoxies appear to be, they satisfy the same psychological and social needs of insecure, alienated modern man (Berger 1997).

THE EXPANSION OF EDUCATION: THE MIDDLE EAST AND THE "LUMPENINTELLIGENTSIA"

"Why open people's eyes? It will simply make them more difficult to control"
(Saʿid Pasha, Wāli of Egypt, 1850s).

"Education awoke absent or slumbering ambitions. It is no surprise that an educated youth wants greater influence on the management and administration of a country."
(E. B. Cromer, British controller-general in Egypt, 1907)

"People don't know Islam here. They prey, fast and make sacrifices. But they have no idea why."
(Omani teacher speaking about his illiterate compatriots, mid-20th century)

"The government wants Islam. But a sterile, controlled, Islam corresponding to their opinions. But Islam is a raging current. It makes no difference between the worldly and spiritual. If the state declares itself to be islamic, it has to harmonise its words and actions and speak in one voice. You can't trifle with Islam." (Algerian teacher)

"Anyone who devotes their time and energy to a study of the Quran and Sunni and becomes proficient in Islamic thought is entitled to speak as an expert in matters pertaining to Islam."
(the Pakistani Islamist Maududi)

"Piety is open and accessible to all. But religion – theology, ethics and dogma – must be left to the experts, otherwise we shall have murder, polarisation, destruction and fear, all in the name of religion. There are traders in religion who want to achieve their objectives in the name of faith and at the expense of Egypt turning into an ocean of blood."
(Mohamed Ali Mahgoub, Egyptian Minister of Religious Endowments /Awqaf/, 1989)

"The failure of Arab education is one of the reasons of the uprising of young people we are witness to at present in the region"
(Ahmed Zewail, Egyptian winner of the Nobel Prize for Chemistry)

"I have read and enjoyed Shakespeare, Dostoevsky, Chekhov and Sartre. I took especially pleasure in Sophocles, whose Oedipus I must have read ten times. And I always wept bitter tears."
(Fathi Shaqaqi, doctor and leader of Islamic Jihad)[28]

---

28   Cited in Starrett 1998: 220, 234 and 9, Kropáček 1996: 128, Roy 1992: 36, Starrett 1998: 185, Zewail 2011: 30, Pipes 1996: 20.

The contemporary Middle East is not a region of illiteracy, spiritually stranded somewhere in the Middle Ages. Nor does the stereotype of ubiquitous Quranic schools and Madrasas dominating the education system do the region justice (Halliday 2005, Hefner and Zaman 2007). On the contrary, during the second half of the 20th century the region experienced rapid modernisation in the sphere of education. Secular, Western-style schools were opened and the primary, secondary and tertiary levels of education all expanded (AHDR 2002, Richards and Waterbury 2008).

However, rising educational standards in the Middle East are not seeing a decline in the importance of religion and its withdrawal from the public sphere in the manner predicted by the secularisation thesis and prejudices inherited from the Enlightenment. Within the context of unequal modernisation, the expansion of education represents more an important factor in the transformation, revival and re-politicisation of Islam, as well as an important factor in the rise of political activism, radicalisation and destabilisation in general. This may sound somewhat counterintuitive, since in the spirit of the Enlightenment we instinctively take education to be the remedy to a problem and not part of the problem itself. The main cause is again the fact that the expansion of education systems is taking place within the context of highly uneven modernisation. The rapid growth in education is out of step with the rate of development in other dimensions of social change. This chapter will therefore examine the interaction between the rapid development of educational systems and other dimensions of uneven modernisation and its wider context with the aim of identifying the causal mechanisms contributing to destabilisation in the Middle East (see fig. 29).

Fig. 29 The interaction of the expansion of education with other independent variables examined in this chapter

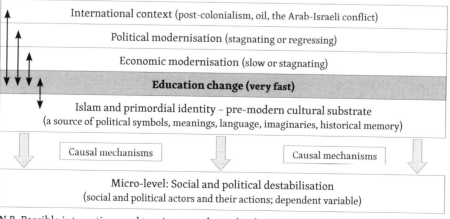

N.B. Possible interactions and tensions are shown by the arrows.

Fig. 30 Adult literacy rates in macro-regions of the world 1970–2015 (in %)

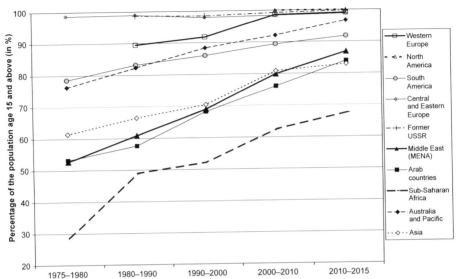

N.B.: The author's calculation of the average literacy rates for individual macro-regions (unweighted by country population size). The primary data is derived from surveys and censuses. For each decade and each country data was used from surveys and censuses conducted within the decade in question. If statistics for more than one year were available, the arithmetic average of the decade in question was used. The oldest data especially (1970s and 80s) is often unavailable for developing countries. As far as MENA is concerned there is data for six countries regarding the 1970s and 13 countries of a total of 21 for the 1980s. Trends within macro-regions and comparisons are therefore for orientation purposes only.
Source: UNESCO

THE DEVELOPMENT OF EDUCATION: AN INTERNATIONAL COMPARISON

The most pronounced trend is the elimination of what used to be a high rate of illiteracy. Statistics in this sphere have to be treated with caution. However, the UNDP states that in 1980, 60% of people were illiterate in the *Arab* Middle East. In 1995 the figure was approximately 43% (AHDR 2002)[29]. After countries achieved independence, post-colonial rulers defined education as a basic human right. The Middle East overcame illiteracy faster than other regions of the developing world, especially Sub-Saharan Africa and South Asia. Although levels of illiteracy in the Middle East are still high compared with East Asia or South America, the rate by which it is being eliminated is faster than these macro-regions (cf. fig. 30).

---

29   This applies only to Arab countries. The graph and other work cited refer to the entire MENA region.

The current young generation (aged 15–24) is thus not only the largest and most numerous in the history of the Middle East, but also the first in history that across the board can read, write and count. The overall literacy of young people in the Middle East is in excess of 90%, though the general impression is spoilt somewhat by less prosperous countries like Egypt (where 73% of young people are literate), Morocco (70%) and Yemen (68%) (Richards and Waterbury 2008).

Tab. 20 Proportion of children attending primary school in MENA countries 1970–2014 (in %)

Country	1970	1980	1990	2000	2010	2014
Algeria	76	97	94	108	115	119
Bahrain	98	105	109	107	---	---
Egypt	65	66	86	93	107	104
Iran	74	94	106	109	106	109
Iraq	68	107	106	94	108**	---
Israel	102	99	95	113	104	104
Jordan	102	110	106	99	91	---
Kuwait	88	103	91	96	103	103
Lebanon	128	108	96	110	105	---
Libya	109	125	108	119	---	---
Morocco	52	79	68	92	112	116
Oman	3	45	83	91	104	110
Palestine	---	---	92*	108	91	95
Qatar	96	103	107	99	97	---
Saudi Arabia	45	---	77	67	99	109
Sudan	35	45	47	47	70	70
Syria	82	95	101	104	122	80
Tunisia	100	101	113	115	107	113
Turkey	103	92	99	98	102	107
UAE	85	89	115	89	100	107
Yemen	22	---	76	74	91	97

N.B.: This is the gross enrolment ratio, i.e. the proportion of the absolute number of pupils attending primary school and the absolute number of children of the relevant age cohort. If the figure is in excess of 100%, the schools are attended by older or younger pupils (e.g. the illiterate adult population, older children who have never attended school because of war, children retaking a year, etc.). This is the primary level as defined by the ISCED.
* The date is from 1995. Older data is unavailable.
** The date is from 2008. Newer data is unavailable.
Source: UNESCO

From a comparative historical perspective it appears that the Middle East reduced illiteracy many times faster than the West. It took Europe two centuries to eliminate illiteracy, while many post-colonial countries of the Middle East accomplished it during the course of one or two generations. The spread of education in Europe was gradual, while the Middle East created secondary and tertiary facilities along with its primary schools. While Europe only developed a system of mass secondary and tertiary education after the second world war as part of the creation of the welfare state and after it had completed its demographic transition, the Middle East created all levels of the education system at once and, what is more, during the height of its baby boom and a numerical increase in the young population. The development of education often barely kept pace with dynamic demographic developments. Finally, the expansion of the Middle Eastern education system took place during a time when the region was not an economic powerhouse. European education, on the other hand, expanded in parallel with economic expansion. The Middle Eastern educational explosion has outstripped the development of the far slower economies, and also diverged from developments on the labour market. However, these historical comparisons must be subjected to more detailed investigation (cf. Kennedy 1996, Lerner 1964).

Illiteracy in the region is these days a phenomenon associated with older generations or with women living in the remaining isolated pockets of the backward agricultural or mountain regions of Morocco and Yemen. The difference in the literacy rates of women and men in the Middle East remains the largest in the world (AHDR 2002, Kropáček 1999). However, the figures differ considerably between individual countries. For instance, in Israel, Palestine and Jordan adult literacy rates are well over 90%, a figure that is fully comparable with many European countries such as Portugal, Greece and Spain. The figure is over 80% in Bahrain, Kuwait, Lebanon, Libya, Qatar and Turkey. However, the situation is significantly worse in Algeria, Egypt and Sudan. The most problematic countries in this regard that defy the overall trend in the region are Yemen and Morocco, where only half of the population is able to read (Richards and Waterbury 2008).

The development of primary school attendance also reveals an impressive dynamic (see tab. 20). As the colonial era drew to a close in the mid-20th century, the network of schools in the Arab world was very sparse. However, by 1970 approximately 82% of boys and 67% of girls of the appropriate age cohort had a place at school. In 1990 the figures were 85% and 78% respectively, while today almost all children of this age cohort attend school (Richards and Waterbury 2008). However, despite the massive expansion of the education system in Arab countries, it is still unable to keep pace with demographic growth. This applies especially to poorer countries of the region and neutralises somewhat the positive impacts of the development of education. As a consequence, the absolute number of illiterate people slightly increased in the Arab world during the 1990s, with 65 million unable to read at the turn of the millennium. The complete elimination of illiteracy amongst Arab men is expected sometime around 2015 and amongst women only after 2040 (according to AHDR 2002)[30].

Secondary and tertiary educational institutions experienced a similar expansion to that of primary schools (see tabs. 21 and 22, figs. 31 and 32). The European colonialists did not encourage the development of education, but favoured simply a small group of the population that helped administer the colony (Starrett 1998). After liberation from colonialism and military occupation (Iran, Turkey, Egypt) there were virtually no secondary schools or universities in the Middle East. If we leave aside the madrasas serving the needs of Islamic scholars, there were only half a dozen Western-style universities in operation throughout the entire region. The situation was just as dismal in the sphere of secondary education (Daun and Arjmand 2005), and the result was a lack of people with a modern education who could form the political, administrative, business, military and cultural elite, run the newly independent state, and plan its long-term future. Therefore, after seizing power new governments needed to act fast in order to create a class that would be capable of running the state. Furthermore, education was perceived as the main force behind Europe's geopolitical and economic dominance. Free education for all became the policy of post-colonial countries in the region, which wanted to catch up with the West as quickly as possible (Richards and Waterbury 2008).

This was not merely rhetoric. The priority accorded education in Arab countries is documented by the allocation of budgetary resources to the Ministry of Education. Between 1980 and 1995 Arab states increased education spending from USD 18 billion to 28 billion (AHDR 2002). Regimes were willing to pump something in the region of 5.2% of their GDP into education, a figure that is higher than in developing or even advanced countries. Other developing regions allocated around 5.1% of GDP to education, and the wealthiest countries (OECD countries) spend around 3.9 of GDP on average, i.e. a smaller share of their total economic output. Of course, this is higher in absolute terms than developing countries, since the economic performance of rich countries from which funds are put aside for education is many times higher (Booth 2002). If we express government expenses on education not as a share of the country's economic performance (GDP) but as a share of the total expenses of the state budget, we again see that Middle Eastern countries are capable of pouring relatively large resources into education: from 8.3% (Saudi Arabia) to 32.8% (Yemen) of the total state budget (Richard and

---

30 Once more it needs to be emphasised that this passage analyses only the Arab part of the MENA region.

Waterbury 2008). However, the last few decades have been marked by a lower rate of growth in school budgets. Because of the faster tempo of population growth, since the mid-1980s there has been a reduction in expenses on education calculated per pupil/student (AHDR 2002).

REGIONAL COMPARISON OF THE DEVELOPMENT OF EDUCATION IN MIDDLE EASTERN COUNTRIES

In terms of adult illiteracy the most problematic countries have long been Yemen, Morocco and Sudan, the poorest countries in the region. Yemen and Sudan, along with Oman, also lag behind other countries of the region in terms of the proportion of children attending primary school. However, while attendance at primary school is at present almost 100% across the region, this indicator does not reliably differentiate between individual countries. It is therefore more useful to compare the share of young people attending secondary schools and universities (see tables 21 and 22).

The lowest proportion of the young generation studies at secondary schools in Sudan (38%), Yemen (46%), Iraq (52%) and Morocco (56%). These are poor countries plagued by civil war. On the other hand, a high proportion of young people study at secondary school in the rich Gulf states (e.g. 97% in Bahrain and Saudi Arabia, 91% in Oman), as well as in Libya (94%) and Tunisia (92%). If we turn our attention to the rate of change, this has been highest since the beginning of the 1970s in Oman, where the proportion of the relevant generation studying at secondary school has increased by a staggering 91 percentage points (from less than 1% to more than 91% forty years later). Similarly impressive growth rates were recorded in the United Arab Emirates and Libya (73%), Algeria (71%) and Tunisia (69%). The slowest growth was in Sudan and Iraq (both on 30%). In the case of Iraq a relatively high proportion of senior school students in the relevant generations fell sharply as a result of the war with Iran (1980–88) and Kuwait (1990–91) and the subsequent international sanctions.

As far as higher education is concerned, the lowest proportion of young people entering university is in Sudan (6%), Yemen and Qatar (10%) and Morocco (13%), while the highest share of young people at university is to be found in Libya (56%), Lebanon (53%), Bahrain (51%) and Palestine (46%). The fastest progress in terms of the expansion of tertiary education over the last forty years is to be seen in Bahrain and Libya (where there has been a rise in the proportion of university students in the generation under consideration of 50 percentage points), and the least amount of progress in Sudan, Yemen and Morocco.

Overall the most backward countries in terms of education system quantitative indicators are Sudan, Yemen and Morocco, while the most advanced

Tab. 21 The share of young people attending secondary school in MENA countries 1970–2014 (%)

Country	1971	1980	1990	2000	2010	2014	Rate of growth 1971 to 2010 (percentage points)
Algeria	11.2	31.2	62.0	75.00	83.20	99.0*	72.00
Bahrain	51.3	57.5	95.1	97.40	96.40	N	45.10
Egypt	29.0	46.2	68.6	75.80	79.30	86.1	50.30
Iran	27.5	48.2	52.1	81.50	83.00	88.4	55.50
Iraq	21.5	51.5	44.9	36.70	51.50	N	30.00
Jordan	46.4	76.4	79.9	87.13	88.20	84.3**	41.80
Kuwait	63.4	77.6	82.6	93.60	89.90	93.6	26.50
Lebanon	41.4	57.8	60.8	75.00	82.14	68.2	40.74
Libya	20.8	74.3	N	108.00	93.50	N	72.70
Morocco	12.6	23.7	37.5	38.10	55.90	69.1**	43.30
Oman	0.2	8.3	39.4	78.20	91.30	101.9*	91.10
Palestine	N	N	N	82.30	87.10	82.2	N
Qatar	36.3	62.1	83.2	87.50	85.20	109.4**	48.90
Saudi Arabia	N	N	N	N	96.80	108.3	N
Sudan	6.9	14.0	20.2	24.80	38.00	42.7	31.10
Syria	36.0	47.6	51.0	41.00	74.80	50.5	38.80
Tunisia	22.7	24.9	44.0	75.90	91.80	87.6	69.10
Turkey	25.8	35.4	46.7	70.50	82.00	100.3	56.20
United Arab Emirates	22.2	48.3	64.1	74.90	95.20	N	73.00
Yemen	N	N	N	43.00	45.70	48.6	N

N.B.: By secondary school we are referring to the upper primary and secondary levels of education in accordance with the ISCED. We are reporting on the gross enrolment ratio, that is on all secondary school students relative to the population size of the relevant cohort. Unlike the net enrolment ratio the values in certain states may exceed 100% if older people also study at a secondary school (study at a second secondary school, retaking a year, requalification in middle age, etc.). These statistics are more accessible in most states. The rate of growth is here given in percentage points, i.e. the difference in the percentage representation of secondary school students in the given cohort between 1971 and 2010.

* The date is from 2011. Newer data is unavailable. ** The date is from 2012. Newer data is unavailable.

Source: UNESCO

Tab. 22 Proportion of young people attending university in MENA countries 1970–2015 (%)

Country	1971	1980	1990	2000	2010	2015	Pace of growth 1971 to 2010 (percentage points)
Algeria	1.8	4.3	10.5	14	31.0	35	29.2
Bahrain	1.4	3.5	17.6	22	51.0	37	49.6
Egypt	6.7	15.7	14.0	35	28.0	32	21.3
Iran	2.8	4.7	5.9	18	36.0	66	33.2
Iraq	4.7	8.4	11.9	11	N	N	N
Jordan	3.0	15.2	21.0	27	41.0	48*	38
Kuwait	4.0	10.9	12.4	23	17.6	27*	13.6
Lebanon	20.4	30.0	27.9	33	53.0	43	32.6
Libya	2.9	6.1	11.8	46	55.7	N	52.8
Morocco	1.4	4.9	10.9	9	13.0	25	11.6
Oman	0.0	0.0	3.8	14	26.0	29*	26.0
Palestine	N	N	N	26	46.0	44	N
Qatar	N	9.6	23.8	24	10.0	16	N
Saudi Arabia	1.6	6.4	9.7	20	33.0	61	31.4
Sudan	1.0	1.5	2.5	6	5.9	17	4.9
Syria	7.4	14.0	18.0	N	N	33**	N
Tunisia	2.6	4.8	7.9	19	34.0	35	31.4
Turkey	4.9	6.1	12.0	23	38.0	79	33.1
United Arab Emirates	N	1.8	6.8	18	13.0	22	N
Yemen	N	N	4.4	10	10.0	N	N

N.B.: By university we are referring to bachelor's and master's level of education in accordance with international classifications (ISCED 5 and 6). We are reporting on the gross level of the representation of all university students relative to the population size of the relevant cohort (*gross enrolment ratio*). Unlike the net enrolment ratio the values in certain states may exceed 100% if older people also study at university (study at a second university, retaking a year, requalification in middle age, etc.). These statistics are more accessible in most states. The rate of growth is here given in percentage points, i.e. the difference in the percentage representation of university students in the given cohort between 1971 and 2010.
* The date is from 2011. Newer data is unavailable. ** The date is from 20012. Newer data is unavailable.
Source: UNESCO

are largely the wealthier states of the Gulf, along with Libya, Tunisia and Lebanon (see tables 21 and 22).

(1) EDUCATIONAL PROBLEMS: POOR QUALITY AND GROWING INEQUALITY AS EVIDENCE OF THE FAILURE OF REGIMES

From an objective *expert viewpoint* then, the main contours of the post-colonial *development* of education can be viewed positively. However, from the subjective *viewpoint of ordinary people* the current state of education in the Middle East is dismal. To most of the population, especially parents and students, the current situation in education demonstrates yet again the incompetence of their governments, which are unable to take society forward. The development and level of education still does not correspond to the growing expectations and demand from the public (Richards and Waterbury 2008). For instance, a qualitative survey of Arab young people found that, when asked to rank seven problems in society, such as corruption or poverty, in order of importance, as many as 23% of respondents cited education as the most pressing problem, hard on the heels of unemployment. Indeed, these two issues are closely linked, since a poor education fails to prepare a young person for the labour market or for life (AHDR 2002).

THE POOR QUALITY OF THE EDUCATION ON OFFER

In the educational sphere the Middle East is confronted by two related problems. There is the issue of the *quality* of public education and the issue of the growing *social inequality as regards access to education*: "Poor quality has become the Achilles heel of education in the Arab world, a problem that is undermining progress in the quantitative expansion of the education system" (AHDR 2002: 54). The Middle East is at threat of being separated and isolated from the global knowledge economy and the creation of new technologies and innovations, this at a time when, leaving aside oil and natural gas, it is poorly off for natural resources. The only capital it can count on in the future is human capital (AHDR 2003).

Problems with poor quality relate to the fact that the pace of developments in education has failed to keep up with the pace of population growth. In Egypt, for instance, the number of pupils doubled over one decade (1953–1963). At the same time the country faced a shortage of school buildings and good quality teachers. According to some authors, only 7% of teachers were university educated, while more than 90% had simply completed the statutory nine years of education, often with below average results.

However, during the following decade (1976–1986) the number of primary school pupils rose at twice the rate of schools and classes (Starrett 1998, Booth 2003).

Although up to the start of the 1970s massive investment in primary education led to reductions in class sizes, the recruitment of new teachers, and an improvement in the quality of education on offer, subsequently macro-economic difficulties and budget cuts ordered by the World Bank and the International Monetary Fund (as part of their structural adjustment programmes – SAPs) has seen the quality of tuition in public schools drop rapidly. The number of pupils has risen and school budgets have been subject to austerity measures. The size of classes has increased. In the oil-rich Gulf States there are 12 to 15 pupils per teacher. However, in poor Yemen or Sudan the official figure is 30 pupils per teacher, and the real figure several times higher. The motivation and quality of teachers suffer as they wee their salaries hovering around the state recognised poverty line. For instance, in Egypt

Tab. 23 Numeracy of 4th grade students. Research carried out by TIMSS 2007 (points average)

Country	Average	Country	Average
Hong Kong	607	Slovenia	502
Singapore	599	Armenia	500
Taiwan	576	Slovakia	496
Japan	568	Scotland	494
Kazakhstan	549	New Zealand	492
Russia	544	Czech Republic	486
England	541	Norway	473
Latvia	537	Ukraine	469
The Netherlands	535	Georgia	438
Lithuania	530	Iran	402
USA	529	Algiers	378
Germany	525	Columbia	355
Denmark	523	Morocco	341
Australia	516	Salvador	330
Hungary	510	Tunisia	327
Italy	507	Kuwait	316
Austria	505	Qatar	296
Sweden	503	Yemen	224

Source: Research TIMSS 2007 (Tomášek et al. 2008)

a teacher's salary is 10% above this line. The rich states of the Gulf are again an exception, so much so that Arab speaking teachers from poorer countries move there looking for work. An Egyptian teacher will earn ten times more in Saudi Arabia than they would at home. The outflow of good quality teachers abroad then becomes yet another problem that poorer Arab countries have to face. The result is that the weakest secondary school students are opting for teacher training courses. The weakest of these then become teachers. In overcrowded classrooms staffed by teachers lacking authority and social prestige, more and more emphasis is being place on rote learning and not on problem solving, critical thinking, creativity, or the ability to discuss and mount robust defences of opinions. This is not to speak of the total absence of adequate teaching aids, since most of the budget of education ministries is swallowed up by payroll expenses for already poorly paid teachers (Richards and Waterbury 2008).

Perhaps the largest deficit in the Middle East in terms of international comparisons is in the sphere of pre-primary education. Recent findings in the sphere of brain development and intellectual abilities place great emphasis on nursery schools in the advanced world. However, the number of children attending nursery schools in the Middle East is negligible (AHDR 2002).

The absence of a pre-primary education system and the critical situation that primary education finds itself in results in pupils with a knowledge deficit and a lack of motivation, a frequent need to retake years, and failure at school. The poor academic levels of pupils in this region are borne out by the reputable surveys carried out by PISA and TIMSS[31]. Some Middle Eastern states are joining in these programmes in order to compare the knowledge and skills of their children with those from other countries. This again suggests that education is a priority for some states in the region (AHDR 2002).

TIMSS INTERNATIONAL SURVEY

The standardised test of the TIMSS survey is defined by the content of the school curriculum and mastery thereof. It tests skills that pupils should have acquired in mathematics and the natural sciences. Nine-year old pupils in Middle Eastern countries (equivalent to 4th grade) came last in the international ranking in mathematics (see tab. 23). Statistically their results are significantly worse than the TIMSS average. Pupils from Iran fared best, though not even their results bear comparison with any Western country. The skills of pupils from Tunisia, Kuwait and Qatar were half those of pupils from the advanced countries of the OECD.

---

31 Acronyms for the Programme for International Student Assessment (PISA) and Trends in International Mathematics and Science Study (TIMSS).

Thirteen-year old Middle Eastern pupils were similarly poor, though many were comparable with pupils of post-communist Eastern Europe. For instance, pupils in Lebanon, Turkey, Jordan and Tunisia had a similar success rate to those in Georgia or Romania. Even here though the overall tendency is clear. And the knowledge of pupils living in Qatar, Saudi Arabia and Kuwait was dreadful, as can be seen in table 24 (Tomášek et al. 2008).

Tab. 24 Numeracy of 8th grade pupils. TIMSS 2007 (points average)

Country	Average	Country	Average
Taiwan	598	Romania	461
Korea	597	Bosnia	456
Singapore	593	Lebanon	449
Hong Kong	572	Thailand	441
Japan	570	Turkey	432
Hungary	517	Jordan	427
England	513	Tunisia	420
Russia	512	Georgia	410
USA	508	Iran	403
Lithuania	507	Bahrain	398
Czech Republic	504	Indonesia	397
Slovenia	501	Syria	395
Armenia	499	Egypt	391
Australia	496	Algeria	387
Sweden	491	Morocco	381
Malta	488	Columbia	380
Scotland	487	Oman	372
Serbia	486	Palestine	367
Italy	480	Botswana	364
Malaysia	474	Kuwait	354
Norway	469	Salvador	340
Cyprus	465	Saudi Arabia	329
Bulgaria	464	Ghana	309
Israel	463	Qatar	307
Ukraine	462	---	---

Source: TIMSS 2007 (Tomášek et al. 2008)

Not even the results of tests of scientific literacy indicate that the Middle East is in any position to compete with the economically advanced countries of European and Asia in the spheres of engineering, science and medicine in the foreseeable future, even though these subjects are very popular with young people in the Middle East. A similar pattern emerges as in the case of mathematics. The differences between individual Middle Eastern countries are relatively large and positive examples are to be found, for instance Jordan, Israel and Bahrain. Overall, however, the region lags behind on a global level. The situation in Qatar, Morocco, Saudi Arabia, Palestine, Algiers and Egypt is very poor. The participation of certain poor states of Sub-Saharan Africa and South America, while indicating that the knowledge and skills of pupils in these regions is also dismal, is not enough to placate Middle Eastern parents. They want the best for their children and compare them with European countries that form their reference group (cf. Tomášek et al. 2008).

PISA INTERNATIONAL SURVEY

The PISA international survey lays emphasis on the practical utilisation of academic skills and knowledge in real-life situations and is not based on the school curricula of the participating countries but more on the demands made by life at the start of the 21st century. Here too the Middle East had nothing to boast about during the testing of fourteen-year old pupils. Relatively respectable results were achieved in reading literacy (understanding and applying texts) by only Turkey and Israel. Pupils living in the United Arab Emirates performed similarly to their Austrian and Eastern European peers. At the bottom of the rankings, along with countries of South America and the former Soviet Union, came Jordan, Tunisia and Qatar (see tab. 25). Middle Eastern pupils were well below the average of OECD countries (with the exception of Turkey and the United Arab Emirates) when it came to mathematical and scientific literacy.

However, it should be noted that Qatar, Turkey and Tunisia are countries that between 2003 and 2009 reported the biggest improvements of all participating countries. The truth is that a rapid improvement is always easier when the initial scores are low. However, there is at least a strong educational dynamic in certain Middle Eastern countries, even though their situation in absolute terms still cannot be compared with the best countries. Conversely, Jordan during the same period suffered a huge deterioration, perhaps because of the influx of refugees and their children from neighbouring Iraq. Not enough states from the region participated in the PISA survey between 2003 to 2009 for us to be able to draw reliable conclusions regarding trends, and the time series is also very short. Any conclusions that can be drawn are therefore for orientation purposes only (cf. Palečková, Tomášek, Basl 2010).

Tab. 25 Scientific literacy of 8th grade pupils. TIMSS 2007 (points average)

Country	Average	Country	Average
Singapore	567	Bahrain	467
Taiwan	561	Bosnia	466
Japan	554	Romania	462
Korea	553	Iran	459
England	542	Malta	457
Hungary	539	Turkey	454
Czech Republic	539	Syria	452
Slovenia	538	Cyprus	452
Hong Kong	530	Tunisia	445
Russia	530	Indonesia	427
USA	520	Oman	423
Lithuania	519	Georgia	421
Australia	515	Kuwait	418
Sweden	511	Columbia	417
Scotland	496	Lebanon	414
Italy	495	Egypt	408
Armenia	488	Algeria	408
Norway	487	Palestine	404
Ukraine	485	Saudi Arabia	403
Jordan	482	Morocco	402
Malaysia	471	Salvador	387
Thailand	471	Botswana	355
Serbia	470	Qatar	319
Bulgaria	470	Ghana	303
Israel	468	---	---

Source: TIMSS 2007 (Tomášek et al. 2008)

The poor quality of Middle Eastern education and the lack of knowledge and skills displayed by pupils of the region then creates problems on the labour market. The education system churns out graduates who have nothing to offer future employers.

THE PROBLEM OF JUSTICE AND SOCIAL INEQUALITY VIS-À-VIS ACCESS TO EDUCATION

One of the roots of the difficulties in the sphere of primary education, in addition to the creeping under-financing of education as a whole, is the emphasis governments place on the development and support of secondary and tertiary education. This attracts the bulk of financing even though it affects a smaller proportion of the population. University students tend to come from the privileged middle classes, whose influence on politics is greater and who are able to assert their interests at the expense of the lower classes. It would be in the interests of the lower classes if, on the contrary, the quality of primary education was boosted and resources redistributed in favour of pre-primary (nursery), primary and secondary vocational education and apprenticeships (Richards and Waterbury 2008).

At present there is even a threat that education in the Middle East will split apart into two mutually separate worlds. The first world will comprise extremely expensive education for a narrow band of the wealthy elite. The second world will be made up of a stagnating public education system intended for the poor majority. Good quality education will become a privilege of the few (AHDR 2002). Poorer countries in the Middle East already exhibit signs of an *educational development crisis scenario*. The diminishing financial resources per pupil and the departure of good quality, overworked teachers is witnessing a deterioration of the level of tuition provided at the primary and secondary levels. This is manifest in the number of pupils to a class, learning by rote, a predominance of frontal instruction, and the overall freezing of innovatory processes in schools. This in turn is reducing the prestige of the teaching profession in the eyes of the public, and talented individuals are then discouraged from enrolling on teacher training courses. Only ageing, burnt-out teachers remain in the system, or the less able, who are unable to create a suitable environment for the self-realisation of more ambitious and motivated colleagues. This all culminates in a further deterioration in the quality of teaching and the entire mechanism enters a negative feedback loop (cf. OECD 2001, Kotásek 2002).

Wealthier urban families are increasingly sending their children to better quality private schools. Though there are still not many in the region, they are enjoying a boom. However, this is impossible for the vast majority of parents, who are unable to afford the high tuition fees. The education at these institutions is better quality, there are fewer pupils in a classroom, the schools are equipped with computers and other aids, and emphasis is laid on foreign language teaching. The result is that social inequality increases, because these pupils attain significantly better results in centralised national examinations (aged 14–15), which are basically an entry pass to the best of the state funded universities. The graduates of these institutions then find it easier to find work than those produced by the system of poor quality, mass public education or of less prestigious and poorer quality universities. If for parents and grandparents graduating from secondary school was a guarantee of rapid promotion, middle class status and relative affluence, this is no longer the case. These days a secondary school diploma is no guarantee of a career at all. It is necessary to have a degree from a good university combined with parents who enjoy good connections (Booth 2002).

An even bigger problem is the arrival of *tutoring* in the sphere of free public education. The quality of primary and secondary public schools is so low that their pupils cannot realistically hope to obtain results in the national tests that would allow them to study the more sought after and better paid subjects, such as medicine and engineering. As a consequence, an alternative to placing children in private schools has become paid afternoon tutoring and individual preparation for national testing. The paradox is that the person being paid for providing this extra tutoring is often the very teacher who should be teaching all students free of charge during regular school hours. However, in this proliferating unofficial and untaxed education sector – a typical illustration of the Middle Eastern grey economy – such a teacher will receive ten times the official salary he receives at the school (Richards and Waterbury 2008).

Education in the Middle East is not a gateway to social mobility and a reduction in social inequality between individual classes. On the contrary, it has turned into an instrument for the maintenance and consolidation of social stratification between the higher and lower classes. The privileged classes have learned to use their resources in such a way that their children make best use of a system based on central testing, which is an entry pass into higher education. The lower classes cannot compete and the result is the reproduction and consolidation of social inequality (AHDR 2002).

These problems in the sphere of education impact directly on the majority of the population, half of which is younger than 25. This contributes to the erosion of the legitimacy of existing regimes and their ideologies. Instead of the progress, reduction in inequality and increase in quality it has been promised, the public experiences at first hand the decline of the educational system. This gifts any opposition group, including Islamist, an opportunity. Islamists are able to offer an alternative vision for education, if only because many of them have long been recruited from the teaching profession and they are well versed in the problems facing education.

(2) THE AWAKENING OF POLITICAL AWARENESS AND THE FAILING MIDDLE EASTERN PANOPTICON

A prerequisite for political conflict is the formation of opposing *interest groups*. A latent, unconscious and unorganised group of isolated, uncoordinated and scattered individuals simply occupying a similar status in the class structure (analogous to Marx's *"class in itself"*) must first be formed into an organised group whose members are aware of their shared interests, values and opponents (a *"class for itself"*).

Many conditions have to be met for the formation of a conflict group that will allow for the recruitment, organisation, motivation and mobilisation of supporters for joint action (technical, political and social conditions). One of these conditions is communication (agitation) aimed at potential members as well as existing members by means of a mission statement, manifesto or graffiti. The increase in literacy and educational standards was one of the prerequisites for the formation of interest groups and an increase in the number of manifest conflicts that persisted throughout the 19th century in Europe (Dahrendorf 1959). The same is true of the Middle East at present.

As Plato observed, illiteracy is the best form of censorship and a guarantee of political stability. As a consequence, at the start of the massive expansion of printing and the industrial revolution that followed, European power elites were forced to rethink the ambivalent political consequences of the spread of literacy. They were anxious to ensure that the education of disaffected working class did not provoke political *revolution* brought on by the reading of banned radical pamphlets and sweep away their power (Kloskowska 1967). Again, it is difficult to imagine the emergence of modern European *nationalism*, non-European nationalism, and the fierce conflicts arising from both variants, without literacy and the expansion of education (Gellner 1993). As Hegel said, national consciousness comes into being over the breakfast table as a wife is making coffee and her husband reads aloud newspaper reports on events within the borders of the nation state (Anderson 2008).

According to some analyses, the *public sphere* of civil society was born in the clubs, salons and cafes of London and Paris at the start of the 18th century. This space represented a pioneering platform operating as the first modern European political forum. The kernel of an urban, literary public oriented on the cultural production of the time (theatre, philosophy and poetry) was gradually transformed into a political public oriented on liberal emancipatory ideals. People met in order to discuss the political developments of the time. They relied mainly on pamphlets and newspapers that were beginning to appear in large numbers and that they were able to read thanks to their education. The intellectuals created gradually expanding islands of the public sphere, spaces where it was possible as equals to have rational, informed debates on issues affecting both individuals and groups, to form an opinion, acquire a political culture of pluralism, and learn the art of compromise. And also to create and interpret politically relevant concepts using which it was possible not only to speak about politics but to think about alternatives and the transformation of the existing political order. These salons did not only create modern public opinion, but functioned as a kind of school of democracy for the refined gentleman. They formed the prototype of a democratic society that then spread slowly throughout the population, since it created and popularised the idea of resolving political problems by means of public discussion among informed, educated and mutually equal citizens (Habermas 2000). However, to begin with access to these clubs and cafes was denied to minorities, the poor and women. The emerging public sphere thus related only to a narrow band of the privileged class (Hefner 2007).

The developing world underwent similar developments as Europe a little later and with similar political consequences. If during the industrial revolution in Europe the general expansion of literacy led to new possibilities for the rapid spread of political ideologies among broad sections of the newly literate population, a similar social change taking place in modern developing countries is having the same politically destabilising impact. Mass education gave people access to politically oriented publications (Brzezinski 1993). As one British politician observed on the threshold of the 20th century: "There is no way to teach a man to read the Bible that does not also enable him to read the radical press" (cited in Starrett 1998: 59).

However, in order that political ideologies were understood by less well read people not privy to cafe culture, it was necessary to simplify them into the form of easy-to-remember slogans and propagandistic dogmas. As a consequence, the attempt to reach out to newly literate populations in the early stages of modernisation led to a certain vulgarisation of political ideals. William Lecky (1838–1903), a historian researching the stormy development of modernising England during the 18th and 19th centuries, described this fact as follows: "Most of those who have learned how to read have never read anything but party newspapers aiming to radicalise and manipulate them. This makes for hordes of semi-educated individuals inclined to political utopias and fanaticism of all kinds" (cited in Starret 1998: 236).

Literacy and education also increase people's ability to search out and classify politically relevant information from different types of media, e.g. radio, television or the internet, and not simply from the press. All of this raises political awareness and the ability of the increasingly educated and informed masses to express themselves ideologically (Brzezinski 1993). In the Middle East this led to the creation and expansion of social groups that, unlike the apolitical, illiterate traditional classes, now held political opinions and wished to see them applied in practice. Rising educational standards also sparked an ability to empathise, which in turn expanded the imagination and enabled a person to visualise themselves in a variety of different roles and positions, as well as to conceptualise alternatives to the social and political order (Lerner 1964).

On the threshold of modernisation, European and Middle Eastern rulers were intuitively aware of the possible political consequences of the expansion of education: it was easier to control an illiterate population than an educated one. As the Egyptian Sa'id Pasha said during the 1850s when discussing educational reform: "Why open people's eyes? It will be far harder to control them" (cited in Starrett 1998: 220). The longer people spend in the educational system increasing their ability to interpret different texts, the more they are exposed to different ideologies and become politicised (Starrett, Doumato 2007).

However, sophisticated post-colonial westernised elites accustomed to thinking in a Western style began to realise in the spirit of the European Enlightenment that centrally organised mass education represented a guaranteed recipe for the control of subordinate populations. Fear of excessive education gave way to fear of the political consequences of a lack of education. Education systems were to become, à la Foucault, an instrument of supervision, discipline, and the modelling of standardised, completely submissive, docile citizens, and hence a tool for a new method of integrating the domesticated individual into society, an instrument for the shaping of the character of entire nations and their pacification. The Protestant Methodists were the first to operate with this idea in Europe alongside representatives of the Enlightenment.

Middle Eastern dictators, like the Scottish Enlightenment political philosopher Adam Smith, began to believe that uneducated, ignorant and intellectually simple masses are easy, defenceless victims of manipulation by political charlatans and charismatic religious leaders. In the eyes of conservatives, the reason the workers rebelled in the early stages of the industrialisation of Europe was their lack of cultivation and education. The same view was taken of the first anti-European uprising in the colonies, namely that it was the fierce rioting of illiterate, irrational and primitive people unable to understand that the colonial "white man's burden" was primarily a sacrifice made by Europe that was only for their own good. Great consternation was provoked by the Mahdist uprising in Sudan (1881), which the British were able to put down only thanks to the first ever deployment of the machine gun. The growing fears of political elites of an eruption of social chaos, rampant crime, political turmoil, unrest amongst workers, looting, epidemics of dangerous diseases, and the spread of indolence, alcoholism, prostitution and poverty led them to believe that these were problems of a moral and not structural character. The cause was to be found in lingering superstitions and the intellectual backwardness of the masses. The solution, it was argued, was education, which would offer people internal order and self-control. Education would teach them respect for authority, work discipline, patience, and the peaceful resolution of conflicts. It would transform irascible and easily manipulated barbarians into decent, loyal citizens. The pacification of the population by means of the education system seemed like a far cheaper and safer alternative form of social control than the permanent deployment of the police and military.

The backbone of the project was a network of modern schools organised along the same lines as modern workshops, factories, barracks, hospitals, psychiatric wards and prisons, i.e. on the principle of omnipresent supervision with an emphasis on "the effective deployment of bodies within the organisation" and the detailed arrangement and coordinated actions of a large number of people in time and space. According to Michel Foucault, the metaphor of this organisational logic was the *Panopticon*, the brainchild of the English Enlightenment reformer Jeremy Bentham, who lived in the 19th century (Foucault 1975). The only drawback to this project was its outcome, which often did not take the desired form. Instead of schools, universities, factories, prisons and barracks being institutions whose inhabitants were thoroughly and reliably disciplined, they often became epicentres of opposition. For instance, to begin with the leadership of the Muslim Brotherhood was drawn from the ranks of teachers and their students. The Egyptian President Anwar al-Sadat was assassinated by Islamists from secular universities and military academies. And the core nationalists fighting for national liberation from European colonialism came together and organised in school classrooms (Starret 1998).

Education was to be the universal panacea. It was to make available to both modernising Europe and the post-colonial Middle East two irreconcilable dividends: a *social dynamic* in the form of social progress and economic development, and *social stability* in the form of political stability, social control, and the loyalty of the population. Political rebellion, Islamism and terrorism were viewed simply as the last vestiges of medieval barbarism, backwardness and ignorance. Therapy in the form of education would exorcise them forever. And if the problems persisted, it would suffice simply to apply even more education (Starrett 1998). "Overall we expect of education something completely impossible – the salvation of society from the consequences of our plans to create it" (cited in Starrett and Doumato 2007: 215). Just as certain modern European regimes attempted in vain to discipline society through the message of the Bible, Middle Eastern dictators are now trying equally unsuccessfully to achieve the same objective by means of the Quran (Starrett 1998).

(3) THE BOOMERANG EFFECT OF RELIGIOUS EDUCATION: THE ISLAMIC REVIVAL AND A CULTURE OF INTERPRETATION

Modern Middle Eastern regimes and medieval tyrannies have always tried to control the prevailing interpretation of Islam and use it for their own political objectives and projects (Mendel 2008, Schulze 2007). Modern post-colonial dictatorships make reference to Islam in order to promote just about anything under the sun, from military or economic modernisation, working hard, constructive enthusiasm, education in the sphere of hygiene, to the consolidation of nationalism, obedience to state authority and attempts to prevent the proliferation of pathologies (alcoholism, vandalism) and oppositional terrorism (cf. Starrett 1998, Hefner 2007). Other political actors also reference Islam when promoting their interests, notably secularists, feminists and Islamists (Eickelman and Piscatori 1996).

To a certain extent the Islamic clergy has performed the same role since the time of the first Muslim dynasties, e.g. the Abbasid Caliphate. These theological and legal authorities, collectively known as *ulama*, occupied the positions of judges, lawyers, imams at mosques, reciters of the Quran, muezzins, and teachers at madrasas. Soon after the creation of Islam, the educated clergy began to modify and distort its ethics, teachings and law to suit the particular needs of political power at any moment in time. In the same spirit they issued a stream of authoritative religious and legal opinions (*fatwas*) regarding important social and political events.

Concerned by the possible internal breakdown of society (*fitna*) and the subsequent risk of external attack, they encouraged the population to respect the imperfect social order, even though they were the only ones who might have declared jihad against blasphemous and unjust rulers. At the same time, however, they attempted to persuade rulers in the name of God to refrain from at least the most egregious, visible excesses and to be fairer to the community of believers. The "bipolar status" of the Sunni (but not the Shiite) clergy meant they found themselves between a rock and a hard place (Kepel 1996). In addition, up until the advent of modernisation reforms the clergy held a monopoly on religious education and thus control over the intergenerational transfer of religious tradition and its interpretation. However, secular rulers were never completely at ease with this situation and were always attempting to intervene and influence the form of religious education in madrasas and curry favour with the teachers through gifts and privileges, or at least avoid antagonising them (Hefner 2007).

TRADITIONAL AND DUAL EDUCATION SYSTEMS

The clerics' loss of a monopoly in the sphere of education at the expenses of the state was slow. For instance, the Ottoman Empire began with the centralisation and political regulation of traditional education on the threshold of the modern era. The initial impetus for *dual education systems* arose as a consequence of military defeats at the hands of European armies and the subsequent attempts made by rulers at "catch-up" or defensive modernisation. Examples would be the Ottoman Empire, Persia or Egypt after the invasion of Napoleon. An example of successful modernisation would be Japan after the Meiji reforms (1868), also imposed on the country on the back of the shock experienced in the face of overwhelming Western military superiority.

At first schools were established for a small group of military experts and technicians. For many regions of the Middle East the next step on the path to the dual system came in the wake of European colonialism, which first opened European-style schools for the education of lower administrators from the indigenous population (Hefner 2007, Berkey 2007). Meanwhile, the European powers opened a network of schools whose form, operations and political objectives corresponded to the pattern and philosophy of the metropolis. For instance, France and Italy applied a strategy of direct influence in the centralised colonial education system with the aim of culturally assimilating and "civilising" pupils from the local population. In contrast, Great Britain opted for the path of indirect influence and decentralisation, encouraging socio-political integration while retaining cultural diversity. Meanwhile, westernisation continued along with the resulting dualisation of education even in those regions that, despite increased interaction and European intervention, were not subject to direct colonial rule. This applied to Ottoman Turkey and Iran, as well as Afghanistan and the Arabian Peninsula (Daun and Arjmand 2005, Lewis 2003a).

In the meantime the traditional education system continued to function. Remnants of it remain visible in many Middle Eastern countries to the present day, almost everywhere within the framework of Islamic civil society and sometimes as a full and official supplement to the public education system. However, this was not a system in the true sense of the word. The traditional "system" was based on primary Quranic schools (*kuttab*) and universities (*madrasas*) and was characterised by substantial decentralisation, fragmentation, informal links and the complete autonomy of individual institutions. These were organised by the local community and financed from local religious endowments (*waqf*). Knowledge was passed from independent teacher to pupils. The Islamic tradition passed down was relatively diversified and fragmented and was impossible to control fully from a single centre of power. At the same time Christian and Jewish schools operated and flourished, which increased the pluralism of knowledge (Hefner 2007, Berkey 2007).

Lower Quranic schools resembled each other by virtue of what in retrospect was the relaxed and unstructured organisation of tuition. They had no system of ascending grades, nor did they employ the systematic testing of knowledge. Every student was able to join in and drop out when they wanted, both during the day and during the year. Children tended not to attend school regularly. The curriculum tried to teach pupils to read and write the Arabic alphabet as a means of later acquainting themselves with the Quran. Emphasis was placed on reciting verses from the Quran, memorising the surahs and acquiring a knowledge of the five pillars of Islam. Students were also encouraged to familiarise themselves with the Islamic tradition (*sunna*), i.e. the words and deeds of the Prophet. They were not encouraged to understand the ethical implications of these words, something that modern state religious education at secular primary schools is obsessed with, and they had no interest in cultivating any criticism or question of religion (Daun and Arjmand 2005). Quaranic schools arose soon after the death of the Prophet Muhammad, immediately after the first caliphs Umar and Uthman finished editing the Quran. Their task was to preserve the divine message and to pass it on from generation to generation, by word of mouth and through records, and in unchanged form (Hefner 2007).

In contrast, the madrasa represents a higher and more specialised training focused on the education of clerics and the preservation, development and oral intergenerational transmission of Islam and other knowledge. The emergence of the madrasa approximately three hundred years after the beginning of Islam was made necessary by the development of an increasingly complex Islamic juridical system as the four basic Sunni schools of law took shape. Mastering their principles meant significantly extending the period of study, and studies end with written authorisation being granted to pass on the knowledge to others (*ijazah*). This is at the discretion of a pupil's teacher, and not the school. As a consequence, the prestige of an academic title is linked to a specific teacher and not the name of the madrasa. The students are usually accommodated and fed by the school. Part of the complex adjacent to the mosque includes accommodation facilities for teachers, and sometimes the tomb of the founder of the school and premises intended for the provision of services to society at large, especially charitable acts (hospitals, spas, observatories, etc.).

The core of the study programme has always been Arabic and its grammar (*nahw*), recitation of the Quran (*qira'a*), legal science (*fiqh*), the Islamic tradition (*hadíth*), personal Quranic exegesis and commentary by the teacher (*tafsir*), theology (*kalam*), and the doctrine of the oneness of God (*tawhid*) and the life of the Prophet (*sirah*). However, in addition the madrasa often provided tuition in arithmetic, geometry, geography, astronomy, Greek medicine, logic, philosophy, poetry or the interpretation of dreams (Daun and Arjmand 2005, Heffner 2007). The top madrasas cultivated the most advanced scientific research of their time, for instance the madrasa al-Azhar in Cairo, al-Quaraouiyine in Fez, al-Nizamiyya in Baghdad, al-Zaytuna in Tunisia and Mezquita in Cordoba (Mendel 2008). Study was seen as a highly valued form of devoutness. The intergenerational transmission of the Islamic tradition by means of madrasas formed the basis of Islamic civilisation (Hefner 2007). It is estimated that in the pre-modern period less than 2–4% of the child population benefitted from a non-unified, heterogeneous and relatively diverse education, the centre of which was to be found in local communities (Egypt circa 1878). This was clearly not a mass phenomenon (Starrett 1998).

MODERN CENTRALISED EDUCATION SYSTEM

However, rapid post-colonial modernisation brought about a fundamental change. With the emergence of centralised states, the creation of state-controlled mass media, and above all the introduction of compulsory schooling and the subsequent expansion of the education system to secondary and tertiary levels, the regimes acquired a powerful and historically unprecedented instrument for the enforcement of their own "correct" version of religion and the widespread suppression of inconvenient, competing versions.

Centrally controlled religious education seemed like the ideal tool for managing the population, a guaranteed means of social control, a political anaesthetic, and even a way of gradually depriving Islam of any social significant and political relevance. The self-confidence of those in positions of power was due to the fact that they had finally managed to get hold of a resource of which previous generations of rulers could only dream: "The government found a way to develop the general morale of the masses, a way of preventing many unfair phenomena that arise only out of ignorance of the true principles of faith and the precise rules of the Islamic religion" (the Egyptian Minister of Education and later the premier, Saad Zaghloul, 1908) (cited in Starrett 1998: 67).

The newly acquired self-esteem of post-colonial states increased by virtue of the fact that for the first time in the history of the Middle East the majority of the up-and-coming generations passed through a state education system (see table 20). It was possible to reach out to and indoctrinate on a mass scale by means of a national curriculum. Religion was a separate subject and in addition was a "cross-sectional" topic since Islam pervaded many other subjects. And this was during the formative years when children and adolescents could be relatively easily manipulated and their opinions, values and character formed in the desired way. For the first time in history the religious education of children shifted away from the family and community with their concept of Islam to state organised schools with their own version of a reconstructed Islam. In the midst of the euphoria brought on by this newly acquired power, states were even convinced that they could retroactively change the concept of Islam in the minds of parents by means of their pupils. Compulsory education then was initially a priority of the state and not parents, who, in rural areas especially, were unconvinced for a long time of the necessity to send their children to school. However, the state gradually acquired a monopoly on primary religious socialisation and "primary education became one of the pillars of national security" (Hussein al-Din, Egyptian minister of education, 1993) (cited in Starrett 1998: 3).

Another powerful tool in the hands of many states (North Africa, Saudi Arabia, Iran, Turkey) was the standaridsed national testing of pupils at the end of primary or secondary school. This was introduced following the example of France and other European countries, and tested a pupil's knowledge of religion. The results of the tests then generally decided a pupil's future path in education, their life opportunities and career direction. Modern mass education with a curriculum organised along Western lines was regarded by the elites as the most influential public institution, if only because, given the demographic situation, every day almost half of the population took its place in the classroom (from primary school to university).

However, this policy turned into its opposite. The state unleashed forces that acquired a life of their own. An unintended consequence of religious education was the current resurgence of religion, its politicisation and the rise of Islamist movements. State initiated propaganda functions similarly to advertising. Though the state had attempted to control the way that people thought by means of an interpretation of Islam promoted by the education system, in fact what it stimulated was a general demand for religion as such. There was now increased demand for the continued study of religion, for "unofficial" alternative interpretations, and above all for religious argumentation and the justification of measures in various different spheres, including the family, social, economic and political spheres. This changed the atmosphere in society, public discourse, and the form of political debate. A generation that had undergone a solid religious education at state schools began to be dissatisfied with the rigid, boring and sterile Islam as offered up by state power and the official clerics and looked for other possible conceptions of faith. The state thus created a demand that it could no longer meet and a vacuum arose that was subsequently filled by new interpretations of Islam, including those of an Islamist character. Opposition Islamists rode the wave of religious revival provoked by the state and received a further boost when they began to attack regimes in the name of Islam itself (cited by Starrett 1998, Heffner 2007).

The causal link between the introduction of general religious education and the Islamic Revival is often demonstrated with reference to the rapid intergenerational change in the concept of Islam within families in the second half of the 20th century, when religiously lukewarm parents found themselves face to face with their zealous offspring. It should however be pointed out that this was more an intergenerational transformation in the way that Islam was understood, and not a change to the intensity of religiosity, which, according to sociological surveys, is roughly comparable across different generations or has increased only slightly (cf. Inglehart and Norris 2004).

MODERN SECULAR EDUCATION AND RELIGION:
THE EXAMPLE OF EGYPT

These developments can be demonstrated in the case of Egypt, which used to be the leading country in the region. During the reign of the secular Arab nationalist Gamal Abd al-Nasser (1952–1970), Egyptian schools became the locus of massive political indoctrination for the first time. Instead of having to learn passages from the Quran by rote, as in traditional schools, pupils were now required, following the model of secular Turkey, to recite the thoughts of the mandatorily beloved president in an attempt to boost his personality cult. In the sphere of religion, schools would emphasise personal, private devotion in order to neutralise the socio-political dimension of Islam supported by the Muslim Brotherhood (founded in 1928). For instance, jihad was interpreted in schools strictly as a personal inner struggle with temptation and evil, while Islam was presented as being fully compatible with the social engineering and experimentation taking place at the time in the name of Arab nationalism and socialism: "Religious education is one of the most powerful tools for the preparation of virtuous young people who believe in God and country and work to the benefit of their society on the basis of socialism, democracy and cooperation, since this is fully in accordance with and confirmed by religion" (preface to a religious education textbook of 1958) (cited by Starrett 1998: 84).

On the other hand, under the presidency of Anwar al-Sadat (1970–1981), religion was used to establish a distance between his predecessor's ideology of pan-Arabism and Arab socialism and to neutralise the supposedly growing Marxist opposition and justify an international political re-orientation from the USSR to the USA. President Anwar al-Sadat first supported and then, by means of education and the state media, popularised the concept of Islam hitherto propounded by the persecuted Muslim Brotherhood. The emphasis was now not only on a strong personal piety, but on a significant social dimension to Islam. This released uncontrollable forces over which Anwar al-Sadat was in the end powerless. Tellingly, he died at the hands of an opposition member of the militant organisation Egyptian Islamic Jihad (1981).

President Hosni Mubarak (1981–2011), although no longer having to worry about left-wing opposition like his predecessor, instead faced pressure from radical Islamic militants, and especially the moderate opposition Muslim Brotherhood. Since unprecedented repression did not work (a state of emergency was called in 1981 that permitted military tribunals to liquidate any opposition), the power elite, in an attempt to neutralise the influence of Islamists, again turned to religious education in schools. This time round they emphasised the non-violent character of Islam, the individual and apolitical character of faith, and the national unity of all Egyptian Muslims, amongst whom conflicts and disputes should play no part. The Egyptian nation (*watan*) was redefined using a key Islamic term, *umma*. Originally this referred to the ideal global community of all Muslims. However, it now began to be used in the sense of "nation" in the strictly political sense of the word (cf. Starrett 1998, Schulze 2007). They also set limits to the responsibility of the individual believer, who was no longer required to shoulder joint responsibility for the unacceptable social and moral condition of society, and decidedly not for finding a remedy. At the centre of attention was again a dispute over who had the right to interpret Islam. The government emphasised the monopoly of the traditional clerics, a monopoly that was to remain untouched. The aim was to use schools in the struggle against opposition Islam and to neutralise the tendency of young people to sympathise with political Islam. At the end of the 1980s the "secular" state again attempted to undermine the influence of Islamic civil society by opening its own network of Quranic schools (*kuttab*), which pupils could attend after normal school hours or during the summer holidays. In an effort to compete with the Islamists in the education of the up-and-coming generations and to demonstrate its Islamic credentials, the regime also introduced highly popular television recitation programmes or general knowledge quizzes relating to the Quran and Islam (Starrett 1998).

THE OBJECTIFICATION AND FUNCTIONALISATION OF ISLAM

In an effort to subjugate religion and promote a generally accepted interpretation through education, Middle Eastern dictators such as the Egyptian presidents initiated the *objectification* and *functionalisation* of Islam.

Objectification means nothing less than squeezing the entire Quran, several collections of hadiths, and fourteen centuries of Islamic tradition into a coherent system of beliefs, practices and precepts that take their place in school textbooks and curricula. Islam with its traditions and rituals then ceased to be viewed by the population as an unchallenged, "natural" part of their lives, and instead became something that must be explained, studied and understood in detail, and finally subject to testing. This difference in the understanding of Islam was described by an Omani teacher working in a traditional rural area shortly after the introduction of compulsory school attendance and religious education: "People here do not know Islam. They pray, fast and sacrifice, ok, but have no idea why" (cited by Starrett 1998: 9).

In order to codify and transform in a modern way the extensive, complex, multilayered, ambiguous and ambivalent Islamic heritage for the purpose of mass consumption in schools, it had to be simplified and systematised. This involved an extremely selective approach that gave rise to a completely new Islamic tradition ("*updated sunna*") that, unlike traditional Islam, was highly homogenous and unified and deliberately disregarded the diversity of Islamic schools of law, regional concepts and local sects. The tradition thus artificially invented was then promoted and reproduced on a mass scale by means of the machinery of the state education system.

And so while in a traditional Quranic school (*kuttab*) a minority of children were taught to recite mindlessly the entire Quran by heart, the modern educational system, which these days almost all children of compulsory school age pass through, encourages pupils to judge the moral and ethical consequences of their behaviour from carefully selected and subsequently canonised fragments extracted from the context of a vast cultural heritage.

A similar process of the codification and unification of Islam brought about by the political needs of powerful interests took place during the course of modernisation in the legal sphere: from the Ottoman Empire of the 19th century or *Anglo-Mohammedan law* in colonial India to many modern-day regimes. Political power attempted to squeeze what originally had been a flexible, elusive, barely controllable and unpredictable tradition labelled by critics with recourse to the metaphor of Sufism as "an ocean without shores" leading to "administrative chaos" into a fixed, closed, rigid system of paragraphs and collections of laws that can be easily learned and applied across the board in state-centralised juridical practice. There is a shift from a flexible traditional Islamic legal system seen as a "general social discourse" to a rigid concept of a positive legal canon based on the European method that can be used whenever and wherever for the needs of modern states, their management and administration. This creates a new approach to Islamic law that is alien to the original tradition (Starrett 1998, Hefner 2007, Berkey 2007).

This brings us to the pragmatic *functionalisation* and *instrumentalisation* of Islam, which explains why the objectification of Islam takes place within a specific political context and in a certain direction. The new religious tradition is tailored to meet the needs and political goals of specific regimes. This usually involves the maintenance of political stability and power, the promotion of various kinds of social projects and economic reforms, or an uneasy combination of both. In other words, it involves the promotion of potentially conflicting reforms while maintaining the status quo as far as power is concerned. It is these political aims that Islam, as created and manipulated by an authoritarian state, has the authority to justify and legitimise in the eyes of a devout, relatively conservative population (Starrett 1998, Hefner 2007).

THE OBJECTIFICATION AND FUNCTIONALISATION OF ISLAM: THE CASE OF SCHOOL TEXTBOOKS

Because the specific interests and aims of individual Middle Eastern regimes differ, so too does the concrete form of Islam presented in school curricula and textbooks of individual countries. This was corroborated by a large international survey that examined the religious education textbooks used in state primary schools (2002 to 2004) in Saudi Arabia, Kuwait, Oman, Syria, Jordan, Egypt, Palestine, Turkey and Iran.

A tendency common to all of these regimes is the attempt to ignore the heterogeneity of different Islamic currents in the name of national unity and social cohesion. Pupils do not learn, for instance, of the existence of the Alawites, Shiites, Druze, Sunnis, Sufism or mysticism. Islam is presented to children as a compact religion without minorities (*"melting pot Islam"*). One exception to this is Shiite Iran, whose textbooks explicitly recognise the Sunni as a respected branch of the same faith and encourage tolerance. Another exception is Saudi Arabia, which lists many Islamic sects and movements in its textbooks, though proceeds to brand them as heretical.

A feature common to all regimes is the attempt to present and promote traditional values along with completely new values as truly "Islamic". For instance, the ritual cleansing before prayer ordered by Islam is presented to schoolchildren in a new guise as a religious justification of good hygiene. Regular prayer is cited as justification of the need for discipline and order in the life of the individual and society, and fasting as a clear Islamic justification of a modern healthy lifestyle. The Prophet's hadith prohibiting the destruction of trees in the desert is to be understood by children as God's prohibition of all forms of vandalism, the need for environmental protection, and justification of an ecological code of ethics.

Children are informed that adherence to these precepts is one of the ways of ensuring personal piety and devotion to the faith. It is a form of individual jihad in the sense of an effort at self-improvement and cultivation. In almost all the countries mentioned children are encouraged to respect their duties and obligations to parents, siblings and old people, as well as to the poor and sick and to guests. In many countries these obligations are now placed on the same level as those toward employer or company, teacher, politician and the state. We see how, unlike the liberal education of the West from the end of the 1960s, in the Middle East the rights of children do not take precedence over their obligations to parents, the needy, the community, and the wider commonwealth.

Moral values are also emphasised, such as obedience to authority, kindness, sympathy and modesty. However, with a nod to political stability and the dangers of excessive radicalism, qualities such as moderation, tranquillity, tolerance of others and the brotherhood of all men regardless of faith are also promoted (with the exception of Saudi Arabia). As far as social and economic development is concerned, the religious education textbooks place an emphasis on hard work, virtuous study, accuracy and punctuality, teamwork, and even the responsibility of the individual for their own faith, which in part flies in the face of the classical Islamic concept of predetermination.

These days, instead of a mindless recitation of the Quran in the traditional fashion, children are inculcated with the correct morals and desirable standards of behaviour with reference to Islam (Doumato and Starrett 2007).

Great efforts are made to popularise science. Children are taught that Islam and science are not in conflict since the knowledge and findings of modern Western science simply confirm what Islam has long known. For example, today's scientific findings regarding the benefits of good hygiene and regular exercise are reflected in the Islamic emphasis on regular ritual cleansing and prayer (see above). Scientific findings claiming that beef and lamb are healthier than pork are again mirrored in the Islamic ban on pork (Starrett 1998 and 2003).

THE BOOMERANG EFFECT AND RELIGIOUS REVIVAL: FROM THE INTERPRETATION OF CULTURE TO A CULTURE OF INTERPRETATION

Religious education became a strategic arena reflecting wider nationwide tensions, in which a crucial political battle was fought for the hearts and minds of Muslims. Westernised authoritarian regimes raised within a European style of thinking and influenced by the secularisation thesis took it for granted that Islam, as a trivial, dependent variable, would allow itself to be easily manipulated in the desired direction. They assumed that the social distribution of the "correct" knowledge informing a subordinate population what was and was not Islamic would reflect the division of political power. However, this power project, which sought maximum control of the population by means of the distribution of an official version of religion and even gradual secularisation, in the end set off a rampant religious revival and the unexpected rise of a religious opposition. The Islamic religion proved itself to be a separate, independent variable that was difficult to control and had a life of its own.

The religious propaganda initiated in schools by a secular state worked in a similar way to advertising: though people ignore ignore particular brands or products, the constant barrage of advertising leads to increased consumerism. It creates new needs and increases the desire for other products. While the state had attempted to control people's thoughts by means of a version of Islam served up by the school system, in actual fact it ended up creating a general demand for religion and religious debate applied to all conceivable topics. And this began to turn on the state itself. While the state had seized the potential ensuing from control of the education system and begun to justify different political projects and values using Islam, in actual fact it ended up popularising the nationwide politicisation of Islam, not its "official" version. Even the attempt to present and promote "apolitical" Islam has become a specific form of its politicisation, since over a longer time span the offer of official Islam and its specific interpretations created a general demand for the further study of Islam and a religious explanation of anything and everything, from questions pertaining to day-to-day life such as raising children or gender relations, to the interpretation of dreams or what policy to take towards Israel. A demand was thus created for unofficial and alternative interpretations. The attempts made by governments to control their populations by means of the *interpretation of culture* resulted in an uncontrollable spread of a *culture of interpretation*.

Governments therefore changed both the social atmosphere and the form of political debate, and this created the conditions for the rise of opposition Islamist movements. The opposition then simply rode the wave of state-sponsored religious education, reinforcing it by means of a rhetoric that attacked the state and its elites using religion itself. This counterproductive policy gave rise to a new *counterculture* of young pupils and students criticising the government and questioning its actions by reference to Islamic and ethical principles. Generations educated in Islamic faith see more clearly than their parents and grandparents that the conduct of regimes is very often antithetical to Islam, Their parents and grandparents incline towards a ritualistic and unexamined traditional Islam, while the educated generations are more adept at revealing the manipulative attempts of dictators to justify their policies with reference to an arbitrarily interpreted Islam. Thanks to religious education at schools, the educated generations also become more critical of official pro-regime clerics.

A battle is being fought over which of the many competing sides will control the newly created religious discourse. Islam has become the common language of political, cultural and ideological battles used by practically all interest groups, social classes, ideological camps, elites and counter-elites. Religious arguments are resorted to by secularists, feminists, the left and right, upper-class businesspeople and the urban poor.

The state education system unleashed forces it was unable to control and a demand it was unable to meet. For instance, while the humanities departments at universities in Egypt recorded an increased in candidates of 8% between 1981 and 1987, the number of young people applying to study Islamic law at Al-Azhar rose by 42%. At the faculty of theology of Cairo University the increase was 70%. Around the same time (1983–1986) Egyptian religious periodicals increased their circulation from 181,000 to 558,000. As has been already mentioned, several scholars note a clear intergenerational shift in religiosity, especially in urban, middle-class families. The more that state power realises that it has unleashed religious forces beyond its control, the more it attempts to seize the discourse of religion and impose its version of Islam on the whole of society. However, it ends up simply further boosting the culture of interpretation and losing control over the religious discourse. Behind these desperate attempts by regimes can be seen a superficial reading of the European Enlightenment: the remedy for any social and political ills must be therapy in the form of the right education. However, Middle Eastern dictators were as mistaken as Michael Foucault, who believed that the citizenry could be subjected to absolute supervision, discipline, indoctrination and control with the aid of modern institutions (Starrett 1998, Roy 2004).

If the official nationalist movements in 19th century Europe deliberately and relatively successfully encouraged a national identity by means of a unified, standardised educational curriculum (the teaching of history, literature and civic education) (Gellner 1993, Anderson 2008), from the second half of the 20th century onwards Middle Eastern regimes, using the same machinery, have inadvertently released the genie from the bottle in the form of a religious revival. The secularisation, privatisation and de-politicisation of religion is not a universal result of the modernisation process following in the wake of the expansion of education systems, as we mistakenly assume on the basis of our Euro-centric experience and enlightenment discourse. The re-politicisation of Islam did not take place thanks to traditional Islamic education with its network of madrasas, but thanks to the expansion of Western-style secular education (Starrett 1998, Starrett and Doumato 2007, Hefner and Zaman 2007). In this way authoritarian regimes created a convenient target group for the propaganda of Islamist movements, which almost always comprise the more modern, educated segments of the population (Kepel 1996, 2002, Dekmejian 1995).

(4) SECONDARY SCHOOL POLITICAL CHEMISTRY: THE REACTION OF DISGRUNTLED TEACHERS AND STUDENTS

The rapid expansion of educational systems in the Middle East has seen ever larger numbers of young people going through secondary school. The majority of the young male population now attends secondary school from Saturday to Thursday, and the participation of young women is also increasing (see fig. 31). The environment of secondary schools is ideal for the successful agitation of the opposition, including Islamists.

The "political chemistry" of secondary schools contributing to increased political instability and the rise of Islamism consists of the mutual "reaction" of dissatisfied teachers and rebellious youth. Secondary school teachers usually have reason to be dissatisfied with the school where they work, and more generally with the current education system and political framework. They have firsthand experience of low salaries, the low social status of the teaching profession, and the pitiful school facilities and conditions for teaching that

Fig. 31 The proportion of young people with a secondary school education 1970–2015

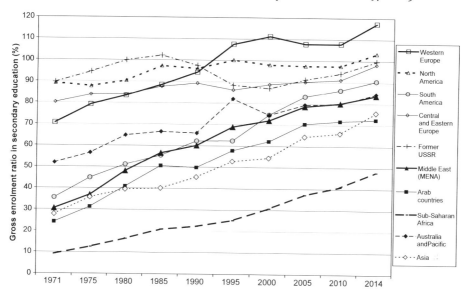

N.B.: The author's calculation of the proportion of secondary school pupils in the population for individual macro-regions (unweighted by state population size). The term secondary school here refers to upper primary and secondary levels of education in accordance with the international ISCED classification. The graph shows the gross enrolment ratio, i.e. total enrolment in secondary education regardless of age expressed as a percentage of the population of official secondary education age. Unlike the net enrolment ratio, values in certain states may exceed 100% if older people are also studying at secondary school (e.g. repeated secondary school study, re-sitting a year, requalification in middle age, etc.). These figures were chosen because they are more accessible in the statistics of most states.
Source: UNESCO

impede professional self-realisation. Similarly, they suffer the unfulfilled as-pirations of upward social mobility and inclusion in the middle classes. For this reason many secondary school teachers sympathise with the opposition, including Islamists.

Islamists consider the educational system to be a key battleground in the struggle for the hearts and minds of students. They therefore make every effort to *infiltrate* all educational institutions, including secondary schools. Furthermore, to the joy of teachers they publicly declare that the sphere of education is a political priority to which they will devote special attention if they win power. The inexorable infiltration of the ideas of political Islam among secondary school teachers is a nightmare for all Middle Eastern re-gimes. For instance, the situation in Egypt was for a long time so serious in the eyes of the elites that the Ministry of Education (2005) resorted to dis-missing en masse "many teachers with Islamic tendencies". The regimes in

Saudi Arabia and Oman also fear the infiltration and radicalisation of the teaching profession. In countries where moderate Islamists have been co-opted into government, they usually control the Ministry of Education and thus the form of the curriculum and textbooks, as well as policy in the sphere of human resources and teacher training (e.g. the role of the Muslim Brotherhood in Jordan) (Doumato and Starrett 2007). We should not forget that Hassan al-Banna, the founder of the Egyptian Muslim Brotherhood (founded in 1928), the prototype of all modern mainstream Islamist movements, was himself a teacher, albeit at primary school.

The second ingredient in our volatile reaction are the pupils. Adolescents the world over incline toward political radicalism and rebellion against authority. However, in the Middle East secondary school pupils are also frustrated by the fact that, though almost all of them aspire to a university degree, given the limited capacity of universities only around a quarter of them can fulfil this dream. Above all, they are dissatisfied because it is extremely difficult for a secondary school graduate to find work, and indeed since the 1980s they have been the most vulnerable group of graduates on the labour market. Their prospects are far from rosy. The formal qualifications, knowledge and skill sets they receive from poor quality education are not sufficient for them to stand their ground in the competition for the scarcity of relatively attractive jobs on offer in the formal economic sector, since here they are competing with better qualified university graduates.

On the other hand, their qualifications are sufficient to stimulate their career and consumer aspirations and arouse a desire to join the middle classes, a desire they share with university graduates. They are reluctant, therefore, to settle for "inferior", poorly paid manual jobs that can be done by people with a basic education. They did not spend years studying in order to end up on a building site or as market porters[32]. However, jobs are in desperately short supply, and so eventually they end up in the informal sector and the grey economy.

Yet another element in our chemical equation is the fact that there is a very small age difference between students and their teachers, and this enables teachers to more easily shape the politics of their pupils. Teachers and students are from almost the same generation, with a very similar life experience, similar feelings and the same language, while a generational chasm exists between representatives of the regime and school pupils.

---

32   However, the subjective benefits of a secondary school education are in all likelihood still significant. Young secondary school pupils are clear on this: it is always better to be frustrated by the very real threat of unfulfilled career aspirations than lack a secondary school education altogether and therefore even the possibility of higher ambitions in life and career (cf. Richards and Waterbury 2008).

Secondary school represents the ideal environment for the spread of opposition ideologies and political activism of all kinds. Like the church or mosque it represents a place where people living in even in the most repressive regimes can meet legally and regularly, socialise and communicate face to face without the need for the mediation of communication by means of anonymous media. Within the context of Middle Eastern dictatorships this kind of relatively free environment is only available on university campuses and in cyberspace. Governments are virtually incapable of banning these political activities and it is very difficult to control and monitor all of them (Richards and Waterbury 2008: 129–130, 143).

This pattern of the political mobilisation of secondary school teachers and the political awakening of their students has been present in the Middle East since at least the 1930s, when decolonisation and the fight for national independence from European domination was the key agenda of opposition activities. All of the nationalist parties fighting against European colonialism – the Algerian National Liberation Front, the Iraqi and Syrian Ba'ath party, the Moroccan Istiqlal or the Egyptian Wafd party – depended on networks of secondary school teachers and the mobilisation of their students in their national liberation struggles in the peripheries outside the main cities. While university students played the main role in the initial stages of the rise of radical Islamist movements, these days the age of activists has fallen and secondary school pupils are playing a more and more important role. However, other opposition movements are also in a position to ingratiate themselves with secondary school teachers and their students.

Authoritarian regimes, often emerging from a struggle for national liberation, are well aware of the political potential of secondary schools, and make attempts to appease both teachers and students. However, this strategy has not proved too successful. In addition, in their fight for the hearts and minds of pupils and teachers, Islamists complement their efforts to infiltrate state schools by creating a parallel network of their own private educational institutions. This applies to Palestinian Hamas, the Muslim Brotherhood in many Arab countries, the Algerian Islamic Salvation Front (during the 1990s), and the Turkish AKP (Ibrahim 1980, Starrett 1998, Richards and Waterbury 2008).

(5) UNIVERSITIES AS CENTRES OF OPPOSITION

As recently as the 1950s and 60s there were no universities in most Middle Eastern countries. For many decades the entire region played host to only a handful of universities: the famous American University of Beirut (founded 1866), the renowned Saint Joseph University in Beirut (founded by the Jesuits in 1875), Istanbul University (1900) and Cairo University (1908), which attracted students from all over the Arab world, the Hebrew University in Jerusalem (1925) and Tehran University (1934) (Hefner 2007, Daun and Arjmand 2005). The European colonial administration was well aware of the potential for political radicalisation stemming from education at institutions of secondary and tertiary education and did not support the idea, with the exception of education for a narrow elite. It was easy to control such a society, which lacked modern centres for the formation of opposition ideas and potential revolt.

The explosion in the number of universities and students only took place in the latter half of the 20th century. For instance, there was not a single university in Algeria at the time it was achieving independence (1962) and students studied in Cairo or France. These days the country boasts twenty-four universities. At the start of the War of Independence (1954) the country had only approximately 7,000 secondary school students and approximately

Fig. 32 The proportion of university students of the relevant age cohort in the regions 1970–2015

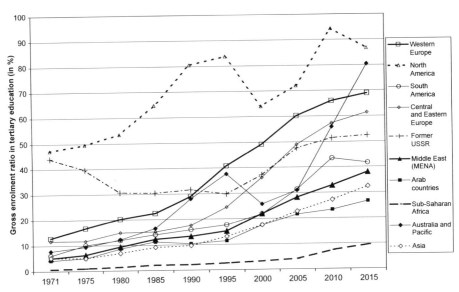

N.B.: The author's calculation of the average ratio of university students in the population for individual macro-regions (unweighted by state population size). The term university here refers to bachelor and master's level of education in accordance with international classifications (ISCED 5 and 6). The graph shows the gross enrolment ratio, i.e. total enrolment in tertiary education regardless of age expressed as a percentage of the population of official tertiary education age. Unlike the net enrolment ratio, values in certain states may exceed 100% if older people are also studying at university (e.g. studying for second degrees, repeating a year and prolonging their period of studies, requalification in middle age, etc). These figures were used because they are more available in the statistics held by most states.
Source: UNESCO

600 people with university degrees, this in a population numbering ten million. Until the mid-1990s the whole of Yemen had to make do with two universities. These days it has fifteen (in all 111 faculties and more than 130,000 students). For a long time Iran had only Tehran University. However, prior to the revolution there were already nine (1975) universities with 60,000 students. Shortly after the revolution (1985) 145,000 students were studying in Iran and at present around 50 universities are meeting the demands of more than 1.5 million students (Richards and Waterbury 2008).

In 1960, less than 4% of this age cohort (18–24) studied at university in the Middle East. By 1980 this figure was 10%. By 1993 it had crept up to 15% and in 2006 more than 20% of the young generation studied at universities (see graph 24, cf. Richards and Waterbury 2008). However, the expansion of universities has been accompanied by an increase in serious political opposition that regimes have been unable to co-opt either economically or politically (Lerner 1964, Roy 1992, Eickelman and Piscatori 1996).

During the 1960s and 70s, universities became one of the first social and intellectual centres whence political Islam began slowly, often with great difficulty, to spread into society. And yet originally universities had been bastions of oppositional Marxism and other secular leftist ideologies (Kepel 1996 and 2002, Arjomand 1986).

In the early days a role in the rise of the Islamists was also played by Middle Eastern dictatorships concerned at a time of tense Cold-War rivalry between the USSR and the USA by revolutions provoked by hyper-critical Marxists and confident leftwing opposition groups. Fearful of losing their power they often supported Islamist movements on university campuses, since they regarded them as being apolitical and a relatively safe counterbalance to an aggressive left. It seemed preferable to divide and rule these camps so that they did not converge into one powerful opposition current but exhausted themselves through mutual enmity. This tactic, known as a "green belt policy", was also supported by the United States with the aim of preventing the global spread of communism. Wherever it seemed that Islamists were opposed to the communists, the United States automatically supported them (Kepel 2004).

A critically minded middle class intelligentsia always suffers, independently of the character of the socio-political system, a universal, permanent and powerful *"opposition syndrome"* in respect of power, and this is doubly true of eternally disaffected, rebellious university students. Their trained intellect and broader perspective ensure thcy have the ability and tendency to compare the reality of life in their own country with the situation in other countries, naturally in those where the standard of living is higher. In addition, intellectually they possess not only the ambition but also the ability to organise and mobilise the masses. From the perspective of regimes this is a dangerous constellation: "The city is the centre of opposition in the country, the middle class the source of opposition in the city, the intelligentsia the most active opposition group within the framework of the middle classes, and students the most radical section of the intelligentsia" (Huntington 2006: 290). This used to apply to European fascism and Stalinism. Nowadays it applies to Middle Eastern Islamism, at the head of which stand disaffected university students. This will come as a shock only to blind admirers of modernisation theories concocted in the spirit of the secularisation thesis (Kepel 1996, Arjomand 1986).

Leading universities also often cultivate an *ethos of responsibility* in the young for the future of the nation and its development. They often support the determination of young people to change the world for the better and concentrate the best minds of a given generation in one place. This can then give rise not only to a scientific and intellectual, but also a political, *synergy* that is difficult to control and predict. Middle Eastern regimes reacted to the risk of this explosive constellation by creating regional universities in remote, peripheral provinces in order to limit the geographical concentration of young, politically active and critically minded people in one place, especially in capital cities, which are also the epicentres of political and economic power and where, therefore, there is a risk that rebellious students might win over other urban classes to their side and bring down the entire regime (Richards and Waterbury 2008).

However, the result of this strategy is debatable. Regional campuses often become "monuments" to the decline and incompetence of regimes. They cannot guarantee a comparable quality of education in the outlying regions as in the capital city. There is a dearth of capable teachers, lecture halls are overcrowded, and the technical equipment needed for top quality teaching and research is lacking. Political activism may have been dispersed into several smaller centres. However, since the 1970s in Egypt, for instance, one of the main factors in the political destabilisation of the entire country is the continuing rivalry among students themselves as well as with the university management and above all with the state police at Assiut University in Upper Egypt, which was founded in 1957 and subject to ongoing expansion. This strategy being pursued by regimes is also aimed at meeting the growing demand for higher education in outlying regions and demonstrates the efforts being made by governments to look after remote areas, reduce regional disparities, and not favour only the inhabitants of the capital city. However, in these respects too the outcomes are doubtful (Richards, Waterbury 2008).

The potential of universities to foster political dissent, including Islamism, is also due to the fact that, under dictatorships that do not respect the right of their citizens to assembly and association, there are not many places to meet legally and to exchange ideas and agitate politically. The university is one of the few public places characterised by relative freedom of communication and organisation. Students can read, distribute and discuss both the banned works of Karl Marx and Sayyid Qutb in relative calm. From here these ideas can slowly spread beyond the boundaries of academia into society at large. As in the case of mosques, secondary schools and cyberspace, regimes are unable to monitor university campuses, dormitories and lecture theatres effectively. They cannot subject these places to complete checks and insist that debates take place only on permitted topics. If a regime wants to thwart a university completely, it has to close it down for good. In repressive regimes universities become one of the few centres of political conflict, because political rivalry is strictly suppressed in other public spaces. The result is that all ideological currents and tactics of political struggle within society as a whole are present on campus, since they have no other outlet. Universities operate as a litmus paper of the distribution of public opinion in the population, where it is not customary to conduct research into public opinion, either in the form of free democratic elections or in the form of surveys. Consequently, elections to academic senates and university management perform this function to a certain extent (Richards and Waterbury 2008, Tilly 2006a).

Political agitation on university campuses is all the more effective for the fact that young people are concentrated here who have only recently left their extended families and the protective circle of the local community where they grew up. Often for the first time ever they find themselves having to stand on their own two feet, without the support of their parents and far from their home village, in the strange, anonymous and radically different environment of a city. They may feel abandoned and helpless, and so they look for new friends and a new orientation, and it is at this point that Islamist circles hold out the hope of reliable, friendly relationships and the familiar language of Islam (Hoffman 1995). It is not simply coincidence that the shift towards political Islam took place for the first time ever amongst deracinated Iranian and Arabic students living and studying abroad (Arjomand 1986). In addition, Islamists view students as their main target group, on which their missionary propaganda (*da'wah*) is to be focused. They themselves are often still students (Dekmejian 1995).

For governments, therefore, control of the universities, along with control of the army, is a question of political survival. Regimes organise competing student associations and create their own propaganda on campuses and attempt to win students over to their side. They arrest the more radical students or conscript them into the army, where they pacify them using military drill and bullying. The secret services attempts to infiltrate informal student groups, install informers and sow fear and mistrust among students. And as part of a carrot-and-stick approach they occasionally offer to co-opt the more talented students into the structures of the regime in order to ensure their lifelong loyalty (Richards and Waterbury 2008).

However, students may opt for *different* oppositional ideologies. Up until the 1970s most inclined towards the revolutionary left. However, in the interim period secular ideologies have been compromised and the *vacuum* left has been filled by Islamism as a new form of political protest discourse (Roy 2004). It is at universities in their role as laboratories of political thinking and activism that Islamists have taken over the political themes and ideological concepts of Marxism. However, they have modified and recast these themes in the language of Islam so as to make them more intelligible and attractive to the majority of the population, and this has facilitated their dissemination throughout society. For instance, 60% of members of Palestinian Hamas are former Marxists, and much the same is true of Islamists in Egypt, Tunisia and Algeria (Kepel 2004, Burgat 2002).

The sympathy of students for Islamism is borne out by one of the few detailed surveys carried out at Cairo University (1988). The results demonstrated the inability of the state to satisfy the demands of university students by means of its offer of official Islam. According to the student respondents (75%) the pro-government clerics did not meet their spiritual needs and ignored the social problems of young people and society as a whole. Students also felt that official mosques should be more involved in the life of society (100%) and should organise religious meetings for young people (87%), schools for religious education (66%), special courses for the illiterate (60%), and health clinics (58%). In short, the students were calling for precisely that which the Islamists already offered. They were pushing for the greater involvement of religious institutions in the public arena and, unlike the state, did not want to reduce Islam simply to the relationship between Man and God.

Students rejected not only the official clerics but also apolitical, mystical Sufism, which they viewed as a primitive, misguided and vernacular version of religion for the rural poor. They believe that Sufism has nothing to offer in the social sphere (75%), does nothing to encourage the spread of Islam (60%), and has nothing whatsoever to say about politics (84%). Having rejected both the pro-government clerics and Sufism, the students were warm in their response to Islamists. They expressed overall sympathy, knew the name of at least one movement and were able to enumerate the points of their political agenda. According to the student respondents, Islamists look after the interests of young people (75%), try to improve the whole of society, and contribute to the spread of the faith and religious revival. For this reason they believe it should not on any account be subject to state persecution, as it has been up till now (82%) (Starrett 1998).

More conclusive proof of the influence of Islamists on college campuses is their position on academic senates. One of the first countries where universities have moved from a predominance of secular ideologies to Islamism is Iran. Other dictatorships then picked up on this trend. For example, between 1975 and 1979 Islamists in Egypt gained control in quick succession of the elected academic senates of all faculties. A nervous President Anwar al-Sadat, ignoring the principles of academic freedom and the independence of universities, responded by banning these senates (Arjomand 1986, Kepel 1996). After this generation of students had graduated and entered the labour market, with its aid the Islamists gained control of the elected leadership of professional associations. They first took over the association of engineers (1987), followed by doctors (1988), pharmacists (1989) tradesmen (1989) and finally lawyers (1992) (Lubeck and Britts 2002). In Pakistan from 1977 to 1982 *Jamaat-e-Islami* took control of the student senates of all twenty of the universities at that time (Hoffman 1995). Similarly, during elections to university committees between 1978 and 1987 Islamists in Palestine received around 40% of the votes on the West Bank. In Gaza this figure was as high as 65–75%. During the 1980s the vast majority of the victims of the repression practiced by the Iraqi dictator Saddam Hussein were university students and fresh graduates (Eickelman and Piscatori 1996). In Malaysia too, far beyond the borders of the Middle East, it has been estimated that during the 1980s as many as 80% of university students were active in an Islamist or missionary organisation (Arjomand 1986).

The overrepresentation of university students among *militant* Islamists was demonstrated in a classic study of two Egyptian jihadi groups active in the 1970s (Ibrahim 1980). A large proportion of the rebels who occupied the Grand Mosque in Mecca in 1979 were university students. After their execution they became unofficial martyrs and informal role models in the eyes of other students at the university in Riyadh (Arjomand 1986).

Probably the most detailed research was carried out in 1984 by El Baki Hermassi into the moderate Tunisian *Mouvement de la Tendance Islamique* (MTI), analogous to the Egyptian Muslim Brotherhood. Approximately 80% of the movement's members were university students, most having grown up in the countryside. They were mostly recruited from the most prestigious and competitive disciplines such as medicine, the natural sciences or engineering. An intergenerational chasm separated them from their often illiterate parents (Hoffman 1995).

THE AVANT-GARDE OF THE ISLAMISTS: ENGINEERS AND DOCTORS AS THE BACKBONE OF THE MOVEMENT

In modernising Iran during the era of secular dictatorship (prior to 1979) a particular pattern appeared for the first time, namely the above average representation of engineers and technicians, doctors and scientists in an

Islamist movement. The movement had significantly fewer members with a background in the humanities, social sciences and theology. Since the 1970s, the predominance of a technical intelligentsia has been repeated in other Middle Eastern countries, and even made an appearance within the context of Christian and Jewish fundamentalism aimed at the re-politicisation of religion in the USA and Israel (Kepel 1996). For instance, in Egypt during the 1980s between 60% and 80% of medical and science students sympathised with the Islamists, while among philologists this figure was only 25% (Arjomand 1986). How is this possible?

The Islamists are attempting to catch up with the findings of modern science and thus reduce the economic and military superiority of the West. The power of Europe and the USA is believed to be their possession of a "secret", namely scientific discoveries and their technical applications. For this reason Islamists are drawn to the scientific and technical spheres and are proud when they manage to embrace the same knowledge as their Western colleagues (Dekmejian 1995, Pipes 1996). Islamists do not reject the technical and scientific aspects of modernity. As Nazih Ayubi appositely puts it, Islamists are not affronted by the fact that aeroplanes have replaced camels. They are simply annoyed by the fact that they cannot sit in these aeroplanes (cited in Hoffman 1995: 208). In a similar vein Gilles Kepel (1996: 29) notes that Islamists "want to taste the fruits of modernity and prosperity but remain marginalised."

Another reason students of technical disciplines are so prevalent in Islamic movements may be the fact that the adoption of science and technology seemingly does not require the adoption of Western values, culture and perspectives, while the opposite is the case in the sphere of Western history, culture, philosophy or literature. Compared with literature or political science, mathematics and anatomy might appear value-neutral (Dekmejian 1995) or might even represent a path to God. In the eyes of modern Muslims, all the findings of modern science have been anticipated on different literal and symbolic levels by the Quran and therefore only confirm, reveal and clarify that which Islam has known for a long time. Older generations of Muslims were unable to see this timeless wisdom so clearly. But these days we can appreciate it by means of the findings of modern science. In this sense at least, Islam anticipates current and future scientific knowledge (Mendel 2008).

Looked at this way science can be viewed as compatible with religion, as a form of knowledge that reliably and retrospectively confirms the prophecy of religion. As a popular *hadith* has it, God gave Man the physical world so that he might learn about it. And by learning about God's creation, Man is better able to experience and understand God the creator himself. A similar approach derives from the principle of the oneness of God (*tawhíd*) meaning the oneness of God and the world, from which is derived Sufism (Hefner and Zaman 2007). For this reason, biology, ecology, mathematics, physics, meteorology and genetics can be understood as the study of God's creation. As religious teachers impress upon their pupils, a Muslim must "read" nature as they read the Quran: "Allah created the world so that everything in it is recycled and reused. Allah has installed a recycling system in nature. Many different recycling systems. And one of them is the cycle of water". Another teacher has said that he wants to demonstrate to his pupils that "God is a mathematician" (Starrett 2003: 99). Study and scientific research can be interpreted as a specific, especially praiseworthy form of piety. Islamists believe that the ideal man (insän kämil) is he who attains inner spiritual transformation through study. The opposite is the jahil, an ignorant person living in delusions and attached to false values. Drawing on the ideas of Max Weber, it could be said that the Islamic Revival is a force leading to the rationalisation of the Middle East as many believe the Reformation and Protestantism were in the case of Europe (Roy 1992). A certain dialectic might be at play here, in which Islamists give precedence to the study of scientific and technological disciplines that in turn serve to confirm and reinforce their faith.

The last and often heard explanation of the prevalence of scientists, engineers and doctors in Islamist movements argues that Islamists yearn for fixed reference points and that they fear relativisation and ambiguity in an increasingly complex, changing world. For this reason they are drawn to the study of the exact scientific and technical spheres, in which only one result is correct and only one solution the best. Conversely, they can be made nervous by analyses that are not black-and-white, ambiguity, and the speculative nature of the social sciences and humanities, where the resolution of a problem leads more often than not to the creation of new problems, and where contradictory competing paradigms exist alongside each other in a certain tension without any one of them coming out the winner (Dekmejian 1995). For example, Jafar Umar Thalib, the Indonesian head of the militant organisation Laskar Jihad, has said that his young Islamists are recruited from the ranks of computer experts, technicians and scientists and appreciate the certainties of Islam and the precision of Islamic law, rather than the social sciences and humanities, which deepen inner confusion, relativism and critical thinking leading to persistent doubts (Hefner 2003).

Unlike science and technology, which study the multifarious manifestations of God, the social, psychological and historical facts uncovered by researchers in the social sciences are taken to be a consequence of human sin. They are not, therefore, signs of an attempt to ascertain the universal tendencies of the life of a society, but a morally low and quite repulsive object of study. For instance, breaking down society into classes, tribes, nations or religions is seen as the consequence of sin, which can be remedied by means of a refocus on Islam. It is not therefore a universal historical tendency.

Indeed, using this form of argument Islamists actually deny history. Apart from the era of the Prophet and the first four "rightly guided" caliphs, history has nothing interesting or inspiring to offer, but simply the tedious story of the gradual degeneration and decline into the modern version of *jahiliyya*. Islamists also deny anthropology and psychology. A man schooled in the virtues can be perfect and without problematic desires and needs. In addition, the Islamists believe that the social sciences unforgivably deconstruct the oneness of God (*tawhíd*) into parts, making it impossible to know him as a solid whole (Roy 1992).

(6) THE BATTLE OVER THE INTERPRETATION OF ISLAM: THE LOSS OF THE MONOPOLY OF TRADITIONAL AUTHORITIES AND THE ARRIVAL OF NEW INTERPRETERS

Along with the expansion of secular secondary and tertiary education, a new social type has emerged in the Middle East: the *Islamic intellectual*. Modern mass education created competition to the traditional Islamic authorities, and since the 1970s the clerics have been losing their centuries-old monopoly on the teaching and interpretation of religion. Increasingly they have to compete with a growing number of self-proclaimed and more and more assertive *laic* interpreters of Islam. It is not that Islam was monolithic and homogenous in the past: far from it. However, the arrival of new Islamic intellectual over the last few decades has deepened the pluralism of Islam, while the current undermining of the authority of the traditional clerics is not leading to secularisation and the decline of Islam. On the contrary, it seems that it is one of the factors in the religious revival. The erosion of the authority of the traditional clerics is also a problem for regimes, since the clerics had been loyal to them and helped legitimise the existing political order using the language of Islam.

The authority of the traditional clerics appeared strong and unthreatened when only a fraction of the population attended lower Quranic schools and madrasas. The traditional cleric represented a generally recognised authority who was the only person with access to sacred texts. They were thus able to provide practical advice to an often illiterate population on virtually any matter. Even back then knowledge meant the ability to influence others, i.e. power. However, these days young people in the Middle East are not only literate and well versed in literary Arabic, the language of the Quran, but around 80% attend secondary school and more than a third university. The *democratisation of knowledge* is taking place and power is being dispersed.

Islamic intellectuals mass produced by a secular tertiary education system are able to read the Quran and study the hadiths for themselves. They

represent a new type of believer who does not have to rely on the oral mediation of sacred texts by traditional clerics, as was the case until the recent past
(Kropáček 2002). They bypass the traditional cleric and now believe they have
no need of them. In this respect they behave similarly to Europeans during the
Christian Reformation. Ellis Goldberg summed up the situation well: "Protestants in their time and Islamists today call upon believers to confront directly
the fundamental revealed texts and read them for themselves, so that they do
not receive them only from religious and political authorities. They believe
that the holy writ is for everyone." Modern Islamists, like Protestants of the
European early modern era, are attempting to dispose of religious authority
and the monopolies of corrupt official clerics, who are compromised by their
links with state power. The Catholic Church and ulamas paid by regimes used
their interpretation of religion to legitimise authoritarian rulers. However,
this rebounded on them and discredited them (cited in Starrett 1998: 231).

It has become popular to confirm the fact that the mediation of Islam via
traditional scholars is not necessary by means of a quote from the Quran:
"God is closer to Man than the jugular vein" (Eickelman, Piscatori 1996: 70).
Appeals to read the revealed texts directly only make sense in the era of mass
education at the end of the 20th century. Mass education opened up a demand
for religious texts of all kinds. This applied to the Quran and collections of
hadiths, as well as simplified and dogmatic manuals and pamphlets, including politically relevant publications produced by the Islamists (Eickelman,
Anderson 2002).

In addition, new Islamic intellectuals confidently believe that, thanks to
their secondary school diplomas or university degrees, they are sufficiently
qualified to understand everything they read as well if not better than the
traditional scholars or Sufi masters. A dispute is now raging as to who is entitled to interpret Islam. For instance, the leading Sudanese Islamist Hasan
al-Turabi claims that "Since all knowledge is sacred, supernatural and religious, the chemist, economist and lawyer are all ulamas". The Pakistani
Islamist Maududi, whose words are cited far beyond the borders of South
Asia, says something similar: "Anyone who has dedicated his earthly time and
energy to studying the Quran and the Sunnah and has become well versed in
Islamic teaching is entitled to speak as an expert as regards Islam" (Roy 1992:
36). Other new Islamic intellectuals draw on the same logic. For instance,
the Libyan President Gaddafi, author of the "Third Universal Theory", which
aims to transcend the shortcomings of capitalism and socialism, says: "The
Quran is in Arabic. We can understand it for ourselves and we do not need an
imam in order to interpret it" (Kropáček 1996: 123).

The greater awareness of a growing number of Muslims regarding Islam has resulted in an explosion of discussion on topics that would appear
absurd to traditional Muslims. What is Islam? How should it be practised?

How strong a believer is this or that person? How should a Muslim behave? What does Islam say about marriage or democracy? What is jihad? Can women work outside the home? (Roy 2004). Newly educated people follow these discussions and select from the competing opinions those that suit them. However, they also join in the debates and offer their own interpretation shaped by their own experience of the modern world (Eickelman, Anderson 2002).

At the core of these discussions is the conviction of the modern educated laity that Islam is a universal religion for all geographic regions and historical periods. However, it must be adapted to changing situations. Traditional clerics are failing in this respect in the eyes of lay Islamic intellectuals. Their ideological rigidity means they lag behind developments in the world. They are too embroiled in power, have abandoned the search for truth, and have nothing to say to today's educated people (Eickelman, Piscatori 1996). As a consequence, new Islamic intellectuals believe that they have the right, not to say the duty, to interpret the revealed texts, i.e. the right to *ijtihad*. Traditional clerics are losing not only their monopoly on the dissemination of knowledge, but the interpretation of that knowledge (Roy 1992).

Ijtihad is a key concept of Islam and refers to independent judgements reached in situations in which neither the Quran nor the hadiths offer clear instructions as to how to proceed. It relates to religious and legal questions, but political issues too, and should be based on a solid knowledge of Islam. The outcome will be a rational, faithful yet sufficiently flexible interpretation. So as to prevent any distortion of the original divine message, the right to independent judgement used to be reserved exclusively for the most erudite legal experts. Moreover, the interpretation of Islam was closed in the Sunni world in roughly the 10th century along with the creation of the four main schools of law: the Hanafiyya, Shafiyya, Malikiyya and the Haanbaliyya madhhab. In contrast, the "gates of ijtihad" always remained open in Shiite Islam. Subsequently there were only partial interpretations within these Sunni schools of law. Consistency was to be maintained with the previous centuries-old religio-legal tradition, which could only be appreciated after many years of study (Mendel 2008, Kropáček 1996, 2002).

However, the gates of ijtihad are still open according to the new Islamic intellectuals and everyone has the democratic right to participate in the rivalry of interpretations. Islam is too serious a matter for it to be left to discredited clerics. However, Islamists claim the right to evaluate everything through their own concept of Islam, and sometimes the right to issue public religio-legal expert opinions (*fatwas*) or to pronounce alleged sinners to be excommunicated heretics and apostates (*takfir*) and to declare armed jihad against them and other enemies. In short, Islamists and other new interpreters claim the right to pursue highly specialist activities that in the past were always a domain reserved exclusively for an elite group of clerics who had devoted their lives to the study of Islam (Roy 1992).

Until recently only traditional authorities showed faithful Muslims the way forward, and these authorities are now facing a crisis. If we use the simplified differentiation between two opposite poles of Islam created by Marshall Hodgson, on the one hand there is Islam as presented by super-literate interpreters in the form of sharia oriented scholars, and on the other there is mystic, vernacular Islam regarded as an "ocean without shores", which is interpreted by non-literate Sufi masters. People always turned for advice and guidance to Islamic scholars (*ulamas*) and lawyers (*fuqahä*), or to representatives of the other pole of Islam, the sheiks of the Sufi brotherhoods (Kropáček 2002, Anderson 2003). However, the authority of these traditional pundits was always locally rooted and was based on recognition of their erudition by the community around them, which was uneducated and looked up uncritically to the traditional authorities with awe. It is precisely between these two established interpretative poles of Islam that new interpreters are springing up today (Turner 2007).

However, if the traditional pundits have completed many years of training, the new lay interpreters of Islam are typically self-taught amateurs. They have usually had a Western-style secular education (Kepel 2002). They are prepared to give an opinion from the perspective of Islam on anything, though their interpretations often result in a vulgarisation of the religion and dilettantism. A few selected concepts, theses, authorities and passages from the Quran are repeated and recycled. This tends not to lead to intellectual originality and authenticity, but more sterility (Mendel 2008, Roy 1992, 2004).

Only certain new Islamic intellectuals come up with original, consistent approaches that constructively develop their inspirations. Unfortunately their ideas tend to be demanding and only other intellectuals display any interest in them (Roy 2004). In contrast, Islamists, the most influential and best organised representatives of the new Islamic intellectuals, offer a simple and inclusive political reading of the Quran. They have a modern education and access to the latest media, they look for answers to modern problems and react to what they regard as discredited modern political ideologies. Their interest in the everyday world outweighs their interest in the sacred.

Their main theme is the non-Islamic character of nominally Muslim societies. The Islamisation of their fellow citizens is the main plank of their programme. The deviation of Muslims from Islam is responsible for the ills that afflict society. Given their educational qualifications they have high career aspirations. However, contemporary Middle Eastern society, in contrast to the historical development of Europe and the United States in the 19th and 20th centuries, is unable to integrate the majority of the newly educated classes into the economic or the political system. It has no future to offer them. And so they become part of the critically minded, opposition "lumpen-intelligentsia", profiling themselves as self-appointed preachers. Their interpretation of Islam leads them to criticise the existing order, to mobilise against it, and to search for alternatives. During the 1960s those members of the intelligentsia excluded from the system turned to Marxism: these days Islam is the discourse of protest (Roy 1992).

(7) COUNTER-PRODUCTIVE REACTIONS ON THE PART OF REGIMES: I SPEAK IN THE NAME OF ISLAM – I HAVE POWER

The outcome of this interpretative struggle is many voices speaking for Islam and the impossibility of anyone having a monopoly over its interpretation. Unlike in the past, these days Islam lends its auspices to anyone that wishes to adopt them. This means not only state power led by secular or monarchist despots or traditional clerics and masters of the mystical orders, but the new secular intellectuals, liberals and Islamists, terrorists and writers, scientists and military generals, tribal leaders and feminists, businesspeople, commanders of armed militias and minorities. More and more voices are entering the religio-political discourse, which have been excluded up till now. As well as the higher educational qualifications of more and more people, the emergence of new discussion platforms made possible by the expansion of the new media as discussed in the next chapter plays an important role.

Everyone is competing for the human imaginary and the promotion of their own interpretations of religious symbols. They try to act as though they were speaking authoritatively on behalf of Islam, and using religious language they promote their own vision of the world and their interests. Obedience to God and his instructions in reality means obedience to the one who best understands his instructions, or rather the one who convinces others this is the case. Everyone claims that their interpretation is the best and that their interests or ideals are nothing other than correctly understood Islam and the best continuation of the Islamic tradition. This leads to the inexorable fragmentation of power through the disintegration of religious authority (Eickelman, Piscatori 1996, Starrett 1998).

A key pillar of the power of dictators is put at threat, since until recently they had relied on the monopoly on the interpretation of Islam enjoyed by official clerics loyal to the regime. In response, dictators are attempting to react to the promotion of alternative religio-political discourses by various means, for instance by emphasising the separation of politics from religion and the alleged apolitical character of Islam. At other times they cleave to Islam in order to maintain a semblance of legitimacy. The Moroccan King Hassan II based the legitimacy of his power on the genealogical origin of the dynasty leading up to the birth of the Prophet Muhammad and on the title "protector of the faithful". However, in 1993 he declared: "Render unto Caesar the things which are Caesar's; and unto God the things that are God's", a reference to the Christian principle of the separation between spiritual and earthly power. The dictators of Jordan, Algeria, Iraq or Tunisia made similarly inconsistent attempts to separate religion and politics in response to the emergence of an Islamist opposition. For instance, in 1977 Saddam Hussein declared of the secular Ba´ath party: "Our party is not neutral in respect of religion. It always stands on the side of faith over atheism. However, it is not and has no intention of being a religious party" (Kropáček 1996: 169). Gradually, however, hand in hand with a growing political crisis Saddam resorted to the justification of power by means of Islam (Kepel 2004).

A key dispute centres on who has and has not the right to interpret Islam and who is an apostate and who misuses Islam to attain their worldly objectives (Roy 2004). As Muhammad Sa'id al-'Ashmawi, the liberal judge sitting on the Egyptian supreme court, said: "God wanted Islam to be a religion, but people have turned it into politics." Regimes warn against the use of religion in political rivalries, something that is dangerous for them. At the same time they emphasise in vain that the interpretation of Islam should be left to specially trained experts, from the ranks of pro-government clerics it goes without saying. As Mohamed Ali Mahgoub, the Egyptian Minister of Religious Affairs, said in an important speech given at a time when militant Islamism was on the rise in the country (1989): "Piety is open and accessible to everyone, but religion – theology, applied ethics and dogma – must be left to specialists. Otherwise we will have killing, disagreement, polarisation, destruction and fear, all in the name of religion. There are merchants of religion who want to achieve their ends in the name of faith and at the price of turning Egypt into a sea of blood" (cited by Starrett 1998: 175 and 185).

Though people are capable of recognising more than one religious authority, the strategy pursued by regimes brings no results. The radical Islamist opposition uses religion to delegitimise regimes, declaring them to be apostates (*kafir*) or at the very least stupid or uneducated (*jahil*). Regimes on the other hand attempt to prop up their power with reference to Islam and to discredit the Islamist opposition deploying the same religious discourse. For instance, after the massacre of 20,000 Muslim Brethren and the bombing of the rebel city of Hama (1982), the Syrian President Hafez al-Assad declared emphatically: "They are apostates. We are defending Islam, the religion and the homeland" (Kropáček 1996: 157). However, this is counterproductive rhetoric. Islamists are able to accuse the government itself of failing to abide by those very principles of Islam to which it appeals. In addition, the strategy adopted by regimes contributes to the popularisation of a political reading of

Islam, since it attempts to join battle with the Islamists using the latter's weapons (Eickelman, Piscatori 1996). An Algerian teacher draws attention to the counterproductive character of the government rhetoric: "The government wants Islam. But it wants an antiseptic, subordinate Islam that kowtows to its opinions. But Islam is a powerful current. It does not distinguish between the spiritual and the worldly. If the state declares itself to be genuinely Muslim, it must reconcile its statements and actions and desist from doublespeak. You cannot mess with Islam with impunity" (cited by Kropáček 1996: 128). The Saudi opposition said something similar: "The Saudi throne cannot be toppled without religious ideology. He who lives by the sword, dies by the sword! And he whose throne was built on a missionary calling (da'wah) will die by the calling! The Saudi throne will not fall until the opposition accepts religious ideology" (cited in Kropáček 1996: 151).

(8) THE WESTERNISED MINDSET AND THE CREOLISATION OF ISLAM: WESTERN IDEOLOGY AND THE INVENTION OF TRADITION

He had read and relished Shakespeare, Dostoevsky, Chekhov and Sartre. He especially liked Sophocles, whose Oedipus he must have read ten times. It never failed to bring tears to his eyes. This was not a denizen of European cafe culture, but a Palestinian doctor named Fathi Shaqaqi. A Muslim, Islamic radical and head of the terrorist organisation Islamic Jihad. Similarly, Hasan al-Turabi, a leading Sudanese Islamist, remarked self-critically: "I know French history better than the history of Sudan. I love your culture, your painters, your musicians". With regret he went on to observe that Islamists were growing apart from their culture and religion and were adopting Western science and culture. According to him, most Islamist leaders came from "Western Christian culture. They speak your languages" (Pipes 1996: 20, 23).

Their familiarity with many different traditions sees the new intellectuals contributing to the "creolisation" of Islam. They connect and combine intellectual and spiritual traditions that had previously been separate: Islamic orthodoxy, Sufism, modern science and Western secular ideology. And just as, thanks to their westernised, secular education, they have a superficial notion of Islamic tradition, so they have become acquainted with modern scientific thinking and Western secular ideologies such as Marxism, liberalism and nationalism, against which they define themselves. However, they tend to pick up fragments of each sphere, and their knowledge is patchy.

Instead of a solid knowledge of the Quran and the collections of traditions, they tend to read simplified, partisan brochures, commentaries, sermons and fatwas, or quotes from sacred texts taken out of context. Instead of insights into Western ideological systems they have but a superficial familiarity with them. Their scientific knowledge is equally fragmentary and random. Then, like typical autodidacts, they attempt to wrap everything up with the aid of common sense into one coherent system. This is eclecticism taken to extremes, with Western inspiration, Islamic tradition, anti-Western rhetoric and their own invention thrown in. What results is a kind of mishmash of newly acquired knowledge full of references to the Quran and the hadiths that begins "The Quran says..." or "Everything is contained in the Quran", and full of references to the findings of modern Western science that begin "Science says..." or "Science shows us...". Sometimes they include references to historical materialism operating with the revealed laws of historical development relevant for today that begin "History always..." or "History teaches us...". However, other authorities are also quoted, including leading media stations like the BBC, CNN or Al-Jazeera (Roy 1992, 2004). One Islamic intellectual described this mix of sources as follows: "I listen to Mozart, read Shakespeare, watch television series on the Comedy Channel and believe in the fulfilment of God's Islamic law (*sharia*)" (Pipes 1996: 20).

The creolisation of Islam leads to the *invention of new traditions* that their creators claim represent the original version of Islam (Eickelman, Piscatori 1996). One should not overlook radical westernisation in the spirit and mentality of secularly educated ideologists of political Islam. Despite their anti-Western rhetoric and obsession with a return to the Golden Age, they promote an *Islamic version of Western modernity*. Discontinuity and a rupture with Islamic tradition often prevails over continuity. A knowledge of and admiration for the West predominates over proficiency in Islamic tradition, culture and their own history. The result is a new Islam retold in the spirit of the West that traditional believers might find hard to recognise (Pipes 1996, Barša 2001).

THE BUREAUCRATISATION OF RELIGION

The organisation of the interpreters of Islam has also undergone a change. In traditional Islam this involved an informal network of clerics without any centre or hierarchy in the manner of a medieval corporation. Decisions were reached on the basis of consensus in a non-directive way, and this approach was probably applied during the editing of the Quran and the creation of the schools of law. Islamists, on the other hand, prefer their interpreters, preachers and supporters to be organised on the basis of Western bureaucratic hierarchies, if possible with an advanced division of labour with many different specialised positions, committees and secretariats. This is more a reflection of the influence of Marxist organisations than the Islamic tradition. The phenomenon of religious bureaucratisation in the Middle East does not have many historical parallels. The initiative was only taken in modern times by Saudi Arabia or the modern Shiite clergy and the South Asian Deobandi reform movement of the 19th century.

WOMEN IN THE PUBLIC SPHERE

As regards the status of women, Islamists also diverge from traditional societies and are closer to the West, and even Western feminism. Tradition states that a woman should remain at home. This opinion prevailed especially in affluent urban families that could afford to hold it. Furthermore, a woman did not have to attend joint prayers at the mosque. The headscarf was seen as a way of harnessing destructive female sexuality. Today, by contrast, female Islamists are visibly active in the public sphere. They study at universities, engage in political activism and seek self-realisation through professional careers. They do not pray at home, but are free to attend public prayers. And they regard the headscarf as a means of protecting and preserving their honour, which could otherwise be jeopardised by a focus on their careers and their involvement outside the home in public spaces full of strange men (Roy 1992, Pipes 1996).

For instance, the Sudanese al-Turabi, addressing the issue of women at the time the National Islamic Front he headed had a share of power, declared: "In Sudan women have the same status as men. They serve in the army, in politics and in the ministries." In his opinion the Islamic movement had helped liberate women. The Egyptian al-Banna, founder of the Muslim Brotherhood, declared at the very start of the 20th century: "Muslim women were free and independent for fifteen centuries. Why follow the example of Western women, who are still so dependent materially on their husbands?" (Pipes 1996: 23). In the 1970s, similarly militant Egyptian groups called for the rights and duties of both genders to be balanced, adding that throughout history men had unfairly overturned this balance to their own benefit so that humanity was plunged back into state of barbaric *jahiliya*. And so they believe that women should be educated. And as long as they are able to handle their most important duties within the family, they should be free to work outside of the home, though they should be segregated from men (Ibrahim 1980). Modern Islamic feminism defends its interests and the emancipation of women by reference to the Quran and sunnah (Burgat 2002). However, the overall attitude of Islamists to the social role of women remains ambivalent, and it is impossible to trace a uniform tendency across all countries, social groups and movements (Mendel 2008).

THE SEPARATION OF RELIGION AND POLITICS

The effects of westernisation on the mentality of Islamist leaders are most apparent in their understanding of politics and law. Traditional Muslims tended to shun politics and the business of government (cf. Lerner 1964), which they associated only with problems, namely conscription into the army, tax collection and public work. For them God and a life led in accordance with their ancestors was the important thing, whereas at the centre of Islamists' interest is politics.

The relationship between politics and Islam is hotly debated in the West. It is stressed that Islam covers all aspects of life, i.e. not only the relationship between Man and God, but also the relationships between people. For this reason, it is argued, it is impossible to separate politics from religion, since both merge into one (Lewis 1990, 2003b). The Western view adopts the concept of *caesaropapism*, which in reality is only propagated by Islamists, who, though the loudest, certainly do not speak for all Muslims. These days, for instance, as well as Islamism, apolitical neo-fundamentalism is growing in popularity, which lays an emphasis on remedying the individual by means of individual effort and not through putting right entire societies. The logic of neo-fundamentalism is illustrated by the Saudi Sheikh Al-Albani: "First establish Islam in your heart, after which it will be established in your country" (Roy 2004: 249). Nor can the fact be overlooked that religion and politics are also linked outside Muslim societies. As far as Islam is concerned, the Prophet, as the model for all Muslims, represented a politician and religious leader in one person. The Quran often adjures obedience to "God, the Prophet and those in authority". However, the separation of Islam from politics properly began after the death of the Prophet, during the era of the first hereditary Umayyad caliphate. A particular class of cleric, independent of political power, broke away. Nominally the caliph was still entitled to continue to lead Friday's prayers and deliver the khutbah, but in practice this role was now taken by the clerics. In history Muslim states did not have a specific character given by religious difference in comparison with non-Muslim countries (Eickelman, Piscatori 1996).

However, Islamists do not define Islam in relation to other religions, something that would be more intelligible to a traditional Muslim, but mainly in relation to secular ideologies they are in competition with. It is for this reason that they present their concept as a kind of "third way": "We are neither socialists nor capitalists, but Muslims". They do not regard Islam in the traditional spirit as a framework for the life of the individual or community, but as a tool for controlling society and the state. When promoting their slogan "Islam is the solution", they believe that Islam is capable of generating an instruction kit for the organisation of political, economic and social affairs that can be applied anywhere in the world. This emphasis on Islam as political ideology and not religion is clear in the letter that Imam Khomeini sent Gorbachev in an attempt to export the Islamic revolution to an atrophying USSR. He appealed to Gorbachev to study Islam as an ideology that the USSR could accept in order to fill the ideological vacuum of the crumbling communist empire. What is striking about the letter, however, is that it contains no encouragement to convert to Islam. Seen in this light, Islam as an ideology is distinct from Islam as a religion. It is not necessary to accept faith in order to apply an ideology: the two are quite separate things (Pipes 1996). Khomeini's major work is on social and political themes, and the reader will learn nothing at all about faith and the relationship with God (Khomeini 2004).

The Islamists sought recourse in Islam after their disappointing experience with secular politics. The first generation of Islamists were often former Marxists (Kepel 2002, Burgat 2002). Their main inspiration for thinking about religion had its roots in the worldly problems they faced, and these inspirations were not therefore primarily of a spiritual character, as was so in the case of traditional Muslims (Pipes 1996).

LAW: CODIFICATION AND TERRITORIALITY

Jurisprudence, too, as commandeered by the Islamists is closer to the character of secular Western law and not the traditional Islamic concept. This shift involved an attempt to *codify* what had originally been an unfettered and semantically open Islamic legal discourse into the form of legal codes and precise paragraphs. The work was begun in the Middle East by French and British colonists and the reformers of the Ottoman Empire. The aim was to find and formulate general norms applicable to a wide range of legal cases. The dogmatism of many Islamists can be traced back to this endeavour to codify Islam. Traditional Islam had worked with a plurality of legal interpretations, and so the fatwas issued by different lawyers on the same issue might well be in conflict with each other. However, the unmanageable plurality of legal opinion was incompatible with the effective exercise of centralised state power, something that mattered to secular dictators, European colonists, and Islamists striving for power. This also accounts for the tendency mentioned above to turn independent experts in Islamic law into civil servants now working for a salary and organised in a state controlled hierarchical organisation.

Furthermore, while traditional Islamic law had always applied to the individual, wherever he might be found, the Islamists, infected by a Western concept of law, now took it to apply anywhere and equally within the territory of the state. For traditional Islam what had been important was what religion you came from. For Islamists what was now important was what territory you lived in. The traditional approach meant that a Muslim could not enjoy a dram of whiskey in Cairo or New York. Wherever he was, he was governed by Islamic law. Christians, on the other hand, could get drunk wherever they choose and Islamic law was not interested in regulating their lives, even if they lived as a minority in a majority Muslim society. According to the traditional legal concept of protected status (*dhimmi*), Christian, Jewish and Zoroastrian minorities were provided legal autonomy and self-rule. These days, on the contrary, Islamists look to the modern Western concept of the across-the-board territorial validity of law and state sovereignty. As the Islamist ideologue Hasan al-Turabi observes: "Islam regards the territory as the basis of legal jurisprudence." This fact impacts significantly on religious minorities, since they are now forced to live according to Muslim standards. For instance, in intransigent Saudi Arabia, Christians must fast during Ramadan. In the Islamist-controlled parts of Palestine, pigs owned by Christian Arabs have been found poisoned (Pipes 1996: 25).

REACTIONS TO MARXISM AND OTHER WESTERN IDEOLOGIES

Like Christian liberation theologians, Islamists have refashioned Marxism, in relation to which they had to define themselves as to a key opposition ideology, in the language of the Quran. A verse from the Quran resonates strongly with Islamists: "And we desired to show favour unto those who were oppressed in the earth, and to make them examples and to make them the inheritors". The revolutionary statement by Imam Khomeini has also attained a legendary status (1979) akin to "Workers of the world, unite!" Hoping to export the Iranian revolution he wrote: "It is my hope that a party will be established throughout the world that will have as its motto "party of the oppressed" (Kropáček 1996: 185). The leader of the Muslim Brotherhood in Syria, Mustafa al-Siba'i (1961) declared: "Islamic socialism acknowledges the legality of private property and allows talented members of society to participate in constructive competition. But this does not lead to class struggle. It is moral socialism."

The Islamists are likewise capable of refashioning other Western secular ideologies to suit the concepts of Islam. The concept of a ruler consulting his subjects (*shura*) can be used to justify the democratic principle of universal suffrage. The functioning of a democracy on the basis of majority rule can also be derived from the Islamic concept of a consensus derived from the opinions of a majority (*ijma*) (Kropáček 1996: 157).

SECULAR OR RELIGIOUS EDUCATION? THE EDUCATIONAL PROFILE OF THE NEW INTERPRETERS

Of the leading non-Islamist new Islamic intellectuals we would mention the Iranian Abdolkarim Soroush (b. 1945). He advocates a new hermeneutic reading of the Quran that distinguishes between the sacred, unchanging revealed religion and the necessarily limited imperfect knowledge humans have of it, which is inevitably influenced by the time and place of its interpreter. Similarly, the Syrian engineer Muhammad Shahrur (b. 1938) proposes a new liberal reinterpretation of the Quran in the spirit of the European Enlightenment, and has been declared a heretic by traditional clerics from Al Azhar. In Egypt a comparable intellectual eclectic combining a variety of sources was the doctor Mustafa Mahmoud (1921–2009). Another important figure in Egypt is the former secular left-winger and now more liberal-minded judge and intellectual Tariq al-Bishri (b. 1933), who in 2011 was commissioned by the army to lead work on a new constitution. He is close to the party al-Wasat, a breakaway group from the Muslim Brotherhood (Kropáček 2002, Eickelman and Anderson 2003, Hesová 2011).

As far as Islamists are concerned, the founder of the Egyptian Muslim Brotherhood (established in 1928), Hassan al-Banna (1906–1949), was himself a primary school teacher. Right from the start, when he would teach children in the state school during the day and offer lectures to their parents on Islam in the evening, he found himself at odds with the traditional clerics. The most influential Islamic thinker and activist of the 20th century, Sayyid Qutb (1906–1966), did a British-style teacher training course before becoming a writer, literary critic, civil servant at the Ministry of Education, and finally the leading ideologist of the Muslim Brotherhood. From 1948 to 1950 he underwent a two-year study trip around the United States. Other leaders of the Egyptian Muslim Brotherhood were also not educated in madrasas but in the secular education system created along European lines. For instance Hassan al-Hudaybi (1949–1973) was a lawyer and judge, as was Umar al-Tilmisani (1973–1986). Mohammed Mahdi Akef (2004–2010) graduated as a PE teacher before going on to study British law. His successor, Mohammed Badie (from 2010) was a vet and university professor.

Smaller and more radical groups advocating armed struggle would regularly split off from the moderate Egyptian Muslim Brotherhood. However, their educational profile is similar. The targets of their attacks were not simply secular representatives of the regime, but also traditional clerics linked with political power (Ibrahim 1980). For example, the agricultural engineer Mustafa Shukri founded the well known sect *Takfir wal-Hijra* (*Jama'at al-Muslimin*), which distanced itself from corrupt mainstream society and lived in isolated communities. Its activities culminated (1977) with the kidnapping and murder of the Ministry of Religious Affairs (Awqaf), Ḥusayn al-Dhahabi. This was a typical cleric from the pro-government establishment employed at al-Azhar, who in the name of Islam was uncompromising in his criticism of Islamists as apostates. Another attempt at a bloody political coup was made (1974) by the radical group of military technicians aptly titled the "Technical

Military Academy Group" (also known as *Shabab Muhammad*) recruited from a military academy. It was led by *Salih Siriya*, who had a doctorate in the natural sciences. The ideological weaponry of another similar organisation, *Jihad*, was the work of the electrical engineer Muhammad abd-al-Salam Faraj. In his popular samizdat pamphlet *Jihad: The Neglected Obligation* Faraj claims that the hidden sixth pillar of the Islamic faith is the duty of every Muslim to fight against Muslim leaders who turn their backs on Islamic law. In this spirit it was not a graduate of a school of religion that assassinated President Anwar al-Sadat in 1981, but an army lieutenant Khaled Al-Islambouli, who had received a secular education (Kepel 2002).

An influential militant to emerge from the Egyptian organisation *Jihad* is the former right hand of Osama bin Laden and Al Queda's ideological leader, doctor Ayman al-Zawahiri. As a new Islamic intellectual he assumed the rights traditionally reserved for religious authorities, i.e. to interpret Islam, issue religious and legal fatwas, and even to call for armed jihad. The Saudi Arabian bin Laden studied at a prestigious secular secondary school and then at university studied civil engineering and public administration, and apart from the Quran his favourite reading included the work of the British Field Marshal Montgomery and the French President Charles de Gaulle (Kepel 2004). The first bomb attack on the World Trade Centre in New York (1993) was carried out by people with a similar secular education. One of them, the young Jordanian Eyad Ismail, studied computer science at the American university and his brother said of him that "he loved everything American, from cowboys to hamburgers", while his parents had always considered him a "child of America". The brains behind the technicalities of the attack and an expert in explosives, Ramzi Yousef, also graduated in electrical engineering in Great Britain (Pipes 1996: 20).

Beyond the borders of Egypt we see the same pattern. Along with the Egyptian Qutb, the most influential Islamist of the 20th century is the Pakistani Abul Al´a Maududi (1903–1979). Though he was partially educated at madrasas, the death of his father saw him complete his education on his own. He immersed himself in Western culture through his study of English. Significant in this context is the fact that his secular party *Jamaat-e-Islami* was always in competition with another party comprised of Pakistani clerics. Similarly, the Algerian leader of the Islamic Salvation Front, Abbassi Madani, trained to be a teacher in England, where he was awarded a doctorate at the prestigious University of London, before going on to be a professor in Algiers. His Sudanese colleague, Hassan al-Turabi, studied law in England at the University of London and at the Sorbonne in France, before winning a scholarship to travel around the USA. The heavyweight of Tunisian Islamists, inveterate critic of the dictatorship of Ben Ali and leader of the *Ennahda* movement, Rachid Ghannouchi, first studied at Cairo University of Agriculture. He then studied philosophy in Damascus before moving to France for a year and continuing his studies at the Sorbonne. The Moroccan Sheikh Abdesslam Yassine, leader of the Islamist Justice and Spirituality, worked as a teacher and inspector for the Ministry of Education specialising in French (Hoffman 1995).

Likewise Laith Shubeilat, chairman of the Jordanian Association of Engineers, has tirelessly promoted the need for a reformulation of the ideal society of the Prophet Muhammad (Pipes 1996). The leader of Hamas and the Palestinian premier, Ismail Haniyeh, studied Arab literature at the University of Gaza. A significant number of his ministers (after 2006) boast university degrees from the United States, Great Britain and Germany (Čejka 2007). The leaders of Turkey's moderate Islamists all received a secular education and are from the ranks of the technical intelligentsia. Necmettin Erbakan, head of the Prosperity Party (Refah Partisi), which won the elections in 1995, studied technology in Istanbul and Germany. Another premier, later president and head of the conservative AKP, Recep Erdogan, studied economics and administration at Marmara University in Istanbul, and for a while was a professional footballer (Roy 2005).

Even in Shiite Iran, where several clerics were in the vanguard of the revolution (1979) and under the constitution now control several powerful institutions, "bearded engineers" and technocrats have made up most of all the post-revolutionary governments. A well known example is the transport engineer and former president Ahmadinejad. It is often pointed out that government ministers in Tehran have more doctorates from American universities than ministers in Washington itself. The informal ideological leader of a faction of the Iranian Islamists prior to the revolution was the Marxist sociologist with a doctorate from the Sorbonne, Ali Shariati (1933–1977), whose revolutionary thinking was moulded during his studies (1960–65) in France (Kepel 2002). Afghanistan is something of a special case. In the internecine civil war unleashed after the departure of the Soviet Army (1989) between the individual factions of the Mujahedeen, the Taliban, which was established in 1995 and made up of students of radical Pakistani madrasas focusing on the millions of uprooted Afghans living in local refugee camps, asserted its presence. However, at the head of the most influential mujahedeen fighting against domestic communists and Soviet soldiers were engineers with a secular education from Kabul University, who during their student years had diligently read the Persian translation of the works of Qutb. Ahmad Shah Massoud held a prominent position and was leader of the organisation Jamaat-e-Islami, along with the less tolerant Gulbuddin Hekmatyar, who established the influential group Hezb-e Islami (Roy 1992, 2004).

It is clear that the core of Islamist movements is dominated by leaders who have received a secular education and possess a significantly westernised mentality. At the end of the 20th century a similar pattern is discernible within Christian, Jewish, Sikh, Hindu and Buddhist religious and political movements far beyond the borders of the Middle East (Juergensmeyer 1994, 2008, Kepel 1996). Although in the Middle East we occasionally observe a certain bipolarity and symbiosis of laics with a secular education and clerics from traditional madrasas, the secular, Western-educated elements generally predominate amongst both mainstream and militant Islamists (Arjomand 1995, Kepel 2002).

(9) GROWTH IN ASPIRATIONS AND THE UNEMPLOYED "LUMPEN-INTELLIGENTSIA"

The expansion of educational systems in the Middle East has outpaced economic growth and with it the absorption capabilities of a labour market incapable of accommodating the ever larger numbers of increasingly educated and ambitious graduates. Similarly, the expansion of education systems has outpaced the absorption capacity of rigid, closed political systems. Graduates have only limited opportunities to establish a professional or political career and to satisfy higher aspirations for upwards social mobility resulting from secondary and tertiary educational qualifications. The economic and political system is unable to integrate them into the social order. This is a significant source of political destabilisation in the Middle East, since frustrated graduates are turning their gaze to opposition, including Islamist, movements.

In 19th and early 20th century Europe increasing levels of education also contributed to political awakening, the rise of political movements, and radicalisation. Better and better educational qualifications created high aspirations that were not always met. This resulted in mass frustration and political radicalisation. Instead of self-realisation within the framework of building a career for themselves, educated people sought an outlet for their energies through the establishment of opposition political movements. Developing countries are undergoing analogous developments at present, with the difference that redundant intellectuals are not seeking recourse only with secular movements, but also with religious opposition movements and ideologies (Brzezinski 1993).

Increasing levels of education stimulate consumer, professional, career and political ambitions. For instance, William Lecky (1838–1903), a historian researching the development of modernising Great Britain in the 18th and 19th centuries, noticed that "education leads to desires that it is incapable of fulfilling". His contemporary, the British administrator of Egypt, Evelyn Baring Cromer (1841–1917), expressed similar concerns regarding an excessively educated population that was difficult to control (1907): "Education has awoken hitherto absent or dormant ambitions. It is no wonder that educated young people are beginning to demand greater influence over the management and administration of the country" (cited in Starrett 1998: 236).

People with at least a primary education expect more from life than illiterate, unqualified people. Those with a secondary school diploma aim higher than their peers with only a primary education. And university graduates expect more than school leavers. Although unemployment is then always a politically sensitive problem, from the point of view of political destabilisation the most dangerous are unemployed graduates. The discrepancy between their high *aspirations* and the bleak reality of unemployment is greatest in their case and results in a feeling of *frustration* that can turn them against the regime. The increased aspirations stimulated by mass education, which outstrip the opportunities of the existing economic and political systems because of the slowness of change in these spheres, can result in a "revolution of rising expectations" (Davies 1962, Lerner 1964, Huntington 1968). This mechanism played a role during the Iranian Revolution (1979), and a similar scenario has long been discussed in connection with Saudi Arabia (Klare 2004).

To begin with university students in the Middle East took as their *reference group* (during the 1950s) the Western middle classes or the domestic economic and political elites (Lerner 1964). In light of the gradual increase in the number of university degrees, which can no longer guarantee acceptance into the top political and economic circles, the reference group now comprises white-collar workers from the secure middle classes. In this post-colonial region a popular profession is that of state employee: a civil servant, army officer, doctor or teacher. Graduating from university was an automatic pass to positions in the public administration or public economic sector. For instance, in Egypt during the 1980s half of those graduating from secondary schools and universities ended up as civil servants (Starrett 1998). However, the swollen state apparatus is no longer capable of absorbing the growing numbers of graduates. States have began to ignore the unwritten rule guaranteeing jobs to school leavers and graduates because established post-colonial mobility channels are overloaded. Educated people are gradually becoming more at threat of unemployment than unqualified people. The highest unemployment rate is recorded amongst secondary school leavers (see tab. 26), closely followed by university graduates (Richards and Waterbury 2008).

Everything is further complicated by the fact that remuneration for work in the public sector is gradually falling and is often insufficient to meet the needs of someone with a family to provide for. As a consequence graduate civil servants are boosting their pay by working as receptionists or taxi drivers and teachers make ends meet by offering private tuition. It also means that women from middle class families are leaving the home and applying for jobs in order to maintain their middle class status and the standard of living they are accustomed to, something their husbands are no longer able to ensure (Hoffman 1995, Lubeck and Britts 2002). The intelligentsia is becoming an unemployed, poorly paid and rebellious "lumpen-intelligentsia" under the banner of opposition ideologies that use their knowledge and intellectual capacities in order to criticise and question the established social order (Roy 1992).

Tab. 26 Unemployment level by education in MENA countries (in %)

Country (year)	Uneducated	Primary school	Secondary school	University	Total
Algeria (1995)	9.6	30.9	30.9	68.4	27.9
Egypt (1998)	4.1	5.7	22.4	9.7	11.4
Morocco (1999)	9.4	26.3	32.4	37.6	15.6
Oman (1996)	5.6	13.4	24.8	2.8	10.8
Tunisia (1997)	10.2	20.8	15.4	6.4	15.7

Source: World Bank labour force data. Cited in Richards and Waterbury (2008: 137).

The main reason for unemployment amongst graduates is *structural* in nature: the number of graduates produced by expanding education systems is rising faster than the creation of new jobs. In addition, if the economy is creating jobs, they tend to be less qualified positions in the informal sector.

However, the *rational strategy* of graduates and their families also plays a role. Graduates feel they have a better chance of finding a decent job than unqualified people. And so they pay a waiting game and do not take the first offer if is not attractive. In addition, they and their families have invested a lot in their education and they want to see a return on this investment. Unqualified people reach decisions on a different basis. They know that they will never be considered for the top jobs, and so are more inclined to accept the first offer they receive. Plus college students come from better off backgrounds. Their parents can support them while they look for work, a process that may continue for several years. The same does not apply to poorer parents, who may on the contrary expect their offspring to contribute to the family budget as soon as possible (Richards and Waterbury 2008).

Nevertheless, despite the situation on the labour market the demand for higher education is still high. An academic title carries with it social prestige and is associated with the opportunity of getting a job in the public sector. Although many countries are facing a shortage of skilled craftsmen, whose salaries exceed those of graduates, interest in apprenticeships is decreasing, while interest in university studies is rising. A job in the public sector is a *status symbol*. A rampant public sector employs up to 70% of the working age population of Egypt. Morocco on 20% is at the opposite end of the scale. The oil-rich Gulf States, where the public sector employs approximately half the workforce, are in the middle. In Saudi Arabia the figure is 40%. The public sector remains attractive despite falling wages because it offers retirement provision. It also offers legally protected lifetime employment, since employees cannot be sacked. The only way levels of bureaucracy can be reduced is by freezing the recruitment of new employees. Although starting salaries are not high, the prospects for promotion and salary increases are guaranteed by the number of years worked. What is more, bribes are on offer from the very start. Employment in the public sector can also be a help on an overcrowded marriage market, since such jobs are regarded as a sign of reliability (Richards and Waterbury 2008: 141).

(10) THE ALIENATION AND RADICALISATION OF THE INTELLIGENTSIA

With the rapid growth in education intergenerational conflict and alienation is deepening. Illiterate grandparents and often semi-literate parents lose their authority in the eyes of their secondary or tertiary educated offspring. As educational standards rise, so life and career ambitions are radically transformed. Parental guidance based on experience of a traditional rural life loses its relevance. The Islam of previous generations also appears in a new light, as a faith full of errors and non-Islamic folklore. A crisis takes place in the intergenerational transfer of the traditional concepts of Islam, and an intelligentsia that has not been integrated into society searches for alternative versions of faith beyond the boundaries of primary groups. Its gaze takes in Islamists (Roy 2004).

A radical counter-elite is always recruited from a disaffected, socially excluded intelligentsia. A *career in politics* becomes the substitute for a professional career, and educated professionals become the vanguard of professional revolutionaries. Only the ideological backdrop changes, while the above-average education and a certain alienation from the rest of society remains. At the start of the 20th century, educated urban counter-elites assumed a position at the head of secularly oriented national liberation and anti-colonial resistance movements and outnumbered members from traditional, rural regions attempting to unify dispersed regions and tribes by appealing to a shared Islam (Juergensmeyer 1994, Anderson 2008).

SECULAR RADICALS AS THE ISLAMISTS' PREDECESSORS: THE SAME PATTERN, A DIFFERENT IDEOLOGICAL BACKDROP

During the post-colonial era political extremists using violence to promote their vision were also recruited from the most modern segments of the population. In the 1950s leftwing and rightwing radicals had an identical sociological and psychological profile. Conversely, they deviated significantly from the politically moderate or apolitical population. They tended to be young men up to 30 years old, who were highly urbanised compared with their peers. They monitored the media intensively and had received a well above average education, even higher than that of the existing political elites, a fact they deemed unjust. The result was that the lower and middle ranks of public-sector or military hierarchies were occupied by ambitious clerks and lieutenants, while the top ranks were occupied by poorly educated civil servants and generals. The radicals were no longer poor, though neither were they rich. However, they were not content with their standard of living: "They speak of the poverty of the poor, but yearn for the affluence of the wealthy". They were highly dissatisfied and most critical of the state of society (Lerner 1964: 368).

Socially and psychologically they were alienated from the values of mainstream society. They did not have families of their own at an age when all of their peers did. Or they were single widowers. They did not attend mosques and neglected other collective rituals. They had fewer friends and usually spent their free time alone. Their alienation from the rest of society ensued from the low value they assigned religion, customs and tradition. Secularised individuals were therefore more willing to accept new, at that time secular, ideologies, which filled the mental space vacated by religion. Social alienation from a traditional, uneducated population resulted in a readiness to identify with a wider range of supra-local reference groups. Categories such as class, nation and political party were more attractive to the new intellectuals, since traditional groups such as family, religion or neighbourhood community no longer played such a role in their lives.

Political extremists were also agitators and ideological leaders who, in their conflict with elites and competing radicals, attempted to win over the masses to their side. If frustration was widespread and there was an absence of established methods for practicing non-violent political participation, i.e. democratic institutions, mass political participation then degenerated into violence (Lerner 1964).

THE RISE OF ISLAMIC EXTREMISTS

We are now witness to a similar profile of extremists and a similar pattern of radicalisation among Islamists. A classic study exists of the environment of two Egyptian militant groups from the 1970s, when President Anwar al-Sadat was in power. The results are summarised as follows: "These are ideal, indeed exemplary, young Egyptians from village or small towns, the middle or lower middle class, highly motivated in their studies and lives, eager for upward social mobility, with a scientific or technical education and from normal, close families" (Ibrahim 1980: 131). They came from rural areas or small provincial towns. However, they usually lived alone or with friends, without the support of parents and relatives in anonymous and aggressive cities such as Cairo, Alexandria or Asyut. Here they tried to find their feet, felt lonely and experienced a culture shock. Intergenerational educational mobility was considerable compared with their parents, though many of their fathers had attended secondary school. Twenty-nine of a total of thirty-four radicals surveyed had a university degree or were still studying. Six were studying engineering, four medicine, three agronomy, two pharmacology, and two military technology. One was a student of literature. None of them studied the social sciences and none attended traditional religious school. And yet students were required to achieve well above average results in the state examinations at the end of secondary school if they wanted to be accepted in the departments of medicine, pharmacy and technology. Eighty percent of the militants had achieved such results in their examinations. As far as the employed radicals were concerned, five were teachers, three engineers, three agriculturalists, and three were doctors. One was a pharmacist and one an accountant. The remaining five members had attended secondary school, which in Egypt at that time also qualified as an above-average education.

Excellent academic qualifications and advanced skill sets result in high aspirations for upward social mobility. However, this was not always possible. Although these bright youngsters did not suffer from extreme social alienation or anomie, the way they interpreted the state of society was crucial in terms of their radicalisation. The secular dictatorship appeared morally corrupt and unsuccessful. They could not identify with it. For example, it lost the war with its smaller neighbour Israel (1967) and the importance of a still proud country dropped on the international stage. These young people were also reacting to problems at home, and so in their manifestos we find an emphasis on justice, the redistribution of resources and the elimination of poverty. They also emphasised the industriousness of the nation and the responsibility of its rulers. However, not even the activities of the Muslim Brotherhood, from which they were recruited, enthused them. They were disappointed by its political passivity and the emphasis the movement placed on personal piety.

One of the two groups studied did not only define itself critically in respect of the power elite but also in respect of mainstream society, which appeared to it to be morally inferior and inconsistent in matters pertaining to

Islam. Sectarian activists therefore often severed their original social links and lived in devout communities separated from the corrupt majority. In the second group too there was a core to the organisation composed of underground cells known as the *usra* (family). Both groups were led by charismatic figures that enjoyed great respect comparable with paternal authority due to their age and moral qualities. A critical view of the world was accompanied by conversion to a strict religious practice. The difficulties associated brought subjective benefits in the form of a positive self-image. This individual project was complemented by a social aspect, since the regular practice of the five pillars of religion on an individual level is insufficient. Islam should also be promoted on a collective level in order to create a just Islamic state through revolution. This is the fulfilment of God's will, to which activists must devote their lives (Ibrahim 1980)[33].

More recent research by Krueger and Maleckove (2002) takes issue with the opinion that there is a causal link between poverty and low education and terrorism. The authors created a database of terrorists recruited from the militant Palestinian Hamas, the Lebanese Hezbollah and the Jewish extremist organisation Gush Emunim. The radicals being researched were mainly from more educated, middle class segments of society. Similarly, sociological surveys of the Palestinian public have confirmed that it tends to comprise middle class, educated people who sympathise with terrorist organisations, while less educated, poorer Palestinians are more restrained and apolitical.

This study, based on a statistical analysis of the social background of "God's warriors", indicates what Middle Eastern terrorism is not linked to. However, it fails to answer the question of what it is linked to. Furthermore, it has many weak spots, and the authors quote one of the leaders of the Palestinian Hamas: "The biggest problem is the crowd of youngsters who come knocking on the doors of our organisation demanding to be sent on missions as martyrs. But we can only choose a tiny handful, and it's no easy matter." The authors implicitly accept the possibility that, even if uneducated people from poor backgrounds prevailed among the candidates for terrorist missions, militant organisations would have the tendency to select mainly recruits of middle class origin with higher educational qualifications, who are more likely to deal with a logistically demanding operation.

---

33   However, the pattern of well above-average educated militants recruited from the middle and lower middle classes is at variance with other research, for instance with the heterogeneous composition of the militants arrested belonging to the Algerian group active in the 1980s (Armed Islamic Group of Algeria). Even here, however, we are talking of a very modern and not remotely traditional segment of the population. The educational qualifications and socio-economic background of the arrested jihadists was as follows: 12 teachers, 7 civil servants, 4 technicians, 1 engineer, 8 university students, 3 members of the liberal professions, 22 retailers, 29 farm workers, 49 industrial workers and 13 unemployed (cf. Beránek 2007: 252).

One of the latest synthetic studies took a sample of more than four hundred known Islamic extremists operating in a number of Muslim countries in recent decades. They came from more than thirty nationalities; nine were members of larger militant groups and twelve of smaller groups, mostly fighting against authoritarian regimes or an external enemy. Approximately 70% were graduates or had at least spent time at universities, a figure far in excess of the average in the corresponding Arab generations – the median year of birth of the terrorists studied was 1968 and in that generation only around 12% had a university diploma. In addition, a fifth of these graduates had studied in the West. The militant university graduates were being recruited from the most elite, demanding and competitive university academic disciplines and programmes. It was extremely difficult to be accepted to study these subjects and even more difficult to graduate in them. Most of those examined were engineers (44%), followed by doctors and scientists. Only around 20% of students attended Islamic sciences, and these were mainly the Saudi Arabian militants (Diego Gambetta – Steffen Hertog 2009).

An identical pattern applies to the specific category of *suicide* terrorism. Under the umbrella of Hezbollah there have been a total of 41 attacks by suicide bombers across the entire religious and ideological spectrum: 8% Arab Christians, 71% secular leftists (the Lebanese Communist Party, members of the secular nationalist Amal movement or Ba'ath party, the Vanguard of Arab Christians in Lebanon) and 21% Islamists from the Islamic Jihad. These ideologically highly heterogeneous groups and individuals are united only in opposition to the Israeli occupation. However, what they have in common is an above average education (75% have a secondary school or university education). The socio-economic status of all Arab terrorists mounting attacks between 1980 and 2003 reveals a similar profile.[34] Approximately 10% had only a primary education, whereas in the adult Arab population as a whole the figure during the period monitored was 40%. Similarly, 54% of the terrorists had completed a secondary school or university education, whereas the figure in the population as a whole is on average only 15%. Terrorists are significantly better educated than is common in the societies from which they are recruited. We can assume that they are therefore politically well informed and aware individuals who will probably be involved in political events on a general level, including resistance to occupation and recruitment into terrorist organisations. The situation was similar in the case of economic activity. Only 17% of terrorists lived in poverty, long-term unemployment or without a permanent job, while this figure is around 30% in the population as a whole. On the other hand, as many as 76% of terrorists were skilled work-

---

34   However, this data was only fully available on 70 of a total of 232 terrorists.

ers or even middle-class professionals, something that is true of only 50% of the population at large. Again, then, we are not speaking of marginalised individuals. There was no difference even in the professional status of secular versus Islamist terrorists. Indeed, Islamists were slightly *better* educated than secular terrorists (Pape 2005).

GLOBAL JIHADISTS

Surveys of global jihadists, i.e. terrorists uprooted and socially alienated from their countries of origin, reach similar conclusions to the analyses of the social, demographic and educational backgrounds of terrorists rooted in their communities (Hamas, Hezbollah). This applies to those who carried out the five largest attacks against Western targets, namely those on the World Trade Centre (WTC) in New York (1993), the American embassies in Kenya and Tanzania (1998), the 9/11 attack on the WTC and the Pentagon (2001), tourist resorts and night clubs on Bali (2002), and the simultaneous suicide bombings in London (2005). These analyses refute the stereotypical idea that the religious schools (madrasas) operate as "factories of terrorism" or "incubators or fanaticism". They also show that the problem is by no means one of the low educational standards of simple, easily manipulated people. Not one of the brains behind the attacks listed above had graduated from madrasa. All the organisers and leaders of these groups had studied at secular, Western-style universities.

Only a tenth of the 79 attackers involved had studied at madrasa. Though three of the four London attackers were shown to have paid short visits to Pakistani madrasas prior to the attack, their plans had already been drawn up and all had studied at British secular schools. Madrasas played the largest role in the case of the attacks in Bali, since Indonesia possesses a high number of madrasas in its education system. Notwithstanding this fact, only nine of the 22 perpetrators of this particular attack had studied at madrasa.

Compared to the minority representation of graduates of religious schools, more than 54% of terrorists had a secular tertiary education at bachelor's level or higher. Two of them held doctorates (PhD) and another two were working on their doctoral theses. The educational qualifications of terrorists are clearly well above the average not only in Middle Eastern societies but in the West too. It makes no sense whatsoever to speak of uneducated terrorists. It is also significant that half of the terrorist university graduates (27% of the sample) studied in the West, either in the USA or Europe. The most popular disciplines included engineering and medicine and the natural sciences (58% of all terrorists). According to the authors of these studies, less educated people or graduates of madrasas are unable to carry out organisationally and logistically demanding operations, which need technical skills and a knowledge of the languages and life and institutions of foreign countries (Bergen – Pandey 2006).

The analysis by Marco Sageman (2004) conducted on four hundred biographies of Islamist terrorists targetting the United States reached a similar sociological profile. Three quarters came from the middle and upper middle classes and knew nothing of poverty. Ninety percent were recruited from functioning, cohesive families and three quarters had their own families and children. These were by no means socially isolated individuals without a sense of responsibility for others. Two thirds had a tertiary education, while in the populations from which they were recruited this figure was around 5%. They were the best and brightest of their generation, most speaking at least three languages. For the most part they had been educated in technology and the natural sciences. Few had an education in the humanities or religion. Most of the terrorists had found work in their fields and built a career. They had often given up a promising professional or scientific career path in favour of terrorism. What is important is that 70% opted for jihad at a time when they were living in a country other than that where they had been born. Similarly they opted for a strictly religious life only after joining a jihadist movement.

RADICALS AND THE SYMPATHY OF THE EDUCATED PUBLIC

As well as the educational profile of the terrorists, we can also examine the same profile of that part of the public that approves their actions. Again this involves more educated, well placed people: the degree of religiosity does not play a great role. For instance, representative surveys into international public opinion carried out by the Gallup Institute (Esposito and Mogahed 2007) proceed similarly to how Daniel Lerner operated fifty years ago when he compared the sociological profiles of political extremists and moderates. Extremists are here defined as those who regard the 9/11 attacks as "completely justified" (7% of all Muslims). Moderate Muslims did not approve the attacks on the USA.

What is the sociological portrait of both groups? Among radically minded people the young slightly outnumber the old and men slightly outnumber women. However, they are not poor, unemployed or uneducated. On the contrary, more of them are employed and they enjoy better qualifications and material comforts than moderate Muslims. There is no evidence to suggest they suffer from chronic frustration. They more often hold down management positions, declare that their standard of living has improved over the last few years, and look to the future with greater optimism than other people. These are not desperate people living in deprivation who have nothing to lose.

In addition, they are only as religious as moderates and do not exhibit signs of fanaticism. The confusing religious rhetoric of "Islamic terrorists" can be explained by the fact that secular ideologies are on the decline in the Muslim world. For this reason Islam provides a banner for all, often antithetical, movements, including militant and terrorist groups.

We cannot even conclude that cultural difference and the ensuing hatred of a Western lifestyle and institutions causes extremism. Radicals, like moderate Muslims, admire the technological developments of the West most of all. They also admire values such as industry, responsibility, cooperation and a rule of law that judges everyone by the same yardstick. Finally, they admire the fairness of Western political systems and respect for human rights. Radicals who perceive the 9/11 attacks as justified are more in favour of democracy than moderate respondents. Talk of a clash of civilisations or a struggle against people who "hate our freedom and our way of life" (the words of George W. Bush) is nonsense.

So how do these "verbal radicals" differ from their moderate fellow citizens? Above all in their perception of the United States and in the degree of criticism of its leaders and the aggressive foreign policy that it has pursued for a long time in the Middle East. Similar results based on an analysis of competing data from surveys of public in the Middle East conducted by Pew Global Attitudes are offered by Najeeb Shafiq (Shafiq 2008, Shafiq – Sinno 2010).

Other surveys also debunk the link between radicalism and a low education and, on the contrary, illustrate the relationship between terrorist sympathisers, antipathy to certain superpowers and the subsequent occurrence of attacks against them when they discover a statistical link between public opinion regarding individual superpowers and data from the databases of terrorist attacks carried out against these superpowers. Middle Eastern terrorists appear to be representative of widespread feelings in the societies from which they are recruited. In nineteen countries of the Middle East surveyed the least popular world leaders are those of the United States and Great Britain, well ahead of those of India and Russia. Attitudes are most favourable towards the leaders of Japan and China, countries that do not interfere in Middle Eastern affairs. It is the United States and Great Britain that have become the frequent targets of terrorist attacks. International terrorism is therefore mainly related to a country's foreign policy, or rather the subjective perception of this policy in individual countries of the Middle East (Krueger and Malečková 2009).

AL-QAEDA'S SECOND GENERATION, ISLAMIC STATE AND A NEW MODEL OF RADICALISATION?

The French political scientist Olivier Roy (2004) points out that a new model of Islamic international terrorism has emerged, with the recruitment of radicals taking place more and more frequently in the West, whence jihad is exported to the non-Arab peripheries of the Muslim world (Chechnya, Central Asia, Kashmir, the Philippines), or to Saudi Arabia. After the invasion of the American-led coalition it was also exported to Afghanistan and Iraq. If Al-Qaeda's first generation comprised mainly people from Muslim countries that travelled to Afghanistan in order to fight against the USSR, the radicalisation of the second generation of global jihadists has taken place in the West. And yet one cannot speak of the role of political repression during their radicalisation, as in the case of home-grown Middle Eastern terrorists (cf. Esposito 2003, Krueger and Laitin 2003, Abadie 2004). It seems that cultural deracination, a personal identity crisis and social exclusion play the main role. Another crucial factor is the foreign policy of the United States in Muslim countries, which is regarded as aggressive, unfair and humiliating.

Sometimes fresh converts to Islam are involved, and other times young Muslims, students from the Middle East or the offspring of Muslim immigrants, who have lost their ties to the culture of their ancestors but have been unable to integrate fully into the new society. They spend the first part of their life in "ungodliness" (street gangs, drugs, premarital assignations), only to throw themselves with even greater passion into faith with a desire to break totally with their previous life and find a sense of fulfilment. Here there is an analogy with the phenomenon of the born-again that we know from Christianity. Generally speaking they do not identify with any specific Muslim state. However, they do not accept their host country as their home, where they feel themselves to be the victim of unfairness and social exclusion. In their rootlessness they then appeal to an imaginary pan-Islamic ummah. A typical example of such a "globalised Muslim" is Ramzí Ahmed Jusuf, one of the perpetrators of the first attack on the New York Twin Towers (1993). He was born in Kuwait to a Pakistani father and a Palestinian mother. He studied electrical engineering in Wales, where he was also radicalised. He left for Afghanistan, participated in the activities of a terrorist cell in New Jersey, and drifted from jihad to jihad, from the Philippines to Pakistan, until his arrest.

Intergenerational conflict is a significant problem amongst second-generation European Muslims. Parents lose their authority. They are perceived by their offspring as epitomising failure and incompetence. They have significantly lower levels of education and life aspirations. They have often failed to learn the language of their new country and have been unsuccessful economically. They have been unable to fulfil their original dream, namely to earn money and return to their country of origin. They have not prospered in the new country, are often without work and unable to support their families. To make matters worse they believe in a "reactionary" version of folk Islam full of ridiculous prejudices and misconceptions that they brought with them from the villages from the Middle East. The intergenerational conflict results in the search for a substitute group and a new home, be this in the form of street gang or fundamentalist brotherhood.

As well as mosques and cyberspace, the re-Islamisation of "born again" Muslims is also taking place in *prisons*, i.e. in an environment in which young people are isolated from all previous ties and reflect upon their life up till now. Allegiance to faith offers them the chance of creating a new identity and new values. Faith becomes a source of positive self-image, a sense of superiority. Their new community of "virtuous" brothers satisfies spiritual needs that were lacking in their previous lives in a materialist environment, as well as the need for close social relations. The concept of Islam among born again Muslims is diametrically opposed to that of their parents. This has little to do with continuing ancient traditions, but more about finding new forms. There is no change of religion but rather a transformation in religiosity, i.e. the relationship a person has to faith. In a "globalised Islam" the trend is analogous to the development of Christian or Jewish religiosity, which is why here too we find a wide range of options on offer, from New Age-style spirituality to strict neo-fundamentalism.

Militant jihadists constitute a marginal current in this trend. Activists from the Middle East play a pivotal role in their recruitment: radical preachers, foreign students and charismatic veterans of the war in Afghanistan. They contact young, rootless and humiliated Muslims from the marginalised environment of European slums. They offer them the possibility of restyling themselves in the role of the vanguard of global jihad against the personification of all evil, the United States or the godless regimes in Muslim countries. However, the main objective of martyrs is not victory in battle but the spiritual journey, i.e. the attempt at radical self-transformation through armed jihad (Roy 2004).

Overall, however, we see that higher educational qualifications are not an automatic cure for political extremism. In the spirit of the European Enlightenment we often regard Islamic radicalism as the rebellion of poorly educated, intellectually simpler and easily manipulated individuals. However, education as such is "politically neutral". What is important is its content and above all its context and interaction with other factors. For instance, over-education and the inability of Middle Eastern societies to co-opt economically and politically graduates has become a key factor in the destabilisation of the region, especially when combined with the government of corrupt, repressive regimes and/or the interventions of foreign powers.

THE BOOM IN MEGACITIES:
A WHIRLWIND OF URBANISATION
IN THE MIDDLE EAST

"Everything was simple. He didn't know of the existence of highways, high-rise buildings, lamps lighting streets where nobody lived. The world was as large as his village. He had no idea what the police got up to behind the walls of their faraway stations. His village was light years from the city."
(Tahar Ben Jelloun, A Palace in the Old Village)

"If people aren't aware of the existence of certain things, they don't desire them and lack them."
(A Lebanese living in a large city in the 1960s)

"The European tendency that does not respect the neighbour and where one person might live for years alongside another without ever knowing who he was did not prevail among us. Everyone in our neighbourhood was a neighbour who knew each other's affairs, names and occupations. They visited each other, expressed their condolences at funerals, attended each other's family celebrations and lent each other money if it was necessary. They were accustomed to visiting and spending entire evenings in the reception rooms."
(Ahmad Amin, an Egyptian scholar)

"I view great cities as pestilential to the morals, the health and the liberties of man."
(Thomas Jefferson)

"Nothing brings us together like our love for Imam Hussein. Religious association unites us and allows us to inform each other who each is getting on."
(newly arrived immigrant, Tehran slum, end of the 1970s)[35]

URBANISATION MIDDLE EASTERN-STYLE:
INTERNATIONAL AND HISTORICAL COMPARISON

"Dream Land", "Utopia" and "Beverly Hills" are among the desirable addresses for the upper classes of Cairo. If you really want to be a mover and shaker in the Egyptian capital, you relocate to one of these gated communities, isolated and protected from their surroundings and guarded by bodyguards from

---

35   Jelloun 2011: 77, Lerner 1964: 117, Robinson 1996: 216, Musil 1967: 26, Arjomand 1986: 97.

private security agencies. The names given these communities, which have proliferated rapidly over recent years in the Middle East, indicate the Western origin of this trend. However, this is not simply a status symbol for rich Egyptians, but also an attempt to separate themselves off from their surroundings (Richards and Waterbury 2008).

At the same time as such Beverly Hills-style earthly paradises are enjoying a boom, a UN report shows that the Middle East is becoming a region of slums. In Cairo itself, home to approximately 15 million people, at least 6 million people live in illegal and spontaneously erected dwellings without access to drinking water and electricity. This is not to speak of garbage collection, heavy smog, sewers and other infrastructure. Another million at least have taken up residence in tombs in the City of the Dead, and the number of those who are resolving the catastrophic housing crisis by living on the roofs of Cairo houses is estimated at more than half a million men, women and children (UN Habitat 2003).

This is a brief summation of the course and contradictory impacts of Middle Eastern urbanisation. Without analysing the urbanisation process and form of Middle Eastern cities, it is impossible to explain the accumulation of political tension, the transformation in political discourse, and the rise of Islamist movements. These movements are mainly urban and do not

Fig. 33 Development of urbanisation in macro-regions 1960–2015 (% of population)

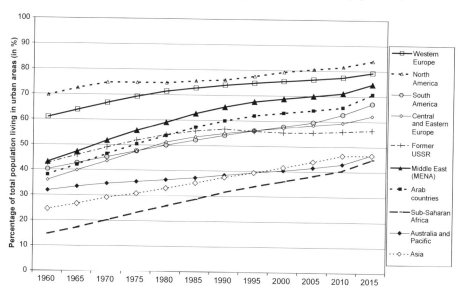

N.B.: The author's calculation of the development of urbanisation for macro-regions and years (unweighted by country population size).

Source: World Bank Development Indicators 2016

enjoy such success in the countryside (Starrett 1998, Lubeck and Britts 2002, Kepel 2002).

The current Middle East is not the domain of nomads or of simple farmers ignorant of life in the city, as cliché would have it (Halliday 2005). On the contrary, it is a region that over recent decades has experienced an urban explosion caused by mass exodus from rural, peripheral regions to cities and by the relatively high birth rates of the already urbanised population. The region has not yet recovered from the consequences of this rapid urbanisation, and the proof of that lies in its ubiquitous slums and chronic housing crisis (Richards and Waterbury 2008).

At the same time it is the rapid *pace* of urbanisation that makes the Middle East a special case (see fig. 33). Urban settlements in the Middle East boast a thousand-year-old tradition. The first city civilisations originated here in the Nile Valley and the plains around the rivers Euphrates and Tigris (Lewis 1997). However, the rapid urbanisation of what has been up till now a predominantly rural population living in tribal communities of settled farmers, semi-nomadic herdsmen and permanently migrating nomads only began after the Second World War (Longrigg, Jankowski 1963). As late as the 1960s only a third of Arabs, Turks and Iranians lived in cities, though by 1990 the figure was up to 50%. During this period Middle Eastern migration from the countryside to the cities was the fastest in the world along with Sub-Saharan Africa. At present more than two thirds of the population live in cities, a figure comparable with Western Europe or the United States. Only in South America is the proportion of people living in cities higher (at approximately 70%) (Richards and Waterbury 2008).

At present the rate of urbanisation is not keeping pace with that of the most dynamic rural exodus in Sub-Saharan Africa and East Asia. Furthermore, the degree of urbanisation in individual Middle Eastern countries differs (see table 27). The oil monarchies of the Persian Gulf lead the world in this respect, where only three generations ago the majority of the population travelled by camel all year round looking for sources of water. On the other hand, the proportion of the urban population in the poorer, more agriculturally based Arab countries of Northern Africa is lower (Kropáček 1999, Bradshaw 2000).

In the West the rise and eventual predominance of an urban population was a long process that took centuries. Even so, European urbanisation was accompanied by many social and political tremors. As far as developing countries in general and the Middle East in particular are concerned, this transformation took only a few decades, sometimes but a mere generation. The annual rate of growth of industrialising cities of early modern Europe was in the region of 1–2%. At present, in developing countries, including the Middle East, it is rising at a rate of 4–5% (Toušek, Kunc, Vystoupil et al. 2008).

The changes that took place to the ratio of city dwellers during urbanisation are not linear but take the form of an S-curve. After an initial phase of slow growth the urbanisation process enters a dynamic phase of rapid growth and then slows down quickly when the urban population reaches around 75% of the population as a whole. The course of urbanisation in developing countries is characterised by rapid growth and a far steeper curve, with the growth in third-world countries being more than twice as fast as it was in early modern Europe (Toušek, Kunc, Vystoupil et al. 2008). As the historian Paul Kennedy (1996) so aptly writes in connection with massive, spontaneous and uncontrolled urbanisation: "The situation in the megacities of the third

Tab. 27 The urbanisation of MENA countries 1975–2015 (in % of the urban population)

Country	1975	1990	2003	2010	2015
Algiers	40.0	52.1	58.8	62.6	65.3
Bahrain	86.0	88.1	90.0	94.4	91.4
Egypt	44.0	43.5	42.2	44.0	44.9
Iran	46.0	56.3	66.6	70.6	73.9
Iraq	---	69.7	67.5	67.7	70.1
Israel	87.0	90.4	91.6	93.0	92.4
Jordan	58.0	72.2	79.1	80.1	81.1
Kuwait	84.0	98.0	96.2	96.7	96.9
Lebanon	69.0	83.1	87.5	92.1	90.1
Libya	61.0	75.7	86.2	89.7	89.0
Morocco	38.0	48.4	57.4	61.7	64.8
Oman	20.0	66.1	77.6	80.8	82.6
Palestine	60.0	67.9	71.1	72.2	75.6
Qatar	85.5	92.2	92.0	94.5	93.6
Saudi Arabia	58.0	76.6	87.6	90.0	91.1
Sudan	19.0	26.6	38.9	45.0	49.3
Syria	45.0	48.9	50.2	55.4	52.4
Tunisia	50.0	57.9	63.7	71.3	68.1
Turkey	42.0	59.2	66.3	69.9	71.9
United Arab Emirates	84.0	79.1	85.1	90.5	87.2
Yemen	15.0	20.9	25.7	28.5	31.3

Source: UNDP 2009; Richards and Waterbury (2008) for 2010 estimates
N.B.: An international comparison of degrees of urbanisation is made difficult by the different definitions used in individual countries (e.g. the size of a settlement defined as a city differs considerably in Egypt and Yemen).

world today is similar to that of the 1880s in Paris, when 100,000 beggars roamed the streets, the only difference being that today's figures are unimaginably higher".

As well as a high rate of urbanisation, the Middle East has another problem. Although most rural folk are now leaving for small and medium sized towns, the region is home to *abnormally large*, overcrowded *megacities*. A disproportionate number of the population, unprecedented anywhere else in the world, is concentrated in one or two metropolises. This is especially true of the oil-producing Gulf States or states with large desert regions (Kropáček 1999, Richards and Waterbury 2008).

What makes urbanisation in the Middle East so special when compared historically with Europe or compared with other regions of the contemporary post-colonial world? While the growth of cities in Europe was caused above all by the migration of the population from the countryside, in developing countries it involves a combination of rapid migration from the countryside *accompanied* by high population growth within the already settled urban population (Toušek, Kunc, Vystoupil et al. 2008). This makes the demographic explosion significantly faster in the case of developing countries. Moreover, there is not such a rapid reduction in the birth rate of the urban population as there was in the case of Europe's demographic transition. Demographic transition and urbanisation overlap in time more than was the case in Europe, where they were out of sync (Kalibová 1997 and 2008). However, both the demographic transition and urbanisation do impact on political instability, and at present are having a mutual multiplication effect. This is creating greater instability in post-colonial regions, including the Middle East, than in early modernising Europe.

Because of the shortage of agricultural land, the "superfluous" rural population created by the European population explosion migrated to other continents. This took place within the context of European colonialism, which coincided with population revolution and urbanisation. Similarly, many superfluous young men hired themselves out or were enlisted in colonial armies. These days migration is not operating as such an efficient safety valve in the case of post-colonial societies. The growing masses of villagers in the Middle East are migrating to cities and not to other continents. The result is historically unprecedented rapid urbanisation and the overpopulation of cities (Lerner 1964, Kenedy 1996).

Another reason for the rapid pace of urbanisation is the extraction of oil and abnormally high raw-material wealth. Approximately 60% of the world's oil reserves and 45% of its natural gas reserves are to be found in the region (Oil and Gas Review 2010). The oil boom has yielded vast incomes for the elites living in cities, especially during oil crises and price increases on world markets. The new billionaires began to spend their acquired petrodollars overnight, and opulent city centres arose in stark contrast to poor rural areas (the Gulf States and Iran). Drawn by their wealth and opportunities, peasant farmers and nomads began to settle in cities (Kepel 1996 and 2002, Kropáček 1999). The expanding urban economy offered former peasants work in the construction sector and services, as well as in the burgeoning extraction industry (Zubaida 2009).

In addition, after acquiring independence governments attempted massive industrialisation in order to catch up as quickly as possible with the countries of the capitalist and communist blocs, which served as their models. What were often megalomaniac industrial operations required large injections of new workforces (Algeria, Syria) (Lerner 1964, Richards and Waterbury 2008). This type of development strategy, inspired by a concept known as growth centres (growth poles), from which prosperity was gradually to trickle out to the rest of the country and the peripheral regions and kick-start nationwide economic development, is now past its prime and has often left behind stagnating industrial giants unflatteringly dubbed "cathedrals in the desert". Nevertheless, many countries are still officially following such strategies (Turkey in Eastern Anatolia) (Blažek 2002, Shumacher 2000).

However, in many countries armed conflict has also played a role in the concentration of the population in cities. These conflicts have forced rural populations to seek security and humanitarian assistance in larger settlements (Palestine, Lebanon, Sudan, Turkey, Iraq and Algeria) (Kropáček 1999). And then over the long term the considerable difference in income between city and countryside (wages in the city are 1.5 to 3 times higher) draws more of the rural population into the cities, as well as increasing the educational levels of the young generations. The aspirations of young Turks and Arabs are rising along with their qualifications, and so their expectations of increased social mobility linked with a career, at the end of which they will become accepted as members of the middle or even upper class, are also rising. For these reasons ever larger numbers of adolescents are leaving their native villages and the security of extended traditional families, even though only a minority of them will ever see this "Middle Eastern dream" come true (Lerner 1964, Arjomand 1986, Richards and Waterbury 2008).

URBANISATION AND UNEVEN MODERNISATION

Over the long term the high rate of urbanisation in the Middle East is outstripping the lower rate of industrialisation and the creation of new jobs in cities. Cities are then unable to absorb the increasing numbers of people migrating from the countryside full of hope and expectations of a new life (e.g.

Lerner 1964)[36]. According to a raft of forecasts, over the next twenty years the highly urbanised populations of most Arab countries will double, while the gross domestic product of 17 of the 22 mainly Arab countries is stagnating or declining (Kaplan 2003). Sober predictions state that in twenty years there will be at least 50 million unemployed people among young Arabs, Turks and Iranians. Most of these will be concentrated in cities (Laqueur 2004).

New housing construction in cities cannot keep pace with the rural exodus, nor indeed can town planning and the building of infrastructure. For instance, during the 1990s Algeria lacked at least 2 million apartments, while the average occupancy of a single apartment was 8.5 people, one of the highest figures in the world. Most of Cairo's 15 million-strong population live in slums. In Khartoum, Sudan, 3.5 million of the city's total population of 5 million live in slums. The district of Sadr City in Baghdad with its 1.5 million inhabitants is regarded as the largest single slum in the world. Alarming information on the proportion of people of the total urban population living in slums in the MENA region is shown in the following table (Richards and Waterbury 2008, UN-Habitat 2003).

Tab. 28 Proportion of the urban population living in slums in 2003 (in %)

Country	Proportion in slums	Country	Proportion in slums
Algeria	11.8	Oman	60.5
Bahrain	2.0	Qatar	2.0
Egypt	39.9	Saudi Arabia	19.8
Iran	44.2	Sudan	85.7
Iraq	56.7	Syria	1.4
Israel	2.0	Tunisia	3.7
Jordan	15.7	Turkey	42.6
Lebanon	50.0	Yemen	65.1
Libya	35.2	MENA total	35.8
Morocco	32.7		

Source: UN Habitat 2003

It should be noted that in developing countries more than 75% on average of the urban population live in slums, which means that the Middle East on 36% is not the worst when compared with other post-colonial regions.

---

36 On the other hand the most important oil producers from MENA do not have sufficient workers. The situation is resolved by means of international migration, mainly within MENA, but also from Pakistan, Bangladesh and India (Kropáček 1999).

However, the situation is not without its problems and is particularly dramatic in countries such as Yemen, Sudan, Iraq and Lebanon (see tab. 28). Another problem is the unmanageable traffic. Levels of atmospheric pollution and noise are usually higher than in European cities. In Cairo there are children with the highest content of lead in their blood in the world thanks to vehicle emissions. On the subject of wretched records, Cairo and Tehran are the winners when it comes to the most polluted capital cities in the world (Richards and Waterbury 2008). The main problem of the urban giants of developing countries tends to be the sheer number of individual problems existing in parallel and the complete absence of any way of dealing with them (Parrillo 2008).

Pathological phenomena spread under these strained socio-economic conditions. Juvenile crime (including organised crime), drug use and the spread of AIDS is clearly on the rise in certain Middle Eastern countries due to mass unemployment, low pay and the high expenses of weddings and having a family, though juvenile crime remains low in comparison with other regions of the developing world. For instance, the poor slums on the outskirts of Turkish, Iranian and Moroccan cities are still relatively safe both night and day. Likewise, these areas tend to be clean, and so a casual passerby might well not recognise that they are located in a district reported in statistics as a slum (UN-Habitat 2003)[37].

The same cannot be said of ghettoes of Latin America, Sub-Saharan Africa and even the USA, where violence, criminality, alcoholism, drug use and prostitution are rife. Likewise, early urbanisation in Europe was no idyll, as a perusal of the works of Charles Dickens or Emile Zola will confirm, and as is attested to by the research findings of the 19th century social reformers Charles Booth and Seebohm Rowntree. Islam operates as a stabiliser during rapid urbanisation. It maintains order, cohesion and social control and keeps pathologies to a minimum in newly urbanised poor districts (Richards and Waterbury 2008). The traditional Islamic value of both settled and nomadic Arabs and Turks is not only monotheism but the solidarity of a family living all year round together and the strict regulation of sexual relationships. The interaction of this pre-modern cultural substrate with modernisation processes associated with urbanisation leads to completely different outcomes than, for instance, the interaction of urbanisation and the traditional cultural patterns of West Africa, which in turn are associated with polygamy and loose family relationships, especially in the environment of West African nomads and herdsmen, where partners traditionally live separately for most

---

37 The UN defines a slum as part of a city combining illegal or below standard accommodation with a lack or absence of services (water mains, sewage system, garbage, electricity, paved roads). Overcrowding is typical of slums (UN-Habitat 2003).

of the year. After being relocated to an urban environment, these cultural patterns result in an expansion of pathologies, whereas in the case of Muslim Arabs and Turks the process is more orderly and is facilitated by the solidarity of family networks (Kaplan 2003, Bastug 2002, Erder 2002). The interaction of rapid urbanisation with other dimensions of uneven modernisation and its wider cultural and international context leads to structural pressures that generate political tension and destabilisation. This chapter will examine what causal mechanisms are responsible for this state of affairs. The main plan of the chapter is shown in fig. 34.

Fig. 34 The interaction of rapid urbanisation and other independent variables examined in this chapter

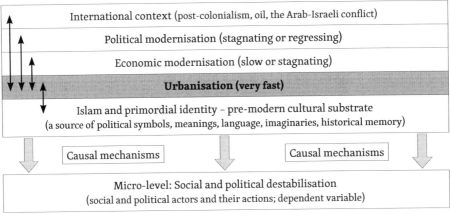

N.B. Possible interactions and tensions are shown by the arrows.

URBANISATION AND (NON)SECULARISATION: EUROPEAN PAST, MIDDLE EASTERN PRESENT

The rise of political Islam took place during Middle Eastern urbanisation. The question posed by this chapter will be whether this is simply coincidence, or whether a causal relationship exists. Western social scientists have not fully appreciated the part urbanisation plays in the increased popularity of religion and the politicisation of Islam, because they have remained captivated by the secularisation thesis, modernisation myths, Eurocentrism, and an erroneous understanding of their own history (cf. Arjomand 1986, Swatos 1999).

The link between urbanisation and religious revival in the form of an intensification of congregational religiosity and strict religious observance (membership of a church, attendance at services) was also apparent in the rapidly industrialising England of the 19th century in connection with the activities of the Methodists. Only during the transition to the post-industrial era was there a significant drop in organised religion within the confines of traditional churches. The current developments in the Islamic world might represent an analogy to this process and follow the same historical pattern (Hamilton 2001, Hoffman 1995).

Rodney Stark (1999) also points to the wealth of historical material undermining the narrative of a golden age of medieval religiosity. There was a lack of churches in the countryside, which was where the vast majority of the population lived. Clerics were also absent in peripheral regions, and those that were present were ignorant of doctrine. The unintelligible Latin Mass was not attractive to the rural population. It was only with early industrialisation accompanied by rapid urbanisation that we see the pinnacle of European Christianisation. More generally, Fareed Zakaria (2008) draws attention to the shift to a Victorian cultural conservatism during the boom of English industrial cities, science and education, i.e. during a period of rapid socio-economic modernisation.

The sociologist of religion Brian Wilson claims that faith is threatened by a loss of social relevance face-to-face with advancing modernisation. At the same time he admits that faith could be saved if, as well as concerning itself with the relationship of the individual to the supernatural, it offered other functions. For instance, that of *cultural defence* against the erosion of ethnic culture and identity – when the Poles and the Irish were dominated by the Russians and the British respectively, they rallied around Catholicism. Or that *of cultural transition*, in which a religious life and communitarian solidarity help people come to terms with rapid social change, the disappearance of a traditional way of life and the security it provides, and a crisis of identity, i.e. with migration to a new, unfamiliar environment. This would apply for instance to the organised religion of Irish and Polish immigrants arriving in the cities of the USA. There was a similar religious revival in industrialising and urbanising England (Hamilton 2001).

A comparison of the relationship between urbanisation and a tendency toward religious orthodoxy is fruitful not only as regards the history of the West, but also in the religious revival of those regions of the modern developing world where there is an exodus from the countryside to cities. For instance, South Korea became an economic tiger at a time when it was experiencing a rise in Protestantism. South America is undergoing a similar development. The growth of Guatemala City is being accompanied by the growth of the Protestant church in the city. The rise of Methodism in 19th century Manchester finds its parallel in the rapid spread of Pentecostalism and other evangelical movements since the 1980s in Sao Paulo. Catholicism has been spreading in Mexico City since the 1950s, when the city began to aspire to the status of the world's largest megacity. A rapidly urbanising Africa is undergoing similar developments. Finally, contrary to the predictions of the secularisation thesis, the most devout believers inclining toward Islamic orthodoxy are the educated urban classes of Malaysia and Indonesia (Arjomand 1986, Hamilton 2001).

Islamists are strongest in the largest cities in the Middle East that are most plugged into the world system. They first established themselves in countries that were the first to urbanise. An example of such a country outside the Middle East would be Malaysia. Islamism is therefore a "modern urban movement drawing strength from the significant changes in the political discourse from secular nationalism to the Islamic narrative that appeal to all urban classes, genders and status groups" (Lubeck and Britts 2002: 308). The backbone of the movement comprises three modern, highly urbanised groups: the urban poor, the religious middle classes, and an intelligentsia with a Western-style education. It does not by any means compromise rural dwellers, traditional Islamic clerics or Sufi brotherhoods (Arjomand 1986, Kepel 2002).

By means of what specific mechanisms has urbanisation contributed to the emergence and spread of political Islam, or, as the case may be, the emergence and spread of other social movements and opposition groups? And why does the exodus from the countryside to the cities lead to social tension and political destabilisation?

(1) UNMANAGEABLE URBANISATION: DISCREDITED REGIMES AND THEIR DOCTRINE OF DEVELOPMENT

The corrupt, authoritarian states of the Middle East were unable to deal with the consequences of the exodus to cities. Welfare systems, transport and housing infrastructure and urban planning collapsed under the onslaught of migration. Uncontrolled urbanisation, accompanied by an explosion in slums, a housing crisis, the collapse of transport, unemployment, a rampant unregulated grey economy, overcrowded school classrooms, mountains of garbage and visible inequality reflected poorly on Middle Eastern regimes and their ideologies and saw a growing call for a credible political alternative.

The visible negative consequences of uncontrolled urbanisation represent one of the main reasons why secular dictatorships and conservative monarchies have found themselves facing a *crisis of political legitimacy* since roughly the 1970s. They are regarded as incompetent, unsuccessful and corrupt by the population, and the models they promote of capitalist or socialist development are deemed wrong. These regimes were successful only in fuelling high expectations of the rapid arrival of prosperity and progress, but impotent in terms of delivering these planned outcomes. Initially ambitious urban planning (cf. Longrigg, Jankowski 1963) degenerated into security measures ensuring supervision of the subjugated populations and facilitating liquidation of the opposition. Old districts and bazaars full of narrow streets, courtyards, underground passageways and cellars where dissidents could hide, were demolished to make way for flat boulevards, large squares and uncluttered marketplaces. The public space created could be monitored more easily and rebellions more effectively quelled (Zubaida 2009). Similar tactics were employed by the monarchies of early modernising Europe facing revolutions. A well known example was the redevelopment in Paris of tough working class neighbourhoods by Baron Haussmann, which were replaced by wide boulevards, parks and open squares where the army could be easily deployed (Parrillo 2008).

The crisis of legitimacy faced by the elites is not always to the benefit of political Islam. It tends to provoke a more general search for ideological and political alternatives. Political Islam represents one of many alternatives to failed governments and their doctrines. However, worried that the crisis of legitimacy would lead within the context of the Cold War to a search for leftwing alternatives, the elites supported Islamic movements as a counterweight to the Marxists. They took these movements to be harmless, conservative and apolitical, capable of neutralising a revolutionary left but not much more. The communist revolution was averted, but the unintended consequence of the strategy was the monopoly of the Islamists on the market for alternative ideas. This monopoly on opposition quickly grew out of control when it became the main critic and ideological contender of regimes. After the change of political discourse the cause of the problems facing states was deemed to be the fact that the people had deviated from God. The blueprint for remedying all problems was a vision of the organisation of contemporary society on the model of the community of the Prophet Muhammad in Medina and the first four "rightly guided" caliphs (Kepel 2002, Lewis 2003b). Islam is neither a religion of the desert nor of uncultivated peasants. It was born in an urban environment (Holliday 2005). This is another reason why it appears to have something to say regarding today's problems related to the negative impacts of urbanisation. This involves the interaction of the negative consequences of urbanisation and a pre-modern Islamic substrate that updates and re-invents the historical memory within a new context.

Many stars of modern political Islam, e.g. the Turkish president Erdoğan or the Iranian ex-president Ahmadinejad, typically began their political careers in municipal politics, in close contact with people and their day-to-day problems. For instance, Erdoğan continues to be praised by the inhabitants of Istanbul for introducing reliable garbage collection. Reacting to the omnipresent smog he abolished local furnaces and created a centralised gas-fuelled heating system. He also reformed the corrupt and non-functional municipal services. As opposed to secular political parties or alienated government elites, the activists of Palestinian Hamas, the Egyptian Muslim Brotherhood and the now banned Islamic Salvation Front in Algeria are in day-to-day contact with people on the street. For instance, in the run-up to the Palestinian parliamentary elections of 2006, a typically vague slogan of the secular Fatah was as follows: "New capacities will be created". Hamas, on the other hand, which knew the needs of the people, offered specific measures: "We will equip clinics and improve the welfare system" (Čejka 2007). Islamists, then, often enter national politics via municipal politics and thanks to their ability to resolve effectively concrete local problems.

(2) SPATIAL CONCENTRATION: THE POTENTIAL FOR POLITICAL AGITATION, ORGANISATION AND MOBILISATION

The mass exodus to cities concentrates large numbers of people in a small space. Political ideologies can then spread more easily and quickly amongst the masses. It is also easier to organise and mobilise the masses for political action. While the rural population consists of a large number of mutually isolated and relatively self-sufficient villages or nomadic communities dispersed around a large geographical area, urbanisation leads to the concentration, connection and interaction of the majority of the population in the confined space of a few large cities. The *spatial obstacle to interpersonal communication and interaction* is negligible. Another important point is that the masses are concentrated above all in the capital city, the centre of political and economic power (Huntington 1968, Brzezinski 1993).

An extreme example of this mechanism would be the situation in Afghanistan from the end of the 1970s onwards. At that time any active, engaged Islamists from the city were isolated from the majority of the population scattered around the countryside, home to more than 85% of the Afghan population. Despite all their efforts, they were without any social influence whatsoever and had no chance of lining up society under the banner of political Islam against the then communist regime. It was only the subsequent rapid urbanisation caused by the flight of the rural population to the cities and refugee camps of Western Pakistan because of the military occupation of the Soviet army that created favourable conditions for the effective political operations of the Islamists amongst broad swathes of the masses (Kepel 2002).

However, the activism of the Islamists could only be effective because the refugees broke free of the influence of fixed tribal communities and moved beyond the reach of hitherto unimpeachable traditional authorities, typical

Afghan social norms and established customs that were often in sharp contradiction to the teachings of the Islamists and their successors, the Taliban (traditional tribal law, kite flying, the breeding of songbirds, dance, the use of opiates, tolerance of Buddhist monuments, etc.). The *deculturation* caused by rapid urbanisation created a vacuum in terms of cultural and social values among the young generation of deracinated refugees. This then allowed for new *acculturation* via the propaganda of the Islamists: the resulting *tabula rasa* was filled by a new identity (Roy 2004).

(3) URBAN UNEMPLOYMENT: VOLUNTARY SIMPLICITY INSTEAD OF REVOLUTION?

Unemployment represents the largest political and social challenge facing the Middle East in the 21st century. Above all we are speaking of *urban* unemployment, since unemployment in cities is persistently higher than in rural areas. This is diametrically opposed to the situation in contemporary Western Europe, for instance, where the centre enjoys the lowest rates of unemployment and the peripheries suffer the highest. For instance, in Moroccan cities the proportion of people without work is four times that of rural areas (20% versus 5% of the adult working population). In Turkey and Jordan the difference is smaller and urban unemployment double its rural counterpart. In Egypt unemployment in cities was approximately three times higher than in the agricultural periphery through the whole of the 1990s. And although the difference has been reduced, the rate of urban unemployment is still around 40% higher than that of rural areas. In Iran unemployment in cities has long exceeded that in the countryside, though here too the gap is narrowing (Richards and Waterbury 2008).

From the very beginning of urbanisation in the Middle East the pace of the exodus of the rural population to cities outstripped that of economic growth and the creation of new jobs in those cities (Lerner 1964). Conversely, during early European urbanisation and industrialisation it would appear that the supply of labour in cities was insufficient. As a consequence labourers saw their real wages rise for a time and migrants poured into cities from rural areas. This situation only changed in the next stage of urbanisation and the industrial revolution, when the number of people living in cities rose dramatically, people began to compete on the labour market, while capital, on the contrary, was concentrated in the hands of a few. The situation of the industrial proletariat became more problematic thanks to the creation of a "reserve army of the unemployed" (cf. Musil 1967, Mareš 1999).

However, the situation differs in individual countries of the Middle East. The small oil-producing states of the Persian Gulf, with the exception of Saudi Arabia, are less affected by urban unemployment and the difference between town and country is not so pronounced. However, the overall picture of the region is clear. Over the last few decades the Middle East has recorded faster rates of growth of urban populations than rural populations thanks to massive migration to cities. This has created greater pressure on the job market in cities, where the supply of labour greatly exceeds the demands of employers, while alleviating the situation in the countryside. The Middle East is "exporting unemployment from the countryside to the cities". Only with the gradual slowdown in urbanisation will a balance be achieved in unemployment between town and country, which is happening at present, for instance, in Iran and Egypt.

The advantage of the peripheral agricultural regions was the character of the local labour market. This was far more flexible thanks to the role played by the informal economy. This was able to absorb surplus labour more flexibly, even though jobs in the informal sector are precarious (seasonal), unattractive and poorly paid. However, at present the informal, non-regulated and untaxed economic sector is expanding in the cities too, and this represents another reason for the gradual blurring of the rates of unemployment between town and country (Richards and Waterbury 2008).

The *social crisis* in Middle Eastern cities is characterised by the long unmet demand for apartments and jobs (lasting from roughly the 1970s). This has encouraged the population to turn to different forms of political Islam that claim to be able to resolve social problems (Roy 1992, Chekroun 2005). What is crucial is that unemployment in highly populated cities has radically *different political consequences* than unemployment in a population scattered around the countryside (Brzezinski 1993). This is borne out by the historical development of Europe and by current events in the Middle East. For instance, Marx and Engels (1973) wrote vividly of the ignorance of the traditional rural dweller, easily domesticated by the bourgeoisie. It was from the urban proletariat that they expected political mobilisation. Samuel P. Huntington (1968), in his historical analysis of the birth of political actors, concedes that, historically speaking, the rural masses are usually the last to be co-opted into political rivalry, even though he does not share the opinion of country dwellers as necessarily a conservative political force[38]. The urban poor and young graduates, i.e. the groups most at threat of unemployment, form one of the main target groups of Islamist propaganda (Dekmejian 1995) and the social base of the Islamists (Kepel 2002). A young citizen of Algiers described the situation he and his contemporaries faced as follows: "You have only four

---

38 Charles Tilly (1983) refuted ideas regarding the passivity of the rural population by showing in the case of France that over the previous four centuries the rural classes had defended their interests and engaged in political rivalry with varying degrees of organisation on a local level.

possibilities: you can remain unemployed and celibate because without a job you can't have a family and acquire an apartment; you can work on the black market and risk arrest; you can try and emigrate to Europe and sweep the streets of Paris or Marseille; or you can join the Islamic Salvation Front and vote for Islam" (cited in Booth 2002: 235).

With the aid of a widely comprehensible, familiar and universally recognised language of the Quran and the hadiths, Islamists manage effectively and clearly to explain the experience of the long-term unemployed and oppressed (*mustadafun*), and to offer solutions. For instance, an unrivalled star in the firmament of 20th century Islamic ideologists, the Egyptian Sayyid Qutb, came up with the theory that orthodox followers of Islam suffer humiliation because they live under the thumb of tyrannical, hypocritical and wicked regimes (*taghut*). In order to improve their lot, they must first mobilise, organise and become cognisant of their common destiny. Then they must join forces in a violent revolutionary jihad, which will not take place without bloodshed, and overthrow the apostate regime that does not rule in accordance with God's revelation. This is why it is illegitimate, and every good Muslim worthy of the name should rise up against it. With the aid of God an ideal and infinitely just Islamic state, a kind of earthly paradise, will be built on the ruins of the old regime. One cannot help but notice the similarities with the Marxist concept of revolution and class struggle, and also the similarity of the term *mustadafun* with the concept of "wretched of the Earth" (Marx, Fanon) or with the description of a humiliated, oppressed urban proletariat (Lenin). The dialectical antithesis and historical rivals of the humiliated classes are the dominant and shamelessly exploitative classes (*mustakbirun*). A key work by Qutb entitled *Milestones* reminds many commentators of Lenin's revolutionary pamphlet *What is to be done?* (Mendel 2008: 160, Roy 1992).

An even more explicit link between Marxism and Islam than that within the framework of Sunni political Islam is to be found in revolutionary Shiism as propounded by the Iranian student guru Ali Shariati, who first sampled leftwing secular ideologies while studying at the Sorbonne. Here he was awarded a doctorate and to the delight of his leftwing French professors developed a Marxist inflected analogy between today's oppression of Muslims by irreligious leaders and the persecution of the first Shiites. More than Marx Shariati was impressed by Franz Fanon, whose book *Wretched of the Earth* (1961) he translated into Persian. However, unlike Marx and especially Fanon he did not agree with the shunting of religion into the sidings. On the contrary, he saw a key place for religion in the global revolution as the source of meaning and motivation of revolutionary efforts. After returning to his native Iran, Shariati turned into a popular revolutionary activist, and to this day the militant secular organisation *People's Mujahedin* that he inspired is still active, believing, like Marx, that philosophers have only interpreted the world, while the point is to change it. However, not even Shariati linked arms with the poor and downtrodden. Instead, he became the darling of the intellectuals and students of technical and scientific subjects, while students of the humanities inclined more to secular Marxism (Hoffman 1995, Kepel 2002).

The terms and concepts of European Marxism resonate in today's Middle East among part of the population because the urban poverty that featured in 19th century Europe was clearly similar to the character, extent and seriousness of Middle Eastern poverty in the second half of the 20th century and the beginning of the 21st. The statistician Charles Booth (1840–1916) concluded that in London at the end of the 19th century, 31% of people lived in poverty[39]. Some 8% represented an extremely poor underclass of people dependent on occasional earnings and hired by the day who were unable to earn an income sufficient to secure their basic needs. One percent of the population comprised a class of tramps wandering the streets and making a living out of begging, rummaging through garbage, occasional menial work and crime. Another class (22% of London's population), though possessed of a steady job and regular income, were poorly paid and under constant threat of becoming outcasts.

European urban poverty was also subject to detailed examination by Seebohm Rowntree (1871–1954), who discovered that in the relatively typical English city of York, 30 to 40% of families were below the poverty line. The situation only improved at the start of the 20th century, when around 10% of the population in England lived beneath the absolute poverty threshold (Mareš 1997). Marx and Engels (1973) went even further. They wrote about overcrowded housing, poor hygiene, disease and alcoholism in working-class neighbourhoods as symptoms of poverty. People occasionally died of hunger, but what guarantee did a worker have that he would not meet the same fate? They spoke of a "concealed civil war", of the accumulation of wealth on the one hand and deepening poverty on the other. History, they wrote, was the history of class struggle, with the impoverished urban proletariat in conflict with the antagonistic class of capitalists. This class exploited the workers and accumulated more and more capital: "The proletariat have nothing to lose but their chains. They have a world to win."

As far as the extent of poverty is concerned, the situation in the modern Middle East is comparable with that of the European proletariat of the 19th century. The Marxists were the first to attempt to make political capital out of the dissatisfaction of the masses by offering the most sophisticated discourse

---

39 He defined the poor as those struggling to acquire the bare necessities though managing to satisfy basic needs. The very poor lived in chronic squalor.

of protest that contained both a critique of the situation as was, as well as holding out the attractive prospect of a classless society in the future. However, they failed to reach the masses and political Islam came along to take their place. It is no coincidence that many first-generation Islamists were former Marxists who refashioned the Marxist perspective in a more intelligible way using religious categories. This appeal remains to the present day: "If unemployment is the prospect that most young people face, jihad holds greater appeal for them than civil liberties" (Kepel 1996: 164). The interaction between the social awareness of Islam and the visible polarisation of Middle Eastern societies leads to a "reading" of this situation as profoundly immoral and unjust. The Islamists' programme offers a fairer distribution of wealth between poor and rich (Dekmejian 1995). Justice often occupies a higher place in the hierarchy of values of Islamist movements than individual freedom. This, at any rate, is the fashionable thesis propounded by many Western analysts (Roy 1992).

Fig. 35 Populations living in absolute poverty in world macro-regions 1980–2005

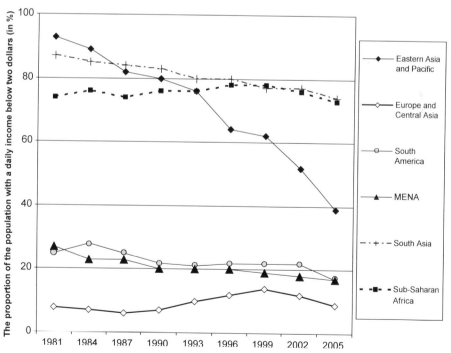

N.B.: The proportion of the population with a daily income below two dollars (converted using purchasing power parity in 2005).
Source: World Bank Development Indicators 2010

These revolutionary concepts are still inspiring many militant organisations in the Middle East, and are widely circulated on the internet and discussed by radical students and opposition intellectuals. However, with the exception of Iran, and despite many attempts (Saudi Arabia, Egypt, Algeria), they have never achieved practical success anywhere. Nowhere else have the Islamists managed to mobilise the lower classes, and not for want of trying. Nowhere else have they managed to form a cohesive revolutionary coalition of the urban poor, the middle classes and intellectuals and seize power through revolutionary means (Kepel 2002, Roy 2004). Moreover, not even the Iranian revolution can be successfully interpreted in terms of Marxist class analysis and the class struggle. Even the Iranian communist party Tudeh reached this very conclusion in a study published after the revolution. The revolution was participated in to the same degree by all classes, from the bourgeoisie to the lumpenproletariat, while the poorest of the clerics were to be found on the side of the dictatorship of the Shah, either as active members of his political party or even as collaborators with the SAVAK secret police (Zubaida 2009).

ABSOLUTE POVERTY: AN INTERNATIONAL COMPARISON

One reason may be the very nature of the social structure of Middle Eastern societies, which in most countries does not move as dramatically in the direction of greater and greater impoverishment of the poorest masses and a widening gap between rich and poor. According to the information available (not always the most reliable, it must be said), absolute and relative poverty are not as extreme in the Middle East as in other regions of the developing world. The authoritarian monarchies of the Persian Gulf (Bahrain, Kuwait, Saudi Arabia, United Arab Emirates) and certain other dictatorships (Syria, Libya) are blank spaces on the map, since statistical surveys have not been carried out. The last years of the reign of several secular dictatorships is another blank space, during which many believe inequality rose significantly. This would apply, for instance, to Egypt during the last years of the government of Mubarak, or Tunisia during the last years of Ben Ali. Again, however, reliable data is unavailable.

However, according to the information available, the proportion of Middle Eastern populations living in absolute poverty has fallen slightly over the last twenty-five years. These are estimates made on the basis of repeated representative surveys of the standard of living of households. In 1981, 27% of the population in the Middle East had to make do on less than two dollars a day (converted using purchasing power parity), while in 2005 this figure was only 17%. This corresponds to the level of absolute poverty in the developing countries of South America, and is not dramatically different to that of the post-communist countries of Eastern Europe and Central Asia. Poverty in South and East Asia or Sub-Saharan Africa has long been immeasurably higher (see fig. 35). However, it should also be pointed out that, while the proportion of poor people of the overall population is gradually falling, the absolute number is not. The number of poor people is still increasing because of sharp demographic growth, from 46 million in 1981 to 51 million in 2005, though the number of people being lifted out of poverty is increasing slightly faster (World Bank 2010).

In a comparison of absolute poverty, i.e. 1.25 dollars per person per day, the Middle East comes out better. In 1981, 8% of the population lived on less than this, while in 2005 this figure had dropped to 3.5%. This is the best out-come of all post-colonial and post-communist macro-regions in the world. The share of genuinely very poor people threatened by famine is therefore relatively low in the region, though because of population growth the abso-lute numbers are falling very slowly, from 14 million in 1981 to 11 million in 2005 (World Bank 2010).

SOCIAL INEQUALITY: AN INTERNATIONAL COMPARISON

Data is often missing on levels of socio-economic inequality in the Middle East (this again applies mainly to the oil-rich monarchies of the Gulf). During the 1990s it was reported that the poorest 20% of the population had to make do on 5% of all income in Egypt, Sudan and Morocco, and on as little as 2% in Iraq (Dekmejian 1995). These days, 20% of the poorest people receive only a 3.9% slice of the cake in Qatar, and this figure is 7% in Yemen, Jordan and Alge-ria, and 9% in Egypt (World Bank 2010). However, Latin America and most of the countries of Sub-Saharan Africa are internally far more polarised than the Middle East. Western Europe, with its relatively well established welfare states, fares somewhat better (Zakaria 2004). According to the infor-mation available (see tab. 29) inequality in many Middle Eastern countries (e.g. Tunisia, Qatar, Turkey and Iran) is fully comparable with that in the United States. Elsewhere it approximates the level common in several states of Europe with strong welfare systems. For instance, inequality of income in Egypt and Algeria is the same as in France. Again, it should be emphasised that between 2005 and 2010 there may have been major changes in the region. However, statistics are lacking for this period (cf. World Bank 2010).

Despite many attempts, revolutionary political Islam has been unsuc-cessful in its objectives. Moreover, social structures are developing in such a way as to reduce absolute poverty, while not even income inequality is particularly shocking in many countries. For this reason, in addition to a violent, revolutionary "*top-down re-Islamisation*", as a consequence of long-term urban unemployment more and more movements are moving over to the opposite strategy of "*bottom-up re-Islamisation*" (Kepel 1996 and 2002).

Tab. 29 Inequality and income distribution in MENA countries (share of total income in %)

Country	Survey year	Gini index	Poorest 10%	Poorest 20%	Wealthiest 20%	Wealthiest 10%
Algeria	1995	35.3	2.8	6.9	42.4	26.9
Egypt	2005	32.1	3.9	9.0	41.5	27.6
Iran	2005	38.3	2.6	6.4	45.0	29.6
Israel	2001	39.2	2.1	5.7	44.9	28.8
Jordan	2006	37.7	3.0	7.2	45.4	30.7
Morocco	2007	40.9	2.7	6.5	47.9	33.2
Qatar	2007	41.1	1.3	3.9	52.0	35.9
Tunisia	2000	40.8	2.4	5.9	47.2	31.6
Turkey	2006	41.2	2.0	5.4	47.1	31.3
Yemen	2005	37.3	2.9	7.2	45.3	30.8
France	1995	32.7	2.8	7.2	40.2	25.1
Germany	2000	28.3	3.2	8.5	36.9	22.1
USA	2000	40.8	1.9	5.4	45.8	29.9
Brazil	2007	55.0	1.1	3.0	58.7	43.0
Kenya	2006	47.7	1.8	4.7	53.0	37.8

N.B.: Data on many countries is unavailable (especially the Gulf States). The Gini index runs from 0 (absolute equality) to 100 (absolute inequality), i.e. the higher the score, the larger the gap between rich and poor.
Source: World Bank Development Indicators 2010

In connection with urban unemployment it would be appropriate to mention those movements that, in reaction to material shortages and subsequent social exclusion, emphasise the simple and modest lifestyle of the Prophet and his companions from the first Muslim community, whom Muslims regard as a role model: the fewer the material demands a person has, and the less he manages to make do with, the more pious and moral he is regarded to be. These movements are critical of the materialism of mainstream Muslim society and a "Western" urban lifestyle characterised by consumerism. They claim that luxury lures people away from God and spiritual values, destroying and deforming Islam. As opposed to the ostentatious public showing off of consumption, possessions and a high standard of living by part of the urban middle classes, they prefer to display publicly asceticism, simplicity, material modesty, austerity and restraint. Simplicity is to be seen in the decoration and design of homes and mosques and unassuming attire. Hijabs should be simple in terms of cut and colour, a feature that in such groups is deemed almost as important as the practice of the five pillars of Islam.

The result is that these movements manage, with the aid of religion, to make a virtue (spiritual and moral) of necessity (material). They offer higher status, a positive self-image and a new confidence to people who are marginalised within society because of unemployment and insufficient income, and help them come to terms with their socio-economic status. As opposed to revolutionary reactions, in which religion is a stimulant and radicalising heroin of the Arab street, in this case it operates more in line with Marx's concept of religion as opium of the people. This reaction is typical of the large modern Moroccan cities, as it is for other Arab metropolises such as Algiers, Tunis, Beirut, Cairo and Khartoum (Chekroun 2005).

In conclusion mention should be made of the analogy between the way some Islamic movements view poverty and the relationship to the poor in Christian pre-industrial Europe. Up until the 17th century the prevailing idea was that the poor were closer to God. Poverty did not represent social stigma but the path to salvation of the soul. Begging was a kind of spiritual contemplation. In addition it offered an opportunity to the god-fearing aristocracy, supporting their own paupers, to secure God's favour through charity. According to this logic the rich are created to save the poor and the poor to save the rich. This state of affairs only changes with industrialisation and the massification of poverty and the need to control the multitudes (cf. Mareš 1997).

(4) SHRINKING OF THE SOCIAL WORLD: VISIBLE INEQUALITY AND THE RESISTANCE OF SOCIALLY SENSITIVE ISLAM

Rural and *urban poverty* usually generates different political outcomes (Kennedy 1996). While rural poverty is regarded for generations as "normal" and acceptable by villagers, the urban version of poverty has strong politically destabilising potential (Kaplan 2003). One of the consequences of rapid urbanisation is a growth in the *visibility* of social inequality in respect of wealth and the availability of good quality education and life opportunities. The legitimacy of the regime falls and this contributes to intensive social tension and political conflict (Huntington 1968).

There exists no society in which all people are equal. However, inequality will provoke resistance when it is not reasonably explained and justified to the members of society. This means that the subjective interpretation of inequality by social actors is more important that its objective form and size. For this reason every society must produce a certain type of broadly acceptable and intelligible legitimisation of inequality. Intensive social conflict for reason of social inequality arises at the moment when the proven schemes justifying inequality collapse and cease to persuade (Keller 1997).

For this reason the relatively new situation to the Middle East caused by urbanisation is destabilising. In traditional agrarian societies the vast majority of the population scattered around the periphery were not aware of the higher standard of living being enjoyed by the wealthy urban elites living in the centre. Now, however, the poverty and lack of prospects of those living in cities conflicts head on with the ostentatious show of wealth on the part of others (Booth 2002, Chekroun 2005).

The theme of social justice and inequality is an integral part of the socially sensitive Islamic religion. For example, alms for the poor *(zakat)* represent one of the five pillars of the faith. Then there is fasting over Ramadan, these days often interpreted as solidarity with the poor. We should not forget the ban on interest, usury and other activities that lead to unbalanced profit for the wealthier, stronger parties to the transaction and the indebtedness and enslavement of the poor and weak. For instance, the first community of Muhammad in Medina is usually depicted as a model of social justice, not only by Islamists but even by secular Arab socialists (Kropáček 1996, Mendel 2008).

The delegitimisation of social inequality and the popularity of political Islam in this case stems from the interaction between widening socio-economic inequality and a socially sensitive Islamic imaginary, which lays an emphasis on solidarity, equality and justice. It is not, therefore, especially relevant how great inequality in reality actually is, but whether it is visible and regarded as justified or not. Islam provides ammunition for its delegitimisation.

(5) URBAN AND RURAL POVERTY: NEW REFERENCE GROUPS, NEW ASPIRATIONS

As I have written above, modern *urban poverty* is qualitatively different from *traditional rural poverty*. The political consequences are also completely different. At present modern urban poverty is beginning to prevail quantitatively over traditional rural poverty as a consequence of urbanisation. This does not only involve *absolute poverty*, but above all *relative poverty*.

It is the urban environment that allows a person to compare their own poverty with the prosperity of others. This stimulates consumer aspirations that are in sharp conflict with the everyday experience of poverty and lack of prospects of the urbanised masses. At this point relative poverty begins to play a more important role than absolute poverty, i.e. the subjective perception of a person's own situation derived from a comparison with other, usually more successful people. This contributes to an accumulation of dissatisfaction and to the threat of the outbreak of revolution due to rising frustration (Lerner 1964, Huntington 1968).

The concept of social deprivation and *relative poverty* (e.g. Peter Townsend) emphasises an ongoing subjective benchmarking of one's own situation and standard of living against a reference group to which a person is attracted. This reference group is usually a more successful social class. However, this group now co-forms the values, expectations, desires and aspirations of the individual. The individual then internalises these values and aspirations and takes ownership of them. How from that point on he operates on the basis of his ongoing comparison with the reference groups influences his satisfaction, identity and self-image. Long-term non-fulfilment of aspirations culminates in feelings of relative deprivation. Relative deprivation and absolute poverty only partially overlap. Only some objectively poor people are also deprived. However, some people who cannot be deemed objectively poor are also deprived. It always depends on precisely what reference group is being used by an individual for the purpose of comparison (cf. Mareš 1999).

In the current urbanised Middle East the relative poverty of large numbers of people results in mass relative deprivation. While the former reference group of the traditional rural population was the previous generation and its lifestyle and preferences, the reference group of the modern urbanised population is the better-off classes. For the poor and newly urbanised classes the reference group is now the more successful, old (bazar) and especially the new (doctors, engineers, merchants and civil servants) urban middle classes. Living in the city means the poor are confronted every day with the lifestyle, consumer habits and careers of these successful classes. The traditional approach of the absolutely poor individual who nevertheless does not feel subjectively deprived in any way can be illustrated thus: "I am satisfied with what God gave me" (a Jordanian Bedouin who had never set foot in a city). On the other hand, a slightly better off Jordanian villager exposed to the influence of the media and intense contact with people from the city expresses the frustration he feels comparing himself with wealthier classes thus: "We live like animals. We know nothing other than work, food and sleep" (Lerner 1964: 318, 338).

At the heart of modern frustrations is a newfound *empathy*, the ability to imagine oneself in various different social roles, relationships and situations. This is a new mentality stimulated by an awareness of the existence of different reference groups. As a young, educated Lebanese living in a city and constantly exposed to the media said: "If people are unaware of the existence of certain things, they don't desire them or lack them" (ibid: 117). While the inhabitants of rural areas in the Middle East have looked to the past and copied the modest needs and ascetic lifestyle of their ancestors, urbanised people are exposed to advertising, consumerism and various different reference groups, and are focused more on the future, from which they have greater expectations. Migration to cities and experience with an urban environment represents one of the factors stimulating consumer, career and political aspirations.

With the advance of urbanisation, the middle class becomes a reference group for the remaining inhabitants of rural and peripheral areas. The lifestyle and standards of the numerically dominant city becomes the cultural norm for the whole of society. An idealised image of urban affluence reaches villages. As a Lebanese farmer said when describing the village youth doing seasonal jobs in the city: "They perform the same function for our villages as camel caravans used to" (ibid: 189). New needs and aspirations arrive in the villages too. If as a consequence dissatisfied farmers decide to migrate to the city, it does not usually have the desired effect. Since the pace of urbanisation is more rapid than that of industrialisation, only a small number of them will find a steady job. For instance, in Egypt only one out of every ten farmers found work paying double what they were used to (Richards and Waterbury 2008).

(6) ISLAMIC CHARITY AND CIVIL SOCIETY: THE URBAN MIDDLE CLASSES AND THE POOR AS CLIENTS

Another possible reaction to high rates of unemployment in cities and other social problems associated with rapid urbanisation is the creation and expansion of charities operated by various different groups of contemporary Islamists. Middle Eastern states have been unable to deal with the social impacts of urbanisation. If they have not collapsed completely under the onslaught of urbanisation, their efficiency, quality and receptiveness is falling behind what Islamic civil society is starting to offer. *Islamic charity* is gradually filling the space left by the state and replacing the social functions of state institutions (Clark 2004). In response to the withdrawal of the state and its institutions from the social sphere the number of non-government organisations rose from 20,000 at the start of the 1960s to an estimated 70,000 during the 90s, this in the Arab world alone (Kropáček 1999).

The role of the Islamists in the social sphere in several countries became even more important in connection with stringent *neoliberal economic reforms* imposed in the 1980s and 90s by the International Monetary Fund. The structural adjustment programmes (SAPs) involved drastic cuts to the budgets for education, healthcare, housing, infrastructure and the abolition of subsidies for the purchase of basic foodstuffs for the poor. This "recovery" package also involved the privatisation of public services and the devaluation of currencies leading to a rise in the price of basic foodstuffs and other daily needs. It also involved many public-sector redundancies and an attempt to boost the role of weak market mechanisms.

These measures were controversial from the perspective of many Muslims. Critics claimed that there should have been a ban on international loans. States have a duty to collect and distribute alms to the poor. They were not impressed by the foreign origin and management of the reforms proposed by non-Muslims. The structural adjustment programmes contributed to the further delegitimisation of unpopular regimes and to the collapse of the fragile social contract between the elites and the masses. The urban classes were particularly affected, creating further beneficiaries of Islamic charity (Lubeck and Britts 2002).

A movement organised around mosques and unofficial prayer rooms thus created a network of people stretching from Tehran via Istanbul to Cairo and Algiers who, though they "want to sample the fruits of modernity and prosperity, remain marginalised" (Kepel 1996: 29). Originally the governments themselves, faced with a rural exodus, selectively supported the seemingly apolitical Islamic charitable activities organised around mosques, or at least suffered them quietly in order to undermine the revolutionary Marxists regarded right up until the end of the 1970s as the biggest threat to Middle Eastern regimes, and perhaps also to undermine the revolutionary branches of the Islamists. And so with minimal expenses they attempted to maintain basic social order, concerned as they were by a rise in crime, alcoholism, drug addition and food riots. Gradually, however, relations between the regimes and the Islamic charities curdled. These charities, the result of "bottom-up re-Islamisation", gradually began to appreciate what power they had and to extend their ambitions to national politics (Kepel 1996).

The creation of a morally minded civil society independent of the corrupt state and the irreligious majority resulted in the ideology of the Islamist group in question being distributed hand in hand with its charitable assistance (Kepel 1996, Huntington 1993 and 2001, Chekroun 2005). The propaganda of these movements came across as trustworthy, functional and superior to the rest, because unlike their political rivals, i.e. despotic regimes and secular opposition groups, Islamists did not offer only words, empty slogans and cheap populism, but tangible acts. Their social institutions pointed the way towards the future form of the promised ideal of an Islamic state. Islamists themselves regard their charitable role as part of a far broader project and as one of many intermediate steps on the road to implementing their long-term vision (Anderson 1998, Clark 2004).

What do the Islamists offer the urban population that is so appealing? Quite a lot is the answer. For the inhabitants of poor neighbourhoods and slums they provide food, second-hand clothes in a non-Western Islamic style, medicines and basic healthcare. They also offer free legal advice and help when dealing with the authorities and complex state bureaucracy and assistance with housing construction. For women worried about losing their honour in congested public transport or overcrowded streets they offer segregated transport services. For nursery school children they provide equipment and extra tuition for weaker or disadvantaged pupils, Quran studies and sports clubs. They also offer summer scouting camps in the fresh air outside the dangerous temptations of the big city, i.e. alcohol, drugs or sexually transmitted diseases. And for tradesmen, small traders, small farmers and the self-employed Islamic civil society offers interest-free Islamic banking.

In the event of earthquake, drought or flooding, the Islamists offer assistance to everyone without exception. It is this type of natural disaster that casts a bad light on dysfunctional, clumsy states that are usually incapable of providing effective assistance or even trying. This is why the popularity of political Islam rose after the earthquakes in Algeria (1989) and Egypt (1992). The role of Islamic charities is crucial in conflict zones and when helping civilian victims and survivors, for instance in the Arab-Israeli conflict. The Islamists also sometimes organise for the collection and disposal of garbage, something official bodies have often given up on

For the devout middle classes participation in an Islamic charity offers the opportunity to live like the true, authentic Islam and be regarded as a good Muslim. Charity offers them the comforting feeling that they are behaving like proper Muslims paying the social tax (*zakat*) intended to assist those in need. The *zakat* is one of the five basic pillars of the Islamic faith that every believer should honour and respect. By paying the *zakat*, praying regularly and fasting during Ramadan, a good Muslim gets closer to God, by no means a negligible benefit. The devout middle class can also derive a warm feeling from the fact that, by being involved in charitable activities benefitting the wider community, they are performing "jihad by the hand" (*jihad bil yad*) as well as possibly "jihad by the tongue" (*jihad bil lisan; dawah*), i.e. spreading the faith through missionary work or through their own example by means of socially oriented NGOs. These two forms of jihad are distinguished in Islamic sharia law from jihad of the heart (*jihad bin nafs/qalb*), i.e. systematic self-cultivation and the overcoming of one's own sinfulness (sometimes known as the greater jihad), and jihad by the sword (*jihad bis saif*), also known as the lesser jihad. At this juncture mention must be made of the fact that many militant Islamist organisations (e.g. Hezbollah and Hamas) have a dual character. In addition to the armed struggle they lay an emphasis on charity and social work (cf. Mendel 2010).

Islamist charity offers middle class professionals financially remunerated jobs, work experience and self-realisation. For instance, teachers and doctors receive a salary, and only some of the staff work on a voluntary basis (Clark 2004). Given the situation on the labour market this is significant. For educated women, work for an Islamist organisation represents one of very few legitimate ways of leaving the home and entering the public sphere without finding themselves in conflict with the prevailing conservative standards. Finally, the middle classes can be attracted by an offer of what are very often far better services than those provided by the state in its overcrowded classrooms, underequipped hospitals and long queues at corrupt government offices.

The internally diversified current of the Islamist movement and its sympathisers has something to offer all urban classes, which means it is concentrated above all in the cities. In contrast, the rural classes are involved in substitution agriculture that, though it does not bring them wealth and social advancement, in clement weather at least satisfies the most basic necessities of life. Furthermore, the cost of living is lower in the countryside and the traditional patterns of social assistance and solidarity within traditional communities, extended families, clans and tribes (*asabiyyah*) still apply. There is therefore not such an acute need for assistance from the Islamists (Anderson 1998, Kepel 2002, Lubeck and Britts 2002).

However, a question mark still hangs over the political and ideological impacts of Islamic charity. On the basis of field research into Islamic charities in Egypt, Yemen and Jordan, Janine Clark (2004) concludes that Islamists are not recording huge successes in mobilising the population on the social vertical by means of social work and are not creating social bonds and trust that would transcend social classes. Their activities are more about self help within the middle and lower middle classes that result only in the horizontal mobilisation of people with a similar social status. The political mobilisation of the poor by means of Islamic charity is therefore limited. Similarly, Sami Zubaida (2009) notes that models of vertical and horizontal solidarity and political mobilisation coexist in the modernising Middle East at various different stages and with different emphases. Islamists genuinely lay emphasis on a unifying cultural and religion tradition common to everyone and thus attempt to bridge social polarisation into class, linguistic and ethnic groups, tribes and rival ideological camps. They are not always successful in this. In addition, there is criticism, not only in the West, of problematic money flows officially intended for charities but in reality used to support militant activities at home and abroad (Beránek and Ťupek 2008)

(7) THE CRISIS OF THE OVERBURDENED URBANISED FAMILY: THE CONSERVATIVE REACTION

Mass migration to cities combined with a housing crisis, a lack of decently paid jobs, and the ever lengthening periods of study of the younger generation, sees young people postponing marriage and continuing to live with their ageing parents in overcrowded households in which one apartment is often occupied by several families. This is creating a historically unprecedented situation and placing huge demands on the traditional model of strong family and kinship solidarity. The traditional model is unable to meet these demands and as a consequence is collapsing under the burden of the uncontrolled rural exodus, as is the state welfare system. The subsequent *crisis and disintegration of the family* (divorce, domestic violence) accompanied by the collapse of traditional family solidarity and possible delinquency (alcohol and drugs) of socially excluded, long-term unemployed unmarried sons and daughters is creating additional demand for the services of Islamic civil society and producing hordes of new clients (Booth 2002, Chekroun 2005). Islamists also win credit by helping to arrange weddings (e.g. the Shukri Mustafa movement). But above all they are highlighting the theme of the family in crisis in conservative societies where the family enjoys the highest value. They do not see the problem as being the consequence of social processes, but as the result of a *moral crisis* (Esposito and Mogahed 2007).

The Middle Eastern family is also in crisis because the urban environment, unlike the rural, represents a far greater threat to traditionally understood *family honour*, especially the honour of its male members, which in many Middle Eastern cultures is directly dependent on the reputation and integrity of wives and the virginity and purity of daughters. It is difficult to defend this purity in a city full of strangers and pitfalls, which is the traditional task of the man (husband, son or brother). This accounts for the obsession that many Middle Eastern urbanised men have with women veiling themselves and with attempting to keep women safely enclosed within the four walls of the home, which is not the rule in the countryside. This part of the programmes of many Islamist movements resonates in harmony with the feelings and nightmares of many Middle Eastern men (Hoffman 1995).

The crisis of the family provokes a sensitive reaction in conservative society and raises the credit of critically minded clerics and Islamists, for whom the family represents a fundamental theme and value, since, as they see it, the health and strength of the whole of society is derived from the condition of the family. Islamists do not regard the origin of the crisis as residing in uncontrolled and unregulated urbanisation. They explain everything simply as the consequence of a generally understood moral crisis, the decline of religion, and laxity regarding values and standards. However, they also focus on the family primarily for the simple pragmatic fact that it is far easier to apply the norms of Islamic law in practice in the sphere of the family than in the economic, political or social spheres. The discredited authoritarian regimes, which are confronted by the opposition of the Islamists, wish to present themselves to their population in a more favourable light and to take the wind out of the Islamists' sails by themselves introducing elements of family law inspired by sharia (Hoffman 1995, Esposito 2003).

Nineteenth-century urbanising Europe experienced a similar conservative reaction when faced with the erosion of the lower class family. Shocked
conservative reformers believed that the resolution of social problems required the rehabilitation of the families of the lower classes: "The thinking of
these reformers was generally extremely conservative. The model of the ideal
family for them was the idealised patriarchal extended family, and the main
enemy was the increase in broken families and divorces and the dismal conditions of proletarian families destroyed by alcoholism and poverty. Their
aim was to protect families against this situation, ideally by returning them
to a patriarchal security that had probably never existed". Conservative theories represented an expression of nostalgia for traditional society, in which a
cohesive form of family was able to stabilise society and individuals and thus
ensure social harmony and peace within a swiftly changing world. There was
a call for the unlimited patriarchal authority of the husband and father and
obedience to the commandments (Možný 1997: 29).

(8) A THREATENING URBAN ENVIRONMENT AND ISLAMIC FEMINISM

Urbanisation also lends powerful impetus to the development of Islamic feminism, which is now involved in a struggle over the interpretation of Islam.
Islamic feminists such as Fatima Mernissi in Morocco (fighting against the
veil and involved in the democratisation of her country) or Nawal Saadawi
in Egypt (fighting for the whole of her life against female circumcision) stand
outside the Islamist movement. However, women also sympathise with and
are active members of various Islamist movements as often as men (Hoffman
1995, Burgat 2002). Mainstream movements (e.g. the Muslim Brotherhood),
though against the distortion of Islam by human innovation (*bid'ah*) in order
to cleanse Islam of these deposits, adhere in the case of gender relationships
to a conservative position and accord women second class status. They defini-
tely do not stand at the forefront of efforts to rehabilitate the status of women
in society following the model of the first community of the Prophet Muhammad, even though for them the first Islamic community (*salaf*) is the main
source of inspiration and a role model (Mendel 2008).
　　On the other hand, Islamic feminism is consistent in this regard and in
its effort to achieve female emancipation takes the Quran and the Sunnah
(*hadiths*) as its main weapon. It would appear that in the Middle East appeals to Islam guarantee success no matter what the debate. This is an urban,
educated and middle class section of the female Islamic movement (Esposito
2003). Literacy and the availability of education has opened up independent
"feminist" reading and thinking about the Quran and the hadiths without the

mediation of a male, clerical or "sexist" interpretation on the part of fathers, brothers and husbands. More and more women are coming into contact with different forms of Islamism during the time they spend at secondary school or university. Indeed, in some countries more women than men study at university (Lubeck and Britts 2002).

For this reason Islamic feminists draw attention to the revolutionary potential of Islam as regards gender relations. For example, they point to the abolition of the pre-Islamic custom of killing the firstborn daughters or killing little girls during times of drought, crop failure and famine, a measure taken by the Prophet Muhammad and praised by feminists. Feminists also point to the personal example set by the Prophet in his relationships with his wives. His first wife, Khadijah, was several years older than Muhammad. Furthermore, it was she who approached him and offered him, as an abandoned orphan ridiculed for his message, her hand in marriage. Their marriage was monogamous. Both before and after the wedding, Muhammad was an ordinary employee of his wealthy wife, who supported him both materially and financially. The last of the Prophet's wives, Aisha (among Sunnis), and his daughter Fatima (among Shiites), are described in many hadiths as the archetype of emancipated and engaged women, as warriors, the sharp-witted partners and wise mentors of their husbands, as well as being devout Muslims who played a prominent role in the political life of the Muslim community (Wadud 2007, Mendel 2008).

For this reason Islamic feminists argue that the inferior status of women in contemporary Muslim societies is in conflict with Islam. In highly religious, conservative societies this is a far more effective argument that anything mustered up by secular feminists, who, on the contrary, argue that the main cause of all the problems faced by women is to be found in Islam, a stance that does not win them many friends in Muslim societies.

One campaign pursued by Islamic feminists is the abolition of the Pakistani legal regulation on rape that is biased in favour of the male perpetrator. They point out that this regulation is at odds with the Quran. Similarly, they campaign against the pre-Islamic custom of female genital mutilation that is widespread in many Muslim societies. In some countries there is an effort to enshrine the equality of women and men in civil law, along with a gender differentiated, though *complementary* and balanced, family law. Demands are also being heard for the equal access of men and women to Friday's prayers in mosques (Esposito and Mogahed 2007, Frouzová 2005).

The effects of urbanisation are most visible in the current trend towards headscarves, veils and Islamic dress. This is taking place against the backdrop of more general debates on the redefinition of the role of women in society and the transformation of gender relationships. While in the countryside women worked on their family farm and lived in an extended household in the local community with high social control, the situation is completely different in the anonymity of a large city. Here there is a high level of contact with complete strangers of both sexes and hence a need to wear the veil as a form of protection and adaptation to life in the city. Because of the housing crisis, people of both sexes who are completely unrelated often live in one overcrowded building or even one room. Women also come into contact with strangers in crowded streets, marketplaces and on public transport. This is also true of educational establishments and in jobs, which women are increasingly entering either from choice or because their husband's income has become insufficient to support a family. By this argument veiling allows women *greater mobility* and *freedom* in urban areas far beyond the boundaries of the extended family (Lubeck and Britts 2002).

In the urban lower middle and middle classes, where a wife's income is beginning to be essential if the family's status is to be maintained, the headscarf and strict Islamic attire is an attempt to regain lost honour. It is deemed shameful to both partners that the man is unable to provide for his family on his own, something long deemed a social norm. A couple can acquire a good reputation by means of a wife's ostentatious conformity with the Islamic dress code, which is taken to be an external sign of the inner moral qualities of a person (Hoffman 1995, Starrett 1998).

The visibly Islamised public space of cities then in itself creates further pressure on veiling and the Islamisation of people who have been religiously or politically lukewarm and hesitant up till now. However, the reasons for this huge trend toward veiling are in reality more diverse. It is often one of the few ways of legally and symbolically demonstrating one's opposition to secular dictators, as well as to Western culture, Israeli policy or upper class women wearing Western clothes. It can also be a sign of poverty and the inability of women to afford expensive make-up and regular changes of clothing to suit the whims of fashion. Sometimes the scarf is simply a weapon in the intergenerational conflict of adolescent girls and their unveiled mothers (Lubeck and Britts 2002, Roy 2004).

(9) INTERGENERATIONAL ALIENATION: THE DECLINE IN THE AUTHORITY OF RURAL PARENTS AND THE SEARCH FOR SURROGATES

If urbanisation is rapid, it intensifies *intergenerational alienation and conflict* and the crisis of the family. Parents and grandparents born and bred in the countryside are accused by their descendants of possessing outmoded skill sets that are of no use whatsoever in the city. Their advice no longer possesses authority and is inapplicable in the modern world. Intergenerational conflict on the level of values and culture arises between the traditional standards of rural parents and the competing demands of the new urban environment, schoolmates, contemporaries and the media. This is often related to different life aspirations. The young generation do not identify with village traditions and with their parents' concept of folk Islam, which they regard as obsolete and infested with pre-Islamic superstition, or, in the worst case, as unacceptably heretical (bid'ah) in respect of the Prophet's original tidings. After many generations, the smooth intergenerational transfer of knowledge and faith is for the first time in history seriously at threat, though the young are also not overly enthusiastic for the aggressive secular culture and materialist values of the city.

What results is a schizophrenic situation in which the young hover between two worlds without feeling fully at home in either. They look instead for substitute sources of authority and knowledge, as well as for replacement sources of recognition and appreciation that would fill the resulting vacuum. They often find these in different religious or political movements that are able to offer something like a surrogate family. Islamists will speak of themselves as brothers and sisters. The basic cells of Islamist organisations are often called families (usra), and the charismatic figure of a somewhat older leader replaces the authority of the parents (cf. Kepel 2002, Roy 2004, Juergensmeyer 1994, 2000). For instance, some middle class urbanised girls whose mothers dress in the Western style prefer the headscarf and strict Islamic dress as part of their adolescent rebellion. The generational conflict is being played out in a relatively conservative environment in which adolescents appeal to religious authorities in conflicts with their parents (Lubeck and Britts 2002).

(10) RADICALISATION OF THE SECOND AND THIRD GENERATION OF MIGRANTS

While the first generation of adult migrants to cities occasionally retain an apolitical, conservative stance, the second and third generations tend to be politically aware, organised and mobilised. They are also radicalised and gravitate towards opposition ideologies and movements. The opposition, including Islamists, benefits from this. Why does the first generation differ from succeeding generations?

The first generation of urban poor, born and bred in the countryside, bring traditional rural conservative attitudes to the city that are above all apolitical. These include fatalism, the absence of political opinions and an inability to perceive the connection between their own poverty and the actions of the government. In addition, they are so taken up with quotidian worries that it is difficult for them to become enthused by abstract ideals and reflections on a utopian future. Their energies are taken up by what they are going eat tomorrow and not by how they might live in ten years time (Lerner 1964). Their identity and patterns of social organisation and trust often end at the borders of their own extended family or clan. They avoid identifying with wider social formations such as political party, class, nation or social movement. For instance, in the slums on the outskirts of Moroccan cities (the *douars*), inhabited in the main (70%) by the families of new immigrants from the countryside, mutual cooperation and assistance across families is not much in evidence. First generation migrants tend to be solitary or even competitive, and each family looks after its own affairs in an attempt to survive (Chekroun 2005). Finally, the horizontal mobility from a backward periphery to the city operates as a psychological substitute for vertical mobility, i.e. as a substitute for social advancement. The first generation of urban poor does not experience such strong frustration because it regards its relocation from village to city as a sign of success, even though in reality all there has been is a shift from rural poverty to urban poverty (Huntington 1968).

Descendants of the first generation of immigrants are born and socialised in the urban environment and so have higher life, career, educational and consumerist aspirations. Unlike their parents, they do not compare their standard of living with their rural grandparents but with the established urban classes. If their demands are not met, the risk increases of political mobilisation and radicalisation. In his classic study *Political Order in Changing Societies* (1968), Samuel Huntington states that the *radicalisation of the second generation* of migrants is a universal phenomenon and can be seen in the urbanised Middle East and in the slums of South American cities. However, it can also be seen in the history of immigration to the US from Europe during the course of the 19th and 20th centuries, which led to a boom in urban criminality and political rebellion. A similar effect was felt by the migration of American blacks from the agricultural southern states to the industrial cities of the north after the Civil War and the abolition of slavery.

The radicalisation of the descendants of migrants from rural areas also took place during the course of European urbanisation of the 19th and 20th centuries, and this gave rise to a similar *second-generation crisis theory*. This states that the first generation of adult urban migrants will not experience disorientation and identity crisis because it possesses a firm value compass formed by its traditional upbringing in the countryside. However, the second generation will find itself in a schizophrenic situation, caught in a conflict between the traditional norms and values of its parents and the opposing demands and values of the city (Musil 1967). At present, a similar mechanism is operating as regards the radicalisation of the second and third generation of European Muslims (Roy 2004, Laqueur 2006).

In addition, the descendants of rural migrants often move from poor suburban slums to the centre of Middle Eastern cities. Here their poverty is in sharp contrast with the lifestyle of the wealthier urban classes with whom they are unable to compete. All around them they see luxury goods that they cannot afford and their frustration increases (Richards and Waterbury 2008).

(11) THE CITY AS THE MODERN *JAHILIYYAH*: THE EPITOME OF MORAL TURPITUDE

At 808 metres tall, the bombastic skyscraper Burj Khalífa, named in honour of the president of the United Arab Emirates, is the highest building in the world. It boasts the highest swimming pool in the world (on the 76th floor) and the fastest elevators. Similarly, the Dubai hotel in the shape of a yacht, Burj al-Arab (the "Tower of the Arabs"), is regarded as the largest, most luxurious hotel in the world, the "first seven-star hotel in the world". No expense has been spared on gold, silver, and other attributes of conspicuous consumption. Neighbouring Saudi Arabia is also using oil revenues to build the second highest building in the world, which will reach a height of 601 metres above the destination of the pilgrimage made by all Muslims, the Grand Mosque in Mecca. Inside is a giant shrine to consumerism and a luxury hotel with the largest clock in the world, reminiscent from a distance of Big Ben in London.

These and similar projects might remind morally minded Muslims of a modern-day Tower of Babel, symptoms of a loss of faith, human ego and self-centredness. At the other end of the same moral criticism are signs of the moral decline being played out every day in Arab streets in the shadow of skyscrapers, in overcrowded slums and anonymous spaces in the city.

A spontaneously expanding and vibrant city, with its inevitable contradictions, paradoxes, glaring deviations and dysfunctions, offers a rich repository of signs of *moral decay*. Offence can easily be taken at contemporary cities by the contrast with the idealised city state of the Prophet in Mecca and Medina. The cause of this decadence is taken to be apostasy, that of both the elites as well as the masses. The therapy is to be found in a more or less vaguely formulated vision of an Islamic state that will seek to enforce strict Islamic law and will oversee the morality of its population so that they do not deviate from the true path. It will promote good and forbid evil as the main programme of state power. The Islamists promise to resolve the complex problems of contemporary cities by creating a parallel to the *idealised community of the Prophet* and the first four rightly guided caliphs in Mecca and Medina. A similarly simple solution to the complex problems of urbanising England in the 19th century was offered by John Wesley and his Methodists (Hoffman 1995).

THE CONTRAST BETWEEN THE TRADITIONAL AND MODERN CITY

The moralistic critique of modern, Western urbanism has much to say that is true, but is partly simply nostalgia for something that did not actually exist. It criticises the degeneration of social life and the anonymity of interpersonal relationships. The centre of Muslim cities always comprised the great Friday Mosque and the adjoining marketplace. The shops and craft workshops always maintained a clear hierarchy in relation to the Mosque; the bookshops and stationery shops were closest and the most worldly goods and the tannery the furthest away. The traditional city centre was an open, accessible area full of cafes, spas and hostels inviting passersby to take the weight off their feet and strike up business and social relationships. However, this was primarily a male world. In contrast, the modern city built by the colonial powers, megalomaniac secular reformers and oil sheikhs does not respect the old urban model. Only rarely is it centred around the great Friday mosques, whose place has been taken by the state authorities, banks, and the headquarters of international corporations. The modern city is full of wide boulevards, cinemas, villas for the rich, hotels full of foreigners, and skyscrapers higher than the tallest mosques, where warm conviviality has been displaced by Western frostiness, bustle and anonymity (Robinson 1996, Longrigg and Jankowski 1963).

A sharp contrast has arisen between the old and the new, tradition and modernity, continuity and discontinuity. At the same time, however, both ingredients blend, combine and coexist. This creates a tension. The city can then be regarded not only as a centre of Western modernity, but also as a centre of the renaissance of Islamic identity and efforts to find a compromise between the old and the new (Fuccaro 2001). Writing of the difference between life in a traditional town neighbourhood as opposed the modern metropolis, Ahmad Amin, drawing on his own experience, writes: "The European tendency that does not respect the neighbour and where one person might live for years alongside another without ever knowing who he was did not prevail among us. Everyone in our neighbourhood was a neighbour who knew each other's affairs, names and occupations. They visited each other, expressed their condolences at funerals, attended each other's family celebrations and lent each other money if it was necessary. They were accustomed to visiting and spending entire evenings in the reception rooms" (Robinson 1996: 216).

The contrast between medieval and modern urbanism can still be experienced in Moroccan cities, where three basic and independent, though immediately physically adjacent, urban and social quarters coexist alongside one another: the traditional Arab *medina*, a somewhat smaller Jewish *mellah*, and the colonial new town (*ville nouveau*) built by the French and expanded by the pro-Western elite after achieving independence. However, Bryan S.

Turner (1974), addressing the contrast posited by Max Weber between the occidental and Muslim city, is somewhat critical of the traditional Muslim city (Cairo, Damascus, Baghdad). He does not share the black-and-white romantic notions of endless social cohesion and the warmth of traditional Muslim cities. On the urban and social side he sees them as to a certain extent captives of their origin – they evolved from Bedouin military tent camps and Arab military garrisons. They therefore consisted of several independent neighbourhoods with their own marketplaces. Members of various ethnic groups, tribes, religions and sectarian groups lived a segregated life separated along the same lines in the countryside. According to Turner, this division of the Muslim city persisted because it was controlled and managed by central state power or its representative in the form of a vizier. It did not therefore possess an independent authority that could organise its affairs, encourage a feeling of shared interest, and represent the city in external relations as in the case of medieval Europe. In addition, the vizier held onto power by employing the divide-and-rule tactic, which meant that mistrust and tension prevailed between individual districts. However, Bryan Turner draws somewhat general conclusions from a particular situation that pertained in Egypt during the reign of the Mamluks from 1216 to 1517.

THE CONTRAST BETWEEN THE CITY AND THE IDEALISED COUNTRYSIDE

Critics of the contemporary city can also draw on medieval Arab social philosophy and history, in which the corrupt city is contrasted with a rural idyll. As far back as the 14th century, Ibn Khaldun (1972) was drawing attention to the dichotomy and mutual interaction between the urban and nomadic populations. According to Khaldun, urban life led to a loss of social cohesion, the accumulation of wealth, intoxication with luxury and an emphasis on a genteel and overly cultivated artistic production. This results in sloth, overindulgence and a loss of resilience, which in turn is the beginning of the end of every city civilisation, which is condemned to being defeated and dominated by tough, tenacious nomads and warriors with high levels of social cohesion and solidarity. However, after attaining and consolidating their power over the urban population these warriors then set off on the same declining trajectory and the entire cycle repeats approximately every four generations. Though Khaldun is a respected Middle Eastern scholar, Islamists are suspicious of him, because he speaks of the splitting up and stratification of society, which goes against their principle of the "natural" oneness of the community, God and all of creation (*tawhíd*) (Roy 1992). Furthermore, unlike Khaldun, Bryan S. Turner (1974) believes that in the urban environment the substitute for tribal cohesion (*asabiyyah*) of nomads was Islamic law (*sharia*), which ensured the unity of urban society and safeguarded social order. The contrast between cohesive rural tribes and fractured urban populations did not therefore have to be so great.

The sect of the *assassins*, shrouded in myth, represents another historical example of a distance from the corrupt medieval city, though modern historiography is modifying the image suffused with exoticism we have long held thanks to the distorted reports of the Crusaders and then Marco Polo. The attacks mounted by the assassins were directed against apostates from among the Muslim elites based in the cities such as political leaders, military commanders and senior civil servants. The assassins themselves inhabited fortresses in inaccessible peripheral regions such as the Alamut Castle in what is today Iran, leading an ascetic, disciplined religious life. And yet no modern Middle Eastern movement refers explicitly to this sect. Even while it existed it was an extreme, marginal sect, and modern Islamists are closer to the social mainstream (Lewis 2003b). If the medieval Middle Eastern city incurred the wrath of moralists of that time, the modern Westernised city is more than capable of arousing similar criticism, accompanied by a nostalgia for an idealised system of smaller communities.

EUROPEAN AND MIDDLE EASTERN ANTI-URBANISM: A HISTORICAL COMPARISON

Just as today the criticism of the moral consequences of urbanisation articulated by Islam is growing, so modernising Europe went through a similar ideological and intellectual reaction. Alongside urbanisation, questions arose in Europe as to whether the growth of cities was a sign of progress and formed the basis for the development of culture, knowledge and the liberation of man from superstition and the hypocritical regulation of rural communities, or whether, on the contrary, cities were pockets of decadence, the moral bankruptcy of individuals, the breakdown of families and the collapse of entire communities (White, White 1962, Musil 1967).

The most radical *anti-urbanism* and cultural pessimism took place against a backdrop of accelerating urbanisation during the industrial revolution in the 19th century: "There was barely a single social evil that was not attributed to cities" (Musil 1967: 31). The complaint was that cities were sucking the smartest, ablest individuals away from the countryside. They were parasites on the rest of society and wasting human lives. Cities were unhealthy and unhygienic, immoral, unnatural and licentious. They led to individualisation, atomisation and anonymity, to psychological malaise, stress, suicide, mental health issues, excessive mobility and subsequent solitariness.

These criticisms brought together both ideology and empirical facts revealing the genuinely negative impacts of European urbanisation. For instance, from 1785 to 1789, Thomas Jefferson, the third American president and philosopher, was ambassador to France, and as well as witnessing the unregulated expansion of Paris had a wealth of experience with overcrowded, filthy London. Regarding the large cities of that time he wrote: "I view great cities as pestilential to the morals, the health and the liberties of man." (ibid. 26). He wrote this after returning, filled with contempt for London and Paris, to the rural environment of small American towns and Puritan settlements where he grew up. The culture shock he experienced was analogous to that experienced approximately one hundred and fifty years later by the Egyptian intellectual Sayyid Qutb in the environment of the burgeoning American cities. However, Qutb transformed his feelings into the most influential ideological tract on political Islam of the 20th century.

Among highly charged moral critiques of cities and urbanisation in Europe, the philosophy of *romanticism* stands out during the 19th century, closest in character to the moral criticism of contemporary Islamic fundamentalism. The permeation of German romanticism and philosophy (Spengler, Heidegger, Rilke) through the modern Middle East was drawn attention to by the Orientalist and historian Bernard Lewis (1990, 2003b). Up to the end of World War II Germany was regarded in the region as a natural ally against British and French colonial expansion. As a consequence, along with the international political alliance of Germany and the Ottoman Empire, the transfer of technology, and military consultancy, German ideology and philosophy also spread rapidly. For this reason, key aspects of 19th German romanticism remain components of the ideology of secular Arab Ba´ath nationalist parties (Syria and Iraq), as well as of both moderate and militant Islamists, to this day. Lewis emphasises the German inspiration behind the moral critique of the West and especially the United States.

European romantic philosophy regarded mass urbanisation and industrialisation as the essence of moral depravity. It accused cities of being unnatural, artificial, overly mechanised, lacking in spontaneity, and characterised by corruption, alienation and the disintegration of warm social relations. In 1853, the German historian Wilhelm Heinrich Riehl spoke in the diction typical of romanticism of the consequences of urbanisation thus: "For the most part the rural population lives communally as one family, while city folk mostly live alone. Isolation increases the larger a city becomes. Immigrants have no fixed employment or household. They come looking for happiness, but because they do not find it they move elsewhere. Our cities are so disgusting not because they have a settled population but because they have a fluctuating population" (Musil 1967: 29). Around the same time the English intellectual John Ruskin launched an even more vitriolic attack on modern cities, which he called "cities of the plain" or "pits of the plain": "Sin begets sin and inequity encourages iniquity in forms so chilling that the eye has never seen nor the ear heard the like, where the foolishness of nations has been whipped up into a fratricidal frenzy and where all the deepest vices of a nation have come together in the most repulsive way, whence the virus of infectious sin and deceit that spreads through the entire country." (ibid: 30). A similarly intransigent stance towards the "depravity" of the city was taken by the American philosopher and inspiration of the environmental movement, Ralph Waldo Emerson: "That uncorrupted behaviour which we admire in animals and in young children belongs to him, to the hunter, the sailor – the man who lives in the presence of Nature. Cities force growth and make men talkative, but they make them artificial." (ibid: 29).

OCCIDENTALISM: THE CITY AS THE ESSENCE OF WESTERN DECADENCE

The European romantic critique of rampant urbanisation is similar to that of modern Islamism. European romanticism continues to inspire Islamists and resonates in the population because the Middle East is undergoing a similar experience of urbanisation as Europe underwent in the 19th century. A *comparative view* of current Islamic reflections on the city was explicitly developed by Ian Buruma and Avishai Margalit (2005a, 2005b) in their thesis on *Occidentalism*[40]. It is German romanticism and its critique of the city that plays a key role here as a *trans-historical* and *trans-geographical discourse* that in a "hateful caricature" offers a "dehumanised image of the West" and demonises the Western version of modernity, listing the following as typical attributes of the West: extreme individualism and an individual deracinated from the transcendent (because of secularisation) and the community (because of boundless freedom, anonymity); lust and a tendency toward materialism, an emphasis on profit and the pursuit of money. In addition it lists mediocrity, weakness, depravity, a lack of spirituality and cold, mechanical rationality, arrogance, hypocrisy, the loss of vitality, prostitution, moral degeneration and decadence. All of these attributes are concentrated within the confines of the city, while in this discourse the traditional rural community is the idealised, exalted and worshiped antithesis. Western man – typically an inhabitant of an anonymous city – therefore lacks soul and roots. He is driven only by carnal lust and the base instincts and sinks to the level of beasts.

The discourse of Occidentalism hostile to the West was born in a Germany humiliated by France and projected into Germany romanticism, fascism and criticism of the Enlightenment. It subsequently influenced the defensively minded Russia, where it was manifest in the worldview of Slavophiles and

---

40 This is the mirror image of the Orientalist discourse, i.e. the deeply rooted and widely held Western stereotypes regarding the Islamic East. It is a continuation of the debate initiated by Edward Said.

Bolsheviks. It also cast a spell on Japan, threatened by the outside world, where it became part of the chauvinist militarism of the Empire of Japan. These days Occidentalism fares best in a Middle East traumatised by rapid change and foreign interference. Generally, then, it is a response to the rapid disintegration of traditional society, precipitous urbanisation and industrialisation, the expansion of predatory capitalism, the rationalisation of an impersonal public administration, and the acceptance of reforms inspired by the West. Very often a society traumatised by rapid internal change is further humiliated from without by the military and cultural pressure of the West.

A common feature of Occidentalism in different historical periods and in various places is a resistance to four mutually interlinked attributes of the West: the *bourgeoisie* representing the soulless machinery of industrialism and the worship of Mammon; an arrogant *rationality* devoid of sense; feminism and the *emancipation of women* from their traditional role in the household; and the *anonymity* of the sinful *city*. This culminates in a view of the West, America above all, as the embodiment of all negative attributes, and in an endeavour to find an alternative; a utopia in the form of a return to the "golden age", an idealised rural idyll, the combination of modern politics and traditional religion, with an emphasis on spirituality and morality, superior values and visions, individual sacrifice for the sake of the commonweal, and the usefulness of occasional wars as an instrument for cleansing society of the deposits of decadence.

The city is therefore one of the main villains of Occidentalism, a cautionary manifestation of Western decadence and the concentration of all evil. In contrast, an idealised image is created of the honesty, simplicity and purity of the pastoral life of the Bedouins or the idyll of the rural agricultural community. Anti-liberal sentiments almost always contain an implacable opposition to the city and to everything that urban civilisation represents: commerce, greed, selfishness, hypocrisy, mixed populations, artistic and sexual freedom, scientific progress, wealth and a corrupting power. Popular films from developing countries work with a similar image of the anonymous, treacherous, heartless, seductive, dangerous and hostile city. These films are accepted by the public because they chime strongly with personal experience. *Slumdog Millionaire* would be an obvious example. In the Judaic-Christian-Islamic tradition Sodom and Gomorrah, brimming over with fornication and abomination, occupy a similar role, or sinful Babylon, a city state aspiring to godlike status whose tower is the symbol of arrogance, hubris and idolatry. According to many authors it was not mere coincidence that the twin towers of the World Trade Center in New York were the targets of the attacks of 11 September 2001.

THE CASE OF MOHAMED ATTA

Occidentalism played a role in shaping the worldview of Mohamed Atta, leader of the Hamburg cell of Al-Qaeda, pilot, and key organiser of the attacks of 11 September 2001. Atta was born in 1968 in what at that time was the small Egyptian town of *Kafrelsheikh* in the Nile Delta. When he was ten his family moved to the vicinity of the old centre of Cairo (the district of Abdeen). In his early teens the family moved (1990) into a large, anonymous, 11-storey pre-fabricated flat in Giza, the third largest city in Egypt and, according to several sources, along with Cairo part of the second largest suburb in the world (after Yokohama, Japan). This experience, combined with his very successful studies of architecture and urban planning at Cairo University and then at Technical University in Hamburg (1992 to 1999), led Atta to a sophisticated, informed and complex moral and cultural critique of the impacts of Middle Eastern urbanisation and the dysfunctionality of local cities.

This became the theme of his academic research and theses. Atta was very concerned by the construction of Western-style high-rise buildings and destructive development projects in ancient cities that he was witness to. He was equally critical of the megalomaniac, impersonal and ugly prefabricated housing estates that had been built in Egypt during the period of Arab socialism in the 1960s and 70s. These estates were displacing and destroying historical buildings, depriving people of their dignity, and robbing them of their cohesive traditional neighbourhoods. In addition, they represented a slavish imitation of the West that had no future. It was in one of these buildings, lacking the human dimension, that Atta lived in Giza with his parents after moving away from the old part of Cairo. In his research into changes made to the ancient Syrian Allepo, Atta reconstructed the historical character of the city and plotted its dramatic transformations in modern times. He showed how modern planning methods and high-rise buildings were destroying the form, atmosphere and panorama of the historical city, and also how the new large-scale constructions were gradually destroying the traditional system of small, shaded streets that for centuries had served as a meeting place for residents. He carried out similar research in the historical quarter of Cairo, and this led him to more general reflections on the conflict between Arab civilisation and the Western version of modernity.

However, it would be wrong to see a direct link between the terrorist act of 9/11 and the cultural, social and moral criticism of Middle Eastern urbanism and Western city planning. In this respect, criticism of Israeli policies played a greater role in the life of Atta, more specifically the foreign policy of the USA, which supported Israel. After Israel's short incursion into Lebanon (1996), Atta drew up his last will and testament and began to reflect upon participating in armed jihad. Furthermore, like his contemporaries, Atta was an opponent of the First Gulf War (1990–1) and the deployment of American forces in Saudi Arabia in the proximity of the holiest places of Islam. He was also a long-term critic of the authoritarian government in Egypt supported by Washington. Politics very much played first fiddle (McDermott 2005, Starrett, Doumato 2007)[41].

THE CITY AS MODERN JAHILIYYA

These days Occidentalism thrives most in the Middle East, above all within urban Islamist movements. Probably the most influential Islamist ideologue of the 20th century, the Egyptian Sayyid Qutb, while a civil servant on a study trip to the USA (1948–50) was supposed to be picking up tips from the education system (Mendel 2013). Instead, he experienced a severe *culture shock*. It was not ideas for reform of the Egyptian education system that he brought home with him, but a sophisticated critique of the morally degenerate American urban society, where market forces applied even in the sphere of religious life. With Americans themselves it was virtually impossible to speak of anything other than money, movie stars, cutting the grass and cars. It was not, therefore, advisable to imitate the West, unless Muslims wanted to fall into an era worse than that of pre-Islamic darkness, ignorance and barbarism (*jahiliyya*) (Buruma, Margalit 2005b)[42].

The state of *jahiliyya* existing prior to the arrival of the Prophet Muhammad was the result of ignorance in which confused people prayed to false gods. They forgot God's tidings to man, being delivered at that time by an ongoing line of prophets (such as Abraham and Jesus), or distorted it in different ways. And so every day saw the abduction and rape of women, the driving away of neighbours' flocks of sheep, attacks on trade caravans, bloody vendettas, debtors falling into slavery because of usury, lawlessness, endless quarrels and intrigues involving individual clans and tribes, lives lived in illusion, the absence of ethics, indulgence in alcohol (see the Arabic *al-kuhul*), or barbaric customs such as the burial of first-born daughters alive and the killing of young girls during times of drought and famine.

---

41 See also the interview with Professor Dittmar Machule, Atta's thesis supervisor at the Technical University of Hamburg-Harburg, available at: www.abc.net.au/4corners/atta/interviews.

42 Sajjid Qutb was inspired by and subscribed to the concept of *jahilíyya* that not long before had been championed by the Pakistani journalist and key lay ideology of the Islamic movement during the 20th century, Abul Al´a Maududi. Qutb distinguished between four types of modern *jahiliyya*: (a) communism, with its blind allegiance to the party and its cult of personality, (b) non-communist idolatrous *jahiliyya* with its cults of nation, race, people, individualism or primitive materialism and consumerism, (c) Jewish and Christian, and (d) that embodied by the hypocritical and false Muslims of the modern Islamic world that had to be reformed (Mendel 2008 and 2013).

With the arrival of the last Prophet Muhammad, Islam was born. It cracked down on barbaric practices and took revolutionary remedial measures. However, according to the rapidly mobilising and moralising modern Islamist narrative, Muslim society is once again in a state of barbarism (*jahilíyya*) and disintegration (*fitna*). Muslims in name only live consciously and hypocritically in a state of delusion, which is far worse. They have received the divine message, but they ignore it, distort it to suit their needs, or reject it completely. They are exposed to many different temptations in the godless environment of the city. They are confused and constantly being diverted from the "straight path" of Islam.

The symptoms of this are manifest not only in a willingness to submit to apostate regimes, internal disunity or an uncritical acceptance of Western models, but also in social breakdown and moral crisis in cities: alcohol, drugs, anabolic steroids in sport, suicide, tolerance of prostitution, pre-marital and extramarital sex, the spread of HIV, the crisis of the family and paternal authority, divorce, abortions in urban clinics, the availability of pornography, crime, undeserved profit, the ostentatious exhibition of luxury by the nouveau riche, and even publicly declared atheism.

As a consequence the urban environment is in stark contrast with the main ethical principle of the community of believers: to do good and to eschew evil and anything abominable. Since the fulfilment of this principle is a sign of faith in God, the spread of abomination and deviancy is deemed proof of the mass apostasy of Muslims from their faith. Urban deviation also discredits the regimes, which, in the eyes of the Islamists, are shying away from their core obligation to suppress and punish everything that is reprehensible. They merely look on as disintegration takes place or even support it (the Islamic discourse loosely cited in Mendel 2008).

ESCHATOLOGICAL VISION

In his bestseller *The Revenge of God* (1996) the sociologist Gilles Kepel examines the way that Judaism, Christianity and Islam have been assuming a more and more important role in politics around the world since the 1970s. The common denominator of the re-politicisation of religion taking place at the same time in many different places around the world is a global reaction to the *crisis of modernity*. Characteristic of this is not only the discrediting of political elites and the draining away of the Enlightenment faith in the progress of mankind, but also feelings of confusion and helplessness caused by visible signs of the breakup of society. The HIV pandemic, ecological crises, rising crime and drug abuse, uncontrolled population explosion, a lack of natural resources, mass poverty and the threat of nuclear war represent phenomena seemingly created for an *image of the coming apocalypse*. Social breakdown on a local level would appear to be accompanied by turmoil on a national and global level. The contemporary Islamic world, compared to mainly Christian or Jewish societies, offers up unprecedented signs of confusion, societal breakdown and helplessness.

The eschatological vision represented in the discourse of the Islamists reflects their experience with developments in the real world. These have been consolidated by the *millennialism* characterising the end of the Islamic 14th century and the beginning of the 15th century (2016 corresponds to the year 1437 in the Islamic calendar). According to one of the hadiths, approximately every one hundred years a charismatic leader (*mujaddid*) will appear who will prevent the further moral decline of society and the degeneration of Islam. This is how, for instance, the Egyptian Shukri Mustafa or the Saudi Mohammed al-Qahtani are regarded by their supporters. Moreover, according to some fifty hadiths, the Mahdi or Jesus is supposed to appear at the end of the world. Shiite Islam awaits the coming of the Hidden Imam; on the eve of the Iranian Revolution this was how Khomeini was often understood in the popular imagination (Dekmejian 1995). However, prior to the end of the world and the Last Judgement there will be a turbulent period marked by confusion, chaos and collapse. This will culminate with the arrival of Gog and Magog accompanied by the Antichrist. They encounter a force for good in the form of Jesus or the Mahdi, or both. After a fierce fight Jesus pierces the Antichrist with his spear and kills the unbelievers. After the victory of the forces of light against the forces of darkness and chaos, order is restored and harmony and justice returned in the form of a vaguely formulated Kingdom of God (cf. Mendel 2008).

Some Islamists believe that it is their religious duty to participate in this *cosmic conflict* that is forthcoming or already underway on the side of God, i.e. on the side of good against the forces of evil. Some Islamists even believe it is their duty to provoke a cataclysm or at least speed up its arrival, since this will hasten the Second Coming of Jesus (or the Mahdi), the Last Judgement and the longed for establishment of God's reign, a kind of Muslim "end of history". Activists expect their sins to be forgiven in return for their sacrifice and to go straight to heaven after their death (Juergensmeyer 1994, 2000). The last to achieve success among some of population of the Middle East with this propaganda was Islamic State in Iraq and Syria (ISIS), which promises a Last Battle between the forces of good, represented by Islamic militants, and evil. According to the tradition of the Prophet this Armageddon is supposed to take place not far from the Syrian city of Dabiq (McCants 2015)

The *interaction* of the negative impacts of rapid urbanisation with the *religious and conservative environment* of the contemporary Middle East and its *Islamic imaginary* (jahiliyya, fitna, eschatology) culminates in a moralistic reflection on and criticism of the expanding cities. This is expressed using the language and concepts of Islam, though often involving intellectual *innova-tion* and an *invented tradition*, an example of which would be the term *modern jahiliyya*, a concept created by the secular intellectuals Qutb and Maududi in the 20th century. This type of invention of tradition is common among Islamists, and approximately 8% of their key concepts represent innovations or neologisms that are not based on classical Islam. And while the remaining concepts are indeed based on classical Islam and its political theory, their meanings are often subject to semantic shift (Mendel 2008: 208). As Hrair Dekmejian so aptly says (1995: 36): "The burden of history rests heavily on Islamic ideologues, who in the current critical context are trying to reconstruct the past in order to shape the future."

CULTURE SHOCK AND CONVERSION TO POLITICAL ISLAM

The biographical narrative of activists and leaders of moderate and militant Islamist movements sometimes features *culture shock* and a feeling of alienation upon arriving in the anonymous and hostile city. Often these luminaries come from rural, conservative and highly cohesive families and stable communities respectful of tradition. The identity crisis and culture shock wrought by leaving the rural community and arriving in an unknown city prompts them to join Islamist organisations. This is so, for instance, in the case of radicals fighting the regime of the Egyptian President Anwar al-Sadat (Ibrahim 1980). However, the life narratives of the founders and leaders of many moderate Islamist movements feature similar tropes. This applies, for instance, to the Pakistani Abul Al´a Maududi, the Egyptian al-Banna, the Sudanese Hasan Al-Turabi, the leader of the Algerian Islamic Salvation Front Ahmad Madani, or the head of the Tunisian Ennahda movement Rachid Ghannouchi. These personalities grew up in a conservative, religious and rural or peripheral environment, but studied and spent the rest of their lives in radically different secular, materialistic and highly westernised urban environments.

For these freshly arrived migrants with one foot firmly in the rural tradition the city necessarily appeared immoral and corrupt. They were aware of the *contradictions* between the social control of the village and the moral laxity of the city, the contradictions between Islamic ethics and the real conduct of people and their social organisation. Part of the *conversion pattern* to political Islam was a dawning awareness of the social and political dimension of Islam. This shift was a reaction to the ubiquitous schizophrenic discrepancy between religion and reality. All it took was the environment of the city to effect a transformation from the apolitical, conservative, ritualistic and unexamined Islam of the peripheries into an activist Islamism with a strong social and political charge. This has to be studied, thought about, developed and finally disseminated and applied (Hoffman 1995). A similar process of religious conversion on the *micro-level of individuals* is being played out within the context of socially sensitive religion on the *macro-level of entire social classes*. For this reason, the newly urbanised segments of the population represent the target group of Islamist ideology (Dekmejian 1995).

This pattern played a significant role especially during the formation of the religious and political identity of the *first generation* of urban migrants and the first generation of the Islamist movement. The second and third generations, already born and bred in the city, experienced and formed their identity differently. It is also important to point out that the pattern applies most strongly to *individualised* migration to cities, during which students or small groups of workers leave their village alone, leaving their families behind. The pattern is weaker in the case of the migration of entire families, tribes or rural communities to the city. These bring their subculture and social support network with them. They are surrounded by family and acquaintances and protected against the worst impacts of life in an anonymous city. I also believe that sharp criticism of the moral corruption of the city played a more important role in the *initial phases* of the creation and rise of the Islamist movement, when the environment of post-colonial cities was more secularised and westernised and therefore capable of more dramatically injuring the moral sensitivities of conservative individuals. Since that time civic public space has become more accommodating to Islam; more women veil themselves, drivers and firms put the Quran on display as a sign of trustworthiness, and people are not afraid to pray ostentatiously. Finally, it seems that it is the transition from countryside to megacity that provokes culture shock and moral outrage. In the case of Egypt, for instance, this entails migration from the rural Upper Egypt to Cairo or Alexandria. The reaction is weaker in the case of migration from the countryside to small or medium-sized towns, which is a new trend in the urbanisation of certain Middle Eastern countries.

(12) THE TRADITIONAL BIPOLARITY OF URBAN AND RURAL ISLAM: A DISTURBED BALANCE

The mass exodus to cities currently resulting in the urban population outnumbering the rural population for the first time ever led to a definitive deviation from the hundred-year-old delicate balance between the two basic and mutually antagonistic poles of Islam: from a diverse rural folk Islam and apolitical mystical Sufism in favour of an orthodox urban fundamentalism or, as we see today, an ever more political Islam (Hodgson 1974, Gellner 1983).

Islam was born in the urban environment of Mecca and Medina and cities gradually became centres of congregational religiosity emphasising strict ritual, piety modelled on the Prophet's community, religious and legal erudition, a literal understanding of the Quran, and strict orthodoxy. A focus on the city was also important in the historical development of Christianity and Judaism (Lapidus 2002). In contrast, folk Islam and Sufism predominated in the Middle East from at least the 11th century to the 1960s. During this long period it played a key role as a kind of vanguard during the geographical and social dissemination of Islam to its geographical periphery and among hitherto non-Islamised classes and segments of the population. Only then did a stricter Islamic orthodoxy begin slowly to penetrate this pre-prepared substrate with varying degrees of success. Rural folk Islam gets on very well with pre-Islamic traditions and alien religious elements. In its innumerable local variants, folk Islam is fully capable of tolerance and integration. This is why to this day folk Islam in Egypt pays respect to the wells and trees inherited from the pre-Islamic era. Likewise there still exists a mystical Islam inspired by elements of Indian Hindu culture. Folk Islam produces with similar ease various local cults centred on holy men, religious pilgrimages to their graves, superstitious practices for healing the sick and many different versions of mysticism practiced by the Sufi order often on the very boundaries of polytheism, apostasy and heresy (Arjomand 1986, 1995).

The long history of Islam can thus be written as the struggle of both its poles, as well as periodical but futile attempts by fundamentalist movements, to cleanse once and for all the only true revelation of Islam of the sediments of human fabrication and delusion from the heads of people who are Muslims in name only. Folk Islam and Sufism have always therefore irritated strictly conceived Sunni orthodoxy because of their tendency toward heresy, though to this list we would have to add Shia Islam, Mahdism, rationalist philosophy, pragmatically based schools of law, and the latest secular ideologies[43]. At the same time the most vociferous critic of folk or mystical forms of Islam is the movement currently deemed Wahhabism or Salafism. This is a direction that is spreading from Saudi Arabia and regards itself as representative of the only true, non-corrupt orthodox Islam.

Only now is the mass dislocation of people from the countryside and peripheral regions under the influence of folk Islam and the local sheikhs of mystical brotherhoods to cities as traditional centres of Islamic orthodoxy

---

43 The famous medieval Arabic historian and philosopher ibnKhaldun (1972) also draws attention to a similar bipolarity of Islam and cyclical attempts at religious reform, though the city and periphery swap roles in his concept. A revivalist movement always arises from stoutly pious, moral nomads who regard their mission to be the rectification of the rich, materialist and degenerate city periodically falling from faith.

significantly skewing the balance of power and dynamising the traditional pattern of fundamentalist Islamic reform, and the conversion to and dissemination of Islam. While there has been a drop in Sufism and traditional folk Islam over recent decades because of the influence of urbanisation, religious orthodoxy has been celebrating success around the whole of the Islamic world (Arjomand 1995, 2004)[44].

(13) PEASANTS INTO ISLAMISTS: SOCIALISING FUNCTIONS AND SURROGATE RURAL COMMUNITIES

Urbanisation leads to the uprooting of people from their natural communities. The individual migrating to the city is torn from his unquestioned tradition according to the rules of which he has reached all his important decisions (whom to marry, how to live, what to believe in) and is faced with the necessity of reaching life decisions on his own. He may feel lonely, and so looks for a new collective and new guidelines for these decisions. In the anonymity of cities, Islamic civil society, Islamist movements and the apolitical Sufi Brotherhood act as a surrogate for rural or nomadic communities characterised by warm, interpersonal relations, a feeling of security and safety, a fixed social anchorage, clear authority, social control and mutual solidarity. Islamic civil society thus functions as a substitute for traditional rural primary groups. It socialises newly arrived migrants from the countryside and helps them to establish themselves in their new surroundings (cf. Chekroun 2005, Kropáček 1996). Middle Eastern urbanisation has therefore not destroyed the primary groups of community character but has led to their transformation, even renaissance, on a religious basis. A new arrival from the countryside is not left alone and at the mercy of an anonymous city (Fuccaro 2001, Zubaida 2009).

Religion can perform this function because it is a social phenomenon. Unlike individualised magic, religious rituals are always practiced in the company of other people and help establish and reinforce group cohesion, identity and solidarity (Weber 1998, Dürkheim 2002). Religion therefore meets not only psychological but also social needs, for instance the need to belong to a community in response to the feelings of alienation, abandonment and isolation experienced in an anonymous and fluctuating city. The rise of modern Christian and Islamic fundamentalism is therefore to a certain extent a reaction to urbanisation (Berger 1997). In this respect Islamic civil society performs a similar function to the municipal associations or secular

---

44 On the indestructible vitality and adaptability of rural and urban Sufism see Kropáček (2008, 2010).

political movements of the era of European urbanisation during the 19th and 20th centuries such as nationalism, fascism or communism (cf. Hamann 1996, Gellner 1993, 1995, Brzezinski 1993).

For instance, during just twenty years prior to the Iranian Revolution (1979) the urban population tripled (from five to fifteen million) and its share rose from one third to one half of the total population. This period also saw a revival in religion and a rise in the popularity of Islamism (Roy 1992). Religious associations of the *lay* faithful came into being that organised religious festivals in poorer neighbourhoods such as the month of Ramadan or the month of Muharram that commemorates the martyrdom of Imam Husayn (*ashura*). However, the associations also organised regular meetings outside the framework of religious holidays. In pre-revolutionary Tehran alone there were 12,300 such associations, the vast majority of which only came into being with the expansion of the city after 1965. Their social base comprised the lower middle classes of artisans and professions linked with the bazaar. They ranged from the "Religious Association of Cobblers and Shoemakers", the "Religious Association of Employees of Public Spas" to the "Religious Association of Street Vendors of Juices". Then came the masses of newly arrived migrants from the peripheries of rural provinces, a typical example of which would be the "Religious Association of Compatriots of the Natanz Region" and the "Religious Association of Natives of Semnan". These associations often provided the only and therefore crucial social activities for poor migrants from the countryside: "Nothing brings us together like our shared love for Imam Husayn. The association unites us and allows us to exchange information as to how people are getting on" (a new immigrant living in a Tehran slum at the end of the 1970s). These networks and associations were mobilised during the revolution against the secular dictatorship, even though their character had originally been apolitical (Arjomand 1986: 97).

The *mosque* became the social hub of the newly urbanised population. During the rapid urbanisation that took place in Tehran, the number of mosques rose at a faster rate than the number of people: over the course of fifteen years the number of mosques increased fourfold from 293 (1961) to 1,140 (1975). The situation was similar in Jakarta, Indonesia, where the number of mosques leaped from 460 (1965) to 1,186 (1979). The number of informal Quran schools and religious associations in cities also multiplied during the course of urbanisation in Turkey. The newly emerging professional associations of migrants supported religious activities. Even the activities of banned Sufi orders increased in Turkish cities along with urbanisation (Arjomand 1986).

Urbanisation can thus culminate in a revival of religion if, during the sensitive transition from rural community to anonymous city, said religion can offer a social function that people long for with new intensity (Hamilton

2001). Islamists offering a political Islam run within a community of "brothers" and "sisters" were able to effect a religious transformation from the Islam of traditional rural communities to its modern urban forms. Indeed, the Islamists failed wherever a majority of the population lived in the countryside and under the control of traditional family and the clerical and tribal authorities and structures (Kepel 2002).

However, through propaganda and the re-socialisation of members the Islamists themselves also actively contribute to the further erosion and disintegration of traditional structures and authorities (Roy 1992). Islamists are not only the effect but also the cause of the accelerating de-culturation of the Muslim masses during the process of modernisation, globalisation and urbanisation. They actively campaign against local Muslim cultures and traditions, and this contributes to the uprooting of Muslims from traditional structures. For instance, they object to the traditional division of Islam into law schools, folk Islam mixed with pre-Islamic customs, local cults of holy men and the traditional pilgrimages to their graves, local elders and non-Islamic customary law. The individual uprooted from their tradition becomes a tabula rasa. *Deculturation* is the prerequisite of new re-socialisation leading to acculturation and the acceptance of a new version of Islam (Roy 2004).

(14) FROM FOLK TO POLITICAL ISLAM: IDEOLOGICAL FUNCTIONS AND AN ORIENTATION FOR THE DISORIENTED

Every society must solve not only the problem of the social integration of its members, but also their meaningful orientation in the world. It therefore has to offer a sufficiently credible and intelligible explanation of why and how society operates and what the meaning of life is (Berger, Luckmann 1999). If society is not capable of this, there is a threat of *anomie*, in which the old interpretations of the world disintegrate without being replaced quickly enough by new ones (Keller 1997, Giddens 2009). In sociological terms early European urbanisation can be described as a state of anomie: "The harsh reality of rapid urbanisation and industrialisation shook the traditional societies of rural communities and small towns, firmly linked with their agricultural surroundings. The intellectual world of the Middle Ages, based around religious faith and the Catholic Church, definitively disintegrated. The normative system and the practical control mechanisms linked with it lost their effect within what was suddenly an unprecedentedly mobile population. However, new cultural patterns had still not been developed for the new method of organising labour and communities." (cited in Možný 1997: 28–29).

However, the impacts of rapid urbanisation are different in the Middle East. They are not leading to a strong sense of anomie. Urban Islam is managing to offer an ideological orientation to people arriving from the countryside in the radically new environment of a large city. It is providing people disoriented and uprooted from an intelligible, predictable rural environment they knew intimately a satisfying and comprehensible interpretation of the new world in which they live. The folk Islam of the village is being replaced by urban Islam, be this urban versions of mysticism, Salafism, Sunni orthodoxy or political Islam. It is political Islam, which reduces Islam to its political, social and economic aspects, that is asserting itself during the course of urbanisation because it resonates with the life experience of the urbanised classes.

In the urbanised classes the rural versions of religion are not being replaced by secular ideologies, something that took place to a certain extent in some European countries (cf. Huntington 1968, Brzezinski 1993). The ideological vacuum left by the decline of folk Islam is rapidly being filled by an urban version of Islam, including political Islam. Islam, therefore, is not on the retreat, as secularisation theses would have it, but is experiencing a revival since it is managing to perform a restored ideological function. What is crucial is the timing of Middle Eastern urbanisation, the culmination of which falls within a period in which secular doctrines are being discredited and are on the retreat (cf. Juergensmeyer 1994). A large global religion with an established doctrine has the potential to offer the dislocated masses an intelligible and credible "cognitive and moral map of the world and the universe". And it is managing this as effectively as secular doctrines (Arjomand 1986, Dekmejian 1995).

Islam is therefore performing both a *social* and an *ideological* function by satisfying the needs of masses dislocated by urbanisation, whom it assists in their new life situation (Hamilton 2001). Religion satisfies *social and psychological needs* that are becoming urgent in an era of rapid urbanisation, fast social change and the *pluralisation* of the world ensuing therefrom. People have to live in this complex world, a world they are unable to understand. They long to decipher its meaning and find a direction (Berger 1997). Fundamentalist movements are a reaction to social changes linked with urbanisation. They offer a selective interpretation of religious tradition and innovation that they pass off as a return to the authentic Prophet's urban community in Mecca and Medina (Riesebrodt 2006).

CONCLUSION

FOUR MACRO-COMPARISONS OF MODERNISATION PATTERNS AND CHRONIC INSTABILITY IN THE MIDDLE EAST

In this section of the conclusion we will systematically examine four possible macro-comparisons of the post-colonial Middle Eastern pattern of the modernisation process using the theoretical model developed in the introductory chapter (see fig. 36).

Fig. 36 A model of Middle Eastern modernisation and its context: the interaction of independent variables

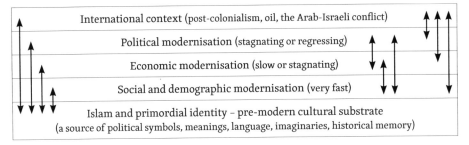

THE INCREASING UNEVENNESS OF POST-COLONIAL MIDDLE EASTERN MODERNISATION AND THE TIMING OF THE ARAB SPRING

The calculations and comparisons undertaken in this book show that instability in the Middle East today is a result of the uneven path of modernisation over the long term. The uneven pace of development of individual dimensions has increased over the last few decades. During the 1950s and 60s this tendency was not so pronounced. However, it gradually intensified and peaked at the start of the 21st century, i.e. a few years prior to the Arab Spring. Uneven modernisation therefore explains in part the timing of the Arab revolutions and the chronic post-revolutionary instability that has affected the whole of the region. What does a comparison of the individual phases of the Middle Eastern pattern of uneven modernisation teach us?

The degree of political repression has been consistently very high in the region since the 1970s, and in the 1990s increased still further. We can only plot the ability of states to govern in their own territory using the data available from the 1990s to the present, and during this period their ability was consistently low. The parameters of political regimes did not change much in time, and weak, repressive political systems were relatively rigid.

The pace of economic development has been very uneven over time. During the 1960s and 70s gross domestic product rose fast, peaking in the 1970s. The 1980s witnessed a sharp drop in the rate of growth, after which it picked up during the 1990s and first decade of the 21st century but did not return to its original level. A similar dynamic is visible in GDP per capita. With the exception of the 1980s, the rate of economic growth kept pace with that of population growth.

The rate of demographic growth was very dynamic. However, the dynamic changed over time, and gradually dropped as the region passed from the first phase (a rapid decline in mortality) to the second phase (a gradual drop in fertility rates) of the demographic transition. While the 1960s saw a rapid increase in population numbers that culminated in the 1970s, the tempo since has slowly but surely dropped. However, in terms of political instability the share of young people (aged 15–24) of the population as a whole is important, which from the start of the 1960s rose continuously until the end of the 1990s, after which it fell slowly so that the population centre of gravity began to shift to older generations during the first decade of the 21st century, i.e. to people in their late twenties and early thirties, which is the generation that rebelled during the Arab Spring.

The most dynamic dimension of modernisation was the social, which did not slow down over time but actually sped up in certain spheres (the expansion of universities and new media). Urbanisation increased from the beginning of the 1960s and its tempo only began to slow from the mid-1990s, by which time the vast majority of the population of the Middle East lived in cities. From the start of the 1970s onwards the literacy rates of the adult population and the proportion of children and teenagers attending primary and secondary school rose dynamically. The proportion of young people attending universities began to rise during the 1990s, and it was the graduates of these years that rebelled during the Arab Spring. By the end of the first decade of the 21st century the saturation of the traditional media (television and radio) was almost complete in the region, though new media (the internet and mobile telephones) also recorded huge gains during this decade.

Overall then we see that while repressive, weak regimes have not changed dramatically, economic development has been volatile and has gradually lost its dynamic. The rate of the population explosion has gradually fallen, the proportion of twenty and thirty years olds has increased, urbanisation has peaked, primary, secondary and now tertiary education has expanded, and the traditional and most recently the new media have expanded very quickly. As a consequence, developments in the political and economic system are coming into increasing conflict with demographic and above all social developments.

I consider this analysis, based on a comparison of the individual stages of the post-colonial Middle Eastern modernisation process, to form the premise of the argument running through the whole of this book. Other comparisons from various different perspectives also show that modernisation in the Middle East exhibits very specific qualities and is characterised above all by a high level of uneven development.

INTERNATIONAL COMPARISON: THE MIDDLE EAST AND OTHER POST-COLONIAL WORLD MACRO-REGIONS

How does the pattern of post-colonial Middle Eastern modernisation differ from that in other world macro-regions, above all post-colonial? The Middle Eastern pattern is characterised by an uneven, escalating rate of development in individual dimensions of social change. Since in other post-colonial regions the unevenness of development tends to drop over time, individual dimensions of social change manage to converge. Above all this has been due to democratisation during what is known as the third wave of global democratisation, higher economic growth over the last few decades, somewhat lower population growth (but not of the proportion of young people in the population), a lower long-term level of urbanisation, or a combination of all these four trends.

While the Middle East has remained under authoritarian rule since the 1970s, Sub-Saharan Africa, Asia and South America have experienced gradual and lasting democratisation since the start of the 1990s up to the present day. In addition, leaving aside Sub-Saharan Africa, Asia and Latin America have never been home to such repressive regimes as such, even if they have been non-democratic. As far as the ability of states and their institutions to govern is concerned, since the 1990s no particular trends have appeared. States in South America and Asia have been somewhat more effective and stronger than in the Middle East, which in turn have been more effective and stronger in comparison with Sub-Saharan Africa (it was not until the Arab Revolutions of 2011 that Middle Eastern states collapsed almost to the same level as Sub-Saharan Africa).

In terms of the basic trends of economic development as measured by GDP growth, all post-colonial world macro-regions reported a similar trajectory in individual decades: relatively fast growth during the 1960s and 70s, a slowdown in the 1980s and in some cases the 90s, but then a pickup in the rate of growth from the 1990s or the turn of the millennium. The Middle East stands out in that, while its growth during the 1960s and 70s was the highest in the world (i.e. not only in relation to other post-colonial macro-regions), during the 1980s the situation was upended and its rate of growth the lowest. Then during the first decade of the 21st century growth picked up somewhat and was higher than in South America, comparable with Sub-Saharan Africa, and lagged behind Asia.

As for the rate of demographic growth, this was highest in the Middle East. It was only in the first decade of the 21st century that it found itself on the same level as Sub-Saharan Africa and lower than that of Africa. However, the proportion of young people (aged 15–24) during the first decade of the 21st century was highest in Sub-Saharan Africa, and in other post-colonial regions, including the Middle East, it was comparable.

Finally, the Middle East differs to some extent by virtue of greater or faster social modernisation. For the duration of the period under examination the level of urbanisation in the Middle East has long been higher than in other post-colonial regions (perhaps with the exception of South America), while its rate has been comparable. The level and rate of the expansion of secondary and tertiary education is comparable with South America and higher than in Asia and especially Sub-Saharan Africa. Finally, the prevalence of the traditional media (television) in the Middle East is comparable with South America and considerably higher than in Asia or Sub-Saharan Africa. The prevalence of new media (the internet, mobile telephones) is comparable with South America and significantly higher than in Asia and especially in Sub-Saharan Africa. There is a significant trend in operation here: to begin with the new media spread relatively more slowly than in other post-colonial macro-regions, but accelerated during the first decade of the 21st century.

This comparative analysis shows, therefore, that Middle Eastern modernisation is a set of sub-processes that when combined result in highly uneven modernisation even in an international comparison: the most repressive regimes in which the most volatile economic growth, fastest demographic change (comparable only with Sub-Saharan Africa) and very fast social changes (comparable only with South America) are played out. As a consequence, modernisation in the Middle East is most uneven and the rate of development in individual dimensions of change is the least synchronised of all post-colonial micro-regions. This explains why it seems that instability in the region has grown in comparison with other macro-regions: we do not need to look to Islam or other supposed specificities of Arab culture.

HISTORICAL COMPARISON: THE MIDDLE EAST TODAY AND EUROPE OF YESTERDAY

There is also a historical comparison to be made between modernisation in the post-colonial Middle East and early modernisation in Western Europe. One of the central claims made by this book is that understanding the Middle

East better requires that we remember our own early modern history. In other words, the more we understand European modernisation, the better we will understand the process in the Middle East, since from the end of the 18th century to the start of the 20th century Europe underwent similar social and demographic processes accompanied by similar political destabilisation. So what in the way of similarities and differences can we find?

First off, while modernisation in the Middle East is currently accompanied by a crisis of most secular ideologies and the rise of various versions of political Islam, early European modernisation was accompanied by a similar escalation of social and political conflicts. However, these were manifest externally by the political language of dominant secular ideologies, while a conservative Christian ideology also played its role; from the French Revolution (1789) via the revolutionary year of 1848 to the arrival of socialism and heightened nationalism at the start of the First World War. However, this is simply a difference in the external ideological manifestations of social conflicts that were of a deeper structural nature.

Secondly, the post-colonial Middle East is full of states that have long been undemocratic and possessed a medium or low capacity to govern. The character of a political regime forms the character of the prevailing repertoires of political contention, which explains why the Middle East generates a high frequency of internal political violence (coups, terrorism, revolution, civil war). The character of the region's political regimes also explains one fundamental difference from the historical development of modernising Western Europe, where there was a gradual transition from weak, undemocratic states to strong, democratic states, accompanied by a slow reduction in the frequency of political violence and a transition to a mainly non-violent form of political contention.

Third, during European modernisation similar social and demographic changes took place: a population explosion and a rise in the proportion of young people, urbanisation, the expansion of education systems and media penetration. However, the rate of social and demographic change is far faster in the Middle East that it was in early modern Europe, where these changes took place more gradually and individual processes were spread over a far longer time frame.

Fourth: nevertheless, the development of the economies and especially the political systems of the Middle East seems to be taking place more slowly than it did in Western Europe, and so the overall unevenness of Middle Eastern modernisation is greater when compared historically with Europe. Although the main dimensions of Western European modernisation also featured unevenness, this was not as pronounced and there was a *stronger link* between rapid social, demographic and economic change (the industrial, scientific and technological revolutions) and political change (the creation of centralised states respecting the rule of law, democratisation). Nevertheless, the politically destabilised post-colonial region of the Middle East is more reminiscent on a *structural* level with its less uneven, Western European counterpart with all its secondary and unintended social and political consequences, than with the European Middle Ages.

Fifth: the geopolitical context of Middle Eastern modernisation is extremely unfavourable in a historical comparison with Europe. Modernisation is taking place on the post-colonial global *periphery* and not at the core of the world system during an era of global colonial expansion, as it was in the case of Western Europe. It was this, for instance, that permitted European colonies in America, Australia, Asia and Africa to absorb the increased numbers of European citizens resident in metropolises caused by population growth. The migration of Europeans to non-European continents effectively let the steam off the accumulating social and political tension in Europe and reduced instability. Another problem relates to the fact that modernisation in the Middle East is taking place within artificially, weak, post-colonial states created by fiat of the European powers during the era of European colonialism, and today's politically awakened population does not completely identify with these states. Finally, a negative role is also played by the existence of significant exportable sources of oil, which distorts the local political systems towards authoritarianism and economic systems towards non-productive rentier economies, and results in the political, diplomatic and military involvement of the superpowers in an already fragile peripheral region. These factors, linked with the historical and geopolitical context of Middle Eastern modernisation, also contribute to the destabilisation of the region.

Finally, a cultural context characterised by the dominance of Islam, which in the case of early European modernisation was obviously absent, operates ambivalently. We *cannot* therefore say that Islam, with its imaginary and institutions, represents a definite factor of political instability distinguishing the Middle Eastern pattern of modernisation from that of the West. Within the context of the region's uneven modernisation Islam is often a stabilising factor. The stabilising potential of Islam and its institutions is seen clearly within the context of the region's urbanisation, a process in which the religion helps maintain normative and social order and restore a feeling of security among the displaced masses. Without Islam, Middle Eastern modernisation would in all likelihood be accompanied by far greater anomie.

REGIONAL COMPARISON: THE MODERNISATION OF MIDDLE EASTERN COUNTRIES AND THE ARAB SPRING

How does the unevenness of the post-colonial modernisation process differ between individual countries within the Middle East? What would a comparison of Arab and non-Arab countries in the region, especially Turkey and Iran, reveal? And can the degree of political stability or instability of individual countries, e.g. during the course of the Arab Spring, be explained by the differing degrees of unevenness of the modernisation process? And can a typology of Middle Eastern countries be created on this basis?

As far as characterising political regimes is concerned, up until the Arab Spring it was possible to divide Arab countries into four basic types. First off, relatively less repressive states with a relatively low capacity to govern: republican Lebanon and monarchical Morocco. Secondly, relatively less repressive states with a relatively high capacity to govern, i.e. monarchical Kuwait and Jordan. Thirdly, highly undemocratic states with a relatively high capacity to govern: the small oil monarchies of the Gulf, i.e. Bahrain, Oman, the United Arab Emirates and Qatar. However, republican Tunisia also belongs here. And fourthly, highly undemocratic states with a relatively low capacity to govern: republican Iraq, Sudan, Yemen, Algeria, Libya and Syria, i.e. republics often teetering on the brink or beyond of civil war. Republican Egypt and monarchical Saudi Arabia are outliers: highly undemocratic states with a medium capacity to govern. It should be said here that in its endeavour to develop a typology of mutually differing Middle Eastern countries, this comparison somewhat overstates the real differences between political regimes. As far as the degree of repression is concerned, they are relatively similar and, perhaps with the exception of Lebanon and Kuwait (hybrid regimes), they are all authoritarian.

From this analysis we see that the hypothesis of a differentiation being possible between Arab countries on the basis of whether they are republics deemed to be unstable within the context of the Arab Spring, or monarchies deemed stable because of different models of legitimacy, must be at least partially revised. Revolutions did not take place in the least repressive Arab countries, i.e. in monarchical Kuwait, Morocco and Jordan and in republican Lebanon. Conversely they took place in the most repressive countries, i.e. Syria, Libya and Tunisia, as well as in the relatively repressive Egypt, Bahrain and Yemen. The group of more repressive monarchies with a relatively high capacity to govern (Saudi Arabia, Qatar, the Emirates, Oman) was able to avoid regime change thanks to a combination of repressive measures taken by a relatively strong, functioning state, and massive economic resources, using which they increased subsidies and created new jobs. Conversely, the group of less repressive monarchies (Morocco, Jordan, Kuwait) reacted to rebellion with dialogue, the co-opting of protesters, and partial top-down political reform.

In terms of economic development, from the start of the oil boom onwards the Middle East has represented a relatively heterogeneous "multi-speed" region. The following countries have long been ranked among low-income Arab economies as measured by GDP per capita of up to USD 3,000 (in ascending order): Sudan, Yemen, Egypt, Syria, Iraq and the relatively dynamic Morocco and Jordan. Among middle-income economies measured by GDP per capita up to USD 10,000 we find Algeria, Tunisia (posting the highest long-term growth figures), Lebanon and Libya. High-income countries include Oman, Saudi Arabia, Bahrain (these three countries have a different dynamic but approximately the same level of income), Kuwait, the United Arab Emirates and the wealthiest country Qatar. If we were to simplify this comparison still further, we could say that most of the smaller and less populated states of the Gulf with large oil reserves have fared better macro-economically over the long term. Conversely, densely populated states without significant oil reserves have been worse off.

As far as demographic developments are concerned, the highest rate of population growth has long been reported by certain rich oil monarchies of the Gulf, i.e. Qatar, the United Arab Emirates and Kuwait, as well as poorer Syria or the extremely poor Yemen. Conversely, the lowest rates of population growth (in ascending order) are reported by Tunisia, Morocco, Lebanon, and Algeria. Other states report a moderately fast rate (within the context of the region) of population growth (in ascending order): Iraq, Jordan, Saudi Arabia, Bahrain, Sudan, Libya, Egypt and Oman.

In terms of urbanisation, the highest level (more than 90% of the population living in the cities) is to be found in the small city states of the Gulf, i.e. Kuwait, Qatar, Bahrain and the United Arab Emirates, as well as in wealthier countries such as Lebanon, Saudi Arabia and Libya. A relatively high level of urbanisation is also to be found in Oman and Jordan (more than 80%), while the lowest is to be found in the poorest countries Yemen and Sudan. Regarding the expansion of education systems, the least developed are those in poorer countries such as Sudan, Yemen and Morocco. The most advanced are in the rich countries of the Gulf and also in Libya, Tunisia and Lebanon. Over the last fifty years these countries have also seen the fastest expansion of the educated population. Finally, above average user ratings of different media (television, newspapers, the internet) prior to the revolutions were typical for Tunisia, Libya and Egypt. However, similarly high ratings are to be found in most of the oil monarchies of the Gulf, where with the exception of Bahrain revolutions did not take place. Conversely, below average exposure of populations to media content is typical of pre-revolutionary Yemen and Syria.

On a very general level we can say that the social dimension of modernisation (urbanisation, the development of education systems, and expansion of the media) is linked to the economic development of a given country. These two dimensions of the modernisation process are relatively interconnected, though we will leave to one side the question of causality. The level of socio-

Fig. 37 Socio-economic development of Arab countries 1980–2014 (Human Development Index)

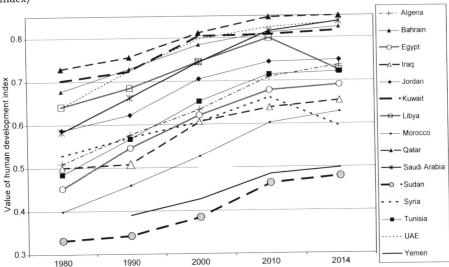

N.B.: The Human Development Index (HDI) is a composite statistic of life expectancy, education, and income per capita indicators. Countries are ranked from 0 (least advanced) to 1 (most advanced).
Source: UNDP

economic development is reliably and clearly and intelligibly expressed by the human development index, which examines economic progress, educational level and the infant mortality of a society. It is also assumed that this index correlates closely with a range of other dimensions of social development, including those used in this book.

The most advanced Arab countries with a relatively high quality of life according to the human development index tend to be the less populated oil states (in the following order): Qatar, Emirates, Kuwait, Bahrain, Saudi Arabia and Libya. They are closely followed by relatively advanced countries: Oman, Lebanon and Jordan. The least advanced countries with the slowest rate of development are Sudan and Yemen, followed by Morocco, though the last is experiencing relatively dynamic socio-economic development. The fastest socioeconomic development between 1980 and 2010 took place in Tunisia, Egypt, Saudi Arabia and probably Oman (reliable data is lacking for this country) (see fig. 37).

Still on the general level, we can say that the socioeconomic dimension of modernisation is linked to the capacity of individual states to govern effectively within their territory: the higher the level of socioeconomic development, the greater the capacity to govern (see fig. 38). These two dimensions

Fig. 38 Socio-economic development and the capacity to govern of Arab state institutions 2006–2010

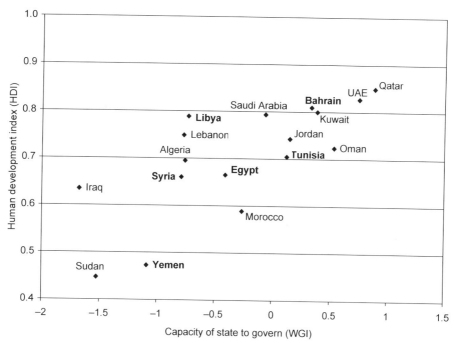

N.B.: The arithmetic average of indices 2006–2010. The author's calculations. The states written in bold experienced revolution or civil war during the Arab Spring.
Source: UNDP, World Bank.

of the modernisation process are relatively interconnected in the Middle East and there are no disproportionate discrepancies. We will again leave the question of causality to one side.

However, in many countries an important structural contradiction can be seen in a *high level* of socioeconomic development accompanied by a very high degree of ongoing authoritarianism: relatively *modern*, prosperous societies are governed by rigid, closed authoritarian regimes (see fig. 39). This mainly involves oil-exporting Libya and the oil monarchies of the Gulf, with the exception of the relatively freer Kuwait. However, revolutions did not break out in most of these countries even though according to our structural model they should have been the most destabilised and prone to various forms of political violence. With the exception of Bahrain, highly polarised along religious lines where the minority Sunnis control the majority Shiites, and Colonel Gaddafi's Libya, highly polarised along tribal lines where approximately three tribes control the remaining almost two hundred tribes, all the other regimes distributed significant oil rent in such a way as to ensure the loyalty

Fig. 39 Socio-economic development and degree of authoritarianism of Arab states 2006–2010

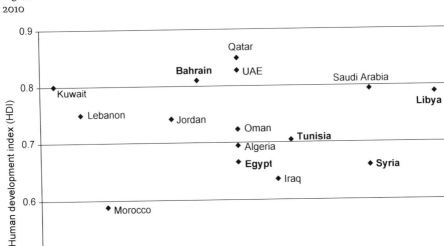

N.B.: The arithmetic average of indices 2006–2010. The author's calculations. The states written in bold experienced revolution or civil war during the Arab Spring.
Source: Freedom House, UNDP.

of the majority of the population. They have therefore avoided destabilisation up till now by virtue of being states with a relatively high capacity to govern and especially because they have extensive economic resources at their disposal that they distribute strategically among the population.

Second, an important structural contradiction relates to highly repressive states over long periods of time where over the last few decades there has been a *high rate* of socioeconomic change: rapidly *modernising*, increasingly prosperous societies are governed by rigid, closed authoritarian regimes (see the graphs). This is true especially of Tunisia, Egypt and Saudi Arabia, and to a lesser extent of Algeria and possibly Oman. However, again we see that destabilisation only resulted in revolution in two of these countries, while Saudi Arabia, Oman and to an extent Algeria were able to use their oil revenue to placate their populations. In addition, the Algerian regime was able to use the population's worries regarding a repetition of the civil war that followed the experiment in democratisation during the 1990s. However, structural causes of destabilisation are present in these countries.

Third, the most stable countries should, on the other hand, be those Arab countries where the structural disconnect between the rate of political and socioeconomic change is smallest. This includes Kuwait and Lebanon, which are relatively highly developed countries with relatively open political regimes by the standards of the Arab world. The rate of socioeconomic and political change has long run in parallel: the demographic, social and economic changes taking place in these relatively prosperous countries are not dramatic, and political rights and civil liberties are being promoted. However, Lebanon's structural problem is the state's low capacity to govern, lower than would correspond to its socioeconomic development (see the graphs). This group would, with reservations, still include Jordan and Morocco. By the standards of the Arab world Morocco is a less repressive regime that slowly but surely over the last twenty years has opened itself up and democratised. And within this relatively favourable political framework lives a relatively underdeveloped society that, however, is developing quite rapidly. The pace of socioeconomic and political modernisation is therefore relatively compatible. In contrast, Jordan is already quite socioeconomically developed, with a lower rate of socioeconomic change and a less repressive regime. However, Jordan's problem is the long-term trend to restrict what at one time were quite respectable political rights and civil liberties, a trend that has continued since the 1990s. This has created a tension between the rate of socioeconomic and political development (see the graphs). We see that, though there was unrest and demonstrations in these four countries during the Arab Spring, there were no revolutions or civil wars. These are therefore stable or at least stabilised countries by Arab standards (see Lebanon).

Overall we see that structural explanations using the concept of uneven modernisation are only partially able to differentiate between Arab countries that have experienced revolution and those that have managed at least in part to avoid revolution. The theory can be used to explain the course of political development in individual countries during the Arab Spring as one of the bases of detailed case studies that, however, must also take into account the specific historical, geopolitical and cultural features of each state and the different constellations and dynamics of the political actors and their coalitions, including patterns of regime legitimacy.

MECHANISMS OF DESTABILISATION: FROM MACRO TO MICRO, FROM STRUCTURES TO ACTORS

I will now attempt to summarise briefly the individual mechanisms identified by which uneven modernisation generates political instability in the Middle East. I will use the theoretical model as a general framework.

Fig. 40 Relationship between the macro and micro levels: from structural change to the actions of individuals

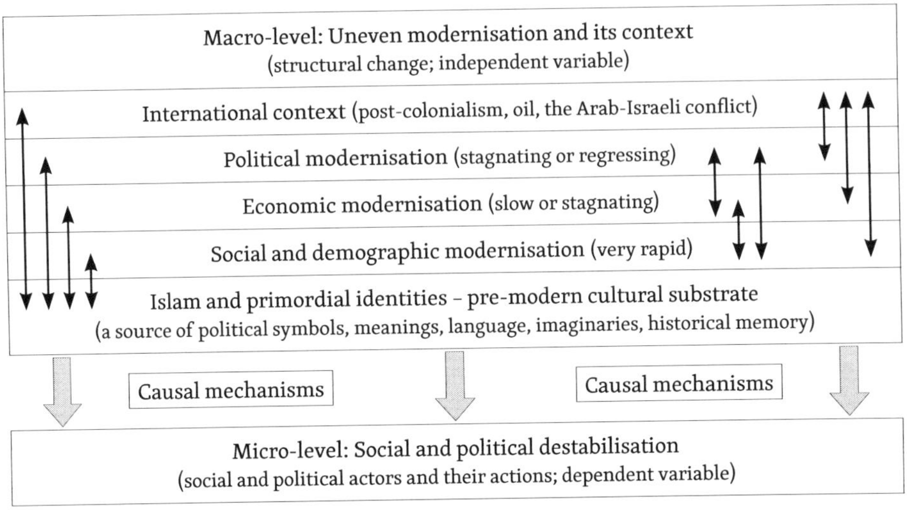

THE POLITICAL SYSTEM: RIGID, DECLINING, HIGHLY AUTHORITARIAN REGIMES

Middle Eastern regimes feature the worst combination of the two basic dimensions of political systems: weakness combined with authoritarianism. A citizen living in such a country cannot rely on a weak, dysfunctional state being able to ensure even the most basic functions and services (security, health, education and infrastructure). On the contrary, he can be assured that the state will not respect the equality of all citizens before the law, will suppress his civil liberties and restrict his political rights.

The escalating tension between rigid, disintegrating and highly repressive political systems with a far higher dynamic of change in demographic, social and economic subsystems of modernising Middle Eastern societies, as well as within their broader geopolitical, religious and cultural context, then generates social instability. What specific mechanisms have we identified that lead to this?

First off, socio-economic modernisation gradually transforms a traditional and apolitical population into a modern and politically mass mobilised population. Socioeconomic modernisation gradually generates new political actors: an intelligentsia, a middle class comprising the liberal professions and employees of expanding state institutions (bureaucracy, the army, education, the health service), students, workers, the urban poor and finally the peasants. In addition, a demographic revolution means that there are more of these new political actors in absolute terms. The mass arrival of hitherto traditional populations on the political scene represents a historically new situation and a fundamental challenge to a regime: politics is no longer the preserve of a narrow political elite alienated from the rest of apolitical society and at most called upon from time to time to engage with a similarly isolated and small counter-elite that threatens to take over. Mass political mobilisation thus comes into conflict with rigid, closed and authoritarian regimes. These are unable to offer institutionalised and established non-violent methods of resolving the proliferating conflicts between groups representing different interests and ideologies. They attempt to suppress conflict, but are not completely successful, because aside from being authoritarian, they also possess a low or medium capacity to govern and assert policy within their own territory. At the same time such regimes have excluded the vast majority of their populations from political systems and political participation. The inability to co-opt new political actors into the political system represents a basic source of political tension and destabilisation in the post-colonial Middle East. The majority of the politically mobilised society is excluded from the political system, and so turns against the regime instead of participating within its framework. This mismatch between the pace of political and socioeconomic change deepens over time. While political systems have been repressive over a long period of time, there has been a relatively rapid demographic transition and socioeconomic modernisation. The result is that different forms of mass political violence are more frequent: terrorism, revolution and civil war. Political violence can be interpreted as a continuation of politics by other means in a situation in which non-violent means of participating in politics are unavailable to the majority of the population. We do not need Islam or "Arab culture" in order to explain this mechanism of destabilisation.

Second, the character of Middle Eastern regimes generates political instability in itself. The consequence of the long-term repression initiated by colonialism and continued by the post-colonial authoritarian governance is the blocking of the development of a political culture based on discussion, tolerance, compromise and participation. An authoritarian political culture and a tendency to political violence on the part of all interested actors, both government and opposition, is thus not the consequence of the historical character of Islam but of modern politics. Arab regimes are confronted by exactly the opposition they deserve, since the political methods of the opposition are determined by the political methods of those in power far more than by religion, culture or ideology. For instance, the state terror of repressive regimes and the terrorism of militant Islamist factions, split off from the mainstream of opposition Islamists, feed off and reinforce each other. This is a perverse symbiosis that regimes draw on in order to justify their power by self-profiling in the role of indispensable defenders of their own people and the international community against terrorism. However, they themselves generate this very terrorism by virtue of their everyday functioning.

Third, there is a disconnect between the clearly pro-democratic and somewhat conservative *preferences* of public opinion in the Middle East and the *reality* of the despotic, "godless" regimes. The consequence is a subjectively perceived democratic deficit and a strong demand for the implementation of constitutional liberal principles and democratic institutions. However, though the chasm between pro-democratic preferences and political reality may be the largest in the world, the Middle Eastern public cannot agree on whether it wants Islamic or secular democracy. The public prefers conservative social values, especially as regards gender relationships and the role of women in society, and lays an emphasis on piety, domestic culture and tradition. The demand for democracy is not accompanied by secularisation and the population remains very religious and relatively conservative. This conflict can be interpreted as a mismatch between rigid, authoritarian regimes and dynamic socioeconomic change generating a modern public and modern public opinion. It is escalating in time as Middle Eastern societies become more and more modern along with intergenerational replacement (the mechanism of "silent revolution"). However, it also involves a tension between rigid regimes and the pre-modern cultural substrate in the form of Islam, the influence of which leads to a preference for conservative values. The greater the mismatch between values and political preferences on the one hand, and political reality on the other, the greater the potential for instability. If public opinion and political reality could be brought into alignment, this would lead to stabilisation.

Fourth, there is a conflict between the moralising political dimension of Islam and the repressive, decadent, corrupt and "godless" reality of Middle Eastern regimes. A political reading of Islam offers a host of black-and-white, highly moralising dichotomies, for instance *haram*/forbidden versus *halal*/permissible, or *jahiliyya*/the age of barbarity versus *hakimiyya*/God's sovereignty. However, these are often invented terms and traditions, unknown in classical Islam, through the prism of which current dictatorships can be discredited and an attractive alternative offered in the form of the ideal Islamic state. Similarly, they can be used to discredit current societies, Islamic in name only, and offer an alternative in the form of an ideal Islamic community. Finally, they can be used to discredit dictators themselves by contrasting their personalities and control methods with the unattainable model of the Prophet Muhammad, offering an attractive alternative in the form of a ruler carefully selected to match the ethical profile and erudition of the Prophet. The benchmark against which existing regimes, societies and dictators are measured is the reign of the Prophet Muhammad in Medina and the idealised rule of the first four rightly guided Caliphs. Early Islam is seen as a golden age, whose principles remain, however, binding upon the present. However, no actually existing regime can attain such an ideal, and this discredits them all. Logically speaking, not even existing Muslim societies can attain such an ideal, and the result is a call for the re-Islamisation of Middle Eastern societies. The re-Islamisation of societies that have diverted from God (*Dar al-Kufr*) has the capacity to satisfy God. God's satisfaction with man is supposed to lead to only the best people governing, and not the worst, as at present. Islam thus plays a destabilising role by virtue of the fact that its political imaginary helps discredit existing corrupt and dysfunctional regimes and calls for a radical socio-political transformation. However, what is important here is not simply a specific interpretation of Islam, i.e. a political reading, but also a critical interpretation of the political reality inspired by such political readings of Islam.

Fifth, the interaction of the religious imaginary and political reality can result in a reading of the world as a place where cosmic war is raging, an implacable, uncompromising and metaphysical conflict between good and evil, light and darkness, God and Satan. Within this metaphysical framework, authoritarian regimes are understood as forces fighting on the side of evil. Opposition challengers see themselves as fighting in defence of good, as employing proportionate self-defence in the face of advancing evil, with which compromise is impossible, but which must be destroyed. This then allows for the use of violent methods of resistance against the regime. This resistance is taken to be a religious duty.

Six, the interaction of the historical imaginary and political reality can lead to a similar reading of the world as a place where legendary historical battles fought by members of particular religious communities in the past are still being fought and even reaching their apex. Within this historical framework corrupt rulers are regarded as successors of the fallen caliphs, barbarian Mongols and godless Crusaders. Opposition challengers then regard themselves as the successor to historical heroes and defenders of the legacy of the great religious and political reformers. In the case of both mechanisms of destabilisation there is an interaction between the bleak reality of political regimes and the imaginary derived from Islam or the historical memory. This is not simply a specific interpretation of Islam or history, but a critical interpretation of social and political reality.

Seven, during the post-colonial period there was a gradual decline of the secular ideologies of Western or Soviet provenance that had predominated for several decades. The ensuing ideological vacuum began to be filled during the 1970s by political Islam, which alongside revolutionary Marxism became the main challenger to republican and monarchist regimes, self-profiling as a domestic, authentic and intelligible alternative. This again involves the interaction between the dynamic of the post-colonial development of Middle Eastern regimes and Islam. This contains a significant political, economic, legal and social dimension and therefore in the event of political and ideological crisis can be seized upon as an alternative and comprehensive ideological doctrine. Originally popular secular doctrines aroused high expectations of the early arrival of justice and prosperity. However, the manifest failures of the regimes that promoted these doctrines resulted in disappointment, the rejection of secular models and the search for functional alternatives. The decline in the attractiveness of secular ideologies was exacerbated by the following: the military defeats of their most important Middle Eastern protagonists; the historical origin of these ideologies and their implementation by foreign colonial superpowers from a position of power; their promotion by post-colonial regimes recruiting from minorities with no respect for the opinions of the conservative minded majorities; and the exhaustion and decline of the appeal of the USSR and the West.

Eight, the post-colonial Middle East became the graveyard of political ideologies. Following the collapse of the caliphate, both interwar liberalism (Egypt, Lebanon) and militant secularism (Turkey, Iran) were gradually discredited, along with post-colonial Arab nationalism/socialism, pan-Arabism, Marxism and even Islamism. In heterogeneous and highly divided societies (Libya, Lebanon, Iraq), democracy was the most recent ideology to be questioned, which contributed to the collapse of these states. The chronic weakness of political ideologies is to be seen in the post-colonial character of Middle Eastern states rather than in the cultural character formed by Islam. The artificial and alien character of states means the population does not identify with them, and so identification with the state finds itself in competition with a strong identification with sub-state communities (the extended family, tribe, ethnic or religious group) or supra-state communities (pan-Arabic or pan-Islamic identities). The weaker the state, the stronger is the identification with these entities. This is the difference between political identities in modern Europe, where identification with nation states predominates. For this reason, modern political ideologies designed for application within the framework of nation states do not work well in the Middle East. However, what results after all ideologies have been discredited is a dangerous vacuum. The fact remains that neither people who need intelligible points of orientation in the world in order to feel safe and secure, nor elites that need to justify political and economic inequality to a subordinate population without relying simply on brute force and coercion, can live without a credible ideology. Regimes thus experience a crisis of legitimacy and societies a crisis of orientation in the world. The result of ideological vacuum is contingency and instability. It is not clear what will fill this vacuum, though what is certain is that everyone yearns for it to be filled.

Nine, discredited regimes suffering a crisis of legitimacy are increasingly turning from secularism to religion for a new source of legitimacy. In the short term this could assist with their stabilisation, but in the long term could on the contrary involve destabilisation. In their everyday functioning regimes are unable to live up to the strict moral criteria that they are propagating by resorting to religion. The unintended consequence of this policy is the ongoing promotion of an Islamic political discourse and the gradual re-Islamisation of society. Opposition groups are then able to ride the wave of this religio-political discourse when criticising regimes. This is a destabilising consequence of the interaction between the crisis of the political system and the attempt by regimes to exploit Islam to their own ends.

Ten, the attempts by regimes to co-opt Islamic clerics as the basis of their strategy to obtain religious legitimacy have similar effects. The traditional clerics become dependent employees of the state. They cease to fulfil their traditional function as the independent moral conscience of rulers when they stop encouraging them to act fairly to the community of believers and avoid at least the most egregious excesses. The collaboration of traditional clerics with power causes their authority in the eyes of believers to drain away. At this point Islamists and other lay interpreters of religion take over the function of moral arbiters, and this puts them in conflict not only with the regime but with the clerics. The erosion of the traditional religious authorities is part of the erosion of authority in general, and the absence of binding authority generates social instability.

Eleven, it is neither Islamic nor Arabic culture that is generating authoritarianism in the region, but oil or other forms of rent. The control of the profits from the export of oil or other raw materials assisted post-colonial regimes to become established and stable. However, over the long term oil rent and its highly unequal distribution in the population generates severe power, socio-economic and identity-based polarisation. Certain social circles are co-opted into the regime, while most are excluded from any share in power. The co-opted circles of power and their cronies then profit most from the redistribution of oil profits depending on how far they are from the first circle of power. Meanwhile, most of society is excluded from the distribution of oil wealth. This unequal division of power and petrodollars thanks to family-based cronyism also means that several groups based around clan, tribe, religion, ethnicity or region profit more from the system than others and some are excluded altogether. This results in a polarisation of power and class that mimics and consolidates the polarisation of tribal, ethnic, religion and regional groups. The power elite wants to hold onto its privileged position and so mobilises its clientele in its defence, whose network copies the tribal, regional or religions segmentation of society. This was how the stability of rentier regimes was usually explained, i.e. through the support of a loyal social base of particular groups. However, tribal, ethnic and religious groups excluded from power and oil profits may attempt to change the disadvantageous constellation. They mobilise themselves politically not only by appealing to shared interests, but also to their shared tribal, regional or religious identity as an excluded social segment. Particular identities then contribute to the internal cohesion and solidarity of those groups in power but also those in opposition. The result is an ambivalent mechanism that stabilises the regime, above all securing it against coups mounted by one of the many excluded social segments. However, in the long term this also destabilises the regime. Above all it generates the threat of revolution led by a broader coalition of excluded segments. This mechanism is the consequence of the complex interaction between mineral wealth, the connection to global oil markets, authoritarian regimes and pre-modern, primordial identities situated within the framework of artificial, post-colonial states.

Twelve, the power elites are alienated from the rest of the population not only because of their power, wealth and particular tribal, religious, ethnic or regional identity, but also because of their culture – an alien, westernised culture comprising a different education, lifestyle, dress, consumerism and language. This overlapping and multiplication of the different identities of both the privileged and non-privileged contributes to a potentially high intensity and violence of political conflict, to the credibility of the opposition's criticism, and to overall destabilisation. The post-colonial power elite is then seen as the main driver of a cultural westernisation that is being forced upon Middle Eastern societies from a position of power. In response, as well as advocating political and economic decolonisation, opposition groups emphasise the need for cultural decolonisation. They take this to be the culmination of the process of national liberation from Western cultural and intellectual dominance by means of a return to a supposedly authentic domestic culture with its values and traditions and an attempt at a new synthesis of domestic and Western influences. This mechanism is the result of the interaction between the domestic cultural substrate and the international context in the form of the historical penetration of Western culture, which, however, is taking place within the context of political contention between (more westernised) privileged and (less westernised) non-privileged groups and within the context of the decline of the legitimacy of the power elite.

Thirteen, the significant resources allocated to the army also contribute to the unequal division of economic resources amongst small segments of the population loyal to the regime. Political control of the army then systematically generates social segmentation and polarisation. This is the result of three basic mechanisms by which the army is co-opted. Firstly, as an important crony of the power elite the army receives a large share of the rent redistributed in the form of generous military budgets. The second mechanism is the provision of economic privileges that allow the army to create an extensive economic empire. Officers redirect their ambitions away from the political or military sphere and into business. This form of co-option is used above all by republics with fewer natural resources at their disposal. The third mechanism of co-option is the recruitment of officers and regular soldiers from specific tribal, regional, religious and ethnic groups, which increases the loyalty of these groups to the regime. This form of co-option is used mainly by regimes recruiting from a minority and controlling a majority (Syria, Bahrain, Jordan). However, to a certain extent most regimes combine all three approaches, which are aimed at ensuring the army has an vested interest in the survival of the regime. Although this assists in co-opting the army into the regime, it also contributes to the polarisation of society and the alienation of the regime from the rest of the population. The effort made by regimes to co-opt other groups linked to the army, though it contributes to stabilisation by successfully eliminating the incidence of military coups, in the long term creates favourable conditions for the emergence of nationwide discontent at social exclusion. Though regimes manage to co-opt certain segments of the population, they alienate the rest. This mechanism, by which the army is privileged, is due to a combination of rent and the existence of authoritarian regimes worried about military coups or recruited from minority groups of the population.

Fourteen, in the second half of the 20th century clienteles seized the reins of power of all Middle Eastern states, were parasitical on them, and used them to their own advantage and to the detriment of the majority. Resources are distributed among cronies rather than invested in education, healthcare, and infrastructure intended for everyone. Unlike traditional medieval or early modern clienteles, they have control over the centralised state and repressive apparatus. They also have the support of the West, are connected to global markets and have monopoles over rents, which then reinforce their power. However, the hypertrophied parasitism of a narrow elite, combined with the sharp polarisation of society into clans and clients, is a theme seized upon by opposition groups, including Islamists. Their ideal is a united *umma* of brothers and sisters derived from the principle of the oneness of God and his creation, including society (*tawhíd*). The current divisions within society remind them of the dangerous and inadmissible internal dissent (*fitna*) that is also contrary to Islamic social sensitivities. The multifaceted polarisation of society and the inequalities of a fragmented *umma* can be critiqued using the language of Islam, and this generates instability. This mechanism of destabilisation results from the interaction between an Islamic derived ethics and political systems based on cronyism leading to fragmentation and polarisation.

RAPID DEMOGRAPHIC CHANGE

The standout demographic feature of the Middle East over the last few decades has been the sharp rise in the population accompanied by an increase in the absolute number and proportion of young people within the population as a whole and the growing concentration of the population within the relatively small space that is realistically habitable within an arid region. This went on against the backdrop of insufficient emigration, which could have ameliorated the population overload. However, the destabilisation in the region is not only caused by the dynamic of demographic change alone. What is crucial is that the rate of population growth over the last few decades has not corresponded to the laggardly pace of economic growth or the negligible rate of change in rigid authoritarian political systems. By what specific mechanisms does this macro-constellation lead to political destabilisation?

First, young people always represent a potentially radical segment of society. If their numbers and proportion increase in society, then so does the potential for destabilisation. This is for many reasons. Young people are more willing to expose themselves to a higher level of personal risk because they have less experience of life than adults. Above all they are freer in their conduct because they do not yet have responsibility for large families or professional obligations. The crisis of adolescence and intergenerational conflict sees them struggling to find a place in the world, to identify an attractive worldview to be guided by, to acquire a feeling of belonging in society and in an attractive group that offers a source of self-respect, and also to find an attractive authority that would replace the shaky authority of parents. This demand can be met by different political movements whose target group tends to be these selfsame impressionable youngsters. Young people can also live the first part of their lives in an ungodly, immoral way, then may yearn to change things and find a deeper meaning: many religious and political movements offer the possibility of such a conversion (see the Malcolm X syndrome). However, in the Middle East the opposite pattern is just as common: the recruitment of perfectly ordinary young people from closely knit, religious, conservative and fully functional families that only when on the threshold of adulthood begin to think critically about the social and political dimension of Islam relegated to the background by their parents, and find many conflicts between these aspects of Islam and the unjust reality of the world in which they live. This mechanism is the consequence of the rapid demographic revolution and its interaction with the slower development of the economic subsystem and the cultural changes running in parallel. Young people do not simply represent a certain statistical category reflecting a particular age group. Adolescence is a social construct that only emerged during a certain period of societal modernisation and the prolongation of school attendance and the period of studies, combined with the forced post-ponement of what previously had been very early marriages because of the situation of graduates on the labour market and the increasingly frequent rejection of traditional marriages arranged by parents.

Second, just as the numbers and proportion of young people began grow-ing in the region, so did their leisure time. Leisure time can be a source of instability depending on whether it is unwanted, forced and frustrating, and on what activities it is filled by. The regimes have attempted without any great success to fill up leisure time with apolitical activities, while opposition groups opt more for political activities. This mechanism is the consequence of the rapid demographic revolution and its interaction with rigid political regimes that have been unable to react in good time and offer constructive, meaningful ways of using free time to young people.

Third, the aspirations of young people in the Middle East are in sharp contrast to the situation on the ground. Young people want to be involved in political, family and working life and want to contribute to their fami-lies, communities and the country as a whole. However, the up-and-coming generation is excluded from economic and political life, which is why a large number of them see no cause for optimism regarding the future given the current situation.

Fourth, the high levels of unemployment in the region are primarily a generational problem, affecting mainly the young generation. This important mechanism of destabilisation is the result of rapid demographic growth and the less dynamic pace of job creation. In addition, unemployment tends to af-fect the educated generation the most, since its qualifications have furnished it with higher career aspirations than previous generations. The frustration ensuing from the inability to find a suitable job is even greater. Everything is exacerbated by the mass entry of relatively well educated young women onto an already overstretched labour market, where they now compete with men. It is also exacerbated by the existence of a dual labour market on which the young, vulnerable generation is squeezed out and into the informal, grey economy, where it finds insecure, poorly paid and unattractive jobs without any legal protection or the possibility of improving qualifications and build-ing a career.

Fifth, there is a marriage crisis. Unlike their parents, the up-and-coming generation are not only failing to meet their professional aspirations, but also the traditional aspirations related to having a family. In conservative societies an individual's social status is derived from their family and children, regard-ing which there is a consensus that they represent the main aim and meaning of life (see point three above). The result is demographic marginalisation, i.e. the uncertain social status of young people who are no longer children but not yet adults. Young, single women especially are subject to stigmatisation.

The result is disaffection and radicalisation amongst young people. This interval between childhood and adulthood is growing and applies to more and more young people. It is the result of the demographic revolution accompanied by the slow pace of job creation within the context of conservative societies whose core values are centred on the family.

Six, the rapid demographic growth of the region is in conflict with its rigid political systems. This opens up yet further the abyss between overwhelmingly young populations and aging political elites. Both groups have different historical memories and employ a different model of communication, they speak at and not with each other and lack mutual respect. The authority of the political elites in the eyes of young population is declining.

Seven, the difference in the rate of population growth of particular ethnic or religious subpopulations living within the boundaries of highly heterogeneous and artificial post-colonial states can lead to a misalignment of the power balance up till now, and the distribution of power and wealth among subpopulations in the state is more and more at odds with the population weight of these individual subpopulations (typically Lebanon is heading towards civil war). This involves the interaction of a different phasing of demographic transition among different subpopulations with the context of this transition created by the existence of artificial post-colonial states.

THE EXPANSION OF OLD AND NEW MEDIA

The massive expansion of the media within society in itself always has a wide range of political repercussions. However, everything in the Middle East is complicated by the fact that the expansion of old and new media is taking place within the context of highly uneven modernisation and its broader international and cultural framework. By what mechanisms does the expansion of the media lead to social and political destabilisation in the Middle East?

First, the expansion of the media contributes to the creation of modern, well informed public opinion. Better informed on a range of issues, people now have their own opinions and are able to perceive the links between their own personal problems and national problems. They are also better able to imagine alternatives to the lives they lead and different ways that society as a whole could be organised. Their desire to implement these opinions can destabilise authoritarian regimes.

Second, the media allows for the simpler, faster dissemination of political ideas throughout a geographically dispersed population. Political and religious agitation is no longer dependent on the spoken word and face-to-face communication. The media makes it possible for hitherto isolated, dissatisfied individuals and groups to communicate and network, which in turn helps in the formation of larger social movements and political parties. At the same time the media allows such people to organise, mobilise and co-ordinate themselves for collective action more effectively. This mechanism was particularly evident during the Arab Spring and involved an interaction between the long held frustrations of the population ensuing from a strongly felt prosperity deficit and democracy deficit, a young, educated population, and new media able to bypass the censorship practiced by the regimes of the old media and serve up universally intelligible stories of the victims of state-sponsored brutality that the general public could identify with and that served as a catalyst of revolution.

Third, generally speaking the media leads to an increase in consumer, career and political aspirations by depicting the lives of members of reference groups. Either this or it presents an idealised image of life in foreign countries enjoying higher levels of wealth and liberty. In reality, however, realistic life opportunities lag behind the growing aspirations awakened by these media images and the result is frustration and discontent.

Four, the media provides information on inexcusably high levels of social inequality that has been concealed up till now by the fig leaf of state censorship and propaganda. This mechanism is the consequence of the inter-action of (new) media, social inequality and the social sensitivity of Islam, which lays an emphasis on solidarity and justice. People then question the legitimacy of economic inequality, which in the Middle East is usually closely linked with inequality of power, and this leads to the legitimacy of regimes as a whole being called into question.

Five, the media shrinks the world, and instead of discredited domestic models of the development and control of society, offers up a wide range of attractive models in the form of successful foreign countries. These days this does not refer simply to the West and the USSR (the bipolar world) or simply the United States (the unipolar world), but a host of successful de-veloping countries such as Indonesia, Malaysia, China and especially Turkey (the multipolar world), which are facing similar problems and challenges to the countries of the Middle East. A comparison of Middle Eastern countries with the more successful regions of the post-colonial world leads to domestic regimes being discredited, because they are shown to be unsuccessful not only in comparison with the West but with countries that were equally or even less developed a few decades ago. This comparison can then lead to an attempt being made to be inspired by foreign successes and models and to use them to fill the vacuum left by discredited domestic models.

Six, the internet and especially satellite television headed by Al Jazeera is helping to introduce to the region a democratic political culture based on tolerance, plurality and the free exchange of different opinions. It has formed a Middle Eastern pan-Arab media public that reacts to the important political events being played out in different parts of the region and not simply to those being played out within a person's own state.

Seven, the possibilities of media propaganda have been very effectively seized upon by the "new interpreters" of Islam, above all the Islamists. Their media output is often highly critical of the established social and political order. It both circumvents and comes into conflict with the traditional clerics.

Eight, the result of the interaction of the traditionally heterogeneous and interpretatively open Islam, a highly educated, active public, and the expansion of new media creating a new public sphere free of censorship is the emergence of a pluralistic religious market on which battles are fought over the interpretation of Islam and on which many new interpreters offer their own concepts. The authority of the traditional clerics is then eroded and their voice becomes simply one among many. They lose the monopoly they have enjoyed for hundreds of years on the dissemination and interpretation of Islam.

Nine, the increasing plurality of interpretations of Islam encouraged by the expansion of the media generates insecurity amongst some of the population. Fear of relativisation and interpretative freedom leads to an inclination in the direction of a single truth, to fanaticism in its advocacy, and to an intolerance of competing interpretations.

EXPANSION OF EDUCATION SYSTEMS

The expansion of education in the Middle East is not leading to a decline in religion and its retreat from the public sphere as the secularisation thesis predicts. On the contrary, against the backdrop of uneven modernisation the expansion of educational opportunities represents an important factor in the transformation, revival and re-politicisation of Islam, as well as an important factor in the growth of political activism, radicalisation and destabilisation. This might sound counterintuitive, since in the spirit of the Enlightenment we tend to regard education as a cure for problems and not as part of the problem itself.

First, the discontent of the population with the deteriorating quality of educational systems and the growing inequality of access to education leads to destabilisation. These two problems represent tangible, widely known evidence of the failure of Middle Eastern regimes and undermine their power. This mechanism is the consequence of the intensifying interaction of rapid demographic growth leading to a stretched education system, authoritarian regimes with a poor capacity to govern, and often the absence of financial resources because of insufficient economic growth.

Second, while to begin with the power elites were concerned that their populations would become overly educated and hence far harder to control, subsequently they began to worry more about a lack of education that would open their subjects to manipulation by dangerous religious and political leaders. And so they set education the same task as the military barracks and prisons, namely the control and mass discipline of individuals and society as a whole and the ideological refashioning of the individual into an obedient, loyal citizen. However, education opened up the possibility of the dissemination of opposition political ideologies within the wider population, and this then created the framework for mass political agitation, organisation and mobilisation for collective action. Furthermore, the longer people remained in education thanks to the expansion of opportunities to study, the more they were exposed to the operation of a variety of ideologies and movements. Paradoxically, then, the centre of resistance to the power elite became the very institutions supposed to discipline and supervise, i.e. the barracks, editorial boards and prisons, along with secondary schools and universities. This mechanism of destabilisation is the unintended consequence of the interaction between the crisis of legitimacy of political regimes and their ideologies, and the expansion of education systems.

Third, a specific manifestation of the previous mechanism is the massive religious revival and its emphasis on a political reading of Islam within society that is taking place in the region. Post-colonial *secular* regimes creating an education system on Western lines believed that they would gradually impose their interpretation of Islam by means of religious education to all generations, and that this would legitimise their power, political projects and ethical principles so ensuring the stability of the social and political order. This was supposed to take place by means of the objectification of Islam, i.e. its summarisation and systemisation into a set of simple rules and precepts that could be squeezed into school curricula and subject to examination, and also by means of the functionalisation and instrumentalisation of Islam, i.e. the creation of a version of Islam that would meet the needs of political power and legitimise its interests in the language of Islam. However, the unintended consequence of this strategy was that, instead of an easily controlled and pro-regime *interpretation of culture*, an uncontrollable and potentially anti-regime *culture of interpretation* was created, i.e. a perception of Islam as something that must be thought about, studied and understood correctly, but also as something by means of which everything, from the life of the individual to the organisation of society, could be correctly justified. And it was open to debate, to say the least, whether official, pro-regime justifications were the most correct. This mechanism of destabilisation was above all the consequence of the interaction of the massive expansion of educational systems and an Islam that regimes had unsuccessfully attempted to instrumentalise.

Four, a specific manifestation of the second mechanism is the potential radicalisation of secondary school students. This is the result of the interaction between the dissatisfaction with the regime experienced by critically minded school teachers who are close in age to their students, and potentially dissatisfied pupils who represent the group of graduates most at threat on the labour market. Many of the latter will never make university because of restricted capacity. This interaction between students and teachers takes place within the relatively favourable environment of secondary schools, which, within the context of repressive regimes suppressing the right of assembly and association, represent one of the few social spaces where opposition ideas can be disseminated. It is for this reason that opposition propaganda is aimed at schools. This mechanism of destabilisation is the consequence of the interaction of the massive expansion of secondary education and unpopular authoritarian regimes that alienate teachers and young people but are relatively weak in monitoring opposition moods in schools.

Five, the radicalisation of university students takes place by means of a similar mechanism, with universities the epicentre of opposition groups, including Islamist. As in the case of secondary schools, the university is one of the few islands of freedom in an ocean of oppression where ideas, including political ideas, can be exchanged and shared with relative ease. Universities sometimes actively promote an ethos of responsibility among young people for improving the world in which they live. However, thanks to their education and awareness, students are able to compare the critical state of their own country with the reality of other countries, or with the promises made by different ideologies. In addition, students are often far from their families and looking for a new source of sociability, and this is offered to them by different religious or political movements. This mechanism of destabilisation is to a certain extent the same the world over and so the simple outcome of the expansion of universities. However, it is partially about the interaction of the generally critical attitudes of students and the extraordinarily critical state of Middle Eastern societies.

Six, the expansion of *secular* education systems has created a class of new interpreters of Islam who no longer need religion to be spoon-fed to them by the traditional religious authorities. Thanks to their education they are able to confront, understand and interpret the revealed texts themselves and no longer have any need for traditional clerics. They regard the official clergy as collaborators debased by their cooperation with political power or as a professional interest group incapable of reacting to the new challenges and themes of modern times. They believe that their lay interpretations of Islam are so convincing that they should be disseminated within society. They then compete in the public space with the interpretations of traditional religious authorities and engage them in debate regarding not only arcane points of Islamic theology, but about whether indeed Islam can be radically interpreted anew and if so, who is entitled to do so. The result of this cacophony of voices is the loss of the centuries-old monopoly of traditional clerics on the inter-generational transmission of religion and its interpretation and the decline of their authority. However, the democratisation of (religious) knowledge leads to a dispersal of (political) power: the elites can no longer claim that they act in the name of Islam. This mechanism of destabilisation is the consequence of the interaction of a highly educated public open to divergent interpretations and a pluralistic Islam, the discrediting of the clerics, and the new themes arising from the rapid changes taking place in the world that the clerics address only inadequately thereby freeing up space for new interpreters.

Seven, this reaction on the part of regimes to the discrediting of the religious authorities and the attempt they make to discredit the new interpreters (often opposition Islamists) simply ends up further popularising religious discourse as such within society. This then strengthens the position of the new interpreters when regimes attempt to beat them at their own game.

Eight, the emergence of a class of new, secularly educated interpreters of Islam results in a process of creolisation and westernisation, the linking up of two formerly separated poles of traditional Islam (orthodox and mystical), modern science, and Western secular ideologies. The result is an escalation of the cacophony of voices and the existence of a large number of highly differentiated interpretations of Islam, including political interpretations. This mechanism is the consequence of the interaction between the increase in education, cultural westernisation, and the discredited political regimes and ideologies for which a substitute is sought.

Nine, increasing educational standards in themselves stimulate higher consumer, career and political aspirations. If an ever more educated population is not integrated into economic and political systems, its aspirations curdle into even greater frustration. This is why increasingly educated Middle Eastern populations are becoming radicalised and turning against the regimes. It is also the reason why the intelligentsia is slowly being transformed into a critically minded "lumpenintelligentsia" and producing its own opposition interpretations of Islamic and other ideologies. This mechanism of destabilisation is the consequence of the tension between the rapid pace in educational improvements and the slower pace of economic and political change, as well as the interaction of Islam and other ideologies with these mechanisms.

Ten, individual groups of political militants, both secular and religious, usually comprise people who, thanks to their education, are well informed regarding political events, have strong opinions, and want to engage on a political and civil level. They are therefore more likely to speak out against the domestic repressive regime or against external occupation. This mechanism is the consequence of the interaction between high educational standards and a domestic and international politics regarded as unfair.

RAPID URBANISATION

First, rapid urbanisation has contributed to the collapse of weak and ineffective state institutions. Corrupt, authoritarian states in the Middle East have mishandled the exodus from the countryside to cities. Social systems, transport and housing infrastructure and town planning have all collapsed under the onslaught of migration to the cities. Uncontrolled urbanisation accompanied by an explosion in slums, a housing crisis, transport collapse, urban unemployment, a rampant unregulated grey economy, overcrowded classrooms, mountains of garbage and visible inequality have compromised Middle Eastern regimes and their ideologies. There is a growing call for a credible political alternative. In this situation political Islam can be seen as a possible candidate. Islam is not a religion of the desert or uncultivated rural dwellers. It was born in an urban environment, and for this reason gives the impression of having something to say regarding the negative impacts of urbanisation. This mechanism involves the interaction of the negative consequences of modern urbanisation and the pre-modern Islamic substrate that is modernising and reinventing the historical memory of the Prophet's Mecca and Medina within a new context. However, the role of Islam is ambivalent on this point. On the level of the city neighbourhoods and slums traditional Islam or bottom-up re-Islamisation can be a stabiliser of the social order, with the institutions and social norms of Islam becoming the backbone of the social organisation of communities.

Second, the mass exodus to cities is concentrating a large number of people in a small space, which means that political ideologies can spread easily and more quickly among the urban masses than among scattered rural communities. As well as agitation, the organisation and mobilisation of the masses for political action is also easier. This is all taking place to the greatest extent in the capital city, the centre of political and economic power. Capital cities are clearly now the centres of instability and resistance, and not rural areas as in the past.

Three, rapid urbanisation is not accompanied by sufficiently fast job creation in the cities, mainly because it has not coincided with any meaningful industrial revolution in the region. Over the last few decades urbanisation in Middle East has resulted in high levels of urban unemployment and poverty. The social question has the potential for destabilisation, since poverty is at odds with socially sensitive Islam. However, here again the role of Islam is ambivalent, both destabilising and stabilising. Though revolutionary Islamists encourage the overthrow of the existing unjust order, there are currents of thought in Islam that pass off material destitution as a moral virtue that helps believers become closer to God.

Four, urban poverty leads to greater political destabilisation than rural poverty. In the city the poverty suffered by one person is visibly confronted with the wealth of another. Social inequality is highly visible in an urban environment with a high concentration, mobility and circulation of people from various different classes, and the contrast between the affluent and the poor is sharper. This delegitimizes inequality no matter how large it is objectively, and it is socially sensitive Islam that offers a framework for criticism.

Five, the urban environment stimulates growing career and consumer aspirations. Completely new needs emerge and existing needs are reinforced. The reference group of the poor urban classes no longer comprises their ancestors as a model worthy of imitation, but more successful urban middle classes, with whose lifestyle, consumption and careers they are confronted every day. However, for the most part these aspirations are not met because of a lack of economic opportunities, and this generates frustration.

Six, while the social function of Middle Eastern states has collapsed beneath the onslaught of the rural exodus, the space vacated has been filled by Islamic civil society with its charities and auxiliary institutions, whose clients are now mainly the urban lower middle class and the poor. However, the question remains as to what extent the Islamists have managed to distribute their anti-system ideology along with their social assistance. The Islamists and Islamic civil society have a stabilising effect, while at the same time presenting themselves as a serious alternative to the discredited states and an attractive seed that will grow into the Islamic utopia they promise for the future.

Seven, the lack of affordable housing and the long-term unemployment of school leavers living with their parents in increasingly overcrowded households creates pressures under which the traditional family and its solidarity is crumbling. This results in more clients for Islamic charities, as well as a conservative reaction that views the disintegration of families not as a social crisis but a moral one and advocates male control over the female members of the family.

Eight, the city with its high concentration of large numbers of strangers of both sexes and its low social control has seen the birth of Islamic feminism. Veiling is a means of protecting women in dangerous spaces and a way of allowing them to move freely around the city far beyond the boundaries of their households, i.e. to study, work and be active in civil society, while upholding their purity and honour in accordance with Islam. This interaction of urbanisation and an adapted Islamic tradition is again more indicative of the potential of Islam to be a flexible stabiliser of societies undergoing a dramatic, profound transformation.

Nine, urbanisation contributes to the intergenerational alienation of parents born or socialised in the countryside and their offspring born or socialised in the city. This undermines the authority of parents, whose values, norms, worldviews and advice make no sense to their sons and daughters, even though they themselves may not yet fully identify with the aggressive urban role models and norms. In this schizophrenic situation young urbanised people seek substitute models and alternative forms of knowledge often to be found in political and religious movements.

Ten, the previous mechanism is related to the universal phenomenon of the radicalisation of second and third generations of (urban) migrants. The first generation of migrants regard their horizontal mobility from the countryside to the city as a substitute for upward social mobility. Even though they often merely exchange rural for urban poverty, they may view their escape from the countryside to be a success in life. The first generation often brings a powerful, if anything conservative moral compass with it. However, subsequent generations have now been socialised in the city. Their dreams and aspirations are higher, and this can create the potential for greater frustration. The second generation is more disorientated, because it finds itself in a schizophrenic situation, caught between the traditional norms and values of its parents and the antithetical claims and values of the city.

Eleven, rapidly and chaotically expanding cities with their visible dysfunctions and deviations are viewed as the essence of moral turpitude. The Islamic imaginary allows for condemnation of the city by contrasting it with the idealised community of the Prophet Muhammad and the first four rightly guided caliphs in Mecca and Medina. The modern city can come to seem like the archetype of modern *jahiliyya*, a sign of to what extent Muslims have returned to the era of pre-Islamic barbarism. Similarly, the godless, immoral reality of large cities full of poverty and injustice can stimulate apocalyptic, eschatological visions speaking of the imminent end of history. The turmoil of life in the city contributes to an emphasis on a political and social reading of Islam amongst Muslims experiencing culture shock.

Twelve, massive urbanisation and the predominance of an urban population leads to a swing away from the centuries-old balance between the two fundamental conflicting poles of Islam, i.e. from a variegated rural, folk Islam and an apolitical mystical Sufism in the direction of an urban orthodox fundamentalism that has always attempted to purify Islam of these unorthodox innovations. While the influence of the urbanisation of the last few decades has witnessed a decline in Sufism and traditional folk Islam, religious orthodoxy has gained ground. However, urban orthodoxy takes various forms, from political Islam in the form of the Muslim Brotherhood, to the less politically motivated Salafists. This involves the interaction of urbanisation and the traditional pattern of the two opposing poles of Islamic religiosity. In the end Islam's effect tends to be ambivalent, potentially stabilising or destabilising depending on the form of orthodoxy enforced in the cities.

Thirteen, urban religious institutions and organisations help during the transition of a deracinated population arriving from the countryside so that it becomes socialised in cities and finds surrogate communities. Islamic civil society, including the Islamists, plays an important role in this process.

Fourteen, Islam, including Islamism, also helps people acclimatise themselves to the city by providing a new worldview that offers orientation in a radically new life situation. Traditional rural Islam is replaced by political Islam or other forms of orthodoxy. These mechanisms are the consequence of anomie: a collapse of or withdrawal from traditional social structures and the collapse of the credibility of traditional worldviews and normative structures. Islam, with its worldviews and above all its institutions and organisations, plays more of a stabilising than a destabilising role. Middle Eastern urbanisation in itself was always going to be problematic, both politically and socially. However, the Islamists actively contribute to the re-socialisation of former rural dwellers by undermining and eroding traditional rural structures, worldviews and authorities. Alongside advancing urbanisation and globalisation, the Islamists thus become one of the causes of the uprooting of Muslims from their traditional structures. An individual uprooted from their tradition becomes a tabula rasa. Deculturation and deracination then become the prerequisites of re-socialisation leading to acculturation and the acceptance of a new version of Islam promoted by the Islamists and other religious movements.

REFERENCES

Data sources and reports

AHDR (2002) *Arab Human Development Report 2002. Creating Opportunities for Future Generations.* New York: UNDP.

AHDR (2003) *Arab Human Development Report 2003. Building a Knowledge Society.* New York: UNDP.

AHDR (2005) *Arab Human Development Report 2005. Towards the Rise of Woman in the Arab World.* New York: UNDP.

AHDR (2009) *Arab Human Development Report 2009. Challenges to Human Security in the Arab Countries.* New York: UNDP.

Center for Religious Freedom of Freedom House (2006) *Saudi Arabia's Curriculum of Intolerance: With Excerpts from Saudi Arabia Ministry of Education Textbooks for Islamic Studies.* Washington, D.C.: Freedom House and The Institute for Gulf Affairs.

Democracy index 2010. *Democracy in retreat. A report from the Economist Intelligence Unit.* Accessible at: www.eiu.com.

FAO: The World Food Situation (2011). Accessible at: http://www.fao.org/docrep/014/i2330e/i2330e00.htm.

Freedom House (2005) The Worst of the Worst. Accessible at: www.freedomhouse.org.

Freedom House (2008) Discrimination and Intolerance in Iran's Textbooks. Special Report. Accessible at: www.freedomhouse.org.

Freedom House (2010) Freedom in the World. Accessible at: www.freedomhouse.org.

Freedom House (2016) Freedom in the World. Accessible at: www.freedomhouse.org.

Human Rights Watch (2010) Country Reports. Accessible at: www.hrw.org.

ILO Global Employment Trends (2012). New York: United Nations.

ILO Global Employment Trends for Youth. A generation at risk (2013). New York: United Nations.

Oil and Gas Review (2009). Alberta Securities Commission, July, 2010. Accessible at: www.albertasecurities.com.

PISA 2003. Accessible at: https://www.oecd.org/edu/school/programmeforinternationalstudentsassessmentpisa.

PISA 2009. Accessible at: https://www.oecd.org/edu/school/programmeforinternationalstudentsassessmentpisa.

Reporters Without Borders. World Press Freedom Index 2010 and 2016. Accessible at: www.rsf.org.

The Economist Intelligence Unit 2011, Population trends in Arab League countries. Accessible at: https://www.eiu.com/home.aspx.

The Economist Intelligence Unit, Democracy Index 2015. Accessible at: https://www.eiu.com/home.aspx.

TIMSS 2007. Accessible at: http://timss.bc.edu/timss2007/intl_reports.html.

Transparency International. Corruption Perception Index. Accessible at: https://www.transparency.org.

UNESCO Statistics. Accessible at: http://uis.unesco.org.

UN Human Development Report 2005. Accessible at: http://hdr.undp.org/en.

UN Human Development Report 2009. Accessible at: http://hdr.undp.org/en.

UN Human Development Report 2010. Accessible at: http://hdr.undp.org/en.

UN Human Development Report 2016. Accessible at: http://hdr.undp.org/en.

UN-HABITAT (2003) *The Challenge of Slums: Global Report on Human Settlements*. London: Earthscan, 2003.

United Nations Population Information Network (POPIN). Accessible at: http://www.un.org/popin.

United Nations World Population Prospects: The 2015 Revisions. Accessible at: https://esa.un.org/unpd/wpp.

United States Department of Agriculture. Economic Research Service. Accessible at: https://www.ers.usda.gov.

Youth Development in the ESCWA Region (2010). New York: United Nations.

World Bank Development Indicators 2007. Accessible at: http://data.worldbank.org/data-catalog/world-development-indicators.

World Bank Development Indicators 2010. Accessible at: http://data.worldbank.org/data-catalog/world-development-indicators.

World Bank Development Indicators 2016. Accessible at: http://data.worldbank.org/data-catalog/world-development-indicators.

World Bank Worldwide Governance Indicators (WGIs) 2016. Accessible at: http://info.worldbank.org/governance/wgi/index.aspx#home.

Works, papers and reports on public opinion (based on surveys)

Dixon, J. C. (2008) A Clash of Civilizations? Examining Liberal-Democratic Values in Turkey and the European Union. *The British Journal of Sociology*, Vol. 59, No. 4, p. 681–708.

Esposito, J. L., Mogahed, D. (2007) *Who Speaks for Islam? What a Billion Muslims Really Think*. New York: Gallup Press.

Inglehart, R., Norris, P. (2002) Islamic Culture and Democracy: Testing the Clash of Civilization Thesis. *Comparative Sociology*, Vol. 22, No. 1, p. 235–264.

Inglehart, R., Norris, P. (2003) The True Clash of Civilizations. *Foreign Policy* March/April 2003. Accessible at: http://www.globalpolicy.org/globaliz/cultural/2003/0304clash.htm.

Inglehart, R., Norris, P. (2004) *Sacred and Secular. Religion and Politics Worldwide*. Cambridge: Cambridge University Press.

Inglehart, R., Welzel, Ch. (2006) *Modernisation, Cultural Change, and Democracy. The Human Development Sequence*. Cambridge: Cambridge University Press.

Inglehart, R., Welzel, Ch. (2008) How Development Leads to Democracy. What We Know About Modernisation. *Foreign Affairs*, 2008, Vol. 88, No. 2, p. 33–48.

Jamal, A., Tessler, M. (2008) Attitudes in the Arab World. *Journal of Democracy*, January 2008, Vol. 19, No. 1, p. 97–110.

Kohut, A., Stokes, B. (2007) *America Against the World. How We Are Different and Why We Are Disliked*. New York: Henry Holt and Company.

Mogahed, D., Rheault, M. (2007) Majorities See Religion and Democracy as Compatible. Accessible at www.gallup.com.

Pew Center (2006). *The Great Divide: How Westerners and Muslims View Each Other*. Washington, D.C.: The Pew Global Attitudes Project.

Pew Center (2007). *World Publics Welcome Global Trade – But not Immigration*. Washington, D.C.: The Pew Global Attitudes Project.

Pew Center (2009). *Little Enthusiasm for Many Muslim Leaders. Mixed Views of Hamas and Hezbollah in Largely Muslim Nations*. Washington, D.C.: The Pew Global Attitudes Project.

Pew Center (2010). *Most Embrace a Role for Islam in Politics*. Washington, D.C.: The Pew Global Attitudes Project.

Pew Center (2010b). *Global Public Embrace Social Networking*. Washington, D.C.: The Pew Global Attitudes Project.

Pew Center (2011). *Egyptians Embrace Revolt Leaders, Religious Parties and Military, As Well*. Washington, D.C.: The Pew Global Attitudes Project.

TESEV (2012) *The Perception of Turkey in the Middle East 2011*. TESEV Foreign Policy Programme.
The Arab Millennials. Understanding the aspirations and attitudes of Middle East youth. 2008 (accessible at: www.arabyouthsurvey.com).
The Silatech Index: Voices of Young Arabs. Gallup, April, 2011.
Zogby International (2006). *Annual Arab Public Opinion Survey*. Power Point Presentation.
Zogby International (2008). *Annual Arab Public Opinion Survey*. Power Point Presentation.
Zogby International (2010). *Annual Arab Public Opinion Survey*. Power Point Presentation.
Zogby International (2011). *Annual Arab Public Opinion Survey*. Power Point Presentation.
Zogby, J. (2012) *Arab Voices. What they are saying to us, and why it matters*. New York: Palgrave Macmillan.

Literary works cited
Aal, G. A. (2010) *I Want to Get Married!* Austin: The University of Texas Press.
Al-Aswání, A. (2002) *Jakobiánův dům*. Brno: Jota.
Alsanea, R. (2008) *Girls of Riyadh*. London: Penguin Books.
Ben Jelloun, T. (2002) *Tichý den v Tangeru*. Praha: Dauphin.
Ben Jelloun, T. (2007) *Posvátná noc*. Praha: Dauphin.
Ben Jelloun, T. (2011) *Poslední přítel*. Praha: Fra.
Ben Jelloun, T. (2011) *A palace in the old village*. London: Penguin Books.
Binebine, M. (2014) *Boží koně ze Sidi Moumen*. Praha: Práh.
Havel, V. (1990) *Moc bezmocných*. Praha: Nakladatelství Lidové noviny.
Malcolm, X: *The autobiography of Malcolm X. With the assistance of Alex Haley*. New York, Grove Press, 1965.
Oz, A. (2006) *Jak vyléčit fanatika*. Praha: Paseka.
Procházková, P. (2003) *Aluminiová královna: rusko-čečenská válka očima žen*. Praha: Nakladatelství Lidové noviny.
Satrapi, M. (2006, 2007) *Persepolis 1 a 2*. Praha: BB/art.
Štětina, J. (2000) *Století zázraků*. Praha: Nakladatelství Lidové noviny.
Šukrí, M. (2006) *Nahý chleba*. Praha: Fra.
Terloeva, M. (2007) *Tanec na troskách. Deník čečenské dívky*. Brno: Jota.

Other scholarly works
Abadie, A. (2004) Poverty, Political Freedom, and the Roots of Terrorism. Harvard University and NBER, October, 2004 (Working Papers).
Abdel-Malek, A. (1963) Orientalism in Crisis. *Diogenes* 11 (44): 103–140 (1963).
Akyol, M. (2012) The Turkish Model. Marching to Islamic Liberalism. *The Cairo Review of Global Affairs*, 4 (2012), p. 68–83.
Al Džazíra. Jiný úhel pohledu (documentary film). Jehane Noujaim, USA, 2004.
Albrecht, H., Schlumberger, O. (2004) „Waiting for Godot": Regime Change Without Democratization in the Middle East. *International Political Science Review*, Vol. 25, No. 4, p. 371–392.
Al-Nakkáš, F. (2004) Fundamentalisté na vzestupu – ženy v Egyptě. In: Frouzová, M. (ed.) *Závoj a džíny. Ženy v islámském světě*. Praha: Vyšehrad, p. 179–189.
Amin, G. (2011) *Egypt in the Era of Hosni Mubarak 1981–2011*. Cairo: AUC Press.
Amin, G. (2006) *The Illusion of Progress in the Arab World*. Cairo: AUC Press.
Amin, G. (2004) *Whatever Else Happened to the Egyptians?* Cairo: AUC Press.
Amin, G. (2000) *Whatever Happened to the Egyptians?* Cairo: AUC Press.
Amin, S. (2004) U. S. Imperialism, Europe, and the Middle East. *Monthly Review*, 2004, Vol. 56, No. 6, p. 2–15.
Anderson, B. (2008) *Představy společenství. Úvahy o původu a šíření nacionalismu*. Praha: Karolinum.
Anderson, L. (1997) Fulfilling Prophecies: State Policy and Islamist Radicalism. In: Esposito, J. (ed.) *Political Islam*. Boulder: Lynne Rienner Publishers, p. 17–32.
Anderson, J. W. (2003) The Internet and Islam's New Interpreters. In: Eickelman, D., Ander-

son, J. W. (eds) *New Media in the Muslim World. The Emerging Public Sphere.* Bloomington: Indiana University Press, p. 45–60.

Ansari, S. (2000) Islam. In: Browning, G., Halcli, A., Webster, F. (eds) *Understanding Contemporary Society. Theories of the Present.* London: Sage, p. 372–384.

Antoňjan, J. M. (2004) Ličnosť terrorista i vaprosy borby s terrorismom. In: Kudrjavcev, V. N. (ed.) *Borba s terrorismom.* Moskva: Nauka, 2004, p. 93–108.

Apter, D. (1968) *Some Conceptual Approaches to the Study of Modernisation.* Englewood Cliffs: Prentice Hall.

Arjmand, R., Daun, H. (2005) Islamic Education. In: Zajda, J. (ed.) *International Handbook on Globalisation, Education and Policy Research. Global Pedagogies and Policies.* Dordrecht: Springer, p. 377–388.

Arjomand, S. A. (1986) Social Change and Movements of Revitalization in Contemporary Islam. In: Beckford, J. A. (ed.) *New Religious Movements and Rapid Social Change.* Paris nad London: Sage/UNESCO, 1986, p. 87–112.

Arjomand, S. A. (1995) *Unity and Diversity in Islamic Fundamentalism.* In: Marty, M. E., Appleby R. S. (eds) *Fundamentalisms Comprehended. The Fundamentalism Project,* Vol. 5. Chicago and London: The University of Chicago Press, 1995, p. 178–198.

Arjomand, S. A. (2004) Islam, Political Change and Globalization. *Thesis Eleven,* No. 76, February 2004, p. 9–28.

Arjomand, S. A. (2006) Thinking Globally about Islam. In: Juergensmeyer, M. (ed.) *The Oxford Handbook of Global Religions.* Oxford: Oxford University Press.

Armbrust, W. (2003) Burgeois Leisure and Egyptian Media Fantasies. In: Eickelman, D., Anderson, J. W. (eds) *New Media in the Muslim World. The Emerging Public Sphere.* Bloomington: Indiana University Press, p. 102–128.

Arnason, J. P. (2009) *Civilizační analýza. Evropa a Asie opět na rozcestí.* Praha: Filosofia.

Arnason, J. P. (2010) *Historicko-sociologické eseje.* Praha: SLON.

Aron, R. (2001) *Opium intelektuálů.* Praha: Mladá fronta.

Ayata, A. G. (2004) „Chci, aby se má dcera měla lépe." Ženy v Turecku. In: Frouzová, M. (ed.) *Závoj a džíny. Ženy v islámském světě.* Praha: Vyšehrad, p. 149–164.

Aydintašbaš, A. (2012) Ankara Looks East. *The Cairo Review of Global Affairs,* 4 (2012), p. 58–67.

Baer, R. (2003) *Sleeping With the Devil. How Washington Sold Our Soul for Saudi Crude.* New York: Crown Publishers.

Bah, U. (2008) Rereading the Passing of Traditional Society. Empathy, Orthodoxy and the Americanization of the Middle East. *Cultural Studies* 22 (6), p. 795–819.

Baňouch, H., Fedorko, M. (2000) *Mezinárodní organizace.* Brno: Masarykova univerzita.

Barak, O. (2011) Studying Middle East Militaries: Where Do We Go From Here? *International Journal of Middle East Studies,* 43 (2011), p. 406–407.

Barr, J. (2011) *A Line in the Sand. Britain, France and the Struggle that Shaped the Middle East.* London: Simon and Schuster.

Barša, P. (2001) *Západ a islamismus. Střet civilizací, nebo dialog kultur?* Brno: CDK.

Barša, P. (2011) Arabská svoboda a obavy Západu. *Lidové noviny,* 12. 2. 2011, p. 24.

Barša, P. (2012) *Orientálcova vzpoura.* Praha: Dokořán.

Batistová, A. (2015) Prvotním nepřítelem je Asad (interview with Su'ád Nawfal). *Respekt,* No. 9, 2015.

Bauman, Z. (1997) *Myslet sociologicky.* Praha: Slon.

Bayat, A. (2010) *Life as Politics. How Ordinary People Change the Middle East.* Stanford: Stanford University Press.

Bazarslan, H. (2005) Kurdish Question. Can It Be Solved Within Europe? In: Roy, O. (ed.) *Turkey Today. A European Country?* London: Anthem Press, p. 79–89.

Beckford, J. A. (ed.) (1986) *New Religious Movements and Rapid Social Change.* Paris and London: Sage/UNESCO.

Belén Soage, A. (2010) Yusuf Al-Qaradawi: The Muslim Brothers's Favorite Ideological Guide. In: Rubin, B. (ed.) *The Muslim Brotherhood.* New York: Palgrave Macmillan, p. 19–35.

Beránek, O. (2007) Soudobé projevy politického islámu v Saúdské Arábii. In: Souleimanov, E. (ed.) *Politický islám*. Praha: Eurolex Bohemia, p. 266–284.

Beránek, O., Ťupek, P. (2008) *Dvojí tvář islámské charity*. Brno: CDK.

Beránek, Z. (2006) Řekni to a zemři! A2, No. 20. Accessible at: www.advojka.cz.

Beránek, Z. (2007) Alžírsko je má vlast, islám je mé náboženství. In: Souleimanov, E. (ed.) *Politický islám*. Praha: Eurolex Bohemia, p. 244–265.

Berger, P. (1997) *Vzdálená sláva. Hledání víry ve věku lehkověrnosti*. Brno: Barrister & Principal, 2003.

Berger, P. L., Luckmann, T. (1999) *Sociální konstrukce reality. Pojednání o sociologii vědění*. Brno: CDK.

Berkey, J. P. (2007) Madrasas Medieval and Modern: Politics, Education and Problem of Muslim Identity. In: Hefner, R., Zaman, M., Q. (eds) *Schooling Islam. The Culture and Politics of Modern Muslim Education*. Princeton: Princeton University Press, p. 40–60.

Besley, T., Persson, T. (2009) The Origins of State Capacity: Property Rights, Taxation, and Politics. *American Economic Review*, 99, p. 1218–1244.

Bičík, I. (2000) *Atlas dnešního světa. Tematický atlas*. Praha: Nakladatelství Terra.

Blažek, J. (2002) *Teorie regionálního rozvoje*. Praha: Karolinum.

Boček, J. (2006) Mluvíme s nepřítelem. Al-Džazíra pouští na obrazovky Izraelce i Usámu a chce anglicky oslovit Západ. *Respekt*, No. 35, 2006, p. 11.

Boček, J., Vlnas, M. (2007) Kdo zaujme televizí, vítězí. Bush, Blair, Putin, Chiran, Al Thání – ti všichni zápasí o Blízký východ. *Respekt*, No. 2, 2007, p. 11.

Booth, M. (2002) Arab Adolescents Facing the Future. Enduring Ideals and Pressures to Change. In: Brown, B., Larson R. W., Saraswathi T. S. (eds) *The World's Youth. Adolescence in Eight Regions of the Globe*. Cambridge: Cambridge University Press, 2002, p. 207–241.

Bowker, R. (2013) Egypt: Diplomacy and the Politics of Change. *Middle East Journal*, Vol. 67, No. 4, 2013, p. 581–591.

Bradshaw, M. (2000) *World Regional Geography. The New Global Order*. New York: McGraw-Hill.

Braizat, F. (2010) What Arabs Think. The Meaning of Democracy. *Journal of Democracy*, 2010, Vol. 21, No. 4, p. 131–138.

Brzezinski, Z. (1993) *Bez kontroly. Chaos v předvečer 21. století*. Praha: Victoria Publishing.

Brzezinski, Z. (1999) *Velká šachovnice. K čemu Ameriku zavazuje její globální převaha*. Praha: Mladá fronta.

Brzezinski, Z. (2004) *Volba. Globální nadvláda nebo globální vedení*. Praha: Mladá fronta.

Brož, I. (2007) *Saddám kontra Chomejní*. Praha: Epocha.

Buiter, W. H., Purvis, D. D. (1983). Oil, Disinflation, and Export Competitiveness: A Model of the 'Dutch Disease'. In: Bhandari, J. S., Putnam, B. H. (eds) *Economic Interdependence and Flexible Exchange Rates*. Cambridge: MIT Press, p. 221–247.

Bukay, D. (2007) Can There Be an Islamic Democracy? *Middle East Quarterly*, 2007, Vol. 14, No. 2, p. 71–79.

Bumbálek, C. (2006) Íráncům zbývá svoboda na internetu. A2, No. 20. Accessible at: www.advojka.cz.

Bumbálek, C. (2007) Politický islám v šíitském islámu a v Íránu. In: Souleimanov, E. (ed.) *Politický islám*. Praha: Eurolex Bohemia, p. 112–147.

Bumbálek, C. (2007b) Libye jde do Evropy. *Respekt*, 2007, 15. července. Accessible at: www.respekt.cz.

Bureš, J. (2007) Koncepce státu v islámu a kritika islamistických postojů. In: Souleimanov, E. (ed.) *Politický islám*. Praha: Eurolex Bohemia, p. 39–61.

Buruma, I., Margalit, A. (2005a) *Okcidentalismus. Západ očima nepřátel*. Praha: Lidové noviny.

Buruma, I., Margalit, A. (2005b) *Okcidentalismus*. Accessible at: http://glosy.info/rejstrik/okcidentalismus.

Burgat, F. (2002) *Face to Face With Political Islam*. London: I. B. Tauris.

Busseová, S., Scheleyová, N. (2004) *Války USA. Kronika agresivního národa*. Praha: Brána.

Cardini, F. (2004) *Evropa a islám*. Praha: Lidové noviny.

Čečáková, T. (2006) *Al-Manár: Televizní stanice Hizbulláhu.* Bakalářská práce. Plzeň: ZČU v Plzni, Fakulta filozofická.

Čejka, M. (2007) Hamás. In: Souleimanov, E. (ed.) *Politický islám.* Praha: Eurolex Bohemia, p. 168–187.

Čejka, M. (2009) Írán mezi osami zla a dobra. *MFDnes (Kavárna)*, 14. 3. 2009, p. D7.

Černý, K. (2006) *Islámský radikalismus v reflexi společenských věd a veřejného mínění v ČR.* Diplomová práce. Praha: Filozofická fakulta, Karlova univerzita.

Černý, K.(2009) Anatomie náboženského terorismu a globální rebelie proti sekulárnímu (ne)řádu. *Historická sociologie*, Vol. 1, No. 1, p. 175–212.

Černý, K. (2010) Pojetí dějin, civilizací a politické současnosti u Mohammada Chátamího. *Historická sociologie*, Vol. 2, No. 2, p. 53–74.

Černý, K. (2010b) Globální náboženské obrození a konflikty na prahu 21. století: Střet mezi civilizacemi, nebo střet uvnitř civilizací? In: Šubrt, J., Arnason, J. *Kultury, civilizace, světový systém.* Praha: Nakladatelství Karolinum, p. 197–230.

Černý, K. (2010c) Dvě tváře S. P. Huntingtona: Od teorií modernizace k civilizacionistice. *Sociologický časopis*, Vol. 46, No. 2, p. 301–311.

Černý, K. (2014) Arab Revolutions and Political Islam: A Structural Approach. In: *Annual of European and Global Studies. Religion and Politics.* Edinburgh: Edinburgh University Press, p. 183–209.

Červinka, M. (2008) *Fenomén popírání holocaustu a perspektivy vývoje této problematiky.* Diplomová práce. Plzeň: Západočeská univerzita, 2008.

Chekroun, M. (2005) Socio-Economic Changes, Collective Insecurity and New Forms of Religious Expression. *Social Compass*, 52 (1), p. 13–29.

Chaldún, M. I. (1972) *Čas království a říší Mukaddima: Úvod do historie.* Praha: Odeon.

Chátamí, M. (2001) *Islám, dialog a občanská společnost.* Praha: Velvyslanectví Íránské islámské republiky.

Chomejní, R. (2004) *Velájat-e Faqíh. Islámská vláda.* Teherán: Institut pro uspořádání a vydávání děl Imáma Chomejního (Oddělení mezinárodních vztahů).

Chomsky, N. (2003) *11. 9.* Praha: Mezera.

Cílek, V., Kasík, M. (2007) *Nejistý plamen.* Praha: Dokořán.

Cirincione, J. (2008) A Middleast Nuclear Chain Reaction? *Current History.* December.

Clark, J. (2004) Social Movement Theory and Patron-Clientelism: Islamic Social Institutions and the Middle Class in Egypt, Jordan, and Yemen. *Comparative Political Studies.* Vol. 37, No. 8, p. 941–968.

Clash of Civilization. *Wall Street Journal.* 11 February 2006. Accessible at: http://www.opinion-journal.com/weekend/hottopic/?id=110007956.

CMIP 2006. The attitudes to „the other" and to peace in Iranian school books and teachers guides. Accessible at: http://www.impact-se.org/research/iran/index.html.

Collier, P. (2009) The Political Economy of State Failure. *Oxford Review of Economic Policy*, Summer, 2009.

Cook, S. (2007) *Ruling But Not Governing: The Military and Political Development in Egypt, Algeria, and Turkey.* Baltimore: John Hopkins University.

Coser, L. (1956) *The Functions of Social Conflict.* London: Routledge.

Courbage, Y., Todd, E. (2011) *A Convergence of Civilizations. The Transformation of Muslims Societies Around the World.* New York: Columbia University Press.

Cvrkal, Z. (2007) *Írán.* Praha: Libri.

Dahrendorf, R. (1959) *Class and Class Conflict in Industrial Society.* Stanford: Stanford University Press.

Davieová, G. (2009) *Výjimečný případ Evropa: Podoby víry v dnešním světě.* Brno: CDK.

Davies, J. S. (1962) Toward a Theory of Revolution. *American Sociological Review*, Vol. 27, No. 1, p. 5–19.

Davutoglu, A. (2012) Strategic Thinking. *The Cairo Review of Global Affairs*, 4, 2012, p. 16–41.

De Blij, H., Muller, P. (2006) *Geography - Realms, Regions, and Concepts.* Hobojem: John Wiley and Sons, Inc.

Dekmejian, H. (1995) *Islam in Revolution.* Syracuse: Syracuse University Press.

Dicken, P. (1992) *Global Shift* (2nd edition). London: Paul Chapman.

Ditrych, O. (2007) Hizb-at Tahrír: Islamismus v euroasijském heartlandu. In: Souleimanov (ed.) *Politický islám.* Praha: Eurolex Bohemia, p. 188–205.

Dohrmann, M., Hatem, R. (2014) The Impact of Hydro-Politics on the Relations of Turkey, Iraq, and Syria. *Middle East Journal,* Vol. 68, No. 4, p. 567–583.

Dorrousaro, G. (2005) Turkey – A Democracy Under Control? In: Roy, O. (ed.) *Turkey Today. A European Country?* London: Anthem Press, p. 27–38.

Dorte, V. (2012) *Adaptation to a Changing Climate in the Arab Countries.* Washington, D. C.: The World Bank.

Droz-Vincent, P. (2011) From Fighting Formal Wars to Maintaining Civil Peace? *International Journal of Middle East Studies,* 43 (2011), p. 392–394.

Durán, Ch., Pohly, M. (2001) *Usáma bin Ládin a mezinárodní terorismus.* Brno: Jota.

Dürkheim, E., Mauss, M. (1913) Note sur la notion de civilisation. *Année sociologique,* 12:46–50.

Dürkheim, E. (2002) *Elementární formy náboženského života.* Praha: OIKOYMENH.

Dürkheim, E. (2003) *Společenská dělba práce.* Brno: CDK.

Ehteshami, A. (1999) Is the Middle East Democratizing? *British Journal of Middle East Studies,* 26 (2), p. 199–217.

Eickelman, D., Piscatori J. (1996) *Muslim Politics.* Princeton: Princeton University Press.

Eickelman, D., Anderson, J. W. (2003) *New Media in the Muslim World. The Emerging Public Sphere.* Bloomington: Indiana University Press.

Eickelman, D. (2003) Communication and Control in the Media: Publication and its Discontents. In: Eickelman, D., Anderson, J., W. (eds) *New Media in the Muslim World. The Emerging Public Sphere.* Bloomington: Indiana University Press, p. 33–44.

Eisenstadt, S. N. (2000) Multiple Modernities. *Daedalus,* 2000, 129, 1, p. 1–29.

Eisenstadt, S. N. (2003) *Comparative Civilizations and Multiple Modernities.* Leiden: Brill.

Elias, N. (1994) *The Civilizing Process: The History of Manners and State Formation and Civilization.* Oxford: B. Blackwell.

El-Nawawy, M., Iskandar, A. (2002) *Al-Jazeera.* Boulder: Westview Press.

Esposito, J. L., Voll (2001) Islam and Democracy. *Humanities,* Vol. 22, No. 6, p. 15–22.

Esposito, J. L. (2003) *Unholly War. Terror in the Name of Islam.* New York: Oxford University Press.

Etzioni, A. (2004) *From Empire to Community. A New Approach to International Relations.* New York: Palgrave Macmillan.

Etzioni, A. (2005) The Real Threat: An Essay on Samuel Huntington. *Contemporary Sociology* 34 (5), p. 477–485.

Favereau, E. (2000) Libye : Six Bulgares accusés d'être à l'origine de 393 cas de sida Assassins d'enfants ou boucs émissaires de la Libye? *Libération,* 2. 6. 2000. Accessible at: www.liberation .fr/php/pages/pageSearchArchives.php.

Fawcett, L. (2009) *International Relations of the Middle East.* New York: Oxford University Press.

Ferguson, N. (2014) *Civilizace: Západ a zbytek světa.* Praha: Dokořán.

Fingerland, J. (2006) Šestka z Bengházi. *Respekt,* 26. 12. 2006, Accessible at: http://respekt.cz.

Fingerland, J. (2011) Putování za jasmínovou vůní. *Lidové noviny,* 2011, 5. února, p. 21–22.

Finke, R., Stark, R. (1992) *The Churching of America, 1776–1990: Winners and Losers in Our Religious Economy.* New Brunswick: Rutgers University Press.

Foran, J. (1997) Discourses and Social Forces: The Role of Culture and Cultural Studies in Understanding Revolutions. In: Foran, J. (ed.) *Theorizing Revolutions.* London: Routledge, p. 203–226.

Foran, J. (1997b) The Comparative-Historical Sociology of Third World Social Revolutions: Why a Few Succeed, Why Most Fail. In: Foran, J. (ed.) *Theorizing Revolutions.* London: Routledge, p. 227–267.

Forbes (2006) Cartoon Tap Into Deep-Seated Grievances. *Oxford Analitica,* 28. 2. 2006. Accessible at: http://www.forbes.com/2006/02/27/middle-east-cartoons_cx_0227oxford.html.

Foucault, M. (1975) *Discipline and Punish.* Harmondsworth.

Foxman, H. A. (2005) The ‚Protocols‘ at 100: A Hoax of Hate Lives On. *The New York Sun,* November 18, 2005. Accessible at: http://www.adl.org/ADL_Opinions/Anti_Semitism_Global /20051118-NYSun.htm

Fuccaro, N. (2001) Vision of the City Urban Studies on the Gulf. *Middle East Studies Association Bulletin*, 2001, p. 2–11.

Friedman, T., L. (2006) Middle East Rules to Live By. *The New York Times*, December 20, 2006.

Friedman, T. (2010) *Horký, zploštělý a přelidněný*. Praha: Academia.

Friedman, T. L. (2011) This is Just the Start. *The New York Times*, March 1, 2011. Accessible at: www.nytimes.com.

Friedman, T. L. (2011b) China, Twitter and 20-Year-Olds vs. the Pyramids. *The New York Times*, February 5th, 2011. Accessible at: www.nytimes.com.

Fromm, E. (1993) *Strach ze svobody*. Praha: Naše vojsko.

Frouzová, M. (ed.) (2004) *Závoj a džíny. Ženy v islámském světě*. Praha: Vyšehrad.

Frouzová, M. (ed.) (2006) *Mříže v ráji: muslimské ženy v Evropě*. Praha: Vyšehrad.

Fukuyama, F. (2002) *Konec dějin a poslední člověk*. Praha: Rybka Publisher.

Fukuyama, F. (2006) Foreword. In: Huntington, S. P. (2006) *Political Order in Changing Societies*. New Haven: Yale University Press, p. ii–xi.

Fukuyama, F. (2011) Political Order in Egypt. How Samuel Huntington Helps Us Understand the Jasmine Revolutions. *The American Interest*, May 1, 2011. Accessible at: www.the-american -interest.com.

Galeotti, M. (1998) *Čas úzkosti: bezpečnost a politika v sovětském a postsovětském Rusku*. Praha: Themis.

García-Rivero, C., Kotzé, H. (2007) Electoral Support for Islamic Parties in the Middle East and North Africa. *Party Politics*, Vol. 13, No. 5, p. 611–636.

Garside, W., R. (1977) Juvenile Unemployment and Public Policy between the Wars. *The Economic History Review*, Vol. 30, No. 3, p. 322–339.

Gause III, F. G. (2011) Why Middle East Studies Missed the Arab Spring. The Myth of Authoritarian Stability. *Foreign Affairs*, July/August, 2011. Accessible at: www.foreignaffairs.com.

Gellner, E. (1983) *Muslim Societies*. Cambridge: Cambridge University Press.

Gellner, E. (1993) *Národy a nacionalismus*. Praha: Hříbal.

Gellner, E. (1995) Fundamentalism as a Comprehensive System: Soviet Marxism and Islamic Fundamentalism Compared. In: Marty, M., E., Appleby, R. S. (eds) *Fundamentalisms Comprehended*. Chicago: The University of Chicago Press, p. 277–287.

Giddens, A. (1971) *Capitalism and Modern Social Theory*. Cambridge: Cambridge University Press.

Giddens, A. (1976) *New Rules of Sociological Method*. London.

Giddens, A. (1999) *Sociologie*. Praha: Argo.

Giddens. A. (2009) *Sociology. 6th Edition*. London: Polity Press.

Giddens, A. (2000) *Unikající svět*. Praha: Slon.

Goldberg, E. (1991) Smashing Idols and the State: The Protestant Ethic and Egyptian Sunni Radicalism. *Comparative Studies in Society and History*, 1991, No. 31, p. 3–35.

Goldstone, J. (1997) Population Growth and Revolutionary Crises. In: Foran, J. (ed.) *Theorizing Revolutions*. London: Routledge, p. 102–122.

Gombár, E. (2001) *Dramatický půlměsíc. Sýrie, Libye a Írán v procesu transformace*. Praha: Karolinum.

Gombár, E. (2004) *Kmeny a klany v arabské politice*. Praha: Karolinum.

Gombár, E. (2007) *Kmeny a klany v arabském Maghribu*. Praha: Karolinum.

Gombár, E., Bareš, L., Veselý, R. (2009) *Dějiny Egypta*. Praha: Nakladatelství Lidové noviny.

Gonzales-Quijano, Y. (2003) The Birth of a Media Ecosystem: Libanon in the Internet Age. In: Eickelman, D., Anderson, J. W. (eds) *New Media in the Muslim World. The Emerging Public Sphere*. Bloomington: Indiana University Press, p. 61–79.

Goodwin, J. (1997) State-Centered Approaches to Social Revolutions: Strengths and Limitations of a Theoretical Tradition. In: Foran, J. (ed.) *Theorizing Revolutions*. London: Routledge, p. 11–37.

Gray, J. (2005) *Al Kajda a co to znamená být moderní*. Praha: Mladá fronta.

Guidére, M. (2012) *Atlas des pays arabes. Des révolutions á la démocratie?* Paris: Autrement.

Gurr, T. (1970) *Why Men Rebel*. Princeton: Princeton University Press.

Habermas, J. (2000) *Strukturální proměna veřejnosti*. Praha: Filosofia.

Hackensberger, A. (2010) Fighting Extremism in A Suit and Tie. New Grand Sheikh at Al-Azhar University. Accessible at: http://en.qantara.de/webcom/show_article.php/_c-478/_nr-1026/i.html.

Halík, T. (2003) Globalizace a náboženství. In Mezřický, V. (ed.) *Globalizace*. Praha: Portál, p. 133–147.

Halík, T. (2007) O Bohu a politice. *Respekt* 2007, No. 51–52, p. 56–59.

Halliday, F. (2005) *100 Myths About the Middle East*. Berkeley: University of California Press.

Hamid, S. (2014) *Temptations of Power. Islamists and Illiberal Democracy in a New Middle East*. New York/Oxford: Oxford University Press.

Hamilton, M. (2001) *The Sociology of Religion: Theoretical and Comparative Perspectives*. London and New York: Routledge.

Hancioglu, A., Ergocmen, A. B., Unalan, T. (2004) The Population of Turkey at the Turn of the 21st Century: The Past Trends, Current Situation and Future Prospects. In: *Population Challenges, International Migration and Reproductive Health in Turkey and European Union*. Istanbul: The Turkish Family Health and Planning Foundation, p. 43–50.

Hashem, M. (2006) Contemporary Islamic Activism: The Shades of Praxis. *Sociology of Religion*, 2006, 67/1, p. 23–41.

Hasso, F. (2010) *Consuming Desires. Family Crisis and the State in the Middle East*. Palo Alto: Stanford University Press.

Hefner, R., Zaman, M. Q. (eds) *Schooling Islam. The Culture and Politics of Modern Muslim Education*. Princeton: Princeton University Press.

Hefner, R. (2003) Civic Pluralism Denied? The New Media and Jihadi Violence in Indonesia. In: Eickelman, D., Anderson, J., W. (eds) *New Media in the Muslim World. The Emerging Public Sphere*. Bloomington: Indiana University Press, p. 158–179.

Hefner, R. (2007) The Culture, Politics, and Future of Muslim Education. In: Hefner, R., Zaman, M. Q. (eds) *Schooling Islam. The Culture and Politics of Modern Muslim Education*. Princeton: Princeton University Press, p. 1–39.

Hejlová, S. (2004) Život ve zlaté kleci aneb ženy ve Spojených arabských emirátech. In: Frouzová, M. (ed.) *Závoj a džíny. Ženy v islámském světě*. Praha: Vyšehrad, p. 61–77.

Herb, M. (1999) *All in the Family: Absolutism, Revolution, and Democracy in the Middle Eastern Monarchies*. New York: State University of New York Press.

Herrera, L. (2009) Youth and Generational Renewal in the Middle East. *International Journal of Middle East Studies*, Vol. 41, No. 3, p. 368–371.

Hertog, S. (2010) *Princes, Brokers, and Bureaucrats: Oil and the State in Saudi Arabia*. New York: Cornell University Press.

Hertog, S. (2011) Rentier Militaries in the Gulf States: The Price of Coup-Proofing. *International Journal of Middle East Studies*, 43 (2011), p. 400–402.

Hendrix, C. S. (2010) Measuring State Capacity: Theoretical and Empirical Implications for the Study of Civil Conflict. *Journal of Peace Research*, 47, 273–299.

Hesová, Z. (2011) Arabské dny hněvu. *Mezinárodní politika*, Vol. 35, No. 6, p. 4–6.

Heydemann, S. (2000) *War, Institutions, and Social Change in the Middle East*. Berkeley: University of California Press.

Hinnebusch, R. (2009) The Politics of Identity in the Middle Eastern International Relations. In: Fawcett, L. (ed.) *International Relations of the Middle East*. New York: Oxford University Press, p. 148–169.

Hlaváčová, S. (2006) Islám a média v USA. A2, No. 20. Accessible at: www.advojka.cz/archiv.

A Hoax of Hate: The Protocols of Learned Elders of Zion. 2010. Anti-Defamation League. Accessible at: http://www.adl.org/special_reports/protocols/protocols_intro.asp.

Hobsbawm, E. (1998) *Věk extrémů*. Praha: Argo.

Hobsbawm, E. (2000) *The Invention of Tradition*. Cambridge: Cambridge University Press.

Hoffman, V. (1995) Muslim Fundamentalists: Psychosocial Profiles. In: Marty, M. E., Appleby, R. S. (eds) *Fundamentalisms Comprehended.* Chicago: The University of Chicago Press, p. 199-230.

Holubec, S. (2009) *Sociologie světových systémů. Hegemonie, centra, periferie.* Praha: Slon.

Homer-Dixon, T., Blitt, J. (1998) *Ecoviolence. Links Among Environment, Population, and Security.* Oxford: Rowman and Littlefield Publishers.

Homer-Dixon, T. (1999) *Environment, Scarcity, and Violence.* Princeton: Princeton University Press.

Horgan, J. (2005) *The Psychology of Terrorism.* London a New York: Routledge.

Hourani, A. (2010) *Dějiny arabského světa.* Praha: NLN.

Howard, P., Hussain M. (2011) The Role of Digital Media. *Journal of Democracy*, Vol. 22, No. 3, p. 35-48.

Hudson, M., C. (2009) The United States in the Middle East. In: Fawcett, L. (ed.) *International Relations of the Middle East.* New York: Oxford University Press, p. 308-330.

Huntington, S. P. (1993) The Clash of Civilizations? *Foreign Affairs*, 1993, 72/3, p. 22-49.

Huntington, S. P. (2001) *Střet civilizací.* Praha: Rybka Publishers.

Huntington, S. P. (2005) *Kam kráčíš, Ameriko?* Praha: Rybka Publishers.

Huntington, S. P. (2006/1968) *Political Order in Changing Societies.* New Haven: Yale University Press.

Huntington, S. P. (2008) *Třetí vlna. Demokratizace na sklonku 20. století.* Brno: CDK.

Hvížďala, K. (2006) Faleš a střet civilizací. *Reflex*, No. 11, 2006. Accessible at: http://www.reflex.cz/Clanek23103.html.

Hybášková, J. (2004) Čekání na válku. *Výpověď odvolané české velvyslankyně v Kuvajtu.* Praha: Rybka Publishers.

Hybášková, J. (2006) Ropa, příčina útlaku arabského světa. *Geografické rozhledy*, Vol. 15, No. 1, p. 4-6.

Hybášková, J. (2006b) Problém není islám, ale ropa. *Lidové noviny*, 2006, 11. března. Accessible at: www.lidovky.cz.

Ibrahim, S. E. Anatomy of Egypt's Militant Groups. *International Journal of Middle East Studies* 12 (4), 1980, p. 423-453.

Idle, N., Nunns, A. (2011) *Tweets from Tahrir.* Doha: Bloomsbury Qatar Foundation.

In quotes: Muslim reaction to Pope, September 16, 2006, BBC News. Accessible at http://news.bbc.co.uk/2/hi/europe/5348436.stm.

Interview with Professor Dittmar Machule, Atta's thesis supervisor at the Technical University of Hamburg-Harburg. Hamburg, October 18, 2001. Accessible at: www.abc.net.au/4corners/atta/interviews/machule.htm (April, 2010).

Introvigne, M. (2003) *Hamás: Islámský terorismus ve Svaté zemi.* Praha: Vyšehrad.

Jazairiová, P. (2004) Cihlářova žena. Muslimky v Indii a Pákistánu. In: Frouzová, M. (ed.) *Závoj a džíny. Ženy v islámském světě.* Praha: Vyšehrad, p. 79-87.

Ježová, M. (2011) Izrale a Palestinská autonomní správa. In: Ježová, M., Burgrová, H. (eds) *Současný Blízký východ.* Brno: Barrister a Principal, p. 118-133.

Juergensmeyer, M. (1994) *The New Cold War? Religious Nationalism Confronts the Secular State.* Berkeley: University of California Press.

Juergensmeyer, M. (2000) *Terror in the Mind of God. The Global Rise of Religious Violence.* Berkeley: University of California Press.

Juergensmeyer, M. (2004) Is Religion the Problem? *The Hedgehog Review* 6 (2004), No. 1, p. 21-33.

Juergensmeyer, M. (2006) From Bhindranwale to Bin Laden: A Search for Understanding Religious Violence. In: Cady L., Simon, S. (eds) *Religion and Conflict in Asia: Disrupting Violence.* London: Routledge, Taylor and Francis Group, p. 21-30.

Juergensmeyer, M. (ed.) (2006b) *The Oxford Handbook of Global Religions.* Oxford: Oxford University Press.

Juergensmeyer, M. (2007) Gandhi vs. Terrorism. *Daedalus* 136 (2007), No. 1, p. 30-39.

Juergensmeyer, M. (2008) *Global Rebelion. Religious Challenges to the Secular State, from Christian Militias to al Qaeda.* Berkeley: University of California Press.

Juergensmeyer, M. (2008b) Religious Nationalism and Transnationalism in a Global World. [online]. Accessible at: http://www.juergensmeyer.com/files/Relig%20natlism-trans.doc.

Juergensmeyer, M. (2008c) Jak myslí teroristé (interview with the author). *Respekt* 2008, No. 47, p. 50-53.

Kalibová, K. (1997) *Úvod do demografie*. Praha: Karolinum.

Kalibová, K. (2008) Populace světa v letech 1950-2007. *Demografie*, Vol. 50, No. 4, p. 288-296.

Kamali, M. (2007) Multiple Modernities and Islamism in Iran. *Social Compass*, 2007, 54, 3, p. 373-387.

Kaplan, R. D. (2003) *Přicházející anarchie. Zborcení snů – svět po studené válce*. Červený Kostelec: Pavel Mervart.

Kaufmann, D., Kraay, A., Mastruzzi, M. (2009) *Governance Matters VIII: Aggregate and Individual Governance Indicators for 1996-2008*. World Bank Policy Research Working Paper No. 4978. Washington, D. C.

Kaufmann, D., Kraay, A., Mastruzzi, M. (2010) *The Worldwide Governance Indicators: Methodology and Analytical Issues*. Brookings.

Kazancigil, A. (2005) Cyprus Question. In: Roy, O. (ed.) *Turkey Today. A European Country?* London: Anthem Press, p. 173-179.

Kedie, N. (1973) Is There a Middle East? *International Journal of Middle East Studies*, 4 (3), p. 255-271.

Kedourie, E. (1992) *Politics in the Middle East*. Oxford: Oxford University Press.

Keller, J. (1990) *Sociologie konfliktu*. Brno: Masarykova univerzita.

Keller, J. (1997) *Úvod do sociologie*. Praha: Slon.

Keller, J. (2007) *Teorie modernizace*. Praha: SLON.

Kennedy, P. (1996) *Svět v 21. století. Chmurné vyhlídky i vkládané naděje*. Praha: Lidové noviny.

Kepel, G. (1996) *Boží pomsta. Křesťané, židé a muslimové znovu dobývají svět*. Brno: Atlantis.

Kepel, G. (2002) *Jihad. The Trail of Political Islam*. Cambridge: Harvard University Press.

Kepel, G. (2004) *The War for Muslim Minds. Islam and the West*. New York: Harvard University Press.

Kepel, G. (2008) *Beyond Terror and Martyrdom: The Future of the Middle East*. Cambridge: Belknap Press of Harvard University Press.

Khaled, A. (2011) Faith and Hope in Egypt. *The Cairo Review of Global Affairs. Special Report: Arab Revolution*, 1, 2011, p. 68-73.

Kholoussy, H. (2010) The Fiction and Non-Fiction of Egypt's Marriage Crisis. *MERIP*, December 2010. Accessible at: www.merip.org.

Klare, M. T. (2001) *Resource Wars. The New Landscape of Global Conflict*. New York: Henry Holt and Company.

Klare, M. T. (2004) *Blood and Oil*. New York: Metropolitan Books.

Klare, M. T. (2008) *Rising Powers, Shrinking Planet. The New Geopolitics of Energy*. New York: Metropolitan Books.

Klofáč, J., Tlustý, V. (1965) *Soudobá sociologie*. Praha: NPL.

Kloskowska, A. (1967) *Masová kultura. Kritika i obhajoba*. Praha: Svoboda.

Knöbl, W. (2003) Theories That Won't Pass Away: The Never-Ending Story of Modernisation Theory. In: Delanty G., Isin E. Handbook of Historical Sociology. London: Sage Publications.

Korotajev, A., Ziňkin, J., Chodunov, A. (2012) *Sistemnyj monitoring globalnych i regionalnych riskov: Arabskaja vesna 2011 goda*. Moskva: Izdatelstvo LKI.

Kotásek, J. Modely školy budoucnosti. In: Walterová, E.(ed.) *Rozvoj národní vzdělanosti a vzdělávání učitelů v evropském kontextu. 1. díl. Teoretické a komparativní studie*. Praha: PedF UK, 2002, p. 8-24.

Kouřilová, I. (2004) Jak prolomit ticho. Televize Al-Džazíra mohla díky podpoře emíra z Kataru vyvolat mediální revoluci v arabském světě. *Lidové noviny*, 24. dubna, 2004, p. 14.

Kouřilová, I. (2006) Televize, která přinesla změnu. A2, No. 20. Accessible at: www.advojka.cz.

Kouřilová, I. (2007) Typologie islámského myšlení ve 20. století. In: Souleimanov, E. (ed.) *Politický islám*. Praha: Eurolex Bohemia, p. 10-38.

Kouřilová, I. (2008) Islamistické strany a hnutí a jejich zapojení do politického života zemí Blízkého východu. Accessible at: www.mzv.cz.

Křížek, D., Tarant, Z. (eds) (2014) *Arabské jaro. II. díl – Sýrie a Arabský poloostrov.* Plzeň: Západočeská univerzita.

Kropáček, L. (1996) *Islámský fundamentalismus.* Praha: Vyšehrad.

Kropáček, L. (1999) *Blízký východ na přelomu tisíciletí.* Praha: Vyšehrad.

Kropáček, L. (1999b) Půlměsíc na severní obloze: muslimové v zemích EU. In: *Variace na Korán. Islám v diaspoře.* Archiv orientální. Praha: Orientální ústav AV ČR, p. 13–52.

Kropáček, L. (2002) *Islám a Západ. Historická paměť a současná krize.* Praha: Vyšehrad.

Kropáček, L. (2006) *Duchovní cesty islámu.* Praha: Vyšehrad.

Kropáček, L. (2008) *Súfismus. Dějiny islámské mystiky.* Praha: Vyšehrad.

Kropáček, L. (2010) Gellnerova islamika. *Historická sociologie,* No. 2, Vol. 2, p. 99–106.

Krueger, A., Maleckova, J. (2002) *Education, Poverty, Political Violence and Terrorism: Is There a Causal Connection?* July 2002. Accessible at: http://www.krueger.princeton.edu/references.html.

Krueger, A., Maleckova, J. (2009) Attitudes and Action: Public Opinion and the Occurrence of International Terrorism. *Science,* 2009, Vol. 325, p. 1534–1536.

Krueger, A., Laitin D. (2003) *Kto kavo?: A Gross-Country Study of the Origins and Targets of Terrorism.* November 11, 2003. Accessible at: http://www.krueger.princeton.edu/references.html.

Krueger, A. (2007) *What Makes a Terroris. Economics and the Roots of Terrorism.* Princeton: Princeton University Press.

Kubálek, P. (2009) *Kurdové a Kurdistán. Moderní dějiny.* Accessible at: http://kurdove.ecn.cz/moderni.shtml.

Kubíková, N. (2007) Muslimské bratrstvo. In: Souleimanov, E. (ed.) *Politický islám.* Praha: Eurolex Bohemia, p. 148–167.

Kunezik, M. (1995) *Základy masové komunikace.* Praha.

Kuznetz, S. (1955) Economic Growth and Income Inequality. *The American Economic Review,* Vol. 45, No. 1 (March, 1955), p. 1–28.

Lafond, N. (2013) Current silend as cleric affirms death penalty for leaving Islam on Al-Jazeera. *Daily Caller,* 12 February, 2013.

Lapidus, I. M. (2002) A History of Islamic Societies. Cambridge: Cambridge University Press.

Laqueur, W. (2004) The Terrorism to Come. *Policy Review,* 2004, No. 126. Accessible at: http://www.laqueur.net.

Laqueur, W. (2006) *Poslední dny Evropy. Humanistická Evropa, nebo islamistická Eurábie?* Praha: Nakladatelství Lidové noviny.

Laqueur, W. (2007) *Měnící se tvář antisemitismu. Od starověku do dnešních dnů.* Praha: NLN.

Laurens, H. (2013) *Arabský Orient za časů Ameriky. Od války v Zálivu k válce v Iráku.* Praha: Academia.

Lerner, D. (1964) *The Passing of Traditional Society. Modernizing the Middle East.* New York: The Free Press and Collier-Macmillan Limited.

Lewis, B. (1988) *The Political Language of Islam.* Chicago: The University of Chicago Press.

Lewis, B. (1990) The Roots of Muslim Rage: Why So Many Muslims Deeply Resent the West and Why Their Bitterness Will Not Be Easily Modified. *The Atlantic Monthly,* 1990, Vol. 226, No. 3, p. 47–60.

Lewis, B. (2003a) *Kde se stala chyba?* Praha: Volvox Globator.

Lewis, B. (2003b) *The Crisis of Islam. Holy War and Unholy Terror.* New York: The Modern Library.

Lewis, B. (2008) Free at Last? The Arab World in the Twenty-first Century. *Foreign Affairs,* Vol. 88, No. 2, p. 77–88.

Lindsey, U. (2011) Revolution and Counter-Revolution in the Egyptian Media. *MERIP.* Accessible at: http://www.merip.org.

Lipset, M. S. (1959) Some Social Requisites of Democracy: Economic Development and Political Legitimacy. *The American Political Science Review,* Vol. 53, No. 1, p. 69–105.

Lipset, M. S. (1994) The Social Requisites of Democracy Revisited, *American Sociological Review*, 1994, Vol. 59, p. 1–22.

Longrigg, S. H. (1963) *The Geography of the Middle East*. London: Aldine Transaction.

Lorenz, Ch. (2006) 'Won't You Tell Me, Where Have All the Good Times Gone'? On the Advantages and Disadvantages of Modernisation Theory for History. *Rethinking History*, Vol. 10, No. 2, p. 171–200.

LSE 2005. Terrorism and Development. Accessible at: www.lse.ac.uk.

Lubeck, P. M., Britts, B. (2002) Muslim Civil Society in Urban Public Spaces: Globalization, Discursive Shifts, and Social Movements. In: Eade, J., Mele, Ch. (eds) *Understanding the City. Contemporary and Future Perspectives*. Oxford: Blackwell Publishing, p. 305–335.

Luciani, G. (2009) Oil and Political Economy in the International Relations of the Middle East. In: Fawcett, L. (ed.) *International Relations of the Middle East*. New York: Oxford University Press, p. 81–103.

Lužný, D. (1999) *Náboženství a moderní společnost. Sociologické teorie modernizace a sekularizace*. Brno: Masarykova univerzita.

Lynch, M. (2007) Young Brothers in Cyberspace. *Middle East Report. The Politics of Youth*, 2007, No. 245, p. 25–34.

Lynch, M. (2013) Twitter Revolutions. How social media is hurting the Arab Spring. *Foreign Policy*, February 7, 2013.

Malá, M. (2004) Butiky, korzo, kavárny – ženy v Libanonu. In: Frouzová, M. (ed.) *Závoj a džíny. Ženy v islámském světě*. Praha: Vyšehrad, p. 139–148.

Malečková, J. (2012) Turecko a Blízký východ – nová podoba orientalismu? *Nový Orient*, Vol. 68, No. 3, p. 18–23.

Malthus, T. (2002) *Esej o principu populace*. Praha: Zvláštní vydání.

Mareš, P. (1999) *Sociologie nerovnosti a chudoby*. Praha: SLON.

Marková, D. (1999) Zelená v záplavě oranžové: islám v Indii. In: *Variace na Korán. Islám v diaspoře*. Archiv orientální. Praha: Orientální ústav AV ČR, p. 87–134.

Massicard, E. (2005) Islam in Turkey: A 'Secular Muslim' State. In: Roy, O. (ed.) *Turkey Today. A European Country?* London: Anthem Press, p. 53–66.

Marx, K., Engels, B. (1973) *Komunistický manifest*. Brno: Blok.

Mauss, M. (1929/1930) Les Civilisations. Eléments et formes. In: *Foundation pour la Science – Centre international de synthese* (eds). Paris: La Renaissance du Livre.

McCants, W. F. (2015) *The ISIS Apocalypse*. New York: St. Martin's Press.

McDermott, T. (2005) *Perfect Soldiers: The 9/11 Hijackers: Who They Were, Why They Did It*. New York: HarperCollins.

McLuhan, M. (1964) *Understanding Media: The Extension of Man*. London: McGraw-Hill.

Mendel, M. (2008) *S puškou a Koránem*. Praha: Orientální ústav.

Mendel, M., Ostřanský, B., Rataj, T. (2007) *Islám v srdci Evropy*. Praha: Academia.

Mendel, M. (2010) *Džihád. Islámské koncepce šíření víry*. Brno: Atlantis.

Mendel, M. (2013) *Sajjid Qutb. Milníky na cestě*. Praha: Academia.

Mendel, M. (2014) *Arabské revoluce*. Praha: Academia.

Merton, R. K. (1957) *Social Theory and Social Structure*. Glencoe: Free Press.

Merton, R. K. (2000) *Studie ze sociologické teorie*. Praha: SLON.

Moghadam, A. (2003) *A Global Resurgence of Religion?* Cambridge: Weatherhead Center for International Affairs, Harvard University.

Montoussé, M., Renouard, G. (2005) *Přehled sociologie*. Praha: Portál.

Montran, R. (2005) Mustafa Kemal Ataturk. In: Roy, O. (ed.) *Turkey Today. A European Country?* London: Anthem Press, p. 119–130.

Mooddel, M. (2006) Shia Muslim Communities. In: Juergensmeyer, M. (ed.) *The Oxford Handbook of Global Religions*. Oxford: Oxford University Press, p. 447–456.

Moore, B. (1968) *Social Origins of Dictatorship and Democracy*. Harmondsworth: Penguin Books.

Moravec, F. (2006) Palestinská mediální intifáda. *A2*, No. 20, accessible at: www.advojka.cz.

Možný, I. (1997) *Sociologie rodiny*. Praha: Slon.

Musil, J. (1967) *Sociologie soudobého města*. Praha: Svoboda.

Myrdal, G. (1944) *The American Dilemma. The Negro Problem and Modern Democracy*. New York: Harper Brothers.

Myrdal, G. (1968) *Asian Drama: An Inquiry Into the Poverty of Nations*. New York: Pantheon.

Myrdal, G. (1970) *The Challenge of World Poverty: A World Anti-Poverty Program in Outline*. New York: Pantheon.

Nafisi, R. (2007) Iranian succession and the IRGC. *Islamic Affairs Analyst*, October, 2007, p. 5–7.

Nešpor, Z., Lužný, D. (2007) *Sociologie náboženství*. Praha: Portál.

Norton, A. R. (2003) The New Media, Civic Pluralism, and the Struggle for Political Reform. In: Eickelman, D., Anderson, J., W. (eds) *New Media in the Muslim World. The Emerging Public Sphere*. Bloomington: Indiana University Press, p. 19–32.

Noueihed, L., Warren, A. (2012) *The Battle for the Arab Spring. Revolution, Counter-revolution and the Making of a New Era*. London: Yale University Press.

Nye, J. (2004) *Soft Power*. New York: Public Affairs.

Olson, M. (1963) Rapid Growth as a Destabilizing Force. *The Journal of Economic History*, Vol. 23, No. 4, p. 529–552.

Ottaway, M. (2010) The Rise and Fall of Political Reform in the Arab World. *Current History*, 2010, p. 376–382.

Owen, R. (2011) Military Presidents in Arab States. *International Journal of Middle East Studies*, 43 (2011), p. 395–396.

Palečková, J., Tomášek, V., Basl, J. (2010) *Hlavní zjištění výzkumu PISA 2009*. Praha: ÚIV.

Panarin, A. (2003) *Iskušenije globalizmom*. Moskva: Algoritm.

Pape, R. (2003) The Strategic Logic of Suicide Terrorism. *American Political Science Review*, Vol. 97, No. 3, p. 1–19.

Pape, R. (2006) *Dying to Win. The Strategic Logic of Suicide Terrorism*. New York: Random House.

Pape, R., Feldman, J. (2010) *Cutting the Fuse. The Explosion of Global Suicide Terrorism and How to Stop It*. Chicago: The University of Chicago Press.

Pargeter, A. (2013) *The Muslim Brotherhood. The Burden of Tradition*. London: Saqi Books.

Parrillo, V. N. (2008) *Encyclopedia of Social Problems*. London: Sage.

Patai, R. (1973) *The Arab Mind*. New York: Schribner's Sons.

Pavlincová a kol. (1996) *Slovník. Judaismus, křesťanství, islám*. Praha: Mladá fronta.

Pelikán, P. (2010) Popírání holocaustu a černé svědomí Západu. *Přítomnost*, 2010, p. 19–22.

Petráček, Z. (2011) Přinese jaro národů násilí a kalifát? *Lidové noviny*, 2011, 12. březen, p. 21–22.

Pfaff, W. (2010) Manufacturing Insecurity. How Militarism Endangers America. *Foreign Affairs*, Vol. 89, No. 6, p. 133–140.

Pipes, D. (1996) Západní smýšlení radikálního islámu. *Proglas*, 1996, No. 3, p. 20–25.

Pirický, G. (2006) *Turecko. Stručná historie států*. Praha: Nakladatelství Libri.

Pope, H. (2011) The Turkish Model and the Middle East. Accessible at: www.transatlantic-academy.org.

Pope, H. (2012) Erdogan's Decade. *The Cairo Review of Global Affairs*, 4 (2012), p. 43–57.

Pongs, A. (2000) *V jaké společnosti vlastně žijeme?* Praha: ISV.

Post, J. M. (2004) *Leaders and their Followers in a Dangerous World: The Psychology of Political Behavior*. Ithaca: Cornell University Press.

Quinn, F. (2008) *The Sum of All Heresies. The Image of Islam in Western Thought*. New York: Oxford University Press.

Rashid, A. (2002) *Jihad: The Rise of Militant Islam in Central Asia*. New Haven: Yale University Press.

Rauch, J. E., Evans, P. (2000) Bureaucratic Structure and Bureaucratic Performance in Less Developed Countries. *Journal of Public Economics*, 75, p. 49–71.

Religion in Global Civil Society. Santa Barbara: University of California Press, 2009.

Riesebrodt, M. (2006) Religion in Global Perspective. In: Juergensmeyer, M. (ed.) *The Oxford Handbook of Global Religions*. Oxford: Oxford University Press, p. 597–609.

Riesman, D. (1964) *Introduction*. In: Lerner, D. The Passing of Traditional Society. New York: The Free Press, p. 1–15.

Richards, A., Waterbury, J. (2008) *A Political Economy of the Middle East.* Boulder: Westview Press.

Robejšek, P. (2006) Po stopách Marca Pola ke světovládě. *Geografické rozhledy*, Vol. 15, No. 1, p. 6–8.

Robertson, R. (2006) Anti-Global Religion? In: Juergensmeyer, M. (ed.) *The Oxford Handbook of Global Religions.* Oxford: Oxford University Press, p. 611–623.

Robinson, F. (1996) *Svět islámu: kulturní atlas.* Praha: Knižní klub.

Ross, M. (2001) Does Oil Hinder Democracy? *World Politics*, 53 (2001), p. 325–361.

Rostow, W. W. (1960) *The stages of economic growth: A non-communist manifesto.* Cambridge: Cambridge University Press.

Roy, O. (1992) *The Failure of Political Islam.* Cambridge: Harvard.

Roy, O. (2004) *Globalized Islam. The Search for a New Ummah.* New York: Columbia University Press.

Roy, O. (ed.) (2005) *Turkey Today. A European Country?* London: Anthem Press.

Rubin, B. (2006) Arab Liberals Argue about America. *Middle East Quarterly*, 2006. Accessible at: www.meforum.org.

Ryan, Y. (2011). „The tragic life of a street vendor". *Al Jazeera English.* Accessible at: http://english.aljazeera.net/indepth/features/2011/01/201111684242518839.html.

Said, E. (1981) *Covering Islam.* New York: Pantheon Books.

Said, E. (2008) *Orientalismus. Západní koncepce Orientu.* Praha: Paseka.

Sageman, M. (2004) *Understanding Terror Networks.* Philadelphia: University of Pennsylvania Press.

Samuelson, P., Nordhaus, W. (1995) *Ekonomie.* Praha: Svoboda.

Šanc, D. (2011) Blízký východ jako politicko-geografický region. In: Ježová, M., Burgrová, H. (eds) *Současný Blízký východ.* Brno: Barrister a Principal, p. 9–22.

Sariolghalam, M. (2008) Iran in Search of Itself. *Current History*, Vol. 107, No. 713, p. 425–432.

Sayigh, Y. (2011) Introduction. Roundtable: Rethinking the Study of Middle East Militaries. *International Journal of Middle East Studies*, 43 (2011), p. 391.

Savoia, A., Sen, K. (2012) *Measurement and Evolution of State Capacity: Exploring a Lesser Known Aspect of Governance.* Effective States and Inclusive Development Research Centre Working Paper 10, 2012.

Schulze, R. (2007) *Dějiny islámského světa ve 20. století.* Brno: Atlantis.

Schumacher, R. (2000) *Malé je milé, aneb Ekonomie, která by počítala i s člověkem.* Brno: Doplněk.

Serebrjannikov, V. V. (1997) *Sociologija vojny.* Moskva: Naučnyj mir.

Shafiq, M. N., Sinno, A. H. (2008) Education, Income and Support for Suicide Bombings. Evidence from Six Muslim Countries. Accessible na http://ssrn.com.

Shafiq, M. N. Do Education and Income Affect Support for Democracy in Muslim Countries? Evidence from the Pew Global Attitudes Project. Accessible at: http://ssrn.com.

Shafiq, M. N., Sinno, A. H. (2010) Education, Income and Support for Suicide Bombings: Evidence from Six Muslim Countries. *Journal of Conflict Resolution*, Vol. 54, No. 1, p. 146–178.

Shaheen, J. (2001) *Reel Bad Arabs. How Hollywood Vilifies a People.* Northamptom: Olive Branch Press.

Shaheen, J. (2001) *Guilty. Hollywood's Verdict on Arabs After 9/11.* Northamptom: Olive Branch Press.

Šisler, V. (2006) Médium, které se nedaří umlčet. *A2*, No. 20. Accessible at: www.advojka.cz.

Šlachta, M. (2007) *Ohniska napětí ve světě.* Praha: Kartografie.

Smelser, N. (1959) *Social Change in the Industrial Revolution.* London: Routledge.

Šmíd, T. (ed.) (2010) *Vybrané konflikty o zdroje a suroviny.* Brno: Masarykova univerzita.

Smith, Ch. (2009) The Arab-Israeli Conflict. In: Fawcett, L. (ed.) *International Relations of the Middle East.* New York: Oxford University Press, p. 231–253.

Soifer, H. (2008) State Infrastructural Power: Approaches to Conceptualization and Measurement, *St Comp Int Dev*, 43, p. 231–251.

Soliman, S. (2011) *The Autumn of Dictatorship. Fiscal Crisis and Political Change in Egypt Under Mubarak.* Stanford: Stanford University Press.

Sorli, M., Gleditsch, N. P., Strand, H. (2005) Why is there so much conflict in the Middle East? *Journal of Conflict Resolution*, Vol. 49, No. 1, p. 141–165.

Souleimanov, E. (2007) Internacionalizace čečenského konfliktu a islámský komponent: Mýty a realita. In: Souleimanov, E. (ed.) *Politický islám*. Praha: Eurolex Bohemia, p. 206–220.

Souleimanov a kol. (2007) *Politický islám*. Praha: Eurolex Bohemia.

Spohn, W. (2001) Eisenstadt on Civilizations and Multiple Modernity. *European Journal of Social Theory* 4(4), p. 499–508.

Springborg, R. (2011) Economic Involvement of Militaries. *International Journal of Middle East Studies*, 43 (2011), p. 397–399.

Stacher, J. (2012) *Adaptable Autocrats. Regime Power in Egypt and Syria*. Cairo: AUC Press.

Starrett, G. (1998) *Putting Islam to Work. Education, Politics, and Religious Transformation in Egypt*. Berkeley: University of California Press.

Starrett, G. (2003) Muslim Identities and the Great Chain of Buying. In: Eickelman, D., Anderson, J. W. (eds) *New Media in the Muslim World. The Emerging Public Sphere*. Bloomington: Indiana University Press, p. 80–101.

Starret, G., Doumato, E. A. (eds) (2007) *Teaching Islam. Textbooks and Religion in the Middle East*. Boulder: Lynne Rienner Publishing.

Stark, R. (1999) Secularization, R.I.P - rest in peace. *Sociology of Religion*, Vol. 60, No. 3, p. 249–273.

Šubrt, J. a kol. (1998) *Kapitoly ze sociologie veřejného mínění. Teorie a výzkum*. Praha: Karolinum.

Šubrt, J. (2001) *Postavy a problémy soudobé teoretické sociologie*. Praha: ISV.

Sutcliffe, B. (2004) World Inequality and Globalization. *Oxford Review of Economic Policy*, 2004, Vol. 20, No. 1, p. 15–37.

Swatos, W. H. (1999) Secularization Theory: The Course of a Concept. *Sociology of Religion*, Vol. 60, No. 3, p. 221–248.

Sztompka, P. (1993) *The Sociology of Social Change*. Oxford: Blackwell Publishers.

Swedenburg, T. (2007) Imagined Youths. *Middle East Report. The Politics of Youth*, 2007, No. 245, p. 3–11.

Tajmíja, I. (2013) *Wásitské vyznání*. Praha: Academia.

The Economist, November 26, 1977. The Dutch Disease, p. 82–83.

The Economist, August 6, 2007. Jihad on the website, No. 29, p. 22–24.

The Economist, March 12, 2011. The royal house is rattled too, p. 44–45.

The Economist, February 5, 2011. The upheaval in Egypt. An end or a beginning?, p. 21–23.

The Food Crises (2011).

Tilly, Ch. (1978) *From Mobilization to Revolution*. Reading, MA: Addison-Wesley.

Tilly, Ch. (1986) *The contentious French*. Cambridge, MA: The Belknap Press.

Tilly, Ch. (1993) *European Revolutions, 1492–1992*. Oxford: Blackwell.

Tilly, Ch. (2006) *Politika kolektivního násilí*. Praha: SLON.

Tilly, Ch. (2006b) *Regimes and Repertoires*. Chicago: The University of Chicago Press.

Tiosavljevičová, J. (2007) Parlamentní volby v Turecku přinesly očekávaného vítěze. *Mezinárodní politika*, Vol. 31, No. 9, p. 4–6.

Tocqueville, A. (1992) *Demokracie v Americe, I. a II. díl*. Praha: Nakladatelství Lidové noviny.

Tocqueville, A. (2003) *Starý režim a Revoluce*. Praha: Academia.

Tomášek, V. a kol. (2008) *Výzkum TIMSS 2007*. Praha: ÚIV.

Tomeš, J. a kol. (2007) *Konflikt světů a svět konfliktů*. Praha: P3K.

Toušck, V., Kunc, J., Vystoupil, J. a kol. (2008) *Ekonomická a sociální geografie*. Plzeň: Aleš Čeněk.

Treblin, A. A. (2004) *Terrorism v 21. věke*. Moskva: Nauka.

Tunkrová, L. (2007) Nová dynamika turecké zahraniční politiky. *Mezinárodní politika*, Vol. 31, No. 9, p. 17–20.

Ťupek, P. (2007) Co je to salafíjský islám? In: Souleimanov, E. (ed.) *Politický islám*. Praha: Eurolex Bohemia, p. 62–87.

Ťupek, P. (2015) *Salafitský islám*. Praha: Academia.

Tureček, B. (2011) *Nesvatý boj o Svatou zemi*. Praha: Knižní klub.

Turek, P. (2011) Jsem hlas lidu. Hudební underground, který vynesl na světlo revoluce v arabském světě. *Respekt*, No. 15, 2011, p. 59–61.

Turner, B. S. (1974) *Weber and Islam. A critical study*. London: Routledge.

Turner, B. S. (2007) Religious Autority and the New Media. *Theory, Culture and Society*, 2007, Vol. 24 (2), p. 117–134.

Yacoub, J. (2003) *Ve jménu božím! Náboženské války dnes a zítra*. Praha: THEMIS.

Velký sociologický slovník (1996). Praha: Nakladatelství Karolinum.

Vulliamy, E. (1994) *Údobí pekla – porozumění válce v Bosně*. Praha: Naše vojsko.

Wallerstein, I. (2005) *Úpadek americké moci. USA v chaotickém světě*. Praha: SLON.

Wallerstein, I. (2008) *Evropský universalismus. Rétorika moci*. Praha: Slon.

Weber, M. (1997) *Autorita, etika a společnost: pohled sociologa do dějin*. Praha: Mladá fronta.

Weber, M. (1998) *Sociologie náboženství*. Praha: Vyšehrad.

Weber, M. (1998) *Metodologie, sociologie a politika*. Praha: OIKOYMENH.

Weiss, M., Hassan, H. (2015) *ISIS: Inside the Army of Terror*. New York: Regan Arts.

White, M., White, L. (1962) *The Intellectual vs. the City: From Thomas Jefferson to Frank Lloyd Wright*. New York: Oxford University Press.

Winterová, B. (2010) Konflikt o vodní zdroje Eufratu a Tigrisu. In: Šmíd, T. (ed.) *Vybrané konflikty o zdroje a suroviny*. Brno: Masarykova univerzita, p. 175–191.

Wucherpfennig, J., Deutsch, F. (2009) Modernisation and Democracy: Theories and Evidence Revisited. *Living Reviews in Democracy*, Vol. 1, No. 1, p. 1–9.

Zahid, M. (2010) *The Muslim Brotherhood and Egypt's Succession Crisis*. London: I. B. Tauris.

Zakaria, F. (2001) The Politics of Rage: Why Do They Hate Us? *Newsweek*, October 2001, Accessible at: http://www.newsweek.com.

Zakaria, F. (2004) *Budoucnost svobody. O krizi demokracie*. Praha: Academia.

Zakaria, F. (2008) *The Post-American World*. London: Penguin Books.

Zakaria, F. (2011) How Democracy Can Work in the Middle East. *Time*, February 2011. Accessible at: www.time.com.

Zaman, M. Q. (2007) Tradition and Authority in Deobandi Madrasas of South Asia. In: Hefner, R., Zaman, M., Q. (eds) *Schooling Islam. The Culture and Politics of Modern Muslim Education*. Princeton: Princeton University Press, p. 61–86.

Zewail, A. (2011) Reflections on Arab Renaissance. A Call for Education Reform. *The Cairo Review of Global Affairs. Special Report: Arab Revolution*, 1, 2011, p. 30–41.

Znebejánek, F. (2007) Ralf Dahrendorf: historické proměny třídních konfliktů. In: Šubrt, J. (ed.) *Historická sociologie*, Plzeň: Aleš Čeněk, p. 266–281.

Zubaida, S. (2009) *Islam, the People and the State. Political Ideas and Movements in the Middle East*. London: I. B. Tauris.

LIST OF FIGURES AND TABLES

List of tables

INDEX

KAREL ČERNÝ

INSTABILITY IN THE MIDDLE EAST
STRUCTURAL CHANGES AND UNEVEN
MODERNISATION 1950–2015

Published by Charles University
Karolinum Press
Ovocný trh 560/5, 116 36
Prague 1, Czech Republic
Prague 2017
Edited by Martin Janeček
Cover and layout by Jan Šerých
Typeset by DTP Karolinum Press
Printed by Karolinum Press
First English edition

ISBN 978-80-246-3427-2
ISBN 978-80-246-3192-2 (pdf)